ZIG ZIGLAR
REACHING THE TOP

ZIG ZIGLAR
REACHING THE TOP

USING THE ART OF PERSUASION TO DEVELOP
EXCELLENCE IN YOURSELF AND OTHERS

SECRETS OF CLOSING
THE SALE

TOP PERFORMANCE

TWO BESTSELLING WORKS COMPLETE IN ONE VOLUME

Galahad Books • New York

CONTENTS

SECRETS
OF
CLOSING THE SALE

To Bill Cranford

Who gave me my start in the world of selling and gently but forcefully pushed me to strive for excellence and reach for new heights. He's my friend, my brother, my mentor, and my golfing buddy. He's a great guy and *one more* fine man.

CONTENTS

Part Four

Imagination and Word Pictures

Part Five

The Nuts and Bolts of Selling

Part Six

The Keys in Closing

PREFACE

Over the past thirty-six years it has been my privilege to be in as many actual sales situations, selling goods, products, services or job opportunities, as virtually anyone who ever carried the title of *salesperson*. Additionally, it has been my privilege to share the platform with and learn from some of the greatest speakers and sales trainers our country has produced. I go back to the days of the late Elmer Wheeler, Charlie Cullen, Frank Bettger, Fred Herman, Charles Roth, Dick Gardner, J. Douglas Edwards, and Percy Whiting. The list includes Cavett Robert, Rod Motley, Ken McFarland, Dan Bellus, Joe Batten, Charlie Jones, Hal Krause, Mike Frank, Ira Hayes, Heartsill Wilson, Judge Ziglar, Thom Norman, Bill Gove, John Hammond, Larry Wilson—and the list goes on and on.

Over these thirty-six years I have been a pack rat. I have taken copious notes from many great trainers. In addition, I have clipped innumerable sales articles from newspapers and magazines, and have learned much by watching salespeople in action. My library includes books and manuals from the greatest writers and trainers of the last fifty years, and I have over a thousand hours of recordings from these and other speakers.

This background presents a rather unique problem. To be completely honest, I sometimes forget the source of my information. To the best of my ability, I have given credit in this book to each individual who has made a contribution via a speech, a personal conference, a book, or an article. Many times, however, I have no idea who my benefactor is. Additionally, I recognize the possibility that in some instances I will credit the wrong author or even claim originality because I learned a technique long ago and have used it so many times that I believe the technique or idea was original. In the event this has happened, I ask the author to forgive me. My objective is to be completely fair with everyone.

Your own personality, conviction, and credibility in the application of the principles and procedures in this book will be the determining factor, but this I promise: The procedures and techniques which I describe have worked not only for me but for countless others as well. Many of them, as I will repeatedly emphasize throughout the book, need alteration or adaptation to fit your sales situation, so you should constantly ask yourself this question as you read the book: "How can I adapt this information to fit my product to my prospect?"

I urge you to become a student as you dig into *Secrets of Closing the Sale*. I'm going to be bold enough to suggest that it has taken me a lifetime to accumulate this information and several thousand hours to assemble and put the information into what I believe is its most effective form. With this in mind, I don't believe I overstate my case to point out that you probably are not going to be able to glean all the information in one reading.

Finally, I suggest that as you read this book you're going to be aware of the fact that it is analogous to the fisherman's lure. Many sales books are written to catch the fisherman—namely, the salesperson—and not to help the fisherman catch the fish—meaning the customer. With that in mind I emphasize that *Secrets of Closing the Sale* was written to help you—the fisherman—catch the fish, and to catch him in such a way that the fish (the customer) realizes he is in good hands—yours.

I firmly believe that if you buy the ideas and concepts covered in this book, as you apply the techniques and procedures, I *will* SEE YOU AT THE TOP—of the sales ladder!

Zig Ziglar

PART ONE
THE PSYCHOLOGY
OF CLOSING

Objectives

To "sell" the importance of the credibility of the salesperson.

To "sell" and teach the importance of commonsense psychology in the sales process.

To "sell" you on why you must learn to use your voice in the sales process.

To familiarize you with the concept that sales training alone won't make a salesperson, but it will make a salesperson more effective.

To introduce you to a real sales pro and a series of professional sales techniques.

Closes and/or Procedures

The "Snooker" Close
The "Ownership" Close
The "Embarrassment" Close
The "1902" Close
The "Affordable" Close
The "Persuasion" Close
The "Want It" Close
The "Bride" Close
The "Alternate of Choice" Close
The "Now or Never" Close
The "Next One" Close
The "Fair Enough" Close

The "New Decision" Close
The "Voice Inflection" Close
The "Fear of Loss" Close
The "Cost" Close
The "Quality" Close
The "Answer for Everything" Close
The "Reverse" Close
The "Shame" Close
The "Extra" Close
The "Add On" Close
The "Gloomy Gus" Close

1

THE "HOUSEHOLD EXECUTIVE" SALESLADY

How Much Should We Invest?

We moved to Dallas in 1968 and I immediately started teaching a class in sales and motivation from nine in the morning until nine in the evening, Monday through Saturday. I was as busy as I've ever been in my life. But it was also house-buying time because we obviously couldn't live in a motel. My Redhead* and I talked about a house in considerable detail until we finally arrived at a "reasonable" figure we would be willing to invest in a home. I know the figure was "reasonable" because she assured me it was "reasonable." (Personally, I felt the price bore a striking resemblance to the foreign-aid bill for the world!)

After we'd arrived at the exact amount we were going to invest in a home, she said, "Honey, suppose we find the dream house. I mean, exactly like we want. How much *more* can we invest?" That brought on a lot more talk. So we talked and we talked and we talked and finally arrived at a figure of an additional twenty thousand dollars. Now in this day and age, when you talk about an additional twenty thousand dollars, you're talking about building a nice carport or a patio if it isn't too big and elaborate. But in 1968, twenty thousand dollars would build an additional two thousand square feet of quality construction. Yes, in 1968 things were quite different.

So, house-hunting that Redhead goes, and I mean she really looked—at two houses. When she walked into that second one, that ended all her house-hunting. She had found what she wanted.

How Much Does It Cost?

That night when I got back to the motel room, there she sat on the edge of the king-size bed. Even though she was *just* sitting there, the bed

---

* When I talk about my one and only since November 26, 1946, I refer to her as "the Redhead." When I talk to her I call her "Sugar Baby." Her name is Jean.

was vibrating! I've never seen her so excited. She jumped up and said, "Honey, I have found our dream home. It's absolutely gorgeous! Four beautiful bedrooms on a big lot, plenty of room in the backyard for you to build that arrow-shaped swimming pool you've been talking about, walk-in closets in every room, and four bathrooms!"

Interrupting her to squeeze in a question I said, "Sweetheart, hold the phone! How much does that house cost?" Sugar Baby: "Honey, you'll have to see it to believe it, but you're going to love it because the den is monstrous and it has exposed beams and a cathedral ceiling. The garage is so big we will have room for the two cars and all our tools. Best of all, Honey, there's an eleven-by-eleven-foot spot for you to build that little office where you can do the writing you've been talking about. And, Honey, the master bedroom is so big we're going to have to get a riding vacuum cleaner! I'll tell you, that is soooooome house!"

Zig (interrupting her again): "Sweetheart, how much does that house cost?" She told me. It was eighteen thousand dollars—*more*—than the *maximum*, which was already twenty thousand dollars more than we had any business investing! Zig: "Sweetheart, there is no way we can buy a house like that!" Sugar Baby: "Well Honey, I know that, but don't worry about it. You know we don't know a thing about real estate in Dallas, so

I invited the builder to take us to the property after your class tomorrow night so we can both look at it and get a benchmark on real estate in this area."

Don't Let the Prospect Fool You

Zig: "Well, I'll be glad to look, but I'll guarantee you that's as far as it's going to go." Sugar Baby: "I know that, so don't worry about it."

When we pulled into the driveway the next evening, I knew I had a problem. When we walked in the front door, I knew I was in bad trouble! The house was beautiful and was laid out precisely as I would have laid it out, had I been an architect. I instantly wanted that house— badly—but what we want and what we can get are sometimes worlds apart.

When I fully realized the situation I was in, as a protective measure I started to treat my Redhead and the builder the same way your prospects have been treating you all of your sales career and will continue to treat you as long as you're in the world of selling.

Even though I was interested, even *excited* about that house, I *acted as if I had no interest whatever*. The reason is simple. I was scared to death that between her and that builder they were going to get me to do something I already wanted to do, was afraid I was going to do, and knew I had no business doing. I'm talking about buying a house which I was absolutely convinced was more expensive than we could handle. To protect myself from myself I acted as if I had no interest.

Many times your very best prospect will almost adamantly refuse an appointment because he doesn't want to "waste your time or his time." He is often the *best* prospect for the very simple reason that he knows he either wants or needs—or both—the product, goods, or services you are selling.* However, at this particular time he doesn't feel he is in a position to take action; therefore, he doesn't want to be tempted by viewing the demonstration or listening to your presentation. He gives you the excuse that he doesn't want to waste his time or yours by looking at something he *knows* he can't buy.

The "Snooker" Close

Don't let him "snooker" you out of position. There is a lot of difference between a prospect's saying, "I'm not interested," and, "I really am interested but don't feel I can get it right now and therefore don't want to

* For simplification I often use "product" instead of "product, goods, or services."

watch a presentation at this particular moment." Many times the prospect is in identically the same position I was in as I walked in the front door of the house that the Redhead was excited about.

Now I would never accuse my Redhead of secretly taking drama lessons, but based on what happened next I strongly suspect that she did. There was a nice chandelier in the entrance hall of the home. As we walked in the front door she didn't say a word, but she did come to a dead stop. It couldn't have been for more than a second. She turned slightly sideways, looked up, grinned, and walked on. That's all she needed to do. Message delivered—message received.

The "Ownership" Close

As we walked into the den, with mounting enthusiasm she said, "Look at the size of this den, Honey, and aren't those exposed beams gorgeous?" Without waiting for an answer she continued, "And just look at *your* fireplace with all those bookshelves around it for *your* books [all of a sudden everything gets to be *mine!* That's good psychology!]. I can just see you watching the Cowboys whip up on somebody on Sunday afternoon out of one eye while watching *your* fire out of the other one."

Without pausing for breath she said, "Look back here" as she took off in a dead run back to the master bedroom. "Just look at the size of it, Honey. There's plenty of room for the king-size bed and we could put our two chairs and table over here. It's perfect for us, because you know how we like to get up in the morning and have our coffee and quiet time together. And Honey, just look in *your* closet. Why, even as messy as you are there's plenty of room for everything."

Still on a nonstop basis, she said, "Look out here," as she opened the back door and pointed to the big backyard. "Plenty of room for *your* arrow-shaped swimming pool. We can put the point of the arrow in the direction of the garage and the diving board on the other end will still be ten feet from the neighbor's lot."

As she stepped off the distance in the direction of the garage she opened the door and said, "Just look. Plenty of room for the two cars, and here's that eleven-by-eleven-foot space for you to build *your* office you've planned for so long." As we moved back into the house she said, "Look at this bedroom. Suzie'll be gone from home in a couple of years and we'll have that guest bedroom we've always wanted."

When the tour was finally over she squeezed my hand, looked me in the eye, and asked, "How do you feel about it, Honey?"

The "Embarrassment" Close

Question: What could I say? Obviously I couldn't say, "I don't like it," because that would not have been true. So I said, "Sweetheart, I like it. There's no question about it; it's a beautiful home, but you know perfectly good and well we can't afford a house like this."

Did this discourage her or dampen her enthusiasm? Not in the least. She looked at me and with a twinkle in those beautiful, loving eyes she said, "Honey, I know that, but I just wanted you to see something really nice—[pause]. Now we'll go look at something *cheap*." (Now come on, you don't *really* think she would try to embarrass me into buying a beautiful home, do you?)

Not much else was said about the house that evening. We went back to the motel and to bed. I got up the next morning and was in the bathroom brushing my teeth (I know you'll agree that when you've got a mouthful of toothbrush you're handicapped, at least from a talking point of view) when she walked in and said, "How long are we going to live in Dallas?"

"Wrmwrmwrmmrr years," I replied, toothbrush still in mouth.

She couldn't understand my garbled reply so she asked again, "How long?"

This time I removed my toothbrush and replied, "A hundred years. I'm forty-two. I'm going to live to be a hundred and forty-two, so that leaves a hundred." Sugar Baby: "No, I mean *really*." Zig: "I do, too."

She's "Closing" in on Me

Sugar Baby: "Honey, do you think we'll be here thirty years?" Zig: "I'll guarantee it! I love Dallas, it's centrally located for my travels, I hate to move—we'll be here at least thirty years, but why do you ask about thirty years?"

Sugar Baby: "Honey, if we live here just thirty years, how much does that eighteen thousand dollars figure out per year?" (She forgets—or ignores—the original price of the house. She forgets about the twenty thousand too much I felt our original commitment to a house had been. She forgets about the interest, insurance, and taxes.)

Zig: "Eighteen thousand dollars for thirty years would be six hundred dollars per year." Sugar Baby: "How much is that a month?" Zig: "That would be fifty dollars a month." Sugar Baby: "How much is that a day?" Zig: "Now, come on, Sweetheart, your arithmetic is just as good as mine. It comes to about a dollar and seventy cents a day, but why do you ask all these questions?" Sugar Baby: "Honey, could I ask you one more question?"

Somehow I sensed as she stood there, all five feet, one and a half inches of her, with a twinkle in her eye and a "Look out, Honey," grin on her face, that I was in the process of being had. But there was nothing I could do about it.

Zig: "Why, sure." Sugar Baby: "Honey, would you give another dollar and seventy cents a day to have a *happy* wife—instead of 'just' a wife?" Guess where we live?

The story demonstrates a lot of points, techniques, and psychology. First, I knew what that Redhead was doing to me, but there was nothing I could do about it short of being obnoxious. Like the vast majority of the people you will be dealing with in a sales situation, I wasn't about to treat that Redhead in any such way. Really good technique, in the hands of a good person (you can't be one kind of person and another kind of salesperson), is almost irresistible.

Translate—to Your Situation

The "1902" Close

I tell the story—which is a true story—because I want you to do a lot of things. First, I want you to translate this story to your specific situation. I call the procedure the Redhead used on me the "1902" Close, because in 1902 a man named Frederick Sheldon described this close in his book. The Redhead had learned that close by sitting in on some of my sales training classes. When she heard that "1902" Close, she took it and applied it directly to her own situation and need.

Don't "Hear" Everything

The second lesson in the story is the fact that for some weird reason the Redhead developed a hearing problem which I had never noticed before. I kept saying, "Too much money, can't afford it, not interested, can't afford it, not interested." To this day I don't think she heard a word I said. She had already decided she wanted *that* house and she wasn't going to listen to any negative talk about not getting it. I believe *most salespeople need to be a little hard of hearing when the prospect says he's not interested.*

Think about it this way. When the prospect says, "too high," or "not interested," he is merely saying or implying that he is not going to give you his "big" stack of money for your "little" stack of benefits. In those cases, be like my Redhead and become a little "hard of hearing."

Another factor which parallels this line of thinking is the fact that not once did that Redhead become defensive, argumentative, or antagonistic. All the way through the presentation she was lovingly and enthusiastically optimistic that she was going to make the sale. She never argued when I kept talking about money and that's good, because arguments often create antagonisms and it's difficult to antagonize and positively influence at the same time.

The "Affordable" Close

Number three. My Redhead is an optimist and knows that I am also an optimist. She was confident I could make a bigger payment by getting another speaking engagement or making another sale. You, too, need to be optimistic that your prospect can handle the purchase. It is an absolute fact that *the salesman's expectancy has a direct bearing on the prospect's decision* in many, many cases. *Expect* a sale on every interview. (More on this later.)

Number four. She asked me a lot of questions and those questions led me to the obvious decision that not only *could* we get the house but we *should* get it. *You* can sell more by *asking* than telling. That's the Socratic (after Socrates) Method and it's used by doctors, lawyers, accountants, detectives, and *successful* people from all walks of life.

Her Objective Was Clear

Number five. The Redhead clearly understood that she needed to make an eighteen-thousand-dollar sale. Before she went house-hunting she had already "sold" the price we could pay. She had even "sold" the idea of going an additional twenty thousand dollars. As a super saleslady she knew there was zero need to discuss what had already been decided.

The issue was clear. She had to make an eighteen-thousand-dollar sale. If you are in real estate and the prospect tells you he can go one hundred and forty thousand dollars for a house, then as a practical matter you have just gotten an order for $140,000. Your "selling" takes place only in the sense that you have to "sell" the prospect on a particular house in a particular location and then you have to "sell" the owner on accepting your buyer's offer, which is almost always lower than the asking price.

Your major selling takes place when you find what the buyer wants and needs, but at a price tag of $170,000 instead of the $140,000 which your prospect says is his maximum price. If you clearly understand that you need to make a $30,000 sale and not a $170,000 sale, your task will be much easier. Actually, your prospect "bought" $140,000, and you had little or nothing to do with it. His *needs* made the purchase from you or someone else mandatory.

The same thinking needs to be applied to any product on the market. If your prospect wants to invest X dollars but his needs come to X-*plus* dollars, then your real sale is the amount beyond what the prospect had already committed, in his own mind, to invest.

As I say, the Redhead had a sales job now of selling just the eighteen thousand dollars. She knew that if we talked about the eighteen thousand dollars *plus* the twenty thousand dollars *plus* the original price *plus* the taxes, insurance, and interest, I would get financial indigestion. With this in mind, she took the *extra* amount, the eighteen thousand dollars, and broke it into such small units that it wouldn't even require a financial Pepto-Bismol. The late sales trainer J. Douglas Edwards called this the "reduction to the ridiculous."

She knew that within reason I would get her just about anything she really wanted and she also knew that I was optimistically confident I could work harder, sell more, or secure another speaking engagement to pay for the house. Finally, that Redhead had worked with our budget long enough to know that regardless of how often you're paid or how you're paid, you spend money on a daily basis in order to live. She simply broke it down on a per-day basis, using figures she knew I could understand and feel confident I could handle. *She did not let the* why *we should buy serve as a stumbling block to the* how *we could buy it.* Point: Break it down into small amounts so your prospects can afford it. Make it *easy* for them to buy.

Know Something About Your Prospects

Number six, you cannot get to know all of your prospects as well as the Redhead knew hers, but you should get as much advance information as is humanly possible. She also knew a great deal about what I wanted. She knew, for example, that as a child one day in a fit of anger I had said I was going to build a swimming pool, a big one. Here are the circumstances.

As a boy in Yazoo City, Mississippi, I was invited one day to go swimming with a buddy at the country club, which had the only swimming pool in town. I rode my bicycle to the club on that hot summer day, and since I had my bathing suit on I was ready to swim. My buddy didn't show. That was more temptation than I could deal with, so into the pool I went. One of the club members was walking by the pool as he was playing a round of golf. He saw me and knew I wasn't a member so he promptly threw me out of the pool. He "invited" me to come down to his office the next day and talk about it. I'd never been so frightened in my life. I was afraid to go and more afraid not to go. I honestly thought I was going to go to jail for my "crime."

He was pretty hard on me. As a matter of fact, I left his office in tears. That day I made a strong statement as children will sometimes do. I declared then and there, "One of these days I'm going to build a swimming pool bigger than the one they've got at the country club in Yazoo City, Mississippi."

I said this in a moment of anger and I didn't really believe it. Later on in life, however, when things started happening to me in a beautiful way and my career took off, the dream was reborn and in 1969 we built a swimming pool in our backyard which is exactly one foot longer than that old original pool at the country club in Yazoo City.

What I'm suggesting is basic. Learn as much as you can about your prospect and capitalize on that information. Learn how to use voice inflections, which we will thoroughly cover throughout *Secrets*. Break the price into small segments. Optimistically sell, and be hard of hearing. Ask questions to identify the problem and lead the prospect to the decision. Find out what he needs to solve his problem, and show him how he can solve his problem with your product.

Three Things the House Didn't Have

The seventh lesson in the sales story is this. When we moved from Columbia, South Carolina, to Dallas, one of the things I shared with that Redhead was the fact that when we bought our next house she could make most of the choices as far as style, location, materials, and the "little extras" which would personalize "our" home. However, I did want to have three things in that house and she could have everything else. First of all, I wanted that arrow-shaped swimming pool which I've mentioned already. Second, I wanted a small office so I could write the book I had been talking about but doing nothing about. And third, I wanted a circle drive.

When we bought our house it had a lot of beautiful features, but there were three things the house did not have. Now, my reading friend, you know what three things were missing. However, the "saleslady," that Redhead, carefully pointed out where we could build the swimming pool, exactly where the office was going to be built, and the exact path for the circle drive.

This truly is a major point. Many times a prospect will ask you for something very specific. Now if you have exactly what he wants, then you should fill that bill. But please remember that *many people do not know what they want because they do not know what is available.* In short, if you cannot fill the bill exactly, do not assume they are so adamant they would not even consider anything else.

From time to time, all of us have gone shopping for a specific item, couldn't find it, and ended up buying something else which we really enjoy much more. Just because the house did not contain those items I wanted did not eliminate the house as a good one to buy. The Redhead simply pointed out that we could add those things later and we could build them exactly like we wanted them and not how some builder might have built them. This really translates into using your imagination to help the prospect get what he wants. Remember:

> *You can get everything in life you want if you will just help enough other people get what they want.*

IMPORTANT

VERY IMPORTANT

The title of this book clearly indicates that it is a book on selling for salespeople. The first chapter even more clearly *demonstrates* that it is a book on persuasion and will be extremely helpful to *anyone* who has to persuade others to take action of any kind (mothers, teachers, dentists, husbands, ministers, coaches, policemen, salesmen—anyone).

In order to most effectively use this book, you need to do exactly what the Redhead did to me. You need to take my words and the product I'm talking about and translate them into your own specific sales situation. This way you have the best of both our worlds—the information I've managed to accumulate from personal experience and considerable research, combined with the knowledge you have acquired which is specifically applicable to your life, your product, your prospects, and your sales situation.

You need—no, you must have—a pen and a stenographer's pad in order to get the maximum benefit from this book. It's easy reading because it contains so many examples, illustrations, and stories. It is not a workbook, but it is a working-book, designed to get you involved in a learning—and not just a reading—process.

Since *Secrets* is written in narrative style, complete with considerable dialogue and humor, the reading will be easy and pleasant. In addition, this manuscript contains over 700 questions and well over 250 sales procedures, techniques, and closes wrapped up in nearly 100 stories, analogies, and anecdotes.

The Book You Never Finish

The first time you read *Secrets*, I encourage you to move through the book quickly, with your pen in hand, underlining or highlighting the things that really "grab" you. Don't analyze, but simply read as quickly as you can so you will get the complete message and the overall view of the book.

For your second reading, you're going to need the stenographer's pad, which is approximately the same size as the book and will be easy for you to keep handy, even if you should be on the road. I encourage you to entitle your notebook the same as I have entitled this book, except substitute your name for mine. Then it becomes *your Secrets of Closing the Sale.*

On the second reading, you will want to stop and commit to writing the ideas generated by *Secrets* which you can specifically use in your own sales career or personal life. The second reading of this book will be lengthy and involved. Your objective is not to see how quickly you can *get out* of the book, but *what* you can *get out* of the book.

The third reading will give you an even broader perspective of the book, and you will add more pages and ideas to your own companion book, *Secrets of Closing the Sale.* Again, this reading will take considerable time to complete; but remember, you are *investing* time, not spending it. Incidentally, I especially encourage you to read this book *early* in the morning, *late* at night, and on weekends. *Do not take the day off from your selling to read.* (The book will stick around—the prospect might not!)

The fourth reading will make you even more aware of the 700-plus questions in *Secrets.* As I wrote *Secrets*—the dialogue and procedures frequently reflecting my own experience in selling—the questions came quite naturally. As I reflected on the manuscript, it was obvious to me that the question approach to selling is a way of life for me. One other advantage in reading the book several times is that this procedure, without your even being aware of it, will become an integral part of you. Your effectiveness will be greatly enhanced.

Even after the fourth reading you will want to keep *Secrets* handy as a reference. Many of the questions, procedures, techniques, and closes will need to be read repeatedly so you can commit them to memory and make them an integral part of your life.

Now, let's get on with the book.

2

MAKING "KING" CUSTOMER THE WINNER

Hold the Phone!

STOP: Don't read another word unless you have that pen I discussed at the beginning. Throughout *Secrets* you and I are going to be involved in a learning-motivational experience that will enable you to sell more of whatever you sell. You need that pen from "hello" to "good-bye," because you will need to circle, underline, mark, and make notes on virtually every page of this book, as well as in the notebook you need for the second reading. *Secrets of Closing the Sale* is an easy, fun-to-read book, but my major objective as the author is not to inform or to entertain but to get you heavily involved in a growth-and-action process that will be stimulating and financially rewarding.

If you have that pen handy, we'll get started because you are ready to grow. If you don't have the pen ready to use, I need to ask you a question. Did you buy the book because you were curious, knew the author, were looking for a miracle, or because you wanted to further your career by effectively making more sales or persuading others to take specific action?

If it was the last—and I surely hope it was—you're in luck, because this book contains *proven* methods and techniques which have worked for others and will work for you *IF* you get involved in the learning and *doing* process. That's a big *if*, but it will play the key role in whether you write "sold" or "missed" on many of your future interviews.

It's Not Easy

It takes work to become a professional salesperson or to substantially improve your closing percentage while building customers instead of just making sales. Work—a lot of work—is required if you are going to fully develop your sales potential.

21

This goes far beyond just reading the script, but to put your mind at least partially at ease, let me assure you that one trip through these pages will definitely have considerable value. You will pick up thoughts, ideas, and feelings which will reinforce many things you already feel and believe, but have not articulated. You will learn power phrases and specific words which will make what you are already using even more effective. You will be motivated to do more and use more of what you already have and *your sales will probably improve before you finish the first reading.* You will pick up new psychological insights which will help you to understand *why* prospects "respond" or "react" as they do to certain techniques and procedures.

This is especially important because if you know how to do something—and then do it—you will always have a job. But if you know *why* it is done you will be the boss or, in this case, the sales leader.

Of even more importance, you will pick up attitudes and feelings about selling and the sales profession which will make an immediate difference in your productivity *and* your long-term career in the most exciting profession (my opinion and that of most *truly* successful salespeople) in America.

Convince—Then Persuade

Perhaps the most frustrating experience a salesperson has is to gain agreement from the customer that yes, the product is good; yes, it will save money; yes, he does need it; yes, he would like to have it; yes, he really could afford the payments; but no, he is not going to buy. Many times this indicates that the prospect has been convinced of the merits—or at least appears to be convinced and "sold"—but he has not been *persuaded* to take action.

Aristotle is considered one of the most brilliant thinkers of all time, but he had one belief which was completely in error. He believed if two different weights of the same material were dropped from the same height they would fall at different rates of speed. This belief was taught at the University of Pisa. Years later Galileo entered the picture, challenged this theory, and started saying the opposite. The other professors and students were astonished that Galileo would dare refute what the great Aristotle had taught. They challenged him to prove his position.

Galileo did so by going to the top of the Leaning Tower of Pisa with two different weights of the same material. He dropped them together and they hit the ground at precisely the same time. He *convinced* the students and professors beyond any doubt that he was right and Aristotle was wrong. But guess what they kept teaching at the University of Pisa?

You're right. They continued to teach Aristotle's theory. Galileo had *convinced* them but he had not *persuaded* them. The questions are: (a) How do you persuade people and (b) what is persuasion? The answers are: (a) You don't "tell" them, you "ask" them and (b) persuasion derives from the French, "to give *good* advice in advance." In the following example I will specifically demonstrate the question-asking technique. Throughout *Secrets* we explore and demonstrate the role the sales professional plays in the process of becoming a "counselor" or assistant buyer who truly gives "good advice in advance." In the process of touching all the sales bases, as I indicated earlier, you will encounter over 700 questions. Now, the example.

The "Persuasion" Close

These questions are ridiculously simple—but it is critical that you answer them because this will clarify your thinking and set the tone for the entire book. What you answer will bear directly on your attitude and hence your success as a salesperson. Please use that pen, which you now have in your hand, and answer these simple questions *one at a time:*

Question:	Do you sell a pretty good product?	Yes_____	No_____
Question:	Do you sell an exceptionally good product?	Yes_____	No_____
Question:	Do you sell a product that solves a problem or problems?	Yes_____	No_____
Question:	Do you feel you deserve a profit when you sell a product that solves a problem?	Yes_____	No_____
Question:	Do you feel you deserve two profits when you sell two products that solve two problems?	Yes_____	No_____

Chances are excellent you answered yes to all of these questions. What you're really saying is you honestly feel that the more problems you solve, the more profit you deserve. That's the way it should be.

Question:	Have you been selling for as long as one year?	Yes_____	No_____

Question: If yes, do you still have all the
             money you earned in your
             last twelve months as a
             salesperson?   Yes_____ No_____

I think it would be safe to say your answer to that last question is no.

Question: Do you have customers to
             whom you sold over a year
             ago who are still using and
             enjoying the benefits of
             what you sold to them at
             that time?   Yes_____ No_____

If you answered yes, and in most cases you probably did, then the next
question is, who was the *biggest* winner, you or the customer _____?
Now if the customer is the biggest winner, who ought to say thank you
to whom at the conclusion of the transaction?

Chances are fairly good that you spent all or most of your profit or
commission shortly after you made the sale (if not before). Chances are
also excellent that your prospect or customer used and benefited from
what you sold him for weeks, months, or maybe even years. If you are
selling a legitimate product that solves a problem and you sell it at a fair
price, the customer makes the best deal.

Question: Is the sales process something
             you do *to* somebody or
             something you do *for* some-
             body?   Yes_____ No_____

[This is one of the most important and profound issues I will explore in
Secrets. Your answer reveals *everything* about where your heart and interests lie in the world of selling.]

If, in your heart, you really feel the sales process is something you do
to the prospect, then you are a manipulator. The dictionary defines
manipulate: "To control the action of, by management; also, to manage
artfully or fraudulently. Manipulation: Skillful or dexterous management, sometimes for purpose of fraud, state of being manipulated." I'll
be the first to admit that manipulators make sales, but in my thirty-six
years in the profession I have never known even one manipulator who
was *successful* in the profession. (As you read *Secrets* you will discover
my definition of *success*.)

If, in your heart, you feel the sales process is something you do *for* the prospect, then this book could represent a significant addition to your sales library. Your benefits will be considerable because you are truly interested in benefiting others.

The world of selling is often the exact opposite of the world of athletics. I fought in the ring for two years. As a matter of fact, the only reason I quit was my hands—the referee kept stepping on them! One of the first things the coach taught me when I got into the ring was, "Zig, find the opponent's weakness and exploit it, find out where his defenses are weak and capitalize on them, take advantage of him." In football, the quarterback is told to probe, to find out where the other team is weak and exploit that weakness. In athletic competition you look for the opponent's weakness so you can exploit it.

In the world of selling you look for the opponent's (prospect's) weakness (need) so you can *strengthen* it by selling him your goods or services. Yes, *the sales process is something we do* for *the prospect and not to the prospect.* Conclusion: If we are truly professional we will seek every legitimate means for persuading the prospect to take action for *his* benefit.

The Winner and Still Champion—"King" Customer

I used the preceding series of questions to establish in your mind that the customer really is the one who benefits the most. (I'm obviously assuming the product is legitimate, is fairly priced, and will perform as expected.) Now let's reverse that process and assume that, instead of asking you those questions, I had simply said to you, "Let's face it, my selling friend. As everybody knows, the customer is the big winner." Many of you would have agreed, but an extremely high percentage of you would have facetiously thought, "Yeah, they are the big winners, all right, but then I didn't do too badly myself!" You would probably have this thought with a satisfied and mildly sarcastic chuckle under your breath.

The method I used, however, is simple and clear because I did not attempt to "tell" or "sell" you anything. If I had, you might have resisted. By my asking you questions, there's no way you can get unhappy with me about the answers *you* give to those questions.

Now let's translate this to your situation with your customers. When you ask or use this particular procedure, the customer is actually persuading himself. There is no resentment and therefore the chance of his taking action—which is your objective—is much higher. Use the question technique. It works.

Here's Why They Won't—or Don't—Buy

There are five basic reasons people will not buy from you. These are: no need, no money, no hurry, no desire, and no trust. Since *any* "reason" or "excuse" for not buying will cost you a sale—and will cost the prospect the benefits he would accrue from the purchase—the missed sale is a loss for both buyer and seller.

Now, because a missed sale is expensive to both buyer and seller, let's look carefully at each reason a prospect does not buy from you. By identifying and then effectively dealing with each of them, our sales effectiveness and hence our service to our prospects will increase. This translates into more profit for you because it means benefits to more people.

One of the five reasons prospects will not buy from you is *they do not feel they need what you are selling.*

If everybody belonged to the old, old, *old* school of thought which says, "We should buy only what we need," then you and all other salespeople would be in serious trouble. I say this because most people have considerably more of everything than they "need." (How many clothes, how much floor space, how much car, how many TVs, how much food do you *need?*) Fortunately for us, and in most cases for the prospect, we buy what we want or desire. I deal with desire or lack of it as the fourth reason the prospect will not buy from you.

Now let's get back to the question of need and what it really means when the prospect says no. In many cases, if not most, the prospect says no because he doesn't know enough to say yes. More on this later.

The second reason most people do not buy is they don't have any money (and there are people who really don't have any—or enough—money). You can use all the techniques in the world and you still are not going to manufacture the money itself. Having made that observation, let me now state that I do not want to disillusion anyone, especially if you are new in the world of selling. When it comes to money, some people will actually *lie* to you when they say they don't have any—or enough—to buy what you are selling. (I'll bet you have a suspicion you've already met some of those folks.)

The "Want It" Close

This little story verifies that point. Many years ago, when I first entered the world of selling, I was calling on a Funderburk family in Lancaster County, South Carolina. They raised chickens and sold eggs. I demonstrated a set of cookware for them and several of their friends. It was a complete demonstration and, since it was in their home, I had a chance to look through their cabinets and see the amount of cookware they did *not* have. Their need for a good set of cookware was obvious. I tried for two solid hours to close the sale, but never came close. Mrs. Funderburk kept saying, "No money, too expensive, can't afford it!" She sounded like a broken record!

Then somehow, somewhere, somebody said something about fine china. I don't know if it was Mrs. Funderburk or me. At the mention of fine china, Mrs. Funderburk's eyes lit up like the proverbial Christmas tree and the following dialogue took place.

Mrs. Funderburk: "Do you have fine china?" Zig (smiling): "We just happen to have the finest china in the whole world!" (At least that's the way I saw it!) Mrs. Funderburk: "Do you have any with you?" Zig (getting up to make a mad dash to the car): "You're in luck!"

A few minutes later I was leaving the Funderburk home with an order for china which involved substantially more dollars than the cookware which I had been trying to sell. Actually, no "selling" was involved. It was just a question of choosing the china pattern she preferred and working out the financial arrangements.

Question: If she bought the china which cost more than the cookware which was "too expensive" and which she "couldn't afford," was she lying when she said she didn't have the money? Interesting question, isn't it? Actually, the answer is yes, she was lying—and I'm one of those purists who believes that a lie is a lie is a lie.

However, the purpose of this book is to help you persuade more people to take action in their own best interests, so let's move over to the customer's side of the table where we can think her thoughts, feel her feelings, and become *an assistant buyer.* (This is important whether you sell china, cars, computers, or anything else.)

When Mrs. Funderburk was saying she had no money and couldn't afford the cookware, she was completing the sentence to herself in this manner: "I don't have any money for that cookware because I *don't want* the set of cookware." Thus she rationalized that she was actually "telling the truth," even though she was telling part of it so quietly no one else could hear it!

The key in situations like this is probing to uncover the real reason she was not buying the cookware. In this case the reason for not buying was no *desire* for ownership and not a shortage of money. I deal with this probing technique throughout this book. Mrs. Funderburk bought the china because (1) she *really* wanted it; (2) she trusted me as a person; (3)

I was courteously persistent in my role as probing assistant buyer and, in the process, she revealed her desire to own fine china and not the cookware.

People Buy What They Want

The minute she saw that beautiful china she said (to herself), *I've got money for that set of china because I* want *that set of china.* Realistically, she desperately needed the cookware and would have used it daily for life. She probably used that china only a few times each year, if that often. BUT SHE *WANTED* THAT CHINA. Critical sales point:

> *People buy what they want when they want it more than they want the money it costs.*

Let me sum it up as we explore the best way to build a sales career. People are going to buy, in most cases, what they really *want*—not necessarily what they need. It is your opportunity *and* responsibility to sell the legitimate benefits of your goods and services in a legitimate manner so your prospect will *want* to buy from you, again and again.

It's Possible to Back Up—and Go Forward

The third reason a lot of people don't buy is: They're just not in a hurry. It doesn't matter to them whether they buy today—or next year. In essence, they are often thinking, and sometimes asking, "What do you mean, I've got to buy today? I'm thirty-nine years old. I've lived all of my life without this earth-shattering product. You're not just passing through town, are you?" Or: "I mean, you *are* going to be here, aren't you? You're not closing your doors, are you? What's your hurry?" Realistically, no hurry is one of the toughest objections to deal with. Since getting prospects interested enough to take action *today* is a major objective, I'll deal with this objection throughout the book.

The "Bride" Close

Here's one effective technique for getting people off dead center. Early in my sales career I learned to agree with the prospect and it has been very productive for me. Here's the way it works. If I was making little or no progress after making a substantial effort to persuade the prospect to take action, I would smile and say, "You know, Mr. Prospect, as I review your situation and think back on my own experiences in life, I believe that perhaps you are right. Maybe you should wait. I know in my own life, when my wife and I got married, we made a financial mistake. Getting married costs money and any time you spend money you might well be making a mistake.

"For example, had we waited just twenty more years, we could truly have had a honeymoon to end all honeymoons! When we started our family, it was a mistake. It did—and does—cost money. Had we waited just another ten or fifteen years, we could have given the children so much more. When we bought our first house, that was a mistake. Had we waited another twenty or thirty years, we truly could have built a mansion. The only problem, Mr. Prospect, with waiting until everything is just right before you take action, is that you might wind up like the two people in this poem":

> The bride, white of hair, is stooped over her cane,
> Her footsteps—uncertain—need guiding.
> While down the opposite church aisle with a wan,
>   toothless smile
> The bridegroom in wheelchair comes riding.
> Now who is this elderly couple, thus wed?
> Well, you'll find when you've closely explored it
> That here is that rare, most conservative pair
> Who waited "till they could afford it!"

From *Timid Salesmen Have Skinny Kids*,
by Judge Ziglar

After the poem I would pause and quietly say, "Mr. Prospect, there is seldom a 'perfect' time to do anything and if you wait until all the lights are on green before you head for town, you're going to stay at home the rest of your life! The Chinese say that a journey of a thousand leagues begins with a single step. You and I both know that ownership of this product begins with the decision to own it. Actually, the only decision you need to make at this moment is whether or not you can handle this first payment, and you've already indicated the first payment is no problem. Since you want it, *can you think of any reason you should not, at this moment, treat you and your family as well as you deserve to be treated?*"

The "Alternate of Choice" Close

In direct sales, smile and ask, "Shall I ask the company to ship it as soon as possible, or would two weeks be better?" In store or service-center sales, smile and ask, "Would you like to take it with you, or should we send it out?" (That's "Alternate of Choice." Never give the prospect a choice between something and nothing. Let him choose between something and something else. This close is used under many circumstances, as you will see.)

They Buy—if They Really Want It

Then there's *the fourth reason* a lot of people don't buy from you: *They do not really want what you are selling.* Most salespeople—and that certainly includes me—find it inconceivable that *anybody* would not want what they're selling. And that's good! If you did not feel that way, I can assure you that with few exceptions you would not be a successful salesperson. (If you're selling caskets, we're going to "need" one eventually but most people will not "want" one at that moment.)

Your belief in your product should be so strong it would be impossible for you to understand how anybody could possibly *not* want what you're selling! Realistically, however, some people don't. When we deal with refusal and rejection, you will be given the details on how to handle this so you will understand that the prospect has refused your *offer* and has not rejected you, personally.

The "Now or Never" Close

When I think of desire, I think of an incident which happened to me early in my sales career. I had demonstrated a set of cookware for a widow living in the little town of Elgin, South Carolina. After I finished the demonstration she asked the price. When I told her, she acted as if she were going to have a heart attack! She loudly moaned, "Oh, I could never buy that cookware! Why, Mr. Ziglar," she said, "I'm a widow. I live by myself. Every morning I eat breakfast with my son and his wife who live in the little house next door. I have lunch at the mill and I don't eat any dinner. I work six days a week. The only time I would really use that set of cookware would be on Sunday." She continued, "I'm getting close to retirement age. The only thing I'm going to have is Social Security, which is not much. It would be the most foolish thing in the world for me to even consider buying that set of cookware!"

She gave me every reason in the world for not buying. Then she looked at me and, giving me one of the most beautiful smiles I've ever seen, said, "But you know, Mr. Ziglar, all of my life I've wanted a nice set of pots. And if I don't order now I know I'll never have them. I'll take them!"

She had given me every reason for not buying. Then she bought because she had that lifetime desire to own a really nice, matched set of cookware. Coupled with that desire for ownership was the very real fear that if she didn't "buy now" she would *never* have the cookware, which meant she would have missed or "lost" something very important to her. It's a psychological fact that "the fear of loss is greater than the desire for gain." (I emphasize this fact several times in this book.)

The only part I played in this scenario was to be in the right place at the right time with the right product. In addition, I kept quiet while she was voicing her objections. This made her feel better and helped her "talk herself" into buying.

Until that moment I thought I believed in the set of cookware I was selling. My meeting with this widow who had *dreamed* of ownership made it crystal clear to me how important belief and the desire for ownership really are. How sad it would be for you *and* the prospect to miss a sale because your own belief and desire to help the prospect own your product is not at least as intense and deep as that of the prospect.

They Buy—if They Trust

The fifth reason the prospect does not buy is the most significant. That one is: *no trust.* This one is very difficult to pinpoint and identify with certainty because very few people are going to specifically say, "Look, Friend, you know you're lying to me. Why don't you go ahead and admit it? You know your product won't do all the things you're claiming."

It's highly unlikely that the prospect will *call* you a liar, but if he *thinks* or *feels* you are lying, the results will be the same. He won't buy. In most cases that feeling of distrust is slight—very slight—but if it's there at all, it could—and probably will—cost you the sale.

According to a study conducted by the New York Sales and Marketing Club, 71 percent of the people who buy from you do so because they like you, trust you, and respect you. The word *trust* includes "us." A bond must be formed between you and the prospect before anything significant will be bought or sold.

Point: You've got to establish that trust and respect with your prospects if you expect to be a sales professional. This should be obvious, but for fear it's not, I'll spell it out. Again, *you cannot be one kind of person and another kind of salesperson. You must be consistent in all areas of life if you are going to achieve maximum results in building your sales career.* That's one of the major reasons we deal with the entire person rather than just the *sales*person throughout this book. This is one of the "not-so-little" things that make the buying difference in the prospect's mind.

Leona M. Helmsley, president of Harley and Helmsley Hotels, says it this way: "I don't hire people who have to be told to be nice. I hire nice people."

Based on *overwhelming* evidence (the Connecticut Mutual Life Insurance study, the Harvard University study by Dr. Robert Coles, *Corporate Bigamy,* by Mortimer Feinberg and Richard Dempewolff, The Forum Corporation Report, The Cox Report, and others) the feeling is strong that corporate America will progressively and *quickly* move toward giving preferential treatment to those job applicants who have a solid moral integrity base on which to build a career. That's *any* kind of legitimate career, but especially a sales career.

A persuasive but immoral salesperson can smooth-talk a lot of people into wanting and buying cheap or useless merchandise or services at inflated prices. When that happens, we have not one, not two, but three losers.

The customer loses money and a certain amount of faith in mankind. The salesman loses self-respect and sacrifices any possibility of a truly successful sales career for temporary financial gain. The profession of selling loses prestige and the confidence of the general public when any of its members betray public trust by using professional persuasion skills in the deceitful practice of selling inferior merchandise at inflated prices to gullible, uninformed, or misinformed buyers.

It is my *strong* conviction that your sales career, or for that matter your career in anything, started when you reached the age of accountability. If integrity is as much a part of you as your head, then success in selling will be much easier and faster, and it will be solid and long-lasting. That's the reason I will repeatedly emphasize that *the most important part of the sales process is the salesperson.*

For Clarification: For simplicity and clarity, when *salesperson* is cumbersome I substitute the word *salesman*. "Man" in *salesman* (or *chairman*) means and etymologically has always meant "person." Even in the Sanskrit *man*, the root *man* means "human being." *Homo sapiens* means male and female alike. Unless limited by context, *mankind* means and has always meant "humanity entire." (Was Paul Revere a "minute-person"?) I am indebted to *Reader's Digest* "Word Power" and the Berkley Publishing Group for this information.

3

CREDIBILITY: THE KEY TO A SALES CAREER

Our Tastes and Wants Are Similar

Salespeople the world over are inclined to say, "Yeah, but my situation is different, my prospects are different, my product is different." That *may* be true but there are a tremendous number of similarities and I believe you will convince yourself of that fact by playing a little game and answering these questions as I ask them:

1. Stop reading and hold up three fingers of your writing hand.

2. Think of a flower and don't change your mind.

3. Now think of a piece of furniture.

4. Think of a color.

5. Think of a number between one and ten.

1. The odds are overwhelming that you held up all but your thumb and little finger (96 percent do).

2. Chances are nearly even that you thought of a rose.

3. Chances are one in three that you thought of a chair.

4. With dozens to choose from, chances are over 60 percent that you selected red.

5. Chances are nearly one in four that you thought of seven.

What I am saying is this: There is a tremendous number of similarities in our habits and our way of thinking as people. There are also many similarities in what all our prospects—regardless of what they do or where they live—want out of life. One thrust of this book is to deal with, and take advantage of, those similarities so we can persuade other people to act in their own best interests.

My good friend and fellow sales trainer, John Hammond, teaches salespeople to stand up, put their hands on their shoulders, and sweep away that little sales-killing devil who is whispering in their ears, "Your situation is *different* so this doesn't apply to you."

I encourage you to literally do the same thing. These methods and techniques are not on trial. They work when you *master* them and use them.

The "Law of Averages"

Unlike most sales trainers, I will have very little to say about the "law of averages." Chances are excellent you have been told by your sales manager almost from the beginning that if you see enough people you will make some sales. "Yes, sir," you were told, "the 'law of averages' will take care of you! You make those calls and you will make those sales." I was even told that you could take an order pad, tie it to a dog's tail, and if he ran around town long enough somebody would stop him and sign the order! I'm certain the author of that statement knew it was an exaggeration, but it makes the point that calls produce sales and no calls produce no sales. So far I agree.

Overall, the law of averages is dependable, but on occasion it is misleading. For example, if you put one foot in a bucket of ice water and one foot in a bucket of boiling water, on the average you will not be comfortable. And obviously, you can drown in a lake which has an "average" depth of six inches.

My good friend and colleague, Mike Frank, who has made, by actual count, over 19,000 "warm" calls (negative folks call them "cold" calls), points out that the key to successfully dealing with averages is to (1) make *enough* calls or presentations; (2) be as effective as possible on every call; and (3) make mental and/or written notes on every call as to what you did right, what you could have done better, and how you can make your next presentation even more effective.

The "Next One" Close

I'm convinced that salespeople all over the world—including you—are not interested in the law of averages. *Question:* What would you like to have happen on your next sales interview? You would like to make a sale, wouldn't you? What about the one after that? And the one after that?

The point is clear, isn't it? You don't care a thing about the law of averages! You are just like this old farmer down home. He did not want all the land—but he did want the land that was next to his! You probably don't want *all* the sales, but you do want the next one. This book was written to help you make that next sale, and to make it in such a way that your new customer is willing and even anxious to help you build your sales career.

How do you make the sale to the person you deal with next? In my judgment, you start and finish with trust on most sales you make and on *all* the cliff-hangers (the tough ones). While I will also deal with no need, no money, no hurry, and no desire, trust and credibility will get a considerable amount of space in this book.

Credibility Is Critical

Here's an example of why I said we would be dealing with the kind of person you are as well as the kind of salesperson you are. I don't mean to upset or offend you, but I can teach the average twelve-year-old many of the techniques and procedures you know and use in sales interviews. However, at this stage of the game, he would not be very effective in selling most of the products you sell.

Here's why: Can you imagine a twelve-year-old saying to a prospect, "Now, Mr. and Mrs. Anderson, our market analysis reveals that the average sales price of the homes in this area for the past twelve months is $96,500. However, our projections convince me that the current trend of the market as well as the movement of the city will give us an average increase in value of 11 percent in this area for the next nine years which simply . . ."?

Can you image a twelve-year-old spouting that kind of stuff and having a prospect sitting there saying "Yeah, that's right, young man, I believe I'll buy that $96,500 house you showed me yesterday"? It's not that the prospect wouldn't believe him, but there's an area of credibility which leaves something to be desired, does it not?

Now an even more serious credibility gap exists if you, an adult, are not the right kind of person. In a nutshell, if you have a character defect, if your integrity is deficient, you will miss a lot of the close ones. (The prospect's *fear of loss is greater than his desire for gain,* and most prospects know that *you can't make a good deal with a bad guy.*) Your product or service has to have overwhelming advantages in order for you to successfully sell with a shortage of integrity. Even then the success is temporary, because a company smart enough to acquire product advantage is too smart to throw that advantage away with character-defective salespeople.

What Is the Commission?

Now before we go any further, you need to answer this question. In your trade area, what is your average commission on the sales you *almost* make? Now, when I say "almost," I mean if you *really* get close with the prospect actually having his pen in his hand to sign. What's the commission?

I'll bet it's the same in your area as it is in mine—and that's a big, fat *nothing!* In other words, close doesn't count except in horseshoes and grenades. You've got to *make* the sale regardless of where you live, if you're going to get the commission. Of course, that's fair because when you just barely make the sale, the company is not going to pay you *part* of the commission because you barely made the sale.

Interestingly enough, the word *close,* as in horseshoes, is spelled the same way as "close the sale," but the difference between being "close to the sale" and "closing the sale" is dramatic. Undoubtedly the most frustrating thing a salesperson experiences is to get *so* close to a sale he can taste it, but still end up missing it. Personally, I'd rather have him say, "No, I don't want to buy it and that's final," and almost run me off, than to get close and miss. Getting close can have you climbing the walls if it happens very often.

Psychology (Common Sense) Is Involved

This is not a book on psychology, but I can absolutely guarantee you that you're going to have to know some psychology (or common sense) if you're going to be a truly professional salesperson. One theme which will repeatedly be emphasized is that

you can get everything in life you want if you will just help enough other people get what they want.

Let me emphasize that if you have ever closed even one sale, I'm not going to be teaching you *how* to close. You already know how to do that. What I would like to do is *improve* your percentage of closes to the interviews, presentations, or demonstrations you conduct. You can improve your closing percentage by understanding three very important things. Number one, *good closing comes from good selling and good selling comes from good people.* Question: Are you a "good people"? Number two, this book is designed to help you develop what I call a "closing instinct." Number three, you will learn many specific new closes.

This instinct or intuition, which women have developed to a much finer point than men, is important in selling and can be developed by men and women. When your prospect gives you those buying signals indicating he is on the verge of making that *yes* decision, you need to instinctively move in and become the "assistant buyer" we will be talking about. You need to assist him in solving his problem, which he can do by buying your products, goods or services.

If you could improve your closing percentage by 10 percent (and I'm confident that if your closing percentage is less than 60 percent, 10 percent is a realistic figure), your additional volume would be substantial, or your time for other pursuits would be dramatically increased.

For example, if you are in direct sales and talk with twenty people each week or one thousand people each year, an increase of 10 percent would be one hundred more sales. The additional volume and earnings would make a real difference in your life-style and your cost of doing business would be almost the same. A 10 percent increase in your closing percentage *could* increase your *net* income 20 percent if you currently close 50 percent of your interviews and 100 percent if you are closing only 10 percent of your interviews.

If you improve your effectiveness 10 percent, the other one hundred sales would represent five solid weeks of work without spending any additional time on the job. This could mean that you would have five extra weeks to do the things you enjoy doing or to prepare yourself professionally to move higher up the ladder with your company. It obviously could also mean additional time with your family, which in our society today is needed more and more and is a *must* if you expect to achieve total success.

There's More to It Than Closing

As we talk about closes, I would like to emphasize something which I consider tremendously important. For some reason, the close has gotten to be the "glamour" part of the sales process. Many people labor under the illusion that if they can just master the right closing technique they can dramatically improve their productivity. Obviously, it would help sales to know how to close and to use those techniques. However, I would like to say that *the close is no more, or no less, important than any other phase of the sales process.*

If you don't have a prospect, how are you going to close? If you don't know how to make an appointment, how are you going to close? If your qualification process or presentation is weak, regardless of how many closes you use, in our sophisticated society you're not going to be able to "pressure" many people into buying. If you do, you will have a cancellation, or even worse, a disgruntled customer. So, in reality, the close is *one* part of the process. Since it is the final part, it has been given a disproportionate burden to carry as far as the sale is concerned. My saying this might puzzle you a bit because of the title and structure of this book. But I simply want to keep things in perspective; you must be effective in all phases of the sales process if you're going to build a rewarding sales career.

I have frequently had salespeople say they could get prospects, secure appointments, and tell a good story, but couldn't close the sale. Interpretation: *they can't sell.* As John M. Wilson of National Cash Register fame would say, "There is no such thing as a good salesman who is a poor closer." Another trainer put it this way: "Selling without closing is like lathering without shaving." Friend, if you can't close you can't sell. *Period.*

When you get a *qualified prospect*, you're on first base. When you make the *appointment*, you're on second base. When you make an *effective presentation*, you're on third base. If you go no further, all you've done is *waste* the time of the prospect as well as your own. Until you move to *home plate with the close*, you haven't done anything constructive for anyone.

In selling, as in baseball, you must touch *all* the bases. Even if the batter knocks the ball out of the park, if he doesn't touch every base he won't score.

The close, to continue the analogy, is the score and it is important because it converts *invested* time to *profitable* time. I insist that the close is no more important than any other phase of the sales process; however, without the close the rest of the process is wasted.

Closing is largely an attitude firmly grounded in solid sales technique. That's the reason so much space is given to the psychology involved, as well as your own mental attitude.

"Little" Things Determine Sales Results

In selling it's the little things that make the big difference in making or missing the sale, just as the "little" things make the big difference in all areas of life. Call a girl a kitten and she'll love you. Call her a cat and you've got a problem! Tell your wife she looks like the first day of spring and you score all kinds of points. Tell her she looks like the last day of a long, hard winter and you're in big trouble!

There *is* a difference in *results* when you have those "little" things working *for* you. Things like a good shine on your shoes; the well-pressed suit, skirt, or dress; the neatness of your hair; the way your tie blends and is tied; whether you are neat and clean-shaven; whether the makeup is fresh and properly applied; whether you are overdressed or underdressed; whether you're smiling and courteous, on time, thoughtful and considerate of your prospect's time; whether you are smoking or chewing gum; whether you are organized and practice good human relations with follow-up reminders and thank-you notes—and countless other "little" things that will mean *missing* or *making* the sale.

The list is endless, but in the final analysis, more often than not, one or more of the little things communicate to your prospect that you do believe in what you're doing, that you are interested in serving him, that you do feel you're offering the best product or service at the best price which will do the most for him and his needs. When all of these things are going for you, the question is not "Will you succeed?" but rather "When, and how big will that success be?"

When Should You Close?

Many times salespeople ask the question "When should you close?" From the beginning I've heard salespeople and sales trainers say: "Close early, close often, close late." If you've been selling for three days, chances are good you've also heard this phrase. In most cases that advice is sound, but there is one glaring exception. You can close or attempt to close too early and lose any real chance of making the sale later. Question: What or when is "too early"? Answer: Too early is when you attempt to close before you have established in the prospect's mind significant value for what you are selling.

Prospects, regardless of the product you sell, *buy the benefits to them* which your product offers. In short, when you convince the prospect that your product scratches where he itches, he will buy. When you make him "itch" for ownership, he will "scratch" around until he comes up with the money.

If you try to close before you establish value, you come across as a high-pressure salesman who wants to make the sale and get on to the next prospect without any real regard for what your present prospect's needs and desires might be. You will appear to be interested only in what *you* want and this will build a wall between you and the prospect. You must climb this wall before you make the sale because the prospect sees you in that "high-pressure" light. That's a tough wall to climb, but if you don't climb it, your career sales register will frequently ring up No Sale.

It is perfectly permissible to inform the prospect early in the interview that you are going to ask for an order. Here's a specific example. When I was in the life insurance business we followed a two-appointment sales process. The first appointment involved getting background information on the prospect and exploring his projected future needs as far as retirement and protection for his family were concerned (that's qualifying the prospect). When I went back for the second appointment (with the proposal) I made the complete presentation, established value, and *then* attempted to close the sale.

The "Fair Enough" Close

I started the second interview by taking out the rather elaborate proposal along with a clean sheet of paper. I would hold the blank sheet of paper, look at the prospect, and say, "Mr. Prospect, as you can plainly see, this is a blank sheet of paper. Because there is nothing written on it, there is nothing to understand or to misunderstand. I also have your proposal, which is quite elaborate. This proposal was prepared exclusively for you and frankly, it is quite detailed. However, Mr. Prospect, I would like to make you a promise.

"I'm going to keep the explanation of the proposal just as simple and clear as this blank sheet of paper. If I fail to do so, I will understand it if you are reluctant to make a decision concerning the proposal. For this reason, I promise you that when I finish the explanation, the proposal will be just as clear and just as simple as the blank sheet of paper. At that point, I am going to ask you to make a decision. If you see that it is in your best interests to say yes to the proposal, I'm going to ask you to say yes. If, however, you think it is in your best interests to say no, then I am simply going to ask you to say no. *Is that fair enough, Mr. Prospect?*"

An interesting thing happened on the way to the bank. My closing percentage improved approximately 10 percent, but my volume of business increased even more because I eliminated, or dramatically reduced, the number of repeat calls, giving me more time to see new prospects.

4

COMMONSENSE
SELLING

Prospects Won't "Change" Their Minds

Think about this. When the customer says no, the odds are at least a hundred to one you're never going to be able to get him to change his mind. Now I know what you're thinking, but I'll say it again. When a prospect says no, the odds are at least a hundred to one you're not going to be able to get him to *change* his mind.

At this point you're thinking, "Now, Ziglar, up until now I've felt you were pretty much on target, but we're going to part company on this one because ninety-eight percent of the business I get comes after the prospect says, 'No, no, no, no.'" I don't doubt for a moment that you are right.

The "New Decision" Close

I asked that Redhead of mine (she is a "decided" redhead, meaning that one day she just decided to be a redhead!) to marry me and she said no. I asked her the second time; she said no. Third time, no. Fourth time, no. Fifth time, no. Sixth time, yes. No, she did not change her mind. What she did was very simple. She made a *new* decision based on *new* information which produced a new *feeling*.

Before you can get a prospect to *change* his mind, you've first got to get him to admit he was wrong, that he made a mistake when he said no. Well, friend, let me ask you a question. How many times in the last twelve months have *you* admitted that *you* were wrong, that *you* made a mistake? Another question: If it's tough for you to admit you were wrong, how are you going to get your prospect to admit he was wrong, that he made a mistake? That will be even tougher, won't it?

When a prospect says no, and you say in one form or another, "Awwwww, go ahead, you know you're going to buy it sooner or later, sign here," all you're doing—in the prospect's mind—is trying to high-

43

pressure him into saying he was wrong, that he was foolish to say no to begin with. Getting a prospect to admit his "mistake" borders on the impossible. All you'll do is irritate or antagonize your prospect. That is *not* the way to persuade him to buy from you.

No *Often Means They Don't* Know

No, the prospect won't change his mind, but he will be delighted to make a *new* decision, based on *new* information. Example: "Why didn't you tell me the property was outside the city limits and I won't have to pay city taxes?" He's in the process of making a *new decision*, based on new information. "Why didn't you tell me we could print on both sides of the paper? Even though it's a little more expensive per sheet, it saves us money because we double the usage." He's making a *new decision* based on new information. "You should have explained that this model comes with 'four on the floor.' My teenager would not want any other model." He's making that *new decision* based on new information. Since prospects *will* make new decisions based on new information, *the sales process demands that you try for the close as soon as you have established value or aroused desire for ownership, but before you give all the information.*

If you wait until you've given all the information before you try to close, that would be an even more serious mistake. Some prospects automatically say no on the first attempt to close so that they won't feel they were "easy"—and that they didn't carefully investigate before they bought. More importantly, they fear they will look foolish if they make a fast decision which turns out to be wrong. Many times these prospects who initially say no are actually saying, "Tell me more. Give me more information. Make me feel *secure* that a *yes* decision is the *right* decision. In short, make it easier for me to buy." Your job as a salesperson is to do exactly that—make it easier for the prospect to buy.

How Much You Pay

As a buyer, my reading friend, let me ask you a question. Would you give a salesman one hundred dollars for a product or service which in your mind you knew was worth no more than fifty dollars? Yes _____ No _____ Obviously, the answer is no, isn't it? Second question: When you negotiate with a prospect, do you honestly believe he will give you one hundred dollars for something which he definitely feels is worth only fifty dollars? Yes _____ No _____ Third question. Back to you: Suppose the salesman uses ten of his best, most effective, most powerful sales closes on you. Under those circumstances, would you give him one hundred dollars for a product you positively felt was worth only fifty dollars? Yes ____ No ____ I'll bet the answer is still no. Actually, that's a ridiculous question, isn't it?

Fourth question: Suppose the salesman got emotional about it, sent you on a guilt trip, insisted that you ought to buy to help him, his family, or someone else? Then would you give him a hundred dollars for a product which you knew was worth only fifty dollars? The answer is still no, isn't it?

Why the Prospect Says No

When a prospect says no, he is saying that he either does not have the money—and all the sales expertise in the world will not generate that— or he is saying, "I am not about to give you more for the product or service than I feel the product or service is worth."

The point is simple. When you use pressure on a prospect and persist in your efforts to get him to buy, all you're doing is antagonizing him or turning the prospect off. When a prospect says no, chances are excellent that in his mind he simply does not feel the product—*for him*—is worth the price you're asking.

Now, in most cases *you can't significantly change or lower the price, but you can dramatically change the value.* But to change that value, you have to give additional information about your goods or services. This generally involves trust and good communications between the prospect and salesperson. With this in mind, a truly professional and effective procedure must include showing how you can raise the value of the product in the mind of the prospect. That's one of the purposes of *Secrets of Closing the Sale.*

Closes Should Be Educational

> *Each close you use should be an educational process by which you are able to raise the value of the product or service in the prospect's mind.*

The minute the value equals the price, you have a prospect. Until the value equals or exceeds the price, *in the prospect's mind* you do not have a legitimate prospect. All the technique, persuasion, and pressure are going to be to no avail.

Once the value of the product or service in the prospect's mind exceeds the price, you have a "hot" prospect *whom you still must close.*

Please remember that you still have to deal with the fear factor in the prospect's mind—the fear he will be making a mistake if he goes ahead and says yes, even though he can see that the value of your offer exceeds the price you ask. This is the reason I constantly stress that the salesperson and his personal integrity will be the determining factor in closing many, many sales. What I'm really saying is that if you are the *right* kind of person, selling the *right* product, using the *right* technique on the prospect with the *right* motive, then your chances of selling your product or service are dramatically increased.

Don't Oversell

One real danger we encounter as salespeople is that sometimes in our exuberance in the presentation, or in our frustration, we attempt close after close with no results. The tendency to oversell on these occasions simply overwhelms some of the weaker salespeople whose integrity is suspect or whose interest is primarily in immediate profit rather than in building a long-term sales career.

When you oversell you will invariably lose. The story of the Roman Catholic girl who dated the Southern Baptist boy says it well. After about the fourth date the girl returned home one evening in a highly motivated, ecstatic, lovesick frame of mind. Her mother instantly saw that daughter was "falling fast," so she had a little talk with her.

Mom pointed out in no uncertain terms that the daughter should terminate the relationship, that Catholics didn't marry Baptists and Baptists didn't marry Catholics, so she should stop dating the boy. The girl tearfully explained that she was in love with the boy and couldn't Mom "do something"?

Mom responded to the tears of her daughter and devised a plan. They would "sell" the boy on taking instruction so he could become a good Catholic, which would make the wedding acceptable and desirable. Together Mom and daughter went to work on making that sale. Actually it was easy because the boy was already sold on the "product." He started taking instructions and the date was set, the church was reserved, the invitations were sent out, and the gifts started coming in.

About a week before the wedding the girl came home one night, shedding those crocodile tears, instructing her mother between sobs to call off the wedding, tell the priest, send back the gifts, cancel the church. Finally Mom got a word in and asked, "Well, daughter, what in the world happened? I thought we had sold him on being a good Catholic." To this the girl tearfully responded, "That's the problem, Mom. We have *oversold*. He's going to be a priest!" Lesson: Don't oversell.

Overselling by Omission

In 1974 I completed one of my dreams, which was to have a really nice office at home for my research and writing. Part of my dream included a genuine leather sofa.

I had vivid memories of trips as a small boy in Yazoo City, Mississippi, to Dr. C. L. Wallace's dental office. In his outer office was an old leather sofa. I still recall sitting on that sofa, squeezing the armrest and getting quite a charge out of the "squish." There is nothing that "squishes" quite like real leather, and I wanted that squish in my new office.

The Redhead and I went shopping at a major store in town with an enormous inventory. The salesman pleasantly approached us, we conveyed our wishes, and he led us to the sofa department. When we saw the first leather sofa that appealed to me, I asked the price. He told me, and I was pleasantly shocked because it was only about half as much as I had anticipated. When I expressed my shock and delight that a genuine leather sofa could be bought at that price, the salesman assured me that it was indeed a remarkable buy and that was one of the reasons they sold so many of them.

I sat down on the sofa and leaned back. It felt really good. I squeezed the armrest and the "squish" was there. I stood up and walked around the sofa, admiring it. It was truly beautiful and again I expressed my delight in finding a leather sofa at such a bargain price. Once again the salesman commented that yes, it was a real bargain and a big seller for them. At this point I told the salesman I would take it.

Next I told the salesman we needed a nice coffee table to set in front of the sofa, so we headed for the coffee table department. On the way we passed another leather sofa, very similar to the one I had just agreed to buy. If anything, I liked this one slightly better, so I walked over, looked it over carefully, sat down, leaned back, and was a little undecided as to which one I truly liked the best. So I asked the price. The salesman told me and again I was shocked, because this one was nearly twice the price of the one I had just ordered. I asked the obvious question: "Why does this one cost almost twice as much?" He explained it in one simple sentence: "This one is *all* leather."

Zig: "Well, friend, what is that one I just ordered made of? I was under the impression it was all leather." Salesman: "It *is* all leather—where the human body comes in contact with the sofa. The tops of the cushions, the armrests, and the part you lean back against are all genuine leather. However, underneath the armrest, underneath the sofa, and the entire back of the sofa are naugahyde." He quickly assured me, however, that no one would ever know the difference, pointing out that even I had not detected the difference. He also assured me that the naugahyde would last just as long as the leather and look just as good.

Zig: "Friend, why didn't you tell me to begin with that the one I ordered is not all leather?" Salesman: "I intended to, but somehow the conversation always changed—but I was going to tell you before you left, because I'm not the kind of salesman who would mislead anyone."

Question to you, dear reader: Which one of the sofas do you think I bought, or do you figure I walked out without buying anything? If you figured I walked out without buying anything, you hit the nail on the head. Not only did I not buy anything that day but in the ten years since then I have never been back in the store.

You might reasonably ask: If he had told me the full story to begin with, would I have bought the sofa? The answer is no, I would not have bought the one which was part naugahyde. All my life I wanted a real leather sofa, and I had just completed a beautiful office exactly like I wanted. Under no circumstances would I have compromised on that sofa. Would I have bought the more expensive leather one? Probably not on the *first* visit, because it was quite expensive. However, I would have shopped around and, based on what I found in the marketplace, I *probably* would have bought the more expensive one. At any rate, I can assure you I would have been back in the store long before now looking for other items.

The point is a very simple one: By omission, the salesman lied to me. It was abundantly clear that I thought the first sofa was all leather. When he did not set the record straight, he misled me. When I saw the real leather sofa and expressed interest in it, perhaps he visualized doubling his sale, but greed or dishonesty cost him a substantial immediate sale and eliminated any chance for future sales.

It's a trite statement, but it's more true than trite that honesty is not just the best policy—it's the *only* policy for those salespeople who expect to build a solid sales career.

Lesson: Don't lie or mislead by omission.

Closing Is Not Natural

Of all the skills we acquire, perhaps none is less natural than the skill of the closer. This is especially true for those of us who are part of another generation, and to a degree this is still true today. Almost from birth we have been told not to ask for everything we see or want. As children we were told that asking wasn't nice, and indicated concern only for self. We were conditioned to wait until things were offered.

However, when we entered the world of selling we were repeatedly told to ask for the order, to encourage the prospect to buy. Since the salesperson obviously benefits from the sale, it appeared to be a selfish move on our part. That's one reason I included the persuasion analogy, using Aristotle and Galileo as an example. This example, along with countless others, makes the point that *you are being selfish, or at least unconcerned, when you don't ask for the order because,* as previously stated, *the customer is the biggest winner in an ethical sales transaction.*

Again, closing is a *learned* skill and not a *natural* one. Fortunately, once your thinking is sound and clear on the matter, a high degree of skill can be acquired, provided you're willing to make the effort.

Miss the Sale and You Both Lose

Actually, salespeople are problem solvers. If you've got the solution to the prospect's problem and he doesn't buy from you then he, far more than you, is the loser. Once you've accepted that fact and understand that *selling is an educational process* for the buyer and *closing represents graduate school* for you, your career will move into high gear. Your personal benefits will be greater because your customers are benefiting greatly.

As a salesperson you need to understand that every close you learn and use should give the prospect *a reason to buy, an excuse for buying,* or *information* so that he can intelligently act in his own best interests. Once you understand and accept this premise it helps you to move closing from being *selfish* on your part to being *helpful* to the prospect.

This important—even critical—adjustment in your thinking will enable you to start closing more of the close ones. This is important to your career because a high percentage of sales hinges on a series of minor things. Your attitude toward that customer is not minor, and I can assure you it will make a great deal of difference in the bottom line of your financial statement at the end of the month. If you do not have that ability to transfer your feelings of belief and conviction to the prospect, you are not going to close those close ones, which means you will not reach your full potential.

As my good friend, sales training and motivational expert Cavett Robert, says:

> *"The prospect is persuaded more by the depth of your conviction than he is by the height of your logic."*

Some Commonsense Psychology From a Psychiatrist

In September of 1980, my psychiatrist friend, the late John Kozek of Dunedin, Florida, was working on his home. John had designed his beautiful home and was the architect and contractor. He was up in the cathedral ceiling working and was covered with dust and perspiration and talking to the crew in Greek. In walked a factory representative of a window company. As the man stood on the floor far below, John called a greeting to him in English. "He ignored me, thinking I was 'only a laborer,' " he said. The salesman went over to Maria (Mrs. Kozek) and started to tell her about stained-glass windows, but she told him he would have to talk to her husband. The representative said he would be glad to. She responded that he'd already missed his chance and the salesman looked puzzled. Then Maria pointed up at the scaffold where John was working.

John suggested that I warn all salespeople to "be nice to everyone, because you don't always know who you're talking to." That's good advice from Dr. Kozek.

Cindy Took the Advice

In January of 1983, while making a cosmetics sale in Sakowitz Department Store, Cindy Oates (who just happens to be my daughter) noticed a customer waiting to be served. Normally when a customer shows up at the cosmetics counter, the salesladies immediately converge on him, but this man wasn't the standard Sakowitz customer. He was wearing run-down loafers and the holes in his socks extended well up over his heels. His hair was greasy and his clothes were dirty and literally hung on his bony frame. All in all he looked (to the idle clerks standing nearby) like he didn't "belong" at the cosmetics counter of a ritzy department store—especially at the Erno Laszlo cosmetics counter—so he was ignored. (Somebody forgot that you shouldn't judge a book by its cover!)

Two things prompted Cindy to quickly and courteously move over to the prospect. Number one, she is a gracious lady (that's an unbiased fact) who is truly a professional saleslady committed to giving *everyone* who approaches the counter a chance to get what he wants and needs.

Number two, she noticed that the man had a piece of paper in his hand. To her that meant he was a husband with a list of things he was going to buy for his wife. She was right on the button. The list was short—just three items—but the sale was nearly a hundred dollars. The purchase was completed in a matter of minutes and the man was extremely nice, with gracious manners.

That book's cover (the man's appearance) wasn't too good, but his pocketbook was in excellent shape. In the final segment of this book I talk a lot about the "Assumptive" Close or attitude. For the moment I urge you to *assume* that everyone you approach is a good prospect with a real problem (need) which you can solve. Be nice to them. *All* of them. You've got nothing to lose and a lot to gain.

Selling Is Like Playing Golf

To be most effective in a sales presentation you should lead off with your very best shot, your Sunday punch; the one you feel has the most persuasiveness and the most power. Save your second-best shot for the final effort. Generally speaking, your prospect hears the beginning and the ending, but often does not hear what's in the middle. This procedure helps insure that your prospect is going to remember the two most powerful parts of your presentation. So if you've got to choose what he hears, you certainly want to choose the most powerful material available.

Underneath all of this is the fact that *your prospect is not going to buy cold, hard facts. He is going to buy warm people benefits.* You also want to remember that selling is like playing golf. In golf, if you're going to score well and win, you must make every shot so you will be in position to make the next one. However, you must remember that if you don't make *this* shot (sale) it doesn't make much difference what position you're in because you might not have a chance to make the next one.

If you miss too many sales you're going to be broke and out of business, so first things first. Concentrate on making this sale, but concentrate on making it in such a way that you'll be in position to make the next one. That's career-building selling.

5

VOICE TRAINING
TO CLOSE SALES

Using Cassette Recorders

Beyond any reasonable doubt, if you're going to build your sales career to the fullest, you've got to do something that 95 percent of all salespeople never do. They never *deliberately* train themselves on how to use their voices more effectively. They don't do any work toward developing voice inflection and voice modulation, so this entire chapter is devoted to selling you on the importance of properly utilizing your voice and offering specific suggestions as to how you can train your voice to improve your sales effectiveness.

In order to develop your voice, let's consider the cassette player and why you *must* use it as a cassette *recorder*.

Many people get marvelous usage out of this instrument by listening to what other people have to say. But salespeople, here's good news for you! You've got something to say as well! You need to—no, you *must*—start utilizing a cassette recorder for the training and development of your voice and sales procedures so you can say what you say even more effectively. You should record not only your presentation but the way you handle objections and close the sale. Then you should listen several times to what you have said and the way you said it.

You're going to be amazed to discover that, your effectiveness notwithstanding, much of what you say is superfluous (you talk too much) and you often speak in a monotone. If it is possible to record your sales call in front of a "live" prospect, I encourage you to do so. If this is not possible, you should definitely record your presentation (role-playing with someone else) in a training-room environment. In either event, you will be shocked at the nonanswers you give to questions and objections, and the number of times you heard what the prospect *said* but missed what he was *saying*. You can correct most of this by utilizing your cassette player/recorder.

52

Would You Buy From You?

Record your presentation, listen to it, and then ask yourself: "If I were calling on me and made that presentation, would I be able to persuade me to take action on the offer?" Many times when I talk to people about recording their presentation they say, "Yeah, but Zig, I don't *sound* that way. That person on that recorder, that's not me!" Well, friend, I've got news for you—it *is* you! Admittedly, there will be some distortion, especially if you use an inexpensive recorder with a poor mike, but the distortion is not nearly as much as you think.

The reason for the apparent distortion is simple. To begin with, when you talk and listen to the sound of your own voice, the primary source of sound is coming through vibrations of the bone. When you make a recording and listen to it, the sound comes into your eardrums through the air. So, record your presentation with the confidence that the way you sound to you is the way you sound to your prospects. In order to develop the most effective methods of dealing with your prospects, you *must* know how you sound *to* your prospects. Recording your presentation enables you to do exactly that.

Voice Inflection Changes Meaning

To demonstrate what you can do with your voice, I'm going to take one sentence which has eight words in it and make those eight words mean eight different things. (I'll admit, this is clearer and more dramatic in a cassette recording.) Take the sentence (1) "I did not say he stole the money." That's a simple, factual statement. (2) "*I* did not say he stole the money," implies that it was said, but by someone else. (3) "I *DID NOT* say he stole the money," is a vigorous denial that you said it. (4) "I did not *SAAYY* he stole the money," hints that you might have *implied* it, but you didn't *say* it. (5) "I did not say *HE* stole the money," implies that someone other than the accused stole the money.

You could also make it say, (6) "I did not say he *STOLE* the money." Here you hint that the accused might have "borrowed" the money but didn't actually steal it. (7) "I did not say he stole *THE money*," implies that he might have stolen *some* money but not *THE* money. (8) "I did not say he stole the *MONEY*," suggests that he might have stolen *something*, but certainly not the money. They are the same words, but with an educated change in your voice inflection you can make those eight words say eight different things.

The "Voice Inflection" Close

The exciting thing is the fact that this is a *skill* which you can learn. It's not as easy as it might appear, but in just fifteen minutes a day for ten days you will have mastered the fundamentals. In my judgment, *this is the most important single undeveloped skill you need to concentrate on in your pursuit of professional sales excellence.*

You start to learn voice inflection by taking your cassette recorder and practicing that one sentence. Once you have recorded it the first time, listen and see if you accomplished your objective. If not, try it again and again until you have recorded it exactly as you want. Go through the entire sequence until you can make those eight words say eight different things. Don't be disappointed or discouraged if it takes you two, three, four, or a dozen nights to get it right.

Once you are satisfied that it is right, give it the acid test. Record the eight words with the voice inflection covering the eight different areas. Let your mate or an associate listen and see if they can pick out what you are communicating. Keep practicing until someone else understands clearly what you are saying. Now the groundwork is solidly laid for you to re-record your sales presentation and procedures. Be certain to save the first recording because you will see a definite improvement in the recording—and more importantly, in the sales results.

I will return to voice inflection several times, and later I'll tell you about a cassette recording which is a must for your sales library. I hope and believe that by the time we are finished, the proper use of your voice will be one of the skills you will be committed to acquire.

Remember—you bought this book to become more professional, so if you're serious, you will follow the suggestions we are making. You are not *trying* something. You are using something that has been tried and proven by thousands of people who have learned the technique in seminars or by using our recordings on the subject.

Final thought. Using voice inflection and change of pace helps to hold your prospect's attention. That's important because if he isn't listening he won't get the message and the information necessary to make the *yes* decision. Under these circumstances, he will be compelled to say no and both of you will lose.

Dealing With the Price Objection

Now let's cover one major objection that can be more effectively handled by properly using your voice. This objection is encountered by virtually every salesperson many times during the course of his sales career. All of us encounter, on a regular basis, the prospect who suggests directly or indirectly that the price is a little out of line or that the product is ridiculously and unreasonably overpriced.

One prospect might belligerently and dogmatically say, "THAT PRICE IS RIDICULOUS!" Another prospect might gently, even smilingly, say, "Well, it seems to me that the price is a little [pause] out of line." I've even had folks put it in exquisite colloquial terms: "You folks kinda proud of that stuff you sell, ain'tcha?"

You Justify or He Defends

To the one who is dogmatic and says, "THAT PRICE IS RIDICULOUS!" you repeat, almost verbatim, what he said: "The price [pause] is *ridiculous?*" (Your voice inflection should make it sound like a question.) Inflection is important because in this example you are, as one of my mentors, the late Charlie Cullen, would have said, "audaciously" challenging the prospect. You're creating a situation that forces him to defend his statement instead of you justifying the price. There's quite a difference. One puts you on the defense and the other puts you on the offense. The difference in results is substantial.

It's simple, but not easy. I challenge you to get your cassette recorder, use the same words, and carefully listen to what you've said. Chances are excellent you're going to have to repeat the process a dozen, maybe even twenty times, to get your voice inflection just right. Trouble? Yes. Work? Yes. Worth it? You betcha!

Suppose the prospect says, "It seems to me the price is a little out of line." The first thing you've got to determine is whether the price really is the problem, or is there another issue? You make that determination by asking questions. Sales trainer John Hammond has *successfully* handled thousands of objections by asking: "If there were a way I could show you that the price is more than fair and the product is worth every dime we're asking, would you go ahead and take advantage of our offer today?"

This forces the prospect to make a commitment based on price when his *real* objection is color, size, style, neighborhood, or something else you could and should identify. If this is the situation, his response is going to be, "Well, no, not really." Then the salesman can say, "Then there must be some other reason you are hesitating. Would you mind if I ask what that reason is?" *This is a superb procedure for smoking out the real objection.*

If price *is* the objection you continue in this way. You: "Let me ask you, Mr. Prospect, do you like the product?" Many times he'll respond,

"Yes, I like the product, but it seems to me that the price is . . . a little out of line." You (softly and gently): "Mr. Prospect, wouldn't you agree that it's difficult to pay *too much* for something you *really* like?" (Now the ball is back in his court.)

Many times, if it's a relatively inexpensive item, your prospect might go ahead and invest, since that question which forces him to think could also lead him to make a *yes* decision. In most cases, if it's a high-ticket item, he will probably think for a moment and say, "Well, I do like it. But yes, I think you can pay too much regardless of how much you might like it. I know I wouldn't give you fifty thousand dollars for a Cadillac, even though I might really enjoy having one."

The "Fear of Loss" Close

Now you're dealing with something which is very basic, so let me repeat. *The fear of loss is greater than the desire for gain.* You need to establish in that prospect's mind the fact that he's safe in dealing with you, that he won't lose (either money or "face") by buying from you, but that he will lose (product benefits) if he doesn't buy from you.

One effective way to do this is to say to the prospect, "Mr. Prospect, you're going to be concerned about price one time. That's the day you buy. You're going to be concerned with quality for the life of the product itself. With this in mind, let me urge you to think along these lines: *Wouldn't you agree that it's better to pay a little more than you expected than a little less than you should?* (Wait for answer.) The reason is simple. If you pay a little more than expected, we are talking about pennies. If you pay less than you should and the product won't do the job which you expected it to do, then you will lose everything."

John Ruskin made an astute observation concerning price: "It is unwise to pay too little. When you pay too much, you lose a little money, that is all. When you pay too little, you sometimes lose everything because the thing you bought was incapable of doing what it was bought to do. The common law of business balance prohibits paying a little and getting a lot . . . it can't be done. If you deal with the lowest bidder, it is well to add something for the risk you run, and if you do that then you will have enough to pay for something better." That makes sense, doesn't it?

Wait—They're Not Worthless—Yet

Let's look at an example that cements this point. If you are a woman or have a wife, sister, or mother, you will relate to this. Question: Do you know anyone who has some unused cosmetics at home in a drawer? Yes _____ No _____ (Betcha you said yes!) Chances are excellent the cosmetics are in perfectly good condition—and nothing is really wrong with them—but they've been in the drawer for several months. They are not being used and they are not going to be used, but these cosmetics are not dried out *quite enough* yet to throw away. So what happens? The owner decides to keep them another six months and at that point, since the cosmetics will be totally worthless to anybody, the owner can economically justify throwing them away.

Question: Wouldn't it have been better to have paid a little more than you expected instead of less than you should to get exactly what you wanted and needed? The extra cost would have been measured in pennies. As it is, you've lost every penny you invested in the cosmetics. If you count satisfaction and personal pride (and you ladies know how much better you feel when you're all dolled up!) then you really are getting a bargain when you invest in quality, aren't you?

This Is a Bargain?

I believe it would be safe to say that all of us (and that certainly includes yours truly) have been guilty of buying "bargains" in the past. You saw the big sale advertisement on ladies' shoes. There they were, I. Miller $169 shoes, special, one-time-only, closeout, inventory reduction, supergigantic, colossal, incredible, unbelievable, magnificent, stupendous sale! Only $59.95! Never before in the history of woman has such a bargain been offered!

It's obviously more than a woman can resist. Down you go to the store, slip on those magnificent I. Millers, and while it is true that you wear a 6½B and these are 6AA's, you begin to rationalize. They will stretch as you wear them, and though they are most uncomfortable as you struggle to take those five or six convincing steps in the store, and even though you know they really are too tight, the lure of buying such a bargain, saving over one hundred dollars, just overwhelms you. Besides, they are exactly the right color to go with your new dress and purse. (Logically you *know* you should not buy the wrong size but *emotionally* the lure of such a "bargain" overwhelms you.)

The sale is made. You pay $59.95, and you walk out with a $169 pair of shoes—carrying them, of course. Since they are so beautiful you save them for church on Sunday. As you slip them on and your feet start to scream, your better judgment tells you not to wear them but you determine to tough it out because, after all, they're so beautiful and such a bargain.

So you do tough it out and you do survive the sermon, though you can't remember a word the preacher said. That's the one and only time you wear those shoes. Sixty dollars to wear them one time is a pretty steep price. Question: Wouldn't it have been better to have paid the regular price and gotten your size and worn them for months to come?

Me, Too

As the old saying goes, I know how you feel because I've done exactly the same thing. The suit was regularly priced (several years ago) at $279.95, marked down to just $149.95. Though at the time I wore a 44 Regular and this was a 42 Regular, I felt confident I was "going to lose the weight," and in the meantime I could suffer a little for such a beautiful suit. You can finish the story, can't you? That's right. I wore it one time and the moths got to the suit before I lost the weight.

Yep. It would have been better had I paid a little more than expected instead of a little less than I did. On the former a few dollars would have been invested; on the latter I lost the entire purchase price (one wearing cost me $149.95 *plus* tax!).

The same line of thinking can be applied when you persuade your prospects to have their teeth crowned, buy a nicer suit, a better dress, a more powerful truck, a better-built lawn mower, or whatever you are selling. Just remember that when you are attempting to move that prospect into a better product it *must* be in the prospect's best interests. Otherwise you both will end up losing.

As the late Dick Gardner often said, "Why settle for the 'get by' when in the long run the good costs less?"

The "Cost" Close

Here's a question you ask when your prospect talks about price: "Mr. Prospect, if you could convince yourself [don't *ever* say, 'If *I* could convince you,' because he's not interested in *you* convincing him of *anything*], that the price is more than fair, would you have any objection to going ahead with a *yes* decision today?"

If that question gets a yes answer, then you ask the next question, which is a very significant one. You eyeball the prospect and say, "Mr. Prospect, since you are obviously concerned about price, let me make certain we're communicating. Are you really that interested in price, or is it *cost* you're concerned with?" The odds are great that your prospect is going to respond with, "What do you mean, am I talking about price or cost? What is the difference?"

Seeing Is Believing

You: "Well, Mr. Prospect, let me explain it this way." (Now get your "talking pad"* ready for use. Prospects are inclined to believe what they *see*. If you write it down, not only are they more likely to believe it but chances are great they will understand it better as well.) When I talk about price and cost, here's the example I use. (You should get your own example, one that's appropriate and fits your situation.)

"Mr. Prospect, in 1971 my six-year-old son and I went out to buy a bicycle. We went to the Schwinn Bicycle Shop and were shocked at the $64.95 price tag. Certainly no prudent parent in 1971, when $64.95 represented a lot of money, could justify spending that much money on a bicycle for a six-year-old boy.

"We headed for the discount store. 'After all,' I reasoned, 'he's just going to tear it up learning how to ride, and a cheaper bicycle will be good enough for that.' We invested $34.95 in a bicycle. Much better—price-wise.

"About six weeks later we went back to get a new pair of handlebars. The cost normally would have been $4.50, but the bike was still in warranty so it didn't cost us anything. Sixty days later, when we went back for more handlebars, the bicycle was no longer in warranty so we had to invest the $4.50. About six weeks later we were back in the bicycle shop because the entire sprocket arrangement had completely collapsed. I've forgotten the exact cost, but it came to $15 and change. A few weeks later we were back in the shop because the wheel bearings were shot, and they wanted another 5 or 6 dollars. At that point I decided there was no way out so I threw in the towel. Then we bought the Schwinn bicycle at $64.95."

"Cheap" Costs More

"Now, let's look at the difference between price and cost. The price of the 'economy' bicycle was $34.95. The price of the Schwinn bicycle was $64.95. Now let's look at cost. The cost of the economy bicycle was $34.95 plus $4.50 plus $15.00 for a total of $54.45. My son rode that bicycle for six months—not counting the down time.

"The cost of the Schwinn bicycle was $64.95 and he rode it for ten years. It 'cost' us $9 *a month* for my son to ride the 'economy' bicycle. It 'cost' us $6.50 *a year* for him to ride the Schwinn—and it's still a good

---

* A yellow or white pad to do your figuring. This procedure clarifies the offer and makes it more believable and understandable. Many people don't buy because they don't *understand*.

bicycle. The only money we've had to spend on it has been for a couple of tires and that has nothing to do with the durability or the quality of the bicycle."

Note: As you talk you diagram it on your talking pad. This one looks like this:

PRICE	PRICE
ECONOMY BIKE $34.95	SCHWINN BIKE $64.95
COST	COST
ECONOMY BIKE $34.95	SCHWINN BIKE $64.95
HANDLEBARS 4.50	NO ADDITIONAL COST
SPROCKET 15.00	FOR 10 YEARS
$54.45	$64.95
$54.45 ÷ 6 MONTHS	$64.95 ÷ 10 YEARS
= $9.00 PER MONTH	= $6.50 PER YEAR
TO RIDE ECONOMY BIKE	TO RIDE SCHWINN BIKE

"Now, Mr. Prospect, let me point this out. The *price* of the economy bicycle was considerably less ($34.95 vs. $64.95), but the *cost* difference was even more ($9.00 a month vs. $6.50 a year). So, Mr. Prospect, may I ask you again, is it price you're concerned with or is it cost? Price is a one-time thing; cost is something you are going to be concerned about for as long as you've got the product. [*If* this next sentence is true, you can and should close with it.] Some companies can beat us on price, but Mr. Prospect, when it comes to cost, we win that battle. Since you are obviously cost-conscious, can you think of any reason you shouldn't immediately start enjoying the lowest possible cost?"

P.S. It goes without saying that you will use an example involving your own product to make this point.

Does This Technique Work?

Bill Egan, the Buick-Datsun dealer in Bradley, Illinois, says yes.

Recently, after returning from a business meeting, Bill was told by his management team that an elderly couple was in a closing office and had been for some time. This was their third trip into the dealership, so they were definitely interested in buying, but they were still hesitating and the salesman was making no progress. Two other salespeople had also tried for the close with no results. Bill had been listening on his cassette recorder to this particular close on price and cost, so he decided to give it a try himself. The following dialogue took place after the introduction and small talk.

Bill: "It will take $9,600 for the exchange." Couple: "The price is too high." (In this particular case the woman was the one who made the statement.) Bill (lowering his voice and adding inflection so the statement became a question): "Ma'am, the price is too high?" Lady: "Yes, the price is too high." Bill: "Let me ask you, Ma'am, are you talking about price or cost?" Husband and wife both looked at Bill with blank stares. Lady: "What do you mean?" (At this point Bill says he knew he had at least made some progress.)

Bill: "Ma'am, do you mind if I tell you a story to emphasize the point?" Lady: "No. Go right ahead." Bill: "Several months ago, I contracted for a large amount of asphalt to be put down on my property. While making the preliminary investigation, just as you are doing now, I wanted to make certain I got the best buy for my money. I believe all of us want that, wouldn't you agree?" (The lady agreed.) Bill continued: "I don't know much about asphalt, blacktop, and construction, but I had learned that the number of inches of gravel you put underneath as a base determines how much the price is going to be. Like a lot of other people, I went with the best *price*.

"To make a long story short, it wasn't two months before I started noticing cracks and upheavals in the surface of the asphalt. Walking around the store I discovered it was happening everywhere. In about a year the asphalt was breaking up and I spent an additional six thousand dollars repairing the job I had originally paid for. Here's my point, Ma'am. *Price* is a one-time thing. *Cost* can go on forever and ever, as long as you have the particular product. Question: Wouldn't it be better to pay a fair price one time and be through with it than to go on paying those little costs you get from a product which is probably not as good as what you're looking at right now?"

At this point Bill paused. The husband looked at her as she looked at him. Without further ado she said, "I'll take it." Bill continues by saying that not only did he close the sale but it was for a product that was several hundred dollars more than she was going to pay for another car somewhere else. The only thing Bill had done was convince her of the difference between price and cost.

Several factors are involved in this sale. Number one, the couple obviously wanted this particular car, or they would not have made the third trip into the dealership. Number two, Bill used voice inflection, a solid business reputation, and a talking pad in the transaction. Number three, he used a simple analogy to make his point and hold the prospect's interest. Number four, he asked a question which led the prospects to come to their own conclusion. Another story with a happy ending because the right man was using the right techniques, selling the right product under the right circumstances to people who were legitimate prospects.

The next point is very simple. Wouldn't it have been doubly unfortunate for everyone concerned had this couple, who obviously wanted the car, and Bill Egan, who obviously wanted the sale, been unable to get together because of the absence of sales skills and persuasion?

The Price Is Too High

In the last segment of *Secrets*, I deal at length with the statement that no salesman is "normal" if he is really outstanding. I now extend that to include the buyers, because they are not "normal" either, at the time they get ready to sign the agreement. There is demonstrable proof that when a person signs an order for a significant amount of money, in almost every case there is a measurable increase in his pulse rate. A change is taking place and he's going through a process that affects him emotionally. When we become completely aware of the extent of the effect, we will be able to more empathetically deal with the prospect and consequently be more effective as salespeople.

In dealing with a price objection, you must remember that many people will automatically say the price is too high, whether they feel that way or not. This is a method many people use because they think that by using it they'll be able to negotiate a better price.

Here is yet another approach to handling the "price is too high" objection: "I'm glad you're concerned about price, Mr. Prospect, because that's one of our most attractive advantages. Would you agree that, as a practical matter, a product is worth what it can do for you and not what you have to pay for it?" (Wait for answer.) "Starting with that premise, let's take a look at what our product will do for you."

Objection: The price is too high. You: "Mr. Prospect, our company had to make a choice between building our product as cheaply as possible and selling it as a get-by product, or building quality into the product for service, durability, and your long-lasting enjoyment. In short, for long-range value and benefit. With this decision facing us, we tried to put ourselves in your shoes. We felt you would prefer to deal with a company that puts everything possible into its product to make it the best and most useful, rather than a company that uses cheap materials and cheap labor to turn out a get-by product. Most people, Mr. Prospect, and I'll bet that includes you, clearly understand that good things are not cheap and cheap things are seldom good. You do want something you can depend on for good service over the long haul, don't you, Mr. Prospect?"

Prospect Forgets Price—but Remembers Quality

As we explore cost and offer suggestions and instructions on the most effective way to use your voice and deal with price in this chapter, it's almost like killing a fly with a sledgehammer, since we give you so many details on this one point. However, it is important and will become even more important in the future, so the objective is to cover *all* the bases.

From your perspective, I think it's important to remember that the customer is likely to forget the price—especially if he likes the product. Example: You probably have several suits or dresses which you *really* enjoy wearing. Chances are good if you've had them very long you have forgotten the exact price of those suits or dresses.

People forget price but they'll never forget poor quality or a poor choice. They generally give the salesperson a generous portion of the blame. Some of that goes with the territory, but too much blame means you won't have the territory for long.

The "Quality" Close

In selling low-ticket items (brushes, soap, cosmetics), your time investment would be too great to cover all the foregoing information on dealing with price, so let's look at a power-packed quick response which is enormously effective. You can also use this one to convince the hesitant buyer who says the price is too high in an over-the-counter transaction in a retail outlet.

Lower your voice, look your prospect in the eye, and say, "You know, Mr. Prospect, many years ago our company made a basic decision. We *decided that it would be easier to explain price one time than it would be to apologize for quality forever.* [Slight pause.] And I'll bet you're glad we made that decision, aren't you?"

If you are selling that low-ticket item, this last one might be the *only* one you will use. In situations involving considerable sums of money, it can be the icing on the cake that moves the prospect into the buyer's chair.

State Farm agent Ab Jackson from Tucson, Arizona, was dealing with a prospect and making no progress. As a matter of fact, Ab was in somewhat of a sales slump and this prospect was mildly antagonistic. After Ab had made his presentation and handled several questions, the prospect was fairly emphatic in his statement that the price was too high.

Specifically as he had learned from the recording which covers this close, Ab looked at the prospect, lowered his voice, and said, "Mr. Prospect, at State Farm we decided many years ago that it would be easier to explain price one time than to apologize for poor quality or poor service forever [pause]—and I'll bet you are glad we made that decision, aren't you?" The prospect said nothing for a few seconds, then firmly said, "I'll take it." The sale was almost exactly twice as big as the biggest contract Ab had ever written.

I urge you to do what Ab Jackson did. Practice, drill, and rehearse until the words and the right voice inflection become a part of you. Do this and you will have developed a powerful tool for persuading your prospect to take the action which will benefit you *and* him.

The "Answer for Everything" Close

Chances are excellent, especially if you are in direct sales, that you have been in a selling situation where you've answered one objection after another. Regardless of what comes up you've handled it effectively. Finally the prospect (in a husband/wife situation) turns to his wife and says, "Oh, Martha, it doesn't make any difference what you say, he's got an answer for everything!" Or, in a more sophisticated environment, he might say to you, "Well, you've certainly done your homework. It doesn't make any difference what I ask; you've got an answer for it!"

Feed Your Ego — or *Make the Sale*

If that ever happens (I should say, *when* that happens), you're faced with a major decision. You can either decide to feed your ego or you can decide to make the sale. You can't do both. When he says, "You've got an answer for everything," you can either grin and say, "Well, as a matter of fact, last month I *was number one in the office . . . and the month before"* — or you can take a different approach and make the sale.

If you give the preceding response, you've just fed your ego and that's all you'll feed. When your prospect makes the statement "You've got an answer for everything," if you want to further your career you need to lower your voice, look him in the eye, and slowly, softly say, "Mr. Prospect, I really appreciate that comment and I'm going to take it as a compliment. But actually I don't have an answer for many of the questions and objections people bring to me. That's the reason I'm excited about selling the product which *is* the answer to your problem. And that's what you really want, isn't it [nodding your head as you talk]?"

That procedure, my selling friend, is stronger than dirt! It will get results, *if* you are sincere *and* believe what you are saying!

Let's elaborate on that last sentence by saying you can take the biggest crook in town and teach him the words, procedures, and techniques that professional salespeople all over the world successfully use. However, the effectiveness of those words and techniques would be seriously limited by the *credibility* of the person using them. It *is* true — the most important part of the sales process is the salesperson.

The study by DeMarco and Maginn of The Forum Corporation of Boston, Massachusetts (page 111), contains much valuable information and supports this credibility contention completely. As a matter of fact, this one factor consistently appeared throughout the report. High performers in the world of selling establish *trust* with customers by one-on-one, eye-to-eye communication skills. They maintain trust by personally assuming responsibility for completing the sale, which means servicing the account on an ongoing basis and utilizing their company support people in the most effective manner. High performers demonstrated great integrity with their follow-through and belief that the sale is not complete until the product is installed and functioning satisfactorily.

6

THE PROFESSIONAL
SELLS AND DELIVERS

My First "Sale"

When I'd been in the sales world about three months in 1947, I used psychology in what I consider my first real sales strategy. Many things were still fairly difficult to get, including good, heavy cookware. We were taking as many orders as we could get, but delivery was sometimes delayed for one to three months. World War II had not been over that long and for about four years no heavy-duty cookware had been available. So there was a backlog of demand. Experienced salesmen were having a field day, but I was a novice and, frankly, I was struggling.

One day I was in Winnsboro, South Carolina, knocking on doors, attempting to sell. I knocked on the door of Mr. Anderson, a highway patrolman whose wife came to the door. She let me in, explaining that her husband and Mr. Boulware from next door were out in the back-yard, but that she and Mrs. Boulware would be glad to look at the cookware. Once I got inside, I persuaded the ladies to invite their husbands in, assuring them that they, too, would enjoy the demonstration. The ladies "coerced" their husbands into coming in.

No amount of persuasion, however, could convince the men to take the demonstration seriously. I put on an enthusiastic cooking presentation, cooking apples without water and on low heat in my set of cookware and some by the old-fashioned way with water in the cookware they had. The difference was dramatic and as I set the apples cooked by two different methods in front of them, both couples were by now impressed with the difference. The men, however, apparently feared they were about to be sold something, so they acted as if they had no interest.

The "Reverse" Close

At that point, I knew the sale was lost so I decided to use a little reverse selling. I cleaned my cookware, packed it back in the sample case, and said to the couples, "Well, I really appreciate your letting me demonstrate. I only wish I could offer you the cookware today. Perhaps it will be available in the future."

Immediately both husbands became vitally interested in our set of cookware. Mr. Anderson and Mr. Boulware both came out of their seats and demanded to know when it would be available. I assured them I did not know exactly, but I would keep them in mind when it was. They persisted, "Well, suppose you forget us, how will we know?" I responded, "Well, I suppose—to be on the safe side—it would be all right for you to go ahead and make a deposit on a set which the company would ship when it's available. It might be a month or it could even be three months." Both of them eagerly reached into their pockets and came up with the down payment. About six weeks later the merchandise was shipped. (It's important to note that throughout the presentation I dealt strictly with the facts.)

There is something about human nature that seems to want whatever is unavailable or difficult to obtain. In this case, I was simply using a little sales psychology to capitalize on this facet of human nature.

Two important points: Number one, reverse selling is a very effective method of persuasion, but number two, you must be scrupulously honest and *very careful* that you always play the game straight. Otherwise it is deceitful and you'll get caught and your prospects will lose confidence in you. More importantly, you will lose respect for yourself and your self-image will suffer, which means your sales will go down. (Part Two of *Secrets of Closing the Sale* explains why.)

Selling a Shoeshine

I believe everyone sells and everything is selling. Here's a story which demonstrates voice inflection and some sales techniques we've been talking about. In the late winter of 1976 I stopped in the St. Louis airport to change planes. A quick glance at my shoes told me I needed a shine and my watch told me I had time. That pleased me, because in my opinion the best shoeshiners in the whole world are in that St. Louis airport.

I walked into the little cubicle and as I stood there the gentleman in the third chair was stepping down. The young shoeshiner said to me, "Come on in, you're next." I climbed up in the chair and while he completed the cash transaction with his customer, I looked over his prices. The prices at that time (they've changed since then) were, "Regular Shine, 75¢. Wax Shine, $1.00. Spit Shine, $2.00." I decided to get the Regular Shine, tip him a quarter, and be on my way.

When Johnny (he had a name tag) came to me after finishing with his other customer, he asked, "What kind?" I responded, "Regular." He took a short step backward, looked up at me, and said, "Regular?!" (His inflection had both a question and a you've-gotta-be-kidding tone.)

I knew then I was headed for an unusual shoeshine, but I wasn't about to let that dude get the best of me. I said, "Yeah, just give me the regular. You guys do such a fantastic job, I know it's going to be supergood!" He never grunted, never changed expression, never said anything. He reached for the saddle soap and started cleaning my shoes by liberally applying it to both of them. Next he got his cloth to wipe the shoes dry.

When he finished wiping the first one, he rubbed the shoe leather and made it squeak so loudly you could have heard it a block away. He half asked, half commented, "These are Ballys, aren't they?" Zig: "Well, as a matter of fact, they are." Johnny: "Man, they are really nice shoes!" Zig: "They ought to be!" Johnny: "They cost a lot of money, don't they?" Zig: "Yeah, they really do, but I'm not complaining because these are the most comfortable shoes I've ever worn." Johnny: "They *are* nice shoes."

The "Shame" Close

By then he had finished wiping the other shoe so he picked up the shoe polish. Before applying the polish he reached up, grabbed a pant leg, and said, "This is one of the most unusual pieces of cloth I've ever felt." He was right. That particular suit *is* most unusual. Doyle Hoyer, the owner of Glasgow Clothiers in Fort Madison, Iowa, sold me that suit and he tells me that particular piece of cloth is from Ireland and will last me at least five years. Actually Doyle was "underselling" because I'm now wearing it the seventh year and you can hardly tell the suit has been worn. It's a marvelous, marvelous suit.

As I was telling Johnny all these things, he asked, "What kind of suit is it?" I told him it was a Hickey-Freeman. "Man!" he said, "that *is* a nice suit! They cost a lot of money, don't they?" I replied that Hickey-Freeman is a relatively expensive suit, but this one was especially expensive because of the cloth. As a matter of fact, I spent over two hundred dollars *more* for this suit than any suit I'd ever bought, but I was very happy with the purchase.

By now he had the polish on the shoes and was really giving it that old cloth-popping job. As a shoeshiner of considerable experience (two years in the U.S. Navy), I know something about shining shoes. One thing I do know is that if the guy doing the shining starts popping the cloth, he is not shining the shoes any better but he is doing two things. First, as the late Elmer Wheeler would say, he is "selling the sizzle," and sizzle does sell, and *keeps* the prospect sold, *if* it's backed with substance. Second, he's letting the folks outside the shine booth know something exciting is going on inside. He's prospecting for that next customer, which is something all *professional* salespeople regularly do.

Just as he finished one of the pops, he stopped, looked me in the eye, and said, "You know, it just seems like a shame! [Pause.] A man will spend over a hundred dollars for a pair of shoes; he'll spend several hundred dollars for a suit of clothes, and all he's trying to do is look his best. [Pause.] And then he won't spend another dollar to get the best shine in the whole world to top everything off!" [Pause.] Zig: "Spit on 'em, man, spit on 'em!" (In a pleasant, humorous way he had shamed me into buying a better shine. He put the *other dollar* into perspective by bringing the price of the shoes and suit into focus.)

Sell It—Then Deliver

He finished the shine and it was a beauty! I don't know how you are, but I personally feel that when I get a seventy-five cent shine, a two-bit tip is fine. But whoever heard of a two-bit tip on a two-dollar shine? People with any class just don't do things like that! I gave Johnny a buck to go with the other two and started walking out (strutting would be more accurate), feeling like the king of the walk while thinking to myself, "What in the world is this guy doing shining shoes?"

Then I looked up at the clock as it flipped to straight up and down, ten o'clock. Now that's very important because when I sat down in the chair it showed exactly three minutes to ten. I was in Johnny's chair three minutes. I gave him three dollars. You don't have to be a Phi Beta Kappa out of M.I.T. to know that a dollar a minute comes to sixty dollars an hour. Do you realize that's what some psychiatrists make?

Now I'm not a mind reader, but I know what you're thinking. Sixty dollars an hour is $480 a day and I know he's not going to make that much, so cut that in half. That's $240. Cut that in half, and its $120. Cut that in half (I'll guarantee that you don't have to cut it that last time) and that's $60 a day. Even if you did, that would still leave him over $18,000 a year shining shoes, and as we'd say down home, if he isn't making over $20,000 a year, there ain't a dog in Georgia!

But hold the phone! There are two things you need to thoroughly understand. Number one, he is a *professional* salesman. As a matter of fact, his name tag also includes his title, "Shoeologist." To the best of my knowledge, he is the only one in the U.S. He is *good*.

Number two, *he delivers everything he sells.* (I'm personally convinced our divorce rate would be reduced 90 percent if men and women *delivered* in marriage what they *sold* while courting. I'm also convinced *your* sales career will be even more rewarding if you deliver what you sell.) In short, Johnny does a fantastic job of shining shoes. Fortunately, this story has not one but two sequels.

The "Extra" Close

I was back in the St. Louis airport about a year after the first incident, so I returned to the shoeshine booth. I had my overnight bag with me so I hung it up before I sat down. By now they'd changed the price structure a little. "Regular Shine" was a dollar, the wax shine had been eliminated, and the name of the "Spit Shine" was "Best Shine." The price was still $2.00. As I sat down, Johnny asked me what kind of shine I wanted. I didn't want to go through the routine again, so I said, "Just give me the best!" He smiled, said, "Okay," and went to work.

I found out a long time ago that people do better when you treat them like a good farmer treats his cows. I don't know how much you personally know about cows, so I'd like to share two things with you. Number one, I can tell you from my experience, dating back to the time I was eight years old, cows don't "give" milk. You have to fight for every drop. Number two, I can tell you the quality and quantity of the cow's milk is directly related to the way she is treated.

Walk into the barn and slap the old cow a couple of times, tell her that her production is down, that the butterfat is lower than ever, and that you feel she's doing a lousy job. Kick her in the side and tell her she's got to get production up or she's headed for the hamburger grill, and two things will probably happen.

Number one, she might kick you back. Whether she does or not, I can tell you with absolute certainty that you will not get nearly as much milk, and the milk you do get will probably be unfit for human consumption. The old cow would get so upset that a chemical change would literally take place in her body and the milk would be sour or so bitter you could not drink it.

On the other hand, walk into the barn and pleasantly greet the cow — no, I don't necessarily think you have to kiss her, but it wouldn't hurt you to kind of rub her a little bit, maybe even put your arm around her. Tell her she's got to be the best-looking cow you've seen all morning, stroke her a couple of times, and tell her what nice, soft skin she has. Brag on her and tell her you're mighty proud of the production she's given you in the past and you just have a good feeling it's going to get better and better. If no one's around you might even tell her you love her. Not only will this approach improve production but it will also improve the quality of the milk.

Compliments Improve Competence

As a boy I saw it happen time after time. My mother loved all animals, but she especially loved cows. When she bought a cow she would name her, pet her, and treat her like a member of the family. I have seen her buy a three-gallon-a-day producer (average for the 1930s and '40s) on many occasions and in a matter of weeks have the same cow producing four or five gallons of milk per day.

Now in case you're wondering what this has to do with shining shoes and selling more merchandise, just read on. I knew Johnny would do a better job of shining my shoes—despite the fact that I already felt he was the best I'd ever seen—if I gave him a little encouragement. With this in mind I started bragging on him. I told him he was doing a marvelous job and the shine looked great. He shined my shoes to a standstill! As a matter of fact, since I was the only customer and I was bragging on him so much, he just kept shining my shoes. I finally told him I had to go, so he finished the job.

As I stepped down out of the chair, I made the observation to Johnny that he obviously enjoyed shining shoes. His response to this was very positive. He explained that he got a lot of pleasure in watching a person come in with grubby-looking shoes and dragging bottom. He said that after a really good shine many times the guys actually seemed to pick up their feet with a new look of pride and enthusiasm.

"Yes," he said, "I do like to shine shoes, but mainly I enjoy people. I meet all kinds and most of them are nice folks so I really enjoy talking with them." To this I commented, "Well, you certainly do a beautiful job, not only as a sales and public-relations man but also as a fantastic professional at shining shoes."

Johnny was beaming all the way through this, but as I stepped down out of his chair he said, "Could I ask you a question?" Zig: "Sure." Johnny: "Didn't I see you with an overnight bag when you sat down?" Zig: "You sure did." Johnny: "Are you spending the night in St. Louis?" Zig: "Yes, I am." Johnny: "Do you by any chance have another pair of shoes in that bag?" Zig: "As a matter of fact, I do." Johnny: "You know, it'd really be a shame—[pause]—to have the most beautiful shine in St. Louis tonight and then look like just one of the crowd tomorrow. It won't take me but a minute and you'll be on your way!"

Deliver What You Sell

I left Johnny with five dollars that time! But again let me emphasize something I stated earlier. Johnny is a professional salesman and *he delivers what he sells*. For some strange reason a certain segment of our population seems to believe the professional salesperson must have on a three-piece suit, carry a fancy briefcase, and sell investments, computers, or some specialized product like real estate trusts or mutual funds.

I've seen many people in those industries who were highly professional, and I've seen some who had only the three-piece suit and the fancy briefcase. By the same token, you can be a highly skilled professional salesperson, as Johnny is, and sell shoeshines. The route salesman who services bread racks or soft-drink racks in rural areas can be a truck driver and delivery boy *or* he can become a well-paid *professional* salesman. Ditto for the clerk in the discount store or the butcher behind the meat counter. The professional learns his product, his job, and his clientele. He learns how to use the right words and body language to persuade people to take action. Then he makes absolutely certain he delivers everything he sells *and then some*.

The "Add On" Close

Of even more importance is the fact that Johnny was not content to make just the one sale. He saw a chance for the second and took advantage of the opportunity. I think you already know I was not the least bit offended that he wanted to sell me the second shoeshine. Actually, once you've gained the confidence of your customers with the first sale, you are in a position to be of real service to them. The first order is an indication of trust. If you have companion products which your customers regularly use, you render a service by saving them time, bookkeeping entries, and inventory problems by *helping* them reduce the number of suppliers they deal with.

I'm not suggesting that if you have a multiple line you should try to sell the entire line on every sales call. I am suggesting that if you believe in what you sell and your customer is using similar products, you will do both of you a favor by offering the other products, especially on the second and subsequent sales calls.

The "Gloomy Gus" Close

Incredibly enough the story has yet another sequel. Just a few months ago on a rainy day, I was back in the St. Louis airport changing planes again. This time Johnny was not there. As I stepped into the chair the shoeshiner (soon to be known as "Gloomy Gus") came to me and said, "Well, I suppose you want the Regular Shine?" I looked at him with disbelief and said, "I can't believe you said that! Why would you offer me the Regular instead of the Best?" Gloomy Gus: "In rainy weather people don't want to spend two dollars for a shine and just get it all messed up." Zig: "Won't the Best Shine give my shoes the best protection?" Gloomy Gus: "Yes, it will." Zig: "Well, why didn't you offer me the best?" Gloomy Gus (or should it now be "Broken Record"?): "People just don't want to spend two dollars for a shine on a rainy day." Zig: "It seems to me that if the Best Shine gives the best protection and your business is down on rainy days, you would work awfully hard to increase the sales of your Best Shine." Gloomy Gus: "Well, I suppose so." (He's hard-core negative.)

Zig: "How would you like for me to give you a few words which would double the number of Best Shines you sell?" Gloomy Gus (with the first sign of a pulse beat): "Man, I would really like that! What are they?" Zig: "The next time a customer comes in and sits down, the first thing you do is look at his shoes. Then you look at his eyes, smile, and say to him, "Unless I miss my guess, you're the kind of guy who is going to want the *best* shine we've got." When he heard those words they apparently struck a responsive chord because he actually showed some enthusiasm as he said, "Man, give me that one more time!" So I repeated the words.

Changing the Status Quo

I haven't seen this guy again so I don't know the rest of the story, but I do know this: You can change everything about your business by changing your *thinking* about your business. In short, *if you don't like the status quo, change the status of your thinking and old "quo" is gonna be all right!* Regardless of what you're selling, a little optimistic addition and positive expectation to your presentation will increase your volume and hence your profitability. I repeat, *if what you're selling is good, why would you hesitate to offer it to the public in an optimistic manner?*

Remember in dealing with your prospects that most people simply do not like to make decisions. They're somewhat like this old boy down home who went to a psychiatrist. The psychiatrist stated, "I understand you have trouble making decisions. Is that true?" The old boy looked at him somewhat puzzled for a moment and said, "Well, yes and no." That's pretty much the way many of our prospects are. They just don't like to make decisions. That's the reason you are a salesperson. You are there to give them information so they can be confident they are making the *right* decision.

Yes, psychology is involved in everything we do. As we conclude this segment on "The Psychology of Closing," I encourage you to develop your sales skills and techniques. I especially urge you—via the use of the cassette recorder—to learn how to effectively use that voice of yours. Get emotionally involved in persuading people to take action, really stay motivated, hone your skills to a fine point, and I will SEE YOU AT THE TOP!

PART TWO

THE HEART OF YOUR SALES CAREER

Objectives

To get the *person* ready to be a better, more productive *sales*person.

To explain selling as a transference of feeling.

To differentiate between sympathy and empathy and help you to think as a buyer and as a seller.

To sell selling and professional preparation for professional results.

To explain the necessity of building physical, mental, and spiritual reserve.

To introduce love as the dominant factor in a successful sales career.

To explore the importance of honesty, conviction, and integrity as absolute musts for an outstanding sales career.

Closes and/or Procedures

The "Believer's" Close
The "Ownership" Close Revisited
The "Get 'Em Smiling" Close
The "Empathy" Close
The "Physical Action" Close

The "Can't Afford It" Close
The "Go Giver" Close
The "Columbus" Close
The "Courtship" Close
The "Testimonial" Close
The "Love" Close

7

THE CRITICAL STEP
IN SELLING

FROM THE BEGINNING we stated that the critical part of the sales process is the honesty and integrity of the salesperson. When I speak of honesty I'm not talking about paying your bills or writing good checks. In today's computerized age, when you give a hot check in Dallas on Monday, they'll know about it in Portland, Oregon, on Tuesday. If you don't pay your bills it becomes common knowledge through the credit bureaus. It's good business to write good checks and to pay your bills.

When I speak of honesty in the world of selling, I go one step beyond that—and that step is significant. The following two stories will spell out exactly what I mean.

Ya Gotta Believe

Years ago (1963), I was the number one cookware salesman in America for the Saladmaster Corporation of Dallas, Texas. We lived in Columbia, South Carolina, and business was fantastic. An associate of mine, selling the same product in the same town, was "starving to death." Once, while visiting in his home, we were in the kitchen having a cup of coffee, talking about his sales decline, when the following dialogue took place:

Zig: "Bill, I know exactly what your problem is." Bill: "What's my problem, Zig?" Zig: "Your problem is simple. You're attempting the psychologically impossible." Bill: "What are you talking about?" Zig: "You're trying to sell a product you don't enthusiastically believe in." Bill: "Zig, that's crazy! Man, we've got the greatest set of cookware on the American market! It's absolutely fantastic! As a matter of fact, Zig, I left the company I'd been with for four years and came with Saladmaster because of the superiority of the product. In addition to that, I was a manager with the other company and started here as a salesman because of my belief in this product."

Zig: "Aw, come on, Bill. Peddle that baloney to other people! I know you and I know you don't believe what you're saying." Bill (a little hot under the collar): "You can say what you want to, but I *know* I believe in our product." Zig: "Bill, I can prove beyond any doubt that you do not *really* believe in the product you sell," and with that, I nodded toward the stove.

Bill: "Awwwww, you mean the fact that I'm cooking in a competitive set of cookware?" Zig: "Bill, that's exactly right." Bill: "Zig, don't give it a thought. Man, that's got nothing to do with it. I'm going to buy a set of our cookware, but you know I've had my problems. We wrecked our car and for a couple of months we had to depend on borrowed transportation, buses, and taxis. Now Zig, you know you can't get the job done in the sales world unless you have transportation you can depend on twenty-four hours a day.

"On top of that, my wife spent a couple of weeks in the hospital and I lost a lot of time and spent a lot of money. Now add the worry and concern I've had and surely you can understand why it knocked us for a loop! And it's not over, because it looks like we're going to have to put the boys in the hospital to get their tonsils out and Zig, we don't even have any insurance! You're right when you say we should have a set of the cookware, and we are definitely going to get a set, but the timing is just not right!"

Selling Is a Transference of Feeling

Zig: "Bill, let me ask you a question. How long have you been with this company?" Bill: "Oh, about five years." Zig: "Bill, what was your excuse last year, and the year before that, and the year before that, and the year before that, and the year before that? [Pause.] Let me tell you exactly what happens when you get down to the 'short rows' (that's Southern for decision-making time), when you ask your prospect that obligating question and he is 'thinking it over.' The decision ball is up in the air; *yes* is full commission, *no* is no commission.

"I can see the scene now, Bill, so let me paint the picture for you. The customer is thinking out loud as he says, 'I don't know, Bill. Boy, we sure need a good set of pots. I don't know how my wife cooks in that stuff she has, but it just doesn't seem like the right time to get 'em now. My wife's been in the hospital, we just wrecked the family car, it looks as if the boys are going to have to have their tonsils taken out, and we don't even have any insurance!'

"Now Bill, you and I both know they're not about to give you exactly the same excuses you've been giving me. But we also know they are going to give you the same excuses you've been giving yourself for the last five years. You are well trained, Bill, so I know exactly what you are going to do every time they give you an excuse for not buying. You're going to sit there with a forced grin on your face, saying to yourself, 'Think positive now, Bill, think positive, Bill!' But all the time, deeeeeep down inside, you're going to be thinking, 'Yeah, I know exactly what you mean. That's the reason I don't have a set of the stuff myself.'

"Let me tell you something, Bill. The smartest thing you'll ever do, even if you've got to mortgage your furniture, is to buy a set of your own cookware. Hear me on this, Bill [and I'm going to say to *all* my selling friends as you read this book, if you stop reading right here or don't believe or follow through on anything else I say in this book, if you will buy—without reservation—my next statement, you will immediately be more effective at selling whatever you sell].

> *Selling is essentially a transference of feeling.*

If I (the salesman) can make you (the prospect) feel about my product the way I feel about my product, you are going to buy my product, if there is any way in the world you can come up with the money.

"Now *in order to transfer a feeling, you've got to have that feeling.* When you're trying to persuade somebody to do something you have not done yourself, that fact comes across to the prospect. Of course, all salesmen can occasionally con a person into buying something he doesn't really believe in, but if you're going to build an outstanding career, you've got to be *committed* to the product yourself. You've got to believe because as Bernie Lofchick from Winnipeg, Canada, the greatest sales manager I know, says, 'Believers are *closers.*' "

The very word *close* starts with a *c*. That *c* stands for *conviction*. Take the *c* out of *close* and you have *lose*, which is what you *and* the prospect do when your lack of conviction and belief influences the prospect in a *no* decision.

You've Seen It Yourself

How many times have you seen a new and untrained person come into your organization? He doesn't know any of the "bear trap" closes; doesn't really know scientifically, psychologically, or technically how to deal with all of the fancy objections, but oh, brother, does he ever believe in the product he's selling! He believes it would be the most serious mistake in a lifetime if a person didn't go ahead and buy immediately and put that product to use. Net result: He sells rings around some of the established pros. In my mind this proves that a green but convicted salesman is better than a blue unconvicted one.

The epitome of this feeling is Willa Dorsey, the great Negro spiritual singer. Until you've heard her sing "Peace in My Soul," you have missed one of life's most beautiful experiences. Willa says something all salespeople can learn from when she talks about belief. She says, *"If you're going to be convincing, brother, you've gotta be convinced!"*

Buy It—and You Can Sell It

What about you? Are you convinced of the merits of your merchandise? If you're selling Fords and driving a Chevrolet, then my friend, it's costing you a great deal of money. Believe in what you sell—or do yourself, your company, your friends, your "victims," and the profession of selling a favor. Change products or get out of the profession. Your failure is predestined, so why prolong the death rattle? The sooner you make the change into something you can honestly and enthusiastically pursue, the sooner you will start climbing the ladder to success. Obviously, there will be some exceptions in buying or using what you sell. For example, if you sell locomotives, million-dollar computers, or 747s, I don't necessarily believe you have to buy one to prove you believe in it!

To emphasize that point I make the following statement without reservation: If you don't believe the customers are the losers when they *don't* buy, you are selling the wrong product. If you don't feel a sense of loss for them, you are not going to be as effective and persuasive as you could be. Selling *is* a transference of feeling and your prospects are persuaded more by your pride and belief in your product than by any "proof" you submit regarding your product's performance.

Until and unless you truly feel that nobody sells a better product value, you really are not completely honest and your performance will not be at the level you are capable of attaining. In that event you are obviously the biggest loser because you will miss too many of the close ones.

The late Charles Roth said that many people feel if they utter the three magic words *business is business* they have license to lie, cheat, steal, and in general rape their fellow man. The fear that those things will happen often exists in the mind of the prospect. Roth pointed out that *a calm, confident, positive, reassuring salesperson working from a base of honesty and integrity is the most effective tool to calm the fears of the prospect and get the sale.* Yes, honesty is more than a moral issue. It is *practical.*

The "Believer's" Close

To make a long story short, I sold Bill a set of the cookware. Don't misunderstand, he wrote his own order and bought it from himself. The exciting "rest of the story" is that the additional sales Bill made that week paid for his own set of cookware! The reason is simple. Every time someone brought up the "can't afford it" objection, Bill could handle it with his head *and* his heart. Bill knew that he had dug in and bought his own product when it hurt to do so. He understood how those prospects felt, but now he was able to deal with them with empathy and not sympathy. (We cover the difference in considerable detail in the next chapter.)

Bill *understood* how the prospects felt, but he did not *feel* the same way because he had bought his own set of cookware. He had made the sacrifice so he could look them in the eye and say, "I know how you feel, but I know from experience it's worth the sacrifice. You'll never regret it." Results were dramatic. *His sales skyrocketed because he was selling from a belief base tied directly to his heart.*

You've gotta believe. I personally feel that *honesty means we believe so deeply, so completely, so fervently in what we are selling that we can't*

understand why other people don't buy. When our belief is that deep, our prospect picks it up. Chances are excellent you've had somebody say to you, "I don't know why I'm listing this home with you, or giving you my business. There have been half a dozen people by here this week and I turned them down." Many times they really don't know, but it gets down to the basic fact that they trust you because of your conviction. They "feel" they can depend on your integrity and fairness. Many times this trust is because of the reputation you have built over a period of years *and* because of that deep belief and feeling you have in and for your product which is *transferred* to your prospect.

One of the major points—if not *the* major point—revealed in The Forum Corporation study was the fact that high-performing salespeople are *trusted* by their customers. They are trusted, over the long haul, for a very good reason. They are *trustworthy*. Like I say, being honest is practical.

"Closers" Own What They Sell

Life insurance companies will tell you they can take a hundred of their salesmen with at least one year's experience and without looking at their sales records predict within five percentage points what these men, as a group, are going to sell for the year. They make their predictions based solely on the amount of insurance these men carry on their own lives. You see, selling is a transference of feeling. *The critical step in the world of selling is this step of honesty which is your total conviction, your complete belief that the product or service you sell is truly the best buy for the prospect.*

When I entered the world of sales training on a professional level, I shared my experience with Bill (own what you sell) in a series of recordings. An enthusiastic young fire-alarm salesman listened to the story and realized he apparently did not believe in his product because he did not own the alarm system himself. His conscience was prodded and he installed the alarms in his own home. Later he wrote me and said, "You know, Zig, the first month I had that set of alarms in my own home I made enough extra sales to completely pay for them."

The "Ownership" Close Revisited

Countless other salespeople, selling everything from cars and cosmetics to insurance and soap, have shared the same experience. Once you've made that emotional *and* financial commitment which says, "I believe in my product so strongly that I bought it myself," then you can transfer that feeling to the other individual. In a nutshell, *closers own what they sell.*

When the prospect brings up a "can't afford it" objection, you can with considerable conviction point out that your product is so good it's *worth* sweating and sacrificing for. Obviously you will be hypocritical and hence not very convincing if *you* have not invested in your own product.

To repeat myself, if you are selling Fords, you should be driving a Ford. If you sell 747s, locomotives, steamships, or multimillion-dollar computers, you don't need to buy one. But generally speaking, if it's feasible, you should believe in what you sell so much that you are willing, even *anxious*, to sacrifice—if necessary—to own it.

By way of emphasizing this even further, if you do not honestly feel the prospect is the loser if he doesn't buy, then you're not going to be nearly as effective in the world of selling. How can you honestly feel the prospect is going to "lose" if you are not "winning" by owning the product? Whatever you're selling should be much in evidence in your home, car, business, or wherever it is used. By its presence you're saying, "I believe." Again: *Closers own what they sell.*

Not only should you believe in the product you sell but you should also believe in and be loyal to the company you represent. Your effectiveness and productivity will be affected by your feelings toward your management and your company. I urge you to read Russell Conwell's *Acres of Diamonds,* which beautifully illustrates the fact that opportunity and "gold mines" are everywhere—including right where you are. You can and will find exactly what you look for in your company and in your life.

As a sales procedure it's smart and professional to praise and build your company everywhere you go. After all, how much confidence do you have in someone who bad-mouths his wife, his city, his company, or any of the people associated with the company?

Believe in your product *and* your company. Transfer that belief to the prospect and not only will you sell more—you will sell it more easily, and those customers will get you other customers. That's career-building selling.

8

THE BIG "E" IN SELLING

PSYCHOLOGIST H. M. GREENBERG, who is president of the Marketing Survey and Research Corporation of Princeton, New Jersey, did a psychological evaluation on 186,000 people and discovered that 1 out of 5 could be trained to be a successful salesperson. He also discovered that if anyone is going to be outstanding as a salesperson, he has to have a special kind of ego. This special ego requires the "food" of acceptance by the prospects he deals with.

When a salesman calls on a prospect and is granted an appointment, the prospect is really saying, "I buy you, so come on in and tell me the story." When the prospect becomes a customer he is saying to the salesman, "I trust you. I believe you're telling me the truth, so go ahead and write the order."

Dr. Greenberg says the top salesman needs to make the sale primarily because each sale is a reaffirmation of his own power, of his own ability, and because failure to close threatens his self-esteem. He likes the conflict; he likes to win; he likes to sell.

To be a truly outstanding salesman you've got to have an ego, but according to Dr. Greenberg, you'd better watch that salesman if *all* he has is ego, because he will do just about anything to make the sale. The result is disaster, for both customer and salesman. The customer is often abused and the salesman will never build the sales career he's capable of building. In many cases he does well on a temporary basis but his shortcuts, misrepresentations, and exaggerations will eventually catch up and he has to move on to another city or another product line. Dr. Greenberg emphasizes if you're going to build a sales career, in addition to ego you've got to have *empathy*.

Empathy vs. Sympathy

Despite the general use of the word *empathy*, many people still do not recognize the difference between empathy and sympathy and their application in the world of selling. This understanding is important because if we tie empathy to ego, there's little danger we're going to oversell, which is sometimes a problem in the sales world.

Sympathy means you feel like another person feels. Empathy means you *understand* how the other person feels, though you do not feel the same way.

Example: When you observe a passenger leaning over the rail of a ship, suffering from seasickness, sympathy is perfectly demonstrated when you join him at the rail. Empathy is when you understand how the passenger feels, so you get him a cold towel and some seasickness pills to help him solve the problem. With empathy you understand and are sensitive to the feedback from the other person. You're not part of the problem so you can back away and become part of the solution.

A marriage counselor with sympathy can get so involved in the other person's problems that eventually he might need counseling himself. An arrested alcoholic with sympathy in trying to counsel a practicing alcoholic will often tragically get back on the bottle. A sales manager with sympathy will end up broke and, in some cases, lose his effectiveness. He will lend his salespeople money and on occasion will end up doing their work for them.

Parents with too much sympathy will let their kids do and have everything they could not do or have as kids, so they often raise spoiled, undisciplined and unproductive children.

The reason most doctors and lawyers don't treat members of their own families or take them as clients is they are so involved in the problem they can't back away and objectively look at the solution.

Empathy is different. You understand the problem, you know exactly how the prospect feels, but because you don't feel that way you can back away from the problem and offer some solutions. In this part of the book my objective is to get you to think both as a buyer and as a seller. To be truly professional you must be able to comfortably move from the seller's side of the table to the buyer's side. If you know how your prospect thinks and feels, you're definitely going to sell more of what you're selling because you will communicate more effectively.

With empathy this little dissertation on business (author unknown) takes on significant meaning.

When we separate the word *business* into its component letters, B-U-S-I-N-E-S-S, we find that U and I are *both* in it. In fact, if U and I were not in *business*, it would not be business. Furthermore, we discover that U comes before I in business and the I is silent—it is to be seen, not heard. Also, the U in business has the sound of I, which indicates it is an amalgamation of the interests of U and I. When they are properly amalgamated, business becomes harmonious, profitable, and pleasant.

Don't Confuse Situations

Much of this is just common sense. Realistically a certain percentage of this is "old stuff." Now before you discount anything for that reason, let me remind you that *the procedure or information is old because it is good.* If the results weren't good the techniques would not be old—they would be dead. We weave the "old stuff" into much of the new material because you personally might not be familiar with all the information and if you are it's still true that *we may not need to be told—but we do need to be reminded.*

As a salesperson it should be obvious to you that you never confuse your situation with your prospect's situation. You must remember that your wants, needs, desires, tastes, and capacity to pay have no bearing on your prospect's needs, wants, desires, and ability to pay.

As an example, you might be a clothing salesperson with personal tastes that are flashy. If a conservatively dressed businessman comes in for a suit, you obviously want to take note of what he's wearing. Then think in terms of what he wants and needs. If he looks at an expensive suit or sports coat which you could not afford, it doesn't mean you should try to talk him down to a less expensive item. Far from it.

If, on the other hand, you could afford something nicer but your prospect cannot, you should not try to sell him something which is completely out of his price range. Be very careful not to turn up your nose at a bargain-basement suit since *you* would not wear such a thing. Remember, for him that suit might be the epitome of luxury.

The same principle applies whether you're selling cars, houses, life insurance, or investments. In short, *don't confuse your situation with his.* Look at the goods, products, or services you sell through *his* eyes. That's empathy—and that's the professional way.

Eager He Was—Professional and Empathetic He Wasn't

Good technique at the wrong time can be disastrous because there is such a thing as the 100 percent wrong time to try to sell even a superb product. Undoubtedly the worst bit of timing I have ever encountered occurred not long after we moved to Dallas. Our son, Tom, was a little less than four years old. Late one afternoon we suddenly missed him. We immediately went to the homes on either side of our house. We looked up and down the street and in the back alley. Then I quickly hopped in my car and drove up to the intersection and through the small shopping center. In the meantime, my wife was busy calling the neighbors and our girls were out scouring the neighborhood and calling at the tops of their voices for Tom. There was no response.

We looked fast and furiously for what seemed like an eternity, but in reality was probably no more than twenty minutes; by then we were getting scared. I called the Dallas police and told them our problem and in a matter of minutes they responded and joined the search. In the meantime, I made another trip to the shopping center, circled the block, went up and down the alleys, rolling down my windows and calling for Tom everywhere I went. In the process I aroused the concern and interest of several neighbors who also joined in the search.

Naturally I checked back by the house every few minutes. During one of these check-ins I encountered one of the local patrol organizations which are very much in evidence in our society today.

I blurted out that my son was missing and asked if he would help us find him. Incredibly enough, the man started trying to sell me his patrol service. As he started his presentation I was in some shock, and when he continued it for a few more seconds I stopped and—partially in disbelief, partially in frustration, partially in anger—explained rather heatedly that if he would help me find my son, *then* we would talk about his services.

His Empathy Was Nonexistent

His timing could not have been worse. Surely no one with enough intelligence to get out of a phone booth without written directions on the side would ever make such a mistake. I use the example only to point out that timing combined with empathy is prerequisite to sales success. Sensitivity to the other person's needs and interests is of paramount importance. For example, had the patrol salesman joined in the search, in just twenty minutes he would have made the easiest sale in his career. You guessed it—we found our boy.

As a rule of thumb, when I call someone on the phone, whether it's for a social or a business call, after the initial greeting I always ask a question in this manner: "Did I catch you at a busy time or do you have four [or seven, nine, etc.—*all* other salesmen ask for five, ten, etc.] minutes to talk?" Not only is this a courteous move but in my judgment it's good selling. If my prospect's mind is somewhere else, my chances of a sale are greatly reduced.

In personal contacts, if your prospect is obviously not with you, I urge you to stop your presentation and say, "Mr. Prospect, apparently I've caught you at a bad time. Would you be freer to discuss this proposal at a later time, or would you prefer that I continue?" It's tough to sell when he's not paying attention. A move like this will bring his mind back to the presentation if he was just thoughtlessly drifting. If he is preoccupied, chances are good he will appreciate your consideration and give you an appointment for a later time. This will partially obligate him to you to the degree he will probably give you his undivided attention when you return.

As you have undoubtedly discovered a few dozen times in this book, common sense and good sales techniques are interwoven so completely it's impossible to separate them.

The "Get 'Em Smiling" Close

As a sales trainer, I'm going to suggest that if you can get your prospects smiling and agreeing with you as you go into the body of your presentation, your chances of making a sale are considerably greater. The reason is simple: *They must buy you before they will buy your ideas or services.* A friendly smile or a laugh is a reasonably good indication they are buying you as a person and will therefore be more likely to buy what you are selling. *And* it is unlikely your prospect is going to have negative *feelings* about your product or services with a big smile on his face or after a good laugh.

As a salesman, I'm convinced it is impossible to be completely wrapped up in what you are doing and *not* in rare instances get a rise out of a prospect who is offended by your zeal and commitment. This could and *should* happen, *but* (now read this carefully) it should happen so rarely that you know, and you know that you know, it's the *prospect* who has the problem. On pages 324–28 I cover the procedure you should use to calm the prospect *and* make the sale.

Now let's look at two examples which clearly demonstrate that *sympathy costs you and the prospect while empathy pays you and the prospect.*

Sympathy Costs

Many years ago, not long after I started my career in the cookware business, I called on a farmer and his wife who had attended my demonstration the night before. We were back in the kitchen when I made my presentation—which I'll never forget.

When I finished he just held up his hand and said, "Mr. Ziglar, this probably won't mean much to you because I know you've got a bathroom *inside* your house. But me and my wife have been married over twenty years and for twenty years I've been promising her 'Next year, honey, we're going to build a bathroom.' Every year it's always 'next year,' because one year we would have a bad crop, another year the baby would get sick, or we had to buy a new tractor."

He continued, "For over twenty years I've been struggling to build that bathroom and I've finally got that money right here, right now." (As he said this he patted his money pocket, which is at the top center of the overalls.) "But," he said, "ain't you or nobody else going to get one dime of my money until we build that bathroom."

Who Sells Whom?

I emphasize this: *A sale is made on every presentation. The prospect either sells you that he can't or won't buy or you sell him that he can and should buy.* In this case and at that time of my career I was badly overmatched. That old boy was a super salesman and he had a fantastic prospect (me) who was far too willing to buy what he was selling. In short, I was sympathetic—and here's why.

When I was a boy we had "running water" at our house, which means that we had to "run and get it," if you know what I mean. When he hinted about those cold, wet trips which you associate with outdoor bathrooms, even though it was August I shivered three times! I had so much *sympathy* for his situation I wouldn't have done *anything* to jeopardize that old boy's bathroom, so I folded my tent and "stole away like a thief in the night!"

I left graciously and pleasantly because my friend and first sales trainer, Bill Cranford, had taught me when you miss a sale you should always terminate the interview in such a way the next salesperson can easily gain admission to that prospect's mind. In show business they tell you to "leave 'em laughing." In sales the professional terminates the interview with the prospect in at least a friendly frame of mind. In this case, I was confident we had parted on friendly terms because he even invited me back for a cup of coffee if I was ever in the neighborhood again.

Two days later I bumped into his sister on the streets of the little town of Lancaster, South Carolina. Even though this was in 1948, I still remember the conversation. (Incidentally, she had a vested interest in the sale because if her brother had bought she would have gotten a premium.)

Sister: "What in the world happened to you and my brother?" Zig: "What do you mean, 'What happened?'" Sister: "He's so mad at you I think he'll whip you if he ever sees you again!" Zig: "Him—mad at me?

A nice guy like me?" Sister: "He sure is!" Zig: "Well, why is he mad at me?" Sister: "Very simple. He wanted to buy a set of pots and you wouldn't even sell 'em to him!" Zig: "Well, I'll go back out there right now!" Sister: "It's too late. He doesn't trust you anymore!"

Hear What the Prospect Is Saying—Not Just What He Says

For a long time I could not conceive of the difficulty. I won't tell you that one day it hit me like a bolt out of the blue, because it didn't. But over a period of time the basic problem became clear to me. I had heard every word the old boy *said*, but didn't hear a word he was *saying*. Let me explain.

I had demonstrated and proved beyond any reasonable doubt that our set of cookware would save money, work, and food value. The farmer and his wife had seven small children between the ages of two and sixteen. It was obvious they had a large family because I don't care how clever you are, you just can't hide seven small children in a little house.

This man had seen and heard the benefits of the cookware at the demonstration. The next day at the presentation in his home he *said*, "I've been working over twenty years to get the money to build my bathroom. I've got it right here, but neither you nor anybody else is going to get one dime of it until we build that bathroom." *That's what he said, but that is not what he was saying.*

He was saying "Mr. Ziglar, for over twenty years I've been struggling, trying to raise the money to build a bathroom, but at long last I've got the problem solved." (He even patted his money pocket.) His body language and home environment were also saying, "Look, I've got seven kids and I want to feed them the best food at the lowest possible price with the most food value. My wife, bless her heart, being the mother of seven children and a farm wife, too, she's working herself to death. Mr. Ziglar, do you have *anything* that would save her some work, my children some food value, and me some money?"

That's what he was saying! That's what his environment was saying. But I was so wrapped up in *sympathy* with a problem *he had already solved* that I lost sight of or failed to recognize his much bigger problem, namely, feeding those kids the best way and taking a work load off his wife. Obviously if you are not completely tuned in to your prospect's major need you are not going to offer a solution. Sympathy cost me the sale, but of infinitely more importance, it cost the prospect the use of a product that would have been very beneficial to him. Sympathy costs the salesperson *and* the prospect.

Or It Could Have Been . . .

There are a couple of other possibilities in this scenario. Number one, my demonstration had been "rigged." The cookware really would not save food value; it would not save the farmer's wife work; it would not save the money which I had demonstrated it would. In short, I had lied to the man. Or the possibility exists that the farmer *thought* those things when I walked out so easily. Had my conviction about my product and my concern for the farmer been strong, he would have had to feel that I would stand my ground and plead my case more fervently for him to buy.

On the other side of that coin is the fact that the cookware was what I said it was. It really would save work as well as food value, and it would save the money. But the farmer could have figured that I, as a salesman, was interested in a fast sale and an easy buck, and when I saw that I was not going to get either of them, in essence I said to him, "Just forget about it, friend. I'll go somewhere else and find an easier sale."

Now please understand. There was no way I could climb down into his mind and know what he was or was not thinking, but I do offer these as possibilities. There's yet another possibility in the farmer's mind. When I stuck my ego out just a little and asked for the order, only to be rejected, the farmer could have thought I was overly sensitive to my own feeling and not sensitive enough to his needs. Thus when he slightly stepped on my ego, I quickly withdrew. Farmer's interpretation: Zig's interested in himself, not in solving my problems. If that was the case it should be obvious that *any salesman who is "wrapped up in himself" makes a mighty small package!*

As I say, there are many possibilities, but they all come out with the same result. I missed a sale and the commission which went with it. The farmer and his family missed the benefits which would have been theirs had I been professional and competent in dealing with this prospect.

Empathy Pays

Empathy is different. Jay Martin, a good friend of mine from Memphis, Tennessee, is the president of National Safety Associates, a company which sells smoke-and-fire detectors. He tells this story: One evening he was working with one of his young dealers. The dealer made a good, solid presentation to a prospect. When he finished he asked the obligating question. Then, Jay said, "Zig, this old boy, who probably didn't finish the first grade, reared back on the hind legs of his chair, folded his arms, and said, 'Well, son, of course you've heard about my wreck!' The young man hadn't, so the prospect proceeded to give him all the details."

This Guy Had Problems

Prospect: "Me and my wife were driving down the highway a couple of months ago and this dude who was passing on the wrong side of the road hit us head-on, tore our car all to pieces, and put us both in the hospital. As a matter of fact, I was in there nearly two weeks myself and it left my ankle kind of stiff. Since I work on a piece-good basis, I haven't been able to get around as well and my income's down and, man, that sure hurts!

"My wife was in the hospital over six weeks and she was gone so long her company phased out her job, so she's not even working. When you've been used to two incomes and all of a sudden you've only got one, man, that sure creates a problem! The hospital bill for both of us was over twenty thousand dollars. Now I know the insurance company's eventually going to pay it, but they sure have us nervous in the meantime!

"On top of all of that, just last week our boy came home from the navy and the first night at home he rounded a curve too fast, went over an embankment and down into a service station, tore up our other car, and destroyed a six thousand dollar oil company sign. Now, I know the insurance is going to pay for the car, but I don't know about that sign. I'll tell you right now, if we have to come up with six thousand dollars, we're really going to be up a creek and I don't know what we'll do!

"If all of that isn't enough, just last night we checked my mother-in-law into the most expensive nursing home in the county. The only other living relative is a brother and I know he won't do anything. He hasn't even been heard from in over a year and he's not worth shooting even if we did know where he was. I know I'm going to have to carry the whole load."

The "Empathy" Close

As you review this old boy's problems the chances are excellent you feel good about *your* situation in life, don't you? I mean, he did have a pretty heavy load to carry. If you were the salesman on this call and you had a lot of sympathy, you would probably say, "Oh, that's just terrible and I'll bet it's even worse than that! You just don't want to make me feel bad and that's the reason you're not telling me the rest of it! But let me ask you a question. Won't the government do something? What about the

Red Cross? What about your neighbors? Won't the church make a contribution? Can't you at least get food stamps?" Now *that's* sympathy, but according to Jay Martin this salesman did not have sympathy. He had empathy.

With empathy you are emotionally detached from the problem so you can offer solutions. *You move from your side of the table to the prospect's side. Realistically that is where the sale is going to be made and the chance of that happening is greatly increased because from his side of the table you can make your presentation from his point of view.*

According to Jay, that's what the young dealer was able to do. He looked the prospect in the eye and said, "Tell me, sir, in addition to those things, would there be any other reason you could not go ahead and protect the lives of your family by installing these smoke-and-fire detectors in your home?"

I don't know if you know what a *conniption* is but that's exactly what that old boy had. He literally roared with laughter, slapped his leg, and said, "No, son, those are the only reasons we couldn't go ahead and buy the alarms today. Ha, ha, ha!" (At that point I believe it would be safe to say that he did not consider himself a prospect.)

The "Physical Action" Close

Strategically the salesman had made a very wise move. You should bring out all the objections as early as possible so you can deal with them in the body of the presentation or early in the negotiating phase of selling.

When the salesman learned there were no other reasons for not buying he never hesitated. He reached down into his sample case (Jay Martin calls this the "Physical Action" Close), and removed one of the smoke detectors. He held the detector up against the wall to let the prospect see how it looked and said, "Sir, as nearly as I can tell, you now owe nearly thirty thousand dollars—[Pause]—and three hundred more just won't make any difference at all." (Pause—followed by the statement that got the sale.) He lowered his voice, looked the man in the eye, and quietly said, "Sir, fire—under *any* circumstances—is devastating. But in *your* case, it would wipe—you—out!" The technique was professional, the logic was sound. He got the sale.

He took the reason the old boy was giving him as to why he could *not* buy and used that as the reason why he *must* buy. *I don't care what you sell, the odds are at least ten to one that the prospect's reason for not buying can be used as a reason he should buy.* That last sentence is quite significant, so let's explore it further.

The "Can't Afford It" Close

In 1978 we had a severe hailstorm in Dallas. The winds blew, the hail fell, and rain came down in sheets. The next morning a nice little artistic design on the ceiling in our living room, den, and kitchen indicated we had a real problem. We called the roofer and his estimate came to something over $5,300. Now if I had said, "Can't afford it!" the salesman, assuming he was a pro, would have said to me, "Mr. Ziglar, if you can't afford to repair your roof, won't it be even more difficult after a few more rainstorms to afford the new furniture, the paint job, the new insulation in the attic, and still have to afford the new roof?"

One more time: Chances are excellent you can use the prospect's reason for not buying as the reason he *ought* to buy. "What do you mean, ten dollars to balance a tire? I can't afford to pay that kind of money!" "Mr. Prospect, if you can't afford ten dollars to balance a tire, then how will you be able to afford the greater expense of the new tire you're going to need much sooner?"

"Premiums! Man, I can't pay any more life insurance premiums now!" You've heard it a thousand times, "I'm already insurance-poor!" To begin with, I would say, "I've never met a widow who felt that her husband carried too much life insurance." That's the first thing. And the second, "If you, working full-time, cannot pay the premium, how will your family pay the grocery bill and the house payment if you are not there to work at all?"

"All that money for storm windows? Can't afford it!" "Mr. Prospect, if you can't afford the bill for the storm windows, what about the ever-increasing fuel bill?" Whatever the reason they give you for not buying, you can generally use that as the reason they ought to buy.

My salespeople (me, too) are confronted with the same objection after a presentation. "I can't afford it!" We teach our sales reps to look at the prospect and with a smile softly say, "Sir, if you are serious when you say you can't afford a few dollars for this training course on closing the sale, may I gently suggest you need to take whatever steps are necessary to get this course? The reason is simple: The techniques and closes will help you close more sales. By the way, sir, how many extra sales would you need to make in order to get your entire investment back?"

As you explore what empathy and ego are all about you'll discover that what I'm really saying is "Move to the prospect's side of the table, *identify* the problem, get involved in the solution, and your closing percentage will increase."

This Attaché Case Looks Like Brother Bern

One day several years ago I received a call from the Redhead, who was doing her (I should say "our") Christmas shopping. She was at Neiman-Marcus and was excited about an attaché case she had just seen. Her observation was, "Honey, this attaché case looks exactly like Brother Bern!"

Now, rather obviously, she did not mean that they had made an attaché case in the configuration of my Brother Bern from Winnipeg, Canada. What she did mean was, had Bernie Lofchick been in Neiman-Marcus shopping for an attaché case, after looking at all of them he would have chosen this one and said, "This one fits me. This one *looks* like me."

Empathy is the ability to get inside the feelings of the other person and look at his wants and needs through his eyes. The Redhead was doing that in the purchase of that particular attaché case. There's an old adage which says *if you're going to sell John Jones what John Jones buys, you've got to sell John Jones through John Jones' eyes.* That's empathy.

Empathy is what you use—or should be using—when you buy your friend, wife, husband, children, boss, or employee a gift of any kind. You should be thinking in terms of what that person would choose or would like if he or she were making the purchase.

Empathy, from the retail salesperson's point of view, can substantially increase sales when you deal with those shoppers who are buying for someone else. Example: Psychologist Erwin S. Weiss of Cleveland, Ohio, suggests that grandparents generally want to give gifts to be remembered, parents give gifts which are practical, and youngsters give gifts to please their immediate interests. Armed with this basic information, an alert clerk can concentrate the prospect's *looking* time and his own sales efforts on those items which most nearly fill the bill for the shopper who is buying gifts.

Empathy Improves Teamwork

Ted Lamb is a successful Chevrolet dealer in Prescott, Arizona. In 1982 (a serious recession year for the auto industry), Lamb Chevrolet increased its unit sales by 69 percent over 1981 and its dollar volume by 68 percent over 1981. From a profitability point of view, 1982 was Lamb's best year as a Chevrolet dealer.

Many factors enter the picture when you start asking the why and how of such a tremendous year. To begin with, Ted is a hardworking optimist who is civic-minded and family-oriented. He is also a creative manager with a "go give" spirit. And he possesses a tremendous amount of empathy.

All successful businesses must have a spirit of oneness and teamwork among the various departments. This is especially true in the automobile business, where cooperation between sales and service rates at the top of the totem pole in importance. On too many occasions, communication breakdowns occur because the sales department can't understand why the service department is unable to give 100 percent instantly perfect service to all reasonable and unreasonable customers. By the same token the servicepeople can't understand why salespeople constantly put them on the spot with "impossible" and often "idiotic" requests for service.

At Lamb Chevrolet those communication problems are few and far between because of a unique procedure initiated several years ago. Periodically the service manager and the sales manager (who incidentally enjoy the same income) swap hats, departments, and responsibilities for a few days. This way each manager literally does walk in the other manager's shoes. He gains considerable insight in the day-to-day responsibilities, opportunities, and yes, even challenges the other manager faces. In the process he develops considerable empathy for his companion manager's role. Needless to say, when each manager returns to his own stand it is with a deeper appreciation and understanding of the role the other manager plays in the daily operation of the business.

This process produces three winners. Each manager gains a new appreciation for the familiar waters of his own job and the unfamiliar waters of the other manager's job, so he wins. The customer wins because of better service in *both* departments. Lamb Chevrolet wins because the team spirit in all departments enables them to serve their customers better, which means they have more customers to serve.

9

THE RIGHT
MENTAL ATTITUDE

As WE CAREFULLY EXPLORE the building of a sales career, one area that stands near the top of the *must* list is the development of the right mental attitude. My book *See You at the Top* deals with attitude in considerable depth, so I'm not going to go into extensive detail concerning attitude as it relates to closing the sale. However, there are four phases of attitude which I feel are critical if you're going to *close* the sale instead of getting *close* to the sale.

First we will look at attitude in general. Second, we will look at your attitude toward you, meaning essentially your self-image. Third, we will explore your attitude toward the prospects you're going to be dealing with; and fourth, we will look at your attitude toward the profession of selling.

Positive Thinking Can Be Frustrating

As an advocate of positive thinking I frequently encounter people who are enormously confused about the subject. They often think we positive thinkers believe with positive thinking we can do anything. That's ridiculous. Positive thinking won't let you do *anything*, but it will help you do *everything* better than negative thinking will.

I don't care how positive I became, I could not whip the heavyweight champion of the world. As a matter of fact, I don't even believe I could take out your appendix and have you live. But this I know, if you and I were isolated on a desert island a thousand miles from everybody and you were to suffer an attack of appendicitis, I personally believe you would prefer I approach you with a winning attitude!

Surely you would feel much better if I were to enthusiastically say, "I'm not a doctor, but reading a lot and watching a lot of television gives me reason to be positive. In the last week I watched three appendectomies and fortunately, I have an extremely sharp knife with me and some powerful medicine that will kill all the infection. My optimistic nature would have me going after Moby Dick in a rowboat and taking the tartar sauce with me!

"Personally I believe that despite my lack of training I can get your appendix out of there, and I just flat believe you're going to make it!" Odds are great you would prefer that approach and attitude over my looking you in the eye and saying, "Man, you're gonna die!"

As a practical matter there isn't one doctor in a hundred who wouldn't agree that the first approach would give you a much better chance of surviving.

You Can Do It—Here's How

Realistically there is a chance that pure positive thinking and motivation without direction can lead to frustration. For example, someone convinces you that you've got what it takes. They say, "Go for it, I know you're going to make it," and then send you out with no training or direction. There is a chance you will fall flat on your face and become frustrated and dejected.

With this in mind, let me briefly identify what I believe. Positive thinking is an optimistic hope—not necessarily based on any facts—that you can move mountains. *I've seen positive thinking move some mountains.* Positive believing is the same optimistic hope, based on reasons for believing you can move those mountains. *I've seen positive believing move far more mountains.*

Secrets of Closing the Sale is a book of positive *believing*. It gives you *reasons* for believing you can move those mountains (make more sales). It gives you the methods, techniques, and procedures which, when applied, will result in more sales. The game plan for *Secrets* is simple: *I will never make a promise—unless I give you a plan and procedure to make that promise possible.*

This book, combined with the knowledge your sales manager or company will provide for you, gives you the information necessary to make more sales. As a practical matter, we can theoretically teach you every situation known to man in a book or in the classroom. Then guess what happens? The first day in the field the theory is shot down by some customer who hasn't read the book or attended our training classes.

He asks some question or brings up some objection which we had not considered. The only way you're ever going to be able to handle those situations is from the personal experience you have out in the field on an eyeball-to-eyeball basis with a customer. The information in this book, combined with the specifics from your company sales trainers, plus your experience in the field, will form a powerful combination to enable you to become the professional you aspire to be.

Your Mental Attitude Makes the Difference

Your mental attitude and everything else about you is influenced or controlled by what goes into your mind. It's safe to say that *you are what you are and where you are because of what has gone into your mind. You change what you are and where you are by changing what goes into your mind.*

Chances are excellent you want most of the things in life everyone else wants: good health, extra money, security, friends, peace of mind, happiness, and all the good stuff. Assuming you either don't have all these things or at least you don't have them in the amount or to the extent you desire them, two possibilities exist.

First, you might be too young and simply haven't had enough time. (If you're over thirty I hope you don't hide behind that one.) Second, and far more likely, your *behavior* is not producing the desired results. This being the case, it should be clear that you need to *change* behavior if you are going to get what you want. What might not be as obvious is the fact that before you can change your behavior you *must* change your thinking. *But* before you *can* change your thinking you *must* change the input into your mind.

If we really do want what we *say* we want—good health, extra money, security, friends, peace of mind, happiness—we must put those positive goals into our minds. This input comes from *positive* friends and associates. Additional input *must* come from reading the *right* kind of books, listening to the *right* kind of recordings, and attending educational, motivational seminars. Through these sources we plant those desirable thoughts of good health, extra money, security, friends, peace of mind, and happiness in our heads.

Buy this next thought and you will *sell* more of what you sell.

> *Your business is never really good or bad out there. Your business is either good or bad right between your own two ears.*

Example: At this moment you are in the best place, at the best time to do the most selling. (Yes, that is realistic. The only time you have and are sure of is the time you have *right now.* Since you are where you are and nowhere else, you can sell only where you are, so you are at the right place at the right time.)

Many "Gloomy Guses" and "prophets of doom" spread their gloom by periodically announcing we're headed for a business slump. Without fail, about every four or five years they announce the coming "recession." Speaker Don Hutson of Memphis, Tennessee, points out the media has accurately predicted eighteen of the last two recessions. (You might need to think about that one.) When they announce the next recession, you've got to make a choice to join or not to join. I'm in favor of joining some clubs like Rotary, Lions, Civitan, and other outstanding service organizations, but personally I'm not in favor of joining the Recession Club.

In my travels I see people in every walk of life selling every conceivable product, from ten-cent whatnots to multimillion-dollar computers. Regardless of the company, industry, or section of the country, some are doing extremely well, some are doing fairly well, and some are going broke. The business is there for all but, everything else being equal, the salesperson with a good self-image and positive mental attitude will get more than his share of business and the salesperson suffering from "stinkin' thinkin' " will get a much smaller share.

The "Go Giver" Close

One excellent example of the right mental attitude is the story of Calvin Hunt from Victoria, Texas. Calvin is one of the really great professional life insurance salesmen in this country. A former Houston Oiler offensive lineman and an extremely creative, civic-minded citizen, Calvin uses a lot of the little extras to produce business. His attitude is certainly one of his outstanding assets. Each year he invites an inspirational speaker as a community service for the town. He reserves the front rows of the auditorium for his clients and invites the general public to occupy the remaining seats. There is no charge to anyone for this.

Calvin is one of those multimillion-dollar producers who writes contracts involving well over $100,000 in premiums. He has a chauffeur-driven limousine and while he's being driven to his appointments, which are sometimes 20 miles or 120 miles away, he is preparing his presentation and taking care of the details of his business.

He explained to me that in 1982 roughly half the insurance people felt business was down and consequently they reduced their efforts. Calvin did explain that business was down a little, but half of his competition was not really working to expand their business. Since there was about 90 percent as much business available and only 50 percent as much competition, Calvin figured his business had to increase substantially. As you might suspect, his business did increase dramatically that year. Yes, attitude does make a difference.

10

YOUR ATTITUDE
TOWARD YOU

IF YOU'RE REALLY INTERESTED in building your sales career, or for that matter any other kind of career, you've got to start by building a healthy self-image. One of my early mentors, Dr. Emol Fails of Raleigh, North Carolina, says *you don't build a business—you build people—and then people build the business.*

When we talk about closing sales we've got to face the fact that many salespeople are colorful. By colorful I mean they're yellow! They just flat don't ask for the order! They talk and talk and talk but they don't ask for the order because they have that fear of rejection. Outstanding sales trainer Chris Hegarty points out that 63 percent of all sales interviews end with no direct effort on the salesperson's part to close the sale.

The salesperson doing all the talking is desperately hoping the prospect will interrupt the presentation and say, "OK, I'll take it." This way the salesman won't have to risk his ego by making a direct closing effort and chancing a direct refusal.

Salesperson or Professional Visitor

In my own career I've been on sales calls and watched the salesperson drone on and on and on and never get around to asking for the order. I've even heard prospects say, "Well, John, you're not trying to sell me something are you?" And the salesman would verbally back away and say, "Oh, noooo, noo, no!" Makes you wonder who he thought he was and what he thought he was doing, doesn't it? Apparently he thought he was a professional visitor. IF that's what you think you are, then this chapter will be quite important to you.

Now, as I understand it, the purpose of the sales interview, whether you go to see the prospect or he comes to see you, is to get the order. Yet, because of poor self-image and this fear of rejection, 63 percent of all sales interviews wind down and drift into oblivion without a *direct effort* to close the sale.

102

So important is your self-image in improving your closing skills and effectiveness that I want to digress for a moment and give you a sales talk on doing something about your own self-image. If you have a problem with yours, and you are the *only* person who *really* knows whether you do or not, I urge you to get busy and do something about it.

One of the many steps you can take toward building a healthy self-image is for you to take a good public-speaking course. The ability to express yourself on your feet is one of the greatest confidence-builders known to man. Chances are excellent your church, community college, or school offers such a course. I have two image-building courses, I CAN and BORN TO WIN. Toastmasters, Toastmistresses, and the Dale Carnegie courses are all excellent image-builders.

Another surefire step in building a good self-image is to become an expert, a real pro, in your chosen profession of selling. A quick count will reveal well over one hundred closes in this book. Learn those that specifically apply to you and your selling situation. Even more important than learning them is to *live them*. Make them a part of you. Adapt them for your own use and you will feel a surge of confidence—your image will improve because you know that in a sales situation the odds are great you are going to come out "smelling like a rose." With improved effectiveness your love for selling will be even greater because an important key to maintaining a good attitude is to *know* what you are doing.

Make Certain the Neighborhood Is Safe

Perhaps this next example will bring to life for you the absolute necessity of building your self-image if you really expect to build an outstanding sales career. In this example I use real estate, but it could apply to any product or salesperson who goes out after business.

Let's assume you have a poor self-image. You're out working your "farm" or territory one morning when you see a FOR SALE BY OWNER sign in the yard. You circle the block three times to make absolutely certain the neighborhood is safe. (You should be careful, shouldn't you?) You finally decide the neighborhood is safe, so you knock on the door (timidly, I might add). The dear lady comes to the door and you start your presentation. After about two sentences the homeowner says, "Just a minute. Let me ask you a question. Do you sell real estate? Just answer yes or no."

You confess that you do sell real estate, so the dear lady says, "I'm just not interested. I'm going to tell you the same thing I told the last two people who came by here selling real estate. I'm going to sell this house myself. I planted every bush, every shrub, every tree in this yard, and I'm not going to give you thousands of dollars for selling my house when I know a lot more about the house than you will ever know. Furthermore, I don't want to hear any more about it!" And she slams the door in your face.

Poor Image Is the Problem

Now remember, you've got a poor self-image. You don't like you and that old biddy *sure* doesn't like you! Chances are a hundred to one you will *react* with, "Poor little me! Nobody likes me!" So what do you do? You do the only thing you can. You go to the coffee shop for a cup of coffee. While you're drinking the first cup you realize what you really need is a second cup. As you slowly drink that second cup of coffee, you come to some "interesting" conclusions.

"Why didn't I think about this before? It is so obvious! What I've got to do is go back to the office, make all the telephone calls I need to make, clean up all the details on my desk, handle all the correspondence, and do all of my service work. After all, you just can't sell with a bunch of nagging details hanging over you. Monday morning I'll get out there with a clean mind and no nagging details so I'll knock 'em dead! Besides, it's already Wednesday!"

Let me tell you something. Ninety-eight percent of the people who procrastinate have image problems. They just don't want to get out and face the possible rejection every salesperson alive faces every time he makes a call. People reject salesmen—desks don't—so, it's safe to go hide behind that desk, a golf club, or, for that matter, *another* planning session. Don't misunderstand. I believe in planning and taking care of details, but after a certain point (like eating alphabet soup in alphabetical order or proofreading the Xerox copy) planning becomes an escape from action to avoid rejection. *If you're overorganized, with more records on less business than you should have, now is the time to take action.*

Good Image Is the Solution

Now let's look at this illustration under identical circumstances, but with one important change. This time you have a good, healthy self-image. You are in the same neighborhood and you see the FOR SALE BY OWNER sign in the yard. So you go knock on the door. The same dear lady comes to the door and after a brief but unpleasant dialogue she slams the door in your face.

This time, however, you *respond* because you have a good, healthy self-image. You understand *it's the lady who has the problem*; you are not personally incapacitated. As a result, you go down the street and find a prospect who does not have a problem!

I'm confident you've heard—maybe even made—the statement "*He* makes me so mad," or "*She* makes me so mad." Let's set the record straight on that one. As my friend Bob George says, "You can't stir soup unless there's soup in the pot." Others don't put "mad" in you, but if it's there they can stir it up, *if* you *choose* to let them. It's up to you to decide whether or not you are going to invite them to come in and tell you how to think, how to act, and how to feel.

From My Sales Notebook

Let me share some personal experiences to emphasize the point that *the salesman's self-image has a direct bearing on his sales success.* As a young salesman, when I was out knocking on doors I would often have a prospect in one house, another prospect next door, and yet another prospect twenty miles down the highway. I would make the call at the first house and if I were rejected by that prospect I used an amazing ability I had. Let me explain. As a young salesman I could actually look at the *outside* of a house and tell you if it were the "right psychological moment" to make the call. In my imagination I could see them eating lunch, taking a nap, having a knock-down-drag-out fight, or 101 other things which I used to justify *not* making the call on the prospect next door.

What would I do? Very simple. I'd get into my car and drive twenty miles down the highway to see another prospect. How could I justify that? Easy. I needed the driving time to "plan" what I was going to say when I got there. (After all, I had been rejected on the previous call because I had not properly "planned" what I said.) I was justifying the fact that I was "working" during that twenty-mile drive.

The point is obvious and hopefully helpful. I had a poor self-image. I had rejected myself. In my mind the prospect in the first house had rejected me, and I wasn't ready to go next door for another rejection. One more time. *Improve your self-image and you will improve your sales performance.*

"They" Can't Make You Feel Inferior—
Without Your Permission

When your self-image is solid, you can go from one prospect to the next many times, almost regardless of the reception you get. (I'll be the first to admit that *everyone* has a limit to the number of rejections he can handle. That's the reason I frequently make reference to building your self-image and listening to cassette recordings regularly, especially after being refused/rejected forcefully several times.)

As a salesperson it will help you enormously from an image point of view to understand that *nobody on the face of this earth can make you feel inferior without your permission.* Once you get your image right—and that's what everything I write or record is directly or indirectly aimed at doing—then your sales world *and* your personal world will improve. The late Dr. Maxwell Maltz, plastic surgeon and author of *Psychocybernetics,* said the purpose of all psychotherapy is to build the self-esteem, that is, the image, of the patient.

Obviously I'm not talking about a superinflated, "I AM THE GREATEST" kind of self-image. (Actually that's the opposite of a healthy self-image. The "I AM THE GREATEST" chest-thumper is, in almost every case, manifesting a poor self-image.) Most people think of that individual as being conceited, which is a disease that makes everybody sick—except the person who has it!)

All great salespeople have strong (not inflated) egos. They cease to be great when the ego has them!

I'm talking about a good, healthy self-image of self-acceptance. When you can accept yourself, with your own faults and shortcomings, it's much easier for you to understand and communicate (I didn't say *agree*) with other people—including your prospects. Your self-image *is* important, so build a good one and you will be able to build your sales career bigger, better, and faster.

Regardless of where you are in your sales career, and regardless of what your self-image might be at this moment, I believe as far as the sales profession is concerned I've walked in your shoes and felt your feelings. I don't believe any one of you who will ever read this, listen to a tape, view a film of mine, or sit in a class I conduct has ever been "broker," "scareder," more uncertain, more apprehensive, or had more doubts about what tomorrow had to offer than I had. I don't believe you have ever been any further down in the dumps or did not like to make that initial approach any more than I did when I first entered the world of selling. I say all of this to give you my personal assurance that there is hope for *you.*

11

YOUR ATTITUDE
TOWARD OTHERS

THE THIRD PHASE of attitude I wish to share with you is your attitude toward others. How do you really view that person you're dealing with across the counter? Is he someone you can "make a buck" by selling to, or does he represent a person with a problem which you can help solve? Are you really thoughtful and considerate of him, or is your main focus on making the sale and reaping the benefits for yourself?

In survey after survey around the country, the number-one complaint from customers is that of rudeness, inefficiency, or plain indifference. Two of these obviously have to do with simple human relations, and if we do not practice those we're not going to have any humans to relate to or sell to as far as our place of business is concerned.

Cavett Robert points out that nearly three-fourths of the population of the world goes to bed hungry every night. He also says that an even higher percentage of people go to bed every night *hungry* for recognition. Of considerable importance is the fact that every merchant and salesperson recognizes the value of every person who walks into your place of business or the importance of every prospect you deal with. Plain, simple courtesy and thoughtfulness will go a long way toward improving your business and building your sales career.

As a practical matter I challenge you to observe the personal qualities and characteristics of the top-performing men and women in the sales and business world as well as the political and religious world. You will discover that almost without exception they are described in two words: Be Nice.

How do you see your relationship with your prospect? Do you think of yourself as a friend, as someone who truly can help and advise the other person, someone who looks after the interests of the prospect? Do you buy the idea that he profits most who serves best? I hope you do, because in the world of selling the way to build customers is to build a winning relationship with the people with whom you are dealing.

Dr. Anthony J. Allessandra, author of *Non-Manipulative Selling,* reports in a December 1982 article for *PMA ADVISER* that in the average business

1. 68% of the customers who quit trading with them left because of indifference and apparent lack of interest on the part of the seller's employees.

2. 14% left because of unadjusted complaints.

3. 9% left because they could buy at lower prices elsewhere.

4. 5% left to buy from a friend or relative.

5. 3% moved to another area.

6. 1% were lost through death.

Normally, a company's or salesperson's annual customer turnover should not exceed 18 percent, and anything beyond that should be cause for concern. Otherwise, in a matter of a few years you will be completely out of business if you don't soon replace your lost customers with new ones. With the exceptions of death (1 percent) and moving (3 percent), a good portion of the remaining 14 percent (9 percent lost to lower prices and 5 percent lost to friends or relatives) can be salvaged by professionally aggressive sales and marketing methods. The customers who are lost because of indifference, lack of interest, and unadjusted complaints (82 percent) can be salvaged with good, old-fashioned human relations.

Everybody, including coaches, dentists, household executives, ministers, builders, interior designers, etc., sells and everything is selling. With that in mind, it simply makes sense to become a highly productive professional. One interesting discovery by The Forum Corporation was that the high performers were just as thorough in their sales-and-service approach with members of the internal staff as they were with customers. Since salespeople—even high-performance ones—generally have no subordinates, they get their work done through others over whom they have little or no direct control. They practice good human relations and sell the support people at the home office on shipping, installing, servicing, and generally just helping them (the high performers) please the customers. This enables the high performer to keep his commitments to the customer and demonstrates to the customer that he, the top performer, is a person who can be trusted and is dependable. This next little dissertation says it extremely well:

I'm Your Customer Who Never Comes Back

I'm a nice customer. All merchants know me. I'm the one who never complains no matter what kind of service I get.

When I go to a store to buy something I don't throw my weight around. I try to be thoughtful of the other person. If I get a snooty clerk who gets nettled because I want to look at several things before I make up my mind, I'm as polite as can be; I don't believe rudeness in return is the answer.

I never kick, complain, or criticize, and I wouldn't dream of making a scene as I've seen people doing in public places. No, I'm the nice customer, but I'm also the nice customer who never comes back.

That's my little revenge for being abused and taking whatever you hand out, because I know I'm not coming back. This way doesn't immediately relieve my feelings but in the long run it's far more satisfying than blowing my top.

In fact, a nice customer like myself, multiplied by others of my kind, can ruin a business. And there are a lot of nice people just like me. When we get pushed far enough, we go to another store where they appreciate nice customers.

He laughs best, they say, who laughs last. I laugh when I see you frantically advertising to get me back, when you could have kept me in the first place with a few kind words and a smile.

Your business might be in a different town and your situation might be "different," but if your business is bad, chances are good that if you will change your attitude the word will get around and I'll change from the nice customer who never comes back to the nice customer who always comes back—and brings his friends.

ANONYMOUS

Making a serious effort to keep our customer makes good economic sense for two important reasons. According to Larry J. Rosenberg and John A. Czepiel, writing in the March 1984 issue of *The Journal of Consumer Marketing*, a lost customer reduces average company profits by $118 compared with a $20 cost to keep the customer satisfied. Despite this fact, it is estimated that the average company spends six times as much to get a new customer as it does to hold a current one.

I might also add that if a customer leaves disgruntled, he will tell an average of eleven other people about the *problem*. That can really be costly.

Incidentally, *losers* think in terms of "replacing" customers; *winners* think in terms of maintaining customers *and* adding new ones in order to build the business bigger and better.

Let me bluntly state if that is your attitude as you deal with your prospect, you're not going to sell or earn nearly as much. Earlier I emphasized the point that selling is a "transference" of feeling. I also made the point that your prospect picks up the feeling of greed and self-interest and you ring up another "no sale."

This story identifies the winning (you *and* the customer) attitude. Several years ago, while bowling in Omaha, Nebraska, I injured my right knee. One of my friends, whose elevator doesn't quite reach the top, made some catty reference to my age. My friend wasn't overly bright or he would have recognized that the left knee was exactly the same age as the right knee, and it was in good shape so, obviously, my age had no bearing on the condition of my right knee!

Not long after I injured the knee I was scheduled to speak in San Francisco to about twenty-five hundred people. After the introduction, as I came hobbling onstage, I could *feel* that audience thinking to themselves, "For goodness sake! Just look at Zig! Bless his heart, he's all crippled up, but I'll bet he's going to do the best he can." As a speaker I could *feel* the feeling of the audience.

To be candid, I'll have to confess that to this day I don't quite understand the therapeutic value of a microphone around the neck as it relates to sore knees. Apparently there is some medicinal value, because when they put that mike around my neck, my knee quit hurting! For the next sixty-five minutes I was up and down, around and about, stooping, squatting, shouting, whooping, hollering, and doing all the things my audiences are accustomed to seeing me do. During the entire sixty-five minutes, I never felt a pain. I finished making the talk, stepped down off the stage, and the knee collapsed, causing me to fall.

Selling Is a Win-Win Situation

I daresay you know exactly what happened. For sixty-five minutes I was not thinking about Ziglar and his knee. I was thinking about my prospects and how I could help them solve their problems. I did not do this consciously, but subconsciously. When I finished making the talk I relaxed inside. It was like I said to myself, "OK Ziglar, you can forget about all those people. Think about yourself." When my thoughts turned inward toward self instead of outward toward helping others, I fell flat on my face.

The same thing will happen to you. Don't misunderstand. I'm highly skeptical of people who adjust their halos and claim, "I sell my product just because I love to help people." (I notice that they always cash their commission checks!) I hasten to add that I like to help people, too, but all of us are alike in one respect. If our company quit paying us for selling, then financial necessity would force us to quit helping people by selling our products or services, regardless of the depth of our belief and regardless of our love for what we do.

When you talk to a prospect you ought to be wrapped up in solving his problem because in the process you will definitely be reaching your own sales and career objectives. This attitude in selling definitely puts you *and* your customer in a win-win situation.

To develop this attitude which leads to building a winning relationship with your customer, let's take a look at what DeMarco and Maginn of The Forum Corporation discovered about how the customers of high performers see the top producer and his role.

As King Customer Sees the Salesperson
(Forum Report)

The customer sees the high-performing sales professional as a person who is genuinely interested in his (the customer's) needs, even while he actively promotes his or her company's own position. This "balance" encourages clients to share confidential information trustingly, knowing the sales representative will try to understand his concerns and be fair in his dealings. The customer sees the high performer as one who *exchanges* information rather than as one who simply gives sales presentations from his perspective.

The high performer is sensitive to the value of the customer's time and is able to spend more *quality* time in front of the customer because he spends more quality time planning strategy and preparing for the call. Customers perceive this and value it highly. He is aware of the personal pressures and needs faced by the customer and sells to these *people*, not to companies.

One myth—that a salesperson should not get involved with customer concerns other than the purpose of the sales call—was exploded, as was the concept that price isn't important and that you should "promise them anything" to close a sale. Customers want and expect their salespeople to be able to act as trustworthy resources who respond directly and provide them expertise, backed by effective recommendations. *One significant characteristic of the high producer is his willingness to explain product drawbacks.*

To customers, the salesperson who is enthusiastic and interested in working with them to solve problems rates as a more successful performer than one who does not. A salesperson who builds relationships and provides a valuable service, whether advice, information, or opinion, is unequivocally considered a high performer by the customer and can penetrate an organization at several levels. Customers feel the basic sales-skills training prevalent in industry today needs to be continued. Product knowledge, competitive knowledge, and the so-called face-to-face skills (selling features/benefits, handling objections, etc.) are still prerequisites for the sales job.

A word to the wise should be sufficient. If you listen to what the customers of the top producers have to say, your chances of joining the ranks of the top producers are greatly enhanced.

12

YOUR ATTITUDE TOWARD THE SALES PROFESSION

SELLING IS THE best-paying hard work and the lowest-paying easy work in the world. For those who "get in selling" and then let selling "get in them," the sales profession offers an exciting, rewarding, and demanding career. What the late Fred Herman entitled his excellent book on selling is true: *Selling Is Simple (Not Easy)*. So let's take a comprehensive look at this profession which has been my life since I sold vegetables and milk door-to-door when I was eight years old.

Large numbers of salespeople are enthusiastic about the product they sell. They believe their company is the greatest and they're pleased to be affiliated with the people who represent the company. However, a high percentage of these salespeople are hesitant to admit they sell for a living. I'm going to make a big deal out of this point because your *total* attitude toward yourself—your prospect, your product, your company, *and* the profession of selling—will often determine whether you make or miss the sale. This is especially true on the close ones. Although this chapter will not include any techniques in selling per se, it will be enormously helpful in closing the close ones.

Be Proud You Sell

I'm proud to be a salesman for many reasons. I believe America is a great nation because we are a nation of salespeople. America was discovered by a salesman. Not by any stretch of the imagination could you accuse Christopher Columbus of being a navigator. History records that he was looking for a short route to India. He missed it by about twelve thousand miles and still went back home and told them he had found it. Where I come from, that's not navigation.

You might say, "Well, that still doesn't prove he was a salesman." True, but think about this: First of all, he was an Italian in Spain, so he was speaking a foreign language. By most territorial assignments he was *way* out of his sales territory. He had only one prospect to call on, so if he missed the sale he would have had a long swim home. To say the least, that's pressure selling!

The "Columbus" Close

He called on Isabella and told his story. After listening to his presentation Isabella said, "That sounds like a good idea, Chris, but twelve thousand dollars for five little ships is ridiculous!" (Till this day many people don't realize they started with five ships—but two of them *did* go over the side!) Columbus heard the money objection Isabella raised, but since he heard what she said *and* what she was saying (page 90), he knew that money wasn't the problem.

He instantly recognized that she was not sold on all the advantages of being the one to discover the short route to India. He knew she felt the cost was greater than the benefit and common sense dictated that neither Isabella nor any other prospect would pay more for something than she felt it was worth. With this in mind, Chris put on his sales shoes and started painting pictures of all the good things that would happen to her nation and the recognition she would get if she were responsible for discovering that short route to India.

Columbus pointed out the colonization possibilities among the lands which were sure to be discovered. He stressed the savings in time, the possibilities of new and unknown foods, spices, gems, and furs. Undoubtedly, Chris reminded her that she would be able to spread the Christian message to the "savages" beyond the horizon. I'm confident he painted the picture of Spain's getting a significant jump on France and England in their competition for world domination.

When the factual/emotional sales presentation had ended and the decision ball was in the air (a *lot* was at stake on this sales call, wasn't it?), Isabella said, "OK, Chris, I'm sold. The only problem is I don't have any money." With this, Columbus looked at her and said, "Look, Izzy" (since I was not there, I'm not sure this is verbatim), "you've got that string of beads hanging around your neck. Let's take 'em down to the pawnshop and hock 'em and we'll finance this deal."

Your history book will tell you they did have to use unusual methods to raise the money to finance the trip. Once the voyage was under way Columbus still had to do a lot of selling. History records that the sailors daily threatened to throw him overboard and sail back home. Since Columbus was selling for his life, I'm confident his daily sales presentation was heavy on the conviction side. Few salesmen in history have had the need to be *trusted* as Columbus had. On a daily basis he had to *sell* in order to *sail*. Then one morning the call came forth, "Land, ho!" And Christopher Columbus had "landed" the most profitable sales call in history.

Tell Your Customers You Love Them

Then Christopher Columbus did what salespeople too often have a tendency to do, and in the process he made the biggest mistake of his sales career. *He did not service the account.* He apparently assumed that since it was *his* idea and *he* had been the one to open such incredible opportunity doors, *he* would be forever remembered—and rewarded.

If you have just started your sales career, I'd like to inform you that it doesn't work that way. If you're an experienced pro in the sales world, I hope I don't need to remind you it doesn't work that way. The reason is competition, the majority of which is legitimate. Competitors are ever-present and they are going to be wooing and courting *your* customers (you do feel possessive, don't you?) with their best foot forward at all times.

When you make the sale you are in the enviable position of being in the driver's seat, but when you take your eye off the road (the customer) and your foot off the gas pedal (service), competition starts selling the idea they are better drivers and have more and better gas.

Service—the Key to a Sales Career

In Columbus's case, the "competition" was Amerigo Vespucci. He started selling and servicing the account. Result: We did not become the United States of Columbus; we became the United States of *America*, because Columbus didn't service the sale.

The "Courtship" Close

I'm personally convinced this is often an important factor in the breakup of many marriages. The guy and the gal put a sales story on each other during the courtship (sales) process like you just flat cannot believe! All during the courtship, each one is on his or her "best behavior" routine at all times. Each one makes and honestly strives to keep commitments and promises. Each one puts, and keeps, that best foot forward. He showers and puts on all that good, masculine cologne, and she bathes and puts on that sweet-smelling stuff. Each one is always prompt, always thoughtful and considerate—until finally they talk each other into the trip down the aisle!

Now Things Change

Then they quit courting. Oh, they don't quit the day after the honeymoon, or even the week or month after, but over a period of time they gradually start phasing out those thoughtful, loving, considerate little actions for each other. They begin to abandon some of their good grooming habits. They gradually fade away from the thoughtful, considerate, loving acts for each other. They start letting other things and other activities enter into the picture. Don't misunderstand—I'm not implying that marriage can maintain the same ecstasy the honeymoon did, but I do believe that courtship and courtesy are absolute musts for the marriage not only to endure but to be exciting and meaningful for each other as well.

We often hear of the "other man" or the "other woman." Actually, there would be no room for the other man or the other woman if the husband and wife simply kept their priorities in order and continued to court each other throughout their marriage. In short, our divorce rate would drop dramatically if men and women "delivered" in marriage what they "sold" while courting.

By the same token, I believe in most cases when we lose a customer to competition it is not because of a better price or a better product, though obviously that can enter the picture. In most cases it is because competition came in and "courted" *our* customer as we had "courted" him before the "marriage" (sale) with better service, more interest, more concern, and by listening more attentively to the needs of *our* customers.

To tie the sales and courtship examples together, someone rhetorically asked, "When should you tell your wife you love her?" And the wit said, "Before somebody else does!" When should you tell your customers you love them? The same answer—before somebody else does! *Then* you should demonstrate your sincerity by showing that love through service.

Columbus did not service the account, but that does not alter the fact that we were *discovered* by a salesman and *named* after a salesman. We were *populated* by a salesman. Sir Walter Raleigh toured the coffee-houses of London selling those ignorant, fearful, superstitious people on the idea they should leave the security of England and come into America where they would have religious freedom and a chance to become landowners. Many of them bought that idea, so America was at least partially populated by that salesman.

George Was a Salesman

We were *freed* by a salesman. Do you fully realize what a tremendous sales job George Washington did in gaining our independence? At that time, America was almost equally divided into three factions. One-third of the colonists wanted their independence; one-third wanted to stay with Britain, and one-third said, "Look, George, whichever side wins is the one we're going to go with. During the conflict we'll stay neutral, but when the danger is passed and the winner is established, we will throw in with that winner. You can depend on our doing exactly that."

George Washington had to get his recruits for the Continental army from the farmers, merchants, backwoodsmen, seamen, laborers, and shipbuilders. He had to be candid and say, "Gentlemen, if we win, I'm probably not going to be able to pay you and if we lose, you'll be hung from the highest tree as traitors." Please remember that only one-third of the colonists actually wanted independence and *all* of them knew that England had the most powerful army *and* navy in the world. Yes, Washington's recruiting (sales) job was formidable.

I mention this again to let those of you who do any recruiting know that your job is simple by comparison. Suppose you had to tell your prospective recruits that every sales call they made would be on a prospect who had never bought anything from anybody. Furthermore, even if they (the new recruits) did make a sale, there would be no funds to pay them, but if they missed the sale they would be shot at sunrise. Yup, George Washington was quite a salesman!

Salespeople Are Important

We became an ocean-to-ocean nation and an international power as a direct result of salespeople. Once we had won our independence, Alexander Hamilton persuaded President Washington to petition Congress for an appropriation so we could study the methods the British had used to set up their colonies and "agents" to merchandise their products and services around the world. At this point, though we had been settled since 1608, in the ensuing 168 years we had made it only to the Appalachian Mountains.

With independence and the benefits of the knowledge acquired because of the appropriation, we were moved to set up trading posts manned by salesmen so that when settlers started moving westward they were able to obtain gunpowder, blankets, and supplies. Because of these trading-post salesmen, just thirty years after we won our independence, America had made it all the way to the West Coast.

Salespeople Make the Difference

Yes, America is the greatest land on this earth because of the salespeople. We definitely are not the greatest because of our size, because Canada, Russia, China, and Brazil are all larger than America. It is not because of our great natural resources, though we have certainly been abundantly blessed in this area. Realistically, Brazil, Russia, China, Canada, and other nations all have tremendous natural resources.

It's not because of our technological superiority, though we are undoubtedly the number-one nation in the world in that area. Still, the Japanese, Germans, Swiss, Russians, and Israelis are our masters in some areas of technological development. In my mind it is crystal clear. We've been able to do what we've done because of salespeople and our free-enterprise structure.

Salespeople Are Secure

I suppose one of the reasons I'm so tremendously excited about the profession is because of the security it offers. Should my own son come to me and ask what I consider the most secure job in the world, I would unhesitatingly say to him that it is a sales job. He, as well as you, might well labor under the illusion that salespeople are the only people who work entirely on commission. This illusion would naturally provoke the question "Does this really offer security?"

The answer is yes, it does offer *real* security, and all jobs are commission jobs. My secretary—and for that matter, every other person in our society—is literally on commission. The salesperson and everybody else, whether he *receives* a salary or is *paid* a commission, is *working* on commission.

Eventually, regardless of what the job might be, if production is not there, then the security of the job is taken away. So whether you are on salary or commission, you are on commission even if you happen to be the president of the United States. As you might have heard, if he doesn't do good even he will lose his job. 'Nuff said.

The sales job offers security, and I remind you of that security with this example. You might remember that back in 1981–82 we had a recession. At that time there were literally tens of thousands of honest, sincere, dedicated, conscientious, hardworking, productive people who lost their jobs. They came from every walk of life—teachers and superintendents, airline pilots and stewardesses, waitresses and secretaries, lawyers, street sweepers, and servicepeople. They lost their jobs not because they were unwilling to work, not because they did not have the ability, but because of the economy.

Here's my challenge: Name one, just one, honest, sincere, dedicated, conscientious, hardworking, productive salesperson who lost his job. If a salesperson did lose his job for reasons beyond his control such as, for example, his company's going out of business, he could in most cases go down the street—or even next door—and almost immediately gain employment.

New Jobs Immediately Available

Never shall I forget an incident in Atlanta, Georgia, when I was conducting a sales seminar. Just before the seminar started, two well-dressed young men in their late twenties came and asked if they could get a refund on their tickets. They explained that they had just lost their sales jobs because of a personality conflict with their manager. Since they had no sales jobs, to learn additional sales techniques would be of little or no value to them (they obviously had momentarily lost perspective and did not realize that they now—more than ever—needed their sales skills and training to *sell* their way into another job).

I asked the two young salesmen two questions. Number one, "Do you like to sell?" They both replied in the affirmative. Number two, "Would you like another sales job?" They again replied in the affirmative. Then

I assured the two young men that before the evening was over I would have a dozen interviews for sales jobs for them if they attended the session.

That evening when I reached this point in the presentation concerning the security of the sales job, I asked the audience two questions. Number one, "How many of you are in sales management?" Roughly one hundred of the five hundred hands went up. Question number two: "How many of you would be interested in interviewing two enthusiastic young salesmen who present an excellent appearance and are sold on the profession of selling, but lost their jobs because of a personality conflict with their manager?" Something like seventy-five hands went up. The two young men were able to pick and choose from a dozen solid offers as to what they wanted to do.

Yes, selling is a secure profession.

> *General Douglas MacArthur defined* security *as* the ability to produce.

As long as you can produce, my selling friend, you have security.

Attitude Makes the Difference

The sales profession has a different attitude about life and business. In the nonsales community, when business drops, management generally calls a "pity party." (That's what Mrs. Mamie McCullough, the lady who started the I CAN course for schools, named them. She also says many pity parties are held on an individual basis.) To zero in on all the difficulties, management explains they are going to have to cut the lights off early and let a couple of the janitors, secretaries, and support personnel go. With a stiff upper lip they explain that despite the fact things are tough, "We're going to fight this—and hope for the best."

The sales world handles recessions differently. When the media announces a recession, management gets everybody together and says, "We know you've been hearing all about the recession, but we've figured out a foolproof way to beat it. All we've got to do is reduce our sales." Right? Wrong!

What management does is simple. They call a management conference to organize a sales meeting to end all sales meetings. The president, board chairman, and sales manager are primed and rarin' to go. They get the troops together, roll out the red carpet, and in a highly excited manner say: "Folks, we know all of you have been hearing the completely unfounded rumor about a recession. Well, let me tell you what we think about recessions. We think they are definitely between your ears! Recessions are like a lot of other things. You can either join them or refuse to join. It is our current company policy not to join.

"Let me tell you what we *are* going to do. We're going to put on a contest like you have never seen before in your life! We're going to put up prizes like you can't believe. We're going to offer incentives to our customers and to you as salespeople which will make everybody so ecstatically happy and excited that they'll end up praying for any so-called recession to continue. We're going to embark on a promotion and advertising campaign that will absolutely blow your mind! We're going to get each one of you involved in a sales training and motivational program which will increase your effectiveness and productivity dramatically. We're going to sell more and better than ever before."

Think About This

Is this approach realistic? Is it effective? I'll answer that with questions for those of you who have been in sales since 1980 or before. Did you make more money in 1981 than you did in 1980? Did you make more money in 1982 than you did in 1981? (Remember now, those were "recession" years.) Are you making more money now than you've ever made before in the world of selling? (Author's note: I've been asking those questions in front of my live audiences since 1976, which followed the recession of 1974–75, and I can tell you there is always a substantial number who are doing better and better, regardless of the national market.)

It's true: If our thinking is stinking our business is going to be in the same shape. *Keep your thinking right and your business will be right.*

The beautiful thing about selling is that it's a democracy. In most cases your company doesn't care whether you're male or female, black or white, tall or short, fat or slim, old or young, introverted or extroverted, or even educated or uneducated. The only thing the company cares about, in most cases, is your integrity and your productivity. (There would be some exceptions in the area of education for some highly technical industries.) You're recognized, paid, and rewarded based on what you—the individual—do.

Good Morning, Mr. Chairman

When you get up in the morning and look in the mirror, you're looking directly into the eyes of your chairman of the board, your president, your secretary-treasurer, and your janitor. You can now make a motivational speech to your entire staff. "You're such a nice guy," or, "You're such a nice girl. You deserve a raise," and the board just met! As Cavett Robert loves to say, "The raise is going to become effective just as soon as you do!" That's what I like about the profession of selling.

I'm always amused when presidential candidates debate about who is going to run this country. I say this because the salespeople of America control the economy of this country. Just in case you question the validity of that statement, read on.

Things Happen When You Sell

Have you, my selling friend, ever really given any thought to what happens when you make a sale? First of all, you make a profit, your manager makes a profit, and if you're lucky, your company makes a profit. That way it can stay in business and you can keep on selling.

To paraphrase Samuel Gompers, one of the founders of the labor movement, "The first responsibility of management is to make a profit, because if you don't make a profit then the company will go out of business. If that happens, the workers not only won't get a raise, they won't even have jobs! Your company *must* make a profit because when they do, everyone benefits."

I'd like to briefly trace what happens when you make a sale. To start the process, you write the order or agreement on a piece of paper. That piece of paper started out as a tree, not as a piece of paper. Somebody had to go out in the woods and cut the tree down. You are the person who paid those people to go into the woods and cut the tree down when you got out there and made that sale.

Many people were involved in hauling that tree to the paper mill. You're the person who paid those people to haul that tree to the paper mill when you got out there and made the sale. In the paper mill there are hundreds of people involved in manufacturing that tree into paper. You're the person who paid those people to manufacture that tree into paper when you got out there and made that sale, but it goes much further than that.

Lots of People Benefit

You take part of your profits, go to the grocery store, and buy a can of beans. The groceryman in essence says, "If you're going to buy my beans, I've got to get some more," so he goes to the wholesaler and buys more beans. The wholesaler keeps the ball rolling by saying, "If you're going to buy my beans I've got to get some more," so he goes to the cannery and buys more beans. The cannery needs more beans so the manager goes to the farmer and buys more beans. This depletes the farmer's supplies, which means he's got to raise more beans. The farmer has a problem because he has worn out his tractor raising beans. Down to the tractor dealer he goes to buy that new tractor. Since the dealer only has one tractor, he has to go to the tractor factory to get more tractors.

When the dealer placed his order for more tractors, the tractor-factory manager said, "If you're going to buy more tractors we will have to manufacture some more because you are taking all our inventory. In order to manufacture more tractors, we have to bring in iron, copper, plastic, steel, aluminum, zinc, lead, spark plugs, and rubber tires. We will also have to let out over one hundred subcontracts for the parts we don't manufacture ourselves." All of those events, all those sales, and all those jobs were created because one day you, my selling friend, got out and made a sale!

Salespeople Make It Happen

If *anybody* should make a negative comment or a belittling statement about the sales profession, you should look that person in the eye and earnestly say, "Friend, you are earning as much money as you are because I and thousands of others are in the sales profession." This is true whether that person is a postman or a postmistress, a private or a general, a teacher or a superintendent. *Our standard of living is high because of the free enterprise system and the salesperson is the heart and soul of that system.*

Several years ago the secretary of commerce of the United States said that what we need in our country today is 1 million *more* professional salespeople. The reason he made the statement is obvious. *When the salesman sells, the wheels of industry turn.* OK, I plead guilty to being prejudiced about this magnificent profession of selling, but let me give you some historical data. I believe this will encourage you in the profession and help to get you more excited about selling, which will be helpful in your career. To do this, let's take a good look at the nation of Cuba.

When Castro took over, nothing was rationed, nothing was in short supply, salesmen were all over the island, and Cuba was completely self-sufficient as a nation. Today, no salesmen are there. Virtually everything is rationed and many things cannot be bought at any price. Today Russia supports Cuba to the tune of over $12 million every day. To my observation that there are no salesmen on the island, some people might say, "Well, Zig, if you don't have surplus you sure don't need salesmen." Interestingly enough, however, when they had the salesmen they had the surplus. The reason is simple. Salespeople create jobs and opportunity. They build industry and prosperity.

Salespeople Are Nice Folks

When the average person understands the role the salesperson plays, our role as salespeople will be much easier. When you as a salesperson fully understand the importance of the sales profession, you are going to be even more excited about your role in the profession. As a group, we truly represent the best of middle America. We have a high percentage of voters, taxpayers, and churchgoers. Our rate of divorce is one of the lowest of all professions and the rate of suicide is the lowest of any of the professions. As a salesperson you are truly privileged to be part of a noble profession.

A natural question or thought on your part at this point could be, "If those facts are true, then why do so many people have a negative image of the salesperson?" In my opinion there are several reasons for this. In the early days the advent of the less-than-professional hustler known as the "Yankee peddler" gave the profession a bad name.

From that point many people got the idea that a "good" salesperson was a person who made someone buy something he didn't want or— even worse—made him want something he really didn't need. In the beginning, the average buyer did not understand (many of them still do not) that a professional salesperson is a counselor who identifies the prospect's needs and then fills those needs through his goods, products, or services.

The Abominable Monstrosity

Our problems were compounded when Arthur Miller wrote that abominable monstrosity entitled *The Death of a Salesman*. Not only did the play enjoy a long run on Broadway but incredibly enough they put it on television—not once, not twice, but three times! Willy Loman, the salesman and central character, was the epitome of a loser. "Professor" Harold Hill of *The Music Man* is the consumate "con man" and received nearly as much publicity as poor Willy. In the minds of millions of Americans these two men are representative figures of the sales profession. Nothing could be further from the truth!

As salespeople we need to be selling at least two items in addition to the goods or services we sell. As a way of life, *we need to sell free enterprise.* We also need to sell the workers and business owners who manufacture our products that it really is in everybody's best interests to put in a full eight-hour day producing the finest-quality products at the best possible prices so that salespeople can sell with even more confidence and solve even more problems. The American public wants—even demands—the best product at the best price, so my family and yours will get the most benefits.

Security, Longevity, and Fulfillment

Career benefits for the professional salesperson are enormous. With the possible exception of the ministry and symphony conductors, salespeople have the longest active career of any of the professions. I started before I was eight years old and expect to continue for many more years.

Victor Christen of South Pasadena, California, is still going strong at age ninety-four. He has been selling automobiles for seventy-eight years and is a top salesman for Colliau Chevrolet. He doesn't even think of slowing down, much less retiring. His health is good. His wife died four years ago, and now there's a chance he might marry his girlfriend, who is a young "chick" of seventy-two. In addition to being a top salesman, Victor is writing a book called *The Birth and Growth of the Automobile Business, I Was There.* His mind and body are both in great shape and he says he has no problems a good meal won't cure.

The exciting thing about the sales profession is the fact the added years could well increase your effectiveness. The mental gymnastics required in selling will keep you mentally alert and the added years give you a better chance to build client loyalty and hence residual income. Since your integrity is the most important factor in building customer loyalty and career stability, the practicality of a totally honest relationship becomes even more obvious. When the salesperson establishes trust and rapport with his or her customers, some magnificently beautiful things happen to that sales career.

You Can Get an Early Start

The beautiful thing about selling is that you can get such an early start in the profession. Larry Hawes, a student at Highland Park High School in Dallas, is a classic case. Larry got his Social Security card at age ten, but at that point he'd already been selling for three years. His mother had paid him off with candy to walk up and down the sidewalk wearing a sandwich board in front of the lighting store she managed. At age eleven he was getting two dollars per hour as a stock boy at the store, but couldn't resist the temptation to sneak into the showroom occasionally to sell a few lamps. During one of these ventures, he sold one shopper a three-hundred-dollar brass lamp.

In January of 1980, Larry's mother, Sandra Jennings, opened her window-treatment shop called "The Blind Spot," specializing in ready-made and custom-made blinds, verticals, draperies, and coordinated fabrics. Larry was fourteen and his brother, Jay, was sixteen but they were the first salespeople she hired. Today The Blind Spot has seven employees and sixteen-year-old Larry is the top salesperson, averaging fifty thousand dollars a month in sales. Store manager Lois Sparks says, "You can depend on Larry to get the job done and done right. He has the self-confidence to sell well and very few of the customers realize Larry is only sixteen because he appears and acts much older."

Sandra Jennings is her entrepreneurial son's biggest booster. "He's plugged into business," she said of the youngest of her four children. "His sixth sense tells him not to let a single customer get away. He's a fast learner, pays attention to everything around him, and loves people. He's incredibly curious and he's done everything—measured windows, installed blinds and drapes, paperwork."

"Selling isn't difficult," according to Larry. "It's really very easy when you know your product and have a purpose. People come into the store either to price, buy, or compare brands and styles. My job is to show them everything so they'll walk away feeling confident in The Blind Spot, and in their final selection."

Larry is a young man with a very definite purpose. "I want to be rich," he says, with great seriousness. "I'd like to be a private investor, buy and sell homes for investment purposes, stocks, oil, own a string of businesses, maybe a department store and chain of restaurants. Working is an upper to me, and I feel incredible after I make a good sale. This is especially true on a Saturday when everybody's working extra hard to reach a particular sales goal." Larry doesn't describe himself as a workaholic, but he does always want to meet or beat the goals he has set and the challenge and excitement of selling are important factors in his work.

At the moment, Larry's working on a salary basis, but he would rather be paid on commission. The situation, however, isn't one that he's discussed with the boss. "I'm not sure my mother would go for that," he laughed, "but I would gladly take five or seven percent of fifty thousand dollars in sales a month as my salary. I'm not afraid of working on commission because it encourages you to hustle."

Larry is understandably optimistic about his future and confidently predicts that in twenty years he will be successful. As I say, that's one of the beautiful things about selling—you can start with little or no investment, at a very early age, and work as long as you wish.

Because of Victor Christen, who's still going strong at ninety-four, and Larry Hawes, who started at age seven, as well as all the salespeople between seven and ninety-four, I'm sold on selling as a career.

If a young man or woman were to ask me what I would suggest as a career which offered the greatest opportunity for personal fulfillment and security, while making a significant contribution to society, I could honestly say, "I don't know of a finer profession than the profession of selling."

Select a product or service that solves problems and in which you completely believe. Make certain the company is morally and financially sound. Become a sales professional and commit yourself to a 100 percent effort and I'll guarantee you can write your own ticket in the world of selling. Be *proud* that you sell! The profession of selling *is* a proud profession. When your attitude toward the sales profession reaches the point that you can look with complete pride at your product, your company, and the service you sell, as well as the profession of selling, when you see the sales profession as a truly glorious one, then you will close more of the close ones. You'll be building a career, which means you will win big now and win bigger later on.

I Am a Salesman

I am proud to be a salesman because more than any other man I, and millions of others like me, built America.

The man who builds a better mousetrap—or a better any-thing—would starve to death if he waited for people to beat a pathway to his door. Regardless of how good, or how needed, the product or service might be, it has to be sold.

Eli Whitney was laughed at when he showed his cotton gin. Edison had to install his electric light free of charge in an office building before anyone would even look at it. The first sewing machine was smashed to pieces by a Boston mob. People scoffed at the idea of railroads. They thought that even traveling thirty miles an hour would stop the circulation of the blood! McCormick strived for fourteen years to get people to use his reaper. Westing-

house was considered a fool for stating that he could stop a train with wind. Morse had to plead before ten Congresses before they would even look at his telegraph.

The public didn't go around demanding these things; they had to be sold!

They needed thousands of salesmen, trailblazers, pioneers, people who could persuade with the same effectiveness as the inventor could invent. Salesmen took these inventions, sold the public on what these products could do, taught customers how to use them, and then taught businessmen how to make a profit from them.

As a salesman I've done more to make America what it is today than any other person you know. I was just as vital in your great-great-grandfather's day as I am in yours, and I'll be just as vital in your great-great-grandson's day. I have educated more people; created more jobs; taken more drudgery from the laborer's work; given more profits to businessmen; and have given more people a fuller and richer life than anyone in history. I've dragged prices down, pushed quality up, and made it possible for you to enjoy the comforts and luxuries of automobiles, radios, electric refrigerators, televisions, and air-conditioned homes and buildings. I've healed the sick, given security to the aged, and put thousands of young men and women through college. I've made it possible for inventors to invent, for factories to hum, and for ships to sail the seven seas.

How much money you find in your pay envelope next week, and whether in the future you will enjoy the luxuries of prefabricated homes, stratospheric flying airplanes, and a new world of jet propulsion and atomic power, depends on me. The loaf of bread that you bought today was on a baker's shelf because I made sure that a farmer's wheat got to a mill, that the mill made the wheat into flour, and that the flour was delivered to your baker.

Without me the wheels of industry would come to a grinding halt. And with that, jobs, marriages, politics, and freedom of thought would be a thing of the past. I AM A SALESMAN and I'm both proud and grateful that as such I serve my family, my fellow man, and my country.

AUTHOR UNKNOWN

Yes, the salesperson and the sales profession are both vitally important to the growth and stability of a free and even greater America.

Good News

Fortunately, the winds of change are blowing in the salesman's direction. Here's what Allan Cox, author of "The Cox Report on the American Corporation," had to say in a copyrighted interview in the December 13, 1982, issue of *U.S. News & World Report*:

> *The loss of status of the salesman symbolizes the distance between corporations and consumers. In the early history of American business, the heads of manufacturing and sales were the twin heroes. Then the salesman lost status even though he was and remains the link between the customer and the company. I see this trend starting to change and expect a revival in status for those in marketing and sales. We are learning that we have to get back to the customer we have neglected.*
>
> *Soon a different kind of chief executive officer will rise to the head of the corporation, someone with his ear to the ground, not the exclusively financially oriented individual who tended to be king between 1965 and 1980. The new breed will be more marketing oriented, in touch with public sentiment and more sensitive to issues of social responsibility. As corporations begin to realize that society and the marketplace are one and the same, they will become more idea oriented and we will see the re-emergence of American business.*

P.S. from Zig: One reason sales and marketing people will return to the chief executive's chair is business has finally learned that selling is the only thing that contributes to profit. Everything else contributes to cost.

13

BUILDING RESERVES
IN SELLING

To repeat what I said in an earlier chapter, the most important part of the sales process is the sales*person*. For that reason, this author deals with the role the salesman plays as well as why and how you must build a physical, spiritual and a mental reserve. Most of the remaining space in this segment will be devoted to the mental aspects of building a knowledge reserve, but first let's look at the physical reserve, which can be enormously helpful in your sales career.

Exercise to Build Physical Reserves

Evidence is overwhelming that you must be in good physical condition if you're going to function at your best in any profession, including selling. For example, psychologists tell me that when I speak an hour I burn more raw energy than a laboring man does in a ten-hour day. (I speak at about 280 words per minute with gusts up to 550.) When I do a four-hour session I've got to be in good physical condition because the audience (my customers) expects me to be just as enthusiastic and energetic the last few minutes as I was the first few minutes. They paid their money to come hear me and they deserve to hear me at my best for the entire session. I feel a strong moral obligation to be physically ready to perform at my mental and emotional best. That's the only way I can "sell" them the ideas, procedures, and techniques which will make them more effective in the sales world or in life in general.

Frankly, my selling friend, you have the same moral obligation to your customers. (We've already decided the customer is the big winner so we *owe* it to him to be in good condition to help him win.) *You need to be just as enthusiastic with the last prospect you talk to every day as you are with the first one.* This is true whether you went out to see him or he came into your store to see you. Each one deserves you at your very best. The last prospect you call on each day has the same basic needs as the first one you called on. You owe it to every prospect to be in the best physical condition possible so you can serve each one best. Obviously, age and physical handicaps are important factors, but you should develop your sales "muscles" so you can give every prospect an honest shot with an energized presentation so he will have the complete story, enthusiastically presented, to make his decision.

There are many books and methods for getting in shape and then maintaining good physical condition. My favorite is *The Aerobics Program for Total Well-Being*, by Dr. Kenneth Cooper. In my case I find jogging the most practical method for staying in shape, since I travel a great deal and can jog anywhere regardless of the weather. I've jogged during torrential downpours and with the temperature as much as forty degrees below zero. (Don't misunderstand—that rain and cold were outside. I was running inside!)

Since I can't measure my distance while on the road, I run by the clock. It usually works out to be about twenty-five minutes per day, five days each week. Until I started my jogging my basic approach to exercise was to fill the tub, take a bath, pull the plug, and fight the current! (Realistically that isn't much of an exercise program.)

In addition to exercise we also need to eat nutritious, well-balanced meals and get a reasonable amount of sleep. If you had a half-million-dollar racehorse, you wouldn't let him stay up half the night smoking cigarettes, drinking coffee or booze, and eating junk food, would you? You *would* feed him the right food and drink, and control his rest and exercise to give him a chance to perform like the thoroughbred he is, wouldn't you?

Since you, too, are a thoroughbred who wants to be a winner, don't you think that you deserve the same treatment so you will have a legitimate chance to win? Additionally, when you take care of your body your mind is more alert and productive. As Vince Lombardi said, "Fatigue makes cowards of us all."

By being in excellent physical condition you will have the energy and motivation to make that one more call toward the end of the day. This is the one which makes such an enormous difference in your career. If you are physically and mentally—as well as emotionally—geared to give your best effort to the very end, you're far more likely to make that sale. You will have the extra edge in aggressively using one more close and making one more effort to take one more step which will take you to the top of the sales heap.

The tired salesperson at the end of the day has a tendency to rationalize away his chances for being a sales champion. If he's had a superb day he's inclined to reason that "after all, I'm not greedy, I have had a good day, why press my luck? By quitting early I can get a good night's rest and be sharp for tomorrow." If he's had a lousy day and he's tired, then he's inclined to say, "The way things are going, no wonder I can't sell! It'll be far better for me to call it quits today and get a fresh start tomorrow, so I'll be sharp."

The successful sales pro will tell you *there is nothing that will get you ready for tomorrow like making a sale on that last call today.* Often the last sale is the one you are doubly proud of because it represents that "extra effort" you've heard so much about. Emotionally it really gets you ready and excited about the next day, so instead of being a reluctant starter the next morning you start the new day like a tiger.

Another factor is involved here, too. According to Dr. William James, the father of American psychology, we not only have a second wind but a third, fourth, fifth, sixth, and even seventh wind. Sometimes after you think you've given it your best, as you make that last call the excitement of the effort gets to you and you feel a renewed burst of energy, excitement, and enthusiasm, and the last call turns out to be the most productive one.

Here's another, very practical, intelligently selfish reason for staying in good physical condition so you will be as enthusiastically effective the last hour of the day as you were the first hour. Insurance salesmen often say that part of what you earn should be your very own to keep and use as you see fit. You and I both agree with that statement, but as a practical matter you probably spend the first six or seven hours every day working for everybody *except* yourself. You *pay* the grocer, the landlord, the utilities company, the service station, the insurance people, the government, the laundry, the clothier, and all the others, *but not yourself.* Now wouldn't it be a shame to go top speed all day until the last hour so that you can pay *everybody* else and then run out of steam when you start working for yourself?

From personal experience I can tell you that for every minute I invest in my exercise program (up to thirty minutes), I get three to five minutes of full-speed-ahead productivity. Frankly, I have so much to do I don't have time *not* to exercise. Take care of your health and that last hour of productivity will not only be your best hour but it will also be *yours* (the money—the satisfaction—the recognition).

All of that is to say, my selling friend, get in shape physically, mentally, and emotionally so you can give it your best. That's the only way you're going to get the best—or championship—results.

Time: Manage It—or Squander It

Sales trainer Don Hutson points out that a study done by S.M.E. International revealed that the second leading cause of failure in the sales profession was the improper utilization of time. Mark Gardner of Houston, Texas, an assistant vice-president with E. F. Hutton and Co., Inc., is of the opinion that the average securities broker spends less than two hours each day in the actual process of selling new or established customers. There are two, possibly three, major reasons for this. First would be a disregard for, or lack of expertise in, the field of time management. Second could be a shortage of energy which causes the salesperson to start the day late, end it early, and go at substantially less than full speed during the day or week.

The third reason could be called reluctance because of a shortage of confidence, a poor self-image, or a bad case of "stinkin' thinkin'." With the exception of time management we are dealing with these problems by offering positive solutions. Most time-management problems are caused by poor habits and lack of direction. The others are caused by lack of knowledge and expertise. The reading I recommend at the end of this book offers positive solutions to this problem.

If you really want to be successful in the world of selling, I encourage you to add these books to your library and their content to your everyday life. It is safe to say that the professional closer, almost without exception, is a time miser. He knows payday comes *only* when he is in front of a prospect, so he handles the necessary details of his profession during those times when he cannot be in front of the prospect. Acquiring the knowledge and staying in shape will put *you* in front of your prospects at least one more hour every day. In a matter of time the bottom line on your financial statement will be substantially better.

One additional way to improve that bottom line is to have your own personal "booster" week on a quarterly, semiannual, or annual basis. A "booster" week is a total-effort week during which you give your maximum effort from early in the morning until late at night. You plan it for weeks in advance so that *nothing* interferes with a total effort on your part to spend every possible moment that week in front of prospects who can make buying decisions. Never will I forget my first booster week after I really got started in the cookware business. The company started promoting it casually about six months in advance and gradually built the tempo until it reached its peak for the scheduled week with one solid "get ready" week to pick up momentum for the major thrust.

For the big week we booked our dinner demonstrations three weeks in advance. We gave extra incentives to our hostesses for having extra couples at their dinners. We booked pancake calls for breakfast starting at 6:00 A.M. It was a busy week. That week I conducted full demonstrations for thirty-nine couples and sold thirty-one sets of cookware. That week had a solid impact on my sales career. My confidence increased substantially as I revised my goals upward.

Total-effort weeks require tremendous physical effort, so again your physical condition is important. You might also consider involving the family in your booster week *and* the week after. Ask your family to do everything possible to remove all your normal responsibilities that week so you can concentrate on selling. Then for the next week plan something extra for the whole family, maybe a short vacation together so you can spend all of your time with them. Personal booster weeks can be good for you, good for your company, and good for your family.

Smoking on Calls Is a No-No!

Since smoking and drinking are both detrimental to our health and are enormously expensive, I personally don't participate in either, but since this book's primary purpose is to help you close more sales, I'll confine my comments to the fact that if you want to sell more merchandise you will neither smoke nor drink on sales calls.

First, let's look at smoking. Even if your prospect is smoking and offers you one, you should turn it down. The reason is simple. It takes time to light the cigarette, a place to put the ashes, and then it takes time to put out the cigarette. Sometime between January 1 and December 31, smoking will cost you some sales. I don't know which ones, nor do I know how many, but based on conversations with hundreds of customers, smoking costs you a lot more than the price of the cigarette. The word is, if you are serious about building your career as fast and solidly as possible, don't smoke and sell at the same time.

What About Drinking With a Prospect?

Many times I'm directly challenged with, "Don't you think it's all right to have a cocktail with your prospects while you talk shop?" My answer is always the same: "Nope, sure don't." Question: Suppose the prospect offers you one? The answer is still no. The questioner often persists, "So what do you say?" (For some reason the inquirer doesn't seem to understand that no *is* an answer! And that "No, *thank you*" is a courteous answer when the prospect insists that you join him in a cocktail.)

In 1972 I took my last drink and since that day less than a dozen people have insisted or offered it the second time. On the second offer, I quietly say, "No, I really don't drink." Would you believe that about half of them reply, "Boy, I wish I didn't!"

I did not lose a friend or a sale and I don't think they respected me any less. As a matter of fact, I believe in most cases they were possibly a little envious and even wished they, too, did not drink. I believe, although this was not my primary objective, that my standing actually improved with most of the individuals. I'm completely convinced that any sales it might have cost me were far more than replaced by the sales I gained.

Your question: "Zig, what am I going to do? Have a Coke?" Not necessarily. From time to time I think you ought to have a Pepsi, a 7-Up, Dr. Pepper, or any number of other soft drinks.

Does a Cocktail Really "Sharpen You Up"?

Many times salesmen tell me, "I take a drink to be sociable and because the drink 'sharpens me up.' I really feel I gain a mental pickup." My comment: "If a cocktail sharpens *you* up, you've got to face the fact that it does the same thing for your prospect, so you still haven't gained any advantage." Unfortunately, many times the salesmen who say a drink sharpens them up actually think they believe what they say.

I say they *think* they believe the drink sharpens them up because they've never really thought about it. An honest answer to this next question will remove that thought from your mind. If you think a drink sharpens you up, you obviously believe it does the same thing for others. Here's the situation: You're facing a major operation and you want the surgeon to be at his *sharpest* best. Question: Are you going to insist that he take a little nip just before he opens you up?

The point is clear. Don't take a drink when you're trying to persuade someone to take action. You're likely to get complacent, lose the mental sharpness and the sale. Liquor is a depressant, not a stimulant.

Build a Spiritual Reserve

To enjoy a balanced success in selling and in life, we need to build a spiritual reserve. I say this without apology or hesitation despite the fact some people feel you shouldn't talk about religion and politics in business. I've weighed my position and that advice many times and have come to the same conclusion which evangelist James Robison clearly states, namely, that religion and politics are the two most important things in our lives and if we don't *choose* to talk about them the day will come when we will no longer have that choice. I'm not going to go into any theological discussion, nor will I devote more than a couple of paragraphs to the subject (I elaborate in my book *Confessions of a Happy Christian*), but I do feel that it's important for you to know where I'm coming from.

If I had never read the Bible or heard a preacher preach, and had only been dealing with young people on drugs, I would have a deep and total faith. I've seen hundreds of youngsters come into drug-rehabilitation programs so strung out on drugs they did not know one day from the next. They had been to psychiatrists and psychologists; they'd been in group therapy and under the care of competent professionals, with minimal results. Once these young addicts enter a program which follows the basic concept of Alcoholics Anonymous, *good* things start to happen.

This Way Out

In simple terms, here is the concept the addicts follow: First, recognize you've got a problem. Second, understand there's nothing you can do about it yourself. Third, accept the fact that you've got to have a Source of help greater than any human being can provide—God, as you understand Him. (In my own case, I'm privileged to say Jesus Christ as I *know* Him.) The addicts are forced to accept the fact there is something greater than man, and they need to look to that greater force.

I don't know who you are as a reader, but whoever you are, wherever you live, whatever you do, I can say this to you. If it hasn't already happened in the past, it will in the future. You're going to have difficulty of some kind which neither you nor any other human being can handle. That's why a spiritual reserve is so marvelous and helpful in selling *and* in life.

What does this have to do with closing sales? Everything, friend. If you are in trouble and have deep personal problems, whether they are of a physical, family, mental, social, financial, spiritual, or career nature, *you are going to be primarily thinking about solving your own problems and not solving your prospect's problems.* One more time, the most important part of the sales process is the salesperson. *And* the most effective salesperson is the one who is balanced physically, mentally, and spiritually.

In 1981 the Connecticut Mutual Life Insurance Company conducted a comprehensive study involving thousands of people and in excess of 1,500,000 pieces of information. They uncovered some interesting and exciting things, including the fact that the three groups in America with the highest moral values were (1) the clergy, (2) businessmen, and (3) the general public.

As a businessman, that information pleased me a great deal, but there is more. The study revealed that people with deep religious convictions are the most productive employees. Here's why. Ninety-seven percent of those who had made strong spiritual commitments carried that feeling of conviction, commitment, and loyalty to their employers with highly productive results. Not surprisingly, this parallels a study involving over 22,000 students who qualified for "Who's Who in American Schools and Colleges." Over 85 percent of these honor students said their faith in God was extremely important to them.

Question: Why are these workers and students more productive and why will you, as a salesperson, be more productive if you have deep spiritual beliefs and strong religious values? Answer: Man is physical, mental, and spiritual—and if you neglect any one of these facets, you will not be a complete person. If you are hurting or empty in one aspect of your life, it's much tougher to be productive in the other areas of your life. On the flip side, if you have taken care of the physical, mental, and spiritual aspects of your life, you can concentrate on the job at hand, which in the world of selling—is selling.

14

BUILDING A MENTAL
RESERVE IN SELLING

THE THIRD KIND of reserve is mental reserve. I'm a fight fan and even fought a couple of years in the ring. I fought just long enough to know that if I ever have any disagreements with anybody, I guarantee you that all I'm going to do is just *talk* about that disagreement.

I love the story of Jack Dempsey and Gene Tunney. When Gene Tunney retained the heavyweight championship in his fight with Jack Dempsey, he did so because he had trained by running backwards. Gene Tunney was anything but a coward, but he knew when he got back into the ring with Dempsey he was going to be hit and probably hurt.

Backing Up to Go Forward

Since Gene Tunney *knew* he would get hit and hurt in the rematch with Jack Dempsey, he decided to prepare for it. He did this by running backwards while doing his roadwork. When his sparring partner clobbered him, he diligently trained himself to back away. He did this many, many times. In my own limited ring experience I learned that when a fighter is hit and hurt, he instinctively tries to "git 'im!" (his opponent.) At that specific moment he's less capable of "gittin' him" than at any other time. That's when he gets his platter cleaned and is often knocked out.

Tunney knew that when he got hit by Dempsey he could be stunned, go on the attack, and possibly get knocked out, so he conditioned himself to avoid this by running backwards. You fight fans probably remember in the second fight Dempsey knocked Tunney down for that famous long count. Later, Tunney said he knew his head was perfectly clear and he could have gotten up and gone back to war, but instead of doing that he remembered his training.

Every fighter who has ever been hurt always says, "I'm OK, I'm OK, lemme at 'im!" I've seen guys who were so out of it they couldn't tell you what city they were in, but they were telling the referee they were OK! Tunney "responded" to his training instead of "reacting" when Dempsey knocked him down. He backed away and fought a holding/delaying action until his head cleared. In the next round he knocked Dempsey down and won the fight going away.

You Will Be Rejected

What does this have to do with you and building your sales career? A lot. Every day you go out to see prospects or prospects come in to see you. On occasion you can anticipate or expect to be "stunned" by firm rejections and caustic comments from prospects. It is an occupational hazard. Question: Why not build up a mental reserve so when you are rebuffed in any way by your prospect you are mentally prepared to handle the incident? Positive mental preparation in advance will help absorb the impact of dealing with negative experiences.

Positive Steps to Overcome Negative Input

By the same token, I'm going to tell you this as a positive fact: You're going to have negative poison dumped into your mind and emotions every day of your life. Events, people, radio, newspapers, and television all participate in the process. Combine this with the fact that in the world of selling, whether you go out to see prospects or the prospects come in to see you, a certain percentage of them will deal with you in a negative manner.

To be at your most effective best in the sales profession, you need to build a substantial mental reserve. This mental reserve of knowledge and right attitude will make a real difference in virtually every sales encounter. The difference will be especially significant to your sales career when you are dealing with the close or borderline cases where the slightest variation in your attitude and knowledge reserve will gain or lose the sale. Generally speaking, all things being equal, the prospect will buy from the salesperson he likes. However, as John M. Wilson points out in his book *Open the Mind and Close the Sale, things are not equal when one salesperson has more knowledge and enthusiasm about the product he sells than a competing salesperson has about the product he sells.*

You build your mental reserve by reading the good books, by listening to motivational and sales training recordings, and by attending professional training sessions and your own company meetings. This really boils down to daily feeding your mind with good, clean, pure, positive input.

I also urge you to join and actively support your SME Club (Sales and Marketing Executives) for sales managers and marketing managers.

For Professionals the Cassette Player Is a MUST

In chapter 5, we discussed the value of recording your presentation on a cassette recorder to make certain you are saying the right words and using the right voice inflection. Now I would like to emphasize the value of a cassette player for you to use in your home and in your car. *If you are in the world of selling and do not have your own cassette player, you are not really serious about selling.* I'm completely convinced, based on literally thousands of letters and individual discussions, that the use of a cassette player can increase your sales effectiveness to the degree that it will be worth many thousands of dollars each year in additional income.

The beautiful thing about cassette recordings is the fact that your time investment is almost zero. Ideally you can listen to recordings as you begin the day, while you are shaving or applying makeup and dressing, and your mind is not otherwise engaged. You can listen to the recordings in the evening as you are preparing for bed. One of the most effective uses of the cassette recorder is for listening purposes as you go from one call to the next. Between those calls you can often pick up an idea or a motivational lift which further prepares you for the next call. Over the years I have had *thousands* of salespeople tell me this procedure was the most important process they followed in order to stay mentally ready to sell. In appliance, furniture, luggage, and other specialty shops you can listen during slow times and keep your attitude right while depositing sales information and inspiration in your knowledge bank.

According to the University of Southern California, if you live in a metropolitan area and drive twelve thousand miles each year, in three years' time you can acquire the equivalent of two years of college education. You can learn every phase of the sales profession from building the right mental attitude to prospecting, handling objections, negotiations, closings, and so on. By constantly feeding your mind via those cassette recordings, you can acquire considerable sales information plus a good feel for the proper voice inflections, pauses, and procedures as demonstrated on the recordings by the independent professional as well as company sales trainers.

Most of the alternatives, as John Hammond suggests, offer one or more negatives. You could listen to the news but much of that is negative; listen to music, but much of that is pornography set to music or some sad tale by a cowboy about how his best friend ran off with his horse, his girl friend, or his saddle. You could play with your CB, but most of that is idle chatter or police reports so you won't get caught for speeding. Even if the alternatives were not negative, while you are in your car on the way to making a call there is *nothing* as productive as preparing mentally and emotionally for that call by listening to those motivational/educational cassette recordings.

Fringe Benefits Are Enormous

There are some fringe benefits from listening each day before you start your day. Psychologists maintain the first person you meet or deal with every day (of any significant nature) will have more emotional impact on your attitude that day than the next five people you encounter. Every day you should select a cassette recording from a motivational speaker, sales trainer, minister, or anyone who gives you a positive lift. Since the whole family is involved in your success, get them together and listen to a few minutes of positive material before you start the day.

In my mind, the most motivating single message you can listen to is exciting music with positive lyrics. I don't believe you could start a day with songs like "Born to Win," "The Magic of Believing," "The Giant Within," "Where But in America?," "The Impossible Dream," "The Battle Hymn of the Republic," the sound track to *Rocky* or *Chariots of Fire*, or any truly great inspirational song, and not feel better for the day.

If you did nothing more than place the cassette recorder in the center of your house and turn it on, you would notice that every member of your family would start "picking 'em up and putting 'em down" in a happier, more excited way. Not only is inspiring motivational music tremendously moving, but it very definitely affects your attitude. I firmly believe if you will start the day by listening to a few of the inspirational songs, you will be emotionally ready to deal with your prospects on a one-on-one basis.

Incidentally, the wrong kind of music is tremendously demotivating and can have a definite negative impact on you. I urge you to read *Behavioral Kinesiology* by Dr. John Diamond to find out which music is good for you, which is bad for you, and why.

Plant Good Seeds—Reap Positive Crops

To repeat myself, your mental attitude is influenced tremendously by what goes into your mind. If you want good "output" you've got to have good "input." If your thinking is good, your business will be good. If you've got "B.O. of the brain," better known as "stinkin' thinkin'," your business is going to be in the same shape. It's true—if you're going to build an outstanding career in the world of selling, you've got to build your mental reserves so that, as Kipling said, you can meet success and failure and treat both these "imposters" the same.

With Mental and Physical Reserves You Can Score

You've got to be able to score in the last few seconds of the first half and the last few seconds of the ball game. The National Football League did a study on scoring in the N.F.L. and discovered that in the last two minutes of the first half and the final two minutes of the game, more points are scored than in any other *twenty* minutes of the football game!

Why? I believe there are three reasons. Number one, the teams realize that in most cases they need to score to get back in the game, to win, or to secure a shaky lead. Number two, they drill, practice, and rehearse the "two-minute drill" more than any other phase of the game so they are loaded with mental, physical, and emotional reserve. Number three, their objectives are clearly defined. They know what they've got to do and because they have thoroughly prepared, their confidence is high that they can reach the objective, which is to score. This results in a fantastic finish of the half or of the game.

The same principles and procedures apply to you in your sales career. Build your reserves, get your thinking right, get your spiritual values in order, get your body in good physical condition, and you will have taken the key steps toward building an exciting and successful sales career. The most exciting thing is the knowledge that *every* individual can do something about these areas.

Building Customer Reserve

There is yet another reserve which truly outstanding salespeople will build, and that is *customer* reserve in the form of testimonials from customers. I remember the first real testimonial I saw not long after I entered the world of selling. I lived in Columbia, South Carolina, and a big divisional meeting was scheduled in Charlotte, North Carolina, for all the salespeople in the Carolinas. One of the speakers that day was an old pro named Ralph Beaver of Greensboro, North Carolina. Ralph was an extraordinary showman who specialized in the spectacular.

The "Testimonial" Close

At the conclusion of his talk that day, Ralph pulled out a roll of adding-machine paper four inches wide. He held it up so we could see that something had been typed on the paper. At this point, Ralph dramatically said, "Now, ladies and gentlemen, even after a spectacular demonstration [he wasn't overly modest] and a strong series of closes, I still *occasionally* have prospects who say no.

"When that happens, I pull out this roll and say, 'Mr. and Mrs. Prospect, since there seems to be a little hesitancy on your part to go ahead and reserve a set of our cookware, let me ask you a question. [With that he held the end of the adding-machine roll as high as he could reach and let one end go. As the roll of paper unwound the entire length of the room, Ralph Beaver continued.] The names on that roll of paper are your friends and neighbors who own the set of cookware you are looking at right now [he had neatly typed the name and address of every customer he had sold to during his twenty years in the business.] Why don't you see if you know any of them?" (As the prospects got down on their knees to look, they always recognized a number of names.)

Ralph: "Mr. and Mrs. Prospect, do you think all of those people made a mistake by investing in a set of cookware which saves time, money, and food value?" Prospect: "Probably not." Ralph: "As you can see, there are three lines at the bottom of the list. Will it be all right if I go ahead and put your name and address on those lines to indicate you took action to get something you've repeatedly said you really wanted?" Prospect: "Yes, go ahead."

The most effective testimonials, with the most dramatic results, are those obtained by Bernie Lofchick from Winnipeg, Canada. Bernie is a Maytag distributor and has achieved the highest level of market penetration of any Maytag distributor in their worldwide network, including over fifty countries. Interestingly enough, Bernie's retail outlet, which is not only a successful profit center but a learning and training center for the other outlets as well, is located next door to a large discount store featuring washing machines, many of which are priced at less than half as much as the Maytag. Bernie considers the store an asset to his business.

He and Maytag sell quality, durability, performance, and service. Recently he sold a new Maytag to a customer who reluctantly traded in her old wringer model, which was still doing a superb job after over forty years of service. She traded it in only because her arthritis had gotten so painful she could no longer operate it.

One of the most effective closes Bernie and his staff use involves telephone calls to satisfied customers who have been using their Maytags five, ten, fifteen, even twenty or twenty-five years. When these customers give their testimonials about service, performance, and durability, somehow the price objection completely disappears and a new Maytag customer joins the ranks.

These two approaches fit special situations, but satisfied customers can be, should be, and in many cases *want* to be helpful to you in selling additional prospects. Let's look at what sales pro Mike Frank has to say about the importance of customer testimonials, how to get them, and how to use them.

Why Use Testimonials?

Whether you and I personally like television, radio, newspaper, and magazine advertising which uses man- or woman-on-the-street "testimonials," recommendations, or endorsements, it is apparent the major corporations feel they are effective or they wouldn't spend millions of dollars per year on "testimonial" advertising. Think of just a few which come to your mind, past or present: American Express, beer companies, paper products, dental products, securities companies, Dale Carnegie Courses, Jif, Charmin, 7-Up, Coca-Cola, Pepsi, etc. (Think further. Do you really think major corporations would continue to pay millions for celebrities to endorse their products if those endorsements did not pay off?)

Most salespeople who have been selling successfully for any length of time often receive testimonial letters on an unsolicited basis. These endorsements will usually compliment the salesperson on his effectiveness, follow-up, or attitude. They express appreciation for the salesperson's extra effort, how happy they are with the product, or how pleased they were with the company's handling of a service problem. Any letters you may have already received serve as a base for your "collection." (Many salespeople who have received such letters appreciate them, but don't realize what a valuable sales tool they can be. As a result, they do a lot of verbal selling when these letters have more credibility than anything the salesperson can say.) Remember: *People believe more of what they see than what they hear.* This is especially true in this case, because the prospect *always* considers the salesperson at least partly biased and often feels that a satisfied customer is just being honest.

Getting Those Testimonials

If you have been selling for a few years, think about those customers you have who have verbally told you how appreciative they are about your product, service, or idea . . . or of you as their salesperson . . . or of your company for any reason. Question: Doesn't it make sense to capitalize on these satisfied customers to find more satisfied customers? Do this. Make a list of all of those who fall into this category, or those whom you think might feel this way but haven't verbalized it to you. Now, either call them or go see them. (Your list might have five or fifty names on it. Make contact with all of them.) Your presentation to them is similar to the following:

"Hi, _____. How is everything going with your _____? (If they have a problem, assure them you will get the problem remedied and do so. If all is well, which it will be about 90 percent of the time, then proceed.) "I'm calling [or I'm here] to ask you an important question and a favor which could help me immensely in my selling career, without my asking you to buy a thing. Is that fair enough?" Smile and pause. (The response is usually positive or encouraging.) "Remember when you told me a few weeks ago how pleased you were with our company [service or me]?" Wait for a response. "Well, believe it or not, we still have a lot of nonbelievers out there. It would mean a lot to me if you would share those feelings in a letter on one of your letterheads, at your convenience, and send it to me. Would you do that for me?" (About 90 percent will say yes. About half of them will do it. Don't ask them again. The 50 percent is sufficient to build your letter file. (If the customer is one who has not verbalized his feelings to you, then of course don't mention that he has told you of his pleasure in the past. Merely ask him his feelings about the company, service, you, etc., and if the response is positive, then ask him to do you the favor by writing you a letter regarding whatever praise he has.)

If the letter is in praise of the product and/or company, that's fine; however, it doesn't have to be to you or about you. You can use letters from fellow salespeople and if you work with others and all of you do this as a team effort, many of the letters can be mutually used.

The next step is to get them copied on a top-quality copying machine. Place them in nice plastic pages and then enter the pages into your presentation manual. If you don't use a presentation manual (and we suggest that 95 percent of all top salespeople do have some type of manual with company information, prices, testimonial letters, guarantees, etc.), then we suggest you get a small three-ring binder for the letters.

Learn the letters. Testimonial letters don't do you any good if you are not completely familiar with them. Use a yellow highlighting pen to emphasize the key points of the letter, which is the message you want delivered anyway. *Take this manual with you on all presentations.*

Testimonials are easy to get. Example: Let's suppose you went to a fine, newly opened restaurant last night in your hometown. You loved the food, atmosphere, and service, and they topped it off by bringing you the check at the proper time. As you left, you indicated your pleasure to the manager, owner, or maitre d'. He thanked you and asked you some of the things we discussed in the previous paragraphs. Would you write him a letter based on his request? Again, 90 percent of you would say you would and 50 percent of you actually would write. You would be happy to help and even flattered that your opinion and *approval* were respected so highly. The request for the testimonial was a testament to your sincerity.

Use Testimonials This Way

To effectively use customer testimonials, you must be able to turn to the right one without delay, because in most cases you will use only one or two in any presentation. Sometimes they can be used to get in to see the prospect. As a general rule they are used in the conviction step or to answer an objection.

Example: The prospect might say to you, "I'm really concerned about service." Your response is, "Mr. Prospect, I can appreciate your concern. Jones Johns at XYZ Company initially felt the same way, but after he had a service need here is what he said." (Now you show him the letter that answers the question or objection.) After he has read it, you continue with your presentation. Example: The prospect might say, "I'm concerned we won't get the tax break you mention." (Now show him a letter that answers his objection.)

You may not have a letter which answers all questions or objections, but if you keep working on building your collection of letters, eventually you will get one to answer almost any question or objection which might arise. Caution: While it is rare that you can have too many letters, I have seen it happen. Replace old letters with better ones and with ones from more credible prospects as time goes on. If you have as many as fifty letters, that isn't too many if you know them and can readily turn to the right one(s). Have them filed in some semblance of order—by industry, or location, or alphabetically, or by type of question/objection, etc. (Don't put them in file folders unless they are just extra copies which you feel compelled to leave with the prospect on rare occasions.)

I know some of the top auto salespeople leave their letter manual with the prospect to read while the salesman has to go into the manager's office for approval. Many of the top real estate salespeople use such letters diligently. Industrial salespeople use them, but in most cases, not to the degree they could and should. Insurance salespeople could be using them much more effectively. Professional speakers use them as their number-one referral source and tool.

I believe a testimonial can be effectively used in almost every presentation or demonstration—either to answer a question or objection, to get in to see the prospect, or as credibility when things are going good or not so good in the interview. Big ticket-retail salespeople should use them *far* more than they do. Testimonial letters from salespeople who may not be with the company anymore may be used in recruitment interviews. If the letter indicates that while the salesperson isn't with the company now, his years with your company were valuable and rewarding, such a good testimonial can sell a prospective recruit.

The uses are unlimited, but the realities of using them are like anything else. Additional effort is required to get them, learn them, highlight them, organize them, and use them effectively as an additional sales tool. Please be assured that the results and rewards are worth the effort—and then some.

15

YA GOTTA HAVE LOVE

You Need to Be Tough

If you are going to make it big in the world of selling you've got to be tough, and easily the toughest, most irresistible force on earth is love. You need to love life, the profession of selling, the prospects you deal with, your fellow man, your God, your country, and your family.

A Love Story

I close this segment of *Secrets of Closing the Sale* with a love story which I believe will be meaningful to you in your personal, family, and sales lives.

This love story is about the game of golf. If you're going to make it big in the world of selling, you've got to have real love and concern for your prospects. This love story demonstrates what I mean.

Playing golf is something I love to do. Several years ago, because of my travels, I didn't get to play very often, so when I did I'd get out there and get after it! I teed that ball up and flat let the string all the way out! I busted that ball and on those occasions when I could find it, I hit it again.

As much as I love to play golf, I love my family infinitely more. And I discovered a good while ago that regardless of the course I play, it still takes about five hours. Since I was away from my family much of the time, I wasn't about to come in from a trip, grab my clubs, kiss my wife and son good-bye, and go play golf.

So I came up with a very creative solution to my "problem." I bought my son Tom and the Redhead a set of clubs. Now golf could become a family affair! Well, my wife and son tagged along with me for a few games, but one day my wife said to me, "I know you love to play golf, Honey. But I just don't enjoy it. It's not my game." And she quit. So much for golf buddy number one.

Then, toward summer's end, Tom said, "I hate to tell you this. I really like to be with you whenever it's possible, but I just don't enjoy playing golf." So much for golf buddy number two. For the next two or three years, I didn't play much golf.

My Son—the Salesman

Then one evening we were out for a ride and drove past a driving range. At that point Tom pleasantly surprised me and said, "Dad, let's hit some golf balls." My sticks were in the trunk of the car and he knew it would be an "easy sale" to get me to stop and hit a few golf balls—and he was right.

After we had hit a few he said to me, "Dad, can I borrow one of your woods?" I handed him the club I was using. He choked up on it and hit that golf ball farther than I had ever seen him hit one before. Then he grinned at me and said, "Dad, when do we head for the golf course?"

The "Bird" Hunter

A few days later, Tom and I were playing on one of the par four holes at the country club where we had been members for several years. He took one of my woods and teed off. This time he must have hit it perfectly because that ball took off straight down the fairway just like the pros hit them. When it hit the ground it rolled a long way and stopped in perfect position, right in the middle of the fairway. From there he used a five-iron for his second shot and hit the ball on the green. Just like on TV! The ball landed softly some forty feet from the hole. Now he was in position to get his "bird."

For the nongolfer, this simply means he would be one under par if he sank his putt. (One under par on any hole is called a birdie.) Now I helped him line up the putt and showed him how to stroke the ball. When he hit that ball it headed straight for the hole. I knew it was good the minute he hit it. And when his ball hit the bottom of the cup my boy grinned and leaped into the air. You talk about excitement! I grabbed my son and hugged him as we did a victory dance for a minute or two.

A "Tainted" Win Is Actually a Loss

Then it dawned on me. I had a problem. My third shot was coming up also and I too was hunting *my* bird. And my ball was on the green much closer to the cup. I knew that if I missed the putt Tom would think I had missed it on purpose, to let him win the hole. But that would have given him a tainted victory, and as far as I'm concerned, that's quite a loss.

With this in mind, I decided to do my very best. Then if I missed it, I could face my son and say, "That's great, son, you beat ol' Dad fair and square." Then the win would not be tainted.

My best effort always includes a measure of providential help—which, I hasten to add, is theologically sound, even on the golf course. I lined up the ball and stroked it into the cup as well as I've ever stroked a putt in my life.

Before I picked up my ball I turned to look at Tom and said, "Now tell me the truth, son, were you pullin' for your dad?"

The "Love" Close

I think you know what it would have meant to him if I'd missed. He was only eleven years old and had never beaten his dad a hole of golf. It would have meant a great deal and yet quietly, but without hesitation, and very firmly, my son looked at me and said, "Dad, I *always* pull for you."

That, my friends, is love. That's pure love. That's what we need more of in Dallas, Texas; Portland, Oregon; Chicago, Illinois; and St. Petersburg, Florida. That's what we need more of in every home and every county in every state in this great land of ours. It's the answer to your personal, family, business, and for that matter, the world's problems.

It's certainly what we need in the wonderful world of selling. When you are on a sales interview, whether you are selling a product or a business opportunity, you must believe deeply, firmly, and sincerely that what you offer is in the best interests of the person you are trying to persuade to take action. If you believe this way you can sincerely pull for your prospect to buy for *his* benefit.

At that precise instant you become infinitely more effective, infinitely more professional, infinitely more productive, and infinitely *more*. It's true, as a wise man said: "People don't really care how much you *know*—until they know how much you *care*."

I guess if I were to sum it up I would say, despite all the information we've been giving you which I'm confident is valid, *in the final analysis you tell people from your head—but you persuade—you sell—from your heart.*

In this segment of *Secrets of Closing the Sale* we discovered that:

H in the heart of your sales career is *honesty*
E is *ego* and *empathy*
A is your *attitude* toward *you*, your *prospects*, and *profession*
R is for physical, mental, and spiritual *reserve*
T is for *tough*—and the toughest thing is love

Now put those beginning letters together and they form an acrostic: HEART, because you see, the heart of your sales career is your very own and *if your heart is right your sales career will be right.*

PART THREE

THE SALES
PROFESSIONAL

Objectives

To learn how to respond, which is positive, and not react, which is negative.

To spell out the differences between the professional salesperson and the nonprofessional salesperson; the high performer and the moderate performer.

To meet some real sales professionals from every walk of life and learn firsthand some of their characteristics, methods, and procedures.

To clearly establish the fact that dentists, builders, waiters, interior designers, schoolteachers, service station operators, children, etc., are *all* salespeople.

Closes and/or Procedures

The "Stood Up" Close

The "Impossible Child" Close

The "Complimentary" Close

The "Abraham Lincoln" Close

The "Previous Purchase" Close

The "Feel Good" Close

The "Tie Down" Close

The "Rainy Weather" Close

The "Spare" Close

The "Puppy Dog" Close

The "Soft Service Sell" Close

The "Accessory" Close

16

LEARNING AND USING PROFESSIONAL TECHNIQUES

Do You Respond or React?

I hope you answered the above question by saying you *respond*, because "respond" is positive and "react" is negative. Example: You get sick and go to the doctor. The doctor gives you a prescription and tells you to come in the next day so he can check on you. When you walk in the next day, the doctor takes one look, shakes his head, and says, "We're going to have to change your prescription because your body is *reacting* to the drugs." Nobody is happy with the *negative* results.

On the other hand, you go back the next day and the doctor takes one look and says, "Looks like we've got the right prescription. Your body is *responding* to the treatment." Everybody is happy with those *positive* results.

Here's What the Judge Does

In the world of selling—or, for that matter, just in the world—everything we encounter is not going to be positive. For example, it would be safe to say that 99 percent of all the salespeople who ever sold—with the possible exception of those who strictly sell behind counters in a retail outlet—have been "stood up" as far as appointments are concerned. This is particularly true in direct sales, life insurance, real estate, and automobile sales. It would be almost as safe to say that most of those who are stood up *react* with anger, frustration, disappointment, or a combination of all three.

My brother, Judge Ziglar, who broke the national sales record at that time for the Saladmaster Corporation in 1964 by selling over $104,000 worth of cookware, had a most unique *response* to broken appointments. He conducted cookware demonstrations, which meant he cooked large meals for several couples whom the hostesses had invited to attend. After demonstrating, he made appointments to see the couples in the privacy of their own homes the next day.

On occasion, when he arrived at the appointed time, no one would be at home. Instead of *reacting* with dismay, despair, frustration, or anger, Judge *responded* by saying, "Oh, boy! That's a sure sale!"

The "Stood Up" Close

The next day, at precisely the appointed hour for the day before, he would again appear at the door. When the host or hostess came to the door, Judge would immediately start with an apology. "I'm so sorry I missed you yesterday. I did everything in my power to see you, but it just wasn't possible." (He was being 100 percent honest. He had done everything in his power to see them. He had been there at the appointed time.)

Judge points out that you would be astonished at the number of grown people who would let him take the blame for their discourtesy. At that point, as he expressed it, he knew the sale was his. Here's why. If they did not have the courage to face him and say no at the appointed time, then they were not psychologically equipped to deal with a highly motivated, enthusiastic, well-trained professional salesman like him. By *responding* with that attitude, it's not difficult to understand why he broke the record.

At this point I need to elaborate and explain that the prime reason he was so motivated was he believed with all his heart that the family he was calling on desperately needed—even *had* to have—his set of cookware. He *knew* it would save them money, work, and precious food value for their children. He truly had a missionary zeal in selling his product. He also understood human nature and the real reason they stood him up. I elaborated on this in the very first segment but basically the couple *wanted* the cookware but didn't think they could *afford* it and *feared* they were too weak to say no to their desires. Solution: Stand up the salesman. Reminder: That's the reason you, my selling friend, need to develop the empathy I covered in chapter 8.

The "Impossible Child" Close

That's not all. Most direct salespeople *react* with frustration and dismay when a small child disrupts the demonstration by climbing into the briefcase or sample case and scattering papers and samples from side to side. Frequently the parents will, in a weak, somewhat pathetic tone of voice, say, "Now, son, you shouldn't bother the salesman's papers."

On occasion the husband will turn to his wife and say, "Honey, that child is impossible! Can't you do something with him?" To this the wife frequently gets up, takes the youngster out, and tells him to stay in his room. Three minutes later the youngster is back in the briefcase or samples, wreaking havoc. Now in despair the father and mother pull their hair, wring their hands, scream at the child, and beg him to behave himself.

It's at this point Judge Ziglar says he knows he has made the sale. Again, if they cannot say no to a three-year-old, how can they say no to a highly motivated, well-trained, professional salesman like him? Judge points out it is obvious to him the parents do not love their child enough to discipline him. He (Judge) loves children, *all* children, but especially the neglected ones. As he expresses it, "Since it is obvious this 'impossible' child will never have the advantage of loving discipline, I feel even more strongly the child must have the best possible chance at good, nutritious food for a healthy body."

Obviously we're dealing with an attitude in selling, but it also involves some knowledge of human nature and just good, common sense. If you think about it, that's what the highly motivated, well-trained professional salesperson uses most often. *And* he certainly works on his thought process and attitude until he can look at his sales situations and *respond* instead of react.

17

CHARACTERISTICS OF THE PROFESSIONAL SALESPERSON

Since I constantly make reference to the fact that the salesperson is the most important part of the sales process, let's take a look at the sales professional. First of all, he clearly understands that logic makes people think, but it is emotion that makes them act. He knows if he uses all logic in a sales presentation, chances are excellent he will end up with the best-educated prospect in town who will go down the street and buy from someone else. If he uses all emotion in a sales presentation, chances are excellent he will make the sale but, unfortunately, chances are also good the prospect will cancel the order. However, he knows that when he uses emotion *and* logic in the presentation, chances are excellent he will end up with a sale today and a happy customer for the future.

The professional understands that logic is aimed at and appeals to the eye. Emotion is aimed at and appeals to the ear. This is why, when humanly possible, we not only tell people what our merchandise or goods will do but we demonstrate at the same time.

We've been conditioned to believe what we see instead of what we hear. The eyes have truly been called the "windows of the soul"—the mind's eye believes what it sees. The eyes are the only one of our sense organs which connect directly to the brain. For this reason, logically we accept more readily what we see than what we hear. However, we are moved into action by what we hear. Remember, our "feeling" brain is ten times as large as our "thinking" brain, so "tell 'em" *and* "show 'em" and your chances of selling them are greatly multiplied.

Extrovert or Introvert

There are probably a thousand different opinions regarding the professional salesperson. The man on the street thinks he is a happy-go-lucky, storytelling, backslapping, extroverted, hail-fellow-well-met type of an individual. The truth is the professional salesperson is far more likely to be introverted than he is extroverted. Not painfully so, but by nature he is quieter and more serious. Obviously there are exceptions to every rule. But let's look at the extrovert versus the introvert.

The extrovert is a person who is more likely to make a good first impression. He is easy to like and establishes rapport fairly well. In too many instances, however, he depends on the force of his personality to get the sale. On a one-call, one-shot item where he's passing through town, that's fine. If he's going to build a career that's a different matter. If he's selling on a continuing basis to the same buyer, that, too, is a different matter.

The introvert is more likely to be *through* in his studies, *precise* in his presentation, and *knowledgeable* about the goods, products, or services his company has to offer. He is better organized. He knows where he's going to be at a given time. He's far more likely to plan his schedule and then work that schedule. He is in most cases a better listener and is a better student at uncovering the prospect's needs.

Of course, the *ideal* professional salesperson is an extrovert who is so serious about his profession he works to develop some of the introvert's characteristics so he can more effectively *serve* his customers. *Or* he is an introvert who is so committed to his profession he develops some of the extrovert's characteristics so he can more effectively serve his customers.

High Performers vs. Moderate Performers

The study by DeMarco and Maginn of The Forum Corporation revealed that highly successful salespeople practice fundamental sales skills, management skills, *and* good human relations to get along with staff members, customers, and other salespeople. *They do not abdicate responsibility for installation, implementation, and service to technical support people.* They continue to maintain a "service" relationship which younger salespeople, interested in building a career, need to learn.

High performers—regardless of the industry—involve others by soliciting opinions, sharing information, and establishing trust relationships *inside* the organization. Indications are extremely strong these high-performing salespeople could move from the sales force into a bank or manufacturing concern and perform at the same level. The revelation was that *ability to sell is not what separates the moderate performer from the high performer.* The other factors—trust, relationships, etc.—were the key. The high-performing sales professionals are *total*, well-balanced people with integrity who are knowledgeable and aggressively caring in their creative approach to solving problems.

A Team Player With Integrity

The high performer is an influence manager of considerable skill and serves as the liaison or connecting link between the customer in the field and the support people in the company. He works with his support people in a way which enhances their productivity and self-esteem while concentrating on issues important to building and maintaining a productive, trusting relationship with the customer.

The high performer helps with related products and services and simplifies the decision-making process for the customer by his willingness to identify other sources of help if the needs of the client extend beyond his expertise and the capability of his own company. Customers value integrity very highly and expect to receive honest as well as knowledgeable responses to their questions.

High-performing salespeople represent the interests of their company and of their clients with dignity, integrity, and skill. They bring added value to the sales task with greater enthusiasm, more sensitive interpersonal skills, and a sense of professionalism. They communicate clearly and sensitively to customers and support staff, which builds customer confidence that they know what they're doing. They also understand that the product or service itself does not build value but that *salespeople build value with every visit to a customer.*

Building internal relationships clearly is a key to the success of high performers. Moreover, the high performer is a team player whose internal-relationship behavior is consistent with the behavior that makes him successful with customers. He also sees his sales managers as a resource to be called upon at the appropriate moment and indicates that his manager is an effective leader who encourages initiative and provides support.

The Professional

He is so other-people conscious he never lets his ego hinder his efforts. He understands his function as a professional is not to attempt to help the prospect decide on buying or not buying, but rather to give information so the prospect will have the facts to make an intelligent decision. He gives some inspirational or motivational input so the prospect will be inspired to make the right decision.

The professional is thick-skinned to the degree that he is not offended easily by what the prospect has to say. This does not mean he accepts abusive language or insulting manners. It does mean he knows that many times the prospect has been abused by other salespeople and he is able to understand the prospect is not rejecting him but is simply refusing the offer he's making.

The Professional Understands

The professional thinks in terms of service, but *he also thinks in terms of his ability to make the sale on a specific call.* He expects to make the sale. He is versatile in his sales knowledge and his approach. He works from a plan and not a can, but as a professional he knows while there are many ways to say things, there is *one* best way. As a result, he includes many verbatim phrases, explanations, and expressions in *every* sales presentation. He feels strongly that it is his responsibility to sell so clearly that the prospect understands it is in his best interests to buy.

He knows when the prospect acts in an abusive manner it is often a defensive measure prompted by a sense of fear because of his own feeling of inferiority or ego inadequacy. He understands one universal rule in the world of selling and applies it with diligence and enthusiasm. That rule is his absolute conviction that *he needs to find out what the prospect wants and then help him get it.*

The dictionary defines the *professional* as "one who has an assured competence in a particular field or occupation." It's *quality* of performance. The professional has a good sense of humor. He takes his profession and his prospects' needs seriously—but not himself.

The Professional Is a Student

He clearly understands that school is never out for him. He studies his prospects, studies his company literature, and studies the art of persuasion. He reads good books, listens to cassette recordings, attends training sessions, and most of all, on every sales interview he studies human nature. He knows if he's going to change his status in life, he must change his performance. To change that performance he needs to change his thinking. To change his thinking he must change the input into his mind, so he selectively chooses the "good stuff" for his mind food. He understands very clearly that his mind is not a garbage dump— it's a temple.

The professional "goes to school" by watching good salespeople in action, whether at the direct, wholesale, or retail level. He constantly asks himself questions like, "How can I take this procedure and translate it into my own sales situation so I can more effectively sell and service my customers?" He knows his prospects will make their decision based on what they understand *and* believe so he undersells, keeps it simple, and makes it believable.

The Professional "Lives" Selling

Yes, he's sales conscious. He wakes up in the morning thinking sales. He goes to work thinking sales. He comes home thinking sales. The only difference is that when he gets home he understands that even though his sales situation is different he will use the same basic procedures and work from the same character base. He remembers that selling is a *transference* of feeling and hypocrisy on these "sales calls" will produce the same negative results they produce with his other "prospects."

From his heart he must sell his children on being the best possible children. From his heart he sells his wife on the idea that he's a good husband, and then demonstrates the point he wishes to make. In short, he is other-people conscious from morning to evening. The beautiful thing is that it's so much fun for him that it gets to be—and is—second nature.

He understands that people buy for *their* reasons and not his. For this reason he studies a great deal about motivation and human behavior, fully understanding that in order to influence behavior you need to understand something about it. He understands that a good idea, procedure, or technique does not care who owns or uses it.

The professional is an optimist. He looks on the bright side of every aspect of life. He knows the average prospect experiences enough gloom and doom in his life and does not appreciate a salesman spreading additional gloom. The professional understands that he—to a very large degree—is in control of the buying climate. With that in mind he does not discuss irrelevant subject matter and does not bring in the latest national or local tragedy. He creates an atmosphere of excitement and optimism so his chances of making the sale are greatly enhanced. He has great singleness of purpose and concentration on the immediate objective, whether it is to make the sale, placate a disgruntled customer, or make a follow-through P.R. call. This singleness of purpose enables the professional to zero in on the customer's dominant buying motive and concentrate his energies and attention on helping the prospect get what he wants. He's highly motivated and transmits his excitement to his prospects, who are motivated to respond by taking action.

The Professional Is Adaptable

He is a thinker, but he clearly understands it is better to emulate genius than to create mediocrity, so he evaluates materials and procedures on the basis of results. If the techniques and methods he is using are getting desirable results, he will stay with them. But he abandons any procedure or technique which proves to be ineffective. He does not permit himself to get comfortable in using a sales process and continuing to use it long after it has lost its effectiveness. He's aware of change in procedure, but he's even more aware of the fact that *principles* do not change.

The Professional Is Career Oriented

Because he is career oriented, every action is taken with the idea in mind of building a career rather than just making that individual sale. The professional fully understands the old cliché that *"words alone will often fail, so he demonstrates to make the sale."* He understands that when the prospect *sees* the product or service demonstrated, the believability factor increases. He also clearly understands that if you hear something you will forget it, if you see it you will remember it, but if you hear it, see it, and do it you will understand and be far more inclined to take action. With this in mind he gets the customer involved in the presentation. He lets that customer feel the cloth as he slips on the coat. He permits him to do the driving in the demonstration. He lets that customer sit down at the keyboard and work the word processor or the computer. He uses visuals and testimonials in his presentation.

He encourages the housewife to take her turn with the vacuum cleaner. She permits her customers to personally apply the makeup so they will have confidence that yes, they can do exactly the same thing. In short, the professional salesperson gets the customer involved in the use of the products, goods, or services he's selling.

The professional possesses conviction, concern, confidence, and courage. His conviction is strong that his product will solve the prospect's problem. His concern is genuine that the prospect buy now for his own benefit. His confidence is strong that he can persuade the prospect to take action, and his courage enables him to ask the prospect to take action now for his own best interests.

The professional has an incurable curiosity! He doesn't just wonder why the grass is greener on the other side, he climbs over the fence to see how the grass is being fertilized and learns the brand they're using.

The Professional Looks and Acts Professional

The professional looks the part of a professional. He is appropriately dressed for the occasion. He knows you can't play the role of success dressed in the costume of failure. He understands that you cannot harvest this year's crop on last year's fertilizer, so he constantly plants the right thoughts and procedures in his mind. In short, he appropriately dresses both mind and body.

The professional is a person of principle. He understands that the man or woman who won't stand for something will fall for anything. He knows if you add one small bit to the truth that you inevitably subtract from it. He buys the statement of Will Rogers, who said, "I would rather be the man who bought the Brooklyn Bridge than the one who sold it." The implication is clear that he will bend over backwards to protect his integrity and to keep from taking advantage of anyone else. He understands, as Ann Landers says, that's an awkward position, but he knows he won't fall on his face while leaning over backwards.

The professional is a hard worker. He understands, as sales trainer Steve Brown from Atlanta, Georgia, puts it, that anything worth doing is worth doing poorly—until you learn how to do it well. And he sticks and studies until he learns to do it professionally. He clearly knows we do not get work done through people, but we develop people through the work. In short, he knows activity precedes accomplishment and learning generally precedes activity. He does his homework and practices at sales meetings and in front of his family. He is eager to get in front of the prospect for the final examination, where he puts his learning on trial and reaches his objectives. As sales trainer Phil Lynch says, *he prepares for tomorrow by performing today.*

The Professional Is on the Grow

The professional builds a beautiful library containing much information about the sales profession, the sales process, and the people he sells. He would never dream of going to a doctor who quit studying when he finished medical school, or an attorney who quit studying when he finished law school. He would be dismayed if he realized the doctor or the attorney had no resource materials to refer to and learn from. With this in mind, he builds his own sales library and adds to it on a regular basis.

He understands that according to 1982 figures the average salesman spends nearly $300 a year dressing the outside of his head—that's for shaves, haircuts and "gook" (sprays, tonics, shaving soap); that he will spend approximately $2,000 dressing his body, and over $4,000 on transportation. Now, after having spent well over $6,000 getting ready to go sell, *he clearly understands that as a professional he needs to know what to say when he gets there.* With that in mind, he constantly fills his library and—more importantly—his head with the new procedures and techniques.

He is able to put the investment in books, cassette recordings, and training seminars into perspective by understanding how much it costs him and/or his company to *make* a sales call—and how much more it costs to *miss* the sale because of inadequate, erroneous, or incomplete information. Incidentally, a study done in 1982 by McGraw-Hill Research involving 605 companies from a number of industries revealed the fact that on an average it cost $178 to make a sales call (salaries, commissions, travel and entertainment expenses). A sale was made for every 5.1 sales calls, which translates into an average cost of $907.80 for every sale.

The *dollar* cost for a sales call is high, but the human frustration and wrecked sales careers because of a lack of sales information, technique, and inspiration is infinitely higher. The cost of acquiring the necessary training information is minute in comparison to the cost of *not* acquiring that training. Like the man said, "If you think education is expensive, just look at the cost of ignorance." Or, to make it personal, how many times have *you* missed a sale and later picked up some information or technique which you *know* would have made the difference (it hurt, didn't it)?

P.S. Congratulations for investing in *Secrets* and getting this involved in the learning process. Keep it up. *You are growing!*

The Professional Pushes Himself

The professional sets internal standards for performance. He has goals which he works on daily. Generally speaking, according to *Psychology Today*, January 1981, he sets his own quotas and goals higher than the company would set them. He is far more inclined to use his spare time in sales-related tasks. For example, when things are slow he writes follow-up or thank-you notes to customers instead of killing time reading magazines, drinking coffee, or engaging in bull sessions.

As times change, the professional changes procedures and techniques but never changes the concepts and philosophy of delivering as much as possible, as enthusiastically as possible, at the lowest fair price.

The professional knows that all the knowledge contained in the books in the Library of Congress won't work without the magic of common sense and judgment. In the final analysis he understands that *his career will depend on what he does with what he knows*, not just on what he knows.

Not a Professional

The professional understands that you don't become a salesperson by answering an ad in a newspaper and grabbing a briefcase with a prospectus in it any more than you become an engineer by buying a slide rule or a doctor by acquiring a stethoscope.

There's far more to being a salesman than simply smiling, dressing neatly, telling some good stories, learning a few good lines, and bang, you're a salesman.

When I speak of the professional I'm obviously not talking about the guy or gal who is a dropout from some other profession, or the ones who simply drifted into selling because it was "easy" ("all you've got to do is talk"—they think—"and since I'm a good talker, I'll be a good salesperson." One of the myths exploded by The Forum Corporation study was the one that a salesperson has to be a glib fast-talker). Nor am I talking about the part-time clerk who went to work six weeks before Christmas to pick up some extra money.

The Professional Gets With It

The professional has *chosen* the profession of selling and stays in school throughout his entire career, consistently working to earn the title "salesman." He works as hard on his attitude, self-image, relationships, and goals as he does on procedures and techniques. He clearly understands that he must get the *person* ready before he can get the *salesperson* ready.

The professional understands that he needs to stay "green and growing," because *a green salesman is always better than a blue one*. He knows as long as he's green he's growing, but when he gets ripe he will rot.

The professional salesman is the story of the high jumper who broke the world's record. Somebody asked him how he did it and he responded, "I threw my heart over the bar and the rest of me followed."

When you really get your heart into the profession of selling and with the company you're representing, you will acquire the skills, procedures, and technique necessary for success. As Dr. Robert Schuller, author of *Move Ahead with Possibility Thinking,* says:

> "*Spectacular achievement is always preceded by unspectacular preparation.*"

The professional's attitude is such that he's grateful for *some* of the difficulties. He doesn't want to be like this old boy down home who stated that he would occasionally like a blessing which was not in disguise. I mention this because when we encounter the tough prospect and the tough sale, we must remember that the tough prospects are our best teachers, and if all sales were easy and "anybody could do it," our commissions would be about one-tenth as much as they are.

The professional understands completely that competition is getting keener all the time, and so he must do the same thing. The professional *has* character; he is not one.

As sales pro Mike Frank says, "The professional acquires and maintains a 'prospecting awareness.' He seeks prospects from current and former clients as well as everyone he calls on, regardless of sales results. He cultivates them at the supermarket, the club, and restaurants, as well as other social contacts. He utilizes information gleaned from radio, TV, and newspapers as well as billboards and bus signs. He 'sees' a prospect behind every bush and tree and around every corner."

The professional keeps records. He remembers what has made him successful and he keeps the same hustle, enthusiasm, and dedication to the job. Those factors which got him started, combined with expertise, experience, skill, and knowledge, are what make him the successful professional. He is a student and reads the good books and publications on selling and motivation.

Question as you read this book: Is this the first one you've read this year or is it the sixth? If it's June or later, I sincerely hope it's at least the sixth one.

Recency—Frequency—Potency—and Recommendation

In the world of professional selling, the professional remembers that if he's going to build a career instead of just selling one customer one time and then having to look for another, he must take seriously the advice of Dr. Joseph Braysich, the "body language" expert from Sydney, Australia.

He advocates the use of the "recency, frequency, potency, recommendation" formula, which is self-explanatory. *Recency* means how long has it been since you were in touch with your customers to let them know you are available to serve, that you appreciate their business, and to inform them about a new addition to your product line or a new use for the products they already have? According to Dr. Braysich, customers, even those who are good friends, need to be reminded of your existence and your eagerness to meet their needs or solve their problems.

Frequency. This will vary tremendously with the product and the practicality of the time investment as it relates to production, but in a competitive world in some shape, form, or fashion, your customers need to be reminded of your existence and your interest. Otherwise, competition which has no feeling of "I've already got that customer" complacency enters the picture and you're short one customer.

The man who is one of the best in the world at keeping his name in front of his customers is Joe Girard, who with Stanley H. Brown wrote the best-selling book *How to Sell Anything to Anybody*. His phenomenal success in the automobile business enabled him to write a book on selling based on his personal experiences. To the best of my knowledge, he holds all the records for selling cars. He sold:

1963–267 cars/trucks	1964–307 cars/trucks
1965–343 cars/trucks	1966–614 cars
1967–667 cars	1968–708 1969–764
1970–843 1971–980	1972–1208
1973–1425 (record year)	1974–1376
1975–1360 1976–over 1200	
1977– over 1200	

For the details on this astonishing performance, you should pick up Joe's book and carefully read what he has to say. There are many remarkable things about his record. First is the fact that over this fifteen-year period of time, he averaged nearly 900 cars per year, and these were all individual sales—no fleet sales at any time. Second, these were sales and not "deals" or giveaways. His company made a profit, Joe made a profit, and the customers obviously "won," too, or they would not have returned time after time. Third, Joe was the number-one automobile salesman in America every year from 1967–77. The magnitude of that feat almost defies description. Fourth, despite the fact there were two recessions during his first eleven years, he sold more cars every year than he had sold the previous year. Fifth, the last six years he sold cars on a full-time basis (before getting heavily involved as a speaker and writer) he averaged over 1300 cars sold each year.

There are many reasons for such phenomenal sales success, but one of them is the fact that once a month Joe dropped a card in the mail to *every one* of his customers. Obvious ones like Christmas, Easter, birthday, and anniversary; not-so-obvious ones like "Happy Fourth of July, Labor Day, Washington's or Lincoln's Birthdays." With cards coming *all the time* his customers consider Joe a member of the family, or at least an old friend. That's the way a real professional does things.

Mike Frank adds his own touch to this process by handwriting a minimum of seven cards every day. Mike uses a notepad which includes his picture because many of his contacts are of a ten-to-fifteen-minute duration, during which time he sells his prospect on inviting him back at a later date to conduct a meeting. The purpose of the meeting is to sell tickets for an upcoming sales and motivation congress. The note reminds the prospect of the date and the picture helps him to put Mike's name and face together. Mike does the same thing with people he did not sell to but who might buy later. He has done this *every day* since 1972. Tough to do—yes. Time consuming—yes. Rewarding—you betcha!

Potency. How strong was your impact? How solid is the relationship? Will your customer distinctly recall your last contact? Are you solidly entrenched because you sold and served well, or did you get in for that initial sale through connections? It's great to have connections to make sales, but it's highly dangerous and erroneous thinking to believe that once you sell to them they are *your* customers.

Recommendation. This one, especially on the initial sale, is critically important. As you will learn in the next chapter, Chuck Bellows sold me a Cadillac because the recommendation was so strong I went to see him prepared to believe him, to trust him, and yes, to buy from him. The professional builds that kind of reputation. Strong recommendations are the easiest—and by far the surest—method of building a sales career.

Finally

The professional is skilled at communicating and reading the prospect's communications back to him. According to some authorities, *what we say only contains 7 percent of the persuasive impact of the message. The way we see it contains 38 percent and our body language the remaining 55 percent.* With this in mind, the professional learns body language and voice inflection. He learns and uses the words that sell, and avoids the words that unsell. (I deal with this phase of the professional in chapter 22.)

The professional is a builder and not a destroyer. He builds his fellow salespeople. He builds his country, his company, his community. He constantly suffers from a case of mild discontent which he instinctively transforms to inspirational dissatisfaction, which is one of the most powerful forces we can harness in professional selling.

18

HERE IS A PROFESSIONAL

LET'S LOOK AT a real professional in the world of selling. I believe this story will cover as many specific sales points, techniques, and procedures as you will ever see covered in a sales story. Not only will it be helpful to all salespeople but the lessons in psychology and persuasion will also be useful for any layman or professional who ever has to "sell" an idea. In short, it will help you—personally and professionally.

This story will "cover the waterfront" since it includes voice inflection, how to ask questions, the importance of sales skill *and* the salesperson, how to effectively negotiate the determining factor in the sale, how to move from the seller's side of the table to the buyer's side, how to lead prospects to new decisions, how to break the price down so it's not such a big factor, how and why you should sell value. It covers the steps you take to make the prospect feel good about unsatisfactory previous purchases, the importance of the follow-through in building a sales career, how to use the Abraham Lincoln approach in convincing the prospect to take action, how to gently chastise the vacillating prospect, and much more.

People Remember Stories

As you have already noticed, *Secrets of Closing the Sale* contains many, many stories. I tell a lot of sales stories for two good reasons. First, you are far less likely to let your mind drift when you are reading a story (provided I tell it well). Second, you remember stories more easily than anything else, and as you recall the story you will also remember the points and techniques taught in the story. Since you *can* use only what you remember, teaching techniques through true stories and analogies is the most effective method ever devised. As you probably know, this was the procedure used by the Carpenter from Galilee, who was the greatest Salesman and the greatest Teacher who ever lived.

171

As a teacher and trainer, I'm completely aware of the fact that if the student didn't learn, the teacher didn't teach. I want this book to inform you, to make you a better person and a better salesperson. I want it to make you more professional and more productive. The only way it will do all those things is if it *teaches* you effective techniques and *inspires* you to use them. That's the reason I tell the stories and use so many examples from life.

In November of 1975, I decided to buy a new car, and since the '76 Cadillac was especially beautiful, I visited two dealerships, shopping for the best overall offer. Since I drive very little, I only buy a new car every five or six years, so I was in no special hurry to "buy today." In a telephone conversation with a business acquaintance, the talk turned to cars and I commented that I was probably going to buy a new Cadillac. He immediately told me that I ought to talk to Chuck Bellows at Rodger Meier Cadillac.

With that comment I said, "Well, you obviously know him. Why don't you give him a call, tell him I'm a nice fellow, that I'm on my way over, and to treat me right?" To that he responded, "I'll be glad to do that and Zig, I'll tell you in advance, you can absolutely depend on Chuck Bellows. If he tells you it's going to rain, man, you can set your tubs out! His reputation for being honest and for having integrity is absolutely great!"

We finished the conversation, he called Chuck, and I got into my automobile and headed over to Rodger Meier. As I was driving down the service road and circling the dealership, Chuck recognized my car because our mutual friend had described it to him. When I pulled into the only available parking slot, Chuck was standing there to open the door.

The "Complimentary" Close

Chuck is an old-fashioned guy and very definitely an introvert. As he opened the door he said, "You've got to be Zig Ziglar." Zig: "Yes, I am." Chuck: "Well, Mr. Ziglar, let me start by telling you I think you're driving one of the nicest cars I've ever seen. It's absolutely beautiful!'

Point number one: Bragging about a recent or previous purchase is not a bad way to start an interview. A sure way to make me feel good about buying something else is to make me feel good about a previous purchase. This is exactly what Chuck was doing. There is an "if" attached. That is, *if* he's telling me the truth. If that car's a dog, if it's a beat-up wreck and he says, "Man, that's a beautiful car!" then I grab my pocketbook and run for my financial life because I know he's trying to get his hands in my pocket.

> **Point:** *Make certain the observation or compliment is accurate and sincere.*

Chuck was telling the truth. It was a beautiful car. It was an Oldsmobile Regency—two-tone brown—with all the good stuff on it which increases the value and enhances the enjoyment of a car. So when he said, "Man, you've got a beautiful car," I responded by thanking him and telling him I had enjoyed the car very much and it had given me excellent service. He reiterated, "Well, it is a beautiful car. Do you mind telling me where you got it?"

Ask Those Questions

It's very important for you to notice these questions because they're completely natural and appear to be casual, despite the fact that Chuck has probably asked these same questions many times over the years. His questions were not "canned," but they were very carefully planned. I responded that my neighbor across the street is a General Motors executive and I got the car through him. Chuck: "Say, did you by any chance get one of the executive cars?" Zig: "Well, as a matter of fact, I did." Chuck: "I'll bet you got a good deal on it, didn't you?" (I don't know how you are, but the odds are great when somebody accuses you of having made a good deal four or five years earlier you're going to modestly admit you did all right in the transaction. I hope you do it modestly; otherwise it's tacky!)

As modestly as I could, I said, "Well, Chuck, to tell you the truth, when I bought this car it was a seventy-six-hundred-dollar automobile." (Remember, this was in 1975.) "It only had twenty-one hundred miles on it and I got it for fifty-six hundred." Chuck: "Say, you *did* get a good deal!"

True. I did get a good deal, but with those words I also did something else. I loaded the first barrel of his sales shotgun. He had asked me for information and I (a prospect) gave it to him.

> **Point:** *When you're talking with a prospect, please remember that in most cases he's delighted to give you pertinent information if you'll just ask for it!*

Chuck continued, "Mr. Ziglar, I'm delighted you're here. Let me get the appraiser to see just how much we can give you for your fine car. I will tell you right now if it is as nice on the inside as it is on the outside, we're going to be able to swap with you today and make you happy in the process, because we have a magnificent inventory." He found the appraiser and they got into the car and drove off.

Think Like a Buyer—and a Seller

They went wherever it is they go when they do whatever it is they do when they appraise a car. They were gone about ten or fifteen minutes. When they drove back into the parking lot, old Chuck was sitting on the passenger side, grinning like the proverbial cat which had just swallowed the canary. I mean, he was really excited!

As a salesperson, let me remind you that you need to be thinking as a buyer *and* as a seller. In this particular case, since I'm buying, I am thinking as a buyer.

When Chuck pulled into the lot with that big grin on his face, I've got to confess to you that an embarrassing thought went through my mind. (Now I want to stress that I didn't let it stay long before I ran it on out of there!) The word *steal* entered my mind. (I figured he was so sold on my four-year-old car that he was going to *pay me* to swap!) Like I say, it's embarrassing, but again I remind you that I was a prospective customer, so I was *thinking* as a customer.

To keep things in perspective I remind you again, again, and yet again that if you want to scale the heights as a professional salesperson *you must always, in every sales situation, be thinking as a seller and as a buyer.*

As a prospective buyer I thought to myself, "He loves my car. I'm going to get an incredible offer on it, I just know I am!" The car stopped and Chuck stepped out. I'm not certain, but I believe old Chuck has had some training in dramatics. When he stepped out of the car he closed the door, backed away, and just shook his head. Then, as if he couldn't believe it, he opened the door and closed it again. He obviously loved this magnificent machine which he was going to have an opportunity to obtain in a trade.

Bring Out Those Unspoken Objections

He looked at me and repeated what he had said earlier. "You know, Mr. Ziglar, this really is one of the most beautiful cars I think I've ever seen! As a matter of fact, it is in even better condition on the inside than it is on the outside. You're to be commended." Zig: "Thank you very much, Chuck." He continued, "As a matter of fact, I'm a little puzzled. Please don't misunderstand, because I'm delighted you're here, but I am a little curious as to why you want to swap such a beautiful automobile at this time."

You readers who are directly involved in the world of selling, especially if you haven't been at it too long, might think this question seems a big negative. Zig brings in a four-year-old car to trade on a new one and Chuck is asking *why* he wants to swap it right now. Instead of it being negative, I believe it is a positive sign of a competent and confident professional.

Here's why. *If there are any objections, it is infinitely better to bring them out early so you can deal with them as part of the presentation rather than at the end of the interview.* If you, the salesperson, can smoke out any objection early, you can sell on the offense instead of on the defense.

Back to Chuck

When Chuck asked, "Why do you want to swap this car?" I looked at him, smiled, and replied, "Well, Chuck, to tell you the truth, we have a family reunion in Mississippi in about three weeks and I think it would really be nice if I drove a new Cadillac over there." Chuck obviously thought that would be kind of nice, too, but he didn't say anything. (He didn't have to—I had just loaded the second barrel of his sales shotgun!) He simply got out his talking pad (I've stressed throughout this book that you need to keep your talking pad handy) and started figuring. He had a big grin on his face, so my confidence that I was going to get a really good offer went up even more.

From High to Low to High

Unfortunately, that feeling was short-lived, because after he'd been figuring a moment or so, that magnificent grin of his started to fade into neutral. As the grin dissolved I looked at him and thought to myself, "Oh, no! He's hit a snag, maybe even found something wrong," and my heart started to sink. He continued to figure and after a few more minutes that magnificent expression of a moment earlier which had shifted into neutral shifted all the way into plain ugly! As a matter of fact, I've never seen such a high concentration of ugly in one small spot in my life! My heart literally went all the way down to my heels. I was thinking (more accurately, talking) to myself, "Oh, no! He's found something bad wrong and I just know I'm not going to be able to get that beautiful new Cadillac I've really set my heart on!"

In retrospect, I should have been more optimistic, especially since I do have a reputation for being a positive thinker. Actually, I was guilty of selling Chuck Bellows short and I shouldn't have done that, because among other things, he is a fighter! I mean he flat hung in there and kept figuring and kept figuring and kept figuring. Finally, that ugly on his face started shifting back into neutral and I caught myself pulling for him, "Come on, Chuck, hang in there, man, stay with it!" And bless his heart, that's exactly what he did.

After a few more minutes of concentrated figuring, that neutral expression went back to his magnificent smile. At that point, Chuck looked up from his talking pad and in an excited voice said, "Mr. Ziglar, I've got marvelous news for you! Because of the remarkably good condition of your car, and because of our wonderful inventory, we're going to be able to swap with you today for just seventy-three eighty-five."

I Almost Had a Heart Attack!

Please don't misunderstand—I'm an educated man. I mean, I watch television and I read the newspapers and everybody knows that's where you get your education. I knew that the price of automobiles had been going up—up—up—UP! Not only that but my friends and all of my relatives had been saying to me, "Zig, you cannot believe what has happened to the price of automobiles! Man, they've gone absolutely crazy!" But my friends and relatives were talking about a different subject.

That's a Lot of Money!

They were talking about *their* cars and *their* money. Chuck Bellows is talking to me about *my* car and *my* money, and that's an entirely different ball game. When he said, "Seventy-three eighty-five," and that's what he said, just as smoothly and easily as anything you've ever heard (he didn't say, "Seven thousand three hundred eighty-five dollars"), I *screamed* like a stuck pig!

"Whooo-whooo! Chuck! Man alive," I said, "that's a lot of money!" Chuck looked me in the eye and quietly asked a very simple question—with just the right voice inflection, I might add. "Mr. Ziglar, is it too much?"

> *Important point:* He didn't argue, get defensive, or try to justify the price. He had quietly and with an almost casual confidence put the ball back in my court.

What Is He Asking Me?

As a player in this game I've got to ask myself some questions and make some decisions. First, what is he asking me? Is he asking me if the price is beyond my reach, is it out of my financial range? Does it represent a challenge? Is he really telling me that if I can't handle the $7385 difference I should act like a man and confess that I just can't handle that much money? Dear reader, if you know anything at all about me, you know that in a thousand years I never would have confessed that I couldn't handle the investment. No way.

Or was his statement/question something of an altogether different nature? Was he simply asking, "Mr. Ziglar, as a wise and prudent businessman, do you feel the seventy-three eighty-five at this time is more than you wish to give in exchange for these two automobiles?"

If the latter is the question, then I have no trouble pleading guilty. I responded, "Chuck, that's just more money than I'm willing to invest in the difference." Pleasantly and gently he stayed on the offensive with another direct but simple question. "Mr. Ziglar, what do you think would be a fair difference to give in exchange between your magnificent four-year-old Oldsmobile Regency and our gorgeous new Cadillac Sedan deVille?"

The "Abraham Lincoln" Close

Please notice that throughout this entire presentation Chuck Bellows never once said anything derogatory or negative about my automobile. He used the Abraham Lincoln approach. Lincoln used to argue both sides of the case when he was presenting it to the jury. He would take the opposition's side, then he would take his client's side. He was very careful to bring out more points in his own favor, but when he took the opposition's side he was always fair, although he was undoubtedly not quite as eloquent as when he presented his client's case.

The "Previous Purchase" Close

Chuck's technique and psychology were "right on." Any attack on my car would have been an attack on me personally. After all, *I* had bought the car and *when you attack the purchase you attack the purchaser and his judgment.* When parents criticize or malign the boyfriend or girl-friend of their son or daughter, they are attacking the judgment, taste, and intelligence of their children. *That's* often the reason the kids rebel. That is not the way to win friends and influence people—or our chil-dren, *or* our prospects.

Be careful *and* tactful when a prospect says something derogatory about a purchase previously made. (Tact, as you probably know, is the art of recognizing when to be big and when not to belittle.) Statements such as, "Boy, they sure took advantage of me!" or, "They saw me coming!" can be disastrous for you if you agree with the prospect.

Example: If you say, "Obviously they were not completely honest with you," or, "I agree they did see you coming," comments like that will lead your prospect to think, "Yeah, *they* got to me, but partner, I'm going to watch *you* and I will guarantee that you are not going to get to me!" You wave a red flag and alert the prospect to be skeptical of you when you say anything derogatory about your prospect's previous pur-chase or a salesperson with whom your prospect previously dealt.

What do you say when your prospect makes a negative statement about a previous purchase? Try this: Look your prospect in the eye and quietly say, "In retrospect, Mr. Prospect, I'm confident that most of us would make some of our decisions differently if we could make them again. However, at the time you made this decision, under the circum-stances which existed at that moment and with the information you had at your disposal, I'm confident that most of us would have made the same decision you did, so I wouldn't feel bad about something which happened such a long time ago."

> *The best way to get a prospect to make a favorable new decision is to make him happy with an old decision.*

Make the Prospect Feel Good

The question is, have you been honest with the prospect? The answer is obvious when you answer the next question: Did you ever buy any-thing and then later wish you had not bought it? Reflect on that for a moment. You bought because you felt you were making the right deci-sion. When you acquire anything of any significance, you do so because you figure it is a "good deal" and in your best interests. Just remember that your prospect felt *exactly* the same way at the time he made his purchase.

By following this procedure Chuck was making me feel good. He was talking about my beautiful four-year-old Oldsmobile Regency, but that's not all he was doing. By inquiring as to what I thought a fair exchange would be, he was also finding out early in the interview if I was a real prospect. He knew that if I offered $500 in exchange for the new car that I was just wasting time and he would do better to terminate the interview.

Same Ball Park—Same Ball Game

A similar situation could exist in the real estate business. For example, a home is listed for $195,000 and the prospect says, "Well, let's make an offer of $95,000." The real estate agent knows he doesn't have a prospect when an offer is so low it indicates they're not only in different ball parks but they're also in different ball games! You need to know this as early as possible so that you can make a sound decision as to whether your time could be more effectively invested with the prospect at hand or with someone else. That is exactly what Chuck was doing.

The question "Mr. Ziglar, what do you think is a fair exchange?" will provide Chuck with the answer he needs so he can decide if I'm a legitimate prospect or not. Zig: "Well, Chuck, I've always believed in dealing in round figures and I personally am convinced that seven thousand dollars would be enough difference to pay between those two cars [pause] including the taxes and costs."

Chuck looked at me in some shock and said, "Mr. Ziglar, you ask the impossible. First, you're asking for a discount of $385, and then you're talking about taxes and costs of about $350. That's $735, and I don't think there's a chance in a million that we would even remotely entertain that idea. [Pause.] But, Mr. Ziglar, let me ask you a question. In the unlikely event we would accept your offer, are you prepared to drive this beautiful new Sedan deVille home with you right now?"

He Is Serious

All of a sudden it dawned on me, "That old boy's serious about selling cars!" It also occurred to me that somebody (me) was a-fixin' to buy something from somebody (him) if somebody didn't do something!

At that precise instant, I did to Chuck what your prospects have been doing to you all of your sales lives and will continue to do to you as long as you are in the world of selling. At the moment of truth, when I had in essence made an offer and Chuck had given me some indication he was going to take me up on it, I started backing away. I crayfished on him and said, "Oh, I don't know about that, Chuck, seven thousand dollars is an awful lot of money and my money just doesn't come that easily."

The Prospect Is Temporarily Insane

You need to understand that if the decision is a major one, at the moment of decision, according to author Charles Roth, your prospects are "temporarily insane." Here's why. On important decisions doubt and fear invariably enter the picture. In my case I was making a seven-thousand-dollar decision, which for a financial conservative is a major one.

The questions—or doubts—which started to pop into my own mind were, "Do I really want this color? Am I certain I want a Cadillac? Do I want to buy it now or wait until the model has been out sixty or ninety days or more? Do I want a Sedan deVille, a Fleetwood, or a Coupe deVille? Can I get a better offer somewhere else? Am I absolutely certain I want to buy, or would I do better to lease a car? If I hang in there, can I get a better offer from Chuck?"

In short, there is doubt and doubt affects your judgment, hence the "temporarily insane" statement. Chuck pinned me down with the question "Mr. Ziglar, if we accept your offer of seven thousand dollars, would you be ready to go ahead?"

The major point I want to make about handling a prospect who has doubts is this: The kind of *person* you are assumes at least equal importance with the kind of *salesperson* you are. Before the prospect buys either your explanations or your product, he must buy *you*. This means he must buy your personality, your sincerity, and your credibility. The bottom line is he must *trust* you.

At this point I would like for you to carefully notice the confidence-building approach taken by Chuck Bellows the man, and the sales procedure followed by Chuck Bellows the professional salesman. I remind you that *the* major reason your prospect does not buy from you is a lack of trust (page 31). For this reason you must understand that your career in sales started when you reached the age of accountability—not when you picked up your first sales kit or stepped behind your first counter.

Skill—or Credibility?

In the sales process you've got to move from one side of the table, where you think and feel as a salesperson, to the other side of the table, where you think and feel as a customer. That's what Chuck must do in this situation. He's got to sit in my seat, wear my shoes, and think my thoughts as a customer. He's got to have *empathy* (page 84) for my situation as a customer if he's going to make the sale.

Combined with this, I want you to notice the negotiation skill he demonstrates and the sales techniques he uses as a sales pro. But again and again I want you to understand that *all the technique in the world you—or in this case, Chuck—might use is of little or no value if the prospect doesn't believe what you're saying and doesn't have confidence in you as a person.*

So what did Chuck do at this particular moment, when I started to crayfish or back out on the counteroffer which I had made? He took his pen, scratched the seven thousand dollars off the talking pad, and said, "Mr. Ziglar, as a practical matter, let's forget about the seven thousand dollars, because I don't think there's a chance in a million our company would even remotely entertain that idea. I'll tell you what let's do. Let's look at the seventy-three eighty-five because I'm certain we would go along with that price." Then Chuck lowered his voice, looked me in the eye, and with just a trace of a smile said, "Because, Mr. Ziglar, we don't back out on *our* offers."

Mildly dangerous? Yes. But only mildly because our mutual friend had said to Chuck, "Zig has been known to pull both legs at the same time," so Chuck knew he could kid me a little. When he said, "We don't back out on our offers," I was amused and not offended. More importantly, I got the message loud and clear that he was a serious negotiator and he expected me to be serious, too.

"So," he said, "let's talk about this seventy-three eighty-five, Mr. Ziglar, because according to the figures you had given me earlier [and again he's using his talking pad], we are offering you within twenty-six hundred dollars of what you paid for your Oldsmobile when it was brand new. Actually, Mr. Ziglar, you have driven your car slightly over four years and if you put your pencil to it, that breaks down to a yearly cost of about six hundred dollars a year." (He's showing me these figures on his talking pad.) Then Chuck lowered his voice, looked me in the eye, and said, "And Mr. Ziglar, you can't even drive a Chevrolet that cheap!" (That made me feel good about my previous purchase [page 178]).

The "Feel Good" Close

I thought to myself, "Ziglar, you clever rascal! You're driving that big, high-powered Oldsmobile for just six hundred dollars a year and those other folks have to pay that much to drive a Chevrolet!" Then all of a sudden it dawned on me exactly what he was doing. I said, "Now, Chuck, hold the phone! Dadgone your hide, I'm not about to give you any seven thousand three hundred eighty-five dollars for that car! I've offered you seven thousand dollars and that's it!"

Chuck has had dramatic training, I know he has! He didn't giggle. He didn't even smile. He simply said, "Well, Mr. Ziglar, it's out of my hands [now he moves over to my side, the customer's side, of the table and *verbally* puts his arm around me], but I'll tell you what I'll do. *I'll talk to the appraiser and see what I can do for you.* You can rest assured I'm going to do everything I can to help you get *your* car at *your* price, because obviously I want *you* driving a car from Rodger Meier."

Earlier Chuck had made me feel like a man of good judgment. Now he was making me feel important. Caution: Be careful. If you can't do this with conviction and sincerity—don't do it.

Chuck is using a subtle version of the assumptive key in closing which I cover in more detail on page 264. When he said "your" car, "your" price, and pointed out that it had cost me only $600 a year to drive my Oldsmobile, he was taking me out of the Olds and putting me in that Sedan deVille. He put me in the seat and behind the wheel. He had already given me ownership.

Now watch him avoid future misunderstanding by repeating our conversation. Chuck: "Before I go back to the appraiser, let me make certain we are communicating. As I get the picture, you're offering us seven thousand dollars in exchange, provided that includes all charges." Zig: "That's exactly right, Chuck."

With that comment, Chuck headed back to see the appraiser. He was gone only about three minutes when he came back and said, "This is a little embarrassing, but the appraiser was called home on an emergency and he's not going to be back until tomorrow morning. My question is, will you be able to sleep tonight not knowing whether or not you're the owner of this beautiful new Sedan deVille?"

The "Tie Down" Close

Zig: "Chuck, I think I can struggle through." Chuck: "Now before you go, let's make absolutely certain we are understanding each other. [Now watch him tie the sale down.] As you know, in the automobile business we don't consider it an offer unless we have a signed agreement, but I've been in this business for a long time and I pride myself on being able to judge men of quality and character. I believe, Mr. Ziglar, that when you say you will pay seven thousand dollars in exchange for the cars, if that includes everything, that's all the agreement I need, that your word is your bond. Am I right on that, Mr. Ziglar?"

What do *you* think I'm going to say to a statement like that? What would *you* have said? I'm certainly not going to say, "No, Chuck, I'm a liar." When someone puts you on a pedestal like that, what are you going to do? So I said (modestly, of course), "That's right, Chuck, if I tell you something, you can depend on it!" Chuck: "I felt confident you were completely dependable, so we'll seal the deal with a gentlemen's handshake and I'll give you a call first thing tomorrow morning, hopefully with some good news for you."

When I walked into the office the next morning at half-past eight, the telephone was ringing. Chuck was calling and he was motivated. "Mr. Ziglar, I've got fantastic news for you! I just talked to the appraiser and we're going to be able to swap with you for just seventy-two hundred dollars, including everything." At that precise instant I knew I had bought the car for seven thousand dollars.

Compromise Leads to—Compromise

As we say down home, "You can put this in your little pipe and smoke it."

> When a company or an individual compromises one time, whether it's on price or principle, the next compromise is right around the corner and you can bet your last nickel on it.

Zig: "Chuck, last night I was impressed with your insight and wisdom in giving me credit for my integrity. I thought you were 'right on,' and since I am a man of my word, I will do exactly what I said I would." Chuck: "Mr. Ziglar, are you saying that you will go no more than the seven thousand?" Zig: "Chuck, we're not eyeballing but we are communicating. That's it." Chuck: "I'll be back to you in a couple of minutes." He called me back and asked, "Do you want me to bring it to you, or are you going to come over here and get it?" Zig: "Chuck, I like to have my cars delivered to me." Chuck: "I'll see you in a few minutes."

Two major points as we conclude the story: Number one, when I started to back out of my seven-thousand-dollar offer, Chuck did not try to resell me. He knew I'd try to get the price even lower if he did. Point number two: Even though I met Chuck for the first time the day before I bought the car, he actually started selling me that car twenty-two years earlier when he made the decision he was going to make his *career* selling Cadillac automobiles.

In order to do this, Chuck knew he had to do two things. First, he knew he had to build customer loyalty so he could sell the same people time after time. Second, he knew he had to persuade his customers to send him other customers. How well he has succeeded is evidenced by the fact that the bulk of his business is repeat business. This is truly remarkable when you understand that we live in a highly mobile society and many of his customers relocate in other cities. My own purchase was initially motivated by one of Chuck's long-term customers.

How he does this is important. Number one, he has built his career on integrity. In my own case, I did not go see Chuck to *look* at a Cadillac. I had already *looked* at Cadillacs at two other dealerships. I was sold on the car. I went to see Chuck to *buy* a car *if* we could work out the financial details. I knew I could trust Chuck, and trust is the most important ingredient in the transaction. Number two, Chuck is extremely professional in his follow-through. Ten days after purchase, he called to see how I liked the car, could he do anything for me, and, "Oh, yes, do you have any friends I should talk to about our new model?"

The first time I was in for service the first man I saw, almost before I switched the engine off, was Chuck Bellows, wanting to know if he could do anything for me. That's not all. Periodically Chuck would call just to say, "Hello, and by the way, do you know anybody who . . . ?" Obviously, he was keeping his name fresh in my mind so when car-swapping time rolled around I would remember him.

Chuck Bellows is a professional. Neatly and conservatively dressed at all times, he creates the image of a friend and adviser who wants to assist you in selecting the right car for you and then working to help you enjoy your selection. That's good selling. That's the way to make every sale so you make more than a sale. You make a customer and a friend. This is the way to sell more now and sell more later. That, my friend, is career-building selling.

19

EVERYBODY IS A SALESPERSON AND *EVERYTHING* IS SELLING

This *Dentist Is a Professional Salesman*

One of the true professionals in selling is my friend Dr. Tom McDougal. Tom is a dentist, and a superb one. He lectures nationally to other dentists on building a successful practice. Like *all* real professionals, Tom practices what he preaches.

On my first visit, the receptionist at the front desk was cordial, friendly, and enthusiastic. An assistant handed me the new-patient forms and encouraged me to take a seat in the reception room. Almost immediately after I completed them, another assistant came to take me into a treatment room for the preliminary examination.

From "hello" to "good-bye," all of them were enthusiastic and professional in what they did. Dr. McDougal, of course, handled the parts of the treatment that only a dentist can handle, but the staff members did their jobs in a professional way. Perhaps the most impressive part of the visit was the fact that not one, not two, but three of them "sold" me on the importance of using dental floss. Each one laughingly said that Dr. McDougal believes you should floss "only those teeth you want to keep."

The point is simple: He believes in preventive dentistry. I left with the strong feeling that everybody there wanted me to keep my teeth. That's practicing good dentistry, good human relations, and it's fantastic service selling!

Words Do *Make a Difference*

When I visited Dr. McDougal I noticed he used *positive words*. Many of these words are taken from the extensive list prepared by dental consultant Gladys E. Cook.

He talked about "restoration" instead of "filling"; about a "change in schedule" rather than any "cancellation" or "postponement." I was in his "reception room" briefly, not his "waiting room." At the end of the visit they wanted to know how I would "take care of," not "pay for" the services. His office called my office to "confirm" or to "verify" the appointment, not to "remind" me of it. I was told to "empty my mouth," not to "spit." They "prepared" the tooth instead of "grinding" the tooth. He gave me an "injection" instead of a "needle" or "shot." I felt a little "discomfort" or "pressure," not any "pain." Yes, sir, words are important. They do make a difference!

Oooops!

Two other things stand out in the relationship. First, two nights later one of the temporary crowns came off. I called Dr. McDougal's office and the answering service responded. Five minutes later my phone was ringing and ten minutes later I was on my way to the office, where one of Dr. McDougal's associates quickly cemented the temporary back in place. That's taking care of your patient (customer).

Second, since Dr. McDougal prepared three teeth for crowns, the visit was lengthy and the work extensive. That evening he personally called me to inquire as to how I was doing. Did I need a prescription? Was I comfortable? Could he be of any help to me? In all the years I've been going to dentists I have never had a single one call me at home to see how I was and ask if I were hurting.

To be candid, I initially thought he was calling because he knew me professionally as a speaker and writer. I checked with other patients of his, however, and discovered that any time he does a significant amount of work on a patient, he always calls him that night to make certain he's doing OK. That's good dentistry—but friends, from where I'm sitting, that's also good selling because that showed me his care and concern for me as a person.

Dr. Hugh Russell from Atlanta, Georgia, points out that often people will buy from us not because they understand our offer but because they feel we understand them. In Dr. McDougal's case, I will buy from him because he's a superb dentist *and* because he understands me and my needs when I sit down in his chair. Every professional salesman should be just that concerned and just that professional in looking after his customers.

This is best verbalized by Dr. McDougal himself in this paragraph which he contributed:

The real secret to "selling" in dentistry or in any other profession or business is to speak from the heart instead of from the head or intellectual base. When the inner man speaks, the deepest form of sincerity is communicated. However, one cannot speak from the heart unless he truly believes in his product and/or service. This means that he must have paid the price by obtaining profound knowledge of his product or service. One must also believe this product/service is unquestionably what the customer/patient needs.

Dr. McDougal is not a "salesman" or "sales trainer" in the eyes of the public at large, but as a salesman you will never read a paragraph any more loaded with sales impact than the preceding one.

A Professional Service Station Operator

Several years ago, when service stations were service stations and not just stands with pumps which you use to fill your own tank, I met one of the supersalesmen of our time. His name is Tom Fountain.

Never will I forget the day I pulled into his station in Decatur, Georgia, with an empty tank. Rain was coming down in sheets as I pulled up to the gas pump, hopped out, and made a mad dash into the station, signaling the attendant not to come out and get soaked because I was not in a big hurry.

I introduced myself to the owner and started the conversation with an untypically negative comment. "Tom, this rain is really tough on the service station business, isn't it?" Tom very cheerfully replied, "No, Zig, not at all. As a matter of fact, this is one of the greatest things that happens to me."

The "Rainy Weather" Close

I responded that in all my years I'd never heard a service station owner get enthusiastic about rain, and I asked him why he said that. He replied, "Well, Zig, while it's raining it is true that my business slows down, but when we have a real gully washer like this it washes hundreds of nails and pieces of glass into the street, and you're going to see a rash of flat tires during the next few days.

"Now, don't misunderstand, Zig, I hate to see anyone have bad luck, but it's a fact of life that when nails and glass hit the street people are going to run over them. And it also happens, Zig, that I have the greatest tire repairmen in this city, and we can do the best and fastest job at the best price of anybody here. That's the reason people come to us. There's nothing I can do about the rain falling, but there is a lot I can do about solving people's problems when that rain does fall." Wow! Was that ever a delightful visit! With an attitude like that no wonder Tom's business was booming!

The "Spare" Close

On another visit into his station we were discussing sales strategy, and Tom shared a fantastic procedure he uses for bonus sales.

When a car pulls into the station, Tom and his crew check the oil, battery, and water as well as the fan belt. When the fan belt is worn and in danger of breaking, Tom says to the owner of the car, "Sir, your fan belt is worn. If you'll get the spare one out of your trunk, I'll be glad to put it on and it shouldn't delay you but just a minute."

Invariably the owner will say, "I don't have one in my trunk." Then Tom responds, "If you'll take a look you'll notice this one is badly worn. I would really encourage you to get a new one because yours could break at any minute and you might be stuck in a bad spot." The owner, in an extremely high percentage of the cases, agrees to do so.

I'll bet you've already finished the story, haven't you? When Tom comes out of the station he is carrying not one but two belts. He not only sells the one belt but in a high percentage of the cases he also sells the second belt. That's the mark of the professional. That's serving by selling—or is it selling by serving?

The Coach Is a Salesman

Everybody sells. And to repeat what Red Motley, the former editor of *Parade* magazine, said many years ago, "Nothing happens until somebody sells something." Never will I forget that hot summer day in 1943 when I walked into the American history class being taught by Coach Joby Harris at Hinds Junior College in Raymond, Mississippi. I was there under protest. I had to have the course in history in order to get my high school diploma, but as far as I was concerned it was a complete waste of time. What possible good would it do me to know what happened fifty years ago, a hundred years ago, two hundred years ago?

I entered the class with the attitude that I would take the class—and I would pass it—because I would learn just enough to "get by." My real interest was in getting the course out of the way so I could take additional math and science courses the following fall in order to qualify for the Naval Air Corps. My dream for several years had been to fly one of the fighter planes. We were in the midst of World War II in that summer of 1943, and I was really gung ho about doing my share. At the ripe old age of sixteen I clearly knew what I wanted to do with my life.

When I walked into the classroom that day, I expected the teacher to introduce himself, make a few light remarks, and get on with the business of teaching us history. The first part was right. Coach Harris introduced himself, made a few casual remarks, and then made one of the most professional sales presentations I have ever heard. By the time the "sales talk" was over, I clearly understood why I absolutely had to know my history. As a matter of fact, before the end of that first hour I was a history major. Not only did I make an A in the class, but it was the only subject in which I consistently made As for most of the rest of my academic career.

Considerably more important is the fact that what Coach Harris said to me that day influenced the rest of my life. My interest in politics, in social conditions, and in doing as much as I can to make our country a better place to live, can be traced directly to that first hour in the history class of Coach Joby Harris.

Since every teacher is a salesperson, wouldn't it be great if we could sell every teacher on the idea that they truly are salespeople, that they need to sell and *can* sell our young people the concepts which made our country great; that they need to sell the students on the idea of doing their best and being their best; to sell them on reaching for higher objectives and making bigger contributions? With this approach, I believe the youth of today will be far more productive in their world of tomorrow.

Professional Builders Sell, Too

As I've said on a half-dozen different occasions in *Secrets,* everyone from the housewife and mother to the professional computer technician is a salesperson. The same is certainly true of builders. In 1981 we initiated an action which had been in our plans for a number of years.

We bought a lot at Holly Lake, which is a pleasant two-hour drive east of Dallas, Texas. It had been my long-range dream to reduce my speaking engagements and concentrate more on writing. My personal objective is to positively influence the maximum number of people. I can do this more effectively through my books than I can through personal appearances.

We found in Holly Lake what we considered the ideal location because it was secluded, quiet, and beautiful. After buying the lot we had to decide on a builder. We never talked to but one man—his name is Bill Tenison. From the beginning Bill's words and actions indicated that he *expected* to build our house ("Assumptive" Close). Bill had many things going for him including an easy, friendly, professional manner and his *reputation*.

When we bought our lot we met the next-door neighbors who were in the process of completing their home. They told us there was only one builder to even consider and Bill was that man.

They enthusiastically pointed out that Bill did superb work, was a man of integrity, and did everything he said he was going to do *and then some*. We talked to people for whom Bill had built a couple of years earlier. They said exactly the same thing. Bill was understandably eager to take us to inspect homes currently under construction as well as those he had built several years before.

The general feeling in the community is that Bill Tenison builds every house so that he can be good neighbors and friends with all his customers. Since Bill was in the process of building his own house at the lake and was going to be fishing and playing golf with all or most of his neighbors, his approach is certainly a wise one. (Can you imagine trying to play golf with fifty angry clients?)

So How Did He Do?

I can honestly say that Bill delivered far more house than I thought we were buying. I know little or nothing about building, but person after person familiar with the industry assured me that Bill had used far more insulation than was required in the specifications and that he added extra reinforcement which was not called for. On countless occasions he used $3' \times 6'$ boards when standard practice dictated $2' \times 4'$.

As the house was going up, since we could not be there for every phase of the construction, Bill voluntarily took dozens of pictures and sent them to us. This enabled us to not only watch the growth of the house but satisfied us completely that we were getting everything we had bargained for—and then some.

The point really is clear. Bill knows when his men drove the last nail into our house he was laying the groundwork for driving the first nail in *all* the other houses his *satisfied* customers are going to sell for him. As a professional, Bill is intelligently selfish enough to know if he does a superb job, delivers more than he's paid for, and satisfies me as a customer, I'm going to be telling people like you that if you ever build a house at Holly Lake, Bill Tenison is the man who should build it. That, my selling friend, is what building a sales career is all about.

Since you don't let a beautiful home sit empty, this story has a sequel and it's at least partially tied to what the late sales trainer J. Douglas Edwards called:

The "Puppy Dog" Close

The close is simple and undoubtedly got its start—or at least its popularity—from the early days when youngsters lured their parents into a pet shop "just to look" at that "doggy in the window" (for those of you who are old enough to remember that song). If the youngster and the pet-shop owner could not gang up on mom and dad and persuade them to buy that cute puppy, then the owner encouraged them to take the puppy home to see how they liked it. You can complete the story, can't you? The most important point is the pet-shop owner let his product (the puppy) sell itself. That's good strategy.

Interior Designers Sell, Too

When Bill Tenison finished our home at Holly Lake, interior designer Joyce Wynn and her beautiful staff (especially Kathy Adcock-Smith, who did a tremendous job of looking everywhere to find *exactly* what we needed) worked carefully with the Redhead and me to make certain it was furnished appropriately and according to our tastes and desires.

Never will I forget what happened when virtually everything was complete except for a large empty space on one of the walls in the great room. Frankly, I thought it looked fine as it was, but Joyce brought in a beautiful wall rug to fill the spot. As you might suspect, it wasn't exactly bargain-basement material. I liked it but there were some reservations about buying it. Joyce casually suggested that we hang it on a temporary basis and see if it "grew" on us. If it did, that would be fine; if not, no problem.

That made a certain amount of sense, even to this stubborn husband. It wasn't until that afternoon while I was jogging that I realized she had used the old "Puppy Dog" Close on me. It was almost all I could do to keep from laughing because it demonstrates exactly what I'm talking about.

Good technique works (yes, I bought the wall rug) even when the person you're using it on is educated in sales techniques and procedures. Actually, if it's really good, the prospect is not completely aware of what is happening. Even if he is, if the need and desire for ownership are there and the salesperson's techniques are professional, there simply isn't a great deal you can or want to do about it. Remember: The prospect *wants* his problem solved.

The professional is so effective you "forget" he or she is a pro. About a year after we moved into our home at Holly Lake, the Redhead and I were visiting with Kathy Adcock-Smith. My wife was sharing with her that many people have remarked how they love the warmth of our home. She also commented that some had expressed surprise that an interior designer had helped us because the home looked so "natural" and livable, whereas many interior designers have a tendency to make homes look artificial and overdone. These comments obviously delighted Kathy, because she knew she had done her job well, that she had "sold" us her furniture, accessories, and ideas so well they had blended completely with our tastes, ideas, and concepts so that her expertise had given *our* home a beautiful added dimension.

The conversation reminded me of an early experience I had in the sales world. After consummating a sale for a set of cookware, I was getting prospects from my new customers. As I sought the prospects, I assured them I would simply demonstrate and if their friends chose to buy that was fine, and if they did not choose to buy that was fine, too. To this statement the wife responded, "Yes, I know that is true because you're definitely not much of a salesman."

Since she had just given me a check for the largest set of cookware our company made, I was delighted with her comment. In the customer's mind she had bought and I had not sold. Ideally, that's the way every prospect should feel at the end of the transaction.

It Works on Million-Dollar Deals, Too

Several years ago, when the corporation was small compared to what it is today, an aircraft salesman called on Rich DeVos, the president of The Amway Corporation, to sell him a jet airplane. Rich is quite conservative and felt the corporation could not justify the purchase at that time. The salesman knew what the jet would do in saving time as well as wear and tear on Rich's body. He also knew the plane would enable Rich to see more of his distributors and substantially increase his effectiveness.

Here's the approach the salesman used: "Mr. DeVos, we have one special jet aircraft which would be ideal for you, and I would like to take you for a demonstration ride." With some reluctance but also with some excitement, Rich took the ride. He liked it but was by no means convinced he should buy, so the salesman said, "Mr. DeVos, we're not going to be using this plane this week, so we want you to take it and use it as if it were your own. Obviously there is no obligation." A deal like that is difficult to turn down since he emphasized there would be no obligation on Amway's part. As luck would have it, Rich just happened to have an especially difficult week, with much travel in front of him.

During that week Rich flew around the country in that jet faster, more comfortably, and more productively.

At the end of the week the salesman came back and tried to close the sale, but Rich was still not convinced the move would be prudent, so the salesman extended the "Puppy Dog" offer with a small string attached. "Mr. DeVos, since we have no specific plans for the jet this next month, why don't you just lease it for the month and continue to use it as if it were your own?" This time Rich was even more hesitant, but the salesman persisted, so Rich made even better use of the plane for the entire month.

By the end of the month Rich was "hooked," so when the salesman came back for "his" jet, Rich DeVos looked at him and asked, "What do you mean, *your* jet?" (By then Rich had grown accustomed to the extra speed and convenience, and it's tough to give up *any* satisfying convenience, especially if you can justify it in any way.) In essence, Rich had no trouble talking himself into an investment which would enable him to serve his corporation more effectively.

He bought the jet because the salesman was able to demonstrate the value of his product. In a nutshell, he let his product demonstrate that it would make Rich more effective in fulfilling his corporate responsibilities, so in the truest sense the product "sold itself" *after* the salesman used the "Puppy Dog" Close.

The Waiter Is a Salesman

Frank Infante was born and raised in Cuba, but when Castro and his Communist cohorts took over he, along with other members of his family, made his exit to the United States. I met Frank for the first time one evening when the Redhead and I were having dinner at Farfallo's Restaurant in Dallas and had the good fortune to draw Frank as our waiter. He's the best I've ever seen. He's thoroughly professional in his every move and is well versed in all the niceties of being a superb waiter. He speaks the languages, knows the words, has the grace, charm, and good manners which are important. He's extremely sensitive to the diner and his every need without smothering him with unwanted, unneeded attention.

Frank starts by greeting us with a friendly, low-key welcome. After we've had a reasonable amount of time to look over the menu and the cocktail waitress has offered her services, Frank—with that innate sixth sense of his—approaches at what seems to be the precise moment after we've arrived at our decision. He smilingly asks if we are ready to order. Generally speaking, there's a little small talk. I always ask about the specialties, and in glowing but not too detailed terms Frank tells us about them. I ask for his recommendation and he seldom hedges. He knows our tastes and will say, "I believe you would enjoy this particular dish. It's very nice."

However, since we are fairly traditional and there are three or four dishes we particularly enjoy, we generally order the Veal Oscar, Red Snapper Sauce Bretonne, or Coeur de Filet Helder (Filet Mignon with Béarnaise Sauce). His description of the salads is also quite elaborate and yet not too lengthy. In other words, he's inclined to "tell us what time it is and not how to build a watch."

The "Soft Service Sell" Close

It's amazing to me that Frank can bring us exactly what we want so quickly when we're somewhat pushed for time and yet time everything to perfection so that we can leisurely and casually dine when it's an evening meal and just the two of us. The tea and coffee are always available and ready; the hot bread is at our fingertips; we never wait more than a minute or so when we've completed one course and are ready to move to the next.

As we finish our meal, Frank asks about dessert and we generally say no. Often, with a twinkle in his eye he will say to us that the cheesecake is particularly good or the cappuccino pie is especially nice and if we split one it would not be too heavy for us. His close is "soft," it's service oriented, and it works. One reason it works is that Frank is truly a "team player" who works with his "busboy" (that's a horrible title which the restaurant industry *must* change in order to help attract more quality people) in a most effective manner. He treats him with respect and courtesy as he requests assistance instead of demanding it. That's class.

From "hello" to "good-bye" Frank Infante is selling. He's doing it in a pleasant, low-key, and very professional way, but he is selling. He recognizes that his income is directly related to the effectiveness and manner in which he serves. However, as you watch Frank and listen to him, you get the distinct feeling that his entire reason for being there is to be the best at his profession. His objective is to make your meal at Farfallo's a true dining experience. Needless to say, we never tip Frank just the standard 15 percent.

As you probably know, the original word was TIPS and it was "To Insure Prompt Service." The tip was given *before* the meal as a reward in advance for the prompt service. The Redhead and I figure the 15 percent is for prompt, courteous service. When we get a "bonus" in the form of helpful suggestions, gracious manners, a pleasant smile, and some friendly enthusiasm, we are inclined to reward our benefactors with more than the 15 percent.

It's a shame that every waiter and waitress can't come in and let Frank Infante serve them a meal. I'm convinced that if they could, and if they were truly interested in becoming more professional, many of them could increase their incomes from 50 to 150 percent almost immediately.

Question: What would you do with this extra income? Answer: You probably could figure it out for yourself, but Frank Infante invested in his own restaurant and is doing well.

One of the mysteries of life is why any waiter or waitress (or any other salesperson) doesn't understand that all they've really got to sell is their attitude and their service. If they would learn some of the simple niceties of being gracious, pleasant, enthusiastic, and helpful, their income would dramatically increase. Yes, a *good* waiter or waitress is a *good* salesperson.

The Three-Year-Old Pro

When it comes to selling, no one—but no one—is as persuasive or effective as a small child. Conviction is total, integrity is beyond question, and enthusiasm is unlimited. Now throw in a completely open manner, combined with the right words, and you have an unbeatable persuader.

Never will I forget an incident with Suzan, my oldest daughter, when she was just three years old. Cindy, our second daughter, had made her appearance just six weeks earlier and I had been on the road much of the time the last three weeks. I pulled into our driveway in Knoxville, Tennessee, slightly before noon on that cold, snowy, February Saturday. After my welcome home from the Redhead, Suzan, Cindy, and our live-in housekeeper, Lizzie Rogers, I was informed that I needed to go to the store to "pick up some things."

Since I was playing with Suzan and holding the baby while talking to the Redhead about the trip, I wasn't exactly thrilled at the prospect of going back out in the cold. However, those "things" were essential so I reluctantly started putting on my topcoat, hat, and gloves. As I was getting ready, Suzan started asking if she could go. I explained that the weather was just too bad to take her out and besides, I would be gone only a few minutes. She responded, "But Daddy, I'll be so lonely." Zig: "Suzan, you know you won't be lonely. Your mother, your little sister, and Lizzie are all here, so you certainly won't be lonely." Suzan: "But Daddy, I'll be lonely for *you*."

It really wasn't a fair fight. I was badly overmatched and never had a chance. Obviously Suzan didn't know anything about "dominant buying motive," or the importance of making the prospect feel important (and really meaning it), but no sales pro with thirty years' experience could have come up with a better line. Needless to say, I didn't want Suzan to be "lonely," so she made the trip.

The Winner and Undisputed Champion

One of the really great professional salespeople in America today is Billie Engman, who sells for the Saladmaster Corporation out of Dallas, Texas. Billie has set and holds more individual sales records than anyone in the history of the company. She sells the complete product line of cookware, china, cutlery, crystal, and flatware. She is now selling to the daughters of the girls she sold to when she started her career with the company in 1950 and is looking forward to selling to the granddaughters someday.

Billie is one of those unusual ladies with a truly professional concept and philosophy. She is incredibly well organized and an extremely hard, persistent, and consistent worker. When she's out "beating the bushes," she has great singleness of purpose.

She's a Sales "Psychologist"

Let's look at some of her concepts, ideas, and philosophies. To begin with, she mildly objects to the use of the term *closing the sale*. She explains that she thinks of closing as someone closing the door and shutting someone out. She feels that when she *opens* her sample case of products and *opens* her storehouse of information which she shares with the prospect, she is really *opening* the sale instead of *closing* the sale.

Billie has some keen insights into human nature and the impact we can all have on one another if we will but take time to learn. Despite her phenomenal success, she is extremely modest and feels that her role as a salesperson gives her the privilege and opportunity to serve. That modesty is best demonstrated by the fact that she has not reported her sales for several years. This costs her a considerable number of substantial prizes and the resulting publicity which is part of the package, but Billie prefers to stay out of the limelight and serve her clients.

According to a company official and her husband, Hal, who works with her and is understandably proud of her, Billie sells so much more than anyone else that her major competition is with herself and her records. Like the professional golfer whose real competition is the golf course itself, Billie can tell you exactly what she sold this same week and this month of the last year. She reaches that goal so consistently that almost without exception this year is better than last year and next year is going to be better than this year. She understands that over the years there have been several recessions. She admits that any talk about recession frightens her, so she gets out and works harder so that her volume of business will continue to climb instead of start to decline. How about *that* attitude!

She's a Smart Lady

Her sales psychology includes getting the entire family involved in a presentation because approximately 60 percent of her business today is with families and only 40 percent with single girls. Initially she had a great fear of selling to men but soon learned they were actually easier to sell to than women. If a small child is present for the presentation, she involves that child and makes each member of the family feel important.

One thing she does to psychologically gear the prospect for the sale is to eliminate tension or feelings of being "closed in" on the part of the prospect. When the closing process starts, if she observes the prospect getting nervous and uptight, she asks him to get her a drink of water. As she explains, it's amazing what that brief interlude will do for the nerves of the prospect.

Billie *never* uses the telephone to make appointments. She believes the telephone is a fast way to burn up a lot of qualified prospects and feels it has put a lot of *direct* salespeople *out* of business, especially in direct sales. She drops in on her leads. She doesn't alert them to her coming and give them the opportunity to think of reasons not to buy. Direct selling is a face-to-face business—not an ear-to-ear business.

Billie keeps meticulous records and takes great delight in tracing her customers into the second generation. She groups her leads into areas and *when she leaves home it is with the sole purpose of seeing as many prospects as she possibly can.* (Like *all* sales pros, she is action oriented and goal directed.) She carries her sample case to the door so if the prospect is home she has everything needed to make a presentation. This procedure eliminates any loss of momentum or a chance the prospect might change his mind during the few minutes required to go to the car and get her samples. Since she goes to the door *expecting* to get in, it would be inconsistent *not* to carry the sample case. Billie is low-key and is not seen as a threat to the people she deals with.

The size of Billie's sales are probably larger than those of anyone else in the cookware and table-appointments field. Frequently her orders run as much as $2,500, and sales of $4,000 and even $5,000 come with amazing regularity.

Each Prospect Is Different

Billie gears her presentation to each individual prospect. Though she gives each one the same basic facts as they relate to the product, she recognizes that the single girl who will perhaps always be single has different interests from the girl who plans to get married, who also is different from the married couple. She personalizes the use of the product to a large degree. She uses what she calls the "mirror of the future," and projects the prospects using and enjoying the beauty and practicality of her products not just in their own lifetime but in the lifetime of their children and even their grandchildren.

She notes with considerable pride that the china and especially the sterling silver which she sold to her prospects thirty years ago is now worth a great deal more than it was when they bought it. She feels that during the years ahead the customer who is investing now will be equally fortunate. She puts that "mirror" into use by letting her customers see themselves using the product in their later years.

Billie is up-to-date on her current events. She ties today's prospect's needs to today's stories and uses that information as a tool or sales prop for getting action today. She sells on love, caring, sharing, and togetherness and the fact that her products contribute to all of these things. She uses warm selling words as she discusses her program with her prospects. Words like *rich, loving, good taste, gracious, comfort, security, investment, caring,* and many other positive words are a part of her, so they are a natural part of her vocabulary. The lowest word on her sales-language totem pole is the word *pitch.* She contends—and I completely agree—that the professional *never* uses that word.

The "Total" Saleslady

Billie firmly believes you "close" (open) the sale by the way you dress, by the neatness of your accessories and attire, by the way you smile, the way you walk, the kind of car you drive. She doesn't believe in being flashy for fear the prospect might think she is being "too" successful, and though Billie could drive a new Mercedes and make her sales calls dressed in mink, she prudently buys fine-quality materials, drives a more-than-adequate car, and gives the appearance of the quiet, confident, success she is.

She never discusses with her prospects how long she has been selling (she started in 1948). She feels this would brand her as a person who was "trying to sell somebody something," when in fact she wants to be regarded as a friend and counselor whose function is to help them make the best possible investment for the future.

She feels the increasing use of catalog buying has been a real asset to her because people can see and recognize that you can buy quality merchandise without having to go shopping to do so. She has the added advantage of being able to show and demonstrate her product with the personal presentation and letting the prospect see, feel, and examine what she is selling.

Billie collects many testimonial letters and constantly updates the ones she has. What a happy customer says today about her product is a strong supplement to what her customers of ten years ago had to say. When she brings out some of the "oldies," it is to let the prospect know that an investment of this type is not a new idea, that years ago investors were doing exactly the same thing she's trying to get them to do today and yes, she really is offering a *provable* lifetime investment. (Conviction *is* essential to closing.)

This "Partially" Explains Her Success

There are many reasons Billie Engman does such an incredible volume of business. I've already touched on some of those reasons, but there are three others which are as much a part of Billie Engman as breathing. First, Billie *expects* to sell everyone she calls on. Not only does she *expect* to sell them, but she *expects* to sell them a large order this time and an even larger repeat order.

Second, Billie feels the order is the result of making a presentation, so she considers the "close" a natural part of that presentation. She gives everyone she calls on a chance to buy by *asking* for the order. If that sounds elementary may I remind you that sales trainer Chris Hegarty points out that 63 percent of *all* sales interviews end with no specific invitation to buy.

Third, Billie keeps records on *all* her customers. She knows *exactly* what they bought, when they bought, and *how* they paid for it. She plans her call-back and prepares the prospect for that call-back when she makes the original sale. Equally important, she prepares herself for the follow-up call. She knows the initial order firmly established the trust of the buyer and puts her in the position of being able to help the customer even more on the second sale.

The "Accessory" Close

Billie's call-back is something else. Before she calls back to complete the order she carefully checks the initial order. Then she prepares three "accessory" offers. Her first offer is the "impossible" one. It's so big, so complete, so comprehensive, and so expensive there is no way the prospect can or will buy it. It's truly a dream proposal in that most people will only dream of owning so many beautiful table appointments. Fortunately for Billie *and* the customer, many of them don't realize they can't have the biggest and the best, so they go ahead and buy the "impossible" dream order. As a pro, Billie has challenged her customers to "go for the gold," to strive for the best, to reach their "impossible" dream, and the prospects respond. It's a fact: *Customer performance is often tied directly to the salesperson's expectancy. Billie's expectancy is high.*

The second accessory order Billie prepares is also beautiful and substantial. It is a big order, designed to perfectly complement the original one. The "average" salesperson would do hand turns to make sales this size, but there is nothing average about Billie. This is her most popular reorder, partly because it is the "middle" offer and partly because realistically, more people can afford it.

The third accessory order which Billie has also prepared in minute detail to complement the initial order is still a substantial order but is obviously smaller than the first two proposals. After looking at the first two proposals, many prospects who initially felt they "couldn't afford" anything become enthusiastic buyers of the "minimum" order and at a later date they follow up with a third and even a fourth order.

VERY IMPORTANT: On the follow-up call to sell accessories, Billie treats the call as a full-fledged sales *and* service call. She gives the customer the "full treatment" *and then some.* She resells herself. She resells the company. She resells the products. She resells the concept of investing for the future. She sells the idea of taking action today—not tomorrow. She has her customer get out her original order so she can check it over. Then Billie either brags on the customer for taking such excellent care of the merchandise or she gently suggests how she can take better care and receive even more benefits. All the time she is reselling herself *and* her products.

She has two legitimate reasons for being there. Number one is the service call, and since Billie had written the customer a thank-you letter immediately after the first sale and had sent him Christmas cards in between, she stands there as a friend. Number two is the fact that the company has a *special sale* which Billie *knows* the customer is going to be excited about. Needless to say, she is almost never turned away on these follow-through calls.

Wish I Had Known This

I personally believe that if I had known this procedure when I was in the business, my income would have been at least 50 percent greater because my customers would have benefited a great deal more. Incidentally, in case you are wondering about Billie's cancellation and delinquency records, it's a fact that her cancellation is extremely low and her delinquency rate for nonpayment is *the* lowest in the company.

Will this procedure work for others? You betcha! Over the years, in addition to her own sales, which put her in first place, Billie has trained numerous others who finished in the top ten nationally. "Will it work for me?" Only if you *use* it. Techniques, procedures, and ideas have no feelings and don't really care who uses them.

One of the real mysteries of life is why more salespeople who work in stores don't "go direct" and generate more business by developing customers who are loyal to them and their stores. Example: In our over thirty-seven years of housekeeping, the Redhead and I have never once been solicited to buy a house, diamonds, furs, furniture, or appliances. Doyle Hoyer, who sells me my clothes (pages 384–87), Tom McDougal, my dentist, Jack Dahlen, my insurance man, and Chuck Bellows, who sold me a car, are the only four who have ever followed through with service and solicitation for future business. During our years together we have bought four homes, more than thirty-five cars, counting company vehicles, and four complete households of furniture and appliances, not counting dozens of major individual items. We've spent thousands of dollars on jewelry and furs, but *nobody* ever tries to sell us those items. They don't even make a serious effort to get us back in their stores!

Question: If you sell any of these items, are you *seeking* business or do you just wait for the business to seek you? When you make the initial sale do you follow through to make certain your customer is satisfied with this purchase, *and* plant the seeds for the next one? In athletics the follow-through is critical. The golfer, pitcher, kicker, boxer must follow through for maximum results. In selling the salesman must follow through with service *and* reminders to buy if he's going to keep his customers (once you sell them you should feel as if they are *yours*) and build a career.

> **Point:** *If anyone makes a "significant" purchase from you, you should put him on your "super customer" list and "court" him as long as you represent the same company or sell the same basic product line.*

In many ways Billie Engman is the epitome of what I speak about throughout this segment. She does all the things, takes all the steps, has learned her lessons, is a constant student, is resourceful and imaginative, has the highest integrity, is absolutely dependable, is an exceptionally hard worker, is loyal to her principles, to her company, to her customers, and most of all to her own sense of what is fair and right. She truly is a credit to the profession.

Question: How do you sum up or in a nutshell explain Billie Engman? Answer: You don't, but if you could you would start with love. She *loves* her family, her products, her company, and her customers. She wants the best for all of them. Then you move to commitment. She's committed to do the best possible job and utilize her talents and abilities to the maximum by utilizing every moment to the fullest. Finally, she sees herself as a person who is going to deserve ("*Serve* is the major part of *deserve*") the big sale, do the big job, earn the big rewards. She knows this is the way her customers, her family, her company, and her country will also win big. She is truly a sales pro.

PART FOUR

IMAGINATION AND WORD PICTURES

Objectives

To open your mind to the importance of developing your imagination for a substantial increase in your sales.

To teach you twenty-four specific closes, *some* of which you can adapt and use in your daily sales life.

To sell you on the value of learning how to use the verbal paintbrush to paint pictures of future customer enjoyment to help you sell more *today*.

Closes and/or Procedures

The "1902" Close
  Revisited
The "Tightwad" Close
The "Diagram" Close
The "20/20" Close
The "Action Now"
  Close
The "No Procedure"
  Close
The "Marriage" Close
The "Imagination"
  Close
The "Click" Close
The "Special Occasion"
  Close
The "Tuit" Close
The "Challenge" Close
The "Twenty-nine-Day"
  Close
The "Front Line" Close

The "Opportunity"
  Close
The "Companion"
  Close
The "Nice People"
  Close
The "Cokes and
  Smokes" Close
The "Corner" Close
The "Time Utilization"
  Close
The "Question" Close
The "Picture" Close
The "Preparation" Close
The "Fear" Close
The "Postselling" Close
The "Repetition" Close
The "Menu" Close
The "Oooh and Aaah"
  Close

20

IMAGINATION
IN SELLING

ACCORDING TO MY GOOD FRIEND and fellow sales trainer Merle Fraser, in the next 24 hours your prospect's heart will beat 103,689 times. His blood will travel 168,000 miles; his lungs will inhale 23,240 times; he'll eat 3½ pounds of food; he'll exercise only 7 million of his 9 billion brain cells. He'll speak 4,800 words of which 3,200 involve something about himself and not a single one will be about you, your products, or services unless you figure out a way to involve him emotionally with your sales presentation. The only way you're going to get your share of his attention and his words is to use that imagination to make yourself a part of his world.

One of the most exciting things I can say to you about the world of selling is that most prospects really do not want to say no. The reason they don't want to say no is that *no* is so final. It ends the relationship. So, rather than saying no, many prospects will say everything from "I want to think about it" to "I've got to talk to my lawyer, wife, husband, C.P.A., etc." This is shocking, but I actually have evidence that some of them will even *lie* to you to keep from saying no.

The "1902" Revisited
(Dramatize Strong Product Features)

As we look at imagination in selling and some of the closes in this section, I'd like to go back to the "1902" Close, which I partially covered in the first chapter.

Years ago, when I was selling cookware, I used this close tailored to fit the cookware business and added a little imagination. I sold an extremely heavy set of stainless steel cookware with a core in the middle to transmit the heat more evenly. This cookware was incredibly durable. As a matter of fact, to demonstrate its durability, I persuaded one of the local police officers to take his .45 caliber service revolver and, using a steel-jacketed slug, shoot our small frying pan from a distance of twelve feet.

The impact from a .45 is enormous. I placed the frying pan against a tree and the slug hit it dead center, but you had to look carefully to see where that slug had hit the pan. Armed with this visual aid and a notarized letter from the policeman, I had no trouble getting customers to listen to me talk about durability. When I said to them, "This is a lifetime set of cookware," they understood and agreed that it would last a lifetime because the average housewife doesn't abuse her cookware to that degree.

As you might suspect, the cookware was expensive when compared to the price of lighter cookware sold in stores. Many times the prospect would raise the price objection, "It costs too much." Zig: "How much too much does it cost?" Prospect: "Oh, it's two hundred dollars too much." (To me that was an astronomically ridiculous figure, but remember, we've got to deal with the *prospect's* feelings.) Again, as I will indicate on many occasions throughout this book, you now use your talking pad.

When the prospect said, "Two hundred dollars too much," I wrote down the two hundred dollars on the talking pad so the prospect could see it, and the dialogue went like this: Zig: "Mr. Prospect, how long do you think this set of cookware will last you?" Prospect: "Oh, it will last forever." Zig: "Well, certainly it would last ten, fifteen, twenty, thirty years, wouldn't it?" Prospect: "No question about that!" Zig: "Well, why don't we settle on a minimal figure of ten years. This means that the cookware, in your mind, will cost twenty dollars too much per year. Is that what you're saying?" Prospect: "Yes, that's what I'm saying."

Break Cost Into Small Pieces

Zig: "Twenty dollars a year is how much each month?" Prospect: "Well, that's about a dollar and seventy-five cents a month." Zig: "OK, that's about right. How often do you cook?" Prospect: "Two or three times a day." Zig: "Let's be conservative and say twice a day, which means that in a month's time you would cook sixty meals [remember, I'm writing all these figures on my talking pad]. So, if this beautiful set of cookware costs a dollar and seventy-five cents a month too much, that is less than three cents a meal too much to have the finest set of cookware on the market."

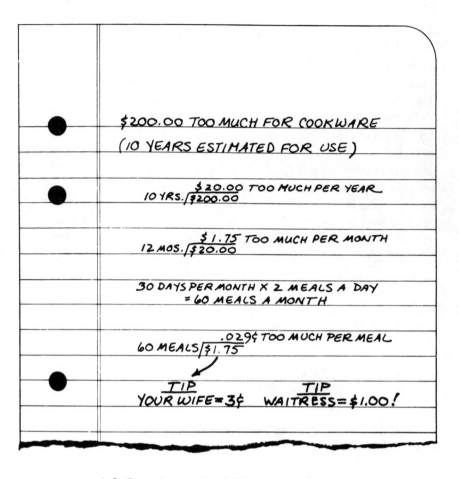

$200.00 TOO MUCH FOR COOKWARE
(10 YEARS ESTIMATED FOR USE)

$20.00 TOO MUCH PER YEAR
10 YRS. /$200.00

$1.75 TOO MUCH PER MONTH
12 MOS. /$20.00

30 DAYS PER MONTH X 2 MEALS A DAY
= 60 MEALS A MONTH

.029¢ TOO MUCH PER MEAL
60 MEALS/$1.75

TIP   TIP
YOUR WIFE = 3¢   WAITRESS = $1.00 !

Ask Questions—Lead Them to a Decision

I continue: "Mr. and Mrs. Prospect, do you ever eat out?" Prospect: "Why sure!" Zig: "How often?" "Oh, once or twice a week." Zig: "Do you ever tip the waitress?" Prospect: "We always tip the waitress." Zig: "How much do you tip her?" Prospect: "Dollar, two dollars, it depends." (Remember, this was 1962!) I'd write "3¢" by "Your wife" and "$1.00" by "waitress." Zig: "Let me offer a thought and ask a question. The waitress takes the order, brings the food from the kitchen to the table, and brings the extras like tea, coffee, and bread. Generally speaking, a busboy cleans the table and carries the dishes back to the kitchen.

"Your wife goes to the store, buys the food, brings it home, puts it in the cabinets and in the refrigerator. Later she takes the food out, cleans, prepares, cooks, and serves it. Then after the meal she takes the leftovers, stores them in the refrigerator, and then cleans up after the meal. Now,

Mr. Prospect, in all fairness, if you tip the waitress a dollar [I'd circle the "$1.00" several times] just for bringing the food from the kitchen to the table, don't you really think your wife deserves at least *three cents* [I'd circle "Your wife" and "3¢" several times] for shopping, cooking, serving, storing and cleaning?"

Imagination, emotion, and logic are all at work on this one. Chances are excellent you noticed the large number of questions asked in this dialogue (twelve). This is significant because it forced the prospect to put pressure on himself. When this happens, your chances for action are substantially increased. In this example, the procedure and the questions undoubtedly helped the husband put the wife's contributions in a more realistic and favorable light. The questions also brought the price into perspective, and broke it down to such a low figure that it was affordable.

The "1902" simply means you break it down to a figure which is so low the prospect can visualize ownership of the product because he now sees it as affordable. Three cents per use certainly put the cookware within reach, especially since we had demonstrated it would save more than that with each use. *This close makes it easy for the prospect to buy, and that's the role of the professional salesperson.*

Concentrate—Establish Credibility

This next close I'm going to share with you is a dramatic one. It's one you can effectively utilize almost regardless of what you sell. *However, I want to emphasize that every close and every procedure which I describe is not going to fit everybody and that in most cases you will have to adapt what I say to your specific situation.* That's the reason you need the steno pad mentioned on page 18 to go with this book. One more time, this book is not a workbook, but it is a *working book* written to teach you *how* to sell more effectively and to inspire you to translate the new "how to" into the old-fashioned *DO IT NOW* approach to sales success.

Many years ago I was working in the little community of St. Matthews, South Carolina. I have always believed in "cluster" selling, so I habitually went into a community and concentrated on a small area and quickly became known to the local people. Not only did this save a lot of travel and time but it also helped me to establish credibility.

In St. Matthews, as in many other communities, after I'd been there a few times I became known as the "Pot Man." (I didn't particularly like the title, but in those days at least everyone knew they were talking about cookware and not dope.) When I'd ride down the street or highway somebody would say, "There goes the Pot Man," and somebody else would say, "Yeah, I'm going to his party [cookware demonstration] next week!"

The "Tightwad" Close

After one demonstration with seven couples as prospects, I was making the call-backs the next day. I sold the first five and when I knocked on the door at the home of the sixth couple, I heard a booming voice which you could have heard all over town, "COME ON IN, MR. ZIGLAR!" I walked in and there stood this giant! (If he had been green, he would have been the "Jolly Green Giant.") He was about six feet, seven inches tall and weighed close to three hundred pounds. A jovial kind of a guy who blurted out, "It's good to see you! Me and you both know I ain't agonna buy no four-hundred-dollar set of pots, but come on in, sit down, and we'll talk, anyhow!"

For the record (and I think it *was* one!), that dude had eaten enough food the night before to feed five normal-sized people. I had bought, cooked, and personally served every bite he ate. Now he started the sales call by saying, "We both know I'm not going to buy anything!"

That's not exactly my conception of an ideal way to open an interview, but I grinned, looked at him, and said, "Well, Mr. Prospect, *you* might know you're not going to buy anything, but I don't." Prospect: "Well, I might as well tell you right now, I'll be glad to talk to you but I'm not going to buy a thing." Zig: "You know, it looks like you and I have a lot in common." Prospect: "Oh, how's that?" Zig: "In my case, my wife spends my money and my neighbors take care of my business, so that leaves me free to work! Now I don't know if your wife spends your money, but I can tell you your neighbors take care of your business!" Prospect: "Why do you say that?" Zig: "Well, today, every time I called on one of your neighbors, after I had talked with them and, incidentally, all of them *did* buy [I wanted to get that little word in at that point], each one would ask, 'Have you called on Mr. So-and-So yet?' I'd say, 'No, not yet, I see him later this afternoon.' Without exception, each one said, 'Well, let me know what *he* does!' "

Your Neighbors Don't Know You

"I finally asked one of them, 'Why does everyone want to know what Mr. So-and-So's going to do?' One of them grinned and said, 'Well, he's known around the community as being fairly conservative.' " The old boy just *hollered*, and said, "They probably said that I'm the biggest tightwad in the county!" Zig: "Well, one of them did say something about 'first dollar,' but I never quite understood what he meant!" The prospect half snorted and said, "You know perfectly good and well what he meant, and he might be right. I *am* a little conservative."

Zig: "Well, they might think you're conservative, but I think it's rather interesting that you were born and raised in this community and yet your friends and neighbors don't know the first thing about you!" Prospect: "What're you talking about?" Zig: "Well, I thought you said you were not going to buy a set of my cookware." Prospect: "I'm not!" Zig: "Isn't that interesting? You were born and raised around these people all your life, and they don't know the first thing about you!" Prospect: "What are you talking about?" Zig: "Mr. Prospect, if I remember correctly—and I believe I do—you told me last night you've been married something like twenty-three years." Prospect: "Yeah, as a matter of fact this August will be twenty-four years." Zig: "OK, let me ask you a question. Were you sincere last night [*don't ever ask a person if he was telling the truth; that's an insult*] when you said you felt you could save at least a dollar a day by cooking in our set of cookware?" Prospect: "With this crowd I've got, I could save maybe two dollars per day. You saw how much I ate last night, and I've got four boys who eat just as much!"

Tie It Down

Zig: "Well, certainly you could save at least a dollar, couldn't you?" Prospect: "At least." Zig: "Well, if it will save you a dollar a day to have the set of cookware, that means it costs you a dollar a day *not* to have the cookware, doesn't it?" Prospect: "I suppose *you* could say that." (Note: Here's where you need to be firm and strong—but gentle. This is where a good, healthy self-image is crucial. If you let him off the hook at this point, he's not going to buy at the end of the interview.) Zig: "What *I* say is not important. Since it is *your* money, what do *you* say?" (In this type of dialogue, voice inflection can be the determining factor.) Prospect: "I suppose I could say the same thing." Zig: "Actually, you can take the 'suppose' out, can't you?" Prospect: "Yes."

Zig: "Instead of saving a dollar a day, if I were to talk about saving fifty cents a day, that would be ultra-ultraconservative, wouldn't it?" Prospect: "It sure would!" Zig: "OK, if this set of cookware will save you fifty cents a day, that means every two days you don't provide your wife with this money-saving cookware, she reaches into your pocket, takes out a brand-new, crisp one-dollar bill, tears it up into a lot of little pieces, and throws it away, doesn't it?" (At this point, I slowly tore up a crisp, new one-dollar bill and threw the pieces on the floor.)

Zig: "Mr. Prospect, you can stand the dollar loss but *according to your neighbors*, you don't get excited about it. And, *according to your neighbors*, even though this beautiful home is yours and not yours and the savings-and-loan's, and even though the eleven hundred acres of land is yours and not yours and the bank's [and I smiled], you don't want to waste anything. Now, Mr. Prospect, do you realize that on the basis of losing fifty cents a day, every forty days you and your wife take a brand-new, *twenty*-dollar bill and literally tear *it* all to pieces and throw it away?" (At this point, I slowly tore up a twenty-dollar bill, but I did put the pieces in my pocket.)

Let Them See and Feel Your Message

Let me digress for just a moment. As you read about me tearing up that money, did you feel a slight hitch in the pocketbook (you might imagine yourself sitting there as the money was being mutilated)? I want to remind you that my prospect was a notorious tightwad. When I was slowly tearing up that money, I was eyeballing him and I can tell you that cold sweat broke out on his forehead.

Questions Make Him Think

I looked at him and asked, "Mr. Prospect, what did you think when I tore up that dollar bill?" Prospect: "I thought you'd lost your mind!" Zig: "What did you think when I tore up the twenty-dollar bill?" Prospect: "Didn't think a thing, I *knew* you had!" Zig: "Mr. Prospect, whose money was that?" Prospect: "I hope it was yours!" I assured him it was and continued, "Yet, *you* really felt physical pain when I tore up that money, didn't you?" Prospect: "I sure did!" Zig: "Mr. Prospect, can I ask you a question?" Prospect: "Sure." Zig: "Don't you feel even closer to money that's your very own?"

Prospect: "What are you getting at?" Zig: "It's really very simple. [Again, I'd go back to my talking pad.] You told me you have been married over twenty-three years. Now, I don't know how to multiply by twenty-three real fast, so let's cut it down to twenty [I wrote "20" on the pad]. You've already told me that this set of cookware would save you fifty cents a day—minimum—which means it costs you fifty cents a day *not* to have it. If we put only three hundred sixty days in the year, that means it costs you one hundred eighty dollars a year *not to have* this set of cookware [I wrote the "$180"]. That means, Mr. Prospect [and I was multiplying this on my talking pad], that in twenty years you have already paid three thousand, six hundred dollars [20 years × $180] *not to have* a set of our cookware, but you won't give three *hundred* ninety-five dollars [I wrote "$395"—that's all it cost] to *have* a set of the cookware—and you say you are conservative! Mr. Prospect, that's government thinking if I ever heard it!"

He's Convinced—*Now Persuade Him*

My prospect got real quiet and reflective, so I smilingly continued, "That's bad enough, but even more amazing is that you are now saying, 'Mr. Ziglar, in the next twenty years I am going to pay another three thousand, six hundred dollars *not to have* a set of the cookware [in large figures I wrote "$3600"], but I'm unwilling to invest three hundred ninety-five dollars to have a set of the cookware.'"

As he thought about this I pressed my advantage by saying, "Mr. Prospect, I don't like to threaten anyone, but with that kind of thinking I believe it's only fair to warn you that I'm going to tell your neighbors all about you [obviously, I'm smiling]. Up until now they have thought you were conservative, but when they learn that you are perfectly willing to pay seven thousand two hundred dollars [I added $3600 + $3600] in losses *not* to have a set of our cookware but refuse to invest three hundred ninety-five dollars to own a set, I fear your reputation as a conservative will be ruined forever."

It got awfully quiet for a few seconds; then he asked me a question which I think is one of the most significant questions I've ever been asked. It revealed a great deal about human nature and had an impact on my thinking as a salesman. Question: "Mr. Ziglar, what would I tell my neighbors?" Now please understand that of all the people in our country, the most independent of the independent are the farmers. This particular farmer certainly fit that role. Additionally, he was a "big man" in the community. He was a wealthy and respected member of the school board, and yet he was asking, "What can I tell my neighbors?"

Get Him Out of the Corner

Why was he asking it? Very simple. When he was invited to the demonstration he had told the hostess, "I'll go, but I'm not about to buy any four hundred dollar set of pots!" He was late for the demonstration and when he made his entrance, one of his neighbors kidded him by saying, "Well, I see you've come to buy yourself a set of pots." To this he had loudly (I heard him from back in the kitchen) proclaimed, "I've come to eat the man's food! I'm not about to buy any four hundred dollar set of pots!" Everybody there heard him, so he had literally painted himself into a corner.

At this point, having seen the demonstration the night before and the financial presentation today, he is sold on the cookware. He wants to buy and he certainly has the money, but before he will buy I've got to get him out of that corner so he doesn't lose face with his neighbors. If I can do this the sale is mine.

Learn This Lesson and You'll Sell More

(Important lesson, my selling friend.) Many times your prospect has painted himself into a corner by promising his wife, brother, friends, or another salesperson that he won't take any further action until. . . . When the "good" prospect is not buying we need to be sensitive to the possibility that he might be in a corner wanting to get out. That's a job the professional salesman loves to take on because it means sales for him.

I looked at him, grinned, and said, "Mr. Prospect, it's not only simple but it will actually make your neighbors love and respect you even more. I'm going to give you a receipt marked "PAID IN FULL," because I know you're not about to pay any high-priced interest since you're 'conservative' [we both smiled]. I want you to take this receipt, go to each one of your neighbors, and say, 'Look what I've got!' I might add that you should prepare yourself for a horselaugh and a little good-natured ribbing. When that happens, just smile and tell them, 'Yeah, I know I said I wasn't going to buy a set of those high-priced pots, but when I said that all I really knew was the price. When I saw that the cookware saved money and food value, as well as saving my wife a lot of work, it just made sense to buy it. Frankly, I love my wife and family too much to let my own stubbornness keep my family from getting something which we would all enjoy.'

"Your neighbors will love you, Mr. Prospect, because it takes a big man to admit he made a mistake—that he made a premature decision. Then it takes an even bigger man to correct that mistake." He got up and as he walked out of the living room to go to the bedroom to get his checkbook, he said, "You're the dadgonest fellow I have ever seen in my life!"

He became a good friend and one of my biggest boosters. From that moment, when people in the community learned that "Mr. Conservative" himself had bought, it made my sales even better and easier. I emphasize that all I did was take him out of the corner into which he had painted himself. That made the sale relatively easy.

The "Diagram" Close

Every product has a maximum price or ceiling. This price is all you can pay. (This is not true of services which are ongoing.) This is not true of benefits. If the product saves money by its use, the longer it is functioning properly and in use, the greater your benefits will be.

If you sell a product which saves money, like the set of cookware I just mentioned, I would diagram the example this way:

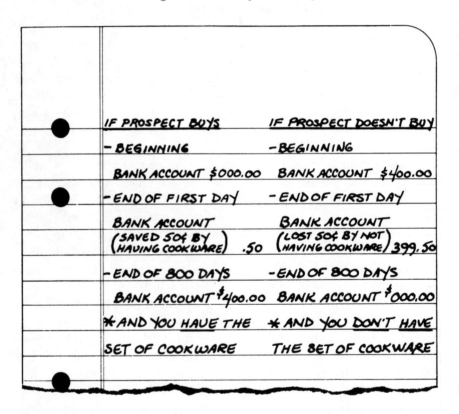

CLOSE: If you buy the cookware the savings will pay for it. If you don't buy it, your daily losses will soon be more than the cost of the cookware. In other words, you can get it and let it pay for itself or you can choose *not* to get it and still pay for it through losses. Since you've got to pay for it whether you get it or not, doesn't it make sense to go ahead and get it?

The "20/20" Close

OR: As you can see, just by saving 50¢ a day, at the end of 800 days the cookware will have paid for itself. If you don't get it, at the end of 800 days you will have paid the $400 through losses and still not have the cookware. So, the choice is simple: *invest* $400 and get the cookware, which will return the $400, or don't invest $400 but still *pay* $400 through losses and still *not* have the cookware. (Pause. Smile.) You're

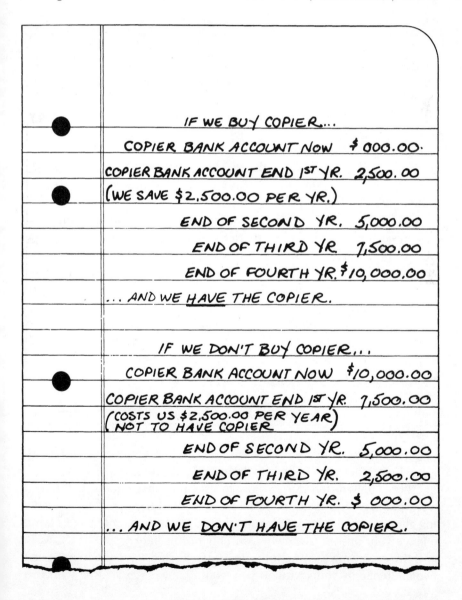

going to love your cookware and we can deliver it on our 20/20 plan, which is $20 per month for 20 months with two $20 deposits in advance. Or you could take advantage of our 90-day cash discount plan. Which would suit your needs best?

Note: Ben Feldman, possibly the greatest insurance salesman ever, says it this way: *"You make the sale when the prospect understands that it will cost more to do nothing about the problem than to do something about it."*

And Another One

In 1977 we invested nearly $10,000 in a new copying machine. By our calculations that machine saves us at least two hours each day. At just $5 per hour (1977 costs), that's $10 per day, $50 a week, or $2,500 per year. Not only does this machine do better work but we have fewer fouled-up copies, so we save money on paper. Because we invested in the machine we have saved enough by using it for the machine to pay for itself. Had we *not* bought the machine we would have paid for it in actual losses and would not be able to show anything for the $10,000.

The point is clear. If you sell goods or services which save money, you should work on your presentation until it is crystal clear to your prospects that they *pay* for your product whether they get it or not. Since they pay for it whether they get it or not, they might as well go ahead and get it. One more time: Don't just tell them—show the figures at the same time. Prospects make the decision to buy based on what they understand *and* believe.

One More Time: When the prospect *clearly* understands that it costs more *not to invest* in a money-saving device than it does *to invest* in the device, he will invest—*if* you ask him to, and help him figure out a simple way to make the financial arrangements.

Not Available in Any Bookstore

Questions for you! As a reader, if there were a single cassette recording which teaches you how to train and use your voice, how to ask questions, how to tell stories, how to use your imagination, paint vivid word pictures, and make more sales, you would be interested in knowing about it, wouldn't you? (If you said no, please go back to page 21 and change your answer as to why you bought this book.)

If this recording was sixty minutes in length and was done in front of a live audience by yours truly so you would know I was sharing with you instead of talking to you, that would be even more exciting, would't it? Yes _____ No _____

If I personally guaranteed the recording would motivate you to *want to* be more professional and specifically teach you *how to* be more professional and sell more, you'd really like that, wouldn't you? (Say yes.) If you could acquire this tape for just three dollars, to cover production, shipping and handling costs, that would be more than fair, wouldn't it? (*See footnote below.)

The "Action Now" Close

If you take action on this offer you'll have to agree that at least one of the techniques in this book works, doesn't it? If you haven't taken action on the offer, let me ask you a question. Are you having trouble with too many prospects who want to "think about it," "sleep on it," "talk to my mate, lawyer, banker, C.P.A.," "check around," etc.? In other words— they procrastinate. You do know that procrastinators bring out the procrastination syndrome in others, don't you?

With this in mind, is it clear to you that the best way to get action from others is to take action yourself? Your next step is clear, isn't it? If you are one of the procrastinators who has decided to become an ex-procrastinator read the footnote and take action now so you can go forward more rapidly in your career.

At this point you are probably wondering why I would make such an effort to sell you a three-dollar cassette. The reason is twofold. First, I wanted to demonstrate another "question-asking" procedure to lead prospects to a decision. Second, and far more importantly, I'm completely convinced this recording, teaching how to train and use your voice, when used in conjunction with *Secrets*, will be the most effective single cassette recording on sales training you will ever own. *I want you to own it.* NOW HEAR THIS: If you *feel* anything less than 100 percent good about my "selling" you so strongly and taking more than a page of your book to do so, here is what I'm willing—even anxious—to do. If you will give us a call and tell us that you want a copy of the recording for *free* we will send you the tape free. This recording *is* important for your career. *I want you to have it.*

Important: This recording is available *only* through our company at the address and phone number in the footnote. (Limit one recording per customer, whether for free or $3.00.)

---

* At this point, you'd be more than willing to call us at 1-800/527-0306 (in Texas 972/233-9191), to order by using VISA, MasterCard or American Express, wouldn't you? If you don't want to use your credit card, you're going to mail your check to The Zig Ziglar Corporation, 3330 Earhart, Carrollton, Texas 75006, aren't you?

The "No Procedure" Close

Sometimes the best procedure is *no* procedure. Example: Recently after an exciting day on the golf course with the president and executive vice president of our company, along with a business associate, we were headed back home. We cut through the Dallas-Fort Worth Airport and took the access road. As I topped a hill, there sat a friendly policeman waving me to the side. I use the word friendly a little facetiously, because at that point he actually had a pretty grim look on his face.

I was honestly surprised because I did not believe I had been speeding. I got out of my car, which generally puts the patrolman at ease, and walked toward him. He asked if he could see my driver's license. I reached for it and as I did, I pleasantly asked him why he had stopped me. He said, "You were doing fifty-one, which is sixteen miles above the speed limit." I replied, in a little shock, "Gracious, I had no idea the speed limit was thirty-five—I thought it was fifty-five." He assured me it was thirty-five. I said, "Then in that case, I am guilty as charged, because I definitely was speeding."

He asked me where I was going. I told him I was going home, but that I was in no hurry and therefore it just didn't make any sense for me to be speeding. He smiled and said, "Well, let me get you to slow it down, if you will." As he handed me back my driver's license, I assured him that I would.

I'm convinced that in this situation, had I attempted to give a "sales talk," I would have ended up with a ticket. I emphasize that what I said was effective entirely because I was genuinely shocked to learn the speed limit was thirty-five. I'm certain there were signs on the access road saying "35," but I had not noticed them despite the fact I'd been on that road a half-dozen times.

This reminds me of the axiom, "When you've laid an egg, step back and admire it as you acknowledge what you have done." That's exactly what I did. I acknowledged without hesitation I'd been speeding. In my own mind I'm convinced he made the final decision not to give me the ticket when I said I was in no hurry, because I really wasn't. My story wasn't fancy or imaginative, but it was effective because it was true.

In the world of selling, as I have indicated many times throughout *Secrets of Closing the Sale*, the completely honest approach is the best approach.

21

IMAGINATION SELLS
AND CLOSES SALES

THUS FAR WE HAVE COVERED a number of specific closing techniques which I believe will increase your closing effectiveness. Now we're going to look at a significant close with a number of sales lessons built into the close. I tell this one in story form because the story is easy to remember and when you remember the story you will remember the close and the lessons. Again, I will be demonstrating the importance of effectively using your voice and applying your imagination to *your* sales situations.

I will also share with you the importance of ignoring certain objections and not taking it too seriously when some prospects say they're just "not interested."

We'll Have to Buy from Someone Else

Years ago when I was in the insurance business, one of the things which frustrated me most was this. After conducting the fact-finding interview, I would go back for the presentation, tell the story, sell the product, the need, and our service, only to have the prospect look at me and say, "Mr. Ziglar, you know I'm embarrassed we've permitted you to come back. Although we recognize our need for insurance, if we buy any we can't buy from you. My wife's second cousin's next-door neighbor's best friend's uncle's son's classmate has a friend whose daughter's husband is in the insurance business [maybe it wasn't *quite* that bad, but it was pretty farfetched!], and if we buy any insurance we'll have to buy from him."

The "Marriage" Close

Obviously it was a stall, and it bugged me that I had sold a need and nobody, including the prospect and yours truly, was going to benefit from it. One day while thinking about the problem, I came up with a solution and developed the "Marriage" Close. This close came from an idea I got from Frank Bettger's book *How I Raised Myself from Failure to Success in Selling.* I read the book in 1948, but it was not until eight years later that I utilized this bit of Frank's information and added a little imagination to develop this close.

I designed a "Marriage Certificate" and had it printed on beautiful parchment paper. When the prospect stalled and said, "I like the idea but I'll have to buy from _____," I looked him in the eye and replied, "I'm confident the individual you mention is competent and the company he represents is legitimate, since it is licensed in this state. [*Never* make a negative or antagonistic comment.] But, Mr. Prospect, I can do something for you at this moment that no other insurance man in America can do." Obviously that's going to elicit the question "What's that?" At that point I would reach into my briefcase, pull out the Marriage Certificate, and say, "I can marry you." [The reaction was interesting.]

"Let me explain this to you." Across the top the certificate said, "CERTIFICATE OF MARRIAGE." Then, "This Certificate of Marriage, issued this 18th day of August, 1970 [or '80 or '90 or whenever], between Zig Ziglar and John and Mary Smith. By this marriage Zig Ziglar agrees to be available in time of need for John and Mary Smith. [I had typed their names in before I made the call.] He agrees to stay abreast of the trends in tax and Social Security developments so he can properly advise John and Mary Smith as to their insurance needs. He agrees to be available for consultation and help. John and Mary Smith agree to give Zig Ziglar the privilege of earning the right to serve. Cancellable for any reason by John and Mary Smith. Noncancellable for any reason by Zig Ziglar."

Is This Legal, Mr. Ziglar?

The close: I would look at them and say, "All that's required to put this marriage into force is for you to put your OK right here." Almost without exception the man would look at his wife, grin, and say, "Honey, what about that? This fellow wants to marry both of us at the same time! Do we want to marry him?" Sometimes she'd laugh and say, "Well, I don't know. It's up to you." Often one of them would say, "Well, he looks like a pretty nice fellow, why don't we go ahead?" Many times the husband would say, "Mr. Ziglar, now this is legal, isn't it? I mean, it's not bigamy. You're not going to get us in trouble?"

I'd laugh and reply, "No, I've already talked to the governor, the secretary of state, the insurance commissioner, and even cleared it with my brother-in-law. Everybody says it's perfectly all right." Many times the man would chuckle and say, "Well, why not?" He'd grab his pen and with a real flowery twist he would *really* sign it. But a funny thing happened on the way to the bank. Never once did I get the Marriage Certificate signed that I did not also get the application blank signed.

By using the Marriage Certificate I'm doing two things. Number one, I'm using a trial close. When they bought the first idea (signing the Marriage Certificate) it made the second one a great deal easier to buy. Number two, I'm saying to the prospect, "I'm not selling you just for today. I'm selling you for the future. I'm going to be part of your life. I'm going to be your insurance man." That's career-building selling.

Now Adapt It

I'm confident you've asked yourself this question many times because I've stressed it from the beginning of the book: "How do I adapt it to fit my situation?" One of the most excited salesmen I've talked with is Jerry Parker. Jerry formerly represented The Extracorporeal Corporation, which is now a division of Johnson & Johnson. Incidentally, the word *extracorporeal* means "outside the body."

For over a year Jerry had been calling on the Los Robles Hospital in Thousand Oaks, California. He was dealing with head nurse Loretta

Davis and was attempting to sell his products and services. For a year Mrs. Davis kept telling him he had the highest price and his company gave the poorest service.

To help you understand the importance of the call, his product is blood-lines. That's the line that transfers the blood from the body to the artificial kidney and then returns it to the body. A person on the system has to go through this procedure 13 times each month, which meant that 156 lines were involved for every patient for a year's usage. Multiply this by 40 patients and as you can see, you're talking about 6,240 lines. This represented a substantial order.

During this year Jerry was doing two things. He was building a relationship of trust and friendship with Mrs. Davis. He was also listening every day to our cassette recordings on selling. He heard the "Marriage" Close, not just once but many different times. Finally one day, half in jest, Mrs. Davis asked Jerry, "Why in the world should I buy from you, since your price is the highest and your service is the poorest?"

Jerry quickly researched his mind, came up with an adaptation of the "Marriage" Close, looked at her, and smiled as he said, "Because I can marry you." With that Mrs. Davis laughed uproariously and said, "Well, what in the world would Willie say about that?" Jerry quickly responded, "Don't misunderstand. Here's what I mean. [As he made the statement he saw a brown paper bag lying on the counter. He reached over, picked it up, and quickly wrote "Certificate of Marriage" across the top. Jerry then explained, as he wrote, the essence of the "marriage" agreement.]

"When you buy our service you also buy me, and I am literally going to be married to this account. I'm going to see to it that you get the best possible service. I will be your personal representative between your hospital and our company. I will see to it that things are handled in an effective and efficient manner so your patients will always be taken care of. The few pennies in extra cost will be far more than compensated with the assurance that not only are you getting the best product on the market but you're also getting my personal interest and attention. This is critical to the hospital because it directly involves the well-being of your patients. That is your *first* consideration, isn't it, Mrs. Davis?" (She acknowledged that it was.)

By this time Jerry had completed his writing, so he handed the "Certificate of Marriage" to Mrs. Davis and said, "The only thing necessary to put this marriage agreement in force is for you to put your OK right here." Mrs. Davis thought about it for a moment and recognized that it made sense. In addition, because of his pleasant and persistent belief that his product was the best, she had developed confidence in Jerry and knew the validity of his argument. He had followed the right procedure, he had used the right words, his interest was in the well-being of the hospital and its patients. Mrs. Davis trusted him. She signed the "marriage agreement" and a few minutes later signed the official order form.

As Jerry was sharing this story with me, I can tell you he was enthusiastic and excited about it. Yes, *these procedures work*—if you will do as Jerry Parker did and adapt them to your specific situation.

The "Imagination" Close

One of the most amazing examples of the use of imagination is that of Paul Jeffers of Sacramento, California. In 1982 Paul made 86 speeches and sold $9.8 million worth of life insurance involving 70 sales and over $250,000 in premiums. Paul is a remarkable man who believes that failure to hit the bull's-eye is never the fault of the target, and failure to buy is never the fault of the prospect.

On February 8, 1975, Paul Jeffers lost his sense of hearing but he laughingly says that being deaf gives him an advantage over other salespeople because he never hears anybody say no.

Not long after Paul suddenly lost his hearing, and before he completely mastered the art of reading lips, he was by himself on a significant interview with two prospects. In Paul's words here is what happened: "I walked into their office, started talking to them, and they answered, and by golly, I couldn't read their lips. So I said, 'Gentlemen, I can't read your lips.' I pulled out my yellow scratch pad and said, 'I'm going to give each one of you a scratch pad and you write out your questions and I'll answer the questions you've written. Is that fair enough?' They both nodded their heads yes, so I handed them the scratch pads and they wrote all kinds of questions on that crazy sheet of paper! They handed them back to me, I looked at the pad—and I couldn't read their handwriting—either one of 'em!

"So I said, 'Gentlemen, I really have a problem. I can't read your lips, and can't read your handwriting. So I've got two choices—I can walk out of here right now and forget about it or, better yet, why don't you let me give you the selling attempt the way I normally would because I have all this material prepared? Let me give you the objections I think you would give me and I will give you the answers to those objections. All you have to do is shake your head up and down if you agree with me and from side to side if you disagree. Is that fair enough?' They both nodded yes to the suggestion.

"I'm charging through that selling attempt, boy, best one I've ever had! I go through the story, the objections, the answers to the objections, the whole thing, get down to the close, and I say, 'Gentlemen, is there anything about this plan you do not like? Is there any reason you can think of that you don't want to get started right now? Is there any problem in giving me a check for $3,800 immediately?' They shook their heads no, so I said, 'Make the check out to Standard Insurance Company.' They did, and handed me the check.

"Now, most insurance people can get an application without a check—I get a check without an app! Now what do I do? How do I handle this? Where is my manager to help me? Obviously, he wasn't there. I was strictly on my own so I said, 'Look, I'm going to give you a blank Part One of the application. Please print in block letters, very plainly. I'm also going to give you another blank Part One for you to sign. I'll transfer the information from the one you've printed over to the one you've signed, it'll be in my handwriting. We'll get you examined by a doctor, and we're both covered, is that fair enough?' They both nodded their heads yes." Paul laughingly says, "That's what I call a controlled interview, and I'll bet you a buck you've never had one like that any time!"

For years I've heard that you could parachute a professional salesman into a strange area where he knew absolutely no one and by nightfall he would be in business. I agree with that observation, especially if that salesman has the imagination, tenacity, will to win, and love for people which Paul Jeffers has.

Another man with imagination and all the other attributes of an outstanding salesman is E. U. Parker, Jr., of Laurel, Mississippi. According to Regional Vice-President Bill Sanders of State Farm Insurance Companies, E. U. has been totally blind since age eight. Despite this fact, he became the first C.L.U. in the Mid-South Region. In Bill Sanders' words, "In the automobile-insurance business, it is very important that an agent see and record prior damage to the automobile at the time it is insured. Our blind agent continues to 'see' and record more prior damage than any of our other agents."

The stories of Paul Jeffers and E. U. Parker, Jr., simply emphasize that "handicaps" are handicaps only when you "see" or "hear" them as handicaps. Chalk up the stories of these two men as another reason I'm so excited about the sales profession.

The "Click" Close

People buy for some incredible reasons. A number of years ago when I was in Nashville, my brother, Judge Ziglar, and I were the home office general agents for a life insurance company. We had joined the company early and helped raise capital through the sale of stock. There was a three-month delay after the stock issue was closed and the company was in full operation. All we had was a rate book and in the competitive world of life insurance programming, if you are going to compete you need to be able to make a full presentation with a complete proposal.

Since we could not afford a three-month income sabbatical, we decided to buy the equipment to print and figure the proposals. One of the things we needed was a calculator. In those days only three companies, Friden, Monroe, and Marchant, manufactured automatic calculators (they were not computers).

We eliminated the Marchant because of the ineptness of the salesperson, but we still had to decide between a Friden and a Monroe. We decided on the Friden for the weirdest of all reasons. *Everything else was equal,* but would you believe we liked the way the Friden "clicked" better? In 1961 that calculator cost a thousand dollars. Despite this, the deciding factor was that we liked the "click" of the Friden calculator the best.

> **Point:** *People don't buy for logical reasons. They buy for emotional reasons.*

That's why you need to be sensitive to some of the "little" things about your prospect and his needs if you expect to improve your closing percentages.

The "Special Occasion" Close

I spent eighteen years in the world of direct selling. During this time I developed a number of "Special Occasion" closes. Many times vacuum cleaner, alarm system, encyclopedia, water softener, and cookware salespeople as well as others will encounter the following or a similar situation. This close, as it is, was originally designed for the direct-sales world, but when you see how effectively a young furniture-store owner used his imagination and adapted it for his business, you will know why I included it in this segment on imagination.

In the cookware business I demonstrated at night for a group of husbands and wives and made appointments to see them together the next day. However, on many occasions only the wife would be at home for the appointment. Generally the wife would assure me she could make the decision, but when I finished the presentation she sometimes attempted to terminate the interview by saying that on second thought, she was going to have to talk to her husband because she now had the information he needed to make the decision. That meant in most cases I was not going to get the sale. Don't misunderstand. If she really *did* have to talk to her husband, I wanted her to do so. I knew from painful experience if she bought over his objections I'd end up with a cancellation or even worse, a dissatisfied customer.

However, I needed to find out if it were a put-off or a legitimate reason for not buying, so I would say, "That's fine. Since he gets home at six [I learned his hours the night before], I'll drop back at seven, or would eight be better?" With this approach I quickly found out if *she* was really interested or if she was just trying to get rid of me. If she gave me the old routine, "Well, you know, we've been married for over twenty years and I know how to handle him," I knew it was a lost cause.

As a salesperson you already know *there is a vast difference between understanding something well enough to buy it as opposed to understanding it well enough to sell it.* She understood the value of the cookware well enough to buy it, but there was no way she could understand it well enough to "sell" it to her husband. I had spent years learning how to explain it well enough to sell it and she had seen *one* demonstration.

When the housewife stalled on giving me the appointment I responded with, "Let me ask you a question. What time does your husband get home with the groceries?" Housewife: "What do you mean?" Zig: "I assume he does buy the groceries." Housewife: "No, he sure doesn't!" Zig: "Well, who does?" Housewife: "I buy the groceries!" Zig: "Have you always bought them?" Housewife: "Why, certainly." Zig: "Boy, groceries are expensive, aren't they?" Housewife: "They sure are!" Zig: "I'll bet you they cost you twenty, twenty-five dollars a week, don't they?" Invariably she'd say, "What do you mean, twenty or twenty-five? You mean a hundred and twenty or twenty-five!" Zig: "You mean they cost more than twenty or twenty-five dollars?" Housewife: "You've never bought groceries!" Zig: "Let me ask you, would fifty dollars a week be a conservative estimate of what you spend on groceries?" Housewife: "It sure would."

After All, Mrs. Prospect, You Picked Him

Zig: "Mrs. Prospect, that being the case [and again, back to our talking pad], you invest fifty dollars a week for groceries [write it down]. Let's take that fifty dollar figure times just fifty weeks in a year. That means in a year's time you spend twenty-five hundred dollars for groceries. Now, Mrs. Prospect, according to what you tell me, you've been married twenty years. Twenty years times twenty-five hundred dollars per year is fifty thousand dollars your husband has already trusted you to spend for groceries. I'm not being unkind, Mrs. Prospect, but I'll bet you can't show me more than a hundred dollars' worth of groceries right now for the whole fifty thousand, can you?"

We would both laugh and she'd say, "Why, of course not!" Then I'd say, "Mrs. Prospect, he has already trusted you to invest fifty thousand dollars for food. Don't you honestly think he will trust you to invest just four hundred more to cook the next fifty thousand dollars worth of food in the *best* and most economical manner?"

Here's Why He Married You

If that one didn't get the order I would add this: "One of the reasons he tells folks he married you is that he admires your judgment, Mrs. Prospect, for selecting him." I'd get real quiet, smile, look her in the eye, and say, "Now you know if he trusted you to pick out your own husband he's going to trust you to invest a few dollars in a set of cookware to cook *his* food." I sold lots of cookware on that particular one!

Don't misunderstand. I personally do not believe any salesperson can sell everybody he talks with. However, I do believe with a little imagination, most of us can increase our closing percentages considerably. I also know the most frustrating experience a salesperson has is to miss a sale he knows he should have made. Not only does this affect his own income for the moment but more importantly it makes it impossible for him to render any service to that person. I simply want to give that prospect every opportunity to make a favorable decision.

In conjunction with this, many times I'm asked the question "Just how long should you stay with a prospect?" There's no set rule or specific answer to that one. It's something you have to "feel" and something you learn from experience. My own barometer was that I stayed as long as the prospect displayed obvious interest or until he emphatically said he was not going to buy.

It Works in Retail Stores, Too

As I was preparing this manuscript to go to the publisher, Randy Cooper, an excited young furniture-store owner (who doesn't believe in recessions!) dropped by my office to see me. Randy owns Cooper's Home Furnishings in Enid, Oklahoma, and was tremendously excited about his business and how he adapted this close to make "one of the easiest sales I've ever made."

In December of 1982, a lady and her daughter came into his store to look for a recliner which her husband was going to buy for her Christmas present. She found exactly what she wanted and the investment was $449. She told Randy she would talk to her husband about it. Fortunately, when the lady walked in Randy had been listening to this "Special Occasion" Close. Here's how he adapted it.

Randy: "Mrs. Prospect, I'm a single parent and keep my two children three days each week. I buy my groceries myself and they cost me about a hundred dollars a week." Prospect: "I buy my groceries, too, and that's about what mine cost." Randy: "A hundred dollars a week is over *five thousand dollars a year* [strong voice emphasis] and I'll bet you don't even talk it over with your husband, do you?" At this point, Randy said, the lady stuck her chin out, looked right at her daughter, and said, "I'll take it!"

Incidentally, Randy started his business without any sales training, and in our brief encounter he expressed delight and a little surprise that these things actually work. A real shocker came on an adaptation of the "Alternate of Choice" Close tied to the "Assumptive" Close. A man and his wife had selected a number of items which came to a substantial dollar amount. The wife told Randy they would go home and "think about it." Randy suddenly became "hard of hearing," looked at the husband, and asked, "Do you want to take this home yourself or do you want us to deliver it?" Husband to wife: "What do we want to do?" Wife: "Shoot, they charge for delivering. We'll take it ourselves." (Remember, this is the same lady who just twenty seconds earlier was going to go home and "think about it.")

One More Time: I'm convinced that *many sales are lost or missed simply because the salesperson doesn't ask the prospect to buy.*

The "Tuit" Close

Many times in the world of selling there are people whom you can nudge over the line, or should I say "on" the line, with a little humor. Never will I forget a company I called on to sell an $18,000 sales-training package. Management was sold on the program and had decided to buy, but they were procrastinating. They kicked it back and forth and back and forth, but always ended up saying, "We will let you know." Zig: "Do you have any time frame?" Company: "Probably within the next thirty, sixty, ninety days." Zig: "But you seem to be sold and you really want it." Company: "Yes, we do!" Zig: "You definitely are eventually going to go ahead and do this, aren't you?" Company: "We sure are." Zig: "In other words, just as soon as you get around to it, then you're going to go ahead and start this training program?" Company: "We sure are."

With that I looked at them, smiled, and said, "Well, gentlemen [there were four of them involved], let me say this. I've thoroughly enjoyed dealing with you because I can see you are sincere. When you tell me you're going to start this training program as soon as you get around to it, I know you are serious, so let me give you my card.

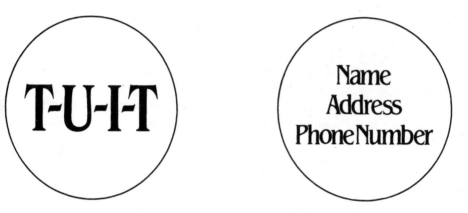

"My card, as you can plainly see, is round and has my name, address, and phone number on one side. On the other side it has the word T-U-I-T. Now that spells 'tuit.' It is round and it's a 'tuit,' so it is a 'round tuit.' Since you said you were going to start our training program just as soon as you 'got around to it,' let me be the first to congratulate you because you've now got your 'round tuit,' so we can get your training program started immediately."

Are You Kidding Me?

Now you might be thinking to yourself, "C'mon, Ziglar, you've got to be kidding! You mean those guys went ahead and bought because you put that one on 'em?" I mean to tell you exactly that, but don't misunderstand. I didn't walk in and say, "As soon as you fellows get around to it, you're probably going to start a good training program, aren't you?" That's crazy. I had done my homework. I'd laid the groundwork; I'd established the need and the fact that our program met their needs. In addition, the work I had done with them previously had enabled us to establish rapport and trust. All the TUIT did was kick them over the top and get them into immediate action.

"Maybe" Will Kill You in Selling

Action Now really is the objective of the sales call. I've said it before and I'll say it a dozen times. The prospects who say yes will not run you out of the sales business. The prospects who say no won't put you out of business. But those prospects who say *maybe* will not only put you out of the business, they'll run you out of your mind, especially if you are in direct sales.

Here's why. If you take each person seriously who says he will "buy later," you will build a backlog of false security which you plan to "cash" at an opportune time. Obviously, if you are in an industry where call-backs are a way of life (like detailing doctors on new drugs, offering a new line to a department store which has carried a competitive line for "umpteen" years, etc.), and you promise to see them on your next trip, you keep that commitment.

The "Tuit" Close, like most closes, fits a specific need at a specific time. It is true there are occasions when you can kid a prospect into doing something you could not seriously talk him into doing. Again, *you need to study your prospect and your situation, throw in a little common sense, and as our Australian friends would say, "give it a go."* P.S. If you would like to try it, send me a stamped, self-addressed envelope and I'll send you a free round TUIT.

The "Challenge" Close

Sales trainer and management development expert Larry Wilson, before he launched his career in the world of sales and management development, was one of the top life insurance men in the country. He developed and used what I call the "Challenge" Close. On his sales calls, Larry took a marble, a baseball, and a beach ball with him. When he started to close the sale, if the prospect gave him a lot of resistance—especially from a financial point of view—Larry would take the marble and ask the prospect to put it in his pocket. Then Larry would say, "Mr. Prospect, the marble is so small and light you are unaware it's there. In a few days you will forget it altogether."

Next, Larry took out his baseball and said, "Mr. Prospect, you could struggle and get this baseball into your pocket. You could carry it wherever you go, but every step you take and every move you make you will know it is there." Next, Larry took the beach ball out of his briefcase, inflated it, and said, "Now there's no way you can carry this in your pocket.

"That's the way it is with life insurance. At your age, if you start today, the premiums will be like carrying this marble. They are so small you soon will forget you carry them. If you wait a few years it will be like carrying the baseball. You can do it but you will always know they are there. If you wait too long, it will be like carrying this beach ball. You just couldn't do it. So, Mr. Prospect, you really are not making a decision today to buy or not to buy life insurance. You're deciding, 'Do I carry the marble? Do I carry the baseball? Or do I carry the beach ball?' I challenge you, Mr. Prospect, carry the marble! It will be easier for you and better for your family."

Many times the response came back, "Well, gee, I had never thought about it quite that way." To that, Larry would say, "By the way, the price of marbles today is just _____ and you can handle it on a yearly, quarterly, or monthly basis. Which would be more convenient for you?" Needless to say, Larry sold a lot of insurance.

The "Twenty-nine-Day" Close

When I was in the life insurance business, one of the things that frequently bugged me was the fact that on occasion I could not uncover the prospect's real objection. I felt confident, in most cases, that I could effectively deal with the spoken objection, but the unspoken one is far more difficult to handle. As a matter of fact, on occasion it borders on the impossible.

Never will I forget one evening when I was calling on a prospect who had a need for more comprehensive life insurance coverage. He was in a financial position to take care of that need and was deeply committed to the well-being of his family. However, I was making zero progress with him as he brought up stalls and objections with little or no validity. It became increasingly obvious that I was not going to make the sale unless I did something imaginative to "smoke out" the real objection.

With this in mind, I searched my memory bank and came up with the germ of an idea which had been planted by a speaker (his identity escapes me) at a seminar several years earlier. I took that idea, altered it considerably, looked at my prospect, and said, "Mr. Prospect, I don't know why you're hesitating to make this decision. You have already indicated your need; you apparently are financially in a position to provide the coverage; and your love for your family is obvious. The only thing which enters my mind is the possibility that perhaps I've been offering you the wrong product. Perhaps we should be talking about our

'Twenty-nine-Day Agreement,' rather than the agreement which I have been discussing with you."

Out Comes the Talking Pad

At this point I turned to my talking pad and said, "Very briefly let me explain the Twenty-nine Day Agreement. First of all, it carries the same face amount of insurance which you've indicated you need. Second, the retirement benefits are exactly the same and that's good because you've emphasized the figure we have chosen is a minimal one. Third, the Twenty-nine-Day Agreement provides both Waiver of Premium and Double Indemnity in the event you become disabled and can't make the payments or are accidentally killed. Incidentally, since we mentioned premium, the premium on this Twenty-nine-Day Agreement is only 50 percent as much as it is on the standard agreement. Would that suit your needs better?"

The prospect looked at me with some astonishment and said, "Well, it certainly suits my pocketbook better, but what do you mean by a Twenty-nine-Day Agreement?"

Frankly, it was all I could do to keep a straight face as I said, "What that means, Mr. Prospect, is that you're covered twenty-nine days out of every month. Since this is April and there are only thirty days in the month, you will be covered every day but one and the company will let you select that day. It might be that you would prefer a Saturday or a Sunday." Then I stopped and said, "No, that would not be a good thing because you will probably be at home and, statistically speaking, home is the most dangerous place for you to be."

Then I looked at my prospect and apologetically said, "In all fairness, Mr. Prospect, if you should elect to ask me to leave your home [or office] at this point, you would be fully justified. I've been doing something which I really have no right to do. I have apparently been making light of the future well-being of your family and you're obviously the kind of man who takes your family responsibilities very seriously.

"I strongly suspect that when I suggested this Twenty-nine-Day Agreement would leave you uninsured one or two days every month, the thought entered your mind that you might well die or be killed on one of those days."

Breathe Easy, Mr. Prospect

"Let me put your mind at ease, Mr. Prospect. There isn't an insurance commissioner in the world who would permit the sale of a Twenty-nine-Day Agreement. I took the liberty of suggesting it, Mr. Prospect, because I knew you would be concerned about even *one* day not being covered. Considering this, I knew you were not about to leave your family's future at the mercy of chance *every* day if you could possibly avoid it. You do feel that way, don't you, Mr. Prospect?

"I believe you're the kind of man who will relate to the agreement you and I have talked about from the beginning. That agreement, Mr. Prospect, will cover you twenty-four hours out of every day, seven days out of every week, regardless of where you are and what you're doing. That's the kind of protection you want for your family, isn't it, Mr. Prospect?"

Not only did I make the sale that night but I used that close many times during my career in the life insurance business. I did not make a sale every time I used it, but there were many sales I did make because I took the germ of an idea gathered at a long-ago sales meeting and tailored that idea to fit my specific situation.

I cannot say this often enough or strongly enough: If you're going to be professional in selling you must read, study, and listen to motivational and educational recordings on a daily basis. You must attend clinics and seminars conducted by the professionals. *Then you must work at adapting and applying these principles and ideas to fit your specific situation. That is the way to stay inspired, informed, and up-to-date.*

Imagination and Common Sense

It seems trite to say, but in the world of selling we need to find out the prospect's major interest and then show him how our product will meet his needs and satisfy his interests.

During World War II, or so the story goes, G.I. insurance was introduced. In simple terms it meant that for a minimal premium of $6 or $7 dollars a month, $10,000 in life insurance was provided. If a serviceman was killed, his beneficiaries received the $10,000. It was a super deal, but like everything else, it had to be sold.

A young lieutenant called his infantry company to attention, explained the policy in great detail, and passed out papers for those who were interested in signing up for the insurance. Virtually no one bought. An old sergeant asked the young lieutenant for permission to explain the program. The lieutenant reluctantly agreed and felt confident that if he could not sell the insurance, the sergeant couldn't.

The "Front Line" Close

The sergeant stood up and in simple eloquence explained it this way: "Men, as I understand it, here's the program. You're going to be sent overseas. If you buy the insurance and get killed, the government is going to send your family ten thousand big, beautiful dollars. If you don't get the insurance and you get killed, the government is not going to send your family anything. My question is this: Who do you think the government is going to send to the front lines first? The ones who would cost ten thousand dollars if they're killed, or the ones who would cost nothing if they're killed?" The men bought the insurance.

In reality I doubt that the story is true. However, as a practical matter, it illustrates the point perfectly. Point: Regardless of what you sell, make it crystal clear that your prospect is better off to buy than not to buy.

Sell Where You Are

In 1952 I was living in Florence, South Carolina, but selling and building part of my sales organization in Wilmington, North Carolina. Late one Saturday evening I was driving too fast on my way back to Florence. A highway patrolman stopped me and proceeded to give me a ticket. Because we had a mutual friend, he let me go without paying the bill that night on the condition that I stop by in Whiteville, North Carolina, on Monday and pay the ticket on my way back to Wilmington.

The "Opportunity" Close

I vividly remember the amount of the ticket. It was $30. In 1952, that was a considerable sum of money. On Monday I stopped by the courthouse to pay the fine. As I gave the money to the single girl who was handling the tickets, the thought occurred to me that perhaps I could recoup my loss by taking advantage of this opportunity. Since I had nothing to lose, the following dialogue took place.

Zig: "I wonder if you'd mind if I ask you a couple of questions?" Single girl (with a smile): "No." Zig: "I just wonder, since you're single and working, if you are saving a portion of the money you're earning?" Single girl: "Yes, I am." Zig: "If you should see something extremely nice, which you definitely will need later on, would you be in a position to save an additional twenty-five cents a day to get it, provided you really wanted it?" Single girl: "Yes, I could." Zig: "Well, if I had something in my car which was really outstanding, truly beautiful, and something which you not only will need but will use for the rest of your life, would you be courteous enough to spend five minutes looking at it?" Single girl: "I'd be happy to." Zig: "Excuse me for a moment."

I quickly stepped back out to my car and brought my cookware samples into the office. I made a short but very enthusiastic demonstration and asked the obligating question. After I asked the obligating question, she turned to a married lady who was about ten years older and said, "What would you do, if you were me?"

Before the other lady could answer, I interrupted and said, "Excuse me for interrupting, but let me ask you a question. If you were in this girl's position, but knowing what you know about all of the expenses and obligations you have as a married person with a growing family, if you had had the same opportunity she has of acquiring this beautiful set of cookware before you were married, in retrospect, what would you do?" Without a moment's hesitation the married lady said, "I would buy it." With that I turned to the single girl and said, "And that's what you want to do, isn't it?" She smiled and said, "Yes," so I wrote the order.

The "Companion" Close

When I finished writing the order I turned to the married lady and said, "Just because you did not have the chance to get it ten years ago does not mean that you should continue to deny yourself and your family this beautiful set of cookware for the rest of your life, does it?" She said, "No, it doesn't." So I said, "I suppose you want the same set, don't you?" She said, "Yes, I do."

I made the second sale because (a) I was aware it was there and (b) I asked for the order. I'm convinced that many sales are missed not because of poor technique but because of *no* technique. *Ask for the order.*

Those sales were two of the easiest I have ever made and my commissions far more than paid for my ticket. As a matter of fact, later that day I encountered that same highway patrolman, but this time I wasn't speeding so I waved him down and thanked him for giving me the ticket!

I tell this story to say you should be so wrapped up in what you're doing you instinctively take advantage of every sales opportunity that comes your way.

The "Nice People" Close

The more commonplace and competitive your business is, the more important it becomes for you to develop and use your imagination. Many times this really boils down to you, the salesperson or merchant, being aware of your customers' needs and concentrating on the best procedure to meet those needs. For example, if you stop at Tiller's Cafe and Shell Station in the little town of Chillicothe, Texas, even though the station is self-service for gasoline you still get a little "extra."

When my wife and I stopped for gasoline, the lady asked for my auto license number. Since I did not know it, I had to walk back to my car to get it for her. She wrote my tag number on a gummed piece of white paper and stuck it on the back of my credit card. As she did this, she explained that now I would always have my tag number with me. *Nice touch.* Then she pulled out a cardboard with a sheet on it and explained that she had listed all of her local customers so when they came in to buy, especially in bad weather, they would not have to go back out to get their tag numbers.

Not earth-shattering, but it is one of those "little things" which bring customers back to the store time after time. That's career-building selling. That is the way nice, considerate, *ambitious* people do things.

The "Cokes and Smokes" Close

One of the most imaginative closes I've ever seen was developed by Hal Krause, the founder of the American Salesmasters, who worked his way through college selling cookware, china, crystal, and flatware to single girls. After completing the demonstration he smiled at the prospect and said:

> The story I'm about to tell in every way is true.
> I'm the only man alive to share this tale with you.
>
> You'll know yourself that I've told the truth
>   the minute I get through,
> Because I never lie or stretch the truth,
>   like some other salesmen do.
>
> If you don't buy a set of pots from me you'll
>   spend all your money on
> Chocolates, Cokes, filtered smokes, fancy
>   clothes, and picture shows,

And then you'll look back and find that Cokes
    and smokes have gone to pot,
And your bankbook will show that your cash is
    shot.

What's worse, you'll find yourself cooking
    out of thin pans and tin pans,
Lead pans and bread pans—
None of which look alike or cook alike.
So everyone says, "Well, what can I do
    but buy some of those from you"—
And most of them do,
And I've got good news for you—
You've got a chance too!

If you think that's too much high pressure,
You can even use your own pen to fill out
    this order.

This combination of humor and imagination, mixed with a lot of hard work, produced championship results.

One of the most creative and imaginative sales trainers in America is Ira Hayes, who served as head of Advertising and Promotion and the Speakers Bureau of National Cash Register (N.C.R.) before he took early retirement in 1980 to form his own company. While Ira was with N.C.R., he did public seminars all over America and, needless to say, his competitors were often in attendance. This didn't bother Ira or N.C.R., because they felt that when you sold *professionally* you were not giving up a piece of *your* pie. You were increasing the size of the pie so that you (in this case Ira and N.C.R.) were still going to get more pie.

Ira also smiled and explained that sometimes he had trouble getting his own people to use the techniques so he wasn't worried about his competitors hearing his ideas. Incidentally, Ira—who is internationally known as "America's Ambassador of Enthusiasm"—believes in the liberal use of one's own picture. He has hundreds of miniature pictures made and when he sends a letter or passes out his business card, he always affixes his picture to the card or correspondence. It works. People recognize him wherever he goes.

Perhaps the most imaginative business card I have ever seen is that of Gerhard Gschwandtner, the dynamic publisher of *Personal Selling Power*, which I also highly recommend. Here is his card, along with what he says about it:

May I present my business card:
"The phone number is on the back. Yes, just turn it around.

Gerhard Gschwandtner Publisher **PERSONAL SELLING POWER®** Your Resource For Sales Success 127 International Parkway Telephone: Fredericksburg, VA 22405 (See Reverse)	Important Telephone Numbers Konstantin Chernenko .... (011) 95-2959051 Ronald Reagan .... (202) 456-1414 Francois Mitterand .... (011) 33-1/2615100 **Gerhard Gschwandtner .... (703) 752-7000** Pope John Paul II .... (011) 39-6/6982 Helmut Kohl .... (011) 49-228/561 Elizabeth II .... (011) 44-1/9304832 **Personal Selling Power .... (703) 752-7000**
(Front)	(Back)

"Why did I put these leaders on my business card?
"There are three reasons: First, it's an icebreaker during the opening.
"Second, it's a reminder that good salesmanship can get you to the top. If you have doubts, just think where these leaders would be without the ability to sell themselves.
"Third, each leader on this card stands for a characteristic that can lead you to the top. Look at the names and see how they relate to sales success:
"A leading salesperson has the ability to be tough like a Russian, persuasive like the president of the United States, diplomatic like the French premier, faithful like the Pope, well organized like the German chancellor, and confident like the queen of England."
SEE YOU AT THE TOP!

The Prospect Won't Change His Mind

Sales trainer Howard Bonnell, formerly the management training director for World Book Encyclopedia and currently a sales consultant and trainer for many different companies, shared this with me. World Book has a lot of policies which are excellent, but one of their best—and one which fascinates me the most—is their policy of sending their executives out in the field with their salespeople every time they introduce a new program.

One day Howard was working with a World Book representative. Howard made the presentation and at the conclusion the prospect said, "Well Mr. Bonnell, let me tell you something. We want the set of books, we need them, and our children can get a lot of benefit from them. However, when we married fifteen years ago, I made a flat statement that I was never going to buy anything on credit except our house and in fifteen years I have never gone back on my word."

All of us have seen people like that, so broke if it didn't cost but fifty cents to go around the world they couldn't get out of sight, but they pay cash for everything. In this particular case the prospect wasn't quite that broke but his pride was at stake and Howard Bonnell, as persuasive as he is, was not about to get that guy to change his mind. There was no way. He'd made the statement and he was dogmatic: "I said I wasn't going to buy on credit and I'm not!" If Howard had tried to sell him by using every sales technique known to man he would have done nothing but back up in the process. As I mentioned earlier, it is virtually impossible to get a person to change his mind.

The "Corner" Close

What Howard had to do was get this man out of the corner and let him be free to go ahead and make a *new* decision. Here's how he did it: He looked at the prospect and said, "Mr. Prospect, let me ask you a question. If I can show you how to get this set of World Book right now, without paying cash, which you've said you don't have, and without going back on your word, would you be interested?" The old boy asked, "How can you do that?" Howard didn't let him off the hook. He repeated. "Here's the question. If I can show you how to get this set of World Book today without paying cash, without getting it on credit, and without going back on *your* word, would you be interested?" The prospect said, "Yeah, how could I do that?" Howard: "It's really very simple."

Then he turned to the wife, looked at her, and said, "Mrs. Prospect, as I understand it, *you* did not make a commitment like your husband did you?" She said, "No, I didn't." Then Howard turned to the husband and said, "Mr. Prospect, will it be all right if I talk with your wife about solving your problem for you and your son?" The old boy said, "Well, whatever you can work out with her is perfectly all right with me. Just go ahead."

Actually, the man was delighted he'd been taken off the hook and was able to get out of the corner. Howard enabled him to save face, which was critical. The man recognized the need for the encyclopedias, wanted to buy them, but would *not* have gotten them had Howard not been astute enough to save face for him and make it easy for him to buy. Much of the sales process is simply figuring out a way for the prospect to buy what you sell.

Howard astutely points out that the prospect's objection was emotional and illogical but *he* wasn't going to buy—period. In order to make the sale, Howard had to appeal to his *emotions. Logically,* whether the man or the wife signed the agreement didn't matter as far as responsibility was concerned. *Emotionally* the prospect could comfortably buy because his wife was *signing* so his *cash* record was intact. Note: His *reason* for buying was for the children's benefit. His excuse: his wife did it—not him.

Many of these closes and procedures involve the use of your imagination, letting your prospect see *logically and emotionally* what you're offering and urging him to make a new decision. I emphasize there is seldom a sales call or interview where everything comes off according to "Hoyle," or exactly as projected on the drawing board. However, if you've got the guidelines and if you build reserves of knowledge which are instantly at your disposal, your imagination is free to work. As a result you'll make more sales, and you'll build your career faster and more successfully.

Imagination in Time Usage

One of the most time-conscious, dedicated, and imaginative salesmen I have ever known is Hal Krause. When Hal founded American Salesmasters he had two major objectives. His first goal was to make the company the biggest and best sales training organization of its kind in the world. Not only did Hal achieve this objective but along the way American Salesmasters was awarded the prestigious President's E. Award, which is awarded to a handful of America's top export companies.

As an aside, I might reinforce what I said in chapter 12 about the sales profession and free enterprise. As a young man of modest circumstances, Hal not only worked his way through college selling hope-chest items to single girls but was also able to accumulate a substantial nest egg in the process. He used this capital to launch a successful business career founded on the principles which made America great. He truly is a wholesome personification of the American dream, and *he got his start in the sales profession.*

Hal's second goal was to sell his company and "retire" before he was forty. Three weeks before his fortieth birthday he reached his second goal. In "retirement" Hal is serving as the Republican National Committeeman for the Republican party in Colorado, looking after some diverse business interests, and conducting financial seminars around the

world. Hal does many things successfully because of hard work, imagination, and time management.

The "Time Utilization" Close

Example: While serving as president of American Salesmasters, Hal
once had about an hour's stop between flights in a large city.

The home office for a major insurance company was close to the
airport, so Hal took a taxi on the chance he could see a decision maker
at the company. He gave the receptionist his card and said, "I'm between planes and I do not have an appointment, but if at all possible I
would like to see the president."

This company utilized a speaker system built into the telephone, so
the receptionist, with Hal listening, called the president and told him
that Mr. Hal Krause of American Salesmasters would like to see him.
Instead of answering back on the telephone so he could not be heard,
the president, slightly annoyed, responded on the speaker system and
said, "Tell the young man I am busy and I work only by appointment."

Hal and the receptionist heard the response and the receptionist was a
little embarrassed. Hal just smiled and asked the receptionist to press the
proper button so he could respond directly to the president's comments.
She complied with the request and Hal said, "Sir, my name is Hal
Krause. May I ask you just one question?" Insurance company president: "Yes." Hal: "In your training program, do you train your salespeople, when they have an hour between appointments, to utilize that time
by making cold calls?" Insurance company president (after a long
pause): "Mr. Krause, because you've asked the right question, I want to
talk with you. Come on in."

Hal utilized the time effectively. On this call the groundwork was laid
and a follow-up call produced a substantial order.

The "Question" Close

Effective sales procedures work everywhere. Mike Bhag, who works with
the sponsor of the Dale Carnegie courses in England, listened to the
Hal Krause example on a cassette recording. Here, in his own words, is
how Mike put the information to work for him:

*It was 1:40 on a hot Friday afternoon. I had just driven into town
for a two o'clock appointment. I had twenty minutes to kill; since
there are 1440 minutes in a day I decided to turn dead time into*

quality time and make a cold call. I spotted a large car showroom, gave myself a pep talk, and walked in.

I asked the salesman, "Is the boss in?" He replied, "No." Not to be deterred I said, "If he were in, where would he be?" "Across the street," he answered. I walked onto the premises across the street, into the reception area, and said to the receptionist, "The boss isn't in, is he?"

"Oh, yes he is, he's in his office in front of you." The boss was in a meeting with his sales manager and overheard the receptionist. He looked my way. I walked in and said, "As managing director of this company, you're probably always looking for ways to increase sales, aren't you?"

I did not get a chance to continue as he said, "Young man, can't you see I'm very busy? It's Friday afternoon! It's lunchtime! Tell me, I'm curious, what makes you call at this particular time?"

I confidently looked him straight in the eye and said, "Do you really want to know?" "Yes, I'm curious," he replied. "Well," I said, "I've just driven in from Reading. My next appointment is at 2:00 P.M. I've got twenty minutes to kill, so I thought I would turn dead time into productive time and make a cold call." Then I lowered my voice and asked slowly, "Isn't that what you teach your salesmen to do?"

At that his mouth dropped, he looked at his sales manager in amazement and awe, smiled, and said to me warmly, "Sit down, young man, sit down!" By the time I finished I had made a large sale involving sales-and-management training for his company.

Fantastic, Mike! Excellent use of your time and your imagination, not to mention the fact that you tailored the script to fit your situation and asked six questions to get into an actual interview.

22

USING WORD
PICTURES TO SELL

MOST—NO, change that to *all*—ambitiously aggressive salespeople are always on the lookout for the magic word, the key phrase, or the new technique that will give them a persuasive edge and leave the prospect powerless to resist them. Fortunately, no such "weapon" exists, *but* there are many words, phrases, and techniques you can learn and use which will enable you to present your offer in a more attractive light. The result is a more persuasive presentation which will enable you to per-suade more—but not all—of your prospects to take action.

To some hard-liners this will sound like heresy, but I am convinced the moment you recognize that not everyone could or should buy your product or services, you will sell to more of those who *can* and *should* buy.

You *do not* enhance your reputation or build your career by overload-ing your prospects or by browbeating a nonprospect into buying some-thing he really doesn't want, doesn't need, or can't afford. Once you clearly understand that basic premise it will be easier for you to forgive yourself for missing a sale you thought you should have made. This frees your mind to give maximum effort to the next sales interview.

Careful. This involves some common sense and mature judgment. Otherwise you might rationalize that everyone who does not buy really isn't a prospect. From a sales-career point of view, *that* would be a fatal mistake.

Now let's look at some words and procedures which the legitimate salesperson, selling a legitimate product at a fair price, can use to per-suade legitimate prospects to take action in their own best interests.

Twenty-four Words That Sell

My friend, sales trainer Thom Norman from Scottsdale, Arizona, is one of the most comprehensive sales trainers in America. Thom's spe-cialty is the telephone, but he's done considerable work and research in other fields. For example, he identifies twenty-four words that sell and twenty-four words that "unsell." Thom has agreed to share these words with us. I encourage you to memorize *and* learn them by getting a good dictionary and finding out *exactly* what each one means. From the list I promise you at least a half-dozen pleasant learning surprises when you pursue them in a dictionary.

The first word that sells is your prospect's name. I think everyone recognizes this as being true. His name is the sweetest sound of them all. You should use it from time to time throughout your presentation. Here are the other twenty-three:

UNDERSTAND	PROVEN	HEALTH	EASY	GUARANTEE
MONEY	SAFETY	SAVE	NEW	LOVE	DISCOVERY
RIGHT	RESULTS	TRUTH	COMFORT	PROUD	PROFIT
DESERVE	HAPPY	TRUST	VALUE	FUN	VITAL

Note: Yale University has added five words to Thom's twenty-four selling words: YOU, SECURITY, ADVANTAGE, POSITIVE, and BENEFITS.

Thom also has researched and come up with twenty-four words that "unsell," and here they are:

DEAL	COST	PAY	CONTRACT	SIGN	TRY	WORRY
LOSS	LOSE	HURT	BUY	DEATH	BAD	SELL
SOLD	PRICE	DECISION	HARD	DIFFICULT		
OBLIGATION	LIABLE	FAIL	LIABILITY	FAILURE		

I encourage you to give these words the same dictionary treatment.

Obviously there are many additional words which are soothing to the prospect's ears, and others which leave the prospect in neutral or even turn him off. I share Billie Engman's dislike for the word *pitch* and most people prefer *home* to *house* and *a fine automobile* instead of *a nice car*. It's easier to get a prospect to OK an *agreement* than it is to sign a *contract* and more people prefer to *invest* instead of *buy*. They find it easier to make a *deposit* each month than to make a *payment*.

Words and phrases which paint word pictures can sell effectively for you and your company. For example, when we ship merchandise from our company, our mailing labels contain these words: "Handle With Pride: Zig Ziglar Material Inside!" Our stamp machine prints our by-line, SEE YOU AT THE TOP. In North Carolina the highway patrol takes a positive and imaginative approach with their roadside signs which proclaim, "North Carolina uses radar to protect you from speeding drivers." The picture is clear, isn't it?

Watch Those Words

One reason I encouraged you to record your sales presentation (*see* chapter 5) is to help you recognize the positive *and* the negative aspects of the words, phrases, and word patterns you use. You know, one of the things, you know, that will drive a prospect up the wall, you know, is the use of *you know*. It's hard to imagine, you know, but some people actually, you know, use the words *you know* as many times in conversation as I have used them in these last two sentences. Nothing is more distracting to a prospect than hearing *you know* in every sentence. And you know that's true, don't you?

Another negative and distracting phrase is the constant use of "Do you understand what I mean?" or "You know what I mean?" Too many of those little goodies and your prospect will start *counting* the number of times you use them. Since he can't count and concentrate at the same time, your persuasiveness will be adversely affected.

Of all the negative words, easily the most negative and destructive are the obscene, vulgar, and profane ones. And a sure way of committing sales suicide with *many* prospects (that would certainly include me) is to take God's name in vain. Question: Have *you* ever heard of anyone buying anything from a salesman *because* he used gutter language or took God's name in vain? Fact: Many people *don't* buy because of the use of those objectionable words. Question: Since the prospect *doesn't* buy because of those profane or vulgar words and *might not* buy because of them, doesn't it make sense to leave them out?

Again, Again, and Yet Again

John Shedd, a great sales manager, said, "We *don't need to be told— but we do need to be reminded.*" Throughout this book I've been painting and will continue to paint pictures in your mind with words. As you think back on what you've read (remember me buying the car, the house, the shoeshine, Columbus's trip, etc.), you will remember the word pictures I've been painting. For the remainder of the book you will be even more sensitive to the number and effectiveness of the word pictures I paint. Another reason I encourage you to read this book *several* times is to saturate your mind with word pictures until their use becomes second nature to you.

In the world of selling you've got to understand two things if you expect to become a real sales professional. First, the mind thinks in pictures. For example, if I say "car," you do not think "c-a-r." In your mind's eye you see a car and it would probably be a beautiful car. If I say "girl," you do not think "g-i-r-l," but fellows, in your mind's eye you will see a beautiful girl. If I say "house," as a reader or as a listener you would not think "h-o-u-s-e," but rather you would, in your mind's eye, see a house. If I say "home," you do not think "h-o-m-e," but you see a home *and* it will have a *family* in it, whereas the house you saw in your mind just two seconds ago was empty. The master salesman takes his verbal paintbrush and instinctively uses *full* words like *home* instead of empty words like *house.*

Number two, if you're going to sell more of your goods, products, services, or ideas, you've got to learn how to take the verbal paintbrush and paint them (your prospects) right into the picture. You have got to put your prospect in the car and show him enjoying the luxury, comfort, or economy of driving your particular car. You've got to paint the picture of satisfaction and gratification of him grilling the steak on his grill on a beautiful spring, summer, or fall evening in the backyard of the home you are showing him. The picture must be (a) in color and (b) in the present tense.

The "Picture" Close in Just Ninety Words

The New York Times printed a story of how a New Jersey housewife's feeling for her home, combined with her sense of what makes good advertising copy, in one day sold a home that five brokers had been carrying for three months. Mr. and Mrs. Lowe decided to sell their two-bedroom home to buy a larger one since space was becoming a problem. The brokers ran typical, standard ads like "Cozy six-room home, ranch style with fireplace, garage, tile baths, all hot water heat, convenient to Rutgers campus, stadium, golf courses, and primary school." Those are facts, but *people do not buy facts or even benefits unless they can see those benefits translated to their own personal use.*

After three months Mrs. Lowe ran an ad herself. She was anxious to get something done and believed she could sell her *home.* Here's the way the ad ran:

We'll Miss Our Home
We've been happy in it but two bedrooms are not enough for us, so we must move. If you like to be cozy by a fire while you admire autumn woods through wide windows, protected from the street, if

you like a shady yard in summer, a clear view of winter sunsets, and quiet enough to hear frogs in spring, but city utilities and conveniences, you might like to buy our home. We hope so. We don't want it to be empty and alone at Christmas.

Out of the six responses the next day, one person bought the home.

Now look back at those word pictures. Block off the first sentence and you can *see* a happy family crowded together in a nice home which is just too small for the *current* owners. You immediately see that there is nothing wrong with the *home*. The problem is *too many* occupants. IMPORTANT: Slow down and take the rest of that ad on a phrase-by-phrase basis. There are *seven* additional pictures, a total of eight pictures in the eighty-six words in the body of the ad. Now tell yourself the truth. Did you see the *other* picture in the heading—or was it so obvious you missed it? That's the reason I keep telling you to *study* this book a number of times.

This ad or "sales talk" painted a beautiful picture of the features *and* benefits the Lowes had enjoyed as owners, but it did even more. It promised the new owners they would inherit the same beauty, benefits, and enjoyment. It painted a beautiful picture of happiness, contentment, and security which the new owners would inherit.

You probably noticed that Mrs. Lowe advertised her "home," not her "house." The difference between a house and a home is *love*. The new owners could undoubtedly sense the love the Lowes had for their "home." They didn't want to *buy* a house to occupy. They wanted to *invest* in a home to *live* in. Yes, words do make a difference, don't they?

Ideally, word pictures should either paint beauty, luxury, love, satisfaction, enjoyment, success, performance, or the features painted by Mrs. Lowe. Obviously, most pictures will paint a combination of features and benefits, but *all* word pictures *must* paint the prospect *in* the picture for maximum effectiveness. Almost without exception, every product or service can be sold by painting word pictures, especially if the pictures are in the *present* tense. As I've previously stated, we *think* in pictures and we *buy* pictures if we are painted into the picture as satisfied customers.

Picture-Painting Selling Is Good Postselling

One of the most effective users of word pictures was the late Fred Herman. Here is a story told by Fred as he demonstrated the use of word pictures in front of live audiences. I had the privilege of seeing Fred do this on several occasions and his widow, Kay Herman, supplied me with a cassette recording of his presentation to refresh my memory. Since I had the advantage of both seeing and hearing the presentation, I'll set the stage as we go, but the words will be Fred Herman's.

Fred (to audience): "People do not buy products or services—they buy pictures of the end result of using the product or service. Let me give you an example. I need somebody who has a boy about five or six years old to come up and help me."

Fred to participant in audience holding up hand: "How old is your oldest boy?" Participant: "Twelve." Fred: "Twelve. OK that's all right, come on up here. What's his name?" Participant: "Michael." Fred: "And your name is . . . ?" Participant: "Bob." Fred: "Bob, I appreciate your coming up here. Bob, we came out here not to talk about insurance or investments but to talk about how to get Michael a college education. You'd spend a few minutes on that, wouldn't you?" Bob: "Sure can."

In this drama Fred explains that the insurance representative describes the insurance program and its benefits. Then he says to the audience: "So we've talked about a program. We've provided the solution. We worked out some sort of a program so there'd be cash value at a certain time, but I'd say, 'Bob, as we've been working together here it's become completely apparent to me that one of the drives inside of you is that Michael will have the tools and equipment so that he can meet life and whip it, is that right?'" Bob: "That's correct." Fred: "Well, this program we've worked out will take care of this regardless of what might happen. Here's what does happen.

"It's about maybe eight or nine years from now. An invitation comes through the mail from the college of Michael's choice. You and your wife go to the graduation ceremonies. You enter the hall, and there's a tremendous babble of voices, a feeling of human warmth; it all hushes down as you hear the graduation processional, hear the swish of robes as you see those little tassels bouncing on the hats. You notice your wife's face. Big smile on it, but there's just the suggestion of a tear in the corner of her eye. And you kind of grab her hand and she holds your hand; you're completely enthralled in the culmination of years of hoping and planning and dreaming.

"It's over now. You watch Mike go across and get his diploma. He's walking up the aisle, he's looking for you and your wife; he spies you. There's a big smile on his face. You feel the warmth of his handclasp, you feel his arm around your shoulder and he says, 'Gee, Dad, I'll never forget you for this.' This is what you want, isn't it, Bob?" "Yeah."

Corny? Only if you, the salesperson, don't really feel the emotion the parents felt. I might also add that this procedure is good postselling, too.

It helps to insure the sale because you are selling the results of the sale. I might also point out that the parents are getting *some* now benefits in peace of mind by *knowing* their son's college education is secure.

Almost regardless of what you sell, you can and should paint a picture the prospect can see and feel. Since many of the benefits, in this case, are delayed for years, it is important that an emotional picture of those delayed benefits be burned indelibly into that prospect's mind. This greatly reduces the possibility of cancellation.

The impact of picture selling is vividly clear and explains why Charles Osgood of CBS News was moved to say, "A camera is a pitiful thing next to words and imagination." To make certain you didn't miss it, I must also point out that the dialogue also contained six questions. Good selling and good closing by good salespeople will always include several facets of the sales presentation.

When Fred was making this presentation, life insurance with cash value was very popular and practical for many young parents. In the world of the '80s we deal with different products (term insurance in combination with mutual funds, common stock, the money market, CDs, etc.), but the technique and procedure are the same. You adapt the procedures to fit your product or service.

As sales trainer John Hammond points out, when a person makes a significant purchase of any kind he generally makes that purchase only *after* he has gone through the picture-painting process in his own mind. As a professional you need to help the prospect with the picture-painting process.

The "Preparation" Close

A good friend of mine, Dr. Emol Fails, a former professor at North Carolina State University, has done a considerable amount of work with many chambers of commerce. He convinced them they needed to have sales clinics for the retail salespeople in stores in their area to teach them how to capitalize on the sales opportunities which many, if not most of them, were missing.

To prove the point that they needed training, Dr. Fails took his wallet, tied it to the back of his car, and dragged it around town for several days until it was in tatters. Then he put his credit cards, money, and driver's license in it. Next he would go into a men's store and buy a necktie which as a general rule is located reasonably close to a display of wallets. He would take his wallet out of his pocket and "accidentally" drop it. Money, credit cards, and wallet would scatter all over the floor.

In one small town the same thing happened in five different stores. The clerks would always help him pick up the pieces. *Sometimes they would look down their noses at that disgraceful thing he called a wallet, but not a single one suggested that in addition to the necktie a new wallet might also be considered.*

The picture Dr. Fails painted was crystal clear. The need for sales training was acute. The benefits to the people, the merchants, and the chamber of commerce could easily be visualized by the chamber official.

It is my firm conviction that by using your imagination you can paint effective pictures for your prospects. In Dr. Fails's case, the preparation (dragging the wallet behind his car and calling on the five stores) for the sales call on the chamber official took ten times as long as the actual call. This supports Abraham Lincoln's statement, "If I had nine hours to cut down a tree, I would spend six hours sharpening my axe." Selling is not easy, but proper preparation makes it *easier* and far more rewarding.

Incidentally, this is true in *all* fields of endeavor. The trial attorney spends hundreds of hours in study, investigation, and preparation for every hour he spends in the courtroom. Ditto for the surgeon, the professional athlete, *and* the professional salesperson. The great racehorse Nashua won over 1 million dollars in less than one hour of racing, but he spent hundreds of hours in training to know how to perform in all kinds of weather and under all track conditions. With proper preparation and by being in great physical and mental shape to run the proper pace, accelerate when needed, and go all out when necessary, he was able to take advantage of every opportunity.

I think you get the picture! When you train in the art of professional closing in relationship to the time a professional football team prepares for Sunday or a boxer prepares for a match (not to mention the championship), you'll begin to realize a tremendous jump in your closing ratio on the regular calls and a good boost in the close ones—which most people in sales have always missed.

The "Fear" Close

Fred Herman used one of the fastest and most effective word pictures I've ever heard of. He conducted a training program for a major oil company and trained their service-station attendants. (This was years ago when service stations gave service!) Fred's primary purpose was to teach the attendants how to sell more oil. (In those days, help was plentiful and service stations were desperately trying to sell more oil.)

When the attendant lifted the hood and checked the oil, Fred taught him to go to the driver and say, "You need five quarts." Fred properly identified this as fear motivation. It paints a vivid word picture, doesn't it? It's easy to visualize the fear in the prospect's mind because the instant the attendant said "You need five quarts," the car owner could visualize a serious engine problem. Most people expect the worst and the thought of his car burning those five quarts of oil was pretty frightening.

Fred said the car owner would come unglued and bound out of that driver's seat in a hurry! "What do you mean, I need five quarts?" Then the attendant calmly said, "Your oil is awfully dirty and should be changed before it damages your motor. It won't take but a minute and you'll be on your way." (That last sentence is another word picture, isn't it?)

You Sell What It Does

You need to paint the picture of your prospect using and enjoying the goods or services you sell. When you become completely aware of this process and the benefits which go with it, you will work at doing it until picture selling becomes second nature for you.

Make yourself a mental note to check the word pictures I paint for you throughout the remainder of this book. Remind yourself in your second and subsequent readings of *Secrets of Closing the Sale* to look for the word pictures. Incidentally, I remind you again that you will glean more ideas, make more notes, and mark the book more on your second reading than you will on your first and still more on your third than on your second.

Throughout the book the picture painted is that of satisfaction and gratification. The reason is simple. *You don't sell what the product is— you always sell what the product does.* Example: Each year over 5 million quarter-inch drills are sold, yet it's safe to say that nobody wants a quarter-inch drill. They want a quarter-inch hole.

Each year billions of dollars worth of cosmetics are sold, yet it's safe to say that nobody wants lipstick, eye shadow, rouge, etc. What they want is a more attractive appearance. They want to smell good, to be glamorous and desirable to members of the opposite sex.

You don't sell what it is—you sell what it does.

Watch the ads on television and you'll hear word pictures and see the actual picture of the users of the products enjoying the benefits of the product.

The "Postselling" Close

Thom Norman paints word pictures with a letter. He trains salespeople to write the customer after the sale is made. This is postselling also, which is often overlooked in sales training. Its importance should be obvious, because once you've made the sale, you need to keep it sold.

Thom encourages his clients to do the same thing he did for many years when he was in the field of direct selling. He urges salespeople to write a letter the evening of, or no later than the day after, the sale has been made, whether the sale was made in a home or office.

Thom insists that the letter be handwritten. It's all right to use company stationery, but it is very important that you hand address the envelope and put a postage stamp on it, since it is more personal than a postage meter.

The letter says, "A personal note to thank you for your courtesy and the trust and confidence you placed in me yesterday [or today, whichever day you are writing the letter]. I very much enjoyed visiting with you and your family. I am proud that you are now using our product or service and know that you will benefit and be pleased with the results. I shall be in touch with you in the future to see if I can be of any additional service. In the meantime, if you should need or want assistance of any kind, please feel free to contact me."

This letter paints a lot of pictures and gives the new customer some sincere "strokes" and assurance that he did the right thing:

> Thank you for your courtesy.
> I enjoyed visiting.
> I am proud of you.
> You will benefit and be pleased.
> I shall be in touch if you need
>   or want assistance.

He was painting the picture of a salesman who cares, who appreciates your business, who is going to look after your needs as they arise. He was assuring the customer that "just because you made the purchase doesn't mean I'm going to lose interest." He was painting a picture of a salesman who is *people-* and *service*-oriented. *That* is the way you make more sales *and* build a solid sales career in the process.

23

PICTURE SELLING FOR BIGGER, PERMANENT SALES

The "Repetition" Close

NOW I'M GOING to stick my neck out just a little, although not very much, because you've heard this one so many times. I'm going to give you a word picture and then I want you to write in the product name before you look below for the answer. "The pause that refreshes." _____ Even though it's been over twenty-five years since they've used it, the picture is still clearly in your mind. Next picture: A group of young people playing, laughing, singing, running, and just having a marvelous time. Which generation are they? _____ Now we see an athlete performing and then sitting down for the "Breakfast of Champions." Which cereal? _____

In each one of these examples the company or product, through repetition and the use of word pictures, has built name recognition while conditioning us to *expect* a particular result when we buy those products. These repetitions and "pictures" are *strong* invitations for us to get a Coke, a Pepsi, or a bowl of Wheaties.

If your presentation or demonstration is fifteen minutes or longer, you need to build in repetitive benefit phrases which suggest that those who buy from you enjoy certain benefits which those who don't buy from you can never enjoy. These phrases should have continuity: "This tightly seals all escapes"; "This keeps the heat out and the cold in"; "Electricity savings are substantial"; "The money you save is yours, not the utility company's"; "Invest your savings in your future."

Every Good Salesperson Paints Pictures

Good mechanics and conscientious doctors all do exactly the same thing. The doctor says, "It's not cancer—yet." The mechanic says, "No, I don't think you need a major overhaul—yet." The word *yet* paints a picture of fear in the prospect's mind.

Question: Would you want a doctor who *wouldn't* put a little fear into your heart that if you didn't do something that benign tumor might become cancerous? Would you want a mechanic who wouldn't let you know that if you didn't get a ring job you might throw a rod and end up spending five times as much money?

Thinking as a salesperson/customer, what do you think about the salesman who is not aggressively concerned enough about the customer to take a certain amount of risk in actively encouraging the prospect to make one or two *more* purchases to increase the effectiveness or enjoyment of the purchases already made? *Motive* is the key word. If you encourage the prospect to buy more merchandise solely because you can earn more, you are a "peddler." If you encourage the prospect to buy more items for his benefit, you are a "professional," and both of you benefit.

When you paint that prospect into the picture and tie the companion selling to it, you're going to sell more merchandise—and cut down on the travel and shopping time of your customer. It is true—you can get everything you want in life if you will just help enough other people get what they want.

The "Menu" Close

One of the most liberal uses of picture-painting words I've ever seen is the menu for the Hyatt hotels. I'm looking at one from Indianapolis, Indiana, and the descriptive adjectives they use really paint beautiful pictures to "close" you on ordering not just this one food item but *more* different items. Their imagination certainly ran rampant on these. Here are a few samples.

The heading is "Sensuous Salads. California Painter's Palate. A colorful array of the season's freshest berries, bananas, melons, pineapple, and grapes surrounding separate scoops of frozen yogurt and cottage cheese on a palaté of watermelon."

Or get a load of this one: "Spinach Supreme. A tumultuous arrangement of fresh spinach leaves mingled with enok mushrooms, crisp chips of bacon, and ripe tomato, with our superb hot honey bacon dressing."

And this one is not bad either: "For Protein Lovers. Mr. Chopped Sirloin conducts an orchestra of fresh vegetables, fruits, and eggs to an audience of shredded lettuce with an accompaniment of frozen yogurt and cottage cheese."

And one more. "The Tivoli. A bountiful garden sandwich of fresh avocado sprouts, Swiss cheese, tomato, and head lettuce on honey wheat bread amidst a symphony of fresh, raw vegetables with our Esquire Sauce for dipping."

The Rusty Scupper® doesn't do badly, either. Just look at the next twenty-nine words. "Crab and Cheddar. A feast worthy of King Neptune himself! A generous helping of crab salad under melted cheddar cheese, all grilled and served open-face on sourdough bread."

This one is short and sweet, too. "Avocado, Shrimp, and Bacon. Tasting is believing! Tempting avocado and Pacific bay shrimp topped with Canadian bacon comes to you open-face on sourdough bread. French fries come along, too."

Yessir, those folks really are word merchants. They know how to throw the words around to describe their food, and since I've eaten at both these places on several different occasions, I'm here to tell you they deliver what they sell. It's good!

The "Oooh and Aaah" Close

During the years I worked with Bernie Lofchick and World Wide Distributors, I was presented with many unusual opportunities. Never will I forget when World Wide started selling fine Bavarian china. Bernie had gone to Germany and negotiated an agreement with a manufacturer of beautiful Bavarian china. He was permitted to select his own patterns and even had some specifically created for his company. This presented a rather unique opportunity for the use of word pictures and imagination.

In selling hope-chest items to single girls, the "romance" or "story" associated with any pattern presented was especially important. Everything was in place and all set for all of the patterns except one, which was a unique and beautiful pattern; but without the proper presentation Bernie felt it would not be accepted in the marketplace.

At the eleventh hour, meaning the night before the convention when the new china was to be presented, Bernie and I finally came up with an idea. On the day of the convention we presented the china to the sales audience and they were wildly enthusiastic about the quality and beauty, as well as the finer points involved with a truly quality product. One by one the different patterns were presented and, since a matter of taste is always involved, the various salespeople responded to the different patterns according to their own taste preferences.

When the magic moment arrived for this one pattern to be presented, I paused, looked at the audience, smiled, and said, "Now folks, just before you take this pattern from your sample case and show it to the girl, here's what you want to say. Look at her, smile broadly, and say, 'Now Mary, this next pattern is what we call the "Oooh and Aaah" pattern. We call it that because when a girl sees this one she either says "Oooh" or "Aaah," which is exactly the same thing your dinner guests will be saying for the rest of your life as you use this pattern.'"

At that point I removed the dinner plate from the sample case, held it up in front of the audience, and sure enough—without exception—everyone there said either "Oooh" or "Aaah." This particular pattern became a runaway best-seller and World Wide Distributors sold more than twice as much of this pattern as they did any of the other patterns. This might have happened in any event, but Bernie Lofchick is absolutely convinced that the introduction of the pattern to the entire sales force with that little touch is what made the difference.

You Can Use It This Way

Again, I urge you to adapt this approach to your own situation. For example, if you're in a ladies' apparel shop and your prospect has been having difficulty choosing the right dress or outfit, I would encourage you to have an "Oooh" or "Aaah" outfit. If you are perceptive, by the time you have spent a few minutes with your prospect you will have a feel for what she really likes. Most of the finer shops have those unique outfits that were "made for" the particular shopper. However, many times the prospect is indecisive and vacillates between choosing one outfit over another. At the right moment—and that definitely is not the first three or four outfits you show—when your prospect shows she is a little confused as to what to purchase, you say to her, "I just remembered something which I believe is what you're looking for. As a matter of fact, let me tell you that when your husband [or boyfriend] sees you in this he's probably going to say either 'Oooh' or 'Aaah.'" Then smilingly say, "So in reality this is our 'Oooh' or 'Aaah' outfit." Obviously, this approach will fit some prospects better than others.

The same basic approach can be used when you have a particularly gorgeous view in a home you're showing or when you're selling a fine automobile with a unique appearance. This approach would also be applicable in the sale of fine jewelry, inspiring paintings, beautiful furniture, or any number of other items which we all merchandise. You could even expand it to a set of golf clubs. The salesperson, in explaining the clubs, can smilingly say to the prospect, "When you hit this driver off the tee, the rest of the foursome will probably say 'Oooh' or 'Aaah.'"

Warm, descriptive words paint pictures, and those pictures and sounds do have a substantial impact on the buyer's decision whether or not to buy. Yes, words do make a difference so you, too, need to be a "word merchant." You must learn to use them in an effective picture-painting process in order to utilize the potential you have and reach your peak as a sales professional.

PART FIVE
THE NUTS AND BOLTS
OF SELLING

Objectives

To sell you on the benefits of objections and teach you how to cash in on them in the marketplace.

To teach you how to identify the different kinds of prospects and how to deal with them as individuals.

To demonstrate the question-asking technique and give you specific questions to use under sales circumstances.

To encourage you to be a little bold—or even audacious—in the sales process under *some* circumstances.

Closes and/or Procedures

The "Assumptive" Close
The "Trial" Close
The "Four Question" Close
The "Talking Pad" Close
The "Safety Valve" Close
The "Alternate of Choice" Close Revisited
The "Wheeler Which" Close
The "Obligation" Close
The "Similar Product" Close
The "Right Experience" Close
The "Deserve It" Close
The "Reason-Excuse" Close
Sixteen "Question" Closes
The "Choice" Close
The "Tie Down" Close Revisited
The "Permanent Customer" Close
The "Disclosure" Close
The "Minor Decision" Close
The "Tennis Racket" Close
The "Ben Franklin" Close
The "Pedestal" Close
The "Hat in Hand" Close
The "Mother" Close
The "Pressure Permission" Close

24

OBJECTIONS—THE KEY TO CLOSING THE SALE

THE VERY WORD *objection* strikes fear in the hearts of insecure and/or beginning salespeople. In reality it should create excitement because, as I will repeat a little later, the indication of an objection is an expression of interest and that's the first thing a salesperson should be looking for.

There are as many different kinds of objections as there are kinds of prospects, so there are many approaches and variations in the way you handle each one of them. The subject is both broad and deep and is one of the most important covered in this book. I urge you to combine and adapt this information with your own company materials and applications, as well as explore the subject with sales leaders in your own industry.

Selling on Objections

I can state with considerable confidence that in most cases involving significant purchases, if you do not encounter objections from the prospect when you make your presentation, you do not have a prospect. When your prospect raises an objection you ought to grin internally and think to yourself, *Oh, boy! I've got a live one today!* Just remember if all the benefits and values of your product were obvious to the prospect, the salesman (that's you) would not be necessary. Also remember that if everybody instantly bought your product, commission rates would drop dramatically.

No Objections—No Prospect

For example, if you were to call on me selling scuba-diving equipment, I'd never raise an objection to the equipment. If you offered to sell me the complete outfit, guaranteed for fifty years for $9.95, I would never object because I have no interest.

If you were to try to sell me golf clubs, I might object by saying, "That shaft is too stiff [or not stiff enough]." A comment like that should bring a grin because then you can say, "What you need is our new graphite shaft." If a person is interested in what you are selling he is, in most cases, going to offer some kind of an objection, so when the prospect raises an objection, you ought to get excited.

As far as objections are concerned, the question most frequently asked is, "When should you answer the objection?" Actually, there are four times to handle objections: (1) before they occur; (2) when they occur; (3) later; and (4) never. On the last one, however, let me explain something. The objection might seem frivolous or irrelevant to you, but if the prospect raises it the second time, you can rest assured it is important to him. You'd better handle the objection at that time or he will feel you are ignoring it, that you either have no interest in him or no answer to the objection.

As we deal with objections, let me emphatically state that I believe a highly motivated, skilled, professional salesperson can strip a prospect of all objections and make him look and feel utterly ridiculous if he doesn't buy. With this procedure a salesman can intimidate or "high pressure" some prospects into buying. I also believe that some salesmen can be so persuasive and charming they can "hypnotize" their prospects into buying products, goods, or services which are not needed or are grossly overpriced. However, no salesman is so hypnotic in his presentation that he can *keep* the prospect hypnotized and feeling good about the purchase until the product is delivered and paid for.

With this in mind, I'm convinced high-pressure or overpriced sales are easily the two worst things which can happen to a sales career. In either case, the sale will probably be canceled and neither approach will build customers, which is a *must* if you are going to build a sales career.

Along these lines, communications and time-management expert Dan Bellus says too many salespeople make the mistake of thinking the sales process is a "win" for the salesman and a "loss" for the customer. With this attitude, Dan says, the salesman gets the feeling he's got to "defeat" the other person. He then raises the question, "Can you honestly expect someone you just 'defeated' to buy something from you?" He points out when the prospect objects or disagrees, the salesperson's objective is to persuade and not defeat.

The communication process demands that we approach the handling of objections in a convincing manner rather than a "defeating" manner. *Our objective is not to defeat but to convince and then persuade.* The point at which we "defeat" someone is the point at which we lose understanding and communication and, hence, the sale. He gives this example:

> A tourist was watching two Orientals in Hong Kong who were really going at each other hot and heavy with language which almost turned the air blue! As they stood there, the observer asked the Oriental guide, "What are they talking about?" The guide said, "They're having a discussion about ownership of a boat." The tourist said, "They're getting so wrought up, aren't they going to start fighting pretty soon?" The guide said, "No, they'll never start fighting because each one of them knows the man who strikes the first blow admits his ideas just gave out."

The same thing happens when we let a conversation develop into an argument. When we start arguing, our ideas have just given out. Communication—or in this case persuasion—no longer takes place.

To properly set the stage for dealing with objections, let me explain by way of analogy what my brother, who is one of the top sales trainers in the country, has to say. Judge explains that some people won't buy because the night train no longer runs from Buffalo to New York City. You might reasonably ask what the night train from Buffalo to New York City has to do with your prospect's not buying from you. Obviously, as Judge says, it has nothing to do with his not buying from you, but *if a prospect does not want to buy, one excuse is as good as another.*

Message: Give every call your very best. Make every effort to extend your goods, products, and services to the person you're dealing with. But if he does not buy, do not beat yourself to death as a result of it. Walk away and mentally prepare yourself to make the next sale on the next call. Remember that *you haven't failed on the sales call unless you let it negatively affect your attitude on your next sales call.*

Answer in Advance

First, let's look at the best time to answer the objection—which is before it occurs. Incidentally, if you are consistently getting the same objections after your presentation, it is a sure sign your presentation is in trouble. You need to analyze the presentation so you will be able to handle *most* objections in the body of the presentation. This approach enables you to answer the objection before it occurs, which means you are selling on the offensive instead of defensively responding. This is far more positive and effective.

Here are a couple of examples of how to handle your objections in the body of the presentation before the prospect verbalizes them.

Years ago I sold a food machine. You probably saw these machines demonstrated on television, at the state fairs and food shows, or in local department stores. After demonstrating the machine for several months I could flat make it talk! I'd put that food in the hopper and it came out about ninety miles an hour, sliced, diced, cubed, minced, waffled, shredded, chipped, curled, shoestrung, etc.

The group of prospects would sit or stand around "ooohing" and "aaahing" as the food came tumbling from the hopper in precise order. However, two objections would almost always arise. Generally one of the husbands would lean over and whisper to his wife in a voice you could only hear about three blocks away, "Yeah, he can make that machine do tricks, but I'll bet if you bought one *you* never could do that!" That was a standard objection, followed in short order by another when one of the ladies would comment, "It looks to me like you'd cut your hand on that thing, too!"

Make It Believable

These objections were so standard we knew we had to deal with them positively and in advance if we were going to sell the machines in quantity. Here is the way Harry Lemmons, the founder and president of The Saladmaster Corporation, taught me to handle this one. When I had quickly and easily cut three or four foods, I looked at the group and said, "Now folks, many times those who attend these demonstrations watch me operate this food machine and ask, 'Mr. Ziglar, if I bought one of those machines, could I do what you're doing?'

"I'm going to be frank with you and say, *emphatically not.* There is no way you're ever going to be as good at running this machine as I am. Now that's not vanity, ladies, that's just a fact. Let me explain. For several hours every day all I do is turn this crank and just look at what's happening [I was cutting food as I talked]. See how beautiful the food is and how easy the machine is to operate? To be fair, ladies, I make it look easy because I am a specialist with this machine.

The "Assumptive" Close

"Now ladies, when you get your machine [there's my first assumptive buying suggestion], by necessity you are going to be a 'general practitio-ner.' While you are using your machine you're also going to have to be looking after the children, answering the telephone, running the vacuum cleaner, chasing the dog out of the house, and doing a hundred and one other things. All I've got to do is turn the crank, so I should be pretty good at it."

Selling What the Product *Does*

They believed what I was saying, but at that point I had not sold a single machine, which was the purpose of the demonstration, so I continued my presentation. "If you won't be as effective as I am with the machine you probably wonder just how good you *will* be at saving time and money plus serving more attractive foods to your family. Here's the answer.

"We could take this lady right here [and I'd always pick out a young lady close to the front], give her five minutes to read the instructions, and with the machine she will cut more food better and faster than any *three* other ladies in the room if I gave them the three sharpest knives in town. Chances are good they've been using knives all of their lives and our machine operator has never used the machine. The reason she will cut more food better and faster with the machine is simple. It's not because she is an *expert* with the machine—but because she has the *machine* which does the work—and that's what all of you really want, isn't it?" (Nodding head.)

The "Trial" Close

That seemed to satisfy that objection pretty well. At this time I would cut two or three other foods, remove the first blade from the machine, and use my first trial close by saying, "Now ladies, as you can plainly see, the machine has five blades. I've used only one blade to cut these first six foods, but let me ask you a question. If the machine had only this one blade [and now I lowered my voice and looked them in the eye], how many of you have already decided you sure would like to have your own food machine? Can I see your hands, please?" Almost without exception 5 to 10 percent of the ladies and even more of the men would nod their heads, hold up their hands, or verbally indicate they wanted a machine.

I've always felt it was cruel and unusual punishment to require a prospect to listen to the entire presentation *after* he told me he was ready to buy, before I took his order and accepted his money. In my judgment, you should be nice to folks and let them buy whenever *they* are ready, instead of insisting they listen to the entire presentation before you permit them to buy. (NOTE: In group selling you need an assistant to handle these impulse buyers while you continue your demonstration.) Caution! Many times a prospect in a group will respond as if he wants to buy when in reality he is just being pleasant and agreeable. It's difficult to tell the difference, so experience and common sense are important.

Humor Can Be Invaluable

At this point I would cut two or three more foods and deal with the second major unspoken objection by saying, "Many times I've had ladies ask me, 'Mr. Ziglar, if I bought that machine could I cut my hand with it?'" To this I would smilingly respond, "Yes ma'am, you can, but we don't recommend it."

(Many times you can do more with humor than you can by being dead serious.) Then I would say, "Ladies, if you want to cut your hand with the machine, it's very simple. All you have to do as you turn the crank is to insert your finger at the very back of the hopper so that it's trapped between the blade and the hopper itself. If you are coordinated, you insert your finger as you turn the crank. This way the red comes out right over here [pointing to the front of the hopper and obviously smiling broadly]!

"Now ladies, if you don't want to cut your hand, *keep it out of the machine!* Any questions?" This approach apparently dealt with the hand-cutting objection beautifully because we seldom heard that particular objection again.

As you know, I dealt with price at great length in the first segment, but since it is an "objection," I want to include one final word on the subject in this section.

Too Much Money

Objection: "Costs too much." Answer: "I'd be inclined to agree with that, Mr. Prospect, because *good things aren't cheap and cheap things aren't good.* Our company had a choice. We could either design the product to do as little as possible so we could sell it as cheaply as possible, or we could design and build it to do as much as possible so in the long run your cost would be substantially lower.

"It is more than just a cliché, Mr. Prospect, to say you should invest in the best in the beginning, or pay for the 'get by' in the end. So why substitute the 'get by' for the best? When our company made the decision to build the best product possible to do as many things as possible, we actually placed ourselves in your shoes and tried to determine what

ADD · BENEFITS OF QUALITY

SUBTRACT · DISAPPOINTMENTS OF CHEAPNESS

MULTIPLY · PLEASURE OF BUYING

SOMETHING GOOD

DIVIDE · COST, OVER PERIOD OF TIME

would be best for you. That's the reason we unhesitatingly recommend this product so highly."

"The price is high." "I don't think there's any question about the price being high, Mr. Prospect, but when you add the benefits of quality, subtract the disappointments of cheapness, multiply the pleasure of buying something good, and divide the cost over a period of time, the arithmetic comes out in your favor."

"The price is high." "Yes it is, Mr. Prospect, however, in the final analysis a product is worth what it can do for you, not what you have to pay for it. If it costs you a hundred dollars but does you a thousand dollars' worth of good, then by any yardstick you've bought a bargain, haven't you?"

Cost Is Not the Determining Factor

On December 16, 1982, pitcher Floyd Bannister signed a five-year, $4.5 million contract with the Chicago White Sox. He chose the White Sox over the Atlanta Braves, who offered him a six-year contract worth $6.3 million. That's $1.8 million *more* than the White Sox offered *and* the Braves had won their division pennant in 1982.

As a prospect, Floyd Bannister obviously considered some things more important than money. Here's what Floyd's wife (in chapter 32 I elaborate on why you should get both husband and wife involved in the decision-making process), Jana, had to say:

The Sox showed interest in Floyd as a person, not as a commodity. Until late in the negotiations, they were not readily in the running, but we kept an open mind. When it came time to make a decision, it was important to us that [White Sox owner] Jerry Reinsdorf and [White Sox pitching coach] Dave Duncan flew to Arizona and took us out to dinner. It also was important that Tony LaRussa [White Sox manager] called Floyd several times, and a couple of White Sox players, Carlton Fisk and Tom Paciorek, also called.

Jerry Reinsdorf commented, "With Floyd we were dealing with somebody entirely different than the average player. The city and his teammates were just as important to him as money. I'd say fifty-fifty."

Other factors in the decision were (1) a spacious home park more suitable for Bannister's fly-ball pitching, (2) an opportunity to remain in the American League, and (3) a city where he has friends and relatives.

All those things were important, but I know Floyd Bannister well enough to know his priorities. He puts God first, family second, and his baseball career third. He weighed the offers of all the clubs and made his decision based on his priorities. I insert Floyd's story in *Secrets of Closing the Sale* because it reinforces what the sales pro has learned throughout his career. Find out what your prospect *really* wants and show him how your goods, products, or services can better help him achieve his objectives, and you will make the sale.

Price *is* important but it is only *one* of many important factors. If you have a price advantage, you obviously utilize it to the maximum. If you don't have it then do what the White Sox did in signing Floyd Bannister—capitalize on your other advantages. Of course, as Sherlock Holmes would say, "That's elementary, my dear Watson."

Maybe You've Got the Wrong Person

Caution: Many times when you've dealt with a series of objections and the prospect continues to bring up other ones, you should understand that maybe you're talking to the wrong person. It could be this man or woman really is not the decision maker. He or she may have to confer with someone else like the purchasing agent, the president, or a mate. Your prospect could be stalling and saving face by not admitting he can't make the decision.

To determine whether or not this is the case, this pleasant but direct approach used by John Hammond is most effective. "Mr. Prospect, I don't want to sound presumptuous, but I honestly believe that because of the versatility of our product and the nature of your need, our product is the answer to any questions which you might raise. But before we go any further, may I ask you a question?" If the prospect says yes, then say: "If I can answer your question to your satisfaction that this is the right product, at the right time and at the right price, are you personally in a position to give me an order for the product today, and would you be willing to do so?"

Chances are excellent if it's handled properly and he cannot make the decision, you will be able to determine this and save yourself a great deal of time. If he acknowledges that he cannot make the decision, then you need to make an appointment—with his help—with the person who *can* make the decision.

Again I emphasize if you are encountering the same objections repeatedly, chances are excellent it is your presentation which is in trouble.

Objections Are Consistent

To repeat myself, the best time to deal with an objection is before it occurs. As a general rule, most of the same objections are occurring after each of your presentations. If this is the case, you need to make a recording of your presentation (covered in chapter 5) so you can carefully analyze the points you are covering and the manner in which you are covering them. Chances are at least ten to one you will discover you are pretty "wordy" and are missing some key points. You are probably elaborating too much on the points which interest you but which might not be of particular interest to the prospect.

It's important you understand that you should already be sold and hence, you're not trying to sell yourself again. You are trying to sell the prospect. It makes sense to *sit on the prospect's side of the table*, anticipate the objections which historically you've been getting, then answer those objections in your presentation.

25

OBJECTIONS
ARE CONSISTENT—
OBJECTORS AREN'T

In no particular order I will first identify the different kinds of prospects and then I will give some basic guidelines in one to five sentences as to how you can deal with them.

First there is the antagonistic prospect; then the skeptical; the gullible; the egotistical; the know-it-all; the procrastinator; the hostile; the indecisive; the dominant "tough guy"; the big spender; the conservative penny-pincher; the critical prospect; the bargain hunter; the good-time Charlie; the stone face. On the humorous side, you have the animal prospect who is going to "bear" it in mind; the insomniac prospect who is going to "sleep on it"; the musical prospect who will make a "note" of it; and the playful prospect who is just "feeling out the market."

Yes, there are many kinds of prospects and I will repeat part of this as I deal with the various ones. There are two things you really need to know about all of them.

Number one, according to sales trainer Thom Norman, they all want to be right and they want to be understood. The second thing you need to understand is that, as the late Charles Roth would say, at the point of purchase all of them are afraid they're going to make a mistake, particularly if a significant amount of money is involved, and as a result, actually they are "not quite normal." It has been proven that at the point of decision a purchaser's heartbeat actually increases. Fear is there and fear affects judgment, so I suppose in the truest sense of the word we could say they're not quite normal. Therefore all prospects want reassurance that they are making the right decision.

Convince the Prospect

Let's also remember as we deal with the prospects that as communications and time-management specialist Dan Bellus says, "The objective is not to defeat the prospect but to convince him if he makes the purchase he's going to be happier and better off as a result."

Another thing to remember is this basic formula which Cavett Robert describes: As objections are raised, regardless of the kind of prospect you have, all the way from the gullible to the hostile, we first of all should act delighted about the objection and assure the prospect this objection is not going to be a problem when he has seen the remaining portion of the presentation (*objections thrive on opposition, but they die with agreement*). Second, we treat the objection as a question and then use that question as the catalyst to get the prospect involved in the sales process. Third, we get the commitment—this is the *only* question, and fourth, when possible, use the objection as the reason he should buy and urge him to go ahead and do exactly that.

Don't misunderstand: No single formula or procedure can or will fit every sales situation or objection you are going to encounter. However, this basic formula or procedure, when completely mastered, will give you a solid foundation which permits you to move easily into those situations which are not tailor-made for the formula itself.

As we delve further into the objections, and as we have already done with some in this book, I hope you notice we generally, but not always, follow that basic formula. I urge you to keep this formula in mind because as we deal with the various objections, it would be redundant to keep reminding you of it.

Prospects Want to Say Yes

I remind you that prospects do not want to say no, because no is final and, as stated earlier, the prospect is just as eager to have his problem solved as you are to help him solve it. This is something most people are reluctant to do. Remember that objections are not a reflection on you and you should not take them personally. Keep your cool and your chances of making the sale are greatly enhanced.

I also encourage you to remember that objections thrive on opposition but basically they die with agreement. That's one of the prime reasons we use some of the techniques which you will observe in the following paragraphs. I also ask you to remember that you are not a lecturer when you are dealing with the prospect. It's not a question of you talking and the prospect listening. The best way to make the sale is to get the prospect involved. That's why the question technique is used throughout this book. That's the technique used by *good* doctors and *good* lawyers as they probe and search for the best ways they can identify the problem so they can come up with solutions.

These Are Easy

Let's start with the easy prospect first. "Gary Gullible" himself. Bless his heart, he's the one who gives all of us hope for mankind because he certainly brightens our day when we encounter him. He's the kind who still believes the moon is made of green cheese. You deal with him in an open, straightforward way. Tell him lots of human-interest stories. He's more likely to buy because he likes and trusts you than for any other reason. He responds to persuasion but is offended with speed and pressure. Deal with him gently but confidently.

The second prospect is "Sidney Skeptical," who demands a bacteria count on the milk of human kindness and is so cynical he thinks someone pushed Humpty Dumpty. Not only is he skeptical but in many cases he will be argumentative as well. I especially remind you on this one that the skeptical, antagonistic prospect wants to be right and he wants to be understood. With this in mind, when he raises a dogmatic objection with a little anger, cynicism, or sarcasm hidden underneath it, you should respond by saying, "I'm delighted you raised that question, Mr. Prospect, and to make absolutely certain I clearly understand what you're saying, would you mind repeating it?"

This does two things: It indicates an honest effort on your part to be fair and it also indicates you place considerable importance on what the prospect is saying. Additionally, when he repeats his objection, chances are good he will substantially reduce the tone of the objection.

In dealing with skeptical, antagonistic prospects, it's important you not try to argue or contradict what they're saying, even if they are wrong. First of all, you let them finish saying what they have to say; get it off their chest; blow off that steam. Once that is out of their system and they've seen that you are interested and concerned about them, your chances of penetrating their minds and closing the sale, as the late John M. Wilson would have said, are increased substantially.

When the prospect brings up a dogmatic or strong statement in objection form, you pleasantly say, "Your question pleases me, Mr. Prospect, because it gets to the very heart of the matter and since that is what I like to do, it indicates we are on the same plane."

The third prospect (soon to be known as "Hostile Helen") is cut from the same bolt of cloth, but one important thing to remember is that she is probably hostile for a reason. It could be because she's been abused or misled by a salesperson in the past. It could be something as simple as a previous sales-man's not listening to her complaint.

One of the secrets is to get "Hostile Helen" talking. As she expresses her anger you fall back on one of the oldest of the old (known to sales trainers as the "Three-F principle") as you say, "I know exactly how you *feel*. Others in the past have *felt* the same way [pause]. They *found* when they had all the facts there was some justification in the procedure which was followed. They felt any mistake which might have been made was a mistake of the head and not of the heart.

"Incidentally, Mrs. Prospect, one of the things that pleases me about what you're saying is this: I have found that most people who are as frank and open [*don't you dare say "angry" or "hostile"*] as you are turn out to be more receptive. They are open and fair-minded when they have their questions answered, so I'm pleased you bring your concerns forward in such an open manner."

He Can't Decide—on Anything

Then there's "Indecisive Ivan," who wanted to start a procrastinators' club but decided to wait till later. Ivan simply cannot make a decision. He's somewhat like the fellow who went to the psychia-trist and the psychiatrist said to him, "I understand you have trouble making decisions." The fellow re-sponded, "Well, yes—and no." The indecisive prospect is the kind of person who is in many ways the unhappiest of all people. He can't decide what to have for lunch, much less decide on a major purchase such as a home, a car, a major investment, or life insurance program. He takes a pep pill to get charged up to do something, then mixes it with Valium so if nothing happens it won't bother him.

The way to deal with him is to win his confidence which you do, as I've repeatedly said, by being the right kind of person. Demonstrate considerable empathy; move to his side of the table; let him know you're on his side; reassure him that yes, he is making the right move. Your own conviction and belief that your product is what he should buy will be the determining factor. Remember, he's having trouble deciding if he should buy. If you have any doubts that you should sell, you can rest assured that he won't buy. Push him—be firm.

Inner pressure is a key factor. You apply this by asking even more questions than you normally would. Later in this segment of *Secrets of Closing the Sale* I will demonstrate in considerable detail exactly *how* you ask questions and I will give you numerous examples. Incidentally, at this point I have used over 500 questions in this book. I'll bet that surprises you, doesn't it? That was another question, wasn't it?

Another type of prospect, identified by my creative associate Jim Savage as "Betty Bargain Hunter" and sometimes known as "Cautious Charlie," always wants a little better deal than anyone else. She considers every purchase a "contest." She's got to feel she is the "winner," and she won't be happy unless she gains some kind of concession. You can handle this one in two ways: First you say to her that one of the beautiful things about working with this company is the fact that you treat everyone in the same manner. She can buy your product with the complete assurance that no one—but no one—is going to get a better offer from the company than she did and that her offer makes her a winner. Generally speaking, that's what she wants—the assurance that she is the winner—that *she* is the smart one—that *she* got your best offer.

Second, you can tie it down if there is something you as an *individual* can do for her personally which not only guarantees no one got a better offer but that she got the *best* offer because she got *you*. It can be a personal service: "One thing I will do for you I normally do not do is I will personally take your order to shipping and see that it is handled—at no extra cost to you—for immediate shipment today." Or, "I will personally walk your credit through and save at least twenty-four hours for delivery." Or, "Since I am going to be heading your way I will personally be present when the equipment is installed to make certain it is to your exact specifications."

He's Painful—Make Him Profitable

The next prospect is "Oliver Obnoxious," the loudmouthed know-it-all. Generally speaking the obnoxious of the world are suffering from serious self-image problems and feel the only recognition they can gain is of a negative nature. Attention is what they crave, so give them attention but in a firm and positive way. You also challenge that individual. Aside from all of his bluster, in many cases underneath he is soft and mushy. He, too, wants to be right—he wants to be understood—he wants to be appreciated.

You challenge him with statements like, "Our research indicates that only three percent of the population is in a financial position to purchase this product." Or, "These payments are going to be large, Mr. Prospect, can you handle one of. . ." Then quote the amount.

These obnoxious, know-it-all people also like to have their pride appealed to. "This is a particularly nice suit," or "an especially beautiful landscape theme. It certainly fits in with your taste and with your character because it puts you in an especially elite group." This is real snob appeal, which is important to them. Along these lines it is good to point out that the local television personality or sports hero also has "this particular model." (Say this only if it is factual. As Bill Gove, one of the real pros in sales training, says, "Never lie or 'loop.' ")

The "I'm in a Hurry" Prospect

To this list add "Heloise Hurry-up," the prospect who doesn't want to be bothered with the details. She wants the "facts, just the facts, I've got things to do, I'm in a hurry!" Many times these people really are more interested in saving time than they are in saving dollars. Be brief; be to the point; be businesslike; close the sale as quickly as you can; assure her that you'll handle the details, you'll take care of the delivery, you'll personally see to it she gets exactly what she wants, then make absolutely certain you follow through.

Next comes "Jolly Jimmy," the playful, good-natured prospect who in many ways can be the most frustrating of all because on occasion he is impulsive and indecisive. He is far more likely to buy from someone he likes and enjoys being around. Make friends with him—laugh with him—be casual. Then—as a *friend*—encourage him to go ahead and take action now so he can enjoy the benefits now.

The Know-It-All Prospect

"Nora Know-It-All" is out to impress you, so let her. You've certainly got nothing to lose. One word of caution: She might want to bend your ear all day, so be aware of the time factor. You might let her impress you by paying cash for the order and, in fact, a challenge to do so could be the key in getting the order.

The same basic approach should be used with "Bobby Big Shot." He wants to feel important, so by all means, make him feel important. He wants to be on center stage, so let the spotlight shine on him. By the same token he likes to know he is not dealing with "one of the boys," but rather someone who is qualified to handle *his* account. If you've set a few sales records or if you have accomplished something significant, work it in in a nonthreatening way so Mr. Big will know he's dealing with someone who is qualified to handle such an important person.

Just as we have the timid procrastinator who can't make a decision, we also frequently encounter "Impulsive Irene" who will say yes or no in pretty short order. Once you've got her agreeing with you and have headed her toward a sale, go ahead and close with conviction and with firmness. Get the order signed while she's at the top of her impulse.

The Toughest of All

Sales trainer John Hammond identifies the toughest prospect as "Agreeable Al," the one who doesn't object at all. He "yeses" you all through the interview, smiles, nods, and agrees with everything. John handles him in this way: When he instinctively feels, early in the interview, this prospect is *that* kind and that he is not going to buy, John stops right in the middle of a sentence, smiles, leans forward, and says, "Mr. Prospect, do you mind if I ask you why you have decided not to accept this opportunity to take advantage of the benefits our product offers?" Then he stops—doesn't say another word.

"Agreeable Al" will do one of two things. He will say, "It's because . . ." and then he will give you an objection which you can deal with, *or* he will say, "What makes you think I've decided not to buy?" If that's the case you just go ahead and write his order. Good strategy, John.

There Are All Kinds of Prospects

I suppose if we made an effort we could list a hundred different kinds of prospects: slow thinkers, fast thinkers, wrong thinkers, and non-thinkers; big spenders, conservative penny-pinchers, criticals, bargain hunters, timid, assertive, impulsive, needler, argumentative; nonlistener, stone face, harassed executive, etc.

Then there are the old, the young, and the middle-aged; the male and female; the black and white and everything between. Regardless of the prospect, everyone wants to be right, to be understood, to be appreciated. All have physical, spiritual, and emotional needs. Our objective is to meet those needs so these prospects will be our customers, instead of remaining under a label as a prospect.

Of course, as Bill Gove laughingly says, "The problem with making a sale is you've just lost your best prospect."

One thing to remember is many times when prospects bring up objections in a dogmatic, antagonistic way, it is often a defense mechanism. Your prospect, for example, might suggest that "all salesmen are a bunch of crooks." The point is that as a salesperson you shouldn't take offense. One or two unfortunate experiences might have led him to this conclusion. Chances are excellent he *wants* to find a truly professional salesperson who will convince him that he has reached an erroneous conclusion. He *might* even want to buy something *now*. That means the chances are excellent he wants somebody to sell him something and since you're there, it might as well be you.

26

THE SALESMAN'S FRIEND

IN HANDLING OBJECTIONS, one of the most important things to do is ask questions. As I've stated on several different occasions, questions help you to persuade the person to take action. Questions enable you to uncover the prospect's dominant buying motive, which you must do if you're going to be effective in selling.

Caution: Many times it is easy, when the customer vehemently brings up a complaint, for you to be too ready to agree with the prospect and take sides against your company. I urge you to proceed with extreme caution in dealing with the complaint. Follow the techniques we've been talking about. Act pleased that he has brought it up. Hear him out. Agree with him that yes, there is a problem. Find out if that is his only problem. Assure him that you, the company, and in all probability the other salesperson want to clear the air and solve the problem to everyone's benefit. Then use that complaint as the main reason he should do business with you and your company.

After a strong complaint say, "Mr. Prospect, would you repeat exactly what happened so I can be certain I understand the situation and we can solve the problem?" You are acting as an arbitrator, as a go-between. You've not denied the right of the prospect, and neither have you put your company in an awkward position. That's good because when all the facts are known, the prospect could be (and often is) grossly overstating the case. If that is so and you make promises which you cannot keep, you will look foolish, the company will be further discredited, and the customer will be even more "anticompany."

With this procedure you diffuse much of his anger without going behind the back of the other salesperson. This keeps his—and the company's—credibility intact.

The more violent the objection the more critical it is that you follow this procedure, because reasonable people generally are not overly belligerent or vehement in their protests.

Objection or Question?

In dealing with objections, we need to make certain we're dealing with an objection and not a question. The way you tell the difference is simple. A question is an inquiry seeking information. How much does it cost? How long will it take me to get it? Do you have it in green as well as in yellow? Do you have a more expensive or a less expensive model? Do you have a bigger one or a smaller one? Those are questions which you answer. Generally speaking, questions are a sign of interest and are asked in the body of the presentation.

Under normal circumstances I've always believed in answering questions when they are asked, provided they do not completely disrupt the sales presentation itself. Example: If in the first part of the presentation the prospect asks, "What does it cost?" you might or might not want to answer it at that point, depending upon whether your product is competitively priced or whether you're the top of the line. Experience, common sense, and judgment should dictate your approach *if* you have a definite price advantage.

If your product has definite quality and feature benefits but is not competitively priced, if possible you should avoid answering the price question until you have explained or demonstrated some of your benefits.

Here Are the Words

A direct answer to the prospect when he asks the price could be this: Smile pleasantly and say, "I'm coming to that in just a moment." Or, "I'm pleased you're interested in the price. In a few minutes when I cover it you'll be glad you asked." If the prospect persists you might say, "I'd be pleased to answer, Mr. Prospect, but it would be somewhat like having to pay for a suit before you saw what you were getting. All I want to do is make certain you see exactly what our benefits are so you can appreciate what a bargain you will be getting."

Yet another answer, provided this fits, could be, "There are so many factors involved in price, such as size, model, terms, and delivery, I hesitate to answer before we have narrowed down the choices I am about to offer you."

When the prospect asks the price before you have had an opportunity to establish value or explain benefit, you could also handle it this way: Look at him, smile, and say, "That's the part you're going to be delighted with. I'm pleased that you are already interested enough to inquire about the price. I'll get to it in just a moment." Then I would move along into the presentation itself.

Stay Tuned in to Your Prospect's Timing

The speed with which you move is important. Don't act like you're on the way to the races, but when you say you'll get to the price in a moment, quickly describe some attractive features and benefits which will justify the price.

Let me emphasize that some prospects by nature are short on patience and if they demand an answer in another minute or two, you could take this approach: "Mr. Prospect, I appreciate your concern and please believe me when I say I am not evading the issue. However, until we determine, as a result of our discussion, what your needs are, it would be impossible for me to give you a figure. My answer at this point might be too high or it might be too low. If it's too high, you might lose interest. If it's too low, then when I give you the true figure you might be disappointed."

At that point you move back into the presentation. If, however, the prospect again demands the price, I do not believe you can stall the issue any longer, so meet it head-on by giving him the highest possible price, including *all* the features, attachments, extras, or benefits which go with your goods or service. Do this by saying, "The highest possible price is," and then quote the figure. "However, chances are good the actual figure will be less when we've determined your exact needs. I suspect your primary concern is that the product meets your needs, isn't it, Mr. Prospect?" Wait for his answer, then move back into features and benefits.

If the prospect indicates the price was about what he had expected or even less than he thought it would be, you ask the closing question. "Since the product meets your needs and is easily within your price range, would you like to have me install the equipment right away or do you have a specific date in mind?"

You Don't Have to Overcome All Objections

Throughout any interview or presentation you must remember that you are not in the "objection answering" business. You do not have to answer all objections in order to make the sale. Realistically there is seldom if ever going to be a situation where your prospect is going to like *everything* about your product, goods, or services. Fortunately, your prospect doesn't have to like everything in order to buy your product. All the prospect has to do in order to be a customer is to like what you sell *more* than he likes what he will have to exchange for it.

Example: I recently bought a suit despite the fact there were two things I didn't like about it. First of all, I wasn't too happy about the price, but with a little help from my friend and clothier, Doyle Hoyer, and my Redhead, I was able to justify the price. (Everything is expensive, quality costs, long-lasting, you need to look successful, etc.) Second, I didn't like the fact that I will have to wear a belt with the trousers, but that was minor.

Despite these two objections I bought the suit because I really liked the color and the way the suit fit. Additionally, when I slipped the suit on, my Redhead, who has got to be the world's number-one hugger, snuggled up real close and said the suit felt good. 'Nuff said.

My major point is this: Often there will be objections you'll be unable to answer. There is even a slight chance the objection or question will have no answer, so don't worry too much about it. When the prospect does bring up an objection, let me remind you that you are in the sales business and the objection, when properly handled, is a friend which can help make the sale.

You Are Not in the Objection-Answering Business

Many times young salespeople (in sales experience, not birthdays), or insecure salespeople acquire the mistaken idea they're in the objection-answering business. As a result of this misguided thinking they actually *encourage* or challenge the prospects to raise additional questions or objections. This is especially true if the salesperson gives a sharp answer (in his own opinion, of course) to a tough question or objection. As a sales trainer, I have seen the salesman almost literally fold his arms and stick his chin out, or by some other body language say to the prospect, "And I'll guarantee you I can handle the next one, too, so go ahead and shoot another one at me, just try me!"

With this attitude the sale is often lost because the prospect invariably gets the feeling the salesperson has an ego problem and is more interested in parading sales knowledge than in solving his (the prospect's) problem.

Rephrase and Soften the Objection

Many times an objection can be softened a great deal by rephrasing it. For example, the prospect might say, "The quality of your product certainly leaves a lot to be desired. I don't believe it would last three weeks, much less the three years your warranty covers!" Pretty strong—but it can be largely neutralized or defused by rephrasing it. You do this by lowering your voice, looking directly at your prospect, and saying, "If I understand you correctly, you want to be certain the product has lasting quality and you're going to get dollar value for every dollar you invest. Is that your question, Mr. Prospect?" Or you could shorten it and say, "So your *question* is. . . . Is that right?" (Never say, "To answer your objection. . . .")

Chances are excellent he will accept the rephrasing of his objection. (Most people *overstate* objections, especially if at that moment they're not really interested. This often discourages the salesperson and causes him to withdraw, which is what the prospect had hoped for.) From this softer, friendlier base you're in a much better position to move in a positive direction toward the sale. This way *you are using your selling skills as a tool to persuade and not as a club to subdue.* This works to the mutual advantage of you and your prospect.

Be Gentle When You Go on the Offensive

The comment most frequently made by the prospect is, "I'm just not interested." Voice inflection and tone will determine whether this is a mild objection, moderate objection, or strong objection.

If the objection is mild to moderate you say, "I'm a little surprised to hear you say you're not interested, Mr. Prospect, because this would [state your product's major benefit]. However, I'm certain you have a good reason for your lack of interest. Would you be willing to share that reason with me?" Once again, the ball is back in his court.

Sales trainer John Hammond says that since he started using this approach in 1957, only two prospects (he vividly remembers the details) have refused to give him their reasons for not being interested. John says this eliminates the *guesswork* as to why the prospect is not interested and enables you to deal directly with the *real* objection.

If the prospect's tone is harsh and dogmatic when he says Not Interested, you should adopt the policy of the late Charlie Cullen and be a little audacious. Repeat the words *not interested* in such a way you are making a statement *and* asking a question. (There's that voice inflection again.) By handling it this way you effectively force your prospect to deal with *your* statement, rather than having to be defensive yourself. It's much more effective.

When the prospect brings up *any* objection and you don't really know *why* he brings it up, instead of guessing you should *ask*, as sales trainer Lee DuBois suggests: "Obviously, Mr. Prospect, you have some good reason for saying that," or "feeling this way. Do you mind if I ask what it is?" Stop—and wait for his answer.

Think About It

Chances are excellent if you've been in the world of selling for three days you've already dealt with a prospect who, after you have made your presentation, states, "I want to think about it." To put this into perspective as well as to reveal something to you about human nature and prepare you to close the sale, let me share with you a procedure I follow when I present this information to a group.

I ask the group, "How many of you consider yourselves reasonably honest?" (All hands go up.) Then I ask, "How many of you reasonably honest salespeople have ever told another salesperson that you wanted to 'think about it'?" (Again, all hands go up.) Then I ask, "How many of you reasonably honest salespeople, after you told the salesperson you were going to 'think about it,' honestly, legitimately, seriously, and carefully thought about the offer which had been made to you?" At this point few, if any, hands go up. Then I ask, "Were you 'honest' salespeople by any chance trying to get rid of that salesman?"

The answer to that question could well be yes or no. Actually, sometimes the prospect does want to terminate the interview or get rid of the salesperson. The statement "I want to think about it," or "talk to my lawyer, my banker, my partner, my mate, etc.," is a simple way to graciously end the sales interview. However, there is another possibility.

Most people hate to use the word *no* because, as previously stated, it is so final. When the prospect says no, that spells the end of that relationship and so, in an effort to avoid the use of the word *no*, they will often come up with a number of made-up excuses. As salespeople, if we can understand this basic fact, it puts us in a stronger sales position because as long as the prospect does not emphatically say no, the possibility of a sale still exists.

At this point it is important that as salespeople we must *always* remember we also are consumers and *we need to be able to think as a buyer as well as a seller.* Obviously, this is the empathy I talk about in chapter 8. With empathy you are not part of the problem, but you understand the problem, which you can help solve if you understand the thinking of the prospect.

Actually He Won't "Think It Over"

Don't overlook this major point. Your prospect who wants to "think it over," in the vast majority of cases will not actually do that, just as you yourself probably will not seriously think it over by weighing and evaluating all the pros and cons of the offer. In short, most prospects who want to "think it over" don't really do that, so in far too many cases they are eventually going to say no.

Obviously circumstances vary. Again, common sense and experience should always be a factor, but as a guideline let me assure you that a *no* today is better than a *no* tomorrow. Obviously, a *yes* tomorrow is better than a *no* today, but I emphasize, when they don't want to make a decision for no apparent reason, in most cases they will say *no* tomorrow.

It's better to have the *no* today than tomorrow for the simple reason it clears your mind. You can now pursue new prospects and not count on that one for a future sale. Once you do, you fall into the trap of not prospecting for new prospects and the sale you miss today will cost you sales tomorrow.

Handle It This Way

There are a couple of ways you can effectively handle the "think about it" stall. First you can smile and say, "That's great! I'm delighted you want to think about it because obviously you would not waste your time thinking about our offer if you were not interested. Therefore, I assume you want to think about it to help reduce the chances of error whether your decision is yes or no. Is that a valid assumption, Mr. Prospect? [Get an answer.] Would you agree that the *length* of time you think about something is not the important point? If I'm reading you right [I use this phrase a lot] and I think I am, your prime objective is to be as certain as possible that you make the right decision, regardless of whether you think about it two minutes or two days. The *right* decision for you is what you're seeking, isn't it, Mr. Prospect?

"Businesspeople and efficiency experts agree that the best time to make accurate decisions is when you have the necessary facts which are unclouded with other issues of the day. This way you can be more certain your thought process is aimed at making the correct decision, based on factual information which is fresh in your mind. Forgotten facts or confused information will almost always lead to a faulty decision. With this in mind, could we think together for a minute to make certain you arrive at the right decision, which is what you want, isn't it, Mr. Prospect?" (Wait for answer.)

The "Four Question" Close

"Actually, there are only four questions you need to answer in your own mind and you've already voted yes on three of them. [Pause after each of these questions.] Do you like it? Do you want it? Can you afford it? The only remaining decision is when do you want to start enjoying the benefits? Obviously, you are the only one who can answer that question, but Mr. Prospect, may I ask you another question? [Pause.] The price will remain constant or probably increase. Since benefits and enjoyment can start only when you acquire the product, your only decision boils down to when you want to enjoy the benefits, doesn't it, Mr. Prospect? [Pause.] With this in mind, doesn't it make sense to vote yes for *now* benefits?"

E. F. Hutton and Company, Inc., Houston, Texas executive Mark Gardner is more direct with this question: "Do you want to think about it, because I may have overlooked some salient point in my presentation?" or "What is it you really want to think about?" "Would you elaborate on this?" (After the answer Mark continues.)

"Mr. Prospect, wouldn't you say that *in order to make an intelligent decision* you must have:

1. good access to the information

2. expertise in order for you to evaluate

3. perhaps a personal acquaintance with the management

"Mr. Prospect, that is exactly what has been done here. What we are discussing are important business decisions.

"Very often people like yourself might say, 'Let me think about it,' or 'Let me call you back.' What they are really saying is that they don't like the idea. Let's speak frankly for a moment.

"Please—don't just be polite. Is there something you feel uncomfortable about? Something else you want to know?

"As a businessman it's important for me to know. . . ."

Here's another approach. If your prospect has a sense of humor and says he wants to think about it, you look at him, smile, and with an exaggerated hand motion, thrust your arm out to expose your wristwatch and say, "Go!" The late Dick Gardner, founder of the National Association of Sales Education (NASE), taught me that one and it generally gets a good, solid laugh. More importantly, it serves as a tension breaker and sales are made. Use this technique with discretion, but it's a safe bet that unless you are selling a life-or-death product, any time you can make your prospect smile or chuckle during the closing process you're ahead of the game.

Here's another, especially if you're selling a lifetime product. "Mr. Prospect, it's just as inexpensive to have it all your life as it is to own it part of your life. With that in mind, it will cost you a lot less per year, per month, per day, to own it from now on instead of waiting five years or even five months and then getting it. With that in mind, don't you think you ought to start enjoying the benefits now?"

Start Logically—End Emotionally

Remember that when you are dealing with a prospect who brings out objections, you need to start with a *logical* answer but you close with an emotional one. Our *thinking* brain is only 10 percent as large as our *feeling* brain. People are moved to buy more from an emotional point of view than they are from a logical point of view.

When objections are introduced and you handle them one by one in such a way the prospect likes you and trusts you, you can generally tell when you begin to make progress toward the sale. The prospect starts getting friendly, goes back for another look, picks up the product one more time. Sometimes he simply gets quiet and starts reading the agreement or some of the promotional literature which you have placed in front of him.

Suppose the prospect brings up a question or objection which you cannot answer. You respond this way: "That's obviously an important question, Mr. Prospect, or you wouldn't have brought it up at this point in the interview. I commend you on your insight, but since no one else has ever raised the question, I don't have the complete answer. Since it is important to you, and quite frankly, to me as well, I'd rather personally get the information from our support personnel at the home office to make certain it is completely accurate. If that's satisfactory, I'll get back to you the first of the week."

Incidentally, *you never say*, "Do you understand what I'm saying?" Instead you ask, "Have I made myself clear?" or "Have I clarified this point to your satisfaction?"

27

USING OBJECTIONS TO CLOSE THE SALE

Many times I am asked, "How many objections should you answer before you attempt to close?" In my judgment two to three should be the maximum number and in most cases it will just be two (remember—there is a difference between questions and objections). When your prospect raises either the second or third objection (it will vary according to the circumstances), look your prospect in the eye (your training in tone and voice inflection covered earlier will be invaluable at this point) and say, "Mr. Prospect, let me ask you a question. Is this the only thing which stands between you and ownership of ____, or is there something else you need to consider?"

If the prospect says, "No, this is the only thing I'm concerned about," at that point you cover the objection and make a positive statement in question form. "I believe that answers your question, doesn't it?" If you get no response or a positive response you continue, "I'm delighted I was able to answer your question because I know you are going to love the product!" You assume the close because the prospect had said only one objection stood between him and ownership and you had secured agreement from him that the barrier (question, objection) had been removed.

The "Talking Pad" Close

Many times a prospect has more than one question or objection, so he could respond to the question in the last paragraph like this: "Well, no, in addition to not being convinced the price is fair, I seriously question your ability to service the account and frankly, your guarantee leaves much to be desired." When your prospect has expressed those three objections, you reach for your talking pad and write them down in abbreviated form as you say, "If I understand you correctly, Mr. Prospect, your prime *questions* are, number one, price." (Write the word

PRICE - PRICE IS COMPETITIVE
SERVICE- PROPERLY SERVICE THE ACCOUNT
GUARANTEE- GUARANTEE MORE THAN FAIR

price.) "Number two, you are concerned about our service." (Write the word *service.*) "And number three, you question our guarantee." (Write the word *guarantee.*)

Now you have only three words on your talking pad: price, service, and guarantee. Look your prospect in the eye and say, "In other words, Mr. Prospect, if you could convince yourself the price is competitive, that we have the ability to properly service the account, and our guarantee is more than fair, you would be comfortable in making a *yes* decision concerning our product. Is that what you're saying?" Get a commitment.

If the prospect says yes, then you go to the price objection and deal with it. I remind you of that in chapters 5 and 24. I have dealt in great detail with how to handle this objection, so at this point you utilize that information. When you complete the handling of the price objection, you look at the prospect and make the statement in the form of a question: "Surely, Mr. Prospect, this satisfies you on the price, doesn't it? If it does, Mr. Prospect, then with your permission I would like to remove 'price' as one of the questions. Is that all right?" (Nod your head as you cross out the word *price.*) Incidentally, "Is that fair enough?," "Does that make sense?," and "Is that all right?" are three of the *strongest* trial closing questions.

Remove the Barriers One by One

Next you deal with the service question or objection. At this point there is nothing more convincing than letters from satisfied customers who have specifically dealt with the service aspect of your business. (These are the testimonials Mike Frank told us about in chapter 14.)

Since this is a question of company stability and integrity, your membership in the Chamber of Commerce and the Better Business Bureau, as well as references to the size, age, and integrity of your company, are important. As you get the verbal and body-language feedback from your prospect, you conclude the service presentation by asking, "Does this answer your question as it relates to our service reputation?" If it does, then ask, "May I then remove the question concerning our service capability?" As you ask the question, you assume a positive answer and literally cross it out with your felt-tip or ball-point pen.

"The third question, Mr. Prospect, had to do with the guarantee which we offer. Let me start by saying that any guarantee is only as good as the company which offers that guarantee. As I have already demonstrated, we do represent a viable, solid business establishment. One thing I emphasize, Mr. Prospect, is that unless the guarantee is fair to both buyer and seller, it has no value. If we, as a company, couldn't live with it, we would be out of business. Then, regardless of how extensive the guarantee might be, it would have no value whatever. Our guarantee protects you from virtually everything but human error and carelessness, as well as abuse of the product. Our product, as I have demonstrated, is built for use but not abuse. We protect you from all manufacturing defects as well as normal use. I believe, Mr. Prospect, that's your major concern, isn't it?"

Parade Your Strengths

Because each company has its own strong points, I urge you to learn what yours are and handle them accordingly. The prime consideration in dealing with objections like this is not to become defensive or in any sense of the word attack your prospect or raise your voice. "Mr. Cool" is the phrase here. Calm, quiet assurance is really what the prospect is seeking. To repeat myself, it is at this point in the negotiation that your qualities as a person are just as important as your sales skills. If you're the right kind of person and have acquired the professional skills, you should lose very few sales because of objections.

After you have covered those objections, including that third one, look the prospect in the eye and say, "I believe, Mr. Prospect, in your own mind you feel pretty good about our guarantee, don't you?" Again, you assume the positive answer and with a big smile, cross out the final objection.

At this juncture, you will have utilized the information provided for you by your own company trainer and your company literature. One more time, *Secrets of Closing the Sale* was written primarily to reinforce your company's efforts, not to replace them.

When you have covered all three of the objections, you look at the prospect and say, "You know, Mr. Prospect, I wish everyone I deal with was as concise with their questions as you are, because if a person knows his own feelings, it makes it easier and more fun to demonstrate our products. I know that you are going to love this product!" With a big smile you extend your hand as you assume the sale.

Caution: Don't "overanswer" any one objection. First, it could indicate, in the mind of the prospect, you are defensive to the point you are uncertain about your product. Even worse, you could so overwhelm the objection that your prospect could be made to feel like an idiot for mentioning it. As we'd say down home, "That ain't the way to sell 'em!"

The "Safety Valve" or "Punt and Pray" Close

In handling objections, I personally believe we all need to have what Dick Gardner called "safety valves." Hal Krause calls this the "Punt and Pray" approach. All experienced salespeople have been asked questions or have been confronted with objections which they know how to handle but, unfortunately, can't recall at the moment of need. When this happens you can't just clam up for a couple of minutes. Nor is it advisable to say, "I know the answer but can't think of it, so give me a minute or two and I'll give you the answer." Since you know the answer (assuming you *do*), you should develop some "safety valves" or "punt and pray" fillers.

Here's the way they work. The prospect asks the question or raises the objection for which you have an answer but cannot immediately recall, so you "punt and pray" by saying, "I'm delighted you raised this question because in my mind it is quite important. I commend you for having the interest and insight to explore this facet of our offer. [Obviously, if you can't sincerely say this then the "pray" part of "punt and pray" needs to be literal.] This interest and insight will enable you to more completely utilize the services which we offer, so you'll get the maximum benefit." By this time you should have recalled the specific answer to the objection, so go ahead and answer it.

The same approach can be taken when you have the answer ready for use but you want to phrase it in the best possible way. For example, a doctor might need to think through the gentlest manner in which to deliver distressing medical news. A loving parent or mate will want to soften distressing or upsetting news, so voice tone, words, and manner play an important part. You know the answer, but delivering that answer is the tough part.

Play It Cool—Use a Safety Valve

Occasionally a prospect will make a dogmatic statement which necessitates a built-in safety valve. For example, your prospect might say, "I wouldn't do business with that outfit you represent in a hundred years!" He's dogmatic, even a little vehement in his statement. Your "safety valve" procedure is simple and effective. Lower your voice, look him in the eye, and say, "Mr. Prospect, it's obvious you feel quite strongly about this issue so you must have an excellent reason for feeling as you do. Would you mind sharing with me why you feel this way?"

Very soft, very quiet, but when you follow this procedure you will remove much of the vehemence and emotion from the scene. Interestingly enough, in most cases you will discover the problem involves a personality conflict, a communications gap, or some insignificant detail. However, regardless of its actual size, if it's big in the eyes of the prospect—it's big.

Regardless of its size or significance, this procedure brings the objection into the open so that you can deal with it. The key to this approach is not to take it personally when the prospect attacks your company, its procedures and policies, or a past incident. Remember, if you lose your cool, you lose the sale.

The "Alternate of Choice" Close Revisited

Much of this has been dealing primarily with the direct or in-house salesperson who has more time and who works under different circumstances from the salesperson who is in a regular retail outlet; hence, the answers and procedures are different. There also is the factor that virtually all direct sales, whether in cosmetics, cookware, life insurance, vacuum cleaners, encyclopedias, etc., are generally sold on a one-call basis. Real estate fits into a different category.

If the prospect is in a retail store, after you have answered the objections you handle the final part in a slightly different way. You assume the close but you do so with an alternate of choice by saying—always pleasantly—"I'm delighted I was able to answer that particular question because it's our function here at ____ Company to give our customers the best possible service. I know you will enjoy this product a great deal, and of course, we're here to service it should there be any need. Now, let me ask you, would you like to take the product with you or would you prefer that we deliver it to your door [assuming it's a product the customer could take with him or merchandise that you deliver]?"

Other alternates of choice on the close: "You seem to be leaning toward the red, or do you prefer it in blue?" Yet another: "Did you want us to use your charge card or were you going to handle it by check or cash?"

The "Wheeler Which" Close

Since I referred to the "Alternate of Choice" Close earlier and will return to it again, let me point out that this close was originally identified during the 1930s by sales trainer Elmer Wheeler, who called it the "Wheeler Which." He was commissioned by the Walgreen Drug chain to help their business. In those days all drugstores had soda fountains which contributed considerably to the profit structure as well as to the flow of traffic in the store.

Malted milks, which sold for fifteen cents, were an extremely popular item in those Depression years. One of the things they added to malted milks was eggs. The price of each egg was an extra nickel, and since Walgreen's bought them for fifteen cents a dozen, the more eggs they sold in malted milks, the greater their profit structure.

When a customer ordered a malted milk, Elmer taught the clerks to hold up two eggs, smile, and ask, "One egg or two?" In the vast majority of cases, though they had not planned to order even one egg, the customers would take the easy way out and say, "One."

Walgreen's discovered that as many customers said "two" as said "none." The number of eggs they sold ran into hundreds of crates each week. The impact on their profit structure was dramatic.

Sometimes the "Alternate of Choice" involves a very simple decision which will carry a major decision. Example: In the sale of a home the real estate person can say, "One of the things I like to provide for my customers is a beautiful door knocker with your name inscribed on it. Tell me, Mr. Prospect, would you want it in Olde English, Modern American, or Corinthian Script?" Automobile salesmen, especially those who sell the luxury cars, can and *should* offer personalized monograms for the dashboard or door, using the same basic approach.

Obviously, no one buys a home or luxury automobile to get a door knocker or monogram, and no close will really work if the customer does not want to buy. What this close, as well as the other closes, does for those people who want to buy and plan to buy is simple. It gives them an additional nudge in the form of a reason or excuse to go ahead and take the action *now*. In short, a good close is designed to get a decision and get the decision in your favor. Really good closing makes every customer feel that he's *buying*, you're not *selling*. That feeling is what makes him a *permanent* customer.

The "Alternate of Choice" Close is used hundreds of times every year by *all* of us. Again, regardless of what your job or profession might be, you *sell every day*.

Parent to child: "Do you want to cut the grass or wash the windows?"

Teacher to student: "Do you want to settle for a B or would you prefer to complete the assignment?"

Physician to patient: "Would you like to live longer or keep smoking?"

Attendant to car owner: "Would you like for me to rotate the tires and give you an extra five thousand miles or leave them as they are?"

Suitor to date: "Shall I pick you up at half-past seven or would eight o'clock be better?"

Waiter to diner: "Would you like soup or salad with your dinner?"

Patrolman to speeder: "Would you like to pay the speeding ticket now or do you prefer to go to court on the first of August?"

Point: Since all of us sell every day, doesn't it make sense to learn how to do it more effectively?

Specific Objections

One question frequently asked in my personal visits with salespeople around the country and during seminars when I'm having an open discussion on objections is this one: How do you deal with a prospect who is currently buying from an old and trusted supplier who offers virtually the same product at roughly the same price, gives approximately the same service, and has the added advantage of being a friend or relative with many years experience in satisfactorily handling the account?

This is a tough one and what I'm going to say will not answer all of the objections, nor will it get the sale every time. But I am absolutely convinced it will enable you to make some of the sales and will always give you the feeling you are at least in the ball park of possibility. In short, hope is there.

When the prospect says basically the things I've mentioned above, the worst thing you can do is attack the credibility of the supplier or the quality of his product. That guarantees you will *never* make the sale, nor will you have much of a chance with a frontal assault. However, I believe the possibility for a sale is good with this next approach. It's the method discussed in two or three different sections of the book, and it involves asking a lot of questions.

The "Obligation" Close

You might convince a person with a frontal assault that you have some advantages, but the only way you are going to get his business is to *persuade* him. As previously mentioned, you persuade only by asking questions, so the prospect literally leads himself into a *yes* decision.

In this particular instance you handle it this way: "Mr. Prospect, if there were a way for you to buy the same product from your current supplier at a better price and get better service in the process, you would be interested in knowing how to do that, wouldn't you?" Wait for an answer which undoubtedly will be, "Yes, how could I do that?" You: "Before I answer, Mr. Prospect, two more questions, please. Number one, at this precise moment do you feel any obligation whatever to buy anything from me, a complete stranger whom you've never seen before?" (Wait for answer. It's going to be *no*.)

"Second question, Mr. Prospect. Do you feel any obligation or inclination to continue buying from your current supplier, who is a close friend and with whom you've been dealing for umpteen years?" (Wait for answer. It's going to be *yes* or *some*.) "Basically, Mr. Prospect, it goes without saying that your first loyalty is to yourself and your family and not necessarily what is best for any supplier. Would you agree with this premise, Mr. Prospect?" (If you can get him to agree with this, you've taken one small step toward the sale. If you can't then obviously you're not dealing with a man with an open mind.)

I'll "Try Harder"

When you get the answer you respond: "Then, Mr. Prospect, since you are not obligated to me but feel obligated to him, does it make sense that I would be willing to work harder, give you better service, and take care of the account in a more anxious-to-please manner? Doesn't it make sense that I would keep you at the top of my list of priorities so that I can earn your business in the only way open to me, which is giving you a good product at a good price with even better service?" (This kind of logic has got to hit a hot button somewhere.)

"Without being presumptuous, Mr. Prospect, would I be wrong to assume you have considerable interest in the bottom line? [Get answer.]

Then if you could get a better price, better quality, and/or better service, any one of those three things would have a direct bearing on your satisfaction and your profitability, wouldn't it? Now, Mr. Prospect, two of them would have a big bearing and three of those factors could make quite a difference in the bottom line.

"With this in mind, Mr. Prospect, and since you've already recognized your first loyalty is to yourself, don't you feel it would be in your best interests to at least give me a chance to prove I can and will give you more for your money? This way I have to *earn* the business, which automatically makes you a winner.

"Please understand, I'm not asking for all of your business. I am simply encouraging you to give me a chance to earn part of your business. You do have a lot to gain and nothing to lose.

"When you receive the shipment, you should display it in a prominent spot so your current supplier will be absolutely certain to see it. When he does, one of two things will happen: (1) He will determine in his own mind that he's got to do a better job or give you a better price in order to keep your business, or (2) you will discover we really can give you better service and/or a better price.

"Could we start you with one gross or would you go for three and the larger discount which goes with it?"

That's What Bill Said

Many years ago Bill Gove, one of my early mentors, covered a simple and effective way to handle this "I'm buying from a friend or relative" objection. However, it wasn't until John Hammond offered it as a suggestion for this book that the real impact hit me. Here it is:

"Mr. Prospect, I understand what you are saying and I can appreciate your interest in maintaining that relationship. I'm not suggesting you take business from him and give to me. However, from time to time I have ideas which I believe will increase your business, which increases the need for my products. If I share those ideas with you, which I'm willing to do, would you be willing to give me the *extra* business which my ideas generate? This way everyone wins. You continue to do business with your friend and your business increases so you and your friend both win. The increase in your business means you must buy more of the product I sell, and so I would benefit because of your increase. Does that sound like a good idea and a fair exchange, Mr. Prospect?"

The "Similar Product" Close

Occasionally a prospect will say, "Your product is just like . . ." and then name another product. When this happens, you don't disagree completely or categorically state that your product is totally different. Instead you find an area of agreement, which is easy to do. You calmly look at your prospect and say, "Yes, I agree with you there are some similarities which I believe is what you are saying, isn't it, Mr. Prospect? [Get answer.] Along these lines, let me state that the visible difference between an original Rembrandt and a reproduction or imitation is small. However, if you put the imitation and the original up for sale there would be a substantial difference in price, wouldn't there? With this in mind, Mr. Prospect, let me show you the little differences which make ours the 'Rembrandt' of the field as far as performance and quality are concerned. You do want the *best* product at the *best* price, don't you, Mr. Prospect?"

If your prospect has a good sense of humor and he states that "your product or service is just like . . ." if you're a sales*man* you go back to the "similar" approach and say, "Yes, they are similar but I might also point out that my wife and I are very similar. Each of us has two arms, two legs, and a head, but there are some intriguing differences. To tell you the truth, it's the differences which got us together and it's the differences which are keeping us together!

"It's true there are similarities in our products, but it's the differences which make our product the best buy for you." Now identify the differences, spell out *why* those differences make your product the best buy, and close by saying, "You do want the best for your money, don't you, Mr. Prospect?"

There are many objections and even more answers, but in the final analysis it boils down to this: If you are the right person selling the right product at the right price and you are convinced the customer is the big winner, then you are in the driver's seat. Now to this add the professionalism of knowing and using the right words with the right voice inflection, the right intent, and the right follow-up, and you will increase your closing percentage.

The "Right Experience" Close

Getting a job obviously involves "selling." This example of handling a major objection is primarily aimed at the teenager entering the job market, but with some variations much of it is applicable to any job applicant.

Since I have emphasized from the opening chapter that the salesperson is the most important part of the sales process, I am going to start with the basic assumption the applicant has been taught the importance of honesty, character, integrity, faith, love, and loyalty. He has also been taught to accept responsibility, to be dependable, and to have a good attitude.

Objection: "What Is Your Experience?"

The typical teenager has had no sales training, so when he is asked, "What is your experience?" he is likely to reply: "I don't really have any regular job experience. I've done some baby-sitting and looked after the neighbors' pets while they were on vacation, but this will be my first job."

A young person may think that is the only answer he can give to such an objection. And as long as he thinks that and replies in that way, he will find it very difficult to secure a job because he hasn't answered the primary objection of this would-be employer.

But the truth is, he does not have to reply as above. If he has received some sales training or attended the I CAN classes we offer in several thousand public and private schools in America, he can say:

"Thank you for asking me about my experience. I realize that's important to you. You want to know if I'm really the kind of person who can do the job so that your customers get the best possible product and service. Do I understand you correctly? [Wait for an answer.]

"Sir, I've had a lifetime of experience which will help me be a better employee. For example, I've learned the importance of being dependable and telling the truth in everything I do. In addition, I've learned the importance of getting along with other people, and I know by experience that everybody does his work better when he's getting along with others.

"I also know that certain things will be expected of me if you hire me. I expect to do the work you give me to do, with a positive attitude and in a responsible manner. I know also that if I want a raise I must be willing to come in early, work a little harder, and stay late if necessary.

"Another thing I understand is that businesses have to make a profit in order to stay in business and pay their employees. It's clear to me that if the employees do a good job, chances are excellent the company will make a profit. In order to keep my job, and get ahead in my job, I am ready to work hard and do my very best. I believe your business and every business needs that kind of experience."

You Told Your Story—Now Close the Sale

Once he has said that—and it only takes a minute or two—this "experienced" teenager can go for the close. I suggest a statement and a question:

"Sir, I need a job and I'll make you a promise. I'll work hard for you and you will never regret having hired me. In fact, you will be proud that you were the one who gave me my first job and training. I'm ready to go to work immediately or whenever it best suits your needs. When do you want me to start? Right away, or would the first of the week be better?" (Say no more. The ball is in his court.)

This "sales talk" won't guarantee a job because that company might not have an opening, but if you give that presentation enough times, I'm confident you'll get a job fairly soon.

Obviously I don't expect a teenager (scared to death) on his first job interview to calmly give that sales talk, but I do believe this: If you, as a teenage job applicant, will convey that information, I don't believe there's an employer in the country who would not be impressed. He might not hire you, but if you work hard enough to learn that presentation I believe he will do everything he can to send you to an employer who will give you a job.

I also believe if you are temporarily unemployed and there are no openings in your specialty or your field, you can use this basic approach to get a job in other fields. You do have the kind of "experience," and *lots* of it, that thousands of employers *need*. They will buy you and your experience *if* you sell yourself to them.

Like *all* other sales jobs this one might require that you make a lot of calls, but this approach will put your name at the top of a number of lists for the next job opening. If you will learn this basic approach (remember, I'm assuming you *have* the characteristics you claim in the presentation), you will be considerably more relaxed and confident going into the interview, which means you will be able to show your product (you) at your best. This fact will dramatically increase your chances of getting the job.

28

REASONS AND EXCUSES
FOR BUYING

Sell on the Tangible—
Close on the Intangible

In overcoming objections it is often necessary to offer the tangible as the *reason* for buying but emphasize the intangible as the *excuse* for buying. For example, you might be selling a beautiful lot on a lake, an outstanding retirement home, or even one of the vacation packages known as "Time Share." Each one of them definitely offers something tangible which they can put their hands on or "sink their teeth into."

However, if the lot on the lake or golf course is typical, it will sell for many thousands of dollars. From a purely logical point of view, to spend that many dollars on a parcel of land which is restricted (to put it kindly) is not really the logical thing to do. The lot is tangible, so there's the reason for buying, but if you're going to get the sale you need to switch it to the intangible, so they also have an excuse for buying.

Example: "In addition to your own beautiful lot, Mr. Prospect, you're getting this marvelous spring-fed lake, which is well stocked with bass and bream. You have the full-time use of the golf course, as well as the peaceful nature trails to either walk or cycle on as your wishes dictate. Perhaps best of all is the fact that you have the quiet serenity of being in an area with people who also wish the quietness of a semi-isolated area such as this. The restfulness and activity at your pace, away from the heat, smog, noise, congestion, and confusion which you encounter in the city, will add years to your life and more importantly, life to your years."

The "Deserve It" Close

You have now taken it from the tangible and moved it into the intangible. More appropriately you have taken a tangible base, the property itself, and given the prospect what he really wants in the package. You've given him a reason for buying (beautiful lake lot—*real* property) and an excuse for buying (gracious living, longer life, etc.).

You close the sale by saying, "All of your life, Mr. Prospect, you have worked and put much into the world and into the future. Don't you think you now *deserve* to start *enjoying* some of the fruits of all those years of labor and effort? *You owe* it to yourself to do this.

"If I'm reading your wife correctly, she is giving her permission; I'm certainly giving my permission; all that's necessary is for you to give yourself permission to enjoy what you've worked for all of your life. What about it, Mr. Prospect? You do like the property and you do enjoy both golfing and fishing, don't you? Can you really think of any reason you should deny yourself the realization of this dream for which you've worked all of your life?"

Remember—He's Scared

As you talk with your prospect, whether he's buying the lot on the lake, the retirement home, the time sharing, or anything else, you need to remember four basic things: First, he needs the reassurance that it's all right for him to take this step, that what he's buying is fairly priced, that you represent a legitimate organization, and your integrity is solid.

The second thing you need to remember is that every prospect, almost regardless of what he's buying in an area which could be defined as nonessential or even luxury, has the haunting fear that he's paying an inflated price and what he's getting is not worth the asking price. You can partially put his fears to rest by having solid evidence of comparative pricing, but ultimately his fears will be put to rest primarily because of his confidence in you as a person. *You are the bridge over which he must cross if he is to move from fearful prospect to confident buyer.*

Number three, you must remember that your prospect's sense of fairness is involved (you are the expert—he is the "innocent lamb"). Perhaps he has been taken advantage of in the past and he certainly does not want it to happen again. Sometimes fear or an unpleasant experience will cause your prospect to act in an unreasonable or antagonistic manner. This is why you, the salesperson, must keep your cool, be completely ethical, and totally believe what you're selling has real value and is fairly priced.

Number four, you must remember your prospect is not only buying for himself but he also is buying with other people in mind. He's concerned about what others will think. This is true regardless of the image he attempts to project. He's concerned about what his family, his friends, his fellow employees, and his neighbors think.

That's one of the reasons little phrases like, "You will be the envy of the neighborhood," "Your family will be proud of you for making this move," "Your fellow workers will be delighted to see you're finally going to give yourself a treat," are so effective. Just remember that there will be some who will kid him about the purchase and you need to arm him with things to say to them, or you might end up with a cancellation.

Remember—Prospect Buys Future Enjoyment

To tie these things down, just remember the prospect does not buy what it is, he buys the future enjoyment of what you're selling, regardless of the product. Remember also that he doesn't buy the house on the lot, he buys the shade of the trees in the yard; the warmth of the fireplace in the cold winter months; the convenience of the telephone in the bathroom. He buys the coolness of the evening on the lake, the exhilaration of the downhill skiing experience with his family, the joy of his motorboat on the lake, the luxury of the dip in the heated pool. Again, all of these are the intangibles made possible by the tangible property which he's buying. Now do this: *Go back four pages, underline and become especially aware of the warm selling words and word pictures I have used.*

Note: At this point you should put *Secrets* aside, pick up your steno pad (discussed on page 18), and write down the *reasons* and the excuses you can give the prospect for investing in your goods, products, or services.

Give Prospect an Excuse and a Reason

If you give a prospect a reason for buying he might buy. If you give him an excuse to buy, he might buy. But if you give him a reason and an excuse for buying, then make it easy for him to buy, your chances for a sale are dramatically increased, as the folks at A. O. Smith Harvestore will tell you.

A Team of Professionals

It's been my privilege to come to know some of the outstanding people at A. O. Smith. Their director of marketing staff services, Carl K. Clayton, is truly one of the real professionals in the world of selling. He has a missionary zeal about what they're selling and he and the professionals around him, including his boss, James Schaap, have developed the most professional agrimarketing team in America.

Before I spoke for their recent national convention, I had the privilege of spending several hours with Carl. Fortunately, I had also spent four days with him in our BORN TO WIN seminar, so my confidence in him as a man was tremendous.

That morning, however, I came to know a new side of Carl as he shared all the exciting information about their Harvestore structure and what it did for the farmer. It actually is a system which farmers use as a storage unit but which has some decided advantages over the old-fashioned silo. This unit enables the farmer to store the grain before it is completely dried.

The farmer gathers the grain from the field when the moisture content is 25–30 percent. He loads the structure with grain from the top of the Harvestore unit. The unit has a pair of "lungs" at the top. This simply means that during expansion and contraction all the outside air is out of the unit and the farmer is able to dramatically reduce spoilage. With the moisture in the grain the livestock will eat less grain, which they are able to digest more completely. This saves from 10–15 percent on the grain while increasing the meat productivity 10–15 percent. It truly is a remarkable concept which is a big dollar saver for the farmer.

The "Reason-Excuse" Close

Another tremendous benefit to the farmer is the fact that by using this system he does not have to bale his hay. He simply gathers it and puts it into this Harvestore system (I mention only one of their products). The farmer knows that having to bale hay has run more young men off the farm than any other single reason.

In the presentation to the farmer the Harvestore salesman can give him some exciting data. Number one, on the average the unit will pay for itself in reduced losses and increased productivity in seven years or less. Number two, the farmer has to work considerably less with the Harvestore system than with other systems where the farmer has to bale the hay or gather the grain after it has dried out or have it artificially dried, which is expensive and causes shrinkage.

To sum it up, they're able to sell the unit because the *excuse* they give the farmer (which he gives to his banker for the necessary financing) is that the unit literally is cost-effective and will save all that money. The excuse the farmer uses is the financial one.

Carl tells me the real *reason* most farmers buy is they've talked to Harvestore customers who testify that the work saving gives them more free time and they can even take vacations. *Best of all, the children they are raising will be far more likely to stay on the farm because it makes for a much easier and more modern operation.*

As I say, give a person a *reason* for buying and he *might* buy. Give him an excuse for buying and he *might* buy. Give him a reason *and* an excuse for buying, then make it easy for him to buy, and chances are substantially increased he will buy.

The Toughies Are the Teachers

Over the years, I suppose I have spent as much time on a sales call as most salespeople. It's not that I'm stubborn or hardheaded, though I confess to a degree of that, nor is it entirely due to the fact I'm that persistent, though I'm guilty of that, too. It's not because I'm so competitive that I just hate to miss a sale, though the Redhead would disagree with that particular statement.

There is at least one other reason I have stayed on some calls as long as I have, and that simply is because the tougher the prospect, the better the teacher. The more objections they give me which I overcome, the better able I am to handle the next sales interview. The more roadblocks which are placed in front of me the sharper I hone my skills. I feel this "firing line" training has enabled me to uncover some great sales truths which I now share with you, because I have been writing this book for thirty-six years. I needed lots of "teaching from the toughies" in order to be able to write this book.

You, too, need lots of "teaching from the toughies" if you are to grow and mature into the kind of salesperson you are capable of being. Howard Bonnell points out that often a prospect will start with an adamant "I won't even consider it" rejection. However, his next objection is weaker and subsequent objections grow progressively weaker.

When the salesman senses the prospect's will is weakening, he is encouraged and his own resolve grows stronger. I want to say again that I'm not talking about "winning" a contest and imposing the salesman's will or merchandise upon the prospect. I established in the beginning that the professional really believes he renders a service and does the prospect a favor when he sells. In my own case I can emphatically state that *the* major reason I made every legitimate effort to sell anybody anything was because I sincerely felt I was morally obligated to sell the prospect a product *which was good for him.*

There is one specific point, however, when I throw in the towel and withdraw my efforts to close. That point is when the prospect makes it clear—after seeing the benefits—that he has no interest and cannot or will not buy. Until that point, however, I am going to make an honest effort to close the sale. As I've already indicated, I do this with pleasant persuasiveness which I will deal with again in the final segment of the book.

As you move into the additional closes, which I share with you, do so in a natural manner. The close is part of the process, just as the hands and arms are a part of you. You should move into the close smoothly, naturally, and above all else, without any hesitation. You do this as you attempt to impart a sense of urgency for "action now" on the part of the prospect. Incidentally, urgency is part of all professionals' repertoire.

The doctor might well say that your gallbladder is not in the best of shape, "but there's no real emergency—yet." What you have to decide is *when* you want to have it removed. Will it be at your convenience, and according to your schedule, or according to when it ruptures and creates considerable pain and an immediate emergency?

The mechanic imparts urgency when he says the brake drums are not ruined—yet. What you need to decide is whether to spend a few dollars now for new lining and pedals and install them safely at a much lower price, or to delay and take the chance of ruining the brake drums and endangering your life. Yes, urgency is a part of the vocabulary of all professionals.

I will continue to remind you that your customers will buy from you because of anticipated future enjoyment or satisfaction. The customer who says yes certainly won't destroy your career, and the one who says no won't destroy your career. However, there are two things which *can* destroy your career: The first is the people you do not see and the second is the people who say "maybe" or "I'll think it over." With that in mind we attempt to so thoroughly cover these areas of selling throughout this book that "think it over" is changed to "sign me up."

29

USING QUESTIONS TO CLOSE THE SALE

QUESTION: How do you persuade people to take action? Answer: You persuade by asking questions which lead the prospect to a conclusion which demands that he take action because it becomes an idea which he (the prospect) originated. This is pressure which the prospect puts on himself. It's internal pressure and it's powerful.

To paraphrase Socrates—who may have said it best—"If you make a statement to which your prospect will readily agree (cannot refute), then ask a series of questions based on that agreement, and ask a concluding question based on those agreements . . . you will force the desired response." This is precisely the method used by successful trial attorneys to transfer their feelings to juries.

Selling Isn't Telling—It's Asking

The ability to ask questions—much like the ability to modulate and use your voice properly—is a skill which is badly neglected and under-developed in the world of selling. It's a skill which we as people have unlearned. I say this because the average six-year-old child, under normal circumstances, will ask something like four to seven hundred questions a day, while the average college graduate will ask approximately thirty. If you know anything at all about life or if you've been around children at all, you surely know the six-year-old child is getting more than the college graduate. Asking questions is an important skill which can be learned.

I'm going to give you a number of questions and some of the circumstances under which they can be used. Again I urge you to adapt these to your situation because all of them will not completely fit you. Nevertheless, in many cases the idea would be appropriate.

Some questions tie in with the assumptive attitude; others have to do with imagination and impending events and any number of other techniques. Example: In the showing of a home you could, after getting acquainted with the family, simply ask, as sales trainer Tom Hopkins suggests you do when you enter the living room, "Where would you place the sofa in this room?" In another room, "Where would you put Johnny's bed? Would you prefer it against the wall or more in the center of the room?" I remind you there is no way the prospect can get irritated with you at an answer he gives you. Another question: "If this beautiful home had only this gorgeous view or if the tour of the home ended with this magnificent living-den and kitchen, it's already exciting to see, isn't it?" Or, "If this house had nothing but this location it would merit consideration, wouldn't it?"

To set up a closing situation for later in the interview, sometimes you can use this as a lead-in: "Mr. Prospect, many years ago Andrew Carnegie, the man who was responsible for developing more millionaires than any man in American history, said, 'Show me a man who can make a decision, act on that decision, and stay with that decision, and I'll show you a man who will succeed.' Successful businessmen are almost unanimous in their agreement on this principle, but what's your personal feeling about this?" Most will agree.

You will use this one when you are talking with a businessman about an investment in equipment, machinery, or efficiency systems. It would not work if you were selling a young couple some furniture for which they were debating the affordability factor.

Sixteen "Question" Closes

Almost identical to a real estate situation, if you're demonstrating a computer or a piece of equipment you can ask, "If this were the only feature this machine had it would be well worth owning, wouldn't it?"

Question: "When we install this equipment, would you like for me to demonstrate the major features again?"

Question: "Would you prefer to accept delivery today or would next week fit your schedule better?"

Question: "Would you like for me to mark this one SOLD while we check on the most agreeable terms to finance it for you?"

Question: "Do you need to consult with anyone else before you place the order?"

Question: "Is the purchase order issued from this department?"

Question: "Would you like to have your own bank finance this or would you like for us to work out the financial arrangements?"

Question: "Since the item is in short supply, would you be willing to wait three weeks for delivery?"

Question: "Would you want to make a large deposit so the monthly deposits are smaller, or would you prefer a minimum deposit and slightly larger monthly deposits?"

Question: "Would you prefer this in green, or does the red appeal to you more?"

Question: "Shall we ship it by motor freight or air express?"

Question: "Do you want the lot registered in your name or your wife's name?"

Question: "Do you prefer the lot on the golf course, or does the one on the lake appeal to you most?"

Question: "If you saw that it was to your advantage to own this product and the terms we work out are satisfactory, would you have any objections to going ahead today?"

Question: "Can you see the financial advantage to reducing the use of those powerful overhead lights which provide unneeded light in some areas in favor of using point-of-impact lighting during certain times of the day?"

Question: "Do you believe it's wise to invest in solidly constructed equipment which will give you long, trouble-free operation for the lifetime of the product?"

Questions for Decisions

Many questions really are "thinking" questions and actually lead the prospect to the decision.

Mark Gardner, an assistant vice-president with E. F. Hutton, like *all* professionals, asks a lot of fact-finding and closing questions. Here are a few which are self-explanatory:

Question: "Are you investing in the stock market at the present time?"

Question: "Are you seeking capital gains or income?"

Question: "Could you give me a measure of the degree of risk you wish to take? Are you aggressive or conservative?"

Question: "What does your portfolio consist of?"

    1. Biggest winner

    2. Largest position

Question: "Please, if you will, give me an example of your last transaction? And when?"

Question: "Usually we are looking for commitments anywhere from _____ to _____. How much capital do you normally commit?"

"Mr. Prospect, I would like to make an agreement with you as one businessman to another. *First,* I'm not going to waste your time. *Second,* when we come back to you it will be with a major strategic suggestion.

For these reasons we want you to give it serious consideration for a major commitment. Now, Mr. Prospect, given all these parameters of the investment, would you be in a position to make a prompt decision?"

This series leads directly to a close:

"Of the stocks you own, do you have any that have not lived up to your expectations? How long have you held the stock? I know I am asking you to make a very difficult decision. Why have you not sold this when it hasn't performed? Why? Because:

1. There is a loss involved.

2. A common mistake by most investors is that you *hope* the stock will somehow come back.

"Wouldn't you agree with this?

"In the real world, not every situation we invest in works out. Isn't it best that we recognize it hasn't worked out, for whatever reasons, and made the decision to rectify this situation by moving out of _____ and positioning into _____?"

These Questions Close Sales

The late Charles Roth, describing how a leasing agent for swanky offices in New York City handled the question-assumption approach, gave this example. The salesman would take the prospect to a beautiful view of the Hudson River and ask, "You love this view, don't you?" The prospect would invariably answer, "Yes, it's beautiful." Then the salesman would lead him to a suite on the other side of the building and ask the question, "Do you like this view as well as the other?" The prospect either did or didn't. Assuming he didn't, the salesman would say, "Then the other suite is the one you want, isn't it?" And the sale was often closed.

The "Choice" Close

When I was in the table-appointments business, selling single girls china, flatware, and crystal, one of our most difficult and important tasks was to lead the girl in the selection of the right pattern and yet make certain it was *her* choice.

We started with china and since we had seven patterns, we handled it this way: The first pattern we offered was one we knew she would like, a "safe" pattern. Whether she necessarily loved it or not was another matter. After we'd displayed and "romanced" it, we reached for the second pattern and demonstrated it. After showing the second one we asked the girl, "Mary, if these were the only two china patterns in the whole world and you had to make your choice right now as to which one you were going to choose, which one of these two would you choose?"

After she made her choice we put the other pattern away.

We followed this procedure through to the last pattern and in most cases the final choice was relatively easy. As she chose that final pattern we gave her one more choice as the close: "Mary, would you want this in the five-piece or the seven-piece place settings?" When we got the answer we proceeded to fill out the order.

My friend Mike Ingram is president of Tufts & Son out of Oklahoma City. I laughingly refer to Mike as "America's Number One Rat Bait Salesman," because he is. Mike and his company have used a number of ideas to promote rat bait sales, but one of the things they promote with their dealers is a .22 rifle. Mike has trained his people to close the sale after explaining the promotion with this question: "Did you want the six-case promotion or would you prefer the one with nine cases and get this beautiful .22 rifle as the promotional gift?" By using this promotional procedure, Tufts & Son broke every sales record in history selling—that's right—rat bait!

Question: "Did you want this single light globe, or would you like three for the 15 percent discount?" In many cases you can move the customer to a larger order by simply asking that or a similar question. The entire questioning process is an involvement procedure, and as Harry Overstreet so eloquently expressed it, *"The very essence of all power to influence lies in getting the other person to participate."* Get 'em involved—your chances of the sale dramatically improve.

Question: "If I show you something that could save you or your firm a great deal of money, are you in a position to act on it now?"

Incidentally, one question you *don't* ask a prospect is, "What do you think about this?" As I said earlier, the "thinking" brain is only 10 percent as large as the "feeling" brain and people generally do not buy logically. They buy emotionally. They buy what they want and not necessarily what they need. Ask, "How do you *feel* about this?" and you've got an infinitely better chance to make the sale.

The "Tie Down" Close Revisited

The late Doug Edwards perfected and taught the following technique, which he called the "Tie Down." He used it with great effectiveness. Frequently a customer will ask a question such as, "Does this come in green?" If you say yes, you still are no closer to the sale. If he asks, "Does this come in green?" you ask him a question: "Do you want it if it comes in green?" When he responds to that question—he's bought. You nail it down with, "We can have it for you in three weeks, or would you prefer that I put a rush on it so you can have it in just two weeks?"

If he asks you, "Do the draperies come with the house?" you ask, "Do you want it if the draperies come with the house?" Or, "Will you take it if I can make arrangements for the draperies to come with the house?" You're tying him down with that question. Doug would automatically or instinctively end his questions or statements with a tie-down such as: "This is beautiful in red, *isn't it?*" "The added weight gives much greater comfort, *doesn't it?*" "The extra horsepower is a real bonus, *isn't it?*" "This extra economy will steamroll the competition, *won't it?*" "The additional color gives it an added dimension, *doesn't it?*" "This evening view should give you a lot of beautiful memories, *shouldn't it?*" Each tie-down is emotionally committing the prospect to taking action on your offer, and when you wrap your offer in an obligating question, the sale is more probable than possible. (Your next reading of *Secrets* will make you even more aware of the tie-downs I've used throughout the book, won't it?)

Of special importance in the tie-down procedure is the fact that you should use contractions to emphasize certain points. Sales trainer Phil Lynch says you should avoid the use of *not* at all costs. Use *isn't, shouldn't, wouldn't, can't, couldn't, doesn't, won't,* etc. Avoid *is not, should not, would not, cannot, could not, does not, will not,* etc.

Now you go to work and start developing specific questions for your product and customers. Remember: The *professional* salesperson *works* at learning how to be more professional. It is not easy—but the psychic satisfaction *and* financial rewards are enormous.

The "Permanent Customer" Close

If you sell in a furniture store, a clothing store, or in any kind of retail outlet where customers come in and say, "I'd like to see a suit," you smile and say, "With pleasure, men's suits are over here." Start in that direction, take about a half-dozen steps, turn and say, "It will be helpful if I know whether this suit is for a special occasion, or would you like for it to blend with the rest of your wardrobe so that you can get maximum mileage out of your clothing dollars?"

This approach not only helps you make the immediate sale but it also plants the suggestion that you are capable of and interested in helping him solve any future wardrobe problems. You are displaying a strong professional approach and a sincere interest in being a problem solver. Your initial question is the opening to the "Permanent Customer" close.

An almost identical approach is effective in most retail outlets (furniture stores, specialty shops, general merchandisers, etc.). In a furniture store the prospect might come in and express an interest in a lamp, rug, or sofa. You smile and say, "I'll be pleased to help you; they are right over here." You start in that direction as you say, "By the way, did you want this as an individual item or did you want it to blend with the rest of your decor so you get maximum mileage from your furniture dollars?" This procedure leads your prospect to make a decision of more significance than just the momentary one of buying the particular item he asked about.

I deal with and use questions in every segment of *Secrets of Closing the Sale. There is no doubt in my mind that your career as a salesperson will move forward faster as a direct result of learning how to ask questions and how to use the proper voice inflection than from any other skills you might develop.*

Most salespeople know the importance of asking questions, but too many of them make a couple of serious mistakes in the questioning process. First of all, they take the "police investigator" approach and are a little too aggressive and assertive. The salesman's attitude is critical. He must remember the service attitude is the one to take. He should never ask the first question without getting permission. You get permission this way: "Mr. Prospect, in order for me to determine how we might be able to help you, I need to ask you a few questions. Do you mind if I ask them now?" This procedure not only gets the positive response but it also tells the prospect *why* you are going to ask the questions. This clears the way for asking the questions and subconsciously obligates the prospect to answer them.

30

FOR DIRECT
SALES PEOPLE

THIS CHAPTER IS PRIMARILY aimed at those who are in the world of direct selling. However, I encourage you, regardless of what you do or sell, to read these next few pages at least once because the odds are good you will get some ideas or techniques which you can adapt to fit your specific situation.

Know What to Do—Do What You Know

Many years ago, so the story goes, a fox and a rabbit were having a "cool one" in the local pub. Talk turned to their common enemy, the hounds of the local hunters. The fox rather boastfully stated he held no fear of them because he had so many means of escape. He pointed out that if the hounds should come he could bolt up into the attic and hide until the danger was safely past, or quick as a flash he could run out the door and no hound alive could catch him. He could head for the nearest stream and run in it for a spell until the hounds completely lost track of him. He could even go in circles and backtrack a few times and so completely confuse the hounds that he could then climb a tree and watch them in their quandary as they sought to find where he was. Yes, his methods were many and his confidence was high.

On the other hand, the rabbit rather timidly and with some embarrassment confessed that if the hounds should come he knew only one thing to do, and that was to run like a "scared rabbit."

As he said those words, they heard the baying of the hounds. The rabbit, true to his word, hopped up and ran out the door like a scared rabbit. The fox hesitated as he debated whether or not to bolt up into the attic and hide, dart out the door and depend on his speed to get away, head for the stream and lose the scent in the water, or take off and confuse the hounds with backtracking and circling before he climbed the tree. As he debated which method to use, the hounds rushed in and ate him.

The moral to the story is fairly simple. It's better to use one effective procedure or close if that's all you know than it is to know *all* the techniques in this book and not use any of them.

Secrets of Closing the Sale includes an extremely large number of closes and procedures for several reasons. For one thing, people who sell—and the products they sell—come from all over the board. Every conceivable kind of person with every imaginable personality sells an incredible assortment of goods and services. Obviously, I can't deal with all of them, but the techniques and principles covered in this book are quite broad in scope and yet specific in objective. Much of what I have written is designed to help salespeople from all walks of life be more professional and successful. Many different approaches are taken because there are many, many different kinds of salespeople selling to an even wider range of prospects.

One thing you have probably noticed is that most of the closes and procedures used in *Secrets of Closing the Sale* are educational. Remember, the prospect will generally say no when he doesn't know enough to say yes, so we need to give additional information containing reasons (logical or emotional) as to why the prospect should, in his own interests, say yes. In the process we need to remember, as Gerard I. Nierenberg said in an interview published in *Personal Selling Power*, "Customers want to learn but they resist being taught."

Since you've come this far in the book, I have every reason to believe you have already learned and are *using* the closes and techniques we've already covered. I also believe you are just as excited about learning *and* applying the procedures and techniques we will cover in the remainder of the book.

Here's a Good Old "Oldie"

This particular close is used primarily by direct sales people, but with certain variations it can also be used for automotive, real estate, appliance, or major-purchase items in department and specialty stores. It is to be used *after* value has been established, but before *all* the information about your product has been given to the prospect. (Don't spill your popcorn in the lobby before the movie starts.) There are several facets to this close.

To begin with, it is educational since it discloses all the details of the transaction. It's another one of the "oldies" which is old because it's good. It works. If it didn't work, it would be dead. When I entered the world of selling it was known as the "Granddaddy" Close. Some sales trainers refer to it as the "Order Book" Close, while others call it the "Basic" Close.

The close is old but Gene Montrose, a sales trainer from Portland, Oregon, renamed it the "Disclosure" Close, and as I "disclose" it to you it will be apparent why this is a much better name.

The "Disclosure" Close

Once the value has been established and the salesperson moves into the close, he does it with these words: "Mr. and Mrs. Prospect, as you know, Uncle Sam is now involved in many facets of our lives. Some of his involvements are good and some of them are not so good. One of his laws which I believe is a good one is the requirement that companies must disclose to each buyer all the details of the transaction. This way there can be no hidden costs. Ethical salespeople and companies applaud this particular law.

"Our company, Mr. and Mrs. Prospect, goes the government one step better by requiring *all* our salespeople to disclose *all* the information— not only on every sale but on every offer for sale as well. That way there can be no confusion in anyone's mind as to what we are offering and what the costs are. Also, if you should discuss our offer with one of your neighbors, you will find the offer we make you is identical to the one we make to your neighbor. It will undoubtedly please you to know you're dealing with a company that is fair and open with everyone."

(Now if you will reread the last paragraph you will note I told him we "disclose" all the information concerning our offer to everyone. Translation: "I am now going to write your order.")

To the Order Form

"The order which you and I have discussed, Mr. Prospect, is number eighty-seven. [At this point your order form is in plain view and on an appropriate portion you write #87.] The investment for this order is three ninety-nine ninety-five. [I say it that way and I do not put a dollar sign by the figure. Not earth-shattering, but it is one of those "little" things which make a difference.] Shipping and handling is twenty, which brings us to a total of four nineteen ninety-five. The government charges us for all their good help, so the tax comes to twenty, for a grand total of four thirty-nine ninety-five."

At this point the prospect will often grow concerned and say, "Now wait a minute, I didn't say I was going to buy anything!" At this or a similar comment you can legitimately respond, "Well of course not. As I explained, I simply want you to see the exact terms of the offer we're making. Personally, Mr. Prospect, I believe you are the kind of person who would never say either yes or no to anything until you knew what you were saying yes or no to. Isn't that right, Mr. Prospect?"

Here's Voice Inflection Again

(It's tough to predict what prospects are going to say unless you're in a training room and role-playing, but generally speaking they will agree with that premise.) You continue by saying, "By the way, Mr. Prospect, *if* [and you really emphasize with strong voice inflection the word *if*] you were to consider this program, would it be more convenient to handle it on our twenty dollars per month investment program, or do you generally handle amounts like this on a sixty-day cash plan?" (Wait for answer.)

In many, many cases he will say, "Well, if—and I did say *if*—I were to buy this, I would put it on the twenty dollars per month program." To this you respond, "Oh, one thing I neglected to mention, Mr. Prospect, is that with this order you're given a choice of the knife sharpener or the floor polisher. [You just moved into the "Alternate of Choice" Close.] Or you can choose between the flatware and the stoneware."

For those companies who do not offer extra merchandise as "buy now" incentives, you still have the "Alternate of Choice." "I neglected to mention this, Mr. Prospect, but this is available either in two-tone brown or solid gray. Which *would* you prefer?" This time the strength of your voice inflection is on the word *would*.

I can personally tell you that in many cases the prospect will say, "Well, if I were going to get it, I would prefer the solid gray." You write the word *gray* on the order form and say to the prospect, "In [and you mildly emphasize the word *in*] getting this, would it make any difference whether the deposits fell on the first or the fifteenth, or would the twenty-fifth be better?"

Again, right out of the book. I cannot tell you how many times I have had the prospect say, "Well, I don't really suppose it makes a lot of difference, but why don't we make it the twenty-fifth?" At this point, for the first time, I personalize the order by asking, "This *is* Mr. J. J. Johnston, isn't it?" and I proceed to finish writing the order.

The "Minor Decision" Close

There are several factors here. Number one, when you move into the "Alternate of Choice," you are getting the prospect to make a minor decision which often will carry the major decision. Number two, *even if the prospect does not buy at this time, your efforts are still significant because you have now educated him by clarifying the order, the terms, and the options available.*

This is important because the prospect needs this information before he can make an intelligent or even comfortable decision. The clarification process gives the prospect confidence he at least knows what he is making his decision to do. Yes, clarification gives confidence.

Also, many times a prospect needs "soaking time." On many occasions I've missed the sale at this point but later, as I was elaborating on other features, the prospect would come back and ask a question relating to the "disclosure" close: "Were those payments for twenty months or eighteen months?" "How long will it take for delivery?" "Suppose I set it up on the monthly program and then elect to pay it off. What's the penalty?" Many times the prospect says no at this stage of the game, but after some "soaking time" and additional information he makes a new *yes* decision.

He's Balancing the Budget

On numerous occasions I have been explaining additional features and the prospect was not hearing a word. He was thinking about other payments which would soon be finished and then he could handle this new payment. That's one of the reasons the disclosure close needs to be used fairly soon *after* you have given the prospect enough reasons to justify a purchase. This close clarifies the prospect's thinking and gives him the solid, basic information for making the decision he needs to make. It *is not* designed to manipulate anyone into buying something he does not need, does not want, or cannot afford. It *is* effective when dealing with legitimate prospects who are hesitant and need a little gentle persuasion to act in their own best interests.

The "Tennis Racket" Close

I'm confident I am accurate with the statement that every veteran salesman has completed a presentation to a husband/wife team only to be confronted with this dialogue: Husband: "What do you think, honey?" Wife: "Well, that's entirely up to you." Husband: "No, you'd be the one to use it." Wife: "Yeah, but you'd be the one to pay for it," and he says . . . and she says . . . and he says . . . and back and forth it goes.

When this happens, you can rest assured that one of three situations exists. Number one, both of them want to say yes; number two, neither of them wants to say yes; or number three, one votes yes and one votes no. However, you can be even more certain that neither one of them wants to make the decision. Each one keeps knocking the ball back to the other one's court by saying, "You make the decision."

Since they are knocking the ball back and forth across the net, we call this one "The Tennis Racket" Close. It's important you understand that if you just sit on the sidelines and watch the "game" and permit them to knock that ball across the net more than a couple of times, one of them (and most of the time it's the husband) will smile and say, "I know we're going to buy your product, but unfortunately, *she* can't make up *her* mind." (As Tennessee Ernie Ford would say, "Bless his little pea-pickin' heart!")

Handle It This Way

Here's how you avoid that situation. After the couple has knocked that decision ball back and forth across the net a couple of times, hold up your hand and say, "Scuse me." (In some sections of the country where people have peculiar accents, they might say "Ex-cuse me," but that is wrong. Yes, for those of you who take everything literally, my tongue *is* in my cheek!) "Maybe I should not say this, but I will. At this point I do not think that either of you folks should make the decision. Now before you think I'm presumptuous, let me explain. At the moment both of you are emotionally involved, and that is the worst possible time to make decisions.

"The reason is simple. If you say yes, sometime later one of you might well say, 'Well, I tried to get you not to buy that thing!' If you say no, sometime later one of you might say, 'If you remember, I tried to get you to go ahead.' Regardless of whether you say yes or no, because of the emotional involvement it could be the wrong decision."

The "Ben Franklin" Close

I include this close in the chapter primarily designed for direct sales people, but to be candid I cannot think of a single sales situation—and very few situations in life—where this approach would not be practical. I challenge you to put your imagination to work on this one and use it in your life. When you are choosing a house, car, job, school, vacation site, church, or anything else, this approach can be extremely helpful. With this lead-in, do I need to remind you that your prospect will also find it helpful in making the right decision? I have no idea where this close was born or who originated it, but my friend Bill Cranford taught it to me in 1947. Now, on with the close.

"Instead of handling the decision emotionally, let me suggest we borrow a page from the life of one of the wisest men our country ever produced. His name was Benjamin Franklin. When he was confronted with a difficult decision, he would take a sheet of paper and draw a line down the center. On the left-hand side he wrote "Reasons For," and on the right-hand side he wrote 'Ideas Opposed.' (This was altered slightly by the late Percy Whiting, author of *The Five Great Rules of Selling.*)

"What I suggest, Mr. Prospect, is that we follow the same procedure, which in its simplest form is to look at the facts for and against the purchase and then let the *facts* make the decision. By following that procedure, folks, *neither* one of you can be wrong and regardless of what you decide, you *both* will be right. Does that idea appeal to you, Mr. and Mrs. Prospect?" (You can depend on it—it does!)

Here's Why You Should Go Ahead

(At this point you take your talking pad and draw a line down the middle and print "Reasons For" on the top left side and "Ideas Opposed" on the top right side.) "There are many reasons you should go ahead."

You say, "Number one, *you like it.*" However, you don't number the reasons for or against the purchase until you sum them up. You do not number the "Reasons For" because it provokes a numbers contest between "Reasons For" and "Ideas Opposed." The prospect might con-

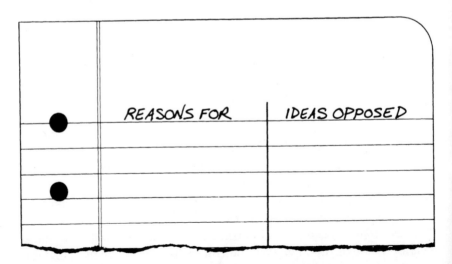

strue this as a challenge to try to come up with more reasons against. Some of the "Ideas Opposed" could be utterly ridiculous, but their very mention creates a ludicrous and therefore potentially losing situation, regardless of which side has the largest number of reasons.

You make "You like it" number one because people buy what they want—not necessarily what they need. "Number two [remember, you say number two, but you don't write the number], you stated you feel our product will *save money*." (Continue this process as you list all the reasons *for* buying.)

Now you go to the "Ideas Opposed." You start this list by saying, "One of the reasons you should not buy today is . . ." (now you list the major objection they have harped on during the presentation). You need to bring out the dominant reason or objection they have been giving you. If you don't, they will—and it removes some of the sting if *you* bring it out. Then you keep quiet and let your prospect list the other reasons why not. If you've done your job, you will have far more *yes* reasons than they will have *no* reasons.

You Assume *the Sale*

Now you add the totals as you say, "Let's see, that's one, two, three," etc. Write the number in a large, bold figure (let's say it's ten) and circle it several times. "The 'Ideas Opposed' are one, two, three," etc. Write the number for the total (let's say it's seven) and circle it several times. At that point, according to Percy Whiting, you turn the pad toward the prospect and ask, "Mr. Prospect, which of these weigh heaviest? The 'Reasons For' going ahead or the 'Ideas Opposed'?" (Let him answer.)

At this point, as the late Charlie Cullen would say, you add a little audacity as you look up from your talking pad and into your prospect's eyes, stick out your hand, and say, "You know, Mr. Prospect, if all the people I deal with used such a logical, commonsense approach to making decisions, my business would be even more fun than it is! You're going to love this product!"

Many times salesmen ask, "Zig, does that kind of stuff really work?" The answer is, "No, not all the time. But it will work *some* of the time." That's the prime reason the presentation or conviction part of the sales process should start with the strongest benefit and end with the second-strongest benefit. This is important because, as we stated earlier, the prospect is more likely to remember what you said and did as you opened and closed your presentation.

A couple of pertinent observations are in order. Number one, the prospect can come up with just one reason why not and still say, "I'm not going to get it, I don't care how many reasons 'for' you've got!" Number two, prospects don't buy anything for ten reasons. In most cases, they buy for one major reason and one minor reason.

This Sells the Kinsfolk, Too

The reason you make the list is so the prospect can see the logic of the concept. This could have a bearing. Also, many times when people buy they need reinforcement, so when they discuss their purchase with husbands, wives, relatives, friends, etc., they have some additional facts to give them. Many people happily buy and then later cancel because their acquaintances either kid or ridicule them for having made what they consider a poor decision. This process of listing these reasons in this "Benjamin Franklin" Close not only helps to make the sale but many times it helps to keep the sale.

Because of this I encourage you to follow the process. Later I cover what I call "emotional logic," and will give you more of the reasons why. I strongly encourage you to use it.

Every close should be an educational process, and although this one does not give any new reasons for buying, it does sum up the ones previously covered. This helps to reassure the prospect and give him added confidence that his new decision (in the event he earlier had said no) is the right decision.

There are two other important factors. First, a prospect can be given all the facts concerning goods, products, or services and still miss the major point. Second, a prospect can get all the facts and still make the wrong decision. The "Ben Franklin" Close helps to make certain the prospect doesn't miss the major point, and the summation process further reduces the chances of the prospect's making the wrong decision.

The "Pedestal" Close

This is one you use in a husband/wife situation when the wife rather forcefully speaks up during part of the demonstration or close and says, "We can't afford it!" When this happens, generally speaking one of two situations exists. She either rules the roost (or as we would say down home, she wears the pants in the family), or she is at the other end of the scale and is completely dominated by the husband.

If hers is the latter situation, she makes the statement for point-scoring and/or self-sacrificing purposes. She is trying to curry favor with her husband by showing him she is willing to "give up" something which he might think she wants in order to gain future favors and benefits which would be worth more to her.

In either event, if you're going to get the sale you're going to have to put her on a pedestal for her husband to see and so you can deal with her from a more advantageous position.

When she says, "We can't afford it," you smile as you turn to the husband and say, "You know, Mr. Prospect, it always excites me when I hear a wife make that kind of statement. I say this because I believe she made that statement because she's afraid you might buy this just *for her*. Frankly, Mr. Prospect, I don't believe your wife wants this product just for herself. It's refreshing to know there are folks like your wife in our country, isn't it? [What can the man say but something nice?] You, Mr. Prospect, are certainly fortunate to find such an unselfish helpmate. Of course she's fortunate, too, because I'm going to bet you're the kind of man who is going to express your appreciation for having such a special wife in a very real and concrete way."

The "Right" Words Plus Good Voice Inflection—Sale

Let's pause now and look at the position in which you have placed both of them. First, you have placed her on a pedestal. From here on in, that lady is going to think you're a very astute salesman. She will be willing to listen to you because you make sense and most importantly, you have made her feel important. You're in pretty good shape with the husband, too, because not only have you challenged him to be his best self by supplying his wife with a want/need but you've also complimented him.

With this thought in mind, you continue the sales process. "Actually, Mr. and Mrs. Prospect, nobody is making any kind of sacrifice for anybody, because even though the wife might be the one to use the product, everyone in the family is going to benefit and it is the entire family we're concerned about, isn't it?

"Yes, Mr. Prospect, it's obvious that your wife wants the product [Now here are the key words. Lower your voice, look the husband in the eye and say], but worse than she *wants* it, *she* wants *you* to *want* her to have it. Isn't that right, Mrs. Prospect?"

I can't tell you the number of times I've had the lady say, "Well, yeah, it would be nice to have," and then before she can say anything else, I offer a handshake to the husband and say, "Mr. Prospect, I'd like to congratulate you twice—first for having married this kind of lady and second for being the kind of man who expresses his appreciation in a very positive way. You are going to love this product!"

Does That Stuff Really Work?

The answer is yes, these procedures work—some of the time. Remember, too, that each close you use gives your prospect another chance to go ahead and make a *new* decision. He now has more facts for a new decision or more emotional involvement, which means the prospect is exerting inner pressure on himself to buy.

I remind you, too, that each close should be a process which raises the value of the product or service in the prospect's mind. Obviously, if you keep raising that value in the prospect's mind, if you know *and* use enough emotional and/or educational closes, you will eventually have value higher than the price, and therefore *theoretically* you will always make the sale.

That is actually what would *always* happen *if* your prospect were a computer. Obviously he is a person and not a computer. So much for the theory. *But* this I promise. The closing procedures I'm describing will increase your closing percentage and in many cases that increase will be substantial. Remember, too, if you are strictly on commission, each 1 percent in increased closing effectiveness will increase your *net* income from 2 to 10 percent, because your costs remain almost exactly the same.

The "Hat in Hand" Close

Many times in the sales world, try as you might, you will be unable to "smoke out" the real reason the prospect is not buying. It's frustrating to sense the presence of a sale and yet miss it because the prospect won't level with you. There is obviously a limit as to how far you can go with a prospect before you not only cause him to not buy but permanently lose any chance of at least having him as a future customer. When it becomes obvious that you are backing up and your probing, persistence, and questioning approach is not producing results, the "Hat in Hand" approach has been known to work. I learned the basic procedure from Bill Cranford, my first sales trainer. Later, Doug Edwards and Dick Gardner added the refining touches. Here's the way it works.

When it is clear you have missed the sale, you "fold your tent" by putting your samples or your papers into your briefcase. In yesteryear all salespeople wore hats so the name "Hat in Hand" Close was born in those days. Today some sales trainers call it the "Lost Sale" Close. As you pack your papers, giving every indication of leaving, you express your appreciation to the prospect for his time and express the hope that at some future date you will be able to do business with him. You get up to leave and as you head for the door, you turn to the prospect and say, "Mr. Prospect, I'm embarrassed to ask you this, but it would mean a lot to my career if you would help me by answering a question [an amazing number of people are willing to help and will indicate this willingness]." You then say, "Obviously, you have not done any business with us today and that's all right. I certainly don't sell everybody. I had hoped you would buy because I thought our product fit your needs. However, you have chosen not to buy and I feel badly about it because I did not explain it thoroughly enough to make the benefits more obvious. It would really be helpful to me, as I call on other people, if you would identify the mistakes I made and where I dropped the ball as a salesman."

You will get an amazing number of answers, but in most cases they will say, "It wasn't your fault at all. We didn't buy because . . ." and at this point they will bring up the real reason. When this happens, you clap your hands or snap your fingers and say, "Oh, boy! Did I ever blow it! No wonder you hesitated to act until now! Had I been in your shoes, I would have done exactly the same thing. How could I have made such a mistake?"

You quickly open your briefcase, give him the answer to the objection, and close by asking if this makes the difference in his decision. This doesn't happen often, but from personal experience I can tell you there is the occasional sale which can be gained with this method. When it happens, it's a total bonus because it was a sale which, for all practical purposes, had been completely lost.

Two things I emphasize: First, make it extremely brief and if you don't *immediately* get the order it's time to graciously make your departure. Second point: If you *truly believe* you and your product can serve the prospect, then you really are acting in his best interests. This procedure requires a degree of audacity or boldness, but *one way to be an "old" salesman instead of an "ex" salesman is to be a bold salesman.*

Suppose the Prospect Says Nothing

From time to time a sales situation arises which can be frustrating and difficult. The salesperson asks an obligating question and the prospect says absolutely nothing. It might have happened to you and if it hasn't, I can assure you that your day is coming.

After asking the obligating question, you sit there and say nothing. He sits there and says nothing. In short, nobody says anything. Years ago there was a school of thought which taught that the one who spoke first was going to lose. Fifteen or twenty years ago that might have been true, but today, with one exception, which I cover in chapter 35, that is generally not true. Here's why:

Number one, the buyers of today are more knowledgeable and sophisticated. Number two, the ask-the-obligating-question-and-keep-your-mouth-shut approach has been around so long that many prospects are aware of it. Number three, there is a good chance the prospect wasn't listening or didn't clearly understand the question. He might have been thinking about other things and suddenly realized you were quiet and wondered why. The fourth reason it might not be sound is that the prospect might feel you are using pressure and he might resent it. Fifth, the prospect might know exactly what you are doing and decide to "wait you out." That could be time-consuming.

The "Mother" Close

Here is a better approach. When you ask the obligating question and get no response, wait a reasonable length of time. How long is that? I have no idea because it will vary. Experience and your commonsense feeling will dictate the length of time but it will generally be from ten to sixty seconds. However, I can tell you this: When you see the red start up the prospect's neck, before it gets to his earlobes it's time for you to say something. Look him in the eye, smile, and say, "Mr. Prospect, when I was a little fellow [or a little girl], my mother told me silence gave consent. Mr. Prospect, do you think my mother was telling me the truth?"

This breaks the silence and puts the ball back in the prospect's court. The question is, what is the prospect going to do? I don't think he will say, "No, your mother was a liar!" You might wonder if this is "pressure selling." Could be—but its primary purpose is to help the prospect put pressure on himself. The next story will be helpful in further clarifying the point while teaching you how to get permission from the prospect to help him apply that pressure to himself.

The Chuck Adkins Story

From time to time, despite our preconceived ideas, pet formulas, and set approaches, along comes an individual who upsets all our theories and ideas. Chuck Adkins was such a man. Chuck didn't "look like" a salesman. He could shave and twenty minutes later look like he needed to shave again. He was not a fat man, but he had an extremely large stomach which hung well over his belt. He wore loafers which had never seen the soft side of a brush or shine cloth. Stealing a line from the old Pepsodent toothpaste commercial, you didn't "wonder where the yellow went" when you saw Chuck smile.

He should never have been hired, because he didn't have a car and he didn't "fit" with the rest of the salespeople. However, he did have a bicycle and the six-dollar bond fee. Considerably more important, Chuck represented a promotion for an ambitious young dealer.

The rules were clear that you had to have five people in production to qualify, and the young man had four and needed only one more. Chuck was given a contract with the full expectation that he would be in and out of the business in about three days. However, Chuck fooled us all. Not only did he stay but in short order he was the leader among the five. Then he quickly became the leader in the entire area, then number one in the state, number one in the entire South, and number seven in the nation.

Despite his physical appearance (actually he "cleaned up" pretty good), Chuck was a hard worker and had this "difficult to put your finger on" quality called "charm." I watched the growth of Chuck strictly through the reports and through phone conversations with his manager. When he took over as the number-one man in the South, I decided it was time to go see what he was doing. By then Chuck had moved to Georgetown, South Carolina, and was working for a dealership promotion himself.

I arrived in Georgetown bright and early Monday morning so I could watch him handle all phases of the business. I observed how he booked demonstrations. I observed him putting on a demonstration, and I watched him closing sales. I tell Chuck's story because there are three lessons which will help all of us be more productive in our chosen field. I'll get to those lessons in a moment.

Never will I forget the demonstration I viewed that evening. Chuck and his helper cooked a full-demonstration meal for several couples. Personally, I was embarrassed to be there. Never have I seen such a messy, sloppy demonstration. I was delighted that I did not have to eat any of the food. Nevertheless, the couples seemed to enjoy themselves, and Chuck did a good job of getting his points across. When the demonstration was over, he made appointments with the couples who had been invited and, when they had made their departure, Chuck sat down to close the sale with the host and hostess.

On the surface, Chuck was friendly, jovial, easygoing, and apparently even lackadaisical in his approach to life in general and business in particular. However, when it came time to close the sale, Chuck went straight for the jugular. I was really amazed that I had worked with the man all day and had not seen even a hint of this "killer instinct" which leaped to the surface. He really sat on the host and hostess and in the process threw common sense and judgment out the window. As a net result, after a few minutes the host almost literally exploded as he slapped his hand down on the table, hopped up, and with considerable heat, proceeded to tell Chuck he did not respond to any such "high pressure tactics," and he would never buy from any high-pressure salesman.

The "Pressure Permission" Close

As I sat there in some amusement, some fright, and some embarrassment, I wondered how Chuck was going to extricate himself from this situation. In my mind there was no way Chuck could do anything other than save his hide. The possibility of a sale was so remote that it was—to my way of thinking—nonexistent.

What happened next was something I'll never forget. Chuck remained as cool as anyone I've ever seen in my life. He simply sat there with a stunned look on his face. Then he slowly shook his head from side to side. Halfway talking to himself and halfway talking to me and the prospect, he said, "Mr. Prospect, I wouldn't have had this happen for anything in the world! I am terribly, terribly embarrassed. Mr. Zig [that's what he called me] is my boss, and I'm afraid he's going to think that I am a high-pressure salesman like you say I am. Actually, Mr. Prospect, I hate high-pressure salesmen worse than you do and if you thought I was using pressure on you, I don't blame you a bit for getting upset. I would have done exactly the same thing. I especially hate it because here I am, a guest in your home, and you were kind enough to invite in your friends and neighbors to see a demonstration as a favor to me, so I am just terribly, terribly sorry and embarrassed about the whole thing. I don't in the least blame you for getting upset, because if I thought somebody was using high pressure on me, I would get upset, too."

This little speech probably took about two minutes, but Chuck's calm manner and sincerity—combined with the fact that he had kept his seat—worked miracles on the prospect. After a moment or two, he sat back down and Chuck asked, "Mr. Prospect, will you accept my apology and can we still be friends?" With that, the old farmer smiled and said, "Well, I don't guess there's any harm done," and with that

Chuck extended his hand and the two men shook on the friendship agreement.

What happened next is one of those things which you see and hear—and please believe me when I say I was *all* eyes and ears—but even after you see it and hear it you ask yourself, "Did I really see and hear what I saw and heard?" At this point Chuck said, "Mr. Prospect, I guess I just got carried away, but would you mind if I asked you a question?" Prospect: "No, go ahead." Chuck: "Mr. Prospect, if I saw that you were about to make a mistake which would cost you money and cause your wife to do a lot of extra and unnecessary work, would you appreciate it if I told you about it or would you just figure it was none of my business?" Prospect: "If you saw me about to make a serious financial mistake which would also cause my wife to do extra work, I'd want you to let me know about it."

At that point Chuck gave him the big ol' Pepsodent grin and, with the innocence of a newborn babe said, "Well, Mr. Prospect, that's exactly what I was trying to do—and you got upset with me. Now, I'm willing to try it one more time if you'll promise me you won't get upset with me." To my utter astonishment, the man promised to keep his cool and Chuck proceeded to close that sale.

In reflecting on the situation, Chuck Adkins, this man who was functionally illiterate, had taught me an important sales lesson. He had literally asked for permission to apply pressure to the prospect—and the prospect had willingly granted that permission. The question "Mr. Prospect, if I saw that you were about to make a serious mistake which would cost you lots of money and cause your wife to do unnecessary work, would you appreciate it if I told you about it, or would you figure it was none of my business?" asked for permission to use pressure. It worked. Chuck made the sale.

The second great lesson I learned from Chuck Adkins was the importance of positive expectancy when you deal with *every* prospect. As I've indicated, Chuck's education was limited. He could fill out an order if the customer gave the standard order with standard payments. If the customer substituted a coffee maker for a juicer, bought an extra utility pan, changed the payments in any way, or made any other changes which were not precisely detailed in the chart, then Chuck was lost. Fully one-third of the orders Chuck sent us did not have a total as far as the size of the sale was concerned. Chuck handled those orders this way.

"Mr. Prospect, I don't know exactly what your total is, but it's about $_____, so just go ahead and give me forty dollars as the deposit and Mr.

Zig will figure out the exact amount of the order." Incredibly enough, virtually no one ever argued with or questioned Chuck. They gave him the money and Chuck wrote the order because Chuck *expected* the customer to give him the order.

The third great lesson Chuck taught me was that *all* of us can learn valuable lessons and techniques from some unlikely people. The fact that Chuck taught how to get permission to use a little pressure does not mean that Chuck knew *more* about selling than you and I know. It does mean that Chuck knew at least *one* technique which was new to me.

Message: Learn whenever and wherever lessons are being taught.

PART SIX

THE KEYS IN CLOSING

Objectives

To sell you a philosophy as it specifically relates to the world of selling and to give you the keys in closing or persuading.

To share additional ideas, methods, techniques, and procedures which will increase your sales effectiveness on a daily basis and enhance your career for a lifetime.

Closes and/or Procedures

The "Sure Sale" Close
The "Neiman-Marcus" Close
The "Assumptive" Close Revisited
The "Kreepy Krauly" Close
The "Smell Good" Close
The "Proper Dress" Close
The "Look and Listen" Close
The "Enthusiasm" Close
The "Presidential" Close
The "Three Question" Close
The "Greatest Salesman" Close

The "Dinner Out" Close
The "Hep 'Em Git It" Close
The "Impending Event" Close
The "Pressure Belief" Close
The "I Can Get 'Em" Close
The "I'll Treat You Right" Close
The "And Then Some" Close
The "Integrity" Close
The "Final" Close
The "Signature" Close
The "Narrative" Close

31

FOUR IDEAS AND A KEY TO SALES SUCCESS

I START THIS FINAL SEGMENT with four ideas which you need to buy.

First Idea: There is not now, there never has been, and there never will be an outstanding salesperson, one who climbs to the top, one who breaks the records and sells more than anyone else, there's never been a real sales champion who was "normal." In every single case they are a little bit "warped" in their belief in what they are selling.

It is beyond their wildest imagination to be able to begin to understand how anybody could possibly even remotely entertain the idea of thinking about saying no. Because they feel this strongly about what they sell, by the very force of their convictions, by the depth of their belief, by their enthusiasm, they are able to persuade many people who are not really hot prospects to go ahead and buy.

However, despite all their zeal, enthusiasm, and belief, they inevitably will encounter that stubborn, hardheaded, nonbelieving individual who is still going to say no. When this happens it could create a problem in the mind of the salesperson. His belief in what he sells is so deep, he rationalizes that no prospect would say no if he clearly understood and believed the salesperson's claims about the product. He therefore rationalizes that the prospect is saying no not to the product—it's too good—but rather the prospect is saying no to the salesperson. In short, with this attitude the salesperson is going to—if he or she is not careful—feel rejected.

Refusal or Rejection

Second Idea: The salesperson must clearly understand the difference between refusal and rejection if he's going to keep his ego intact and be able to effectively sell his product. My son has clearly understood this difference from the time he was about three years old. When he asked for something and I said no, he did not feel rejected. He simply felt his dad had missed the question. He waited two or three minutes and gave me another chance to correct an obvious mistake.

When the prospect says no to you, you should be as nice to him as my son was to me and as your children probably are to you (if you have children). Give him (your prospect) the benefit of the doubt; give him a chance to correct what surely is an obvious mistake. In your mind, when he says no you should definitely feel it is a mistake and proceed from there, giving him a chance to correct that mistake by saying yes.

No "Born" Salesmen

Third Idea: You do not have to be a "natural born" salesperson in order to be a good one. As a matter of fact, I've traveled almost all over the world and I have seen that women have given birth to boys and I've seen that they've given birth to girls, but thus far I've never seen that a woman has given birth to a salesman. Now, I've seen that salesmen die, so if they're not born but they do die, then obviously somewhere between birth and death—by choice and by training—they become what they decide to become, namely trained professional salesmen.

Message: Don't come up with the "loser's limp" that you are not a "born salesman." That's true. But you definitely can be trained to sell and this book is playing a part in that training.

Fourth Idea: You must remember who wins in the sales transaction. I covered this in the second chapter. If you recall, I asked if you still had all the money you had earned in the last year of selling. Next, I asked if you had prospects who still owned merchandise you sold them more than a year ago. The answer was obvious. Hopefully you recall that you came to the conclusion the prospect was the big winner. When you fully understand and believe the prospect *is* the big winner, you can close more enthusiastically and forcefully.

Tie Logic and Emotion Together

Seldom is any effective close or procedure going to utilize only one technique or principle. Here's an example which ties emotion and logic together with a "reduction to the ridiculous" procedure.

Remember, when a person brings up a logical objection you answer it emotionally, and when he brings up an emotional objection you answer it logically.

At one time I represented a bicycle company and was responsible for much of the training of their salespeople. A common objection was the price of the bicycle, which was about twenty dollars higher than other bicycles which were approximately equal in quality. This particular company emphatically claimed their bicycle had the finest brakes in the industry.

When the price objection arose, we taught the salespeople to focus on the brakes, explaining their effectiveness, durability, and most of all, their dependability. Frequently the customer still came back to the price objection. At that point we instructed the salespeople to get involved in this dialogue: Salesman: "Mr. Prospect, approximately how long do you think your child will ride this bicycle?" Prospect: "I don't know. Several years; probably five, maybe even longer." Salesman: "OK, let's take five years—and if this bicycle only costs twenty dollars more, that means it's costing you four dollars per year for the best brakes in the industry." (We also taught the salespeople to bring out that familiar little talking pad, so the prospect could *see* that the price was four dollars per year.) "Since there are three hundred and sixty-five days in the year, Mr. Prospect, you're talking about little more than a penny per day for the finest brakes available for your child's bicycle."

The salesperson was instructed to pause for several seconds, then quietly say, "If these brakes were only effective one more time in a five-year span, they would be worth far more than twenty dollars, wouldn't they?" The procedure was effective because the salespeople were absolutely convinced of the truth of the statement—or was it a question? There was logic in the approach that a penny a day was certainly insignificant, but the emotional impact was even greater. In the prospect's imagination, he could visualize his child *always* being able to stop his bicycle quickly to avoid danger.

The Keys in Selling

There are eleven keys in selling which will make you more professional and help you close more sales. These keys involve attitudes, procedures, and techniques. In some cases, all three will be involved and in *rare* instances none of these will fit you or your situation (if I could think of even one, I'd share it with you).

As we look at the keys in closing, the very first key we're going to look at is what I call the "Key of Positive Projection." I want to emphasize as

POSITIVE PROJECTION

strongly as I know how that your business is never either good or bad—out there. Your business is either good or bad between your own two ears. *In your mind you should have made the sale before you even talk to the prospect.* Whether he comes in to see you or whether you go out to see him, you've got to understand, you've got to sell him in *your* mind before you actually physically sell him.

Just Looking!

If you work in a retail outlet, chances are good you've had a prospect come in, slowly look around, and as you approach him he says, "I'm just looking." The question is, did you believe him when he said he was "just looking"? I hope you did because that's exactly what he was doing! Just looking.

I didn't realize that fact for a long, long time, but in 1973, Julie, our youngest daughter, graduated from high school. For graduation we had promised her a new automobile and buying that car was an exciting event.

Now let me confess that I've never sold automobiles, but if you were to ask me to write a description of a super-good automobile prospect, here's the way I would describe that prospect: "A daddy with a daughter who had just graduated from high school. He publicly announces he's going to buy her a car and gives some indication he has the money to do it." From where I sit, I'd say that's a pretty good prospect!

Don't Offer Charity

I had been at work when we went down to look at cars, so I was dressed in a business suit. My daughter hadn't been to bed the night before because she had been getting dressed for the big event.

This was to be her first car and she was all dolled up in her "Sunday go to meetin'" best. I was driving a fairly new "Ninety-eight" Oldsmobile, so between the two of us we gave some indication of being at least mildly prosperous. When she got out of our car, Julie wasn't walking—she was floating—into that dealership.

Despite that fact, the young salesman came to us and offered charity. He asked, "Can I help you?" Despite his charitable offer, we were in a hurry so I did not beat around the bush. I responded, "My daughter just graduated from high school and we're looking for a car for her as a graduation gift." Word of honor, he looked at us and said, "Well, if you see anything you like, let me know," and he turned around and walked away.

I have no idea if the young salesman stayed in the business another day. I do know that regardless of how long he stayed in the business, he never had a better prospect. Like most prospects, we had started with the dealership which sold the cars my daughter was interested in.

The young salesman "blew it." I thought he was pretty bad until we got to the next dealership. This salesman said exactly the same words, and in addition he had B.O. The third dealership was almost as bad, but when we went to the fourth dealership we got lucky.

Yes—They Are "Just" Looking

What do I mean, "we got lucky"? Very simple. My daughter had dated the salesman so we had a connection with the dealership and were able to buy a car. This helped me to understand two things which I had not previously understood: First, I understood why we were having a recession. We couldn't get waited on! The second thing I understood was that when a prospect comes in and says, "We are just looking," or "I'm just looking," you can bet your last nickel they are "just looking"—but it's *desperately* looking! For a salesperson! To sell them something—so they don't have to keep on looking!

Think: As a Buyer and as a Seller

Now let me go back to chapter 8 on empathy and sympathy. You want to hear what the prospect says *and* what he is saying. I want you to think as a seller and as a buyer. When you go shopping, would *you* rather find what you want in the first store or the tenth store? Odds are about forty-three to one you would much prefer to find what you want in the first store, wouldn't you? As a seller, the next time somebody comes in to see you and says he's "just looking," it should bring a smile instead of a frown. Careful—don't overreact. Don't grab and hug—just smile.

If the shopper seems to be shy and introverted, as you smile take a step backwards (you *must* come across as nonthreatening and nonpushy) and say, "We're delighted to have you with us. Look as long as you like. My name is _____ and if you would like some help it will be a pleasure for me. [And as an afterthought] Oh, and incidentally, if we don't have *exactly* what you want, I could probably tell you where to find it. *Is that fair enough?*"

If the customer is *obviously* an outgoing, extroverted, hail-fellow-well-met kind of person you should smile broadly and say, "Congratulations! You have just found someone who is interested in helping you find exactly what you want. If we don't have it, I'll suggest the place or person who can solve the problem. *Is that fair enough?*"

"Is that fair enough?" is a very vital question to ask. Our nature is such that we have a wish, even a need, to be fair. The "is that fair enough?" question will almost always bring a *yes* answer, which means you have just scored your first points in a sales game designed to produce two winners: you and the prospect. To repeat myself, when the prospect says he's "just looking," you really ought to be grinning all over.

The "Sure Sale" Close

This next story dramatizes the power of the Key of Positive Projection.

Several years ago a small east coast printing company started an expansion program. Every six months a new salesman was hired and started his training in the office with product knowledge and procedure. Next the new salesman went into the field with an experienced sales trainer who taught him sales skills and technique. Finally the new salesman got his sales "wings" after an interview with the company president, who gave him that last little pep talk.

On one occasion the company hired a young salesman who was especially green and lacking in self-confidence. As a matter of fact he was so scared the boss figured he'd better give him a little extra help. After the fairly standard "you can do it" pep talk, he said to the salesman, "Son, I'll tell you what I'm going to do. I'm going to send you across the street to see a 'sure sale' prospect. This is where I always send our new salesmen for one very simple reason—that old boy is a buyer. He always buys something. But son, let me give you a word of warning. He's mean, nasty, ornery, and foulmouthed. He's going to make you think he's going to bite your head off, chew it up, and spit it out in little bitty pieces.

"Put your mind at ease, son. He's all bark and no bite. Regardless of what he says, I want you to hang in there and say, 'Yes sir, I understand, but I have the finest printing offer in this entire city and this is what you ought to get.' It makes no difference what he says, you stand your ground and come back at him. Remember—he *always* gives our new salesmen an order."

Go Get 'Em, Tiger!

Our charged-up hero crossed the street, walked in the door, introduced himself and his company, and for the next five minutes those were the only words our young salesman had a chance to say. That old boy really tore into him. He told him how the cow ate the cabbage in no uncertain terms. He introduced that young man to a segment of the English language which he had never known existed. However, our hero, because he had been prewarned, hung in there. He said, "Yes sir, I understand, but this *is* the finest printing offer in this entire city, *this* is what you ought to have." Back and forth they went and after about thirty minutes he made the biggest sale in the history of the printing company.

Naturally the young salesman was excited about the order. He picked up his briefcase, made a mad dash across the street, threw the order on the boss's desk, and said, "You were right about that old man! He is mean, nasty, ornery, and foulmouthed, but I'll tell you something else about that *nice* old buzzard [our attitude *is* affected when the prospect buys, isn't it?]—he *is* a buyer! I've got the biggest order in the history of this company, just look!"

The boss looked at the order in astonishment and said, "Oh, my goodness, son! You called on the wrong man! That old man *is* the meanest, nastiest, orneriest, most foulmouthed old goat we have ever dealt with! We have been trying for over fifteen years to sell him something and he's never bought a dime's worth of anything from any of us!"

Make the Sale—in Your Mind

Question: Where did he make the sale? Now I don't think there's a doubt in your mind, is there? You *know* the salesman made the sale *in his mind* before he crossed the street. He was using the Key of Positive Projection. All the young man did was go across the street, totally prepared, even willing to take some abuse because he *knew* he was going to make the sale.

Suppose the boss had said, "Now, son, I'm going to send you across the street, but I don't really know why. I've been sending my best people over there for fifteen years and that old buzzard's been chewing them up and nobody has ever sold him a dime's worth of anything!" How much chance do you think he would have had to make the sale? None whatever. All I'm saying is that you *must* make the sale in your mind before you ever talk to the prospect. This is true whether you solicit your business on a direct basis or you run a retail business with your customers coming in to see you.

Drill-Practice-Rehearse-Project

Your planning, preparation, and projection *before* you see the prospect will determine, to a large degree, what happens *after* you see the prospect. It's more than just a cliché that *spectacular performance is preceded by unspectacular preparation.* In the classroom a sales wreck (mistake) is an *inexpensive* learning experience. The same wreck (mistake) with a good prospect is not only expensive for the salesman *and* his company but is discouraging as well. If it is repeated too frequently or over a long period of time, it will end the career of the salesman. Physical and mental preparation, complete with drill and rehearsal, will get you technically *and* emotionally ready to sell.

This is practice without pressure. To go with this you need that mental projection of making that sale in your mind before you see the prospect. The beautiful thing about mental practice, as Dr. Maxwell Maltz said, is that you gain perfection on the playing field of your mind. You do everything exactly right, respond to every question with the best possible answer, meet every objection in the best possible way, and end up with the sale.

On this playing field of your mind you can develop enormous confidence and courage. If there is anything consistent with all of the super-salespeople in the world it is that they do have confidence they can succeed. They put this confidence into action with courage.

If you're going to be a successful closer, you've got to mentally see yourself as a closer before you physically close the order. You write the order in your mind when you first get out of bed every morning. You start writing and you continue to write those orders in your mind all day long. The professional salesperson is observing, thinking, selling, and closing all the time. Closing becomes a part of him. He burns it into his subconscious mind. On *every* sales interview he projects successful results so that inevitably the end results are a foregone conclusion.

Just in case you think I overstate the importance of making the sale in your mind *before* you see the prospect, let me point out that a study done by S.M.E.I. (Sales and Marketing Executives International) revealed that the number-one reason salesmen fail is their tendency to prejudge the prospect and decide in advance that he might not or even will not buy. As I stated earlier, you *should* prejudge the prospect, find him *guilty*, and convict him of buying *before* you see him.

I'm not certain the saleslady in the next story "saw us coming," but based on the way she handled the transaction, I'm convinced she "tries and convicts" every prospect who walks into her department and "sentences" them to buy.

The "Neiman-Marcus" Close

Several years ago my Redhead and I were at a department store doing some Christmas shopping. We rode the escalator to the mezzanine floor and as we stepped off and turned left we saw a beautiful fur coat on a mannequin. I looked at the fur and at the Redhead. She looked at the fur and at me. Both of us knew without either one of us saying a word that we were looking at *her* coat. We both stopped at the same time to give it a good once-over. I looked at one part of the coat and she looked at another part. I'll bet most of my readers can tell me which part each one of us examined. The Redhead grabbed the sleeve and looked at the price tag. I unbuttoned the coat, looked at the lining, felt the fur, and said, "Sweetheart, this is magnificent." By then she had seen the price and said, "It ought to be!" And with that, she turned around to walk away.

When she turned around she literally bumped into one of the sharpest salesladies I've ever seen anywhere. She was a short, pleasant, grandmotherly type whom you would instantly like and trust. She looked right at my wife and with a twinkle in her eye said, "Honey, that is a beautiful coat, isn't it?" Sugar Baby: "It ought to be!" Saleslady: "Well, you apparently only looked at the price tag. Let me show you what you should have looked at." Very quickly she took physical action (I cover the physical-action key in selling in chapter 29) as she opened the coat and said, "Look at the Eliot label. When you see that name, especially when combined with our reputation, it means quality and satisfaction. This coat will be with you a long time and it will be beautiful and practical every day you wear it." Then smoothly and easily she slipped the coat off the mannequin as she said, "Let's try it on, just for size." (Now she is physically getting my wife completely involved.)

My Redhead (protesting ever so mildly) slipped the coat on and the saleslady asked, "How does it feel?" Sugar Baby: "Well, it feels good, but it *ought* to!" (She's still thinking about the price.) Then the saleslady did something which was truly beautiful and professional as she said, "Well honey, what you ought to do [and she didn't have a pad to talk with in this situation] is take that price tag and divide by ten. You will wear that coat five or six years and then your husband will probably have a clutch cape or jacket made from it and you'll wear the new garment another five or six years. Actually, you can wear this beautiful fur for less than a cloth coat would cost, since you would have to buy a cloth one every three or four years. And," she said, "Honey, this is quality and on you it looks natural." (*Love* that word in this situation!)

Pressure? Sure—but So Gentle It Felt Good!

Then she looked right at my wife and then at me. As she took her eyes off my wife to look at me, she glanced back and caught my wife gently stroking the fur. When she saw this she broke out in the biggest grin you've ever seen. She knew, and she knew that she knew, she had the sale. (Despite her verbal protests, my wife's body language—which *cannot* lie—had revealed her true feelings.)

She looked back at my wife and said, "You know, honey, you're one of the lucky ones. There are an amazing number of wives who come in here and drool over a coat like this. Unfortunately, their husbands are not cut from the same cloth as yours [I hadn't said a word, but apparently my body language had also given me away] and are unwilling to get something this nice for their wives."

Guess who left there with a coat? That's exactly right! That dear lady had put me on such a high pedestal I just couldn't let her down, could I? It wasn't too hard to convince the Redhead that she should "let me get it for her."

Does It Work?

Even though the entire transaction lasted less than five minutes, there were several important principles involved.

Number one, the saleslady was alert, on her toes, and in love with her job. She observed the little twenty-second drama that took place as my Redhead looked at the price and I looked at the fur. She might have heard me comment on the coat, but I can't definitely state that she did.

Number two, she immediately got my wife physically involved (she saw that I was sold, so she figured it was one down, one to go!). Number three, she knew my wife really wanted the coat but apparently didn't feel it was practical. Number four, she broke the cost down on a "reduction to the ridiculous" approach so both of us could see it was practical and affordable.

She gave us an excuse to buy (it was practical) and a reason to buy (my Redhead really did want the coat). One more time. Any time you can give a prospect an excuse *and* a reason for buying, and make it easy for him to buy, the odds are great the sale is yours for the asking.

32

SELLING AND COURTING
RUN PARALLEL PATHS

THE SECOND KEY in closing the sale is the "Key of the Assumptive Attitude." As a starting point for this key, let me suggest that selling and courting run parallel paths. For the ladies who read this, I apologize in advance because this analogy won't have as much value to you as it will have for the guys. Actually, you are the ones who could write the book on this particular subject. But fellows, let me urge you to stay tuned in because I honestly believe this will have considerable value for you.

I'm convinced if you know anything at all about courting, you already know a great deal about selling. Question for the guys: When you were single and courting (or if you still are), did you ever ask your date, "Honey, can I hold your hand?" "Do you mind if I put my arm around you?" "Is it all right if I kiss you? Just one time, that's all I want, just one kiss?"

If you did or do court that way, chances are pretty good you are still single. Next question: Did you ever kiss a girl? Chances are good if you are a guy you answered in the affirmative, which means you kissed her without permission.

Question for the distaff side: Did the suitor in the above example kiss you without permission? Yes _____ No _____ Note: In a seminar situation, when I ask this question the girls will invariably respond with a big, laughing yes. At that point I playfully call them a bunch of liars and they all laugh.

Actually, in most cases the guy probably had permission to kiss the girl ten minutes before he took advantage of it. Chances are even better, however, that the girl didn't pucker up and say, "OK, partner, now plant it there!" That's not the way it's done!

To tie this courting example directly to the sale of a product or service, I can guarantee you that when you knock on a prospect's door, whether it's his home or office, he's not going to open the door and enthusiastically proclaim, "Oh, thank goodness, you finally got here! I've been waiting for one of your people to come by for years! Come on in!

341

THE ASSUMPTIVE ATTITUDE

I'll go get my checkbook while you start writing the order!" You couldn't pay the light bill on the profits from prospects who "bought" like that.

In Selling and Courting You Assume and Imagine a Lot

Then how does the prospect say yes? Exactly the same way the girl said yes. Fellows, did you ever try to hold hands with a girl and she said, "No!" then a few minutes later you were walking down the street holding hands? What she was saying initially was, "Based on the information you've given me thus far, I can see no justification whatever in indulging in a hand-holding exercise with you."

Obviously she didn't verbalize that, but that's what she was *saying*. By her actions she was saying, "Now look, Charlie Brown, the night is young. Be patient. Take your time—and SELL!" In selling we can sell more if we transfer what we learn in the world of courting to the world of selling by remembering that in the world of courting and in the world of selling, you do a great deal of assuming *and* imagining.

In courting you *assumed* when you asked the girl for a date she was going to say yes. You *assumed* if you treated her properly on the date when you got her to the front door you were going to get the good-night kiss. However, you didn't get her to the front door and say, "Honey, I'll tell you what. It's getting late. Why don't I stop by tomorrow afternoon at half-past five on the way home and get my goodnight kiss then?"

Here's Why

There are two basic reasons you would not do this: Number one, you are "motivated" by being with your date and you've spent an entire evening hoping to get her in the same condition. To bid her good-night at that point would negate the effort you had expended for that evening. The second reason is *you know* that the next day you would have to start all over. As a matter of fact, after thinking about it overnight, you might be further behind than you were when you started the day before, because your date might have had those second thoughts about granting that good-night kiss. There are a lot of guys and gals in the world of selling who make that mistake in the sales process. After making the full presentation and going through the demonstration, completely establishing value and covering all the sales bases, when the prospect brings up one lousy little objection or excuse the salesman often panics, backs away, and says, "OK, I'll see you tomorrow or next week or next month."

Let me tell you something, my selling friend. In the world of courting *and* in the world of selling you *must* assume from the beginning when you approach the prospect he's going to be delighted to talk to you. You *assume* you're going to get the appointment. You *assume* you're going to put on a powerful, professional presentation. You *assume* he's got the money to buy and you *assume* he is going to buy from you *now*. From "hello" to "good-bye," in courting *and* in selling, if you assume a lot you will sell a lot.

You should *see* the prospect signing the order and transferring a portion of his monetary resources to your estate. You should *see* in your own mind the transfer of your goods or services to him. In every step of the sales process you assume and see the desired end results.

Visualize and Assume

Selling and courtship do run parallel paths. You guys undoubtedly remember when you were young and single and first started your dating lives. You vividly remember exactly what you planned to say when you approached that pretty little girl about going out with you. You rehearsed it in your mind a thousand times and changed your "sales talk" just as often. However, in your excitement and enthusiasm you visualized her nodding and agreeing after a slight demurral that yes, she would honor you with her presence that evening.

You remember, fellows, how you planned exactly what you were going to wear and exactly what you were going to say when you picked her up. In your mind you vividly painted the picture a thousand times as to how she was going to be dressed, how she would greet you when you arrived for the big occasion. You drew the picture of that initial little squeeze when you extended your hand to her, and how she would smile and say she was glad you had gotten there. You clearly saw yourself opening the front door for her and chatting as you walked out to the car and then opening that door for her.

You had already carefully planned where you were going to go and what you were going to do. You planned, or should I say "plotted," how you were going to stretch after you were seated in the theater and let your arm kind of "naturally" end up on the back of her chair and ultimately, "accidentally," end up on her shoulder. Then you were going to pat her a couple of times and leave your arm there (you clever rascal!).

You carefully planned the event after the movie, how you would stop by for a Coke, an ice-cream sundae, or a pizza. You visualized the slow drive back to her home and yes, you visualized, as a result of all your graciousness, wonderful conversation, sparkling personality, enthusiastic appreciation of her, and all the other good things, that you were going to be able to—maybe—on that first date, get a good-night kiss. Yep. You planned it all. You visualized it all. You could see it happen. You were on a very important sales call.

You, Too, Girls

And girls, with few exceptions you were doing the same thing from your side of the fence (on occasion you do go out with a guy because you have no "better" or "other" offer and going out with Charlie Schmo beats watching TV). For the guy who made your pulse beat faster, you did a little subtle maneuvering as to how you could regularly, "accidentally," be at the same place as your dream guy. You carefully planned *exactly* what you would say when he asked you out. Then you visualized what you were going to wear and how you would greet him. You visualized how you would respond when he "accidentally" found his arm around your shoulders. You visualized how you would plant those subtle little hints and suggestions through all of the little maneuvers you girls learned at the knees of your mothers. Actually, it's a sales process for the boy and the girl, with the girl being more adept because she, from an early age, learned to think as both a buyer *and* a seller.

Just Keep It Up

Question: Now that you're selling products, goods, or services, why don't you follow identically the same procedure? Oh, I understand the prospect will not be quite as cooperative as the girl and will certainly not "plot" to aid you in your sales effort. However, need I remind you if what you sell solves a problem or fills a need for him then he, like the girl, is just as interested as you are in "getting acquainted" with that solution. If you really believe the sales process is something you do *for* a prospect and not *to* the prospect, and if our sales technique is as sound and as carefully planned as our courtship process, then more and more of the prospects will enter into the process I discuss.

Now let's take the courtship process (as in boy/girl) and translate it into the sales process (salesperson/prospect). In the sales process you need to clearly visualize, memorize, drill, and rehearse exactly what you are going to say in the initial approach. You need to visualize the prospect's response. If you are new in selling, the chances are excellent your company has already given you the approach to use and the expected response of the prospect.

In your mind you need to see the prospect responding with a *yes*, you can make your presentation. You need to visualize the presentation as you're going to make it as well as the response of the prospect. You need to see him nodding and agreeing that yes, he does have a problem and yes, your product will solve that problem. You need to visualize him enthusiastically receiving the good news about the service you can render.

Yes, the sales process—like the courtship process—is a visualization procedure. If you think the sales process through and apply the same enthusiasm, imagination, and visualization that you applied on those first few dates you had, I can assure you your sales results will substantially improve.

Throughout the entire process, whether you are "selling" your date or selling your prospect merchandise, you assume the ultimate end result. That's easy and natural in the courtship process, but apparently it has to be relearned in the sales process.

Most proposals are not in the form of "Will you marry me?" and most sales are not in response to "Will you give me an order?" The end results are brought about by a far more subtle assumptive approach. In courtship the suitor, after he has made his presentation, drops little thoughts like, "When we're married we won't have to be in so early," or "Our children will be even prettier than those," or "One of the things I'm going to get you when we're married is _____." The list is endless but the phrases are all aimed at the same target. They are assumptive closes.

The "Assumptive" Close Revisited

One of the most effective assumptive closes I've ever experienced involved my pastor, the venerable Dr. W. A. Criswell.

In late 1981, some members of the church approached me about teaching a particular Sunday-school class known as the "Auditorium Class."

This class is held in the main auditorium between the two Sunday-morning sermons. It is a large class and represents a significant commitment on the teacher's part. I had serious reservations about my qualifications as a Bible teacher.

With this in mind, I expressed my gratitude to the church members for the invitation but also expressed some of my doubts. I told them I would give it careful consideration and would be much in prayer about it. They told me this was the message they would deliver to the pastor.

The next day (I've never seen Uncle Sam so efficient) I received a letter from our pastor thanking me for accepting the assignment and expressing his confidence the class would be an outstanding success. That's the "Assumptive" Close, and in this case it worked to perfection because I wasn't about to say no to Dr. W. A. Criswell, especially since I really wanted to say yes.

Point: Assume the prospect *wants* to buy because he probably does, then assume he is *going* to buy and he probably will. The "Assumptive" Close makes it easy for him to buy. As a professional, that's your job.

The "Kreepy Krauly" Close

In the summer of 1983, Tom Brickman, an enthusiastic young Kreepy Krauly salesman (you read it right!), came knocking on our door. I was jogging and as I passed in front of our house, I saw Tom and my Redhead busily engaged in serious conversation, so I aborted my jogging for the day to see what was going on. Tom quickly explained that the Kreepy Krauly was a robot with only one moving part and he was demonstrating its effectiveness in cleaning swimming pools.

A few questions, a little chitchat, and the appointment to clean our pool was made. The key to getting the appointment was Tom's enthusiasm and sincerity, combined with a few well-placed questions: (1) Would I be interested in a device that dramatically reduced algae buildup in my pool while saving up to 50 percent on my pool chemicals? (2) Would I like to have the cleanest pool in the neighborhood and spend less than ten minutes a week in the process? Both questions produced the expected answers and the demonstration was arranged.

Tom brought a new Kreepy Krauly, so the assumption was clear that he *expected* to leave it in our pool. He used a dialogue guaranteed to arouse interest ("invented by an engineer from South Africa who grew tired of cleaning his own pool or using ineffective devices." The engineer part assured the acceptance and credibility. The South Africa part and "just being introduced in the Dallas area" gave it an aura of intrigue and snob appeal. "Tired of cleaning his own pool" rang an empathy bell). I give Tom an A for opening effectiveness. Incidentally, he covered these points while he was taking "Kreepy" out of the container.

During the demonstration, Tom talked about Kreepy almost as if it were a person. He explained that we would soon regard Kreepy as a silent, hardworking member of the family (a little corny, but Tom's infectious grin made it very effective). Throughout the demonstration, Tom was answering questions and showing me exactly what to do to keep Kreepy functioning effectively (*assuming* all the time). The single step that *really* stood out, however, was the way he used the "Assumptive" Close:

Tom: "Best of all Mr. Ziglar, we keep a permanent record of the shape and dimensions of your pool so if, for any reason, Kreepy is not keeping *all* of your pool clean, a telephone call to our service department will solve the problem. Now let me make a sketch of the exact size and shape of the pool so our service department can give you the best possible service" (this is a completely natural assumptive close). He quickly drew a sketch, asking me the dimensions as he drew. When he had finished he asked if it was accurate. I assured him it was. Tom: "Mr. Ziglar, as you can see, Kreepy is doing a thorough job on your pool and this one is new, but I'll be glad to take this one out and put in a brand-new one. Would you like for me to do that?" Zig: "No, this one is fine" (I had bought). Tom: "Do you want to give me a check or do you prefer to put it on a credit card?" (two of the "Alternate of Choice" Closes in succession).

Remember **Why** *They* **Buy** *or* **Give You the Kiss**

At this time I'd like to share my own courtship experience with you — up to a point. I learned very early in my courtship career the girls I was dating were not kissing me for *my* benefit. As soon as I realized they were having fun, too, I started kissing more girls! (For what it's worth, I never kissed my wife until *after* we were married. Of course, she wasn't my wife until we got married, was she?)

As a salesperson you need to understand that nobody's going to buy from you so you can win a trip to Hawaii (oh, your mother might, but you can't make a career of selling to Mom), nobody's going to buy from you so you'll win the new car, nobody's going to buy from you so you'll be Number One. People are going to buy from you because of the benefits to them as a direct result of buying what you're selling. So, from "hello" to "good-bye," you assume they're going to buy from you *now*.

The "Smell Good" Close

The third key to help you close more sales is one which I desperately hope you are already using. It's one which I'm embarrassed to mention, but painful experience and observation tell me I must. I'm talking about the "Key of Physical Action." It's the first part of this key I'm embarrassed to talk about.

The Key of Physical Action starts with physical cleanliness. You start every selling day by taking a bath or shower (especially if you're using this new twenty-three hour deodorant. The company which makes it figures everybody's entitled to some time to themselves!) After the bath or shower you use a good deodorant. You need to smell good and you also need to make certain you do not have halitosis. (Some people say that halitosis is better than no breath at all, but don't bet the family jewels that the prospect would agree with that!)

It's terribly difficult to offend people and influence them at the same time. You should use a mint or some kind of breath freshener about every hour so you do not offend the prospect. Physical action begins with physical cleanliness.

No Bath—No Sale

In 1969, the company I represented and served as vice-president was approached by an organization selling executive retreats and seminars. The primary concept was that anyone who qualified to attend was a chief executive officer of a company or earned in excess of $100,000 a year. The seminars featured lectures by outstanding people, and each one was structured so there was a considerable amount of free time for these executives to visit with each other for brainstorming and sharing of ideas. The salesman who called on us wore an expensive, tailor-made suit, drove a luxury automobile, and wore a large diamond ring. He was persuasive and articulate but he never came close to making the sale. His body odor was so offensive that after a few minutes in a room with him we simply could not tolerate the odor. The interview was terminated in short order and the salesman missed the sale.

I'm not certain we would have bought under ideal circumstances, but we were intrigued with the idea. The salesman never had a chance to make the sale, even though his sales knowledge and basic procedures were excellent. His preapproach was good. He knew something about us. He was professional in his introductory remarks, was enthusiastic about his product, and did many things right. His lack of personal hygiene completely eliminated any chance of the sale.

On the other side of the coin I have seen some salespeople go to the other extreme. I have been in the company of some who used such an overwhelming amount of an expensive after-shave or cologne the odor nearly knocked me over. Some of the girls use entirely too much perfume and/or makeup. Taste and judgment enter the picture. In this case, as in all cases, I'm convinced that most salespeople who are guilty of halitosis, B.O., or too much after-shave or perfume are simply careless and unaware of what they're doing. There is no excuse for this. Be aware—and you'll sell more.

P.S. to husbands, wives, or sales managers: If your mate or salesperson is ever guilty of being "odor offensive," you need to *gently* suggest that something be done about it.

The "Proper Dress" Close

Physical action includes how you dress. There are no "set in concrete" instructions on this one. The dress will vary according to the time of year, section of the country, and product or service which you sell. You start by dressing within the structure of the industry and part of the country in which you live. Obviously an individual selling computers, securities, or estate planning would dress differently from the salesman who sells feed and fertilizer on a direct basis to the rural areas of the country.

As a speaker, I follow one rule which makes sense to me: I try to dress so my audience does not notice what I'm wearing. If you leave one of my presentations raving about that "beautiful suit he had on," I believe I have been improperly dressed. If you leave thinking to yourself, "Gee, you would think the guy could do better than that!" then I have been improperly dressed. In my judgment I should dress so your focus is on my face and what I'm saying rather than on the clothes I'm wearing. That's a pretty good guideline for you. If you are too elaborately dressed or too shabbily dressed, you distract from your presentation. In the case of you ladies, if you are seductively dressed it's going to cost you as a professional saleslady. You will, perhaps, get extra attention, but it will not be the kind which leads to more sales and the building of a sales career.

Get Help—It's Available

Your dress is so critically important I urge you to do two things: First of all, buy a book such as *Dress for Success* or *Women's Dress for Success* by John Molloy, *Winning Images* by Robert Shook, or *Dress With Style* by Joanne Wallace. You will find many excellent guidelines in these books.

Number two, make contact with a professional clothing salesman in a good clothing store. Get to know him; seek his advice; work with him on a wardrobe concept; make friends with him and encourage him to keep you informed about any style changes or sales which will enable you to dress more professionally.

The same advice obviously applies to professional salesladies, but if anything, it is even more important for you. Here's why: There is a fine line between good taste and being overdressed and an equally fine line between casual and careless, gaudy and imaginative. Also, quality and style are not as clearly defined for the lady business professional as they are for the man. By all means, you should make friends with sales professionals in several department stores and specialty shops. Encourage them to keep you informed about sales and style changes. This approach is to your advantage as well as to that of the salesperson from whom you are buying, but it is *especially* to your advantage.

The August 1979 issue of *Psychology Today* reported that a study done by Edward Young of Emory University revealed that when salesmen in a Montgomery, Alabama, men's store wore suits, the average value of their sales was 43 percent higher than when they wore shirtsleeves and ties, and 60 percent higher than when they wore open-collar shirts.

The old cliché is still true: "You never have but one chance to make a first impression." You want to make absolutely certain that impression is a good one. It is true you don't judge a book by its cover, but if the cover isn't appealing you probably won't bother to find out what the book is all about.

If you're selling a legitimate product or service at a legitimate price, you need to concentrate on being dressed so you "blend" rather than "offend." You will also want to remember that *the people you go to for advice* (doctors, attorneys, C.P.A.s, minister, bankers, financial consultants, etc.) *are almost always neatly and conservatively dressed.* As a matter of fact, how would you feel about their credibility if they were wildly or sloppily dressed? Would you take them *or* their advice as seriously?

POINT: If you want your prospects to take your advice ("buy my product"), you should dress as an adviser.

You have probably noticed that on several different occasions I have suggested you "look your prospect in the eye." You can't do this very effectively if you are wearing dark glasses. Since childhood the statement "I don't trust a man who won't look me in the eye" has been ingrained in most of us. With our ever-increasing drinking and drug problems, the average person wants to see "the whites of the eyes" of any salesman who is trying to persuade him to take action and buy something. On unusually bright days, slightly tinted glasses *might* be acceptable while you are outside a building with your prospect, but once you sit down at the negotiating table, those glasses *must* come off if you are to be most effective.

In Golf and Selling, Position Is Important

Physical action, according to sales consultant Donald Moine, includes establishing trust by reflecting the customer's personality. If the customer talks fast, the salesman will increase his own conversational speed. If he talks in a whisper, the salesman's voice will quickly drop to a whisper. "His voice and manner say, 'I'm like you. You're safe. You can trust me,'" says Moine.

Physical action also means being physically in *position* to sell. If you're selling a high-ticket item, if it's humanly possible to have your prospect seated, then by all means do so. Psychologically your prospect will be more comfortable making a decision when he's seated than when standing. When the decision involves a substantial sum of money, you want everything going for you.

Physical action means having the right seating arrangement. For example, if you (the salesman) are calling on a man and his wife, you should be *next to the wife* or in front of both of them. Every time you speak to the husband, you should have to look past the wife or at the wife in the process. Now if it's true the husband is the head of the family, it's just as true the wife is the neck. Since the neck is what turns the head, you want to make certain she is in a position to turn it properly.

This procedure has another advantage. By including the wife in the complete presentation, you are covering one more sales base. On many occasions a salesperson will have a tendency to do most of the talking to the team member who is giving him the responses he wants and needs. Generally speaking, this is the one who is most enthusiastic and who is agreeing more with the salesperson. The problem with this procedure is many times this "agreeing" prospect has little or nothing to do with the decision. By including both husband and wife in the presentation, as this Physical Action step will do, you are touching one more sales base which gives you a better chance of making the sale, which I repeat is the purpose of the call.

Those Jealous Hearts

In a sales presentation you should be careful not to get too close to the prospect's wife. He might be a jealous man and if you either deliberately or accidentally touch the wife, the prospect might think you're trying to sell something other than merchandise. I can guarantee you under those circumstances you're not going to sell him anything.

Incidentally, age does not enter the picture in this particular situation. Whether the wife is twenty-five or seventy-five makes little or no difference to a jealous husband. The one exception to this might be the man who is married to a wife much younger than he is. In this case, he would be inclined to be even more protective and more jealous.

The same advice goes to you salesladies. We're in a society which is more open today than ever before, but that does not eliminate the fact there are many women who are protective and very jealous of their husbands. To have a saleslady use her sex appeal to try to persuade the husband to buy something is not going to endear that saleslady to the wife. In many cases, it will cost you a sale and you'll never know why. All of this simply says use good judgment—be careful of where and how you sit and physically deal with your prospects.

Remember even if one member of the team, whether it's a business team or a husband/wife team, is a dominating one and is the primary decision maker in most cases, the other member, as sales trainer Don Hutson says, can still veto the sale. Don't take that foolish and unnecessary chance.

When you deal with two or more prospects in an office or at a restaurant, be careful not to sit between them or you will either look, act, and feel like a referee at a tennis match or you will give one prospect more attention than the other. If you are talking to the "boss" in the office and he is hidden behind his desk, it will be difficult to communicate with him especially if you work with visual aids or a prospectus. In these cases, according to John Hammond, you need to get permission to move a chair to the side of the desk. Here's how: "Mr. Prospect, I have some things I need to tell you as well as show you. To do that I need to move this chair to the side of the desk. Will that be all right with you?"

If you work in a specialty shop or a small store, it is almost always good strategy to move from behind the counter and get on to the prospect's side. This eliminates a "barrier" and helps to establish trust. Two exceptions to this procedure occur when the shop is busy with customers or your prospect is still in the selection process and you need to take additional items from the display case.

If you are in direct sales, if it is humanly possible (without making an issue of it) to get the prospect seated at the kitchen or breakfast-nook table, you are in the ideal spot to sell. There is something about sitting at the table where bread is broken that makes the prospect more responsive. Generally speaking, most people invite *company* to visit in the living room; friends and acquaintances visit in the den; and *family* sits down at the kitchen table. When you sit at that kitchen table you become, in the prospect's subconscious mind, a member of the family. And we do *trust* our family, don't we? We also *buy* from those we trust, don't we?

Physical Action Should Put Prospect at Ease

Physical Action means your samples are clean, well cared for, and in good order. Physical Action means that in the beginning of the interview (primarily in direct sales) you have your order pad in plain view with your presentation book.

In the case of a real estate presentation, I urge you to have the legal document which you fill in to complete the sale in plain view on the front seat of your car. As you get into the car, hand the husband and wife a copy of the sales form and say, "In our city and state, this is the standard agreement which we use. During our drive to the various properties you might want to glance through this and see if there are questions which you need to ask."

This is a simple way of getting the agreement into the prospects' hands and, more importantly, putting them at ease as you drive to the homes. It gives them a chance to look it over and is handled in such a matter-of-fact, nonthreatening manner it eases the closing process.

Instead of coming across as a "pressure" sales approach it presents you, in the prospect's mind, as somebody who wants him to have all of the information so he can make a good, sound decision. If there are any questions he obviously wants them answered, and this approach showcases you as one who is willing to answer.

Physical Action also means letting your product "sell itself." The next story by Janet Corning, taken from *Cheer*, a monthly publication of realtor Larry Fargher and Realcom Associates of Santa Clara, California, illustrates the point beautifully.

"The Best Salesman Ever"

   Shortly after Christmas I almost stumbled over a little boy in the middle of the sidewalk who was so busy playing with a toy computer-controlled spaceship and a walking man that he was oblivious to the crowd milling around him. His obvious pleasure made me think the same toys would delight my own youngsters. I asked the little boy where he got them.

"In there," he said, pointing to a shop behind him.

I went in and asked for the toys the small boy was playing with. "Who is he?" I remarked, as the proprietor wrapped my purchases.

She smiled. "You might say he's my Christmas present. A few days ago he came in and stood, staring longingly at the spaceship. 'Would you like it for Christmas?' I asked.

" 'Mother says there isn't any money for Christmas this year. We lost Dad last spring,' he explained, and turned to go.

"It had been a lean season for me, but it was a week before Christmas. I gave him the spaceship, and he was so delighted that he got no farther than the sidewalk before he sat down and inserted the batteries.

"Then the most amazing thing happened. People stopped to talk to him, and I've never had so many customers. I kept count of the spaceships I sold and when he got up to go I called him in and gave him a commission. I asked him to come back the next day and added the walking man to his playthings. Yesterday his commission amounted to twelve dollars!"

The story also makes a pretty good point for generosity, "going the extra mile," "having a heart," investing in sales promotion, etc. I hope it's not necessary to remind you that the little guy was "The Best Salesman Ever" because of his obvious ecstasy and sheer delight with the toys (products) he was playing with (demonstrating). He believed in his product and even though he had no idea as to what a sales technique might be, he "sold" very effectively because he transferred his feelings to the prospects.

33

THE "LOOK AND LISTEN" CLOSE

PHYSICAL ACTION MEANS you physically *listen* to what the prospect is saying, not just with your ears alone but with your eyes as well. You do this by observing him. Physical Action comes from watching what your prospects are physically doing. For example, a prospect might say no, but is busy stroking the back of the chair. His mouth says no, but his body language says *maybe*: "This is really nice," "Tell me more," or even, "I'm interested and will buy if you will go ahead and close the sale."

When this happens just remember a prospect *can* lie with his mouth but he *can't* lie with his body. For example, you are demonstrating a home and the prospect keeps giving objections such as, "It's too expensive, don't like the corner lot, too far out of town," etc., but all the time he's standing looking at the beautiful neighborhood or gazing out a back window at the view, admiring the master bedroom or the kitchen cabinets. If he walks back to take one more look at anything, you can be assured that in his mind he is buying the property. You're in an excellent position to sell. The body doesn't lie and that's just one of the reasons *you should learn to lean forward with the complete expectancy of making the sale when you ask for the order.*

When the prospect for the automobile says he would never pay $12,000 for one of the "low-price three," but is stroking the upholstery or looking at the performance figures, then you need to understand what his mouth is saying and what his body is saying are two entirely different things. One more time: He can lie with his mouth; he can't lie with his body.

This is much like kissing the girl good-night. When you try to kiss her good-night, if she says no but stays right where she is, what she really is saying is, "Look, why don't you try just one more time?" Now if she says no, slaps your face, turns around, walks in the door, and slams it behind her, you can generally assume that what she really means is *no*, or at least, "Not tonight, Charlie Brown!"

When a prospect says no with his mouth but ends a sentence with a *but*, you know you've got a prospect. "No, I don't think so, *but* this really is nice." If you are tuned in to what he's doing by watching his body language, you're going to be able to persuade more prospects to take action—*now*.

The next key in closing the sale is the "Key of Enthusiasm." This key, along with the Key of Persistence, is the most misunderstood key of them all. Many people think that enthusiasm means you're loud. Obviously you can be enthusiastic *and* loud, but in its truest sense, enthusiasm has nothing to do with being loud. Enthusiasm comes from the two Greek words *en theos* and literally means "God within." Look at the last four letters in *enthusiasm*. They are I A S M and are an acronym for "I Am Sold Myself." If you are sold yourself on the product, goods, or services you sell, then you are going to be enthusiastic as you make your presentation and close.

The "Enthusiasm" Close

Enthusiasm sells. As I have said from the beginning, we sell because we transfer the feelings we have for what we're selling to our prospects. Sometimes—and I need to warn you about this—too much enthusiasm can cost you a sale. However, if I'm going to miss a sale I prefer to miss it on the positive side rather than on the negative side. I also believe that *for every sale you miss because you're too enthusiastic you will miss a hundred because you're not enthusiastic enough.* With odds like that I'll stay with the enthusiasm.

I have no earthly idea as to why this is true, but there are some people who misunderstand what enthusiasm really is. They equate enthusiasm with pressure or an overpowering compulsion on the part of the salesperson. The prospect might feel because you're enthusiastic you're trying to dominate or force your feelings, beliefs, and product on him, and therefore he rebels or resists. I emphasize, this doesn't happen often, but it does happen. But I still feel if I'm going to miss, I'd rather miss because I'm too enthusiastic rather than because I'm not enthusiastic enough.

This Is a Lotta Bull

With an abundance of enthusiasm, you might be just like this young fellow down home whose enthusiasm caused him to miss. Here's the situation: It was courting night and he was running late. He knew if he was too late his girl friend would not go out with him. This was in the days before everybody had automobiles and he was one who didn't, so he had a choice to make. If he walked all the way around a large pasture which separated him from his girl friend, he'd be so late, she wouldn't go out with him. If he took a shortcut across the pasture he might *never* get there because in the pasture was twelve hundred pounds of BIG, BAD BULL.

It was a difficult decision but he decided the prize was worth the risk, so he took the shortcut across the pasture. He didn't want to go too fast and attract too much attention, but he didn't want to stay there any longer than was absolutely necessary—so he was running at a slow trot. All of a sudden he heard the thundering hoofbeats of twelve hundred pounds of BIG, BAD—and now, very MAD—BULL! Our hero shifted into high gear and was doing the hundred in about 6:4, but the bull was doing it in about 4:7. It was a losing situation and the bull was picking up speed with every step.

Our hero knew he'd never make it to the other side of the pasture so he desperately looked around for a means of escape. Halfway between him and the other side was a big tree. The tree had only one limb on it and it was twenty-two feet off the ground. Our hero shifted into higher gear; the bull was gathering steam and gaining ground with every step he was taking. As a matter of fact, he could literally feel the bull breath on his heels. Now, I don't know if you have ever felt bull breath or not, but it's got to rate as one of the most awesome, frightening, fearful feelings of all time!

At the last moment, when it appeared he was going to be gored and trampled, he got within jumping distance of the tree, so he made a desperate leap for that limb—but he missed it! Fortunately, however, he caught it coming down!

If You're Gonna Miss—Make It a Positive One

Chances are excellent that on occasion you'll make a desperate effort for a sale—and miss it. If you do miss, it's better to miss on the positive side because you might still make that sale—coming down.

Enthusiasm sells. Chances are excellent that on at least one occasion this last month you've had eggs for breakfast. The odds are even better you ate hen eggs instead of duck eggs, despite the fact that duck eggs taste better and are more nutritious. One reason you didn't eat duck eggs is probably that they were unavailable.

The reason they are unavailable is a lack of enthusiasm and no organized sales presentation on the part of the duck. When a duck lays an egg her entire sales presentation is wrapped up in one short "quack," and off she waddles. End of sales talk! Now when a hen lays an egg, she tells the whole world what she's done in a highly motivated and enthusiastic manner. No wonder we eat duck eggs by the dozen and hen eggs by the billions.

Enthusiasm sells—but enthusiasm without direction is like running in the dark. That's the reason I sell enthusiasm enthusiastically but I sell knowledge, procedure, and technique even more enthusiastically—because those skills will increase your enthusiasm, which increases your effectiveness.

I don't believe this book will have a single reader who hasn't on occasion bought something and later had a friend or relative ask why. The response invariably is, "It's a marvelous product!" The questioner will insist on more of an answer. "What will it do?" Chances are good you've said, "A lot of things." The questioner persists, "Name one." And suddenly it dawns on you that you can't really name any specific benefit you received by buying the product, goods, or service. What happened was simple. You bought an enthusiastic salesperson. You bought the idea and the feeling this other person had for the product. You bought *his* belief in this product. You were sold because the salesperson was sold. It's true. Enthusiasm sells.

Yes, there are over a hundred closes in *Secrets of Closing the Sale*, but I fervently believe an enthusiastic salesperson who passionately believes in his product is going to sell more if he uses only a few of them than the salesman who knows all of them but who is not enthusiastic in his presentation of these closes.

Ask—and You Shall Receive

The next key in persuading people to take action is the "Key of the Subordinate Question." A subordinate question is any question the answer to which, if positive, means the prospect has bought. If it is not positive, it does not mean he has not bought. My friend Hal Krause used this subordinate question as he headed into the close. "Well, Mr. Prospect, have you sold yourself or should I tell you more?" Two points: Never ask "Have I got you sold?" People don't want *you* to sell them anything. They'll be pleased and even delighted to buy if they have sold themselves. The framework of the question is important because prospects don't want you to *sell* them anything.

The answer to the question makes you a winner, regardless. If the prospect says, "Well, no, I'm sold," then you write the order. On the other hand, if he says, "No, I'm not quite sold, maybe you should tell me more," that's really all any good salesperson wants—a chance to tell his story. This approach provides you with that chance.

Many years ago I was scheduled to speak in Greenville, South Carolina. I had written for a hotel reservation. I assumed I had one but when I walked into the lobby of the Holiday Inn, I knew I was in trouble. A sign at the back of the lobby read, "Traveling Men—Avoid Greenville, South Carolina, the week of October 11 through 15. It's Textile Week."

During that week you cannot get a room within fifty miles of Greenville. Rooms are booked from one year to the next. Nevertheless, I walked up to the counter, reached for the room registration, and boldly

THE SUBORDINATE QUESTION

said to the clerk, "My name is Zig Ziglar, would you check my mail, please?" The lady was not impressed. She asked: "Do you have a reservation?" Zig: "I certainly have—or, at least I wrote for one." Clerk: "When?" Zig: "A long time ago." Clerk: "How long?" Zig: "Oh, it was three weeks—and would you please see if I've had any phone calls?" Clerk: "Mr. Ziglar, I might as well tell you—"

Zig (interrupting her): "Now, just a minute, ma'am," and about that time another lady stepped out from behind the counter. The first clerk was apparently new on the job so with some relief she turned to the second one and said, "This is Miss Fortune and she will help you." I looked at Miss Fortune, grinned, and said, "She doesn't *look* like 'misfortune' to me, she looks like good news all the way!"

The "Presidential" Close

She good-naturedly smiled and said, "Mr. Ziglar, ordinarily I am good news, but tonight—" I interrupted, "Just a minute, ma'am, don't say another word. I've got to ask you two questions." Miss Fortune: "OK." Zig: "Question number one. Do you consider yourself an honest woman?" Miss Fortune: "I certainly do!" Zig: "OK, question number two: If the president of the United States were to walk through the door and come up to you and say, 'I want a room,' now tell me the truth, would you have one for him?"

She smiled and said, "Now, Mr. Ziglar, you and I both know that if the president of the United States were to come in here, I'd have a room for him." Zig: "OK, ma'am, you're an honest woman and I'm an honest man. You can take my word for it. The president of the United States is not going to come through that door. I'll take his room!" I slept there that night—not because of what I *told* her but because of what I *asked* her.

As an interesting aside, the organization I was speaking for that evening had tried to get me a room and had failed, despite the fact the secretary to the innkeeper was the wife of the man for whose organization I was speaking. The point is simple: The use of questions often leads to the sale.

I used this identical procedure to get a room at the Royal Sonesta Hotel in New Orleans. My wife and I, at the last moment, decided we wanted to celebrate one of our anniversaries in New Orleans, but everything was booked. Via long-distance telephone I used this procedure on the manager and got the room. It works!

Question: Will it work for you?

Answer: I can't say with certainty it will, but Larry Nichols, the training manager for the Kirby Company of Cleveland, Ohio, was pleased that it worked for him. Here is the situation: The Kirby Company had a managers' meeting scheduled at the Industry Hills Sheraton in City of Industry, California, on July 21, 1983. Larry arrived late at night, but when he attempted to check in the clerk told him he did not have a reservation and there were no rooms available.

Larry is a person who believes if something works you shouldn't fix it, so he followed the procedure exactly as I had described it on the cassette recording. When he asked the clerk if the president of the United States walked in, would there be a room for him, a pleasant surprise was the result. The clerk smiled broadly and told Larry he would not have a room for the *current* president, but he would have one for the *former* president. "As a matter of fact," the clerk said, "we do have the Gerald and Betty Ford Suite and they are not going to be using it, so it's available for you."

Two points: First, the procedure works. Larry had a *nice* place to stay. Second, the clerk *honestly* had forgotten about that suite and Larry's questions jogged his memory. Need I remind you this procedure can be adapted and slightly changed when you seek an item which is in short supply, or when you need a service favor on a holiday or weekend?

My good friend and "brother" Bernie Lofchick instinctively answers every question with a question. One time I asked, "Bernie, why do you always answer questions with questions?" His response: "Well, why not?"

The "Three Question" Close

One of the simplest and most effective closes is the "Three Question" Close, which you use after you have convinced your prospect your product or service will save money, time, work, etc. As an example, if you've been demonstrating the money-saving feature, the three questions are:

1. "Can you see where this would save you money?"

2. "Are you interested in saving money?" (Wait for answer.)

3. "If you were ever going to start saving money, when do you think would be the best time to start?"

The last question ties it down and gets the decision. If you've done your job and the prospect is honest, you just made a sale.

If you're selling on health you use the same three questions. "Can you see where this would be better for your health?" "Are you interested in better health?" "If you were ever going to start taking care of your health, when do you think would be the best time to start?" On convenience: "Can you see where this would save you some time and work?" "Are you interested in saving time and work?" "If you were ever going to start saving time and work, when do you think would be the best time to start?"

In our company everything we produce is essentially geared to improve production in one form or another. When our sales representatives are dealing with a salesperson, we teach them this adaptation of the "Three Question" Close: "Can you see how using this sales training course would increase your sales?" "Are you interested in increasing your sales?" "If you were ever going to start increasing your sales, when do you think would be the best time to start?" It's effective.

The Minister "Sells," Too

(The next example is taken directly from the inspiring book *The Secret of Supernatural Living*, by Dr. Adrian Rogers, and is used with permission of the Thomas Nelson Publishing Company.)

A man came to see me concerning his wife. She was suicidal, and he wanted me to counsel with her. I said I would if he would come with her to my study. This man worked in the space industry at Cape Kennedy and held an important position.

The wife poured out her story of a broken heart. She wept as she spoke of her husband's cruelty, infidelity, drunkenness, and gambling. I turned to him and asked, "Sir, are you a Christian?" Mind you, I was not asking for information but turning the conversation toward Christ.

He threw back his head and laughed scornfully. "No, I am an atheist," he said.

"Well," I responded, "an atheist is one who knows there is no God. Do you know all there is to know?"

"Of course not," he shot back.

"Would it be generous to say you know half of all there is to know?"

"Yes, that would be very generous," he muttered.

"Then if you only know half of all there is to know, wouldn't you have to admit the possibility that God may exist in the body of knowledge you do not have?" I asked.

"I never thought of that," he said. "Well, I am not an atheist, then. I am an agnostic."

I said, "Now we are getting somewhere. Agnosticism means you don't know." (I didn't tell him that the Latin equivalent for agnostic is ignoramus.) "An agnostic is a doubter," I said.

"Well, that is what I am and a big one."

"I don't care what size as much as what kind. There are two kinds of doubters, you know—honest and dishonest. The honest doubter doesn't know, but he wants to know. The dishonest doubter doesn't know because he doesn't want to know. He can't find God for the very same reason that a thief can't find a policeman. Which kind of doubter are you?" I asked.

His face softened. "I never really thought about it. I guess I never really wanted to know," he said.

"Did you know that there is a promise to the honest doubter in God's Word?" I asked. I then read to him the words of Jesus Who was speaking to the doubters of His day. "Jesus answered them, and said, 'My doctrine is not mine, but his that sent me. If any man will do his will, he shall know of the doctrine, whether it be of God, or whether I speak of myself' " (John 7:16, 17).

I continued, "In plain English that says that if a man will surrender his will completely, God will reveal Himself to that man." My friend was getting interested.

I then asked him, "Would you be willing to sign a statement like this: 'God, I don't know whether You exist or not, but I want to know and because I want to know I will make an honest investigation and because it is an honest investigation, I will follow the results of that investigation wherever they lead me regardless of the cost.' "

After a time of soul-searching, he said, "Yes, I would be willing to sign a statement like that. I will do it. How do I go about making such an investigation?"

We shared together, and I got him started reading the Gospel of John with the commitment that he really wanted to know the truth and would follow any truth revealed to him regardless of the personal cost or consequences.

In a matter of weeks, this same man came back to my study, got on his knees, and gave his heart to Christ. That was many years ago. I had lost track of him until recently, when I received a letter from him. He is now living in a northern state and is an excited witness for Christ.

In his letter to me, he said, "Dear Friend, thank you for being willing to spend time with this general in the devil's army."

Now where was this man's real problem? It was not in his head as he first thought, but in his heart. When he surrendered his will, faith followed. Unbelief reveals a wicked heart.

As you can see, Dr. Rogers asked seven questions which resulted in the decision. He also dealt with the man's head *and* his heart.

The next example is a case study on how to effectively ask questions to lead even distraught prospects to a favorable decision.

Selling a Service

In 1982 and '83, our daughter Julie worked for the Beneke Company as the only female public insurance adjustor in the state of Texas. Her job was essentially that of selling, so she and I took advantage of many opportunities to discuss sales technique and procedure. I was thrilled with her professionalism and the number of questions she developed to lead the prospect to favorable and mutually advantageous decisions.

Obviously, the company training program provided her with many techniques, procedures, and questions, but she generated some key ones on her own. Her primary prospects were those who had suffered major losses due to weather, fires, floods, or any other natural or man-made catastrophe. Most of her clients and prospects had suffered losses from fires and the damage exceeded $20,000.

When Julie arrived for her "sales call," the first question she always asked was, "Did everyone get out OK?" Please understand that nearly 100 percent of the people she dealt with were emotionally upset. Not only are fires hazardous to your health but they are also messy and expensive. Many times the victims had also lost personal items, irreplaceable keepsakes, and family heirlooms. Their need for someone to share in their grief and give them some measure of empathy and understanding was enormous. Julie's opening question demonstrated real concern for the victim and helped create a favorable climate for the interview. That opening question also brought the victim face-to-face with his good fortune in suffering only the loss of "things" and not a loved one (she never had a client who suffered that loss).

Establish Rapport—Then Ask Questions

Once the prospect had assured Julie that everyone was OK, she made a few comments expressing her relief and her sincere regret for the property loss. Once rapport had been established, Julie asked the second question: "Have you ever had a major property loss before?" (Most of them had not.) "Did you ever have a claim on a car wreck or damage?" If the answer was affirmative, she would ask, "How did it go?" If the answer was "Satisfactory," she responded positively by saying, "Generally speaking, on small losses the treatment is usually fair." If the answer was negative, she responded, "Then you are already familiar with how insurance-company adjustors work in order to minimize the settlement amount?" (Her voice inflection made the statement a question.) She would generally wait for a comment.

Julie: "Did you know you have a right to a professional representative when you suffer a loss such as this?" Prospect: "No, I didn't." Julie: "Do you understand, Mr. Prospect, that whether or not you want to be, right now you are your own claims adjustor?" Prospect: "I hadn't really thought about it." Julie: "Do you feel knowledgeable enough to negotiate with the expert the insurance company will send out to adjust your loss?" Prospect: "Probably not." Julie: "Do you have as high a regard for your money, Mr. Prospect, as the insurance company does for its money?" Prospect: "Yes, I do." Julie: "Do you realize they're going to send out a professional to protect their money?" Prospect: "I hadn't thought about it in those terms." Julie: "Their claims adjustor is a professional, so do you think it would be in your best interests to have a professional protecting your money?" Prospect: "Yes, I probably should." Julie: "You do understand that the insurance company is not simply going to say, 'Send us the bill and we'll pay it,' don't you?"

Each of these questions is designed to make the prospect think in terms of using a professional because the insurance company is also going to have a professional. This is not to imply that the insurance company wants to cheat anyone or is going to be unfair. Realistically the homeowner, in most cases, does not understand his rights and in virtually every case forgets many of the items which are destroyed in a fire.

Other questions Julie often asked: "Mr. Prospect, would it be a problem for you and your wife to take time away from work and family to sift through, sort out, write down, and price everything you lost in your home, from the brushes in the closets to the number of socks in your drawers?" Prospect: "Yes, it would." Julie: "Would it be convenient for you to meet with the adjustor, restoration people, dry cleaners, and others who need access to your home and belongings?" Prospect: "That depends on when and where." Julie: "In a court of law, you have an attorney to represent you and in front of the I.R.S. you have a C.P.A. to plead your case. Doesn't it make sense that you would do better to have a professional adjustor plead your case in this loss?" Prospect: "Sounds reasonable."

Julie: "When you get down to negotiating the loss, will you feel comfortable the figures being presented are just and fair to you?" Prospect: "I'm not sure." Julie: "Mr. Prospect, did you know that our average increase, after the insurance company's first offer, is thirty percent?" Prospect: "No." Julie: "Mr. Prospect, our fee is only ten percent, so you still realize an additional two hundred dollars per one thousand dollars by making the right decision to hire a professional. In simple terms, on a loss of twenty thousand dollars this will bring you four thousand dollars extra; on fifty thousand dollars it would be an extra ten thousand, which is in reality your money, which you will need to rebuild and replace your loss. These figures are net to you, after our fee. Does that extra money—which *is* yours—appeal to you, Mr. Prospect?" Prospect: "It sure does!"

Julie: "The exciting fact, Mr. Prospect, is that we guarantee our work. If we don't secure a settlement large enough to cover your repairs *and* our fee, there will be no fee. In other words, Mr. Prospect, there's no way you can lose. Is that the kind of situation you'd like to participate in, Mr. Prospect?" Prospect: "Yes, it is." Julie: "Would you like for us to start working for you today so you can move back into your home at the earliest possible moment, or is there any particular hurry?" Prospect: "We don't have a place to live, so the sooner we can move back in, the better it will be." Julie: "If you will go ahead and OK this agreement, we can get the process started so that despite the grief of the loss, you will not be faced with a financial burden to go along with it. That is what you want, isn't it, Mr. Prospect?" Prospect: "Yes."

If you count, you'll discover that in the process she asked over a dozen questions. Her results were excellent because the questions were designed to lead that person to take the action step to solve his problem.

You Can—You Must—Learn to Ask Questions

Many times people ask me how they can learn to ask questions. The first thing I'm going to tell you is obvious: *Study*—don't just read—this book. Take all of the questions (there are over eight hundred in this book) and rephrase them so they relate directly to your business. Then record those questions with the right voice inflection and listen repeatedly until they are firmly embedded in your subconscious mind.

This will clarify your thinking to an amazing degree. It will enable you to zero in on your target, which is to help crystallize your prospect's thinking which helps him in making the right decision. This is critical because *your* success *and* the solution to his problem are ultimately dependent on his making the right choice.

Additionally, you should learn how to ask questions by talking with the top salespeople and sales trainers with your company or by asking other salespeople who sell similar products. Ask them the specific questions they use to (1) arouse interest, (2) sell benefits, (3) get appointments, (4) secure prospects, (5) close the sale, (6) tie the order down, and (7) convey conviction. Keep your eyes and ears open when you go out to shop or when a salesperson comes calling on you.

Build a sales library and become a student of selling. Develop the power to concentrate on one thing at a time. In this case that one thing is how to ask questions. Any time you see or hear an effective sales question, write it down in the question section of your sales notebook. Remember—the truly professional salesperson *always* keeps his inner ear and his sixth sense tuned in to good sales techniques. He has that true missionary zeal to learn as much as he can so he can spread the word to as many people as possible about his fantastic product or service.

The "Greatest Salesman" Close

Since I am often asked about sources for learning more about asking questions, I'll simply anticipate your question.

There is a Manual available in every good bookstore which will be enormously helpful to you in learning how to ask questions. The Manual you'll want to pick up is called the Holy Bible. At this moment this has nothing to do with religion, but any fair-minded person has got to admit that the Greatest Salesman who ever lived was the Carpenter from Galilee.

Get a red-letter edition (Christ's words are in red), and you will discover that *every* time somebody asked Jesus Christ a question He always answered with a question or with a parable. So if you want to know how to ask questions, that's the place to learn! (Everything He said in the Bible can be read in about three hours, so He was obviously going right at men's hearts with every word.)

He was also the greatest sales and marketing Manager who ever lived. He took just twelve salesmen—and one of them (Judas) was a loser— and spread the Good News everywhere in short order.

Many times I've heard people say, "You know, I've read the Bible, but I don't understand it!" Personally, I don't think it's the part they *don't* understand that bothers them! Actually, the Bible is very, very clear. For example, I'll bet you've noticed He didn't call the Ten Commandments the "Ten Suggestions."

As long as you are reading the Bible to learn how to *ask* questions you might as well read on and learn the answers. One of these days He's going to ask you a question and if you get it right, you get to stay! My friend, that will be the biggest sale you will ever make! You really should read your Bible. Not only will it give you peace of mind now but to tell you the truth, it'll help keep the heat off you later!

The "Dinner Out" Close

Questions are especially effective if you can tie customer benefits to the question. The "customer" is the person who is buying the idea, concept, goods, service, or product from you, whether it is a sale or a social situation. Never will I forget one Friday evening when I returned from a tough week on the road. The Redhead met me at the airport and she was dressed fit to kill. As usual, she had on some of the good, sweet-smelling stuff that I especially like.

As we were waiting for my bag to come down on the carousel, she snuggled up real close, slipped her hand into mine (she's powerful friendly, anyhow!) and said, "Honey, I know it's been a long, tough week for you, so if you want to we can stop by the store on the way home and pick up a nice steak or some seafood. While you relax with the paper I'll prepare a nice dinner for two. Tom is spending the night with Sam, so we'll be by ourselves. Then, honey, after we've had a nice dinner I'm certain you won't want to get involved in cleaning dirty dishes and greasy pots and pans, so you can watch television while I take care of that.

"It shouldn't take me more than an hour, hour and a half, two hours at the most. [Pause] Or, the thought occurs to me, honey, that you might be more comfortable and enjoy the evening more if I were completely free to devote all of my time and energy to you. I could do this in a really nice restaurant. Of course, honey, it's entirely up to you. What do you prefer?" (And they call them "the weaker sex"!)

I don't really think it's necessary to tell you we did not stop by the grocery store or cook that dinner at home. That Redhead "sold" me by asking questions. It is effective *persuasion* when you ask questions which lead the prospect to a decision that is in his best interests.

34

LISTEN–REALLY LISTEN

THE NEXT KEY in closing sales is a very significant one. It is the "Key of Listen." Most salespeople do not really listen to everything the prospect is saying or asking. Many times the salesperson interrupts the prospect and attempts to anticipate what he is going to ask. Solomon covers this one in the Book of Proverbs when he says, "He who answers a matter before he hears it is not wise" *(see* Proverbs 18:13). And when you listen—*listen*. Don't just "hear him out" so you can take the initiative and "say something which is really important." Chances are excellent if you really *hear* what he says *and* what he is saying, he will give you the key to making the sale.

An inexperienced or insecure salesperson is the one who asks the question and answers it in the same breath. Example: "Can you see where this would save you some money—of course you can!" "Can you see where this would help you save some work—obviously you can." The salesperson is afraid he's going to get the wrong answer and therefore he does not permit the prospect to give him any answer. When you ask a question, listen for the answer. It will give you the proper direction to close the sale.

If the prospect raises an objection, that's great! As a matter of fact, any good presentation should be designed—especially in the early part—to bring out objections. The earlier you can deal with them the more likely you are to close the sale.

Hear Everything—*Register* Some *Things*

You need to listen and hear everything, but when the prospect says no, you don't want to register it. Merlie Hoke, a good friend of mine from Great Falls, South Carolina, worked with me for several years in the cookware business. She had a peculiar hearing "problem." I've seen a prospect from a distance of three feet almost shout, "No, Merlie, I don't want to buy!" Merlie wouldn't blink. She didn't "hear" a word. I've also seen a prospect whisper yes at thirty feet and Merlie clearly heard the good news. Merlie understands when a prospect says no he doesn't really mean it. It's only when he says yes that she takes him seriously.

The "Hep 'Em Git It" Close

Merlie Hoke has a technique which is truly beautiful. As she starts to close the sale, from her seated position in front of the couple she makes this statement (as she moves her chair to the side of the lady): "Oh, this is so beautiful . . . and you deserve it . . . and I'm gonna hep (that's h-e-p) ya get it."

As I sat there watching this master saleslady at work, I got the distinct feeling I was witnessing a conspiracy. It appeared that Merlie and the little lady were going to gang up on that big old cookware company because they've got thousands of sets of cookware and bless your heart, little lady, you haven't got even one! "And I'm gonna hep ya get it!"

Good Salespeople Help *Prospects to Buy*

I got the strong feeling that Merlie Hoke had become an assistant buyer. *She had moved to the customer's side of the table and was interested only in helping that customer own the set of cookware.* Now obviously she was going to be using the customer's money. In all the years I worked with Merlie, I never heard her say, "I sold" anybody anything. She always said, "I helped her get it," or "I let her have it."

In the final analysis, what we as professional salespeople want to do is find people with a problem which our products, goods, or services will solve. We want to become assistant buyers and move to their side of the table. We want to feel their feelings so we can assist them in solving their problem by acquiring our goods, products, or services.

Your careful preparation, sincere interest, and action expectancy will determine to a large degree whether it's a sale or an "I'll let you know later."

Listen With Your Eyes

As we deal with our prospects we particularly need to listen with our eyes. The eyes are the only sense organ connected directly to the brain. Every other sense organ has to make a round trip before it gets back to the brain, but the "eyes are the windows of the soul," and an impulse on the eye is transmitted directly to the brain. That could be one of the reasons all of your life you've heard the two phrases "You can't believe everything you hear," and "I saw it with my own two eyes—and seeing is believing." With this in mind we definitely need to listen with our ears *and* with our eyes.

Here's a simple little formula for listening with your eyes: It's called the "CHEF Method" of listening. *C* stands for "chin" or "cheek." When the prospect begins to rub either his chin or cheek or holds either one in his hand, it is a satisfaction/gratification sign. In his mind he's already using and enjoying the benefits of the goods or services you're selling. It is a buying signal, telling you that now is the time to close.

H is for "hands." Watch your prospect's hands. If they are gently massaging palm against palm, or palm against the back of the other hand, in his own mind the prospect has already assumed ownership of whatever you are selling. He's telling you he is ready to buy.

E stands for "eyes." Watch them. It's a fact that the wider the eyes are open the more intently he is listening, the more he's understanding, and the more he's buying. To magnify this one a bit, many of the advertisements you see today on television have been checked by the use of cameras. The commercials are shown to a group of people who are never questioned about their sentiments concerning the commercials. Instead, high-powered cameras focus on the eyes of the individuals who are watching. The degree of dilation of the pupils of the prospect determines whether or not that prospect is really buying the idea in the commercial.

Interestingly enough, the prospect might say he loved the commercial, but if the pupils are not dilating the commercial is rejected. As I say, body language doesn't lie.

You also want to watch the prospect's eyes as they begin to open wider. If there are crow's feet and they begin to relax, you are getting your message across—you're communicating and selling. It's a visual signal to close the sale.

F stands for "friendly." When the prospect smilingly uses such statements as, "John, you dirty dog! Jesse James used a gun but you're using your pencil, trying to get my money!" he's buying.

He is also probably calling you by your first name; he crosses his legs, leans back, and relaxes. On the other hand he may suddenly become quiet, get up, and walk around the item without even speaking. He may get busy looking at the item you offered or he simply might look out the window, light a cigarette, or get a cup of coffee. Those are buying signals. *Close the sale.*

Act on the Signals

As the prospect gives you these "buying signals" (a "visual" buying signal is defined by John Hammond as anything the prospect *does* that indicates he has accepted the product), you want to take advantage of them. You do this by *quietly* asking questions. For some reason, according to Will Rogers, people seem to listen more intently and believe more completely anything which they hear in a low tone voice or a whisper.

Obviously, as you observe these visual buying signals (anything the prospect *says* that indicates the prospect has accepted the product), you do not want to overlook them. He might, for example, ask you to go over exactly what he gets with the purchase. Comments like, "I've never had this particular style [size, model]." Questions like, "How long is the warranty?" "When would the first payment be due?" "How much is the deposit?" "How long will it take me to get delivery?" "What is your service policy?" "Where do we get spare parts?" "Do you have a warranty?" "How much did you say the deposit was?" "I've never used this brand." "What do you think, dear?" What is the *real* rate of interest?" "How long would it take to get it installed?"

Yes, the Key of Listen is a critically important key. The ability to be a good listener is vitally important in communication. Many people will buy primarily because you display an interest in them as individuals. They buy because you listen to some of their hopes and ambitions and apply your product or service benefits directly to them.

The Key of the Impending Event

The next key is the "Key of the Impending Event." What is an "impending event"? It's something that is going to happen in the future and has direct bearing on the price, performance, service, desirability, or availability of the goods or services you are selling.

I'm convinced that, almost without exception, I can assure everyone who reads this book that whatever they're selling today will be more expensive tomorrow. There will be some notable exceptions in the future, as there have been in the past (computers, televisions, refrigerators, etc.), but by and large things *are* going up. With this fact as a base, once we've committed ourselves to serve our customers, we need to offer them the most goods at the best price with the best possible service. Since price increases are inevitable, if we can persuade our prospects to take action today we will be acting in our prospect's best interests.

Actually, we have a moral obligation to acquire as much professional expertise as possible to enable us to persuade more people to take action today for *their* benefit. If we do help them (our prospects), then obviously our sales will go up.

When I entered the world of selling one of the first things my good friend and sales manager, Bill Cranford, told me was that if I could effectively deal with the "I'll buy it later" stall I would be successful in the world of selling. Over the years I came to realize and appreciate the value of that observation. I also saw convincing evidence as to why prospects hesitated and wanted to "think it over." They feared they would lose financially or look foolish for having bought.

That's the reason that, in the early pages of the book and on several other occasions, I have pointed out that *the salesperson is more important than the sales process*, though the process is certainly important. To repeat myself, if you're sincere about building a career and helping others you will protect your integrity at all costs while learning as much technique and process as possible so you can more effectively persuade your prospects to take action.

The Key of the Impending Event is a key which you can use to help your customers, which obviously means you'll be helping yourself as well. This is especially true when you're selling a product to the customer which has resale value and hence the prospect is investing for profit or investment purposes. Typical, of course, is real estate, fine arts, securities, commercial-grade diamonds, stocks and bonds. Obviously your sales effort will be to convince the prospect the economic trends are such that the investment he makes today will be worth more in the tomorrows of his life.

The "Impending Event" Close

Here is an example of the "Impending Event" Close. Prospect: "The price on this house is too high." You: "Yes, I'd be inclined to agree with you. The price on this home—like most everything else—is too high. But you, Mr. Prospect, are the one who set the price." Prospect: "What do you mean, I set the price?" You: "Actually, it was you *and* all the other people who are in the market for homes who really set the price of the homes. For example, if ninety percent of the people who are in the market for a home were to suddenly stop looking, I can assure you that in a matter of six months the price of this house would be considerably less. However, everything indicates more—and not fewer—buyers will soon be in the market for a home and the law of supply and demand sets the price.

"As you well know, real estate has consistently increased in price. It's my firm conviction that a year from now or ten years from now, should you elect to sell this home, you will be able to get substantially more for it than the current price. If you go ahead and invest in this home today, you will profit from the *impending increase* in price brought about be-cause of the demand for homes created by you and thousands of others."

Another Impending Event opportunity is the fact that anyone who lives will have more birthdays and consequently they need to look at retirement or taking care of their old age. Your prospect *is* going to want to enjoy some good things in the future when he will not be working quite so hard. As an example, if you're selling a retirement home, beach, or lakeshore property, the close could go like this: "Mr. Prospect, since you've been putting so much into life for so long, don't you think it's time you prepare to let life put something back in you? This property I'm talking about will do exactly that."

Don't Let Them Dazzle You With Their Footwork

Mental alertness is a critical necessity if you expect to scale the sales heights, so let's take a little test to see if you're with it. (It's OK to figure in the margins.) Here we go.

You're a bus driver and you're headed south with fifty-five passengers on the first leg of your trip in your bus. You go four and four-tenths miles, then you turn east in your bus on the second leg of your trip and you go three and three-tenths miles. On the third leg of your trip in your bus you turn back to the south and this time you drive your bus exactly two and two-tenths miles. On the last leg of your trip in your bus you turn east and you go exactly one and one-tenths miles.

On this trip you've driven your bus in two directions but you've made three turns for the four different legs of your trip in your bus. You actually drove $4.4 + 3.3 + 2.2 + 1.1$ miles, which comes to exactly 11 miles.

Here's the question (no fair looking back!): Based on the information which I've just given you, please write the bus driver's age in this blank _____. (I repeat, it's OK to figure in the margin.) Go ahead—participate. Figure it out. That is the way we learn.

Question: Did you put your own age in the blank? If you didn't please prepare to be a little embarrassed, because I told you twenty-four times, "*You're* a bus driver on the first leg of *your* trip in *your* bus *you* are going south," etc.

Don't Let Them Lead You Astray

If you missed it the chances are good you did because I dazzled you with my verbal footwork. I kept you diverted by talking about unrelated items such as "Turn east, south, and east again." I talked about 55 passengers, 4.4, 3.3, 2.2, 1.1 miles, etc. At this point, you've got to be wondering, "What does this have to do with closing a sale?" Answer: A lot. Many times when you've got the prospect motivated and interested in what you're selling, he suddenly realizes he is headed straight for a purchase and it hits him that this purchase is not in the budget.

This is a problem. He fears he is now going to make a *yes* decision and he's not certain he should. Solution: Divert the salesperson's attention and thrust by talking about the presidential election, crime on our streets, violence on television, etc. So what do you, the salesperson, do? Two things: First, never lose sight of your objective, which is to make a sale. Second, when the prospect changes the subject you acknowledge the change, comment briefly, and tie it to the diversion, for example, "Yes, the presidential election is really exciting and so are the benefits which go with our product or service."

When I was a child I would occasionally see a bird which was apparently injured, so I would try to catch it. However, as I made my move the bird would struggle into the air and fly a few feet. Again I'd run after it and say, "I'm going to catch that bird." A little later and a mile away, Mama Bird would take off and go back to the nest. What Mama Bird had done was to lead me astray.

Message: Don't let your prospects lead you astray by changing the subject and leading you away from the issue at hand. Keep in mind that it might be nice to talk about other things, but you don't help anybody unless you can leave that prospect with a solution to the problem he has. Your goods or services should offer that solution.

Zero in on the Target

Keep that issue focused. The story is told of a father in the Swiss Alps who sent his three sons out into the world. Before they made their departure he took them to a mountainside and instructed them to bring their crossbows. He said to the eldest one, "Aim your crossbow at the bird sitting on the ground some fifty feet away." The son did as instructed. The father asked the question, "What do you see?" The son replied, "I see the beautiful skyline, the gorgeous clouds, the majesty of God's universe." The father said, "That's good. Now, lower your bow."

The second son was instructed to raise his crossbow and aim at the bird and he did. The father then asked the same question, "What do you see?" The second son said, "I see the beautiful mountains, the rolling valleys, the beautiful scenery with the rich grass." The father said, "That's good. Now lower your bow."

The youngest son was then instructed to raise his bow and aim it at the bird, which he did. The father said, "What do you see?" The youngest son said, "I see where the wings join the body," and with that he released the arrow, which flew straight to the mark.

Point: When you're on a sales interview you have only one target, which is to serve your customer by selling your goods or services.

35

THE KEYS IN CLOSING—
CONCLUSION

OF ALL OF THE keys in persuasion, undoubtedly the one which is *the* most misunderstood is the "Key of Persistence." Many people think the persistent salesperson is the one who "sits" on the prospect and says, "Aw, you know you're going to get it sooner or later, SIGN HERE!" Or, "You know you want it, go ahead and SIGN," or, "The only way you can get it is to SIGN HERE, so SIGN HERE." That's not persistence, that's just plain, unadulterated pressure. All you do is irritate people when you take that approach. I thoroughly covered that subject in chapter 4, so let's now look at what persistence really is.

Persistence is a good word, but I believe a better word is *belief.* I'm absolutely convinced if you really believe the product you're selling will solve a problem for the person you're dealing with, you will be reasonably insistent he take action in his own best interests. You'll do it professionally—pleasantly—politely—but you *will* persist.

The "Pressure Belief" Close

The word *persistence* took on a new meaning for me several years ago. I was on a speaking tour of Australia and met John Nevin, who at that time was the managing director for World Book Encyclopedia. His story is the classic "rags to riches" one. He started his World Book career as a part-time representative. He had a milk route and sold World Book in the afternoons and evenings. His dedication, hard work, and mental agility enabled him to quickly move up the management ladder to the position of managing director.

Early in his World Book career, John made a call on a recently arrived German immigrant, his wife, and son. The couple really looked more like grandparents than parents. They married late in life and their first and only child came along when the wife was forty-two years old.

"Tank You, Young Man"

John arrived for the appointment at about eight o'clock and it was after midnight when he finally made the sale. Many salespeople would never stay with a prospect that long. That's persisting too much! But John said to me, "You know, Zig, after I finally made the sale the little lady escorted me out through the front gate because they had a big dog in the yard. Outside the gate, the short, stocky mother reached up and put her hand on my shoulder and in that guttural German accent which was difficult to understand she said, 'Tank you, young man, for staying till we understand what these books do for our boy. Tank you, tank you, tank you!'"

John and the couple had a serious communications problem because of their unfamiliarity with the English language. They understood some things, but it was necessary for John to talk very slowly and repeat himself many times. Finally it got through to the couple that the World Book Encyclopedia would make a difference in the education of *their* son. Later John said, "You know, I hate to think I ever missed a sale because I was not communicating and the prospect was not properly understanding what my product would mean to him." Message: *The true professional wants the prospect to own the product so badly he strives for the yes decision again and again.*

As a salesperson you must also understand that many times the prospect is sold on what you're selling but he's been had before. He's made mistakes earlier by acting too quickly and what he really wants to know is, "Do *you* [the salesperson] really believe what you are selling is for *my* benefit, or are you just trying to sell me so *you* will benefit?"

Make Certain You Pass the Test

Many times the prospect will ask you some questions which really don't make sense. He's trying to find out if you're going to stick to the story you told him earlier. He's checking you out. Many times I've made the sale (and so have you) after I'd been with the prospect a long time, only to have the prospect look at me, grin, and say, "I was going to buy this all the time. I just wanted to find out what you would say."

That's what they *said*, but I'm convinced they were really checking the depth of my own conviction as to what the product would do for them. One more time. From Cavett Robert, *"The depth of your belief is far more important than your oratorical eloquence and sales phraseology."*

Some Persistence Ideas

It has been said—and I believe it's true—that many times the prospect will literally test you at least three times just out of curiosity to see exactly what you will say. Obviously some people—particularly those who are not knowledgeable about selling—will label it as "pressure" if a salesperson doesn't take the first *no* as the final word.

In chapter 30 I discussed how to get permission to use "pressure," so I won't repeat it here. Let me point out, however, that over the years I've asked hundreds of people to identify pressure and I've gotten answers from all over the ball park. Salespeople themselves say they don't like high-pressure salesmen, but then seem to be unable to identify what the word means.

I'm convinced it's not so much what it means to us as salespeople but what the prospect we're dealing with at the moment feels about it. That's another reason I keep saying you need to be sensitive to the other person. One prospect might feel terribly uncomfortable if you give him the second reason he should buy. Another one thrives on that very thing and loves to see a salesperson who is gung ho about what he's doing and who so fervently believes the prospect benefits from the purchase that he will try again and again to make the sale.

The Best I've Heard

Frank Bettger, in his magnificent book *How I Multiplied My Income and Happiness in Selling*, explained pressure this way: "I don't want to give anyone the impression that I am a high-pressure salesman. That is if I understand what the term 'high-pressure' means. Just so long as I can forget myself and what I am going to make out of a sale, and keep my mind on the other person and what he will get out of the sale, I have no fear of creating the impression that I am high-pressure."

Is this pressure? You're in the real estate business. You've just shown a couple a home which they obviously love. It's exactly what they've dreamed of owning but they are procrastinators who hesitate to make decisions. They're gracious, pleasant, and friendly but hesitant to decide. From your perspective you positively know at least one other couple is also seriously interested in that home. Are you doing the current prospect a favor by smiling and saying, "Well, I don't want to rush you into anything and I certainly don't want to pressure you into making a decision, so as soon as you make up your mind let me know." The couple responds that they really appreciate your consideration and they'll be back in touch the next day.

Problem: That very afternoon the other couple who were interested come in and buy the home. I'm convinced that you would have been far more loving, caring, concerned, *and professional* if you had taken this approach: Truthfully point out to the prospects you want them to make the right decision and you don't want them to feel rushed. However, if they are sincerely interested in the home they should put a binder on it to secure it, because another couple is also interested in the home and for exactly the same reasons they are.

You actually flatter your prospect when you do this because you're complimenting them on their judgment—that they like the home for the same reason the other people like it. In short, both couples have good judgment.

Go Ahead Doctor, Do What Is Best

In 1981 a close personal friend and business associate went to his dentist. The diagnosis was that, because of some problems with his teeth as a young boy, he needed nine crowns. As you know, that involves a considerable amount of time and money, so my friend asked if some teeth needed crowns more than others. The dentist replied that five should be done right away, but there was no immediate rush for the other four. With this information, he decided not to have all nine done, but did go ahead with the five.

As we go to press, my friend still has not had the other four crowned. Question: Was his dentist practicing either good dentistry or good selling? Answer: No, on both counts. As a professional salesman, one simple question would have revealed that my friend's dental bill was covered as one of the company benefits which he enjoys. As far as dentistry is concerned, my advisers point out three very significant facts concerning the delay for the other four crowns.

First, they say piecemeal dentistry is never attractive or effective as a complete masterpiece. In short, the dentist can do all nine at the same time and have a better chance of a more complete success with matching colors and results than if he crowns five at one time and the other four at a later date. Second, although the possibilities are slim they do exist that a tooth deterioration could occur quite rapidly and my friend might end up losing one or more of the other four teeth. Admittedly, the chances are small because he has had his teeth checked since he received those five crowns. At that point the dentist rather casually mentioned that he still needed those other crowns but did not suggest setting a date. Since the dentist was casual about the need, my friend was just as casual about getting the crowns.

From a dentistry point of view, the odds are great that the price of crowns, like everything else, will have increased substantially during the intervening time period between the first five and the final four, whenever that might be. Additionally, the time involvement for one project, namely having nine crowns, as versus two projects, meaning five crowns on this go-round and four crowns for the second series of visits, will be considerable. Total additional time involved will be somewhere between three and four hours. For a busy executive, that is a pretty healthy slot of time.

Obviously, there is some risk involved when a professional encourages a patient to take action. However, when your prospects or patients *depend* on you for your professional advice, you should be willing to take some risk.

Now You Have Two Problems

If there is some indication the prospect is growing uncomfortable with your persistence, you might smile and say, "You know, Mr. Prospect, when you and I started talking you had one problem. Now you have two, because you've got to get rid of me." Smile as you say this and continue by saying, "Now the second problem is easy to solve. All you've got to do is ask me to leave and I'll be gone in the twinkling of an eye. But that would still leave you with the first problem. So why don't we spend a few more minutes together and see if we can solve that problem as well. *Is that fair enough?*" or "*Does that make sense?*"

Another approach: "Don't misunderstand, Mr. Prospect, I'm not here to put the monkey *on* your back—I'm here to take him *off* your back. That's what our goods or services will do and that is what you want to have happen isn't it?"

One excellent reason for persisting is that's where you really learn to sell. After all, *the toughies are the teachers.* The ones who resist are the ones who force you to use your imagination, skill, and knowledge reserve which you've been accumulating over a period of time.

There's another side to the coin. Sometimes your prospects are confused about their belief in what you're selling and their desire for ownership. They're not sure they really trust you so *they* persist by asking a number of questions which are not consistent with whether or not they've been listening to you.

On occasion some of these skeptical prospects will ask some shallow questions just to see how you will respond. They want to see if they can "get under your skin." They want to check you out to find out if you're going to tell them the same thing you did earlier in the interview. I urge you to be cautious here.

If a prospect asks you the same question, you don't smile and say, "Well, as I explained earlier. . . ." When you do that, what you have done is call him an idiot for not listening and there is no way you can graciously call another person an idiot. When the same question comes up again you need to act a little astonished and say, "Oh, my goodness! No wonder you've hesitated until now to go ahead and make the decision, because that's one of the most important points. I'm pleased you brought it up because when we clarify this one, all doubt will be removed." You clarify it, lean forward in your seat, and say, "That removes the only obstacle between you and ownership of the product, doesn't it? Would you like me to ship this air freight or by truck?"

Yes, persistence is an important key. Learn to use it—then use it but don't abuse it. Remember, in selling, those who hang in there often win because they believe in what they're doing, and as you have already learned, *"The will which weakens first strengthens the other."*

The Key of Inducement

The next key in closing the sale is the "Key of Inducement." Chances are good if you have ever spent a few minutes with me you have seen my arrow-shaped diamond cuff links which the Redhead gave me on our twenty-fifth wedding anniversary. I confess to a degree of prejudice, but I honestly believe they're the most beautiful (not the biggest) cuff links in the whole world.

When she gave me those cuff links, French-cuff shirts were not very popular. I went to a dozen different stores in Dallas, Texas, looking for French-cuff shirts and I could not find them anywhere. Not only could I not find them but I was virtually invited to take my future "looking for" business to other stores. A typical conversation went like this. Zig: "Do you have any French-cuff shirts?" Clerk (certainly not a salesman!): "No, we don't." Zig: "Do you know where I might find them?" Clerk: "No, I don't. Besides, didn't you see me talking to this other clerk? I'm busy!" That little interchange is almost a literal truth.

The next spring I was in Burlington, Iowa, speaking for the Chamber of Commerce. After my talk I saw a gentleman in a white suit which I really liked, so I asked him where he got it. He told me he bought it from Doyle Hoyer, who runs Glasgow Clothiers in Fort Madison, Iowa. I commented that I was going over there the next day and get one just like it. With that he said, "I've got to go over there tomorrow morning, too, and I'll be glad to take you."

After I met Doyle Hoyer the next day, the following conversation took place. Zig: "Doyle, do you have a white suit?" Doyle: "What size?" Zig: "I wear size forty-one." Doyle: "Zig, I've got one in stock." With that he walked over, took the suit off the rack, and slipped the coat on me to check the fit, which was perfect. All he needed to do was cuff the trousers and I could walk out the door in that suit of clothes.

As Doyle measured me I asked, "Doyle, how long will it take me to get this suit?" Doyle: "Well, Zig, you don't leave until two o'clock, do you?" Zig: "No, I don't." Doyle: "Man, you're going to take this suit with you!" He gave the suit to a young man who worked with him and said, "Take it upstairs to the tailor and tell him I want this suit of clothes right away."

I Bought a Suit—Doyle Sold the Rest

Then with a twinkle in his eye, Doyle looked at me and said, "Now Zig, I've got something I really want to show you." Before I left there I bought two suits of clothes, five pairs of slacks, and all the good stuff that goes with them!

Today, despite the fact that Dallas has over one hundred men's stores for every one Fort Madison has, I buy 98 percent of my clothes in Fort Madison, Iowa. The fact that Doyle's a nice guy and a super salesman is important, but that is not why I buy from him. In a moment you will know the major reason.

When I finished my shopping spree, almost as an afterthought I said, "Oh, by the way, Doyle, do you have any French-cuff shirts?" Doyle gave me an answer which was entirely different from the one I had been getting in Dallas.

The "I Can Get 'Em" Close

He said, "No, I haven't," but he said something else. "But I can get them!" As a frustrated French-cuff-shirt seeker, those were beautiful words to me! As a follow-up a couple of weeks later, Doyle called and asked, "Did you get your shirts?" Zig: "I sure did!" Doyle: "How do you like them?" Zig: "Doyle, I love them!"

About two weeks later I was in the airport in Kansas City and I saw a fellow wearing a beautiful suit of clothes. (You are now going to find out how I select some of my clothes.) I walked over to him, complimented him on his suit, and asked him about it. He was delighted to give me all the information concerning the brand and his source for the suit. Armed with this information, I called Doyle and asked if he had this particular suit. Doyle: "No, I don't . . . but I can get it." A couple of weeks later he called me again and asked, "Zig, did you get your suit?" Zig: "I sure did." Doyle: "How do you like it?" Zig: "I love it!"

About a month later I called Doyle again, but this time when he picked up the phone he excitedly asked, "Zig! Are you still at the same phone number?" Zig: "Yes, I am." Doyle: "Man, I was just going to call you!" Zig: "Yeah, and I know exactly what you were going to tell me, too!" Doyle: "You do?" Zig: "Sure! You're going to tell me you just got in a magnificent new shipment of suits and at least half a dozen of them are especially made for me. You've put my name on them and are shipping them to Dallas so I can choose the ones I want and send the rest of them back to you." Doyle: "Zig, you are a genius!"

Now I need to make an important point. I am not color-blind, but I am color ignorant. I simply do not know which colors go together. Doyle picks out a suit, selects a shirt, chooses a tie and socks, and sends them to me with a note which says, "Zig, these go together." Now, I can understand that kind of communication! Fortunately the Redhead understands color combinations, so when I forget or get fouled up in general about what goes with what, she straightens me out.

My tailor is just a short distance from my house. Doyle Hoyer sends me my clothes and when he has a sale (which he says is always), he'll call and say, "Zig, I've really got something nice for you. I'm going to send you some suits and sports jackets. Choose the ones you really like and send the rest of them back."

The "I'll Treat You Right" Close

I'll never forget the time he called me and raved about a beautiful new navy blue cashmere sport coat. By the time he finished his eloquent and enthusiastic sales talk, I had a fear the price tag would bear some resemblance to the foreign-aid bill to Lower Slobovia, so I asked the obvious question: "Doyle, how much does this magnificent creation cost?" Doyle: "Don't worry about it, Zig, I'm going to treat you right." Actually, I don't know why I bothered to ask because he *always* gives me the same answer. I hasten to add that he has *earned* the right, over a period of many years, to give me that answer.

Now what does "treat you right" mean to me? It means he's going to be fair, he's going to be honest, he's going to be aboveboard. It does not mean he gives me his profit. You see, I happen to believe Doyle Hoyer needs and deserves a profit. But it does mean he's going to deal with me in such a way that he wants me to come back and buy from him again and again.

I probably buy as many clothes as 98 percent of the people you know because I generally have to travel in the suit I'll wear for the speaking engagement, and since I'm on stage my clothes must be smart and in good shape all the time. I buy a lot of clothes, but I don't believe I spend more than two hours a year selecting my entire wardrobe. Doyle Hoyer does most of my work for me. He's a super salesman who serves his customers.

So the *major* reason I buy my clothes from Doyle Hoyer in Fort Madison, Iowa, is that he offers me quite an *inducement* to do so. *The inducement is he saves me time* and for me, that is quite an inducement. Doyle tells me he also saves me money on the clothes and he probably does. As long as Doyle keeps treating me the way he's treated me thus far, old Doyle's got himself a good customer, although I'll be the first to admit I haven't bought anything from him in nearly a week.

The "And Then Some" Close

Doyle understands the three greatest words in selling are: *and then some.* He keeps every promise he makes—*and then some.* The clothes he sells me are exactly what he says they are *and then some.* In a nutshell, Doyle Hoyer delivers more than he sells—he doesn't sell more than he delivers. *That* is the way to sell more in the tomorrows of life.

There is a second point which is important: There is no such thing as a *little* sale. When Doyle got the six shirts for me he had no way of knowing how much business it would generate. I was a complete stranger who lived eight hundred miles from his store and he had never heard of me. Yet he went out of his way to make certain I got what I wanted and that I was happy.

At the moment I have no idea how many clothes Doyle has sold to me and because of me, but he says he gets from one to ten calls every week because of my references to him in my speeches and recordings. I would be comfortably confident in saying that his sales—because of the initial "little" sale—must exceed a quarter of a million dollars, and who knows what will happen now that this story is in print!

To quickly elaborate on that "no little sale" point, here's a "little" real estate story which also makes the point: A young couple contacted several real estate agents in Georgetown, Texas, seeking a place to rent. Since rentals at the time were almost nonexistent, no one paid any attention to them. Finally they walked into the office of McLester & Grisham. Instead of being laughed at, they got a bit of encouragement from salesman Dennis Robillard, who said he'd try to help them.

After making two dozen phone calls he found a suitable apartment and helped them move in. They were so appreciative they asked him to find them a permanent home—in the $400,000 price range. The couple had an income of about $10,000 a month from a newly established trucking firm, plus an inheritance of 46,000 acres of land rich with uranium.

Message: Treat everyone as if he is a valuable customer. He is—or he *could* be if he's treated like one.

The Key of Inducement is tremendously important. It can be as little as a smile or pleasantness in dealing with your prospects, or it can be as significant as a cash discount. In my mind I see it as the personal touch, the little courtesies you offer which make it easier for your customers to function in their business and personal lives.

The *Most Important Key*

The next key is, without a doubt, the most important of all the keys. It is the "Key of Sincerity." Chances are excellent if you are a successful professional salesperson you've had this experience. Someone bought from you and then said, "You know, I don't really know why I bought from you. I've had three or four people trying to sell me the same product," or, "I don't know why I'm dealing with you because for years I've been dealing with someone else." What he's really saying is, "I *trust* you." He is confirming what I've repeated several times in this book. *The most important part of the sales process is the salesperson.*

If you'll recall, very early in this book I made it clear we would be dealing not only with the sales *process* but infinitely more important, we would be dealing with the sales*person*. Trust is critical and sincerity is the key that opens the "I trust you" door.

Know the Author

Many years ago Charles Laughton, the famous English actor, was touring America, giving Bible-reading demonstrations. He was a Shakespearean actor with considerable dramatic skill. I personally never had the privilege of hearing him read the Bible, but indications were great it was a very moving, spiritual experience.

Once, after reading in a small midwestern community in a large rural church, Laughton's audience was totally and completely silent. It was almost as if God had made a special trip and was there among the congregation. After what seemed like an eternity but probably involved no more than a minute, a man who must have been about seventy years old stood up and asked for permission to read the Bible. It was granted and as the old man started to read, it was apparent he was no Shakespearean actor. He did not have the voice, the elocution, or the diction of the great Charles Laughton. As he read, however, it became completely obvious to everyone present that if this had been a Bible-reading contest, the great actor would have finished a distant second. When the evening was over, a reporter went to Charles Laughton and asked how he felt about having participated in such an event; what was his reaction to the old man's reading of the Bible? The English actor thought for a moment, looked at the reporter, and said, *"Well, I knew the script and I knew it well, but this old man knew the Author."*

The point is clear and very simple. The old man had the added advantage of being totally sincere and totally convincing because he had that deep personal belief. With a deep personal belief in what you're selling, you will be able to communicate and transfer that feeling to the prospect, and the Key of Sincerity will help you sell a lot of merchandise. By now it should be crystal clear the sales world is no place for a phony. He just won't make it in the world of professional selling.

Just Like the Little Boy Across the Street

Of all the sales closes in *Secrets*, this next one—even more than the preceding ones—absolutely demands sincerity.

I've never seen sincerity and integrity more on display than they were in a personal experience my son and I had several years ago. A few days before Christmas, Tom and I went down to get a new bicycle for him. Many years ago I could speak bicycle but today "bicycle" is an entirely different language. If you don't believe me just listen to a teenager or go down to a bicycle shop and listen to the chitchat which takes place.

On this occasion Tom and I went to the Schwinn Bicycle Shop on the corner of Valley View and Coit Road in North Dallas. The owner was busy with a grandmother and her little grandson, who were looking at a bicycle. The grandmother didn't speak bicycle either, so she had a precise list of exactly what she wanted on a specific bicycle, including the size. The owner of the shop looked at the list and said, "Yes, we have this bicycle and it comes in two sizes. Is the bicycle for this little fellow here?" The grandmother said, "Yes, it is. The little boy across the street has one like it and I want one exactly like his for my grandson."

Owner: "Ma'am, your grandson is too small for this big bicycle and it will not be safe for him to ride. You should get him the other bicycle, which is identical in every way. It is the same price and quality but it is smaller, and your grandson can handle it much more easily. It will be at least three years before it will be safe for him to ride the larger bicycle."

Grandmother: "No way. I want exactly the same bicycle the little boy across the street has. I want the very best for my grandson." Again the owner tried to explain that it *was* the best, it was just smaller, and if her grandson were riding the larger bicycle he'd have to move so far from side to side he would be unable to control it. The owner patiently pointed out that her grandson could lose control and might fall and if he happened to be in the street, it could result in a very serious accident. The grandmother was adamant. "No sir, I want *that* bicycle, right there, exactly like the one the little boy across the street has. If I can't have the one I want, I don't want any."

Then the owner did one of the most beautiful things I've ever seen a *professional* salesman do. It set the standard for what I consider the "professional" in the world of selling. He looked at that grandmother and said, "Ma'am, you're probably going to think I'm crazy, but I cannot sell you the bicycle you want. It would not be safe for your grandson to ride, and if anything should ever happen to him because I sold you a bicycle he could not control, it would be on my conscience." Incredibly enough, the grandmother left in a huff.

The "Integrity" Close

I hope you don't think the owner carried his integrity too far, and deep down I don't think anyone who is interested in building a sales career will feel that way.

Here's a man who can be trusted. I would be willing to send my son into his shop with a check made out to him with the amount left blank. This man has integrity and he really does care about his customers. It's true that the owner missed that sale, but as a direct result of "missing" that one, he has probably made countless others.

The "Final" Close

Now let's look at the "Signature" Close, which I think is the most powerful close in use today. Since I claim originality, I don't suppose that statement sounds overly modest, but I do hope you will indulge me in a little pride of authorship.

I want to explain that this close will not work for everyone. It would be absurd to use it for low-cost items such as cosmetics, household items, or brushes. However, most companies which sell those items do a lot of recruiting and, with a few changes in terminology which I share with you, this is a powerful approach to get the procrastinator to make a decision.

This close is the final one to use in an interview. It is ineffective if you've been laughing and joking throughout the interview. You must be sincere and come across as a sincere person. It will not work if you use it at the beginning of the interview before you establish value. You must use a number of other closes before this one in order to properly prepare your prospect. This is the final effort to get the sale, and when you use the "Signature" Close there is nothing left. It's now or never.

Feel—Felt—Found

Here's one you *must* practice, drill, and rehearse *before* you use it on a prospect. I call this procedure the "Signature" Close because many times a prospect will say he doesn't *sign* anything until he talks to his wife, lawyer, banker, or sleeps on it, thinks about it, etc. You respond with the oldest lead-in of them all: "I know exactly how you *feel* because for a long time I *felt* exactly the same way. [Pause.] When I analyzed it I *found* that everything I have or own which has any value to me I acquired only after I *signed* my name" (feel, felt, found).

(At this point I want to emphasize that I'm going to use a smorgasbord approach and give you far more examples to choose from than you should use. Don't ever use more than three, and if one doesn't fit your own personality or belief system, then don't use it. Caution: Virtually anything new in a tense situation such as closing will make you a little uncomfortable until you master it and make it your own. Don't be *too* judgmental in deciding what to use. Try it—you might like it!)

Voice Emphasis on "Signed"

(Now the words after the feel, felt, found introduction.) Here's the way I use it: "Over thirty-seven years ago, God gave me a beautiful woman and I'm one of the truly fortunate men in that I love her infinitely more today than I did the day I got her. I got her because one day, in the presence of witnesses, the minister, and Almighty God, I *signed* my name.

"I have four beautiful children—three grown daughters and a nineteen-year-old son. They're all mine, but the doctor would not even let me take them out of the hospital until I had *signed* my name."

Nothing Happens—*Until Somebody Signs Something*

"I own a lot of life insurance. I bought it because I wanted to make certain if anything happened to me my family's standard of living would not decline and my wife would not have to go to work unless she wanted to. I was able to protect my family's financial future because on several different occasions, in the presence of a competent salesperson, I *signed* my name.

"I have some investments. I own some real estate, some CDs for emergencies, a little piece of an oil well, and a couple of other investments. I made those investments because I wanted to make certain when the day comes that I am unable to do what I'm doing, I will be able to sit back and take life easy without being a financial burden to anyone. I'll be able to do that because on many different occasions, in the presence of a salesperson, I *signed* my name."

Now I repeat myself as I say, "As a matter of fact, Mr. Prospect, I've never made any progress of any kind, anywhere, or an acquisition of anything of value until I committed myself by *signing* my name. Mr. Prospect, if I'm reading you right—and I think I am—you're the kind of man who not only likes to make progress but who also likes to do things for your family. You can do both of those things right now by *signing* your name." (Point to the line on the order blank and hand him the pen.)

You Feel Good—Even if You Miss

If the "Signature" close is properly used, there is nothing else to say. This is that *one* case where you do not speak until the prospect speaks. There is total silence, but in this specific case, the longer the prospect remains silent the better your chance of making the sale. If there is a significant objection, your prospect will make it known almost immediately.

In every case when I've used the "Signature" Close, whether I made the sale or missed the sale, I've felt good. Obviously, I feel better if I make the sale, but even if I miss it, I feel good because I know I have done everything I can to get a positive decision. That's good because it's important to the ego and feelings of the salesperson to *know* you've done everything you can to get it, so you feel good about *you*. That's important for those future sales interviews.

The "Signature" Close for Recruiting Purposes

In this case you've thoroughly interviewed the prospect and are convinced he can successfully handle your business, but he seems uncertain and wants to "think about it" before he "signs up." You: "I know exactly *how you feel* and I'm delighted to see you take such a thoughtful approach to this decision, because as a practical matter, if the decision is not right then both of us lose. As a matter of fact, I *felt the same way* you do just _____ years ago when I was confronted with the same decision. [Pause.] I *found* there were many people in the company who had fewer qualifications than I had but who were doing extremely well simply because they had said yes to themselves. They didn't have better skills or abilities but they did have a better opportunity.

"Think about it, Mr. Prospect. You've never made a single career advancement by standing still and saying no. You didn't acquire your wife, your children, your home, or your savings account until you *signed* for them. Each step forward—regardless of what you do—involves a commitment on your part. In this particular case your signature, along with my signature, says we are both committed to *your* success. The instant you sign your name the opportunity door swings open, but until you sign it the door is closed and nothing can or will happen. In short, Mr. Prospect, you can open that door right now by *signing* your name." (Be quiet. The ball is in his court.)

There are hundreds of closes and variations of closes which can be used whether you are selling goods, services, or recruiting. Again, especially for recruiting purposes, they will have to be adapted to fit your special situation.

One thing I have emphasized throughout *Secrets* is that as you acquire technical expertise and the right words to persuade your prospect to take action, the most important thing is your *intent*. Why do you want to make the sale? Is your heart as well as your head completely in the transaction? Do you really believe it's in your prospect's best interests to buy what you are selling? That's important—nay, critical—because that very belief is your best, maybe your *only*, vehicle to outstanding success in this magnificent sales profession.

36

THE "NARRATIVE" CLOSE

To SUMMARIZE and tie a lot of things together, I'm going to tell you a story which will involve all of the keys we've been talking about. This is the "Key of the Narrative Event." A narrative key or narrative story is the most effective way to use third-party influence to persuade your prospect to take action. These are short vignettes which paint pictures of people or companies that had problems "just like yours [the prospect] and solved their problems by using our goods or services." (Implication: You can buy our goods or services and solve your problem.)

My purpose in telling this particular story is to give you, in story form, an overview of this segment of *Secrets of Closing the Sale*. This review is designed to trigger your imagination and memory so you will be able to recall and use more of the information I have shared with you.

One Saturday morning in Columbia, South Carolina, when my son Tom was three and a half years old, I walked into the den and said, "Let's go to the grocery store. I've got to buy some groceries." He said, "OK, Daddy," hopped up, slipped on his little boots, and we drove down to the store. As we walked into the store, I turned right to pick up a grocery basket, but Tom had seen a display of rubber balls, so he made a beeline for them. He grabbed one of those rubber balls, ran over, and popped it into the shopping basket.

Four Keys in Four Seconds

Now I've never talked at great length to my son about this particular little trip, but I've got an idea that when I said, "Son, let's go to the

THE NARRATIVE EVENT

grocery store," one of the reasons he was so enthusiastic about going was he had an idea. In his little mind he figured if he got his daddy down to that grocery store, he was going to get himself something. He probably didn't know what it was going to be, but he figured it would be something. He was using the "Key of Positive Projection." Once we entered the store my son also used the "Key of the Assumptive Attitude," as well as the "Key of Enthusiasm" and the "Key of Physical Action." He "assumed" he was going to get that ball, so he took "physical action" with a great deal of "enthusiasm." In five seconds he used four more keys on me!

What Would You Have Done?

I took the ball out of the basket and said, "Son, you've already got a dozen balls and you don't need another one, so take it back," and I put it into his hands. With that my son looked straight at me and said, "Daddy, can I just hold the ball?"

Question: What would you have done? Remember, now, my son was just three and a half years old. What kind of daddy would I have been to say, "No, son, you can't even hold the ball, now take it back!"? The boy did not want to buy the ball; he just wanted to hold it and all he had done was ask me a very simple "Subordinate Question." (You don't ask for the sale, you ask for the appointment. On the appointment you ask for the sale. You don't ask for the good-night kiss, you ask for the date. On the date you sell the good-night kiss.)

So I said, "OK, son, you can hold it, but don't get any ideas. You're not going to buy it. You've already got a dozen and you just don't need another one." We walked around shopping for a few minutes and came back by the display of rubber balls. I took the ball out of my son's hands, put it back in the display, and said, "Son, that's long enough, you're going to fool around, drop it, get it dirty, and then Dad'll have to buy it and you simply do not need another ball."

That's Quite an Inducement

Apparently my son was not listening when I said no because he ran back around me, took that ball out of the display, and popped it right back in the basket. He was a "Persistent" little salesman, any way you look at it. Well, I'm kind of persistent myself, so I took the ball back out of the basket and headed for the display to put it back, talking as I was walking. "Son, for the last time, Dad's already told you you've got a dozen balls; you just don't need another one." As I was walking and talking, I looked down and there he stood—all thirty-nine pounds of him. He looked up at me and said (at that time he talked with a slight lisp), "Daddy, wis you buy me that ball. I'll give you a tiss."

When you think about it for a moment, he was offering quite an "Inducement." He was offering himself. What else could a three-and-a-half-year-old give his daddy but a part of himself? Since it was in the immediate future, it was an "Impending Event." And "Sincere"—in all of my years of selling, I have never known a more sincere salesman than that three-and-a-half-year-old one.

I don't think it's necessary to tell you this, but I will. In the Ziglar household today we've got thirteen rubber balls!

At this point I need to correct something. In chapter 31 I said to you I had never seen that a woman had given birth to a salesman. Actually, that's not *quite* true, because on February 1, 1965, in Columbia, South Carolina, the local paper carried a small headline which read, "Birth of a Salesman Announced. Mr. and Mrs. Zig Ziglar announce the birth of a salesman, John Thomas Ziglar, born February 1, Provident Hospital, 9:08 P.M." Now I don't want you to get the wrong idea. I am not trying to influence my boy's career. I mean, he can *sell* anything he wants to!

That's my message to you. If you will buy these ideas and use the keys, procedures, and techniques we've been sharing, I sincerely believe you can sell more of the goods or services you are selling.

To Build a Career

A lot is involved in building a sales career. I love this story Elmer Wheeler told before his death. Once while across the border in Old Mexico he cut his finger and it had become infected. A bartender looked at the finger and said, "Man, we had better do something about that infection!" He took some tequila, put it into a shot glass full of ice, squeezed some lemon juice in it, and said, "Now if you soak your finger in this several times a day, it'll solve your problem."

I'm certain the medical community would not give its 100 percent approval to the procedure, even though the astringent effect of the lemon might contribute to the healing process. The old farmer would say, "Yup, the ice is going to reduce the swelling, so there is a certain amount of common sense involved." The poet would testify that the juice of the maguey plant would certainly have some value. A couple of days later all the swelling had disappeared and there was no soreness in the finger.

What all of this really says is, "Take a little common sense, add some scientific knowledge, throw in a little poetic philosophy, and you'll get results."

To build a sales career, you need to acquire the knowledge made available through sales trainers, books, recordings, and seminars. With that knowledge you should weave in a poetic philosophy of life which says that "you can get everything in life you want if you will just help enough other people get what they want."

To the knowledge and poetic philosophy, add the common sense of the old farmer which says, "Friend, I don't care what you do, know you've got to work and work hard at seeing new prospects and servicing old customers." You have a moral obligation to work so hard at building your sales career and becoming truly professional that as my friend John Nevin from Australia says, "If anyone ever sees you coming and says, 'Here comes a salesman,' you won't let him down."

THANK YOU

Secrets of Closing the Sale has made me even more aware of my indebtedness to the tens of thousands of salespeople who have gone before me. These pioneers blazed new frontiers, opened new doors, learned new procedures, and established the credibility of the profession. To a large degree these men and women left me a heritage which I proudly claim.

When you start to say thank you in a book of this kind, you invariably leave out some important contributors. If I have overlooked you, and others who have meant so much to this work, it's simply an indication of another of my human frailties. Please know that your efforts and help are appreciated and I apologize in advance for not including you.

I start with my friend Bill Cranford, to whom I have dedicated this book. He taught me the first principles of professional selling. Mr. P. C. Merrell also taught me some important sales principles and "sold" me the idea that I could be a sales champion. My surrogate father, Mr. John Anderson, and my first free-enterprise mentor, Mr. Walton Haining, taught me a great deal about getting along with people and communicating with them on their level. I believe that *Secrets of Closing the Sale* qualified as a unique book if for no other reason than the fact that I have been so ably assisted by a number of truly outstanding people and one major company which unselfishly shared a considerable amount of its research.

Heading that list would be Mike Frank of Columbus, Ohio; Billie Engman of San Mateo, California; D. John Hammond of Phoenix, Arizona; and Bernie Lofchick of Winnipeg, Canada. I say without hesitation that with the aid of the four of them I must have made a minimum of three hundred changes in what I have written. Not only were they generous in their praise but more important, they were constructive in their evaluation and enthusiastic with their positive suggestions to make the book more effective for you. In several cases their help enabled me to keep some egg off my face. Though I do mention each one several times, I want to emphasize that without their help, combined with the significant contributions of the others, this book would not be as effective as I am convinced it is going to be.

When the manuscript was roughly 80 percent complete, I sent these people copies and asked them for evaluations, suggestions, and additions as well as corrections. Each went above and beyond just being close friends in their zeal and enthusiasm for helping. I asked them specifically because, without exception, they have outstanding sales backgrounds and a combined knowledge that surpasses any group with which I've had the privilege of working. Each one made not just one or two but literally dozens of invaluable suggestions.

I am also indebted to Mrs. Juanell Teague of Lubbock, Texas, and Gerhard Gschwandtner, publisher of *Personal Selling Power*, as well as Phil Lynch and Bryan Flanagan of Dallas. Their suggestions and insights were extremely helpful.

I'm deeply indebted to The Forum Corporation of Boston, Massachusetts, for making the study done by William M. DeMarco, Ph.D., and Michael D. Maginn, Ed.D., available to me. These researchers did a study involving twelve "Fortune 1300" companies with large sales forces from six industries (high-tech, banking, petro-chemical, insurance, pharmaceutical, and communications). The study involved 341 carefully selected salespeople—173 high performers and 168 moderate performers. They acquired 44,741 pieces of data over a period of fourteen months. Information from their findings is scattered and identified throughout the book.

No list of thank-yous would be complete without a special one to my younger brother, Judge Ziglar, whose book *Timid Salesmen Have Skinny Kids* gave me some invaluable ideas which I utilized freely throughout the book. Jim Savage, our vice-president of Corporate Training, my right and left arm at The Zig Ziglar Corporation, was extremely helpful with his editorial comments, sales suggestions, and creative ideas.

My thanks also extends to the entire staff of The Zig Ziglar Corporation, who carried double burdens while I secreted myself at our lake home and wrote much of this book. Of necessity, several members of the staff handled their regular jobs as well as some of the things I should have been doing myself. Thank you to Ron Ezinga, president of The Zig Ziglar Corporation, and Denny Roossien, executive vice-president, who relieved me completely of most of my responsibilities and helped make this book possible.

A double-special thank-you goes to my administrative assistant, Laurie Downing. If any man ever hit the jackpot in an assistant, the author of this book certainly did that. Not only did Laurie do the work beautifully and skillfully but she mastered a new word processor in order to do so. I include an entire segment in *Secrets* on "Professionals"—no book could be completed without professional help—and Laurie Downing is certainly professional in every respect. It's also significant that her "bragging" on the book as she typed the manuscript kept me excited and encouraged. Thank you, Laurie.

If you are even casually familiar with my work, you undoubtedly know that I never undertake any major project without the knowledge, support, and enthusiastic help of "the Redhead," my wife and my life for over thirty-seven beautiful, fun-filled years. Thank you, Sugar Baby, for being you, for being mine, and for always being there.

To the salespeople of America, who are in my mind the real heroes of this century, I also want to say thank you. We still have much to do regarding our profession, but much progress has been made. I'm fervently convinced that as you read and apply the principles in this book, you will be more professional and the net result is that all of us—including the salesmen of the future—will benefit from it.

Zig Ziglar

RECOMMENDED READING

Sales Training and Sales Motivation
(Listed alphabetically by author)

Selling is an exciting profession and in many ways a complex one. There are many specialists in the field and no one person has a monopoly on all the information. I encourage you to read the books listed below to get a broader, more thorough approach to the profession. I do not necessarily agree with and approve of every concept, technique, and procedure in every book. However, I am completely convinced that you will glean some useful ideas and information from each one which will broaden your scope and deepen your thinking and appreciation for the sales profession and its incredible possibilities.

Non-Manipulative Selling, Anthony J. Allesandra, Ph.D., Reston, Virginia: Reston Press, 1981.

How I Multiplied My Income and Increased My Happiness in Selling, Frank Bettger, Englewood Cliffs, N.J.: Prentice-Hall, 1982.

How I Raised Myself from Failure to Success in Selling, Frank Bettger, Englewood Cliffs, N.J.: Prentice-Hall, 1975.

A Motivational Approach to Selling, James F. Evered, American Management, 1982.

Power Selling, Willie Gayle, Englewood Cliffs, N.J.: Prentice-Hall, 1959.

How to Sell Anything to Anybody, Joe Girard and Stanley H. Brown, New York: Warner Books, 1979.

Selling Is Simple—Not Easy, But Simple, Fred Herman, New York: Vantage Press, 1970.

How to Master the Art of Selling, Tom Hopkins, New York: Warner Books, 1982.

The Selling Heart, Jack and Garry Kinder, Indianapolis: R. & R. Newkirk, 1974.

How to Be a Supersalesman, Art Linkletter, Englewood Cliffs, N.J.: Prentice-Hall, 1974.

The Greatest Salesman in the World, Og Mandino, New York: Bantam, 1974.

Dress for Success, John Molloy, New York: Warner, 1976.

The Woman's Dress for Success Book, John Molloy, New York: Warner, 1978.

Nido Qubein's Professional Selling Techniques, Nido Qubein, Rockville Center, N.Y.: Farnsworth, 1983.

Secrets of Closing Sales, Charles B. Roth and Roy Alexander, Englewood Cliffs, N.J.: Prentice-Hall, 1982.

Winning Images, Robert Shook, New York: Macmillan, 1977.

The Feldman Method, Andrew H. Thomson, Rockville Center, N.Y.: Farnsworth, 1980.

Dress With Style, Joanne Wallace, Old Tappan, N.J.: Fleming H. Revell, 1982.

The Selling Power of a Woman, Dottie Walters, Englewood Cliffs, N.J.: Prentice-Hall, 1962.

Sizzlemanship, Elmer Wheeler, Englewood Cliffs, N.J.: Prentice-Hall, 1983.

Tested Sentences That Sell, Elmer Wheeler, Englewood Cliffs, N.J.: Prentice-Hall, 1983.

The New Psychology of Persuasion and Motivation In Selling, Robert A. Whitney, Thomas Rubin, and John D. Murphy, Englewood Cliffs, N.J.: Prentice-Hall, 1965.

The Best Seller: The New Psychology of Selling, Ron Willingham, Englewood Cliffs, N.J.: Prentice-Hall, 1984.

Open the Mind and Close the Sale, John M. Wilson, New York: McGraw-Hill, 1953.

Timid Salesmen Have Skinny Kids, Judge Ziglar, Martinez, Ga.: Action Now, 1978.

The Strategy of Successful Retail Salesmanship, Allen E. Zimmer, New York: McGraw-Hill, 1966.

Special Note: The Forum Corporation report is available for the asking. Write:

Wm. M. DeMarco, Ph.D.
The Forum Corporation
53 State Street
Boston, Massachusetts 02109

Inspiration and Self-Help
(Listed alphabetically by author)

The salesperson is one of the few professionals who goes to work with the understanding that his chances of rejection by some of the people he deals with is pretty high. With this in mind, our commitment to the profession, the image we have of ourselves, and our own personal motivation will often be the determining factors as to whether we "make it" in the profession or not. The following books have been very meaningful to me and I believe you will glean some useful ideas and inspiration from them.

How to Win Friends and Influence People, Rev. Ed., Dale Carnegie, New York: Pocket Books, 1982.

Acres of Diamonds, Russell H. Conwell, Old Tappan, N.J.: Fleming H. Revell, 1975.

The Aerobics Program for Total Well-Being, Kenneth Cooper, M.D., New York: M. Evans, 1982.

Positive Power for Successful Salesmen, Glass, Kinder, and Ward, Dallas: Crescendo, 1972.

Yak! Yak! Yak!, Ira Hayes: Ira M. Hayes, 1978.

Life Is Tremendous, Charlie Jones, Wheaton: Tyndale House, 1981.

Psycho-cybernetics, Maxwell Maltz, New York: Pocket Books, 1970.

The Greatest Miracle in the World, Og Mandino, New York: Bantam, 1977.

The Power of Positive Thinking, Norman Vincent Peale, New York: Fawcett, 1978.

Tough Times Never Last, but Tough People Do, Robert H. Schuller, Nashville: Thomas Nelson, 1983.

The Magic of Thinking Big, David J. Schwartz, St. Louis: Cornerstone, 1962.

Success Through a Positive Mental Attitude, Napoleon Hill and W. Clement Stone, New York: Pocket Books, 1977.

Seeds of Greatness, Denis Waitley, Ph.D., Old Tappan, N.J.: Fleming H. Revell, 1983.

See You at the Top, Zig Ziglar, Gretna, La.: Pelican, 1975.

For Your Continuing Education

Personal Selling Power, published monthly, Gerhard Gschwandtner & Associates, Post Office Box 5467, Fredericksburg, Virginia 22403.

Success magazine, published monthly, Success Unlimited, Inc., Post Office Box 2240, Boulder, Colorado 80322.

INDEX

TOP
PERFORMANCE
with Jim Savage

To P.C. Merrell

A Top Performer
whose leadership by example
had a lifetime impact on my performance

ACKNOWLEDGMENTS

In many ways, this is the most unusual and exciting book I have written. *Unusual* because for the first time, I worked with a coauthor. As a matter of fact, without the contribution and assistance of Jim Savage, our vice-president of Corporate Training, this book would not have been written. *Exciting* because this book makes practical tools out of the motivational principles I have shared for many years and which Jim has tested and applied in his career. He truly is the classic example of the axiom "If you do more than you are paid to do, you will eventually be paid more for what you do." He exemplifies the principles *Top Performance* teaches.

When Jim Savage joined our organization in January of 1981, it marked the end of his three-year pursuit of an opportunity to work with us. Initially, because we had no other opening, we hired him in a capacity which was considerably below his experience and capabilities. He had served as both a teacher and coach for eleven years, had worked as a scout with the Washington Redskins (two governors of the State of Texas and the Dallas mayor have issued proclamations forgiving him for that), and had functioned in an executive capacity with another human resource development company.

Initially, Jim traveled with me and was responsible for on-site activities, including sales of our products wherever I spoke around the country. Jim handled every assignment with complete commitment and with great enthusiasm. It was obvious to us that we had to utilize his talents and energies in other areas. For the last five years Jim has, among other things, authored training materials and manuals to enhance our product line and developed and implemented a comprehensive recognition-and-incentive program for our corporate staff. In addition, his abilities as a speaker and consultant have led to well over three hundred speaking and training opportunities with corporations of all sizes over the last three years. Thank you, Jim, for a job well done.

As always, Laurie Magers, my ever-faithful, always dependable administrative assistant, did a magnificent job; when called upon, Kay Lynn

Westervelt, who works so closely with Laurie, also did a beautiful job. I owe a particularly heavy debt of gratitude to my friend Fred Smith, whom I hold in such high regard, for his willingness to contribute thoughts and ideas throughout the book. A very special thank you to Leo Presley, assistant state director of Business and Industry Services, Oklahoma State Department of Vocational Education, who encouraged us and gave important direction on getting involved on a larger scale in corporate America. Leo is one of the brightest young men I have ever known.

Also, to the president of the Zig Ziglar Corporation, Ron Ezinga, whose steady hand at the helm and encouraging guidance has kept us at least partially on course in meeting our guidelines. Then, of course, there's my wife, "the Redhead," whose willingness to tolerate some intolerable demands on our time together, combined with her loving support, has made the book not only possible but an exciting experience. To the other members of our staff and to the numerous authors who contributed through your articles, thank you.

Zig Ziglar

CONTENTS

FOREWORD

Fifteen percent of the reason you get a job, keep that job, and move ahead in that job, is determined by your technical skills and knowledge—regardless of your profession! That's what human engineer Cavett Robert says. What about the other 85 percent? Cavett quotes Stanford Research Institute, Harvard University, and the Carnegie Foundation (which spent one million dollars and five years in the research) as having *proved* that 85 percent of the reason you get a job, will keep that job, and move ahead in that job has to do with your *people skills and people knowledge!*

I'm completely convinced he's right. As I travel around the country sharing ideas on personal growth, sales training, and the corporate concepts we teach at the Zig Ziglar Corporation, I become more and more aware of the critical need for specialized instruction on how we can *manage* ourselves and others for maximum effectiveness. As I visit with professionals from all walks of life, I see common problems in many—if not all—of the different situations men and women are facing . . . and the common denominator in these problems is always the same: people.

So obviously, "managing people" (starting with yourself) becomes a high priority if we are to be successful. In this book, we have three primary goals relating to understanding people management skills:

1. We will identify the key factors in people management, including helping managers to identify potential sources of conflict.

2. We will offer solutions to help overcome these potential sources of conflict.

3. We will share how you can apply the principles and ideas other managers have used successfully, thereby taking this book out of the realm of "theory" and making it applicable in the "real world."

According to *Megatrends* author John Naisbitt, "For the reinvented, information-age corporation of 1985 and beyond, the challenge is retraining *managers*, not retraining workers." With this in mind, the ultimate goal of *Top Performance* is to develop excellence in managers and to provide management with teaching procedures and inspiration to effectively develop and utilize team members.

Make Them Want Your Leadership

The foundation for developing yourself and others is wrapped up in this principle:

> *You can have everything in life you want if you will just help enough other people get what they want!*

I have used this statement for nearly thirty years as a foundational truth, and never is the concept more accurate than when managing yourself and others. However, it is important for you to understand that I'm talking about a *principle* and not a *tactic*. As a tactic the words would be crass and ineffective. As a principle the concept works because it makes others *want* your leadership.

The great managers from all fields *know* that when they put people first, their effectiveness and efficiency improve. Zoltan Merszel, who left Dow Chemical to become president of Occidental Petroleum, said, "My philosophy is that *people* make business; technology is a distant second."

Use All Your Strength

Chances are excellent you agree that one basic definition of *management* is "getting things done through people." The story is told of a little guy valiantly but futilely trying to move a heavy log to clear a pathway to his favorite hideout. His dad stood nearby and finally asked him why he wasn't using all his strength. The little guy assured his dad he was straining with all his might. His dad quietly told him he was not using all his strength, because he hadn't asked him (his dad) to help. Successful managers use *all* their strength by recognizing, developing, and utilizing the physical, mental, and spiritual talents of their subordinates. They learn what makes people tick, and they transfer their own feelings of excitement and enthusiasm to those who follow their leadership.

That last sentence is true whether you are a sales manager, a supervisor, a trainer, a corporate executive, a parent, a doctor, a teacher, a coach, or any number of other professionals "on the grow"! Chances are good that if you are not already doing well in your chosen career, you are on the verge of a breakthrough to becoming more successful. Regardless of your chosen profession in life, *Top Performance: How to Develop Excellence in Yourself and Others* is written specifically for *you!*

By now you should be ready to go, so hold on to your hat and grab your marking pen, because you and I are headed for the most action- and information-packed book you have ever *worked* through!

INTRODUCTION

Several years ago, this old boy down home won a bass fiddle in a drawing. It came complete with an instruction book, but unfortunately every page—except the first one—had been torn out. All that was left was a single picture showing the left hand in one position at the top of the fiddle and the other hand with the bow in a position across the strings near the middle of the bass fiddle. The old boy thought that was *the* position for playing the bass fiddle, so he carefully noted the position of each hand and started pulling the bow back and forth. Obviously, he was "Old Johnny One Note." Back and forth he drew the bow and the gruesome sound came forth. He was diligent in his practice and did it every single day.

Needless to say, his wife was soon climbing the walls. Then one day she went to a concert and, as it happened, sat next to the orchestra within a few feet of the bass fiddle. She was intrigued with the way the fellow moved his left hand up and down the strings while repeatedly changing the bow position. He made fast strokes and slow strokes and he pulled the bow all over those strings. The music was beautiful, so the wife returned home all excited about what she had seen and found old Johnny One Note playing his fiddle.

Knowing his nature and not wanting to upset him, she gently said, "Honey, can I ask you a question?" Without breaking stride or slowing down, he said, "Sure." Wife: "At the concert I noticed that the bass fiddle player kept moving his left hand up and down and left and right, while his right hand moved slowly on occasion and rapidly on occasion, and he moved it in a number of different spots. I'm just curious as to why he was moving his hands and the bow in so many different ways and places, while you hold both your hands and the bow in the same spot." The old boy never broke stride; continuing to play, he simply said, "The answer's easy. That old boy's still lookin' for his place and I done found mine!"

Now, my friends, obviously this story never happened, but I do fear it happens many times in life and in the business world, where many people "find their places" and don't want to make any changes. I know that's not your attitude in and about life or you wouldn't be reading this book! I share the story because you will have to deal with those who do have that kind of attitude. Hopefully, the suggestions we offer will help you in your own career, as well as give you some guidelines to help others open their minds to develop and use their abilities.

PART ONE

THE ART OF
TOP PERFORMANCE

The object of art is to crystallize emotion into thoughts and then fix it in
form.

Delsarte

1

CHOOSING TO BE
A TOP PERFORMER

We are free up to the point of choice, then the choice
controls the chooser.

Mary Crowley

OUR SUCCESS IN LIFE is determined by the choices we make. You are
going to be making choices that will determine your success as you
learn to manage yourself and others. To be effective in making proper
choices, you must understand the difference between *reacting* and *responding*.

On January 23, 1981, I was in Kansas City, Missouri. It had been one
of those weeks. As we'd say down home, "I'd been drove hard and hung
up wet!" I wasn't just whipped—I was *whupped!* And there is a difference.
That particular morning I had a lengthy recording session—four
solid hours. When I record, of necessity I must turn my volume and
tempo up a couple of notches. The only means of communication I
have on a recording is my voice, so I must utilize it to the fullest or the
people who listen to the recording might let their minds drift and miss
the message.

That morning for four solid hours the session was wide-open, full-speed
ahead, no holds barred. (I speak at about 280 words a minute with
gusts up to 450.) I finished at exactly one o'clock and since we had a
three o'clock departure time for Dallas, we had to hurry. The airline had
told us to get to the airport at least an hour early to secure our recording
equipment, which is very heavy and bulky. My son-in-law, Chad
Witmeyer, who is the general manager for At the Top, our recording
and cassette-duplication corporation, packed our gear as quickly as possible
and the two of us made a mad dash for the airport, which is a thirty-minute
trip from downtown Kansas City.

We pulled into the airport at exactly two o'clock. There were two long
lines and we selected the shortest of the two. I noticed almost immedi-

ately that one of the ticket agents was walking around behind the counter and I saw a POSITION CLOSED sign at one end. My experience told me she would remove POSITION CLOSED and replace it with POSITION OPEN, so I mentally and physically got ready to make a quick dash to the counter when she opened the other line. In a matter of minutes she walked over the POSITION CLOSED sign, flipped it to POSITION OPEN, and smilingly announced to the group, "Those of you who have a seat on the three o'clock flight to Dallas come over here."

Surprise, Surprise!

Quick as a flash, I ran to her position and was first in line. The ticket agent looked at me, smiled, and said, "The three o'clock flight to Dallas has been canceled." To this I enthusiastically responded, "Fantastic!" When I said that, the ticket agent, with a puzzled expression on her face, asked, "Now, why in the world would you say 'fantastic' when I've just told you the three o'clock flight to Dallas has been canceled?" I smiled back at her and said, "Ma'am, there are only three reasons why anybody would cancel a flight to Dallas, Texas. Number one, something must be wrong with that airplane; number two, something must be wrong with the person who is going to fly that airplane; number three, something must be wrong with the weather they're going to fly that airplane in. Now, ma'am, if any one of those three situations exists, I don't want to be up there. I want to be right down here! Fantastic!"

Hot Dog, I've Got Some Bad News for You!

Have you ever noticed how some people seem to delight in delivering bad news? It's as if they just can't wait to let you know that life is tough and you're in for a tough time. To my response, the ticket agent put her hands on her hips in an authoritative, "I'm not through with you yet" kind of position and said, "Yes, but the next flight doesn't leave until 6:05." To that I responded, "Fantastic!"

By now the other two lines of people were looking in my direction and undoubtedly wondering, Who is that nut who says everything is fantastic? The lady herself looked at me in complete shock and said, "Now I'm really puzzled. Why in the world would you say 'fantastic' when I've just told you that you've got a four-hour wait in the airport in Kansas City?" I smilingly said, "Ma'am, it's really very simple. I'm fifty-four years old and never before in my entire life have I had a chance to spend four hours in the airport in Kansas City, Missouri. Why," I said, "do you realize that at this moment there are literally tens of millions of people on the face of this earth who not only are cold, but who also are hungry? Here I am in a beautiful facility and even though it's cold outside, it's comfortable inside. Down the corridor is a nice little coffee shop. I'm going to go down there, relax for a few minutes, and enjoy a cup of coffee. Then I've got some extremely important work which I need to do and here I am in one of the nicest buildings in the whole area. It is easily the biggest, most comfortable, rent-free office I've ever had at my disposal. Fantastic!"

That's Pretty Strong—Even for Positive Thinkers

Now, I'm reasonably confident you may be saying to yourself, "Ziglar, I'll go along with a lot of this 'positive thinking' stuff, but man, that's a little strong!" You might even be saying to yourself, "I wonder if he *really* did say that?" As we'd say down home, "On my scout's honor, that's exactly what I said."

To this you might well say, "Okay, Ziglar, you said it. But now tell me the truth—did you *really* feel that way?" To this I respond, "Of course not!" At least initially I didn't really feel that way. Like most travelers who've had a tough week on the road, I would have preferred to have been on my way home, but for the next four hours I did not have that option. However, I did have two other options to choose from. I could have chosen to *respond*—which is positive—or I could have chosen to *react*—which is negative. I chose to respond.

If *react* and *respond* sound like the same things to you, let me explain the difference. You go to the doctor, who gives you a prescription and tells you to come back the next day. When you go back, if he looks worried and tells you he needs to change the prescription because your body is "reacting" to the medicine, you're probably going to be concerned. On the other hand, if he tells you your body is "responding" to the medicine, you're going to smile because you know you're on your way to recovery. So, to react is negative and to respond is positive—the choice is yours! It's a fact that *you can't tailor-make the situations in life, but you can tailor-make the attitudes to fit those situations before they arise.*

When the ticket agent told me my flight had been canceled, I could have reacted sarcastically and said, "That's great! That's just great! I've had reservations for this flight for over a month and I've had the ticket for two weeks. I've done everything you've told me to do, including nearly breaking my neck to get here an hour early. All I need is my boarding pass and my seat assignment, but without explanation and without apology you tell me some dodo has canceled my flight! Well, I want to know why the flight was canceled! As I drove up I saw several of your airplanes sitting out on the runway, not doing a cotton-pickin' thing. Why can't you take one of them and fly us to Dallas like you are supposed to? What are they doing out there, anyhow? Who made the dumdum decision to cancel my flight to Dallas, Texas?" I could have reacted in that sarcastic manner. *And the next flight still leaves at 6:05!*

Respond—For a Better Tomorrow

Now, my reading friend, there are some things you simply are not going to change. If you were born white, you're going to stay white. If you were born black, you're going to stay black. I don't care how much thought you give it, you're not going to add a single cubit to your height. You're not going to change when you were born, where you were born, how you were born, or to whom you were born. As a matter of fact, you're not going to change one single whisper that's taken place in the *yesterdays* of your life.

Tomorrow is a different subject. Regardless of your past, your tomorrow is a clean slate. You can choose what you want to write on that slate. You make that choice each time you decide to *respond* to negative events or *react* to those negative events. As a manager, when your employees act in a rude, thoughtless, and inconsiderate manner and are impossible to deal with, please understand you can still *choose* to respond or react. Your choice will play a major role in your relationship with your employee. Obviously, this doesn't mean that to lead others you, the manager, must be "perfect" and never blow your cool. That's not only unrealistic, it is impossible—and maybe even undesirable. After all, managers are people, too, and our employees need to know we are human and have feelings. On balance, however, we need to be careful we choose to respond far more often than we choose to react, and that when we react it is under control and is to the *action* the person took and not to the employee personally.

My friend Fred Smith, one of the truly outstanding consultants and management experts in America, gives us some helpful advice on this matter in his excellent book *You and Your Network*. Fred says that when others deal with us in a dogmatic or even in a mean and vicious way, it doesn't necessarily mean they want to hurt us. It could mean, and generally does, that they are acting that way because *they* are hurting. If you will remember that

---

every obnoxious act is a cry for help,

you are way ahead of the game. Recognizing and accepting this fact makes it much easier for us to take a calmer, more levelheaded approach to our functions as managers and as people.

It's Up to You

All of life is a series of choices, and what you choose to give life today will determine what life will give you tomorrow. You can choose to get drunk tonight, but when you do, you have *chosen* to feel miserable tomorrow. You can choose to light up a cigarette today, but when you do, you have *chosen* to die fourteen minutes early. You can choose to eat properly today and when you do, you have *chosen* to be healthier tomorrow. You can choose to be overweight, or you can choose to be the right weight. You can choose to be happy or you can choose to be sad. You can even choose, according to some authorities, to be insane—and *some* people make that choice to escape the responsibilities of dealing with life on a daily basis.

For twenty-four years of my adult life, by choice I weighed over two hundred pounds. I say this because in my lifetime (at least since infancy) I have never *accidentally* eaten anything! Every bite is carefully planned and deliberately taken. I even set aside at least three times *every* day when I concentrate almost exclusively on taking those bites of food. When I choose to eat too much today, I have chosen to weigh too much tomorrow. In 1972, I *chose* not to be overweight and took the appropriate steps to reach and maintain the correct weight. It was one of my better choices.

Never will I forget the night my wife (to whom I affectionately refer as "the Redhead") and I were in our favorite ice cream parlor when a young man and his girlfriend walked in. He appeared to be about twenty-three or twenty-four years old. I gently nudged the Redhead and pointed out the couple and the following dialogue took place.

Zig: "Do you see that couple?" The Redhead: "Yes, I do." Zig: "Wonder what happened to him." The Redhead: "What do you mean?" Zig: "Well, just look at him! He's been in some kind of accident. He's hurt!" The Redhead: "Aw, honey, he's not hurt! He's been to the barbershop." Zig: "You mean he paid money to look like *that?*" (In my lifetime, I've never seen a human being that badly mutilated from the ears up. It was awesome!) The Redhead: "Sure, honey! He's trying to be different and original, so he's chosen to imitate some rock star."

Don't misunderstand, one of the things I love best about my country is the fact that we are free and can *choose* to look any way we please. The major point I wish to make is that when that young fellow chose to look that way, he also chose to eliminate 98 percent of all employment opportunities. For example, we could not consider hiring him at our company. He would be a total distraction and we'd have to spend half our time just explaining him!

When a young person chooses to sit up late at night watching television or socializing, he has chosen to be sleepy in class the next day and, consequently, absorb less of the information he needs to know in order to be successful in the competitive world in which he lives. When we choose to be mean, nasty, and ornery to other people, we have chosen to be treated in a mean, nasty, and ornery fashion by others. By the same token, when we choose to be thoughtful and considerate of others, we've chosen to be treated in a thoughtful and considerate manner. The list is endless, but the message is always the same: *You are free to choose, but the choices you make today will determine what you will have, be, and do in the tomorrows of your life.*

You can choose to take the necessary steps to help you succeed as a manager, or you can choose to ignore the experience of successful managers and take the consequences for you and your employees. We must teach our employees that they are responsible for their attitudes and their conduct and that in life,

> *every choice we make, whether it is good or bad, has consequences!*

Once those consequences are thoroughly understood, it's easier to make the right choices. As Mary Crowley, an outstanding Christian businesswoman and author, says, "We are free up to the point of choice, then the choice controls the chooser."

Back to the Airport

At the airline counter I had another choice. I could have ranted and raved and whooped and shouted and snorted and screamed and hollered. I could have made an absolute idiot of myself and embarrassed everybody around me as well as myself by screaming, "That's crazy! That's idiotic! I'm tired! I've been gone all week! My family wants to see me and I want to see them! Who made this decision, anyway? Who runs this outfit?" Yes, I could have chosen that as the second reaction. *And the next flight still leaves at 6:05!*

The Choice Is Yours

I chose to respond as I did for one simple reason. I don't have, need, or want ulcers, high blood pressure, a heart problem, or any of the negative consequences that go with reacting. I have chosen to *respond* to negative situations in life instead of *reacting* to those situations. Even if this does not benefit anyone else, I'm persuaded that it is the best thing I can do for me. When it's the best thing for me, then obviously that puts me in a far better position to do my work, which basically is designed to help other people. That, my friend, is exactly the same position you are in. When you *respond*, you are making real progress toward living a healthier, happier life and developing effective, efficient, and happy employees.

As a practical matter, I do not know anyone who works for that monstrous airline. From the chairman of the board to the people who handle the baggage, I cannot give you the name of a single one. However, it is their airline and *if they choose to do so, they can cancel my flight. But they can't cancel my day!* It's mine. God Himself gave it to me with written instructions on how I am to use it. He told me to "rejoice—and be glad in it."

The problem with letting others "cancel your day" is that they just might want to cancel a second or even a third day (you know how folks are!). Then they might want to cancel the whole week or even a month. Some people have even permitted others to cancel a lifetime. As we go through *Top Performance*, we are going to look at specific steps and usable formulas that will help you make the right decisions while helping those for whom you are responsible to also make the proper choices!

Innocent—Or Guilty?

Question: Have you ever been heading for work, driving along, minding your own business, your mind "in neutral," when suddenly somebody cuts sharply in front of you at an exit? You manage to avoid him by hitting your brakes full force while at the same time sounding your horn, shaking your fist at the offender, and even yelling, "You dummy! Why don't you watch what you're doing? I could've been killed and so could you!" Have you ever gotten upset about an incident like that and taken your anger to work, where you proceeded to tell everybody in earshot about this idiot who pulled in front of you and almost killed you? Did you wonder out loud why they allow people like that to get licenses? How could anybody have made such an idiotic mistake? And you go on and on and on as you describe in angry terms the idiot who almost killed you. "They ought to keep people like him off the streets!" you declare with righteous indignation.

In the meantime, the man who committed the dastardly deed rides merrily on, completely oblivious of the fact that you even exist or that anything unusual has happened. And yet, he is in complete control of your life. He is in charge of your mind and your emotions. He is affecting your productivity, your relationships with others, even your very future, and (once more) *he doesn't even know you exist!* One of our greatest gifts is the ability to choose the way we think, act, or feel, and the ultimate personal put-down is when we permit someone like the above-mentioned driver to take charge of our lives and our attitudes.

Think with me for a moment. If you are the way you are because "when your mother was pregnant with you she was scared by a runaway horse, and consequently you have been scared of big, brown animals ever since. . . ." If you are the way you are because they "snatched you off the potty too soon. . . ." If you are the way you are because of someone else, then here's what you do: You take the person who's responsible for the way you are to the psychologist, the psychologist will treat him or her, and *you* will get better! See how crazy that is? If you fall and break your arm, you don't send a friend to the doctor to have his arm set. You don't even send the one who pushed you! You go yourself—you take personal responsibility! It's the same for your mental and emotional health. You must accept personal responsibility.

Yes, I know that *your past is important,* but as important as it is, according to Dr. Tony Campolo, *it is not nearly as important to your present as the way you see your future.* Ralph Waldo Emerson was right when he said that what lies behind you and what lies before you pale in significance when compared to what lies within you. This is especially true when you learn to respond and not react to life's daily challenges.

It's been said before and it will be said again: You cannot change the past, but your future is spotless. You can write on it what you will. In order to do so, however, you need to learn to *respond* to the positive *and* the negative. Fortunately, you have far more control than you realize. For example, all of us have on occasion been guilty of saying, "He/She makes me so mad!" That simply is not so. As a wise man said, you can't stir the soup unless there's some soup in the pot to stir. Nobody can make you *act* mad unless there is already some mad in you. Mad reactions are *learned* behaviors and consequently they can be *unlearned.*

You can watch a person go about his or her daily activities for days or weeks and learn a great deal about him. However, you can watch a person under adverse circumstances for five minutes and see whether he has learned to respond or react. Actually, you can learn more about him in a few minutes under trying conditions than you can in days of just watching him involved in daily activities.

Your response—or reaction—to the negative reveals what's inside of you. It exposes your heart and shows the kind of person you really are. The problem is that most people have a tendency to react instead of respond. They have a tendency to blame everything and everybody for the difficulties and reversals in life.

It Started in the Beginning

The reaction—tendency to blame someone else for your difficulties—procedure is not new. It started back in the Garden of Eden. You undoubtedly remember the story. God placed Adam and Eve in the Garden of Eden; He gave them everything a human being could possibly desire or even imagine. It was the whole world, including the mineral rights (talk about a real estate deal—WOW!). However, He specifically instructed them not to eat the fruit from one special tree. But you know what happened: They ate the fruit.

When God came walking in the garden that evening, He called out, "Adam, where are you?" (This won't be verbatim.) Adam responded, "Over here, Lord," and the Lord asked Adam, "Did you eat the fruit of the forbidden tree?" Simple question. All God wanted was a yes or no answer. But Adam's answer set the precedent of pointing the finger of blame at someone else for our own difficulties, which the world has followed ever since. He said, "Lord, let me tell You about that woman You gave me!" The Lord then asked Eve if she had eaten the forbidden fruit and Eve replied, "Lord, let me tell You about that serpent!" (And of course, the serpent didn't have a leg to stand on!) I might not be completely right theologically with that last observation, but I am right when I say *you* don't have a leg to stand on when you blame other people and other things for your difficulties. Point: Don't waste time placing blame. *Fix the cause!*

Question: Do You Respond or React?

I've been beating the bushes a long time, but I seldom hear anyone make a habit of blaming someone else for his success. He doesn't say, "It's all my manager's fault. He/She spent a lot of extra time with me and made me study, drill, and prepare. He's/She's the reason I'm successful today." Most of the time we don't even say, "It was my spouse's or parents' fault. They kept after me night and day until I did what was necessary, and that's the reason I've been successful." No, most of us have a tendency to *blame* somebody else for our difficulties, but keep appropriate credit for our success to ourselves. What about you? Do you *respond* to the negative and make it better, or do you *react* to the negative and make it worse?

To be a Top Performer, you must make the proper choices. Now, if you have never had instruction on HOW to respond positively or WHAT Top Performers do to become Top Performers, then you have a "built in" excuse. But wait a minute! I'm not going to let you hang your hat on that excuse. Together, we are going to look at HOW, WHAT, WHO, WHY, WHEN, AND WHERE to make the proper choices so that you can get the most out of yourself and others!

PERFORMANCE PRINCIPLES

1. Regardless of your past, tomorrow is a clean slate.

2. Every obnoxious act is a cry for help.

3. Don't waste time placing blame; fix the cause!

4. The choices you make today will determine what you will have, be, and do in the tomorrows of your life.

5. Top Performers *learn* to make the proper choices.

2

CAUSING OTHERS
TO *WANT* YOUR
LEADERSHIP

> Leadership: the art of getting someone else to do
> something that you want done because he wants to
> do it.
>
> Dwight D. Eisenhower

IN JULY OF 1984, I was on a media tour of the country promoting my book *Secrets of Closing the Sale*. Now it just happens that I thoroughly enjoy this phase of my life. The schedule is generally hectic, but over the years the media, with few exceptions, has been extremely kind to me. Bookstores have been delighted to sponsor autograph parties because they generally sell lots of books, which is why they are in business. On this particular occasion, I ended up in a beautiful Houston, Texas, hotel at 2:30 A.M. I was really excited, since I had experienced a truly incredible day where *everything* had gone exactly right. Wonderful interviews, friendly people, lots and lots of sales, and my first interview the next day wasn't until 11:00 A.M.

A Sense of Humor Will Help

As I approached the desk to register, a quick glance at the night clerk told me things had not been going well for her. Her facial expressions indicated she had not only lost her last friend but had also had some M & M's melt in her hand, and might even have received some junk mail with the postage due. Despite her melancholy countenance, I enthusiastically approached the registration desk and the following exchange took place.

Zig: "Good morning, how ya doin'?" Night Clerk: "Oh, I suppose I'll make it." Zig: "I bet you not only make it, I bet you are going to win!" Night Clerk: "Well, you certainly feel good though it's so late!" Zig: "Yes, I do. When I woke up this morning I knew I was ahead of the game, because *some* people did not wake up this morning." (She *almost* smiled at that.) Night Clerk: "Well, I suppose that's the best way to look at it." Zig: "It definitely is." Night Clerk: "I suppose so, but I need to get you to fill out our registration slip." As I handed the slip back to her she said, "Now I need a major credit card." Fortunately, I was able to comply with her request and so I handed her this version of a truly major credit card.

When she saw the card she burst out laughing and even demonstrated some real enthusiasm as she said, "You know, I'm delighted you came along. I definitely feel better—but I'm going to need some other form of identification." With that comment I turned the card over and when she saw what you are now looking at, she almost did the proverbial roll on the floor:*

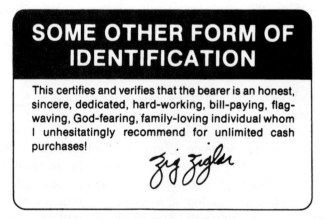

* If you would like one of these "Major Credit Cards," send a stamped, self-addressed envelope to
The Zig Ziglar Corporation
3330 Earhart
Carrollton, Texas 75006

Question: Do you think she was a better employee the rest of her shift? I'll answer it for you. You betcha! Question: Why? Answer: A change of attitude.

I include this little episode because I believe that in our high-intensity world a sense of humor can play a major role in our physical and emotional health. Humor helps us relate to others and will help make them want to know us, to please us, and to want to follow our leadership and direction.

Robert DeBruyn has written an excellent book called *Causing Others to Want Your Leadership*. While this book is designed specifically for educators, I recommend it highly. There are so many practical and usable concepts in the book that it is worthwhile reading for all Top Performers. After all, one of the manager's most important functions is *teaching*.

Actually, I believe management goes beyond leadership, because management is that special kind of leadership where the goals of the organization must be combined with the goals of the individual for the good of both. If the individual's goals are more important than the organizational goals, or are in conflict with organizational goals, the organization will suffer. Similarly, if organizational goals overshadow individual goals or are in conflict with individual goals, the person will suffer. Excellent managers of people *cause* others to *want* them to channel energies for the maximum benefit of both.

This obviously applies whether we are talking about an office, an athletic team, a church, a home, or any situation where two or more people are gathered with a potentially common interest. Our objective must be to foster this common interest and be sure that individual and organizational goals complement each other as much as possible.

Leaders Deserve—And Get—Cooperation

No matter how brilliant or how technically capable you are, you won't be effective as a leader unless you gain the *willing cooperation of others*. For example, let's think together about the number of people you can really "force" to cooperate. Eliminate the boss because he is over you. You can't force those at your level because they are equal in authority. You can't even force a subordinate to obey without his filing a complaint, quitting, or developing so much resentment that his output will suffer, directly or indirectly. Realistically, if you have a subordinate who always agrees, watch out! It's probably because he lacks self-starting qualities, the ability to think for himself, or both. *Cooperation is not getting the other fellow to do what you want. Rather, it means getting him to want to do what you want.* And there's a great deal of difference by the addition of this one word *want.*

True cooperation generally depends on certain feelings that have been established over a period of time. It's the responsibility—and opportunity—of the leader to understand and develop these deeper feelings and then to work *with* them, rather than against them. Now let's look at some basic rules and thoughts for getting cooperation.

1. The sensitive, effective leader knows that to get real cooperation he must understand he probably doesn't have all the facts *or* feelings about anything.

2. Dynamic leaders understand that *anyone* can get along and work with those who agree with them. Real leadership involves getting along, working with, and getting maximum production from those with whom we disagree.

3. Effective leaders develop the ability to see things from the other person's perspective. They *sell* the advantages of cooperation instead of demanding it.

4. Organized leaders carefully plan their projects and choose the time and place when their ideas are most likely to be accepted, and then present those ideas in a clear, concise manner.

5. The successful leader starts with the basic premise that the other person is probably at least partially right and, consequently, doesn't let his own prejudice stand in the way of accepting valid counterproposals and ideas. He knows ideas don't care who owns or uses them, so he wins cooperation with an open mind.

Why Should Anyone Want to Follow You?

I hope that once you get past the "attention grabbing" value of the question you can turn your interest and attention to the point: Have you taken a personal inventory of your strengths as a manager? Come on, now, there must be some reason you have your position. This is not the time for false modesty. Try to recall those positive statements you have heard from others. The fact that we have trouble remembering positive reinforcement is a terrible indictment of our society and should emphasize to each of us the importance of sincerely pointing out the good we see in others. However, now is the time to honestly face some facts about yourself and your future as a manager of people. Look at areas such as Planning, Organization, Communication, Listening, Decision Making, Delegation, and Motivation. Before we go any further, right here and now list at least ten *strengths* you have as a manager of people.

Significant Reasons Others Should Want to Follow Me

1. _____

2. _____

3. _____

4. _____

5. _____

6. _____

7. _____

8. _____

9. _____

10. _____

Regardless of the length or strength of the list you made, you can become even more effective as a manager of people. John D. Rockefeller stated, "I will pay more for the ability to deal with people than any other ability under the sun." To cause others to *want* our leadership and management we must become experts in the kind of people skills to which Mr. Rockefeller was referring. According to Emerson, *our chief want is someone who will inspire us to be what we know we could be.* Dan Rather, "CBS News" commentator, took Emerson's idea a step further when he said, "The dream begins with a teacher who believes in you, who tugs and pushes and leads you to the next plateau, sometimes poking you with a sharp stick called 'truth.'" As a manager, you must embody all that these men are speaking of and more. If this sounds like an overwhelming task, it is not. Actually, becoming an expert in the people business can be very simple. I did not say "easy" . . . nothing in life is easy, but managing people should not—*must* not—be made complex.

Question: As a manager, if someone with the following qualities applied to you for a job, would you find a spot in your company or department for him or her? This individual has the evidence and can *prove* that he/she is honest, enthusiastic, intelligent, disciplined, dependable, caring, knowledgeable, humble, hardworking, persistent, loyal, organized, motivated, dedicated, patient, ambitious, energetic, friendly, goal-directed, personable, responsible, loving, and thoughtful. Not only that, but this individual has a positive mental attitude, is wise, has faith, is a good listener, has a marvelous sense of humor, a fine character, and shows integrity.

Question: Do you think this person would have a fair shot at success with your company? Two things: First, we both know this person could succeed with your company or with proper training in just about any job or profession he/she chose to enter. Second, odds are long that you think such a person doesn't exist—but I urge you, if you have that thought, *think again.*

Actually, the person with all these winning characteristics is *you.* Now before you protest too loudly, I challenge you to go over the list characteristic by characteristic. Think about it. You have *some* honesty, *some* enthusiasm, *some* intelligence, and so forth. You truly have *some* of every one of those qualities. You truly are a remarkable person—and so are the people in your company or department. Your challenge and responsibility is to further develop and use what you have and motivate your people to use what they have because they, too, have these characteristics. This short story makes a point about what you need to do to further develop these characteristics in your people.

Years ago in a remote Eskimo village, dogfights were the only diversion and "sport." One old Eskimo owned two particularly strong and vicious dogs who fought each other every Saturday. One dog won one week, but invariably the other dog won the following week. Interestingly enough, the owner of the dogs *always* bet on the winning dog. After the dogs got old and unable to fight, they were retired. At that point someone asked the Eskimo how he had always picked the winning dog. With a twinkle in his eye, the old Eskimo replied that each week he fed only one dog and that week he bet on the one he had fed. Makes sense, doesn't it? As a manager I can tell you something which makes even more sense. To develop your abilities and further your career you need to "feed" your mind on a regular basis with good, clean, pure, powerful information.

Doesn't it make even more sense to take these extremely good, winning qualities you *and* your people have (admittedly, in some of them your inventory might be fairly limited, but remember that the mighty oak from the acorn grows), and *daily* feed your mind via good books, seminars, and cassette recordings the information and inspiration needed to make these "acorns" of good qualities and characteristics grow into the "mighty oaks" which will carry you to your objectives?

Powerful, powerful suggestion: Write the list of qualities and characteristics identified on page 439 on a three-by-five-inch card and read them in the first person, present tense every day. This will be especially effective if you do it in front of a mirror while looking yourself directly in the eye. Be enthusiastic and convincing. Do this just before you go to sleep so your subconscious mind can work with it all night.

> *I am honest*
> *I am enthusiastic*
> *I am intelligent*
> *I am disciplined*

Do You "Rush" to Judgment?

A family counselor once said that what most wives want is a man they can look up to but one who will not look down on them. A manager's or leader's team members want *exactly* the same thing. Someone they can truly look up to—but someone who does not look down on them. This is the goal every manager should strive for in dealing with his people. This next page out of my own book of life makes the point quite well.

Several years ago, while on my way to a small town in Ohio for a speaking engagement, I had to stop in Pittsburgh to make a connection. I had a little over an hour on my hands and so, as I walked toward the connecting gate, I was in no particular hurry. Two young men had a booth and were shining shoes.

One of the guys was "Mr. Personality"—outgoing, jovial, pleasant—the kind of guy who could brighten up any party. The other was the exact opposite—somber, quiet, absolutely nonexpressive. He was "just there." I wanted the "Personality Kid" to shine my shoes, but he was still working on his customer when I arrived and the quiet young man was available, so I had no option.

As I stepped up into the chair, I cheerfully greeted the young man with, "How ya doin'?" He simply looked at me as if I did not exist and said absolutely nothing. I could not help but think that his behavior was certainly strange for somebody who was working with the public and who, to a very large degree, depended on his income from tips. However, since I am the "incurable optimist," I started rationalizing that in all probability I had gotten the one who was the best at what I wanted done—namely, shining shoes.

As the young man applied the saddle soap to clean the shoes, I immediately noticed he was very meticulous—extremely careful not to get any of the soap on my socks or my pant leg—and I was pleased with that. As he dried the shoes I again noticed how extraordinarily careful he was and how efficiently he worked. By the time he finished applying the polish, I was convinced I had come out ahead by getting him. He was very thorough and careful. As a matter of fact, he's the only guy I've ever seen who looked around at the back of my shoes to make certain he was applying polish everywhere.

When he started brushing the shoes it was obvious that he was using the artist's touch. He was very good and I was getting more enthusiastic all the time. When he applied the cloth to the leather, he had to use a little pressure to get the high gloss he wanted. It was at this point that, for the first time, I really *looked* at the young man. Since the enthusiastic kid in the next stand had finished, there was no one in the other chair, so things were extremely quiet and for the first time I heard an almost inaudible "uh-uh-uh." At this point I realized the young man was seriously handicapped.

As you can well imagine, I felt like about two cents. Here I, in my high-and-mighty judgmental way, had decided I was going to "honor" this young man by "letting" him shine my shoes! In my own mind, I was even going to be bighearted and give him a nice tip—*if* he was pleasant, courteous, gracious, outgoing, and also gave me a magnificent shine!

Needless to say, it was a very humbling experience and also needless to say, this young man got the biggest tip I've ever given anybody for shining my shoes.

I've often thought about the young man's parents and what a magnificent job they had done of raising him. He was neat and clean and he was using an extremely high percentage of his abilities. In short, his parents, or whoever raised him, were exceptional people and outstanding managers.

As managers, our job is to further the abilities our people have and then lead them to productively use those abilities. As my friend Fred Smith says, a manager "is not a person who can do the work better than his men; he is a person who can get his men to do the work better than he can." In many cases our employees have much more talent than we realize they have. It's also true that some people are a little slower than others at developing and manifesting their abilities. I think of people like Grandma Moses, who got such a late start in life; Albert Einstein, who was four years old before he could walk or talk; Thomas Edison, who was considered slow and dumb; George Westinghouse, who was labeled "impractical" and "dull," and was asked to leave college because his teachers didn't think he could make it—and yet he was awarded a patent for the rotary steam engine before he was twenty!

The point I'm making with this is—or should be—obvious. Most people have considerable ability, often undeveloped, which is not always immediately noticeable. Many others, like the young shoeshine boy, are more than willing to use what they've got to do a marvelous job. As managers, we need to be ever alert to find and develop whatever talent is available in our company or department.

A Formula for Success

I think you will agree that the responsibility of your unit—whether it is you and one other person or you and one hundred other people—is to function together for a common cause or purpose. Unquestionably, the 1984 Olympics held in Los Angeles were a great triumph. One of the primary reasons was Peter Ueberroth, the man in charge, the MANAGER. Mr. Ueberroth was successful, according to many of those who worked closely with him, because he made everyone believe they were involved in a *cause* that was bigger than the individual. The way he involved everyone in his (and their) cause was by using excellent PEOPLE SKILLS. He developed a team spirit and had everyone working together for the same end result. You can do the same thing with smaller or larger units by understanding a simple formula for success.

Much has been written and said about team effort. It's important for the family, for the athletic team, and for the workplace. Recently a friend of mine was discussing a basketball team for which his son plays. The team was functioning quite well early in the season. There were no "superstars" on board, but they had learned considerable discipline and a series of plays which were enabling them to beat teams which actually had greater individual talent. They had a good record. Then two guys who had been ineligible regained their eligibility and joined the team at the change of semesters. As individuals, these two guys were bigger, stronger, faster, and better shooters, but unfortunately they did not have the discipline, nor did they know the plays. The net result was, though they had the talent, they actually were liabilities instead of assets to the team. Important point: They were liabilities because the coach did not have the courage to keep them on the bench *until* they learned the plays and developed the discipline to function as team members instead of individual talents. That coach (manager) let himself, his team, his supporters, *and* the two individuals down.

As managers we frequently have similar situations arise in which an individual might have great talent and ability, but because of certain personality traits, annoying habits, or refusal to function as part of the team, they became liabilities instead of assets. The most important function a manager has is to bring the individuals together as a team—in other words, to make them "GEL."

In athletics we often hear coaches talk about team spirit. They sell their units on the importance of playing together for a common cause: WINNING! One of the catchwords that coaches use to describe unity is *gel*. They will say that the offense is just beginning to gel; or to be successful the defense must gel. Of course, they are talking about playing *together* and not as individuals; putting the objectives of the unit ahead of personal gain so that when the unit wins there will be great gain for each member of the team.

Some reporters have spelled *gel* with a *J* because of the television commercials about Jell-O, but actually *gel* (a derivation of the word GELATIN) means "to congeal or come together." For our purposes, let's take these three letters and use them as an acrostic to remind us how to be experts in the business of managing people.

The next three chapters will take each of these letters individually and give specific instructions on how we can use this formula to become Top Performers.

PERFORMANCE PRINCIPLES

1. A sense of humor is vital to good leadership.

2. Common goals plus a common cause equals greater success.

3. Cooperation must be earned, not demanded.

4. Face up to your strengths as well as your weaknesses.

5. You have some of every quality necessary for success.

6. All resources are not obvious; great managers find and develop available talent.

3

LOOK FOR THE GOOD

How far you go in life depends on your being tender with the young, compassionate with the aged, sympathetic with the striving, and tolerant of the weak and the strong. Because someday in life you will have been all of these.

George Washington Carver

Goodfinders

Expect the Best
Loyalty

THE *G* IN OUR GEL formula stands for *Goodfinders*—those who are experts in Top Performance learn to look for the good in each person they manage.

Andrew Carnegie said, "No man can become rich without himself enriching others." He went on to live this philosophy, as evidenced by the 43 millionaires he had working for him. A reporter interviewing Mr. Carnegie asked how he was able to hire that many millionaires. Mr. Carnegie patiently explained that the men were not millionaires when they came to work for him, but had become millionaires *by* working for him. When the reporter pursued the line of questioning as to how he was able to develop these men to the point they were worth that much money, Mr. Carnegie said, "When you work with people it is a lot like mining for gold . . . when you mine for gold, you must literally move tons of dirt to find a single ounce of gold. However, you do not look for the dirt—you look for the gold!"

It works the same way when you want to develop people to their full potential. You must look for the gold (the good), and when you find it you nurture it and bring it to fruition. Another wise man expressed it this way: The greatest good we can do for others is not to share our riches with them, but to reveal theirs to them.

Bill Hewlett, one of the founders of Hewlett-Packard, said, "Our policy flows from the belief that men and women want to do a good job, a creative job, and that if they are provided with the proper environment they will do so." Since people want to do a good job, why shouldn't we point out their success as it occurs?

The next illustration, which comes from my childhood, tells about an effective method of dealing with your people when they don't do their jobs as effectively or professionally as they can and should. As you read this, I encourage you to remember some wise words from Dr. Norman Vincent Peale: "The trouble with most of us is that we would rather be ruined by praise than saved by criticism."

Criticize the Performance—Not the Performer

Some of you will recognize the following story from my book *Raising Positive Kids in a Negative World*, but it so vividly makes the point, I wanted to repeat it here. When I was a small boy down in Yazoo City, Mississippi, things were pretty tight during those Depression years and everybody had to work smarter and harder. As a leader, and as a manager, I honestly believe my mother, despite her fifth-grade education, would rate close to the top.

Dad died when I was five years old and there were six of us too young to work. Remember, now, that this was in the heart of the Depression and things were tough for everyone. We survived because we had a very large garden and five milk cows. I was milking and working in the garden by the time I was eight years old and, for what it's worth, let me interject the fact that cows don't "give" milk—you have to fight for every drop!

Two things we always knew when Mother gave us an assignment. Number one, we knew what she *expected* (our very best). Number two, we knew she was going to *inspect* to make certain she got what she *expected*.

I'll never forget my first solo assignment in the garden. On this particular day, because my mother was also a good teacher, she showed me exactly what I needed to do to properly hoe those beans. When she finished her lesson, she pointed to three long rows of beans—which were about three and a half miles long (well, would you believe three?). But to an eight-year-old boy they looked more like ten! Anyhow, Mother instructed me that when I finished I was to call her so she could inspect what I had done. When I finally finished I called her for the inspection.

As she looked the job over, she did what she always did when she was not pleased with something. She folded her hands behind her back, ducked her head, cocked it slightly to the right, and started that little left-to-right motion which I knew all too well. As she was doing this, I asked her what was the matter. She smiled and said, "Well, son, it looks like you're going to have to lick this calf over."

Now in the corporate world that might seem like a strange term, but in rural Mississippi during the days of the Depression, it simply meant that what I had done was unsatisfactory. Obviously, I knew what she was saying, but—hopeful for an escape—I smiled and said, "Mama, I wasn't botherin' the calf—I was hoeing those beans!" With this my mother chuckled and said, "Well, son, what I mean is this: For most boys this would be perfectly all right. But you're not most boys. You're *my* son, and my son can do better than this."

What Mother had done was extremely wise. *She had criticized the performance* because it badly needed criticism, *but she had praised the performer* because he needed the praise.

Effective management, whether in athletics, education, family, or business is measured by your effectiveness in managing your personnel to get maximum productivity and benefits for all. To accomplish this objective there are two things which great managers always do. Number one, they always *ex*pect every member of the team to do their best; and number two, they always *in*spect to make certain they get what they expected. (There is almost *nothing* as demotivating to a subordinate as having a completed project ignored or taken for granted after heart and soul have been poured into that project.)

Question: Suppose your inspection reveals that the project is either unsatisfactory or not up to the standards you feel that individual is capable of attaining. Do you "brag on him" or "fuss at him"? Answer: Neither. To brag on any project which represents less than a person's capability is to encourage mediocrity and the corporate world is already oversupplied with that commodity. You *owe* that person more than that. To "fuss" at him or to be harshly critical could well destroy the subordinate's confidence and stifle his initiative for future projects. You also owe that person *and* your company more than that. So what do you do? Answer: You use a page from my mother's notebook. Criticize the performance . . . not the performer!

Effective leadership demands that kind of approach. Extend the hand of encouragement to the person while making it clear that you expect— even demand—that he or she use their ability for maximum results. In short, have that person reaching for more, but do it without challenging or questioning his worth as an individual. Assure him or her that you *really* respect and appreciate their ability—and that's why work which is not consistent with their ability is unacceptable.

The ABC's of Management

Ken Blanchard has worked with several other outstanding authors to compile a series of "One Minute" books. These books are easy to read and have really simplified some foundational concepts. Dr. Blanchard worked with Dr. Robert Lorber on a book called *Putting the One Minute Manager to Work*. In this outstanding book, these men identify the ABC's of management and reveal some startling facts.

A = Activators . . . what a manager does *before* performance
B = Behavior . . . performance, what someone says or does
C = Consequences . . . what a manager does *after* performance

For example, according to Blanchard and Lorber, "Most people think that activators have a greater influence on performance than consequences. And yet, only 15–25% of what influences performance comes from activators like goal-setting, while 75–85% of it (behavior) comes from consequences like praising and reprimands." What happens *after* a person does something has more impact than what happens *before!* To use another "one minute" phrase, "Catch them doing something right!" If you can catch people doing something well, no matter how small it may seem, and positively reinforce them for doing it, they will continue to grow in a positive direction.

Does this mean that we are to ignore the mistakes of those for whom we are responsible? Of course not, but there is a correct way to handle these errors or deal with the person whose overall job performance is unsatisfactory or begins to slip. I will address these issues later in this chapter. For the moment, however, let me simply state that the *best managers make finding the good in others a priority.* Too many managers do exactly the opposite.

Action Often Precedes the Feeling

Most of us, in our daily managerial duties, don't feel like Good-finders. As a matter of fact, we often become the exact opposite and function in a role similar to school disciplinarians or police detectives. Den Roossien, executive vice-president of the Zig Ziglar Corporation, uses a slightly different technique I would like to recommend to you. Den is responsible for the daily operations of our company and is our chief financial officer. He comes from an accounting background. Den would be the first to tell you that people skills are not emphasized in accounting courses, and that he really has had to study and work on this area of his professional expertise. I can proudly report to you that Den Roossien has (by his own hard work, study, and dedication) become an outstanding "people" manager and communicator.

One technique Den uses, which I believe you will find extremely helpful, is to keep a running list of the minute and sometimes seemingly insignificant successes of the people who fall under his responsibility. This may include things such as staying late to see that a "rush" package gets out in the warehouse, or coming in early to set up the chairs for our Monday-morning devotions—the little things that make the big difference. He will verbally point out the fact that he appreciates the effort—*as soon as possible after the behavior.* This follows one of the most important rules of positive reinforcement: *it should be immediate.* In addition, he notes the behavior in a notebook so that at the end of the year, or at quarterly review times, he can share with our People Building Team a series of seemingly inconsequential behaviors that have worked together to dramatically impact the bottom line of our company.

The time involved in doing this is really worthwhile when compared to the goodwill and positive reinforcement benefits. Sure, it takes discipline to remember and follow through, but Den is committed to a disciplined approach when it comes to the factors and procedures which positively impact our company. Discipline and organization are both involved and fortunately, Den has developed both these characteristics in spades (there is even a persistent rumor that he is so well organized he periodically proofreads the Xerox copies).

Does he always *feel* like doing this? Certainly not, but action often precedes the feeling. When it comes to giving positive feedback, we sometimes may not *feel* like doing so; that is why it is even more important that we do so immediately. If griping and complaining can become a habit, why can't goodfinding become a habit? One reason is that we have not been trained to look for the good. Another obvious one is that we don't fully comprehend the motivational impact a word of encouragement can have on an employee or co-worker.

Finding Fault as if There Were a Reward for It

Jim Savage, my good friend, chief research associate, and coauthor of this book, tells a fascinating story about a retired professor at Louisiana State University in Baton Rouge. He was a psychology professor and though he was Chinese, he communicated beautifully in English—

unless he wanted to have a little fun with his classes. Then he would do the best "Charlie Chan" imitation you have ever heard! Early one semester, a student had an examination paper returned that looked like the one in the illustration—it had only one mark in each corner of the paper. Frustrated that his paper was not graded properly (as all the other papers had been), the student stood up to demand an explanation. "Sir, I don't understand! Everyone's paper is graded properly except mine—all this test has is one mark in each of the four corners! What does that mean?" The professor got that big smile on his face that let you know his best "Charlie Chan" was coming, paused for dramatic effect, looked out over the auditorium class of three hundred students, and said, "Zero so big, not fit on paper!"

After thinking about this story, it dawned on me that as managers we often play similar games. While the professor's joke was done in fun, it still had an impact on that embarrassed student. Part of the reason we are tempted to play these deadly games is that we have been trained or conditioned to do so. You remember how it was when you were in school. You got that paper back and even though you scored 85–90 percent, the paper had so much red on it that it looked like it was mortally wounded and was in the final stages of bleeding to death. Remember? The markings screamed, "YOU MISSED THESE TWO,

YOU BIG DUMMY!" I'm confident you and I are alike in at least one way. If we get 85–90 percent of our work correct, we would like to have somebody point out some of *that* part in addition to the parts we fell short on.

When I work with teachers I often tell them I'm going to ask the principal to take away all their red marking pens and replace them with blue marking pens and instructions to mark the correct answers on all exams. Now, I understand a test is not only an evaluation tool but a reteaching tool as well. And I understand that when we correct somebody we work with it's an evaluation and is designed to teach that person. But I also understand, as you do, that recognition is one of the most important tools to teach and motivate in every job. We must point out the good as well as the things that people do wrong. Instead, we too often get involved in the terrible game of "Gotcha!" You do 99 percent correct work and you may be completely invisible, but make one little mistake and . . . "Gotcha!" The manager jumps on the employee with both feet. Like a cheap suit or an ugly rash, he's all over him! One little mistake and "Gotcha!" That is unwise and unfair and is devastating in its impact on productivity.

A Tool to Teach and Motivate

One of the most effective tools you can ever use to teach and motivate is a sincere compliment—with the emphasis on *sincere*. The more sincere the compliment, the more effective it will be. Unfortunately, too many of us pass out those sincere compliments as if each one were skin off our backs, or as if we had a limited supply which we were saving. In our business, personal, and family lives, we continue to play the "Gotcha!" game. You come in at the end of the day, walking kind of proud, wearing your new coat and tie, and your loving spouse greets you at the back door. Her eyes grow large as she zeros in on your new attire and your proud bearing and she says, "Honey, I like your coat and tie . . . [pause] . . . hang on to them—I hear they're coming back in style." Gotcha!

But you get back at your loving mate. As you sit down at the dinner table you look over the meal she has slaved to prepare for you and announce to the entire family, "What a magnificent meal! Why, this food is fit for a king . . . [pause] . . . here King, here King!" Gotcha!

Don't get caught up in the humor of these illustrations because that's exactly what happens in real life. We give a compliment and humorously "pull the rug" from under our "victim," thinking that no harm is done. Evidence is solid that even one nasty "gotcha" can do serious

BADARACO

damage and a continuous barrage of them can do irreparable harm and adversely affect an entire department.

Part of our hesitancy in sharing compliments comes from the fear of being misunderstood. If a man greets an attractive lady at a business or social occasion with, "That's a beautiful dress," she might wonder about his motive. If you compliment a male acquaintance with, "That's a great looking watch you have on," he might well think you're trying to set him up for a future favor or even a small loan. So even though both compliments would be sincere, we often don't share them because of the FEAR of being misunderstood. This results in two people losing because *you cannot receive a sincere compliment without feeling better . . . and just as important, you cannot give a sincere compliment without feeling better yourself!* Sharing the compliment results in a Double Win!

A Right Way—and a Wrong Way

As an optimistic Goodfinder with many years experience, I'm convinced that with commitment and persistence you can find *something* good about any person, performance, or situation. After all, even a stopped clock is *exactly* right twice *every* twenty-four hours! To illustrate the point, let's look at a wrong and a right way of handling a coaching situation. The example is from athletics, but it could just as easily have been from business, education, family, or the church.

The offensive line coach of the football team had a player who did a great job of accelerating out of his stance, but he didn't roll his hips into the block, so the coach—in a loud voice—said to him, "Dummy, roll your hips!" When he said "Dummy," the player visibly slumped and his ears shrank to the size of a pinhead. He didn't want to hear anything else this misguided coach had to say. He was on the fourth team, he knew he was on the fourth team, but his mama and daddy knew he should be on the first team. His girlfriend was telling him he should be first team, and he knew full well that if he didn't have an idiot for a coach he would already be on the first team. When this "coach" addressed him as "Dummy," he didn't want to hear anything else the man had to say.

On the other hand, suppose the coach had said to him, "Man, that's a *great* job of coming out of your stance [remember, it really *was* a great job of accelerating out of the stance], now if you will just roll your hips, we can win with that block!" When the coach said *great*, and *win*, the player brightened perceptibly, smiled broadly, and made better use of his ears than Dumbo, the Walt Disney flying elephant hero with the huge ears. He wanted to hear everything his coach—obviously a combination of Vince Lombardi, Tom Landry, and Don Shula rolled together—had to say! And the coach was able to get in his correction quickly, painlessly, and far more effectively because the player listened more attentively to the coach, who was observant enough to see the *great* way he had come out of the stance.

There are two things you must remember if you are going to use this technique. Number one: *The compliment must be sincere.* If not, the people you work with will know it faster than you do and you will lose all credibility. Number two: *You cannot follow every compliment with a correction.* When this happens, the technique is viewed as manipulative because *it is.* This results in the Double Lose in the long run.

How do you feel when you get a memo or phone call and the boss says, "I want to see you, and *right away!*" Ninety-five out of one hundred people get that "glitch" in their stomachs and that *How did he find out?* thought in their minds. We have been trained to expect the worst in that type of situation. However, imagine that your boss is the kind of people manager who looks for the good and normally compliments you. When you get the call, you actually look forward to your time together—it's a whole new mind-set. The real question is, *How do you want your work-*

ers, friends, spouse, children, and others to feel when they get the call that you want to see them?

A Tool for Written Feedback

Some people really do have trouble verbalizing feedback, but have no fear because this is an acquired or learned skill. However, until you learn the skill, you need a practical tool for feedback. Here is a great one for you, whether you have excellent verbal skills or are just learning. In our Zig Ziglar Corporation seminars, we use a tool or concept called the "I LIKE . . . BECAUSE" pad. Each participant is given a pad like the one shown in the illustration and asked to note things they like or appreciate about class members during the seminar. This is an original idea, given to us by the Bay City High School in Bay City, Texas. It has an enormous impact on seminar participants as well as on numerous homes and businesses across America where it is used.

The I LIKE . . . BECAUSE pad teaches us to look for the good and causes us to point out the positives we see in others. The comments run from the simple, such as complimenting the way a person smiles, to the more complex ideas, showing deeper levels of appreciation.

When we first introduced the concept in our three-day BORN TO WIN seminar in Dallas, there was one participant who used his body language to express his obvious disapproval. He squirmed, turned to the side, folded his arms and legs, and in general said, "I'm not having any part of this silliness!" Well, our seminar facilitators watched this man's comments carefully as they distributed the sheets to the participants. The first comments were seldom more than a few words. On day two,

I like _____

because _____

_____

_____

_____

You Are A Winner!!!

his comments gradually got longer, and on day three he was filling up the front and back of the sheets. At the end of class, he stood up and said, "When these I LIKE . . . BECAUSE pads were introduced, I thought it was the silliest idea I had ever heard, but it's amazing how much you people have changed over the last three days!" Obviously, the people had changed because BORN TO WIN really is a life-changing experience, but even more obviously, this man had also changed because he was learning to look for the good in others.

We have a two-day seminar called EFFECTIVE BUSINESS COMMUNICATIONS, in which we coach people on their communication skills. Over the two days, the people are videotaped a dozen times and given private coaching and feedback on how they might improve their communication skills. In addition to American Airlines, DuPont, and others, world-famous Neiman-Marcus department store had our instructors "in house" to train some of their key personnel. They liked the I LIKE concept, adapted it, and printed YOU ARE WHAT WE'RE FAMOUS FOR! on their pads. Under this great heading they write their positive comments about their peers.

Does Anybody Ever Really Use Those Things?

Laurie Magers is my administrative assistant, and one of the most efficient people you will ever meet. In over nine years of working together, I think she made three mistakes (and two of those were my fault!). The error she probably felt worst about was forgetting to tell me (again) about a television interview. You can imagine how badly she felt, and despite the fact that I pointed out this was no major catastrophe and that it was at least 50 percent my fault, she was feeling very down for the biggest part of that day.

The next day when Laurie arrived at work, there were over thirty-five I LIKE . . . BECAUSE notes hanging from the air conditioner vent above her desk. Some of her friends at the office had noticed that she was down, found out why, and decided to do something to cheer her up. Someone had written, "I LIKE LAURIE BECAUSE SHE CAN LEAP OVER A TALL BUILDING WITH HER TYPEWRITER UNDER HER ARM!" and someone else wrote, "I LIKE LAURIE BECAUSE SHE TYPES AT THE SPEED OF LIGHT!" And there were others that said, "I LIKE LAURIE BECAUSE SHE IS ALWAYS WILLING TO LISTEN!" or, "I LIKE LAURIE BECAUSE SHE IS THE MOST CONSCIENTIOUS PERSON IN THE ZIG ZIGLAR CORPORATION!" Laurie was literally moved to tears by the thoughtfulness and encouragement of her fellow employees—and talk about motivated—

man alive, you should have seen her productivity! She was back to normal in no time flat. The thoughtfulness of others, the fact that others were willing to look for the good and then point it out, helped Laurie through a difficult time.

Now if you are having a little trouble with the concept, this probably means you are zeroing in on the wrong word. The key word on the sheet is not LIKE. If that word bothers you, simply scratch it out and insert *appreciate* or *respect*. The key word is BECAUSE! This word moves the concept out of the superficial and general into the sincere and specific.

All of the effective management books on the market today encourage us to give feedback to employees. Giving feedback successfully means pointing out *specific and observable behavior.* "I LIKE JOHN BE-CAUSE HE BROUGHT IN THE PROJECT ON TIME AND UN-DER BUDGET!" Not, "I LIKE JOHN BECAUSE HE IS A GOOD EMPLOYEE." "I LIKE JANE *BECAUSE* SHE WORKED OVER-TIME FOR THREE STRAIGHT DAYS TO FINISH AN IMPOR-TANT PROJECT!" Not "I LIKE JANE BECAUSE SHE WORKS HARD." Remember: *Catch them doing something right!* When you do, you build on what's right instead of what's wrong.

Unless you have written or received an I LIKE . . . BECAUSE note, you cannot fully comprehend the impact of such a simple idea. Let me offer you a challenge right now: I want you to think of someone you need to tell that you appreciate, like (love), and/or respect. Please, think of that someone and make a commitment to yourself to stop read-ing and share a verbal or written I LIKE *immediately!*

Our course for schools is called the I CAN course. Developed by Mrs. Mamie McCullough, it is based on the principles in *See You at the Top.* One of the assignments we give the students is to go home and tell their parents they love them. You would be shocked, but your heart would also be warmed, if you could read some of the letters or listen in on some of the phone calls we get from parents in tears because, for the first time in their lives, a twelve- or fourteen-year-old child has said he or she loves them. There's somebody in your life you need to let know you appreciate. You really need to make a commitment to *you* to do that today! Go ahead. The first time is by far the most difficult or awkward. In short order, because of the wonderful feedback, it will be fun and extremely rewarding.

Unusual Commodities

Love and respect are possibly the two most unusual commodities in our society today. Unfortunately, they are also among the rarest. The reason they are unusual is that the *only* way we can *get* them is by *giving* them away. If you are not as loved or respected as you would like to be, you should give yourself a "gut" check and see if you are giving either of these items away. An important fact to remember is this:

> *You cannot give away something you do not possess!*

In other words, the love and respect you should give to others is something you must have within yourself!

"There are high spots in all of our lives," wrote George Matthew Adams, "and most of them have come about through encouragement from someone else. I don't care how great, how famous or successful a man or woman may be, each hungers for applause." If you will just recapture how good *you* feel after you have encouraged someone else, no other suggestion is necessary to persuade you to seize every opportunity to give encouragement. "Encouragement is oxygen to the soul. Truly great work seldom comes from a worker without encouragement. No one ever *lived* long, happily or productively without it."

Along these lines, an article in Dr. Mortimer Feinberg's superb *Management* newsletter reinforces the point.

William James, the noted psychologist and philosopher, said without qualification: "The deepest principle in human nature is the craving to be appreciated." *By helping to preserve the rival's self-respect, the effective leader brings him closer to alliance by demonstrating a shared* concern in a major area of personal values.

This approach is desirable *in dealing with opponents; it is* vital *in dealing with subordinates. The constant objective of higher-level executives must be to strengthen the competence and commitment of those who, in the last analysis, are responsible for implementing organizational objectives.*

As Dr. Alan C. Filley writes in his important book Interpersonal Conflict Resolution, *the portrait we draw of ourselves is a major determinant of how we behave:*

Various studies indicate that those low in self-esteem (1) are more likely to feel threatened in a situation, (2) are more vulnerable and dependent upon a power laden situation, (3) have greater need for structure, (4) inhibit aggression, (5) are easily persuaded, and (6) yield more to group pressure than those high in self-esteem.

Not to be ignored is the importance of encouraging members of the group to respect each other. Acknowledging individual achievement should be done in ways that not only strengthen relationships between superior and subordinate but between the latter and his peers. Praise given to one person should never be stated in terms that criticize other members of the group. And wherever the achievement was in fact accompanied by help from others, their contribution should also be acknowledged. Any other approach is likely to lead to group tensions rather than increased cooperation.

Essentially, the key principle is the importance of sharing the credit, both with and among subordinates. In a rare moment of self-revelation, Casey Stengel once said in perfectly literate phrases: "Ability is the art of getting credit for all the home runs somebody else hits." But the surest way to keep the team from hitting home runs is to take the credit for yourself and never administer the athlete's salute—the pat on the base-runner's behind.

But Isn't There a Time When We Must "Come Down" on Others?

Yes. Of course all feedback is not going to be positive. Some of you are thinking that I have overemphasized the concept of "goodfinding"—and you are partially correct. You really cannot say too much or find too much good in others, as long as each comment is sincere. The reason I have spent such an extended time talking about pointing out the good is that we (as a society in general) are so negligent in doing so. Now that the point has been emphasized, exactly how do we go about letting others know we are *not* pleased with their performance?

Answer: We start by really understanding what Jean Paul Richter meant when he said, "A man takes contradiction and advice much more easily than people think, only he will not bear it when violently given, even if it is well-founded. Hearts are flowers; they remain open to the softly falling dew, but shut up in the violent downpour of rain."

Bryan Flanagan, an outstanding speaker and sales manager of our Corporate Training Division, holds the honor of being recognized by our staff as one of the most outstanding I LIKE . . . BECAUSE writers in our office. Everyone looks forward to getting feedback from Bryan because he is so kind and so specific. He carefully validates every compliment he gives. Many times he will give verbal feedback to support the written I LIKE and will do this in front of the supervisors of those he is complimenting—always sincerely.

Bryan also uses all the proper tools and techniques when it is time to give instructive feedback to those for whom he is responsible. On one occasion, Jim Savage, Bryan's longtime friend and immediate supervisor, observed a "less than highly motivated" employee exiting Bryan's office. Naturally, he was interested in what happened. Here is what Bryan told Jim:

> *You know, Jim, that young lady is one of the best workers we have in our division. She is at work on time every day and is more than willing to stay late when necessary. She is pleased to do just about anything that will benefit our organization. Why, just last month I asked her to take on a project that is somewhat outside her area of expertise and interest and she not only took on the project but she also performed extremely well. Actually, however, this project was what demotivated her. The project I assigned took her off track from her normal duties, and since returning to these duties she has been less effective than before the project began. I simply pointed out that her productivity was not up to her usual standards and asked why . . . and listened. She shared her concerns and during the conversation we were able to determine the specific behaviors and factors which were decreasing her productivity. With this information we were able to come up with a plan of action, which she agreed with and felt good about, to increase her productivity. I reminded her that she is not only a valuable employee but a valuable person as well. We also set a date when we would get together again to review the program on our plan of action. She actually was relieved to discuss the concerns we both had and while she was a little nervous about the meeting, she realized she needed direction and was glad I cared enough to give her the time and direction.*

Bryan Flanagan is a role model for excellence in this particular scenario. I know you were picking out the key points as we went along, but let's go back together and be sure we have analyzed carefully.

1. *The feedback was given in private.* Nothing can be more devastating than public censure. Some managers are prone to tease or "dig" at an employee in front of others about a real concern as a way of hinting that they are displeased. All this does is destroy the seeds of trust between the people involved. *All* instructive or critical feedback must be given in private.

2. *The feedback was about specific, observable behavior.* The individual involved was never under personal attack. If there is to be criticism, it must pertain to the performance, *never* the performer.

3. *The feedback was immediate.* As soon as he recognized the problem, Bryan confronted the situation.

4. *Bryan asked questions and listened to the answers.* Rather than rushing to judgment, he asked questions for which, for the most part, he already had answers. He wasn't looking for the answers as much as he was looking for the employee's perspective on the answers. As a bonus, try closing your next instructive feedback session with this question: "How do you think I feel about this meeting?" After you get the answer, follow with, "How do *you* feel about this meeting?" The answers will often surprise you and will generally give great insight about what has just transpired at your meeting.

5. *A cooperative plan of action was developed.* Bryan did not mandate what action was to be taken to correct the situation; rather, the two people involved discussed a mutually agreeable plan. The employee contributed and "shared ownership" of the plan.

6. *A date for a follow-up session to inspect to make sure Bryan got what he expected was assigned.* Too many excellent Plans of Action fall victim to the "tyranny of the urgent." With all good intentions, we try to get back to the employee, but "things" pop up and we forget. Establishing a specific date and setting an appointment creates a sense of urgency for the plan and helps prevent failure as well as hurt feelings from neglect.

7. *Praise was used throughout the session.* There is much debate about "sandwiching" criticism between praise. Some managers think they must start or end every session with praise. I will leave the decision on when to use praise up to you. However, to measure success, you must be able to answer this question affirmatively: "Did the person leave my presence feeling good about himself?" No one should ever leave an encounter with a manager doubting his or her personal value or self-worth!

To be a Goodfinder we must often *teach* those for whom we are responsible to do something good. That is the objective of the instructive feedback session. The great managers give others instructions on how to be more successful—always giving direction *within* the ability level of the employee. The great manager does not ignore mistakes. Permissiveness is neglect of duty. For as Dr. Michael Mescon, dean of the College of Business Administration, Georgia State University, says, "When a store clerk is rude, don't blame the clerk, blame the manager. The manager is ultimately responsible and accountable for actions of subordinates." If you will look for the good, point it out verbally and in writing, give instructive feedback in the manner outlined, and accept responsibility for those who answer to you, you are well on your way to becoming an excellent manager of people!

Marshall Field, American business leader and philanthropist, said, "Those who enter to buy support me. Those who come to flatter please me. Those who complain teach me how I may please others so that more will come. Only those hurt me who are displeased but do not complain. They refuse me permission to correct my errors and thus improve my service."

As leaders, we need to hitchhike on what Marshall Field said as a method for improving performance and assisting in the personal growth of our people. Remember, if we only flatter the people, we are pleasing them. If pleasing them is all we do, we are participating in a conspiracy to prevent their further growth and opportunities for themselves, as well as service to the company.

A Positive Reminder

One of the most important aspects of motivating a force has to do with praise and recognition. That's the reason the I LIKE . . . BECAUSE approach is so effective. Before we close this chapter on "goodfinding," let me share one last story which has a different twist.

A company sent four couples to one of our recent BORN TO WIN seminars. At the end of the first day they were tremendously motivated and excited about the I LIKE . . . BECAUSE idea. That evening they went to a late dinner at one of Dallas' most exclusive restaurants. They hit the jackpot. The food was exceptional and the service was superb. Their waiter was a professional with twenty-five years of experience, and over twenty of those years had been at that one restaurant. He was there when he needed to be, but he did not join the party. He served effectively and efficiently but did not smother them with attention. He was intimately acquainted with the menu and was able to answer their questions and give them concise information about the specials of the day. It seemed he miraculously appeared at their instant of need and then made his exit so that he did not intrude upon the party. Friendly yet not familiar. In short, to repeat myself, he was a pro.

The four couples were all personable and friendly and soon on a first-name basis with the waiter. The meal was particularly delicious and was greatly enhanced because of the waiter's gracious and effective service. The diners left him a 25 percent tip which, in an expensive restaurant, is substantial. Each of the guests also left him an I LIKE . . . BECAUSE slip, detailing why they liked him. After they had made their exit and were about a hundred feet from the front door, they heard him calling for them to wait a minute.

The waiter briskly walked up to them and, with the eight slips of paper in his hand, started to speak but broke down with emotion and for a moment or so literally could say nothing. When he finally regained his composure, he told the four couples that in his twenty-five years of being a waiter, this was far and away the most meaningful thing that had ever happened to him. Imagine!

That waiter was living proof of something my friend and fellow speaker Cavett Robert says: Three billion people on the face of the earth go to bed hungry every night, but four billion people go to bed every night hungry for a simple word of encouragement and recognition.

Do you think that with this kind of input this already effective waiter is going to be even more conscientious in his efforts? Do you think he benefited from the experience? Wouldn't you have loved to have been seated at the next table he served? Most important, who do you think were the biggest winners? Was it the waiter, who received the I LIKE . . . BECAUSE slips, or was it the eight individuals who wrote those notes? It doesn't take much imagination to answer that one, does it? I'm confident you agree that those who wrote the slips were the biggest winners.

That's what this concept is really all about. I would like to stress that we are talking about a *principle* and not a tactic. The Bible itself says, "Give and it shall be given unto you." However, if we give or do for others with the expectation of having them do something for us, then our action is a tactic and is certain to either backfire or become entirely ineffective. However, if you buy into the concept that you can have everything in life you want if you will just help other people get what they want, and then set about helping your people become more effective and more productive by giving them honest, sincere praise, not only will they benefit but you and your organization will also benefit tremendously. The magic thought is this:

> If it's a principle, it's a winner—if it's a tactic, it's a loser.

Don't forget that William James of Harvard said a deep need in human nature is the craving to be *appreciated*. When you, the manager, fill that need, you have taken a mammoth step toward becoming a more effective manager.

Remember: the G *in our formula stands for* Goodfinder.

PERFORMANCE PRINCIPLES

1. Look for the good in others.

2. Catch them doing something right.

3. Remember that action often precedes the feeling.

4. Seize the opportunity to share a sincere compliment.

5. Praise in public, censure in private.

4

EXPECT THE BEST

If you want to get the best out of a man, you must look
for the best that is in him.

Bernard Haldane

Goodfinders

| Expect the Best |

Loyalty

THE *E* IN OUR GEL formula is for *Expect the Best*. I was sharing some of
the ideas I've been explaining to you in a seminar awhile back and a
man in the audience came up to me during the break and said, "This
information is fantastic. I wish some of those *morons* back at my office
could be here!"

My question to you is this: Do you think there is a chance he missed a
very important point?

Now let's bring it home to you. What kind of co-workers do you have?
What kind of employees? What kind of children? What kind of spouse?
So many times we get from others EXACTLY WHAT WE EXPECT! In
short—the way we see them affects the way we treat them and the way
we treat them affects the way they perform.

Several years ago, Rom J. Markin and Charles M. Lillis published an
article in *Business Horizons* called "Sales Managers Get What They
Expect." This article probably does as precise and concise a job of
summarizing the Pygmalion Effect (sometimes called the "echo effect"
or the "mirror effect") as I have read. Let me hit some of the main
points of this excellent article.

*Expectations can influence behavior: therefore, a manager may get
better staff performance if he expects better performance. This be-*

464

havioral phenomenon is called the Pygmalion Effect. . . . According to Greek Mythology, Pygmalion was a sculptor and the King of Cyprus who fell in love with one of his creations. The ivory statue was created out of the desire of his own expectations. After Pygmalion's repeated prayers to the gods, Venus gave life to the statue . . . the concept rests on the premise that what we see reflected in many objects, situations, or persons is what we put there with our own expectations. We create images of how things should be, and if these images are believed, they become self-fulfilling prophecies. . . .

The Evidence

The feelings and tones which surround us can be changed if we work to change them by sending out the kind of signal we want reflected or echoed. Comedians as well as dramatic performers succeed in creating the kind of mood or atmosphere they want to prevail by sending out the kinds of signals they want mirrored or echoed. . . . "Once you begin laughing," a drama coach explains, "it is easy to continue, for the action and the emotion mutually stimulate each other." *. . . We all have an audience of individuals and colleagues whose day, including their moods, feelings, and dispositions, will be influenced by the way we start it. Hence, sales managers are perhaps the most important "signal generators" for field salesmen, and the expectations of the manager will profoundly affect the performance of the salespeople he leads and supervises.*

Science vs. Folklore

The Pygmalion Effect has met the test of scientific analysis and hence the value of the theory is borne out both in terms of usefulness and truthfulness . . . a cross section of carefully validated scientific studies reflects their significance:

• *A study showed that experimenters could raise the IQ scores of children, especially on verbal and information subtests, merely by expecting them to do well. . . .*

• *A study showed that experimenters could improve their subjects' performance on a task requiring them to drop as many marbles as possible through one of several holes in a tabletop by expecting them to do well. . . .*

• A *study showed that worker performance increased markedly when the supervisor of these workers was told that his group showed a special potential for their particular job.*

How Does It Work?

The paramount question is, how can managers implement the technique and improve their own performance while at the same time improving the performance of others?

William James, the father of American psychology, concluded that we become how we act . . . so if we wish to conquer undesirable emotional tendencies in ourselves, we must go through the outward movements of the kind of tendencies we wish to cultivate. Alfred Adler, another well-known psychologist, later reaffirmed this no- tion by proving that if we make ourselves smile, we actually feel like smiling . . . *in short, our moods match our posture and more important, people around us tend to feel as we feel.* Mood is contagious.

B. F. Skinner, the foremost disciple of the psychological school of behaviorism, contends that our behavior operates on the environ- ment and behavior is shaped by consequences. When a sales man- ager, for example, sends signals to his sales personnel that he regards them as highly competent, effective, capable, and mature, and that his work and theirs is meaningful, significant, and worth- while, the sales personnel who receive his signals will respond in many instances by performing more competently and effectively.

And they respond further by perceiving their work as more re- warding, gratifying, and self-fulfilling. The self-image is the key to human behavior. Change the self-image and we change the be- havior. Even more than this, the self-image sets the boundaries of individual accomplishment. It defines what one can or cannot do. Expand the self-image, and we expand the area of the possible.

Through the power of expectation, a sales manager (or any man- ager) can develop an adequate, realistic self-image in personnel that will imbue them with new capabilities and new talents, and literally turn failure into success.

Whew! I'm Not Sure I Wanted to Know That Much About It!

I give this much detail on the self-fulfilling prophecy because many people give the concept lip service but really don't buy into the proven facts. If man has suspected that the Pygmalion Effect does in fact work, and science has *proven* that it works, then why are we so unwilling to take advantage of the obvious benefits of application?

Successful Performers do *buy in and they* apply *the principles!*

If the Pygmalion Effect is going to work for you, you are going to have to help others by:

A. Encouraging achievement by providing a constant flow of positive feedback (which also creates a positive "climate").
B. Allowing for regular learning and growth opportunities for the people you expect to be Top Performers.
C. Providing activities and information that help people to understand their efforts are meaningful and productive.
D. Generating desirable and rewarding consequences for others (remember that 75–85 percent of behavior is determined by consequences).

A. Positive Feedback

We have already spent a great deal of time and energy on the importance of positive feedback and I am confident that you are sold on the importance of this vital area. Remember: Be a Goodfinder!

B. Regular Learning and Growth Opportunities

The importance of training cannot be overemphasized. According to Tom Peters, coauthor of *In Search of Excellence,* one of the companies he researched spends four full days training a teenage employee whose life expectancy on the job is only five weeks! The company: Disneyland. The job: parking lot attendant. The reason: the parking lot attendant is often the first person park guests meet, therefore these teenagers set the tone for the guests' visit.

IBM requires forty hours of training per year for management personnel—one solid week of the work year is spent in training!

The Arthur Andersen Company in Dallas, Texas, spends 10 percent of their *gross* revenues on training.

Too often in times of tight finances, training programs are the first area cut. This is the exact opposite of what should happen. In times of financial difficulty, training budgets should be sharply increased.

To quote Tom Peters, "The excellent companies view extensive, pragmatic training as a necessity, not as a boom-time nicety . . . you gotta trust 'em, and train the livin' daylights out of them." When asked how he justified large amounts of training dollars, Peters replied, "Management from Excellent Companies would not ask a question like that!"

C. Activities and Information That Prove Our Efforts Are Meaningful, Productive, and Appreciated

I usually make every effort to stay away from absolutes such as "never" or "always," but in this case I am going to make an exception. Never under any circumstances at any time downplay the role of a Recognition Program in your organization, home, church, or any area of interest. In Part II, "The Science of Top Performance," we will get into the specifics of developing a Recognition Program. However, let me emphasize right here and now that you must never overlook the importance of this vital area.

When we look at activities and information that prove our efforts are meaningful and productive, we look at a very important area for Top Performers. This is the area in which the manager must make one of the most important "sales" ever made. Others must have a concept or a vision—an idea of what the "big picture" is all about—and how they personally fit in and contribute. The great managers regularly paint vivid word pictures showing their people exactly how this is happening now and what is in store in the months ahead.

This is important because one of the greatest problems faced in society today is the problem of "unrealistic expectations." In business, we set unrealistic goals or expect our progress within the organization to happen much too quickly. In relationships, we expect others to do certain things for us or act in a certain manner and if they do not, we are devastated. Now before you say, "Wait a second, Ziglar—a minute ago you were saying that if we expected the best, we could get the best . . . and now you are saying that 'unrealistic expectations' are a problem!" Let me finish.

Actually, this apparent discrepancy is the primary reason for the problem. Under the heading "Activities and Information That Prove Our Efforts Are Meaningful and Productive" is where we will solve this dilemma.

It seems as though no self-respecting management book could be published without dealing with Douglas McGregor's "Theory X and Theory Y" concepts. This is the appropriate place for us to look at these schools of thought. In his book *The Human Side of Enterprise*, Mc-Gregor developed two opposing views of worker attitudes based upon different conceptions of human nature:

Theory X Assumptions

*Work is inherently distasteful
*People prefer close supervision
*Most people are lazy and their work must be carefully structured
*The principle worker incentive is money
*Typical workers are uncreative
*Workers need to be coerced or bribed

Theory Y Assumptions

*Work is as natural as play
*People like to work
*Self-control is oftentimes essential
*Workers at all levels are creative
*Workers respond favorably to mature, favorable treatment
*Recognition and self-fulfillment are as important as motivation and money

According to the Pygmalion Effect, if we expect the Theory Y Assumptions to be true, more often than not they will. The Pygmalion Effect also says that if we expect Theory X Assumptions to come true, more often than not they will. The dilemma comes from the point of view of *worker expectations!* Because of expectations that have been placed on them in the past, many workers are operating under a set of consequences or within an environment (climate) that is more closely aligned with Theory X. How do we overcome this past conditioning effectively? By providing activities and information that prove worker efforts (or spouse, children, etc. efforts) are meaningful.

Unfortunately, *there are very few workers today who know when they are successful on the job.* Oh, they have quotas and some guidelines as to what their activities are supposed to be, but how will they know when they are successful?

What about the manager? If we are supposed to give regular feedback to our people, and keep them apprised of how they are doing, and paint the "big picture" for them, how can we determine what information to pass along?

<hr>

The Performance Value Package

I believe the answer is in the three-step Performance Value Package. Step #1 is *Foundational Performance*. This is the level of performance the person must achieve to continue to work with the organization (or in the case of children, to avoid punishment). I call it Foundational Performance rather than *Minimum Standard* because I don't want people even *thinking* minimum, much less working toward a minimum. With Foundational Performance thinking, not only do people maintain their positions but they also build a foundation upon which they can build future successes. We will discuss the specific "how to's" of each step in the Performance Value Package in "The Science of Top Performance," but for now let's simply say that the Foundational Performance is determined by mutual agreement of the manager and employee. The employee shares ownership in the ideas and does not feel "put upon," and the manager can lead the employee to better understand the "big picture" during the discussion. If you have never used this technique or a similar one, you will be surprised that rather than having to encourage employees to "reach" for objectives and standards, more often you will have to work to get them to be realistic and conservative about their Foundational Performance.

Step #2 in the Performance Value Package is *Successful Performance*. The Successful Performance is the level of performance that might reasonably and realistically be expected by both manager and employee. Again, the manager and employee determine this level of performance by working together and looking at past history and all data available about the position. By working together, and through discussion, both employee and manager get a reasonable understanding of what each is looking for as far as a Successful Performance is concerned. Again, let me remind you that the specific "how to's" are in chapter 8 in "The Science of Top Performance."

Step #3 in the Performance Value Package is *Value Performance*. The Value Performance is the level of performance that might be expected if everything goes according to plan and the employee excels in all areas. This level provides Top Performers with a target. Again, Value Performance is determined through sharing and discussion. The manager must be sure Value Performance objectives cause the individual to really "stretch." After having established Foundational Performance and

Successful Performance levels, the manager will be able to direct the employee toward Value Performance quite successfully.

The advantages of this three-level system are numerous:

1. The manager spends directed time in specific discussion about job performance.

2. The manager and employee get to know each other and identify expectation levels through the discussions.

3. The manager can identify the performance level the employee *wants* to reach. Too often we make the mistake of classifying employees; this system allows employees to classify themselves and the manager to help them move through all levels to the extent of their comfort and desire.

4. Achievement ceilings are removed. As the self-image grows, employees have room to grow, too.

5. A basement or foundation level is established so that neither the employee nor the company is placed in danger.

6. By using this system properly, the manager will almost never have to fire an employee—some make the decision to terminate themselves, but the manager is seldom placed in this painful and awkward position.

Chances are excellent you raised your eyebrows somewhat on #6. One of the most difficult things any manager ever has to do is terminate an employee, and to think this will seldom if ever happen again is a real boon! If you will combine the Value Performance Package with what I call *Due Process*, firings will largely be a thing of the past. Due Process leads us to:

D. Generate Desirable and Rewarding Consequences for Others (Remember That 75–85 Percent of Behavior Is Determined by Consequences)

My understanding of Due Process is going to seem somewhat simplistic to some of you, but a system does not have to have 16 graphs and 189 pages of "legalese" to be workable. To me, Due Process means "three strikes and you are out." When an employee makes a mistake, we should be really *pleased!* Why? Simply because we learn much more from mistakes than we do from victories. We should do everything we can to congratulate people when they make an error . . . we should be delighted (well, almost) with ourselves when we make an error. Once we get over this initial euphoria, we need to analyze *why* the mistake was made, and *what* we can do to see that it rarely occurs again.

When we make the *same* mistake a second time, we must confront this mistake with a slightly different attitude. The process of analysis is the same in that we ask *why* and *what* can be done. If, after analysis, we decide that the determined performance level is fair to *all* parties involved, and it is within our control to prevent a recurrence, we design an action plan to do so. However, everyone must understand that *the same error* a third time will result in termination.

The person *repeating* errors is making a value statement about his feelings and his ability level. The statement he is making is one of two things: (1) "What happens on the job is really not a high priority in my life. My enthusiasm and commitment levels are just not very high." (2) "I do not have the ability necessary to handle this position." Our responsibility in helping ourselves and others to become Top Performers is to discover which of these statements is being made and take the appropriate action. In the case of statement #1, the proper action for employee and organization is to help the individual relocate. If this can be done within your company, so much the better. If it must be done by moving to another organization, then this is best for all concerned. To ask a person to continue performing tasks he does not enjoy, is not committed to, and fails to perform satisfactorily, dooms the individual to unhappiness and decreased productivity. Often the most helpful thing we can do for a person is to help him discover that his strengths may lie in another job or another industry. It may be a tough decision, as management consultant Fred Smith says, but the earlier the decision is made, the less actual waste.

If statement #2 is the case, then our responsibility is to help him get the training needed to handle the position. If the skill level needed is beyond the capacity of the employee, you don't have an employee problem, you have a *hiring procedures* problem. You can best help the employee by helping him find a position in which he can use the skills and abilities he already possesses—or be trained to more fully develop these skills so he may be successful.

To Generate Desirable Consequences, Add PVP

When we establish that Due Process as I have outlined it is standard operating procedure, then we need only add the Performance Value Package concept to have a fail-safe system that allows you to manage efficiently, effectively, emphatically, and with results that please both employee and organization. The Foundational Performance level is the primary key. Remember: You and the employee have agreed that the Foundational Performance level is the *minimally* acceptable level to continue employment . . . *and* if it is established properly (with employee participation), you and the employee have a foundation upon which to build. With Due Process, if the original Foundational Performance standards are not met, the manager and the employee go back and analyze by asking *why* and determining *what* can be done to assure that those Foundational Performance levels will be met in the future. When these levels are not met for the second time, and the manager is certain the burden of the responsibility lies with the employee, then a probationary period must be established. The length of this probationary period could be from two weeks to six months, depending upon the plan of action to correct the mistakes, and the position of the employee. Some assembly-line employees can show their improvement (or lack of) in a matter of weeks, while some executives may have "start-up products" that need to be on probation for as long as two years.

When Foundational Performance level is not met within a reasonable period of time (that manager and employee arrive at together), the employee has signaled that the current position he holds is not the position he should be in. If the process is handled properly by you, the improperly positioned employee will terminate himself or at least agree with you that another job would be in the best interests of both parties.

Does That Stuff Really Work?

Let's look at a specific incident where this concept was applied. Recently my colleague Jim Savage spoke to a group of dentists, their spouses, and entire office staffs, and they taught him this system really does work. According to Jim, they were a delightful group with which to work—very professional, very receptive, and anxious to find ideas that would help them become even more successful in their chosen profession. After the program, they were having lunch together and Jim sat with the doctors at a large round table and had one of the most interesting luncheon conversations ever.

One dentist said, "I cannot get my receptionist to make 'tension' calls." He went on to explain that "tension" calls were the daily calls to confirm appointments and/or remind people it was time to have their teeth cleaned. Jim "innocently" asked, "Then why is she still working for you?" Obviously, Jim had touched a sore spot because the dentist responded with a touch of heat, "Well, good employees are not that easy to come by!"

Then Jim asked, "How good an employee is she?" After spending several minutes rationalizing and justifying, the dentist stopped in mid-sentence and said, "I am being silly . . . she really is a good employee but I haven't given her the proper direction." Jim said it was exciting to see him come to the conclusion on his own. If Jim had said, "It seems to me you are not giving her enough direction," the doctor really (and rightfully so) might have become defensive. By answering questions, this man was able to discover that:

1. He must *establish* and *sell* the concept of the importance of making these calls.

2. He must *train* the people to meet his expectations.

3. He must *inspect* to make sure he gets what he *expects*.

The good doctor went back to his office and called a conference with his office manager and receptionist. He started the meeting by saying, "It is my goal to pay each of you more money! Would you be interested in discussing how this might happen?" He definitely had their attention! After their enthusiastic nods of approval, he continued, "As both of you know, our office handles sixty to seventy-five percent of our capacity (based on hours of the day and potential clients) each month. To give you both a substantial raise, we need more clients. One very good way to get additional clients is through appointment confirmation, which will cut down on our cancellations and no-shows. Another way is to make 'business building' (that's a much better name) calls. In the past, these have been called 'tension' calls because the emphasis has been on the one making the call. From now on they are 'business building' or 'helping' calls because the emphasis will be on the one we are calling. We have services these people desperately need, and it is our *responsibility* to help them by letting them know when they should be in our office." He went on to say, "Now I know these are demanding calls and I don't want you to make them all day, so let's start by figuring out how many helping calls it takes to encourage a client to visit our office."

The conversation continued and by drawing out the ideas of both the office manager and the receptionist (by asking questions), the following resulted:

1. The receptionist would make sure that 100 percent of all appointments were confirmed by starting seven days ahead on calls. She would make calls in the morning, afternoon, and even one call from home each evening, if necessary. She devel-

oped a follow-up system that allowed her to organize her time so these calls could be made during slower times of the day. In this case 100 percent of appointments *contacted* was her Foundational Performance level, Successful Performance level, and Value Performance level.

2. The office manager and the receptionist divided the "helping" or "business building" calls into two equal segments. Five calls each day was Foundational Performance; eight calls each day was Successful Performance; ten calls each day was Value Performance level. (Remember that all three levels were the same because 100% of the appointments must be contacted during the seven days before the appointment.)

3. A single sheet record report was developed by the office manager that enabled everyone involved to gather and compute the information they needed to see how the program was working. The report was submitted to the dentist weekly.

4. In only sixty days, appointment no-shows were almost entirely eliminated (a side benefit was the excellent public relations created); the office was operating at 85–90 percent capacity, and the office manager and receptionist had received their substantial raises. Note: The dentist got what he wanted (more clients) because he helped his assistants get what they wanted (a raise). The assistants got what they wanted (the raise) because they helped the clients get what they wanted (more beautiful, healthier teeth and gums).

The primary tool used in this example is what I like to call "tracking down." When a hunter is in pursuit of game, he tracks down his prey . . . meaning he divides the activities that will lead him to success into small, bite-size pieces. The hunter determines: game, geographic area, date, weapons, time of day, mode of transportation, and so on. When we hunt for Top Performance, we must do the same thing. We must "track down" success activities that take us to our goal—SUCCESS! When we break our goals into bite-size pieces and set Foundational Performance levels, Successful Performance levels, and Value Performance levels, we know *when* we are successful and *how* to get to our Top Performance level. One excellent manager stated: *"If you can't measure it, you can't manage it."*

Obviously, not all Performance Value Package programs will have the positive results this one had. In our own organization, we had a telemarketing representative who was not performing well. He and his supervisor agreed that on a daily basis he needed to average 80 attempts (numbers dialed), 20 completed calls, and $600 volume in sales as a Foundational Performance level; 90 attempts, 25 completed calls, and $800 sales volume were determined to be a Successful Performance level; and 100 attempts, 30 completed calls, and $1200 sales volume would be Value Performance level. After thirty days, the representative averaged 60 attempted calls, 12 completed calls, and $200 in sales volume. When confronted by his supervisor, the salesman had no really good reasons as to his lack of performance. In an hour-long planning session, they came to the agreement that the Foundational Performance level could be changed to 60 attempted calls, 15 completed calls, and $500 sales volume for the following week. At the end of the agreed-upon time period, the results were 58 attempted calls, 10 completions, with $180 sales volume.

These were the questions asked by the supervisor in their next meeting:

1. Do you feel that our Foundational Performance level agreed upon in our last meeting is fair? ("Yes.")

2. Is there anything I can do to help you be sure you reach this level? ("No.")

3. Do you understand that if you don't build a solid foundation level on this job you might be better off somewhere else? ("Yes.")

4. Do you understand that if you don't meet these minimum standards we will have no option other than to find something better for you to do with your time than work here? ("Yes.")

5. Is seven days a reasonable period of time to allow you to meet this standard? ("Yes.")

6. How do you think I feel about this meeting? ("You seem concerned about my success.")

7. How do you feel about this meeting? ("Good . . . and informed.")

Two days later the salesman came in and asked for a transfer to another part of our company.

The time periods and numbers may change, but the process does not! Let me tie down the point with one final example:

"I Hate My Job"

One day, just before I was scheduled to speak in Birmingham, Alabama, a lady came backstage for a brief visit. She was attractively dressed, but she had completely forgotten to put on a smile before she left home. She walked in and started her little talk—which was apparently well rehearsed. "Oh, Mr. Ziglar, I'm so glad to see you! If somebody doesn't help me, I don't know what I'm going to do! I just hate my job! My boss never says anything encouraging. Nobody in the company likes me and I don't like any of them. It's a bad, bad scene and I want out!" She was the kind of lady who could brighten up a whole room— by leaving it, if you know what I mean!

As Cavett Robert would say, "She looked like the Cruise Director for the *Titanic!*"

I quickly got the strong feeling that it was a little speech she had given about eleven thousand times for all of her friends, relatives, neighbors, and complete strangers. She seemed to have a lot of experience in dumping a full load of garbage on anyone who would sit still. I got the impression that she expected me to sit there and let her dump all that garbage on me. I even felt she figured when it was all over I was going to say, "Oh, that's terrible! Boy, that's just awful! But, my dear, you must be brave. There are those who are destined to carry the burdens of the world for others. It's just a cross you're going to have to bear and you must bear it bravely and willingly and in the by-and-by everything is going to work out for the best."

I even have an idea that in her mind she expected to leave our interview wiping the corners of her eyes with a little handkerchief, saying, "Oh, you've just helped me so much! I'm so glad you had time to share this with me!" But if I had taken that approach I would have betrayed everything in which I believe. The *last* thing she needed was sympathy. She had spent a lifetime wallowing in self-pity and as Mrs. Mamie McCullough, the I CAN Lady, would say, "holding her own private 'pity party.' " She needed empathy, not sympathy. She needed someone who was not part of the problem but who could help her find a solution.

Unfortunately, It Will Get Worse

When she finally took a breath of air so I could slip in a quick word edgewise, I looked at her and said (firmly, but not unkindly), "Yes, your situation doesn't sound very good and the unfortunate thing is that it's probably going to get worse!" If I'd hit her in the face with a bucket of ice water she could not have been more surprised.

She obviously expected that "nice Mr. Ziglar" to be entirely different. I know she did because she reacted by jumping back and asking, "What do you mean?" Zig: "It's very simple: Your situation's going to get worse because there is a good chance you might lose this job, and jobs, even bad ones, aren't that easy to find." Lady: "What are you talking about?" Zig: "Ma'am, there's not a company anywhere that can have that much negativism in one concentrated spot and survive."

A few tears started to form and she asked, "Well, what can I do?" Zig: "I've got an idea, if you're really interested in solving the problem." Lady: "Please tell me what it is because I'm definitely interested."

In my mind, it's critically important to determine whether or not a person really is interested in solving the problem. Many people appear to be seeking help when in reality all they want is a listening audience and someone who will agree with what they're saying and doing. My time frame was such that I did not have the time to be just a listener. I had to feel my time was going to be utilized in solving the problem rather than just beating the problem to death.

The woman assured me she was definitely interested in solving the problem, so I agreed to share a couple of ideas which I thought would help.

Start Looking for the Good

Zig: "The first thing I want you to do tonight when you go home is to take a sheet of paper and list everything you like about your job and your company." Lady: "That will be easy because I don't like anything about it!" Zig: "Now hold the phone and let me ask you a question." Lady: "All right." Zig: "Do they by any chance pay you for the work you do or do you work there for benevolent reasons?" Lady: "Certainly they pay me for the work I do!" Zig: "Don't you like that?" Lady: "Of course I like it!" Zig: "Well, the number-one thing you like about your job, then, is they pay you for doing it, so go ahead and write it down. We'll start our list right now.

"Number two, do they pay you below average, average, or above average for what you do?" Lady: "I've got to confess they pay me above average." Zig: "Don't you like that?" Lady: "Of course I like it!" Zig: "Okay, the second thing you like about your job is that they pay you above average, so write it down.

"Number three, do you ever get a vacation?" Lady: "Why, of course I get a vacation!" Zig: "Don't you like that?" Lady: "Of course I like it!" Zig: "Okay, you get a vacation, you like it, so write it down.

"Number four, do you have a retirement program?" Lady: "Everybody's got a retirement program, including us!" Zig: "Don't you like that?" Lady: "Of course I like it!" Zig: "Okay, you've got a retirement program and you like it, so write it down."

As we continued the process we discovered a host of things the lady "liked" about her job (hospital and life insurance, five days annual sick leave, all the national holidays, a profit-sharing plan which vested upon retirement, only a ten-minute drive from her home to the office, a full hour for lunch, participation in employee/employer relations, a beautiful building to work in with protected private parking spaces, and so on).

By actual count, there were twenty-two things she liked about the job which she had hated and liked *nothing* about just a few minutes earlier.

Remember: You Find What You Look for in Life

I could go into Mobile, Alabama, Albany, New York, or Fresno, California, and *find* drugs, crime, prostitutes, and in general the most negative, objectionable people in the world. Or I could go into Mobile, Alabama, Albany, New York, or Fresno, California, as I actually have done in times past, and *find* some of the most beautiful, loving, caring, dedicated, God-fearing, flag-waving, family-loving people in the world. You will *find* what you are looking for.

You can take the most outstanding man or woman, husband or wife, boy or girl imaginable, nitpick them to death, and manage to find some fault with them. Or you can take the average man or woman and start looking for the good qualities, and you will find them in abundance. It depends on what you're looking for.

Husband, if you treat your wife like a thoroughbred, you will never end up with a nag. Wife, if you treat your husband like a champ, you won't end up with a chump.

You can take your job or your company and find many good things you like or a number of things you don't like. It depends on what you want out of life, because *you are going to find what you're looking for.* Significantly, the more good *or* bad you find in yourself, your mate, your job, your kids, your country, or your future, the more good *or* bad there will be to find.

Message:
Look for what you want—not for what you don't want.

Accentuate the Positive

I encouraged the lady to take her list of twenty-two positive things about her job and, just before she went to bed, get in front of the mirror and slowly, firmly read the list out loud. This would plant positive thoughts in her subconscious mind before she went to sleep. The next morning she was to read the list again before she left for work.

She was also to take the list with her because in just twenty-four hours she would be adding to it, having started conditioning herself to look for the positives about her job. During that day and in the days ahead, she was to add the positives to that list. I encouraged her to follow this process for a minimum of twenty-one days, because it takes that long to substitute a *bad* habit (finding fault) with a *good* habit (finding something positive).

After about thirty-five minutes this lady left in an entirely different frame of mind. When she walked out, she was actually *striding!* She didn't walk out a beaten and defeated person. Don't misunderstand. I'm not implying that in thirty-five minutes we were able to overcome a lifetime of her making an overdraft on the bank of right mental attitude. However, we did give her some hope and a plan and those are two powerful ingredients. As a matter of fact, winning managers never make promises to their people unless they give them a plan to make the promise possible. And when managers make demands on anyone, they extract a plan *from* that person as to how they can realistically meet that demand.

Six weeks later I was back in Birmingham doing a follow-up sales training session. The woman was seated right in the front row, grinning like she had walked through a swinging door on somebody else's push. I chatted with her briefly and asked her how she was doing. She responded, "Well, to tell you the truth, I'm still not completely out of the woods, but you would be amazed at how much the company and the people who work there have changed!" Her world changed because her attitude changed. *Yours* will do the same.

Expect the best from yourself and others!

PERFORMANCE PRINCIPLES

1. We generally get from others what we expect.

2. The difference between good and excellent companies is *training*.

3. You find what you look for in life . . . and career.

4. Never a promise without a plan.

5

"WAIT FOR ME,
I'M YOUR LEADER!"

An ounce of loyalty is worth a pound of cleverness.
Elbert Hubbard

Goodfinders

Expect the Best

Loyalty

THE *L* IN OUR GEL formula stands for *Loyalty*. Loyalty, very simply, is the desire to help other people become successful.

Grant Teaff is the football coach at Baylor University in Waco, Texas. He is an outstanding man and a winner as a football coach. I once heard him share a story which says quite a bit about loyalty.

Baylor won their first conference championship in fifty years during Coach Teaff's third year. The first two years they struggled to establish a solid foundation and were not as successful as they would like to have been in the "win column." Just prior to the beginning of the third season, Baylor's offensive coordinator came to Coach Teaff and asked him to go hunting with him. It seems that a farmer out in west Texas had offered to let them hunt on his property. Seizing the opportunity for one last break before the beginning of the long (fourteen- to sixteen-hour workdays are typical) football season, they placed their guns in the truck and departed.

Upon arrival, Coach Teaff asked his assistant to wait in the truck while he let the farmer know they were there and would be hunting on his property. As Coach Teaff knocked on the door he had no idea of the enthusiastic greeting awaiting him! "Coach Teaff! Man alive, it's great to see you! You fellas are doing a great job with our Baylor Bears! I know

482

you've not won as many games as you'd like these first two seasons, but I believe we are prepared for a championship season!"

The coach was both pleased and humbled by what the farmer said. "Thank you so much," he replied, "and if we can ever do anything for you, just let me know."

"As a matter of fact," said the farmer, "I do need your help! If you notice, about fifty yards in front of where you parked your truck is an old mule. That old mule has been in our family for nearly twenty years and, frankly, Coach Teaff, she has become just like a member of the family. Recently she contracted a disease which is most painful and she needs to be put out of her misery. I just can't bring myself to do it and my wife has never fired a weapon and wouldn't step on an ant. Since you have your hunting rifles, would you be willing to put our mule out of her misery?"

"Well, it seems like the least I can do, considering you're being nice enough to let us hunt on your property," said the coach.

"Thanks," said the farmer, "the county will remove her later and when you and your assistant finish hunting, you come back here and we'll have a big supper together."

As Coach Teaff started back to the truck, he got an idea which, as he says, "can be a dangerous thing for a football coach." His face turned to a scowl and he bit his tongue until a trace of a tear appeared in the corner of his eye. The assistant coach saw this and asked, "Coach, what's wrong?"

"Oh, that old farmer infuriated me!" Coach Teaff replied. "Can you believe he said Baylor would never win another game while you and I coached there?"

"What?" was the incredulous reply.

"Not only that, but he said we were probably the worst coaching staff in the history of football!"

"But we were supposed to hunt on his property."

"Not only did he say to get off his property immediately, but if we don't he is going to call the law on us!"

"I cannot believe it," said the dumbfounded assistant.

"Yep, makes me so mad," responded Coach Teaff, "I think I'll shoot his mule!"

"Oh, Coach, no! You talk about trouble with the law! We'll really be in trouble if you shoot his mule!"

"Trouble or not, I'm tired of people bad-mouthing Baylor . . . this is it!"

Trying hard to hide his ever-widening grin, Coach Teaff pulled his gun off the gunrack, lined up on the poor old mule to do her a great favor, and squeezed the trigger. *Bang!* the shot rang out. As he turned to see the reaction of the assistant coach, *Bang—Bang!* two more shots rang out from the other side of the truck and the assistant coach shouted, "I got two of his cows, now let's get out of here!"

Now obviously, had this happened it would be taking loyalty too far, but if you are going to be a Top Performer, there can be no question about your loyalty in three areas. You must be loyal to yourself, to those with whom you live and work, and to your organization.

Be Loyal to Yourself

To be loyal to yourself, you must *work* to maintain a healthy self-image. This is not an overinflated ego or the kind of self-confidence that the wit says, "generally occurs just before we really understand the situation." Loyalty to yourself means looking for the evidence that supports *why* you should believe in you.

In *See You at the Top*, I wrote, "You cannot consistently perform in a manner which is inconsistent with the way you see yourself." I cannot stress too much the importance of "seeing" yourself successfully completing your daily tasks. Do you think the heavyweight boxing champion of the world goes into the ring questioning his ability? Absolutely not! The champion steps into the ring *believing* in himself and his ability to win! The quarterback of the world championship Super Bowl team does not step into the huddle and timidly ask for advice from his teammates! Chris Evert Lloyd expects to win the majority of her tennis matches, Nancy Lopez expects to be among the top money winners in the Ladies Professional Golfers Association. Johnny Carson has been in front of more people, more often, than anybody in the entertainment industry, yet in an interview he reported that he still gets nervous before he performs. Believing in yourself and being loyal to yourself will help you move toward becoming a Top Performer.

A Gallup Poll revealed that the self-esteem of workers and managers plays a substantial role in economic productivity. Dr. Robert Schuller, pastor of the ten-thousand-plus member Crystal Cathedral of Garden Grove, California, commissioned the study which was paid for by an anonymous donor. Initially Dr. Schuller was not primarily concerned with productivity, but simply with the general importance of self-esteem in Americans. However, the answers in the fifteen hundred personal interviews convinced him that the relationship between self-esteem and productivity is of profound importance to business and government.

The study showed:

- Persons with a high level of self-esteem feel productive.
- Those with a low self-esteem do not feel themselves productive and seem to lack productive incentives.

Dr. Schuller concluded that "nurturing human capital, the people who make decisions and operate the tools of our increasingly industrialized society," has been allowed "to take a backseat to machinery" and this adversely affects productivity. The study showed that 37 percent of Americans have high self-esteem and 30 percent have very low self-esteem. In this low self-esteem group only 17 percent considered themselves very productive and 20 percent said they were not productive at all. Dr. Schuller concluded from the survey results that the 30 percent low-esteem group are a "drag on themselves, their employers, and American society in general."

Noting that economists and the federal government generally prescribe capital investments and new plants as the solution to the problem of static or falling productivity, Dr. Schuller said it seems that raising people's self-esteem may be nearly as important. The study showed that the elements usually conducive to high self-esteem are good family relationships, good moral standards, religion, close friends, financial well-being, hobbies, and status. Married persons tend to have more self-esteem than divorced, widowed, or single adults. Education also contributes to high self-esteem. Persons with high self-esteem are inclined to view success in personal terms; those with low self-esteem tend to look on success as a strictly material matter. One of the most important findings was that *persons with low self-esteem tend to suffer from a lot of physical and emotional stress and to have high absentee rates on the job, which definitely diminishes productivity.*

Obviously, your self-image will play a major role in how high you go in your company, because it plays a major role in your ability to develop leaders who will follow you up the ladder of success or, in many cases, pass you on the ladder of success.

The following article by James L. Hayes, former president of the American Management Association, says a great deal. The title of the article is "The Art of Self-Promotion," which might turn off someone with low self-esteem or one who does not understand what self-esteem is all about. But the article will definitely turn you on and help you develop your own potential. The last sentence in the article really gets to the heart of the matter:

Many competent managers fail to rise within their organizations because they overlook a vital career consideration—the need to "promote themselves."

According to a recent survey conducted by Henchy & Co., a New York placement firm, it was found that 83 percent of fired executives shared one common trait—not calling attention to their abilities and achievements. The end result: they were perceived as not having any.

On the other hand, a second study by a Boston research firm found that successful managers know how to intensify their images through self-promotion.

Unfortunately, many executives conceive of self-promotion as simply meaning game playing and ego-exercising. In their conscious efforts to avoid that type of image, they go too far to the other extreme.

The executive suffering from lack of self-promotion may not approve of the behavior of the high profile executive. But he will grudgingly recognize the benefits that successful self-promotion can bring.

Since there are limited opportunities in any organization, managers who promote themselves usually have the best chances of getting better career opportunities—leading to quicker advancement, more interesting work, better pay and easier access to top management.

Managers who are skilled in promoting themselves know that it is a delicate art. There is always the risk of promoting too much. Nonetheless, there are certain promotional constants that can be applied to some degree anywhere and at any time. These techniques include:

• Compliment colleagues. You can demonstrate confidence and security in your own abilities by drawing attention to the achievements of others. Such reinforcement can establish you as an overall "positive" individual, and this attitude will be reflected back to you.

• Praise subordinates. *When a subordinate does good work, tell him or her. After all, a subordinate's success is yours also. Frequent positive reinforcement will make your subordinates work harder. And your reputation as a good supervisor will grow as a result.*

• Circulate memos. *If you come across information of interest to your colleagues, circulate it in a memo. Your efforts and consideration will be appreciated.*

• Implement creative innovations. *If you develop a better way of doing something, implement it. Your efforts to improve operations will be recognized and your value increased.*

• Volunteer. *Special projects or committees will probably demand more of your time. But participation in such activities will identify you as someone who cares beyond the paycheck.*

• Talk up. *Sometimes you may be privy to information that others are not aware of when making a decision. If so, talk up. You may complicate matters, but if you are right, you will be thanked later.*

• Know all. *Don't be content in knowing what you are expected to know. Find out as much about your organization as you possibly can. You can never tell when such information will pay off.*

• Observe and respond. *Be aware of whatever goes on around you. If something happens that calls for a response, act upon it immediately. The longer you wait, the less chance you have of exerting control. If you wait too long, in some cases a situation may fester and grow out of proportion.*

As you can see, none of the above suggestions prescribe loud, flamboyant, attention-getting self-promotion. On the contrary, they are sensible techniques for developing an image of even-keeled competency. For the point is not to be perceived as the most visible, but as the most capable.

Steps to a Healthy Self-Image

If self-esteem really is important to Top Performance, what can we do to improve our self-image? In *See You at the Top*, I listed fifteen steps to a healthy self-image . . . and I would strongly recommend that you review those steps. For our purposes here, I would like to suggest three steps the manager may take to improve self-esteem in himself and others.

Step #1   Make Out Your Own Victory List

When looking for evidence that supports *why* you should believe in *you,* make out your own victory list. The items listed do not have to include things such as "Developed the cure for cancer." List the simple everyday victories, like helping a senior citizen across a busy intersection (assuming he wanted to go across that intersection!).

Unfortunately, our human nature is such that if I were to ask you to recall your most embarrassing incident in the last two weeks, you might be hard-pressed to decide *which* incident to share. However, if I asked you to share your greatest victory in the last two weeks, you might have difficulty coming up with one. This is human nature—to hang onto the failures and forget the victories. To combat this natural tendency, you need to make out a victory list.

This list is not a "brag" list. As a matter of fact, no one should see it but you. This list has nothing to do with conceit. As I often say, "Conceit is a weird disease that makes everyone sick *except* the one who has it!" This list is to help you remember you are a person of worth.

This is not a "comparison" list. You do not build yourself in comparison to others. There will always be someone more powerful, more helpful, better looking . . . less powerful, more selfish, or less attractive than you. When you make positive or negative comparisons, you are on dangerous ground. To build a healthy self-image, you can make only one comparison: *Compare your actions to your ability.* If you will make this comparison only, and realize that even this is somewhat unfair because your abilities can be enhanced by training and growth, you will have taken a giant stride toward a healthy self-image and Top Performance.

Remember, success is not measured by how you perform compared with how others perform. You might have twice their ability—or half their ability. Success—*real* success—is measured by how you do compared with what you could be doing with the ability God gave you.

You should also have a victory list for those people you are managing or supervising. Why not keep a running record of occasions when you "catch them doing something right"? If you do, both you *and* your employees will win.

Step #2   Determine to Live Until You Are Dead

Will Rogers made this comment in the very last speech he ever gave: "Lord, let me live until I'm dead!" Of course, he was referring to those "walking zombies" who make their way through life never wanting to be confused by the facts. You will recognize them as having been born in the 1940s or 1950s, died in the 1970s, and they will be buried in the 1990s! They are stuck in a rut, which is, you know, nothing more than a grave with the ends kicked out. The way we get out (and stay out) of the rut is by understanding that happy, successful people don't go through life, they *grow* through life!

When I think of growth, I think of the story Robert Schuller told on his *Hour of Power* television program about Sir Edmund Hillary. You will remember that Sir Edmund was the first man to climb Mount Everest, the tallest mountain in the world. He failed in several of his early attempts and on one occasion left five associates dead on the side of that great mountain. Parliament wanted to recognize these valiant efforts, so they invited Hillary into their chambers. They even placed a picture of Mount Everest at the front of the room. When Sir Edmund Hillary entered the room, Parliament rose as one to give him a standing ovation, and when he saw these great legislators standing and applauding his good effort, tears filled his eyes. Many members of Parliament noticed the tears and must have thought, *Ah, look, the tears of happiness that we are recognizing this good effort he has made.* But they were not tears of happiness and joy—they were tears of anger and frustration! For Edmund Hillary had not set out to make a "good effort" at climbing that mountain, and he certainly had not set out to leave five associates dead on the side of that mountain.

As Hillary walked to the front of that room, he recognized something that many of you have recognized and that is, yes, he had made a "good" effort to climb that mountain, but

---

the greatest enemy of excellence is good!

Sir Edmund Hillary walked to the front of the room and literally pounded on that picture and actually screamed at the mountain: "You defeated me! But you won't defeat me again! Because *you have grown all that you can grow . . . but I am still growing!*"

You see, my reading friend, if you are in a growth posture—regardless of what you have already accomplished or have not accomplished— there are still great things left in front of you! With that last statement, as positive and optimistic as it is, I need to remind you of what Emerson said: "What lies behind you and what lies in front of you pales in comparison to what lies inside of you." He was right, of course.

When employees move into the management role, they often feel they must know *everything* about their new position. This is an overwhelming burden to be forced to carry. You were not hired to be an encyclopedia or a computer . . . you were hired to manage. Managers must know where to find information, not have total recall. Those who can think are much more important than those who can regurgitate facts. Remember: *It's very difficult to be overtrained!* So, get involved in continuing education, seminars, books, and tapes. Your thirst for knowledge and understanding must never cease—but you don't need to memorize the manuals for every seminar you attend. Determine that you will continue to grow and learn as a manager, and you will greatly improve your self-image.

We must never overlook the fact that our company can spend millions and millions of dollars on buildings, computers, electronic gear, fixtures, communication systems, and so forth, but the full utilization of these monumental expenditures is entirely dependent on the growth, training, attitude, and capability of the people in the company. The responsibility for that growth, training, attitude, and capability rests squarely on the shoulders of management.

Step #3   Focus Your Attention on Those You Are Responsible to and For

One of the fastest ways to improve our own self-esteem is to focus our attention on others. Often, the more we think of ourselves, the less self-confidence we have. Forgetting about *us* and becoming sincerely interested in *them* will lead us directly to a healthy self-respect. When you give your full and undivided attention to others, and concentrate on making them feel comfortable, you become less self-conscious.

Dr. Alfred Adler said that we can be cured of depression in only fourteen days if every day we will try to think of how we can be helpful to others. David Dunn wrote a wonderful little book entitled *Try Giving Yourself Away*, which gives some marvelous insights as well as some simple, practical steps on *how* we can be an encouragement and help to others. When we are sincerely interested in others, we don't have time to direct negativity toward ourselves.

"Mr. Ziglar, I Heard What You Said"

One Saturday afternoon several years ago, my wife and I were scheduled to play golf at a beautiful course in the Dallas area. On this particular day we had a one o'clock tee time. However, on Saturdays the course attracts many local residents as well as people from other cities, so we were delayed a few minutes. The foursome in front of us consisted of two couples, and one of the young men was on the tee box getting ready to tee off. As my wife and I sat in our cart, I could not help but notice the young man.

He was about thirty years old, something like six feet, three inches tall, and weighed about 220 pounds. However, as the young man stood there addressing the ball, it was obvious to me that he was not a golfer. He looked a little uncomfortable and was addressing the ball in an unorthodox manner. He picked his club up, wiggled it a few times, then put it down and repeated the process for what seemed like an eternity.

Finally, I muttered under my breath that he obviously was not a golfer. My wife quietly asked how I knew. I responded I'd been playing the game a long time, had watched a lot of golfers, and just *knew* he was not a golfer. In the meantime, the young man kept wiggling the club and picking it up and putting it down. Finally, he pulled his club back and proceeded to bust that ball about 240 yards, right down the middle. So much for my expertise in evaluating golfers!

After the young man hit the ball, he walked over to his cart, put his club in his bag, and walked straight back to me. He was neither smiling nor frowning, but as he walked up to me he said, "Mr. Ziglar, I heard what you said . . ."

(Now, my reading friend, I want you to think with me just for a moment. Had you been in my position, what would you have thought—and done? I felt some apprehension and wanted to pull a disappearing act, but fortunately the young man continued.) ". . . when you spoke in my hometown three years ago, and it completely changed my life. I just want you to know, Mr. Ziglar, that it is an honor for me to even be on the same golf course with you."

Needless to say, I breathed a deep sigh of relief, thanked the young man profusely, and was grateful at the sudden unexpected and delightful turn of events. I also made a resolution that day to be far more careful in my judgmental attitude when I am observing or dealing with other people.

I've often thought of how tragic it would have been, had the young man actually heard the cutting, unkind, and, as it developed, untrue remarks I made about him. It undoubtedly would have adversely affected him and certainly would have lowered his opinion of me. Not only that, but it would have been virtually impossible for me to have positively affected him in the future from an inspirational and instructional point of view.

As managers and leaders, one of the things we cannot escape is the fact that when people look to us we have a responsibility to let them see we deserve to be in that position of leadership. They evaluate and respond to us to a large degree based on the way we see them, feel about them, *and* treat them. That's why it's so important for us to look for the good, expect the best, and always remember that as managers we are role models for many of the people in our group or company. It is at least reasonably important that they like us. It is critically important that they respect us. It is difficult, if not impossible, for them to either like us *or* respect us if we make snide, judgmental, unkind, and/or untrue observations about them as I did the young golfer.

Don't misunderstand. Each one of us — including that young man — is responsible for his own actions and conduct. By no stretch of imagination am I responsible for what he does. However, I am responsible *to* him to be fair, honest, objective, and exactly what I appear to be. As managers in your organization, you are not responsible *for* your people, but you are responsible *to* your people.

Honesty + Courtesy = Loyalty

Top Performers are loyal to those with whom they live and work. Mamie McCullough, the I CAN Lady, says her idea of Judgment Day is that the Lord is going to line up everybody we have ever said anything ugly about and make us repeat it to their faces. That's a sobering thought, and I'll bet it will make all of us think twice before we say anything unkind about others, won't it?

There is a statement you have heard since you were a child that is no less true today than it was when you first were told: "If you don't have something nice to say, don't say anything at all." I know the admonition has become a cliché and may seem oversimplified, trite, and worn out, but wouldn't we all be better off if we took this bit of sage advice?

The Forum Corporation of Boston, Massachusetts, did an in-depth study of 341 salespeople from eleven different companies in five different industries. Of this group, 173 were top salespeople and 168 were average salespeople. The primary difference between the two groups was not skill, knowledge, or ability. The 173 super salespeople were more productive because their customers *trusted* them, and customers are far more likely to *believe* the honest salesperson. They discovered that people do not buy based on what you tell them *or* what you show them. They *do buy* based on what you tell them *and* show them, which they believe. The same principle applies in directing the activities of those under your leadership. They will "buy" and act enthusiastically on your leadership based *only* on what you show and tell them, which they believe. Anything less than that trust and confidence simply means they will give it less than their 100 percent support.

In managing people, trust and honesty are commodities we can take to the marketplace and cash in at any time. Top Performers in management learn to create trust in others by *complete* honesty in all dealings. The second characteristic these supersuccessful salespeople possessed in spades, according to the *Forum Report,* was plain, old-fashioned courtesy. These salespeople are just as nice and courteous to the switchboard operator and file clerks as they are to the office manager and accountant. They are as pleasant with the shipping clerk and service personnel as they are with the president of the company. The reason is simple: They clearly understand that the sales process is not complete—and future sales are in jeopardy—until the current sales order has been delivered, installed, serviced, *and* paid for. For this reason they *know* they need the cooperation, effort, and goodwill of the entire team back at the home office.

In any business or family where two or more people are involved, there is always going to be a certain amount of discussion and conflict about who does what. One of the best opportunities for teaching trust and honesty is in the area of responsibility or doing what needs to be done. Unfortunately, in most businesses and homes the battle cry is, "That's not my job!" Top Performers, however, are loyal to those with whom they work and live and show this loyalty by doing what they are supposed to do, when they are supposed to do it. They give strong verbal support, and never say negative or unkind things about their associates. They clearly understand that when you're slinging mud, you're not doing anything but losing ground. Top Performers also are willing to go the extra mile and do the extras because they instinctively know that the more successful their company or department is the more likely they are to move ahead in their own careers.

Burke Marketing Research, Inc., asked executives in one hundred of the nation's one thousand largest companies, "What employee behavior disturbs you the most?" The result was a "hit parade of things that stick in the boss's craw, the kind of behavior that hits a nerve," said Marc Silbert, whose temporary personnel agency commissioned the survey. "They can blind employers to employees' good qualities. They become beyond redemption," he said. Liars, goof-offs, egomaniacs, laggards, rebels, whiners, airheads, and sloths—these are eight banes of a boss's existence, according to the survey, with *dishonesty* and *lying* topping the list. "*If a company believes that an employee lacks integrity, all positive qualities—ranging from skill and experience to productivity and intelligence—become meaningless,*" said Silbert, vice-president of Accountemps. Loyalty to those with whom we live and work is a prerequisite to Top Performance.

Be Loyal to Your Organization

When I say that loyalty to your organization is important, I do not mean you should accept every thought that comes from upper management as if it had come down from the mountain on tablets. No one expects you to leap with joy when the commission structure has been changed so that there is more for the company and less for you. You are not expected to thank ownership when the working hours are changed and you are allowed to work more hours for the same or less pay. Loyalty to your organization means handling these aggravations in the proper manner.

Let's take a "negative break" and talk about how *not* to handle these situations. You do not complain about your areas of concern over coffee with a co-worker who has no authority to change the situation. You do not identify internal problems externally—meaning to someone outside your organization. The person who takes either of these avenues becomes a cancer to the organization. As you know, a cancer is a cell that lives within the body independently of the other cells of the body, and unless it is removed it will eventually lead to the death of the body. There are few diseases that will affect your organization in a more deadly manner or will creep up on the company with less notice than lack of loyalty. I have already mentioned that I feel very strongly about the importance of Due Process, but if there were ever a reason for dismissal without Due Process, it would be a lack of loyalty.

How, then, should the loyal employee manage the situation? The proper method of handling any situation that concerns you is to take the "problem identified" to someone who has the authority to handle the situation. Present it and several "potential solutions" for consideration. If after a realistic amount of time the company takes action on your recommendations or another satisfactory solution, you should congratulate yourself for working from within the organization to make it stronger.

However, if after a realistic amount of time the company fails to take action to change the situation, you now have two options: (1) shut up; (2) move on. There are no other options! If you continue to identify a problem over which no action is going to be taken, then the cancer grows. Continuing to identify a problem on which no action is going to be taken is beating your head against the proverbial brick wall. I believe that ulcers, serious headaches, burnout, stress, and even heart problems often begin in this very manner. Dr. David Schwartz, in his book *The Magic of Thinking Big,* says that over 80 percent of our hospital beds are filled with people with "EII," or Emotionally Induced Illness. This does not mean that the people are not sick, just that their illnesses *began* in their minds.

You owe it to *yourself*—as well as to your organization—to either support what is happening or find another company to work for. Now some of you are saying that jobs are not that easy to come by, and I agree. Neither is the human body that easy to come by—at least, spare parts are in great demand! The answer is simple but not easy: Get with the program or find another program to get with!

This Coin Has Two Sides

Loyalty to the company is important, but the other side of the coin is that management and the corporation owe that same loyalty to their people. A classic example is Ross Perot and EDS. First a little background. His story is one of those rags-to-riches American stories with which many are so familiar.

In 1958 a young man drove into Dallas, Texas, in a 1950 Plymouth automobile. He had virtually all of his possessions in the backseat and his wife and baby in the front seat. He was a top producer with IBM in 1958, but later he came up with a better idea in the use of computers. The idea was so good that he decided to start his own company. I don't believe there are many people in the United States today who don't recognize the name of Ross Perot and EDS (Electronic Data Systems).

Now remember, Ross Perot is one man. With a limited amount of money of his own plus some from his family and friends, he started his own company. EDS has made a major contribution to the computerized age of which we are a part. And in 1985 EDS was purchased by General Motors for more than three *billion* dollars.

One interesting and encouraging side to this story is the fact that although EDS deals in computer services, it is a very "human" company. Its management feels that qualities such as loyalty to country and family, high business ethics, and a sense of fair play to one's fellow man are all more important than job skills in a "total man, total company" growth concept.

The purchase of EDS by General Motors made Ross Perot one of the wealthiest men in the world. However, the key for Top Performers is to understand *why* he was able to become so successful. The following incident will give you some real insight into the character of this very successful man.

Just How Far Can You Go With Loyalty?

When the American Embassy in Iran was overrun in 1979, two of Ross Perot's key executives were captured by the Iranians and put in prison. Ross Perot is known as a man of decisiveness and a man of action. He is even better known among his employees as a man of intense loyalty. He stands by his people and supports them and they, in return, are intensely loyal to him. The problem in this situation was what to do about these two men who were in an Iranian prison. The answer—as far as Ross Perot was concerned—was fairly simple. He had little confidence (because of the political ramifications) that his men would see the light of day for a long, long time. He even feared their lives were in jeopardy. He quickly called a conference of his key executives in the United States. They mapped out a daring plan for the rescue of their co-employees.

The details are so exciting and so involved that space does not permit their being told here. However, I encourage you to read *On Wings of Eagles*, by Ken Follett, and get his full and exciting account of the story. In a nutshell, Ross Perot was able to organize a campaign to get those men out. He created a false riot situation, hired his own loyal people, and they freed those two men from that Iranian prison. Is there any wonder his people are so loyal to him?

Obviously, most of us will never be called on to get involved in such a situation, but

> *every day we have an opportunity to be loyal and to stand by our people.*

A Final Word on Loyalty

We began this chapter with a quote from Elbert Hubbard, and now let's close with some wise words from the same man.

> *If you work for a man, in heaven's name, work for him. If he pays you wages which supply you bread and butter, work for him; speak well of him; stand by him and stand by the institution he represents. If put to a pinch, an ounce of loyalty is worth a pound of cleverness. If you must vilify, condemn, and eternally disparage— resign your position, and when you are outside, damn to your heart's content, but as long as you are part of the institution do not*

condemn it. If you do that, you are loosening the tendrils that are holding you to the institution, and at the first high wind that comes along, you will be uprooted and blown away, and probably will never know the reason why.

PERFORMANCE PRINCIPLES

1. Loyalty begins with loyalty to self.

2. You cannot consistently perform in a manner which is inconsistent with the way you see yourself.

3. Make every effort to be perceived as the most capable, not the most visible.

4. The greatest enemy of excellence . . . is good.

5. If you don't have something nice to say, don't say anything at all.

6. Support your organization or go to work for an organization you can support.

6

"PEOPLE JUST DON'T
CARE . . ."

One learns peoples through the heart, not the eyes or
the intellect.

Mark Twain

UNFORTUNATELY, as managers of people, we often feel like the speaker
who was met with less than a resounding welcome and said, "In the
words of William Shakespeare, it's nice to be among friends . . . even
if they are somebody else's." So many times managers and their employees almost seem to work at developing an adversary relationship. Instead,
we have to be like the small boy who was confronted by the three big
bullies, any one of whom could have obliterated him. (They even gave
some indication they were going to do exactly that.) Like a lot of us, the
little guy wasn't too well qualified to fight, but like *all* successful managers, he was qualified to think. (In this case, his physical well-being depended on it!) With this in mind, the little guy backed up dramatically,
drew a line in the dirt with the toe of his shoe, looked the leader of the
group in the eye, and said, "Now you just step across that line." Well, as
you might imagine, the big bully confidently—even arrogantly—
stepped across the line. The small boy then smiled broadly and ex-
claimed, "Now we are both on the same side!" If we are going to be
successful in managing people, we have got to remember that the manager and the people he manages *are* "on the same side."

You probably recall that Sir Edmund Hillary and his native guide,
Tenzing, were the first people to make the historic climb of Mount
Everest in 1953. Coming down from the mountain peak, Sir Edmund
suddenly lost his footing. Tenzing held the line taut and kept them both
from falling by digging his ax into the ice. Later Tenzing refused any
special credit for saving Sir Edmund Hillary's life; he considered it a
routine part of the job. As he put it, "Mountain climbers always help
each other." Can we, as managers, afford to be any different? Aren't we

obligated to work with our people to direct their energies and help them to develop their skills and talents to the fullest?

Your Billion-Dollar Asset

It is my firm conviction that if you could take only one thought or one idea out of *Top Performance*, it would be the thought I will share with you now. If you would really be an expert in the "people business" (that determines 85 percent of your success), then you should look into this statement:

> *People don't care how much you know, until they know how much you care . . . about them!*

Chances are great you have heard that phrase before and as an achiever, you really don't need to be told . . . but it doesn't hurt to be reminded. You see, whether we are talking about parents, brothers and sisters, children, spouse, friends, associates, co-workers, employees, or employers—people don't care whether you are a Phi Beta Kappa from MIT, or if you got your Ph.D. from Harvard. They don't care if you have twenty years of experience (or one year of experience repeated twenty times!), sold more units for more dollar volume than anyone else ever has, or set every record the company keeps . . . *until* they know how much you care about them.

Anyone can do a job; anyone can do a *good* job. But it's not until there is love in a person's heart for a job that the results are something which others will call GREAT! Love is caring—caring enough to invest your life, caring enough to give it your all, to stick it out, to do the best you possibly can.

Love comes forth to contribute, to invest, to help, to be a loyal part of an effort or enterprise. Love will draw out from a person the very best he can do, which is often more than he himself or anyone else thought he could do. Love motivates one's entire potential for that individual's total success. But love also serves to inspire others to motivate the ones who follow them.

Several years ago I heard this story, which comes from Dr. George Crane's daily newspaper column "The Worry Clinic," but its real impact hit me much later and I think it applies to what we are discussing here.

Jimmy, age ten, was devoted to his little sister, age six. One of the older staff doctors at Wesley Hospital told me of this case. It occurred about 1910 when blood transfusions and other medical miracles were not yet common.

Jimmy's sister had fallen off her bicycle and cut a large artery in her leg. Bleeding was profuse, so by the time the doctor arrived at their house, she was failing fast.

Quickly, the doctor managed to clamp the cut ends of the artery with his hemostats, but her heart was failing. In desperation, the doctor turned to Jimmy and said, "Jimmy will you give your blood to help save your little sister's life?"

Jimmy swallowed hard, then nodded his head, so the doctor lay him on the kitchen table and began withdrawing blood from one of his veins. Then he injected the blood directly into the little girl's vein.

For the next thirty minutes the doctor and family watched the little girl anxiously and prayerfully. The doctor kept his stethoscope over her heart to note its beating. Finally it showed she was over the crisis, so he wiped the perspiration off his forehead and turned around. Only then did he notice that Jimmy was still stretched out on the kitchen table, tense and trembling.

"What's the matter, Jimmy?" asked the doctor. "W-w-when do I die?" Jimmy replied through his clenched teeth.

That's when the doctor realized that Jimmy had misunderstood what the request for his blood really meant. For Jimmy had imagined his sister was going to need all his blood! Which meant that Jimmy, though hesitating a moment and swallowing hard at the doctor's original request, had silently agreed to die for his little sister!

The doctor had tears in his own eyes when he reassured Jimmy that he had extracted only a little of his blood and that Jimmy was not going to die. The doctor's tears demonstrated Descartes' comment about those divine sparks that God places in the brains of all of us. Jimmy's willingness to die that his sister might live is the type of thing which you empathetic readers will find makes your own divine sparks glow just from reading about Jimmy's sacrifice.

Now sacrifice and giving part of ourselves is not a popular concept in our society today, but think with me for just a second. When you come in at the end of the day and your spouse greets you at the door, chattering like a magpie about something in which you are totally disinterested, and you stop and give him or her your undivided attention, aren't you giving your loved one a part of your life? Aren't you giving up a little bit of yourself?

When you have been dealing with people — not always successfully — all day, what you really want is a few minutes of peace and quiet in front of the evening news or with the newspaper. Just as you settle down, your children, whom you dearly love but want to do so from a distance for the next few minutes, come climbing on you as if you were a jungle gym. At this point, when you either turn the TV off or put the newspaper down so that you can give them your love and undivided attention, you are investing a part of your life in theirs and giving up a little bit of yourself. When you are dead tired because it's been "one of those days," and an employee needs an empathetic ear and counseling and you take the time to listen, aren't you giving up a part of yourself?

If you would be an expert in the people business, read the Performance Principle at the end of this chapter, brand the words on your heart, and live them every day of your life.

PERFORMANCE PRINCIPLES

1. People don't care how much you know, until they know how much you care . . . about them.

PART TWO

THE SCIENCE OF
TOP PERFORMANCE

Science is organized knowledge.
                    Herbert Spencer

7

"BUT I THOUGHT
YOU SAID . . ."

Precision of communication is important, more important than ever, in our era of hair-trigger balances,
when a false or misunderstood word may create as
much disaster as a sudden thoughtless act.

James Thurber

EVERY MANAGER has heard about the importance of *communication.* Yet,
we all need to be reminded occasionally just how important it is, and we
need some specific suggestions on *what* we can do to be more effective.
*We also need to remember that miscommunication, poor communication,
or no communication can create incredible problems.* For example, take a
look at this legislative summary of a bill introduced by California Assem-
blyman Alister McAlister (D-San Jose):

"The existing probate code does not expressly provide that its provi-
sions are severable, in the event any of them are held invalid; that the
singular number includes the plural, and the plural, the singular; that
the present tense includes the past and present, and the future, the
present; or that designations of distinct portions within the code, without
specific reference to the code, means such portion of the probate code.
This bill would make specific each such provision."

Yes I know this is an extreme example, but isn't all communication,
when it's *mis*communication, extreme?

In this chapter we will examine some of the problem areas that inhibit
communication, review some of the rules for better communication,
and take a closer look at specific situations, such as public speaking and
meetings, in order to maximize effective communication. Finally, we'll
see how communication plays a part in creating a work environment
that is conducive to productivity.

According to the *Harvard Business Review,* the most promotable
quality an executive, manager, salesperson, or anyone can possess is the

ability to communicate. Alan Loy McGinnis, in his excellent book *Bringing Out the Best in People*, tells why:

> *Motivators always use words lavishly and intensely as they outline their dreams to prospective supporters. Such diverse leaders as Lyndon Johnson, Winston Churchill, and Lee Iacocca have all possessed something in common: a mesmerizing ability to talk. Some may have had their shy sides, but when the occasion presented itself, each could pour out a profusion of words. "The inspiring talker produces zeal," said Aldous Huxley, "whose intensity depends not on the rationality of what is said or the goodness of the cause that is being advocated, but solely on the propagandist's skill in using words in an exciting way." Words are a remarkably powerful vehicle. Much of Franklin D. Roosevelt's success was due to his ability to coin a phrase and use slogans to summarize his dreams, and those slogans became a part of the fabric of our national life. Gandhi and Martin Luther King, Jr., both knew that if one speaks long enough, there is an uplifting and elevating, almost intoxicating power in words. Most of us have experienced it hundreds of times—listening to another speak, either before an audience or in one-on-one conversation, until the sound of their words and the sheer weight of their flow eventually persuades us.*

> *You can gain a considerable following if you are willing to relate your message to enough people and not be deterred by the large numbers who will not buy it. Instead, you pick up your idea and present it to the next prospect. Eventually, with enough presentations to enough people, a few people become enthusiastic, they join the parade, one by one, and soon a movement is on its way. Talk may be cheap, but the right use of words can generate in your followers a commodity impossible to buy . . . hearts on fire!*

Yet, every day in our business and home life we encounter examples of miscommunication that bring grief and despair. This little bittersweet story could be true, and says much about life's communication problems.

An elderly couple were celebrating their fiftieth wedding anniversary. Their children, grandchildren, and great-grandchildren, as well as the townspeople, really rose to the occasion and recognized them in every conceivable way. The mayor gave them the key to the small town; there was a brunch at the country club; an afternoon tea; a banquet that evening, and all the townfolk as well as kinfolk came by to extend their congratulations. Finally, at about ten o'clock that evening the public celebration was all over. As was his custom, the husband headed for the kitchen to prepare the buttered toast with jam and the small glass of milk which he and his wife always enjoyed just before retiring.

Perhaps it was exhaustion from the long day, but when the husband called the wife into the kitchen for their little snack, as she sat down she broke into tears. Naturally concerned, the husband rose, walked around the table, embraced his wife, and asked her what the problem was. Through teary eyes she proclaimed that she thought on this most special of all occasions he would not have given her the end piece of bread. In some shock and surprise, the husband replied, "Why, sweetheart, I thought you knew that was my favorite piece!"

Isn't it ironic—and tragic—that for such a long period of time the husband had been giving what he thought was the best, but his wife had been receiving it as what she perceived to be the worst. Unfortunately, many of us have had similar miscommunication in our lives.

What Inhibits Communication?

As this story illustrates, one of the greatest inhibitors to effective communication is the simple word *assume*. The husband *assumed* his wife knew he was giving her what he considered the best piece of bread. The wife *assumed* the husband was deliberately giving her the least desirable piece of bread. In the family setting, that leads to family dissension with dire consequences. In the corporate world, the consequences can have a disastrous effect on productivity. Any time you think, *They probably know,* let that be a red flag to remind yourself that they probably *don't* know—and seize the opportunity to *remind* them of what they should know.

According to AT&T, the lion's share of time spent in any office is spent communicating: listening, talking, chasing down stray facts, dealing with mail, etc. Were you to keep a log you'd be appalled at how little time you have for actually producing work (par for senior executives is about 15 percent of the workday).

In addition, communication can be very difficult, and it takes a constant, concise effort to make sure you are understood. For instance, the five hundred most commonly used words in the English language have about fourteen thousand different meanings. And then there is the tendency to compound the problem by using words that don't fit together at all and force them into the same phrase. Take these examples:

"It's the *same difference!*"
"I would like the *jumbo shrimp.*"
"He worked with *military intelligence.*"

Word meanings and usage can complicate your life. Take the story of the woman who went to her pastor for counseling concerning her marriage. After a few preliminaries, the pastor said he had a few questions that would help identify the problems if she would just answer his questions as openly as possible. When the lady agreed, he began by saying, "Do you have any *grounds?*" To which the lady responded, "Why, yes we do, we have about ten acres just north of town." "No, ma'am," the pastor replied, "that's not what I mean. What I mean is do you have . . . well, do you have a *grudge?*" "Oh, no," she replied, "but we do have a nice little carport!" "No, ma'am," said the pastor, "that's not what I meant. One more question: Does your husband beat you up?" "Beat me up? Oh, no, I get up before he does just about every morning!" In complete exasperation the pastor said, "Lady, you're not listening to me. Why are you having trouble with your husband?" "Well," she said, "the man just doesn't know how to communicate!"

Communication should be as crisp and to the point as the sign I saw when I was in Chicago recently. It read WARNING! GUARD DOG ON DUTY—SURVIVORS WILL BE PROSECUTED! Now that communicates! I didn't want any part of that fence, that dog, that yard, or anything to do with that house. To be effective communicators, we should always be just that clear, though not necessarily that threatening.

As Easy as EBC

The problems in communication in the management area, and in society, for that matter, are so great that we at the Zig Ziglar Corporation have developed a seminar for companies and individuals called EFFECTIVE BUSINESS COMMUNICATIONS, which we are tremendously excited about. Our corporate staff instructors will spend two days helping your middle- and upper-management people become more effective in all-important communication skills.

Seeing yourself as others see (and hear) you is important, so participants are videotaped a dozen times, given private coaching sessions, and instructed in twelve Vital Skill Areas. EFFECTIVE BUSINESS COMMUNICATIONS is an extremely strong skill builder because approximately 30 percent of the time is spent in instruction while 70 percent of the time is spent in practicing skills each individual needs and can use *immediately* upon returning to the job. Now this is beginning to sound a little bit like a commercial because it is . . . a commercial for gaining communication skills! Let me give you a sample of some communication skills and ideas from our seminar that you can use immediately.

Did You Know That . . . ?

You have about four minutes to be either received or rejected when you first meet someone. You gather 87 percent of your total lifetime information by sight; 7 percent by hearing; 3.5 percent by smell; 1.5 percent by touch; 1 percent by taste. So when you encounter a prospect or an employee, what they *see* is vitally important. Listeners need visual stimulation—a point of activity to focus on. Gestures, body language, and facial animation, in addition to other visual stimuli, are crucial. The average person *speaks* at about 150 words per minute but *thinks* at about 600 words per minute—or about four times faster. You may think your mind wanders, but in fact it often is *galloping* ahead of you like a runaway racehorse. As a communicator you must do everything possible to hold the listener's attention, including keeping your thoughts in order and paced with your speaking.

People respond 55 percent to your body language and expression, 38 percent to your vocal inflection, and only 7 percent to what you say. And, because of TV, the average person's attention span is now said to be from about seven to eleven minutes. Then it's time for the commercial. As communicators we must work to overcome these habit patterns which have become ingrained in our listeners' minds.

The Dazzling Dozen

You can become a more effective communicator by becoming aware of what we call the twelve Vital Skill Areas of communication. These areas are: Appearance, Posture, Gestures, Eye Contact, Facial Expressions, Voice, Padding, Involvement, Handling Questions, Humor, Introducing Others, and Visual Aids.

Appearance means your clothes, plus the way you groom, the way you carry yourself and your accessories. Your appearance makes a statement about you; it tells others what you think of yourself. Does it add to or detract from the message you wish to communicate? What does *your* appearance say?

Posture means body language. Does your body language say that you are confident and in control, that you really care about the person you are communicating with, and that you are comfortable—or does it communicate just the opposite?

Gestures are the specifics of body language as it relates to arm and hand movement. You have heard people say they couldn't communicate if they were tied up and couldn't use their hands, and that is at least partially true. Natural arm and hand movement allows the communicator to express himself or herself much more clearly.

Eye Contact is to the eyes what the handshake is to the hands. When we "clasp" eyes with someone, we either send positive signals of confidence, courage, interest, and concern or negative signals of boredom, irritation, disgust, antagonism, or even anger.

Facial Expressions include the smile and frown. Your face is one of your greatest assets to effective communication. With controlled facial expressions, you set the tone for conversations and let people know what's coming. You also show what you mean, and make your thoughts easier to follow.

Voice includes not only the pitch of your voice but also volume, inflection, and pace. When you vary the volume level, place emphasis on certain words and phrases, and speak at a varying pace, you become more effective and are far more likely to be understood.

Padding is the nonworking words that we so uh, often um, insert ah, into you know, our—well, like our, uh, um, ah, spoken conversation. Just for fun, record a telephone conversation (your side of the call only) and count the number of nonworking words. You may be surprised.

Involvement means active listening both on your part and the part of those who *might* listen to you. Using a person's name, asking questions, and listening to the answer, and speaking in terms of others' interests are examples of how we involve others in communication.

Handling questions is especially important in business conversations. All too often we do not listen to the question or do not answer the same question that is asked. If integrity and trust are important in business (and they are), then the way you handle questions can increase your "trust level" with those with whom you work.

Humor can be used to relax your audience (of one or ten thousand) and make friends with them. It can also be used as a bridge when you are shifting into other perhaps more serious subject matter, and to give your audience a mental stand-up. It can be especially effective in lengthy presentations to bring a tired or drifting audience back to the session. Careful—don't overdo it. Too many would-be communicators sacrifice message for humor. Incidentally, the rule in sharing questionable humor of an off-color nature is this: If you have to ask the question "Should I share this?" you already have the answer: *No!* (I've never known a speaker to get a speaking engagement, an employee to get a promotion, a salesperson to make a sale, or a politician to win votes *because* he or she used profane language or told off-color stories. However, I do know of countless instances when extremely negative reactions were the result of profane language or tasteless stories.)

Introducing others may not seem very important to you, but someone very wise said, "You never get a second chance to make a first impression." In introductions, you have the opportunity not only to make an excellent first impression but also to make others feel important through sincere recognition of their strengths.

Visual aids are not only used in board meetings but may also be used in one-on-one conversations as well. Anytime you can impact more than one of your listener's senses, you are ahead in the communication game.

By just being aware of these Vital Skill Areas, you will move ahead in communication skills . . . and if you spend time working and studying these areas, you can substantially increase your communication skills.

Differences Between Oral and Written Language

Even though you may be an excellent writer, you will not be an excellent oral communicator if you use the same approach in speaking you do for the written word.

- Spoken language must be easily and instantly understandable to the listener. If the listener misunderstands, he cannot go back and reread.
- Spoken language should be more repetitive. It is important to rephrase several times key ideas you want the listeners to take away with them.
- Spoken language should be more idiomatic. Otherwise, it sounds somewhat stilted and stuffy.
- Spoken language should be simpler in structure than written language.
- Figurative language adds life and color to spoken words. Colorful, descriptive words can turn an otherwise colorless phrase into a memorable one. Lincoln described a nation "conceived in liberty . . ." Kennedy spoke of freedom as a "torch passed to a new generation . . ." J. F. Bere, chairman of the Borg-Warner Corporation, described untapped human assets as "waiting like a coiled spring to release enormous potentials . . ." Problems were called "smoldering fires . . ." and new programs being developed as "a brick here and a brick there."

Communication: Manager to Employee

Let's take an overview of how a Top Performer creates an environment for communication by looking at several points which I think are excellent guidelines for Top Performers.

Openness sets the basis for knowing your employees personally. *Communicate the desire to know your employees, and then make the effort to know them personally as well as professionally. The personal goals, interests, hobbies, family relationships, thoughts, and beliefs should be known as openly as possible so that the employee becomes more than an object. Managers should recognize employees as dynamic, unique individuals. Openness communicates dignity. No longer an object, the employee can enjoy the benefits of involvement and commitment, a platform for an exchange of trust. Mutual honesty and confidence create a model of behavior that becomes a positive emotional and mental support system.*

Listen and communicate. *To know employees openly, listen to what others say and encourage them to communicate their motivation, concerns, personalities, and unique mental sets. Listen to their ideas. Doing so makes possible the sharing of responsibility not only for work but also for the quality of personal relations.*

People carry out their own ideas best. Your responsiveness generates employee responsiveness: mutual responsiveness sets the stage for growth and training. Commitment to such evolution is a grand design to help people recognize their own capabilities.

Communicate compassion and recognition. *By listening carefully, you come to know your employees intimately. The human condition is vulnerable to both joy and pain. The manager who communicates compassion for the strength and potential of others can generate a friendship that brings about maturity and mutual acceptance of responsibility. The opposite is probably true as well. Being a friend is preferable to the adversary relationship of "us and them."*

Communicating compassion is a kind of recognition, a key ingredient of people development. Good performance is an evolution of people development.

Communicate co-management. *The trappings of authority inhibit human growth and stunt organizational development. Co-management is the key to each individual's opportunity to become interwoven with a dynamic organization's progress. Together, in an informal and intricate away, commitment becomes a working definition of the quality of life possible for everyone.*

Communicate fallibility and involvement. *No one is perfect. When you make a mistake, admit it and ask for help. If you've taken the preceding steps, employees will not mistake your humanity for weakness. Communicating fallibility communicates involvement. When the manager admits a mistake, everyone can err. With that freedom, shared decision making, authority, and responsibility are possible. People become committed because they can afford to do so. The axiom "Management is getting things done through people" becomes reality.*

Communicate initiative through "parenting." *We "parent" everyone, including ourselves, when we are striving to become viable human beings. Like a good parent, a good manager implements organizational mechanisms so that decisions are forced down the chain as far as possible, thus fostering initiative. Authoritarianism for its own sake destroys initiative; people will want to be told what to do. The manager as parent can foster the evolution of autonomous, responsible workers who are involved and can expend initiative for furthering the organization.*

Communicate trust, missions, and expectations. *The manager as parent shares the responsibility and decisions of work, and in turn, the meaning in work. Sharing meaning in work inspires commitment. When trust and meaning generate commitment, communicating missions and expectations is possible. Attainable, clearly understood objectives shared synergistically in organizational missions are the results.*

Communicate confidence. *The freedom to bring missions to fruition should be sustained by confidence in employees and the courage to stand back and let them make mistakes that can lead to modified objectives. Proper parenting includes giving credit where it is due, suggesting and requesting, not ordering and driving. People will know the reasons for your suggestions and requests. Praise in public. Reprove in private. Do both constructively.*

Communicate fun and happiness. *Be positive. Self-esteem, confidence, and happiness beat their alternatives for generating both productivity and quality of work life. A child's enjoyment of life comes from the hope and joy of tomorrow and the potential of numerous opportunities. Maturity is becoming the parent of the child within yourself. That simply means that you nurture the child's natural abilities, the greatest of which is the ability to "have fun."*

Communicate expectations. *Treat people as what they* can become. *New missions are natural outgrowths of expectations when dignity and responsibility are shared. People perform according to what is expected of them. Building in employees a sense of the importance of their work will give them goals, a sense of direction, something to strive for and achieve. They can become what they choose to become. [These points were made in the August 1985 issue of the* Training and Development Journal *by Gerald D. Baxter and John K. Bowers.]*

To the thoughts expressed by these authors, I might simply reinforce the fact that the Baby Boomers of today, who constitute 48 percent of the work force, are vastly different from the work force of forty years ago and, to a large degree, even of twenty years ago. The Baby Boomers were raised in permissiveness and have rejected authority figures, to a large degree. Not only that but they are more outspoken and have a real desire to participate in the decision-making process. Most of them have attitudes which would have appalled their fathers, and that's not all bad. They do not respond to dictatorial managers or leaders but are far more responsive to those leaders whom they perceive as having an interest in their personal growth and development.

According to Glen Raschick in a January 1986 article in Air Canada's magazine, these new members of the workforce are more "people oriented" and respond more to the gentle approach than they do to harsh discipline. Results indicate that this nonpunitive approach has positive effects on these Baby Boomers, such as less absenteeism, dismissals, disciplinary action, an increase in morale, and a reduction in wrongful termination.

Now let's take another look at the new work environment.

A recent survey showed that the number-one job of top executives is to communicate successfully. Aside from communicating—including speaking, writing, listening, reading, and thinking—company presidents and chairmen of the board do virtually nothing.

"Which courses best prepare one for business leadership?"

This was the question posed by the University of Michigan graduate school to 1,158 newly promoted top executives. Business communication was the most common response, with 71.4 percent rating it as very important. Finance was the second highest, with 64.7 percent.

Bruce Barton, congressman, author, and ad agency founder, said, "In my library are about a thousand volumes of biography. A rough calculation indicates that more of these deal with men who have talked themselves upward than with all the scientists, writers, saints, and doers combined. Talkers have always ruled. They will continue to rule. The smart thing is to join them."

Communicating to Two or Two Hundred

From time to time, most of us are forced to stand up and address some kind of meeting somewhere at some time on some subject. Inevitably, that experience will happen in every leader's work environment. Since all of us—especially leaders and managers—are judged by our peers, underlings, and supervisors by the way we present ourselves, our ability to communicate on our feet is extremely important. Since you might not have the time or inclination to join the National Speakers Association, take the Dale Carnegie Course, join Toastmasters, Toastmistresses, or come to Dallas for our specialized training, I'd like to give you a few additional tips and reminders that will offer some immediate benefits for you.

Chances are good you know that former Vice President of the United States Alben W. Barkley died in the process of giving an address. I mention that simply because to the best of my knowledge, he is the only person who ever passed on while making a speech. Since the beginning of time there have been ten or twelve billion people to walk this earth. Mathematically speaking, therefore, I can tell you with considerable confidence that public speaking is easily the safest occupation on the face of this earth. Although your knees might knock, your heart race, your palms get sweaty, your mouth feel like cotton, and your blood pressure go up considerably, the odds are dramatically in your favor that you are going to survive. That should give you added confidence.

As Bruce Barton said:

I never want to speak if I'm not scared; when I'm not scared I tend not to care enough about what the listener thinks. I don't care whether I get the subject across or not; all I want to do is get done and go home. But if I'm scared, I know I'll have the proper tension to do the right kind of job. I know of nothing that will give the energy and creativity that healthy tension and stress will give.

Let me remind you that if you should lead an old mule—or, for that matter, even a young one—in front of the group to whom you're going to speak, he would look as if he were bored to tears and might even stand there and go to sleep right in front of the group. However, if you were to lead a beautiful thoroughbred horse in front of the group, he would be extremely nervous and fidgety. So, if you are "scared to death" or nervous and fidgety when you stand in front of a group, just be grateful you're a thoroughbred and not a mule! As Toastmasters International is fond of saying, "Effective speaking is not the result of eliminating those butterflies in your stomach, but simply getting them to fly in formation."

Real vs. Imagined Fear

But the fear of speaking is anything but a laughing matter. In fact, in the *Book of Lists*, speaking before a group was listed as the number-one fear among Americans. It ranked ahead of the fear of death by fire or death by drowning. So the fear of speaking is a legitimate one. The way to overcome fear is by taking action on that fear, and that's how training can benefit you. Let me give you some specific hints on successful speaking.

First, remember that speaking is a safe thing to do. More people die getting out of the bathtub daily than have died in the history of the world speaking. (I don't say this to discourage bathing, rather, to encourage speaking.)

Second, if you don't like public speaking, don't do it. Stick to private speaking because chances are excellent that since you're this far into *Top Performance* you are doing a lot of private speaking in small meetings for the people under your supervision. Yes, I know you're thinking, *But I often have to address a significant number of people.* I still insist that you stick to private speaking. On occasion I have addressed as many as twenty-three thousand people—and that's a bunch! However, I can honestly tell you that it was a private speech. What I do is select certain individuals in the audience and key on them most of the time. I pick friendly, responsive, supportive people whose body language tells me they agree with what I'm saying and they even like me for saying it. If there's a sourpuss in the crowd who looks like his ancestors descended directly from Attila the Hun, I do not play hero and try to win him over. I ignore him and concentrate on the supportive, friendly people. In most cases, if I'm effectively doing my job, the sourpuss eventually joins the meeting, but in the meantime he has not been a drain on my own enthusiasm and energy. (I'm responsible *to* him so I give him my best effort, but I'm not responsible *for* him, his attitude, and the way he receives my message.) I encourage you to select one friendly person (in your own company there should be lots of them), look him directly in the eye, and talk to him. Then move to another friendly person and do the same. You'll find this to be helpful and a tremendous confidence builder.

Third, I can tell you that in my many years as a speaker and teacher, I do not believe I've ever come across any one thing which builds self-image and personal confidence as much as the ability to communicate on your feet. I encourage you to become skilled in this area. Once the initial fright subsides, you will probably discover that you actually enjoy speaking! And if you are ever called on to give a presentation, and feel those butterflies flying radically out of formation, just think of this little story:

Back in the days of the Roman Empire during a circus in the Colosseum, a Christian was thrown to a hungry lion. As the spectators cheered, the wild beast pounced. But the Christian quickly whispered something in the lion's ear and the beast backed away in terror. After this happened several times, the emperor sent a centurion to find out what magic spell could make a ferocious lion cower in fear. A few minutes later the guard returned and said, "The Christian whispers in the lion's ear, 'After dinner you'll be required to say a few words.'"

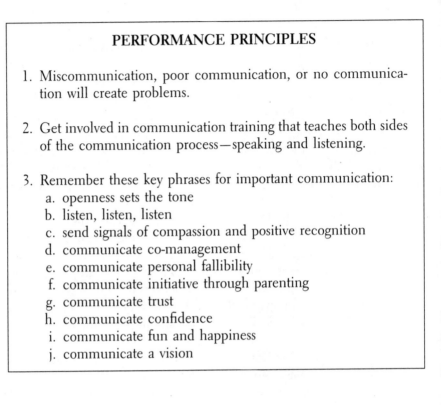

PERFORMANCE PRINCIPLES

1. Miscommunication, poor communication, or no communication will create problems.

2. Get involved in communication training that teaches both sides of the communication process—speaking and listening.

3. Remember these key phrases for important communication:
   a. openness sets the tone
   b. listen, listen, listen
   c. send signals of compassion and positive recognition
   d. communicate co-management
   e. communicate personal fallibility
   f. communicate initiative through parenting
   g. communicate trust
   h. communicate confidence
   i. communicate fun and happiness
   j. communicate a vision

SPECIAL BONUS SEGMENT
ON COMMUNICATION

SINCE SO MUCH information is communicated in meetings, we decided to include a bonus section dealing with all facets of a meeting. As our company has grown so much in the last ten years, I have personally seen the importance of effective meetings.

Meetings, like certain forms of wildlife, are protected under the law. The First Amendment to the Constitution of the United States says in part that "Congress shall make no law . . . abridging . . . the right of the people peaceably to assemble." Under this guarantee, meetings seem to have multiplied like rabbits . . . until today it seems that everyone is on his way to or from a meeting. But remember this simple definition of a *meeting*: "A meeting is a group of people who have come together for a common purpose." The challenge for a Top Performer is to see that that purpose is accomplished. Because meetings are so vital to business communication and hence productivity, I want to give you a few tips, hints, and secrets for maximizing their effectiveness.

Ten Commandments to End Meeting Madness

Prior to the Meeting

1. *Meet only if necessary.* If a decision can prevent a meeting, make it. If a substitute will do (like a conference call), do it. If it's not of maximum importance for you, delegate participation to a subordinate.
2. *Limit attendance and attendees.* If you're needed for a minute, stay for only a minute. Invite only those people who must be involved . . . and then involve them.
3. *Pick the best time and the right place.* If you don't base your schedule on every attendee's schedule, you'll end up holding another meeting. Make sure everything you need is in the room before starting.

4. *Make your agenda their agenda.* Be sure everyone knows the purpose of the meeting, the items for discussion and decision, and the time requirements involved. Number the items on your agenda in order of priority so the most important gets done first, and the least important may be sacrificed.

During the Meeting

5. *Assign a time watcher.* No one keeps time . . . so watch it! (Often your best time watcher is your keeper of the minutes.) This person is a key and objective observer of the agenda and of meeting dynamics. Your time watcher starts on time, calls out time segments, drives you toward completion.
6. *Steer the meeting along the agenda track.* Control digressions, delays, and denouements while you drive toward your destination: the action that accomplishes your stated purpose.
7. *Conclude, assign, depart.* Sum up what you did or how you're going to do what you decided to do. Remind whoever is going to do it to do it (and tell him when it should be done). Then leave.

After the Meeting

8. *Make sure that attendees get minutes in hours, not weeks—twenty-four or forty-eight maximum.* Nothing is more frustrating than receiving minutes for a meeting you can barely remember. They won't be read. Use minutes to reinforce assignments, and as a checkup at follow-up meetings.
9. *Assign someone to report to the person in charge.* Establish a reporting method to assure that decisions are executed and progress is being made.
10. *Evaluate meetings and abolish standing committees that are sleeping.* Did your meeting *work?* Did it actually do the *work?* Did it make subsequent *work* easier? If not, fire it! Evaluate meetings, all committees, and any important get-together regularly. Was the meeting well prepared for, well run, a creative, communicating session that accomplished its purpose and involved people in a meaningful way? If the answer to any of these questions is no, go back to the First Commandment and start all over again.

To help you prepare for meetings that really work, I'm including a checklist for planning meetings, one for controlling participation in a meeting for maximum effectiveness, and another for evaluating meetings. By using these instruments you can help your team, company, or group be a Top Performer.

Checklist for Planning Meetings

Prior to the Meeting

Publicity
___Notices
___Letter of invitation
___Bulletin boards
___Personal contacts
___News release
    (if apropos)

Agenda
___Plan agenda
___Plan for involvement
___Contact people on
    agenda
___Previous minutes
___Committee reports

Space and Equipment
___Place reserved
___Equipment reserved
___Materials needed

Just Before the Meeting

Space
___Room arrangement
___Seating arrangement
___Extra chairs
___Climate control

Equipment and Supplies
___A-V equipment set up, checked
___Extension cords
___Microphones
___Gavel, felt pens, pencils, pads
___Newsprint
___Visual aids
___Agenda, other handouts
___Name tags

At the Meeting

___Meeting, greeting, seating participants and guests
___Greeting and seating latecomers
___Handing out materials
___Operation of equipment
___Recording equipment

End of Meeting . . . and After

___Collect unused materials
___Return equipment
___Clean up

___Thank helpers
___Read and analyze evaluation, feedback
___Remind people of follow-up commitments
___Make plans for next meeting—date, etc.

Dealing With Individuals in Meetings

In every meeting you will find basically two kinds of people—those who talk and those who don't. But within those broad classifications, there are several types you as a presider or presenter need to know how to handle.

BEHAVIOR	SOLUTION
Talks too much	Cut across their talk with a summarizing statement and direct a question to someone else. If they continue to talk, say, "Let's hear what Jerry thinks." If they're difficult, get other participants on your side by asking what they think about what the talker is saying.
Quick, helpful	Even though this type often has the right answer, it keeps others from participating. Thank them and direct a question to someone else. Be sure they understand that you appreciate their help. Suggest, "Let's get several opinions." Use them to summarize.
Rambler	When they stop for breath, thank them, rephrase one of their statements, and then move on.
Arguer	If they are naturally troublesome or trying to make trouble, get them placed in your blind spot right next to you. Pretend not to hear. But recognize legitimate objections and side with them when you can. Sometimes the group will take care of them if they persist. If all else fails, talk to them privately and ask for their help.
Obstinate	This may be someone who really doesn't understand what you're driving at. Reflect or ask them to say more. Get others to try to help them see the point by stating it a different way. If that doesn't work, tell them you'd like to discuss the question further after the meeting.
Wrong subject	Focus on the topic. Say something like, "That is interesting. I'm sorry, though; it's beyond the scope of our meeting."
His own problem	Tackle the problem if it is pertinent to the subject under discussion. Otherwise, acknowledge the value of the problem and ask to discuss it privately.
Racial or political question	Frankly state what you can or cannot discuss. Say something like, "Problems do exist, but our meeting can't deal with them."
Side conversations	Pause and let others listen to the conversation. Draw them into your discussion by asking for their opinion.
Poor choice of words	Their ideas may be good, but they just don't know how to express them. Help them out by putting their idea in your words. Say, "In other words, you mean . . ." Protect them from ridicule.

BEHAVIOR	SOLUTION
Definitely wrong	Comment, "Well, that's an interesting way to look at it," or "Of course, you're entitled to your opinion." And go on.
Clashing personalities	In the midst of dispute, cut across with a direct question on the topic. Bring another participant into the discussion. If it still continues, frankly ask that personalities be left out.
Question you can't answer	Redirect the question to the group. If you don't know the answer, say so. Offer to find out.
Bored	Try to find an area of interest. Call on them for their experience.
Never participates	Use direct, provocative questions.
Shy, unsure of self	Ask direct questions you are sure they can answer. Ask if they agree. Build them up in the eyes of the group.

How Did It Go?

To avoid having meetings that "self-destruct," evaluate them afterward. Here are some of the more obvious problems and a few tips to prevent falling into common meeting traps.

Lack of involvement in the planning by those who will be at the meeting. Members need to feel "ownership" and will support what they have a part in planning and developing.

Same plan, same place, same time. While sameness gives security to some people, it bores others. Participants can add spice and zip to meetings by using different methods and techniques.

Equipment that doesn't work. Check equipment beforehand. Have extra bulbs and cords. Have an alternate plan.

Illegible visual aids. Prior to meeting, check visuals to make sure they can be easily seen and deciphered.

No planned agenda. Make sure that the purpose and plan of activities are defined and participants know what is to happen.

Inappropriate seating plan. Formal classroom-style seating is all right for an audience. Semicircles, seating around tables, and other less-formal arrangements, however, invite and facilitate communication.

Long, drawn-out speakers. Give the speaker a specific topic and a time block, and keep the meeting moving.

No record. Keep a history of the meeting, the plans, discussions, and commitments made.

Neglect to carry the group "into the future." Plan for who will do what and when.

"Show" run by only a few. Get the total group involved.

These tips are adapted from Eva Schindler-Rainman and Ronald Lippitt, *Taking Your Meetings Out of the Doldrums.*

8

"THE FIRINGS WILL CONTINUE UNTIL MORALE IMPROVES"

Every man takes the limits of his own field of vision for the limits of the world.

Schopenhauer

THE PARAMOUNT RESPONSIBILITY of every manager is to obtain successful results, which can be done by getting the proper performance from the people we manage. As we just learned, communication is an essential element. So is establishing standards for evaluating performance. Question: How can we supervise or plan performance if the parties involved don't understand *and* agree on what is to be done? The answer to this question lies in mutual goals and mutual understanding. The process of developing these mutual objectives and this common understanding is called the Performance Value Package. We discussed this in chapter 4 in "The Art of Top Performance," and in this chapter we need to get into the specific how and why of the Performance Value Package (PVP).

As a reminder, let me repeat:

The Foundational Performance level is the level of performance a person must achieve to continue to work with the organization. It is called Foundational because when this level is achieved the person not only maintains his or her position but he also lays a foundation upon which he can build future successes.

The Successful Performance level is the level of performance that might reasonably and realistically be expected by both manager and employee.

The Value Performance level is the level of performance that might be expected if everything goes according to plan and the employee excels in all areas. This provides overachievers with a target.

When introducing the employee to the Performance Value Package, you are really introducing him or her to a three-level goal-setting or management-by-objective concept. The idea that makes PVP so valuable is that the employee participates in the decision-making process rather than being dictated to. This "shared ownership" principle is a powerful motivator. The one possible exception is the Foundational Performance level. Since this is the basic level at which an employee can function and maintain his position, it is often dictated by the company and by historical data about the position.

For example, here at the Zig Ziglar Corporation, our telemarketers must average six hundred dollars in volume per day to cover their overhead (including phone time, salary, commission, product cost, building maintenance, employee benefits, and so forth). We have learned that to average six hundred dollars per day over a thirty-day period, the telemarketer must make a minimum of eighty attempted phone calls per day. This number of attempted phone calls will yield twenty completions (opportunities to make a sales presentation), which will result in the correct volume. This is our break-even point. These numbers are carefully studied and constantly monitored to see if they are changing.

However, we know that if a telemarketer cannot achieve these quotas, we cannot afford to have him on staff. This leaves little room for negotiation on Foundational Performance level, so the supervisor introduces the new employee to concepts during the initial interview.

The Successful Performance level is a different story. To determine the Successful Performance level, the supervisor will start with the salesperson's goals. We set goals in primarily two ways at ZZC: (1) number of people helped (sold); (2) dollars earned, keeping in mind that dollars earned is a yardstick for success and not our only objective. However, we do know that the only way we can stay in business is to operate at a profit, so we do not apologize for being fairly rewarded for delivering an excellent product. When the employee has determined the number of people he wants to help (sell) and the amount of money he wants to earn, it is fairly simple to "track down" his Successful Performance level goals. The Value Performance level is figured last and serves as a real "stretch" goal.

What happens when I don't meet my Foundational Performance level?

One of the concerns about PVP is what happens when minimum standards are not achieved. This is the really exciting thing about the program. By following a three-step outline, everyone wins.

I. Consultation. The manager must have the courage to confront the employee with his or her concern. If the manager does so in a nonaccusatory, nonpersonal manner (attack the problem, not the person) by attempting to see the situation the employee's perspective, then the manager and employee can work together to solve the problem and not be on opposite sides of the situation.

II. Problem definition. The manager and employee must agree on *exactly* what the problem is. If they cannot agree, they must at least have an agreement that there is a problem and they must agree to identify the "pieces of the puzzle" so that they may define the problem.

IIA. Brainstorming alternatives. The manager and the employee work together to contribute ideas for solving the problem. There must be no "value judgments" on these alternatives since to judge them at this point would stifle creativity.

IIB. Choosing the best alternative. The manager and employee work together to evaluate each alternative and identify the one that will be most effective for solving their problem.

III. Plan of action. The manager and employee agree on a specific Plan of Action including timetable, activities, and outcome for immediate implementation.

IIIA. Inspection. The manager and employee meet regularly to assess progress. If the alternative selected is not working, it may be that the problem was not properly identified. Or, if the alternative solution is not working, the manager and employee may need to select another alternative.

The Scientific and Analytical Approach

Let's take each step in the process and break it down into small, digestable parts and use the scientific and analytical approach to problem solving.

I. Consultation. One of the most difficult aspects of management is confronting employees who don't seem to be getting the desired results. We often confuse sympathy with empathy and end up sympathizing with them instead of managing them with empathy. Because this is such an important aspect of the process, I want to deal with it in a more detailed manner.

> *Every manager comes up against the problem of someone whose progress is being blocked by some deep-seated attitude or behavior. It might be a person who can't organize his time effectively; or someone who is always fighting with others. Or, it might be one of those people who will never admit that he has made a wrong decision and bridles at the slightest criticism. . . . The precise nature of the problem is usually immaterial. The real difficulty is*

Adapted and reprinted by permission of the publisher, from PERSONNEL, May-June 1963 *that the individual concerned sees nothing particularly wrong with his behavior.*

Everyone has blind spots but no one can continually and profitably evade reality. In the final analysis, it is what others think of a person that determines his or her acceptance and progress in life.

For such problem people, there is only one remedy. You must guide them to reexamine their values and behavior. Admittedly, this is not easy, but it is not beyond the capability of any manager with empathy and an honest desire to help people develop their fullest potential. And it is a vital part of every manager's job, for it is in guiding and influencing the behavior of his subordinates in such a way as to make them better and more effective employees that the manager fulfills one of his key roles—the role of performance counselor.

Effective counseling is not only fundamental to the development of people, it is synonymous with it. Yet the chief reason so few managers succeed in mastering the art of counseling is that they fail to understand their true role in the counseling process. Asked to define this process, many people would say that it meant "having a heart-to-heart talk." Others might define it as "giving fatherly advice," while still others might call it "constructive criticism." However, true counseling is really none of these things. A manager's object in counseling is to change the attitude and behavior of a person by changing the thinking. . . .

In short, the aim of a manager's counseling, or coaching, is to clearly present to a person a behavior or attitude that negatively affects performance in a way that convinces that person to change.

Here are some pointers for every manager who needs to coach a person about his performance:

1. Remember that counseling is a routine management responsibility and should be treated as such. It should not be regarded as, or allowed to become, a psychological exercise or a major emotional crisis.

2. Recognize that the essential work of counseling goes on within the counselee. It is there that changes must be brought about and it is there that the drive to change must be developed. In this process you can rely on a person's desire to succeed.

3. *Acquaint yourself with your employee's background, work history, and relations with others in the organization.* Much of this information is available in personnel files and previous evaluations. Sometimes it is helpful to record observations about the person's behavior over a given period, such as the year between formal evaluations. You must have a clear understanding of the problem you are trying to resolve.

4. *Pick a comfortable place to talk, preferably, a routine business setting, either your office or your subordinate's, if there is sufficient privacy.* Managers supervising a field sales force might find suitable opportunities in the course of driving with their salespeople. Wherever the discussion takes place, make every effort to give the employee the feeling that he or she is in a relaxed and confidential setting, thus enhancing the feeling of security.

5. *Remember that people differ in their ability to see their personal biases.* Those who are mature and used to viewing themselves critically can be brought to such realizations fairly quickly; others, particularly if they are immature and burdened with deep emotional needs to avoid the truth, often take considerable time. You need to make a decision about the pace he should employ in a particular case.

6. *Focus on the barriers to the person's "progress."* Try to show him that he is working against the very thing he really wants to achieve. It often helps to proceed from a person's remarks, since this reduces the possibility of friction, and keeps the emphasis on his values. As we saw earlier, if the man has some attitude or behavior problem that he has failed to recognize for what it is, he is overlooking facts that have a direct bearing on his business success. The uncovering and cautious evaluation of these facts is in itself a most potent therapy.

Finally, there is the question of follow-up. You should do this as unobtrusively as possible. If no change takes place, or the change is temporary, you should try again. If after a few attempts the problem is still unresolved, it is time to consider other action, including termination.

Make Certain You Are—Or Want to Be—A Manager

Some managers will balk at the thought of having to "counsel" employees. To those of you who feel this way, I want to challenge you to consider whether management is really for you. If you are so caught up in activities that you cannot spend time with your people, then I submit that you are *not* a manager. If you will go back to the first pages of this book you will see we agreed that *management is getting things done through people.* To impact people's performance, we must be willing to confront, counsel, lead, and direct. The next steps in the PVP process are *problem definition* and the action which follows.

II. Problem definition. Very few problems are singular in nature. They probably consist of several aspects. What you usually see are a variety of symptoms of a problem. Long hair was not a problem in the 1960s, it was a symptom of the problem: unwillingness to conform to established standards.

To effectively identify the problem of a person you manage, you must list on paper the "parts" or primary "factors" of the problem as you see them and ask the employee to do the same. On paper, some of the factors will not be as pertinent as you originally perceived them to be. Stick with the specific observable facts when listing the facets of the situation. You can support facts with evidence. If there is little or no evidence, you may not have many facts.

Together, you and the employee must determine the answers to the following questions in identifying the problem:

1. In what areas do you feel you are performing proficiently?

2. Why are you doing so well in these areas?

3. Could you give me some specific examples?

4. Where do you feel (think) you did an acceptable but not necessarily commendable job?

5. Why was this work only average?

6. Could you give me some specific examples?

7. In what areas did you perform below Foundational Performance level?

8. Why?

9. Could you give me some specific examples?

10. Are you interested in developing a Performance Improvement Program?

11. How do you think the performance might be improved?

12. How can I help implement *your* plan?

While these questions may seem somewhat obvious, this list should result in over one hour's worth of counseling and conversation. There will be important points along the way where you will need to interject your own point of view and shape or guide the direction of the session. The manager must help the employee to *see* the situation. Then the manager must help the employee develop the *desire* to make the improvement and a *plan* to overcome any obstacles. You are not sitting in judgment, in your long black robes, waiting to render your verdict; instead, you become a partner in helping another Very Important Human Being become a Top Performer!

Is It Always as Easy as It Sounds?

Absolutely not! Most management books make the coaching and problem identification sessions between manager and employee sound like the easiest part of the job, when in fact it is often just the opposite. Just asking the list of questions I shared with you takes a great deal of courage and considerable skill to come across as a concerned manager instead of a prosecuting attorney. Combine this with the fact that many times employees see no problem, and the result is they often don't cooperate and give the answers you hoped for. So what do you do? Well, I'm glad you asked, because that's the next agenda. As I've said before, we need to break each situation into its smallest components. The same is true for problems. Here are some guidelines and questions for exposing and defining a problem.

A. Beware the potential for problems and don't ignore danger signals.
   1. What changes have occurred in your areas of responsibility?
   2. What facts led you to notice the change?
   3. Exactly what has changed? What has not changed?
B. Identify the crucial elements of the problem.
   1. What first led you to notice a change?
   2. What are the problem indicators in concise terms?
   3. When did you first notice these indicators?
   4. Who is involved?
   5. Where do these indicators occur?

6. Are the problem indicators causing members of the team to
   fall short of their objectives?
7. Are there any similarities or patterns to the indicators?

C. Identify the obvious causes of the problem indicators.
   1. Which indicators have you seen before?
   2. What are the causes of the indicators?
   3. What action must be taken to eliminate the indicators?
   4. What would happen if you did not take any action?

D. Expose and define the problem.
   1. Write out the problem in one clear and concise sentence.
   2. List the evidence that indicates this is a real and not imagined problem.
   3. Who, What, How, When, Where, and Why?

Poor Performance Indicators

It seems almost too simplistic to list some of the indicators that managers should be on the lookout for in dealing with poor performance. However, if we will recognize the earliest indicators, we can avoid big problems down the road. The attitude of poor performers is one of defensiveness, and they often become disinterested and fail to communicate with you or their peers. They have a tendency to take very little initiative and when forced to take action that doesn't work, they will blame failure on others instead of accepting personal responsibility. They often keep to themselves and seem to have no real enthusiasm for their work. This will result in poor performance as indicated by making careless errors and appearing disorganized. They may turn in work incomplete or not at all. If you have established some time limits for work, they rarely meet a deadline. These poor performers avoid the difficult tasks and spend enormous amounts of time on the easier aspects of their jobs.

When you suspect any of these indicators, do the right thing for both you and your employee: confrontation. Remember:

> *Permissiveness is only neglect of duty.*

The rationalizations you have been using for procrastinating on facing the poor performer—"It's tough to get replacements; if my predecessor didn't help them how can I; I simply don't have the time [the worst excuse of all]; I don't want to hurt her feelings"—will eventually come back to haunt you in the worst ways. Take courage and action! Know that if you have answered the questions in "tracking down" the problem, then you have sufficiently prepared to work positively to eliminate the problems and not the employee.

IIA. Brainstorming alternatives. Before your session with the employee, look over these key points:

1. Make no value judgments on ideas. To criticize *any* alternative will diminish creativity and render the session ineffective.

2. Wait to discuss the alternatives. The purpose of this portion of the meeting is to generate a large number of possible solutions, not to discuss implementation.

3. List all alternatives on paper or flip chart.

I can't emphasize too much how important it is to consider *all* alternatives. If you and your employee feel comfortable in letting the ideas flow, the "creative juices" are released. No matter how ridiculous the idea may seem, encourage sharing. As a matter of fact, I sometimes start these sessions with a humorous or ludicrous example just to make the point.

IIB. Choosing the best alternative. This is the all-important step where you determine the best of the alternatives. Evidence and specific reasons must be given for making the choice. This is a good time to use the Ben Franklin "Plus and Minus" method. When considering each alternative separately, use the form shown in the illustration. This helps keep your ideas on the specific and not the speculative. Write out:

POSSIBLE ALTERNATIVE SOLUTIONS

Positive Reasons (+)	*Negative Reasons* (−)

III. Plan of action. When developing this plan of action, we must be sure to not only "track down" our activity, but we must also be sure that these activities are measurable and inspectable. Daily, even hourly, activities may need to be planned. If you start with the desired outcome and track the result down to its smallest component, *only then* do you have a realistic plan of action.

In *See You at the Top*, I explained how I lost 37 pounds in a ten-month period. Thirty-seven pounds was the desired outcome. That tracks down to 3.7 pounds per month and 1.9 ounces per day. While thinking of losing 37 pounds is overwhelming, 1.9 ounces per day is conceivable. The next question I must answer is: "What must I do now—today—to lose 1.9 ounces?" Some ideas (specific, measurable, inspectable) include: eat only the correct foods (chicken, fish, salads, fruit); leave off the extra bread and butter and desserts; drink only unsweetened tea rather than soft drinks. I think you see what I mean, but let me give you an example from the business community.

A successful real estate agency manager noticed that one of the women who worked for him was not as enthusiastic about her work as she had been when she was hired eighteen months before. During the last thirty days Mary had been late in attending meetings, seemed to be somewhere else mentally during the meetings, and in general had kept to herself. This was quite unusual since she had previously been a real people-oriented person. While she had never been his top performer, her results had always been consistent and had improved steadily. Her performance in the last thirty days had been miserable. The one sale she had the opportunity to close had to be postponed due to careless errors on her part in the paperwork.

Realizing that he had to take some action or lose a very solid performer, the manager called Mary into his office. As soon as he closed the door, she started to cry. "I know you're going to fire me," she sobbed, "and I don't blame you one bit!" (Right then and there the manager knew he had waited too long to call the meeting and vowed to himself that he would never wait that long to confront a problem again). "No," he said, "I have no intentions of firing you. I just want to see what can be done to help you regain the level of productivity you have enjoyed for so many months. Has something happened to upset you?"

After regaining her composure, Mary went on to explain that she was embarassed by the fact that her automobile was the oldest one driven by any of the agents and that she had set her goal several months earlier to buy a new car by the beginning of the current month. She was devastated that her earnings had not allowed her to do so. "So, you see," she said, "my problem is that I have a car I am embarrassed to drive and it is limiting my productivity." Her manager thought for a minute and replied, "Is that really your problem, or could it be a symptom of your problem?" He went on to take her through the series of questions we have already shared on pages 530–31.

1. In what areas do you feel you are performing well? ("None.")

2. Why? ("I'm not meeting any of my Foundational Performance level goals.") The manager worked with each agent to establish all three levels of activity for each agent based on their personal goals. This lady knew what her Foundational Performance level was to be as well as her Successful Performance level and Value Performance level. The manager had "tracked down" the success activities needed for each level.

3. Give me a specific example. ("My Foundational Performance level calls for me to knock on five doors per week in looking for possible listings; I have knocked on none.")

This response allowed the manager to skip questions 4 through 9 and get right down to business. He asked Mary, "Are you interested in developing a Performance Improvement Program?" She said, "What I am really interested in is driving a new car!" They both laughed and agreed that they needed to delve more deeply into the problem. The manager took the agent through the series of questions for exposing and defining a problem which we outlined on pages 531–32. Under part A. *Beware the potential for problems and don't ignore danger signals,* they were able to agree that the problems had begun when her activity levels had decreased. Under part B. *Identify the crucial elements of the problem,* they were able to agree that not reaching her goal seemed to be the crucial element since her activity had been good with the same car up to that point. Under part C. *Identify the obvious causes of the problem indicators,* the manager and the agent agreed that her goal setting had been unrealistic and she had not allowed herself a realistic amount of time to reach her goal of having a new automobile. Under part D. *Expose and define the problem,* they wrote out the problem as follows: "Mary did not understand the goal-setting process well enough to set a realistic goal to purchase a new automobile." The evidence that indicated the problem was real and not imagined was the seven-year-old car in her driveway. The positive action step that needed to be taken was to get the proper input on how she could realistically set the goal. So the manager and the agent began to work together to develop a Plan of Action.

They started with the desired result—a new automobile. Mary knew exactly what kind of car, what color, all the options, and the price, down to the last penny. By carefully studying Mary's performance records for the first seventeen months she spent with the company, they were able to determine that to purchase the automobile she wanted would take nine months instead of the four months she had originally allowed. They also discovered that she could reduce that time to six months by improving some of her activity levels.

Next, Mary and her manager got involved with the final step.

IIIA. Inspection. This step is not a subversive activity that requires you to go through subordinates' desks at night or plant listening devices on their phones. The employee must know *when* to expect the inspection and *what* to expect from the inspection.

Mary and her manager set a weekly appointment to monitor her progress. By doing this, Mary's manager not only let her know that he was interested in her career but also that he was going to hold her accountable.

Next, Mary and her manager evaluated alternatives to her not improving her performance. Mary agreed that she could not afford to keep her position if she did not improve, and her manager assured her that though termination was a possibility, it was *not* his first choice. The manager assured Mary that through their regular meetings she would be kept posted on progress so that termination would not come as a surprise to either of them and that she could be confident that Due Process would be observed.

In reality, the Performance Value Package is nothing more than goal setting on three levels. The seven steps in determining a goal, an objective, a standard, or whatever you want to call it, do not change. You may not be able to tell me what 782×411 is; however, you do have a formula that you can use to determine the answer. The seven steps in the goal-setting process are the steps in the formula that you can use to establish each performance level.

The Seven-Step Goal-Setting Formula

1. Identify the goal.

2. List your personal benefits for achieving the goal.

3. Identify the major obstacles you must overcome to reach this goal.

4. Determine what skills or knowledge are required to reach this goal.

5. Identify the individuals, groups, companies, and organizations you must work with to reach this goal.

6. Develop a specific plan of action to achieve the goal.

7. Decide on a realistic time limit for achievement.

MY GOAL IDENTIFIED:

_____

MY BENEFITS FROM ACHIEVING THIS GOAL:

_____

I, _____ , COMMIT MY FULL EFFORTS TO

ACHIEVING MY GOALS NO LATER THAN _____ ! I AM BORN TO WIN!

_____   _____
(signature)   (date)

In our three-day BORN TO WIN seminar, we not only teach this formula but we also practice using it. We have developed a format which contains all seven steps and helps you to organize the steps on a single sheet of paper which we call a "Detail" sheet.

With a realistic goal in mind and her boss's support, Mary's productivity (and results) took an immediate turn for the better. Eight months later she was driving a new automobile. She hadn't improved her performance to the level that would have allowed her to get the car in six months, but she had improved it so she could have the new car in less than nine months. Both she and her manager were extremely happy.

This manager had done what all good managers do in a similar situation. Let's recap the major points.

1. He confronted the poor performance.
2. He helped the employee come up with well-defined and clearly understood goals.
3. Together they determined a time frame for goal attainment.
4. Together they determined a means to *in*spect to make sure they got what they *ex*pected.
5. They scheduled meetings regularly to assess progress.
6. Together they determined the specific assistance needed.
7. They examined alternatives if the improvement was not achieved.

When they were looking at the time factor, they considered: her prior history with the company; the time required to reasonably meet her goal; what contributed to her poor performance; and just how unsatisfactory her performance was. By putting all these ideas together, the manager was doing exactly what a good manager should do:

1. Provide performance standards that are realistic, understandable, and measurable.
2. Identify as soon as possible the poor performance.
3. Criticize the performance, not the performer.
4. Pay attention to specific observable behavior, not hearsay.
5. Clearly express the consequences of failing to meet the agreed-upon performance level.

Outstanding managers give their employees every opportunity to succeed. They view employee failure as personal failure and use every means possible to help their employees succeed. They are intolerant of losing behavior on the employees' part as well as their own. Great managers demand excellence . . . and use the Performance Value Package as a success tool!

PERFORMANCE PRINCIPLES

1. The Performance Value Package consists of three levels of goal or objective setting:
   a. Foundational Performance level—minimum standard
   b. Successful Performance level—realistic goal
   c. Value Performance level—stretch goal

2. These are the steps in the PVP process:
   a. consultation/confrontation
   b. problem definition
   c. brainstorming alternatives
   d. choosing the best alternative
   e. plan of action
   f. inspection

3. Outstanding managers often ask questions they already know the answers to in an effort to understand employee perspective.

9

RECOGNIZING, REWARDING, AND ROLE MODELING FOR TOP PERFORMANCE

The greatest humiliation in life is to work hard on something from which you expect great appreciation, and then fail to get it.

Edgar Watson Howe

BRINGING OUT THE BEST in people means appreciating what they do, rewarding them for it, and giving them the role models they need to become Top Performers. In this chapter we'll take a look at these three important aspects of successful management.

Recognition

Several years ago I was scheduled to speak at a banquet in Dallas for an insurance company. During the meal, I was seated at the head table between two company vice-presidents. We were chatting amiably as the meal was being served. When our waitress placed a salad in front of me, I said, "Thank you." A few minutes later, when the bread was placed in front of us, I again said, "Thank you." When she brought the entree I not only said, "Thank you," but added, "you know, I want to tell you how much I appreciate the good service you're giving us. It's amazing how you work so efficiently and yet don't seem to be in any kind of hurry. More important, you're so pleasant and gracious and I just want you to know I appreciate your efforts." She beamed broadly, thanked me for my comments, and said I had made her day.

While all of this was going on, the two vice-presidents on either side of me were ignoring her or acknowledging her service with a grunt. They directed all of their comments and attention to me and our conversation. Dessert time was quite an eye-opener. When the scoop of ice cream with chocolate syrup was delivered, the two vice-presidents received a scoop about the size of a golf ball with their syrup. I received one about the size of a baseball. The difference was so obvious that both of them simultaneously commented, "Well, Zig, I see you know this lady." I laughingly said, "No, I've never met her before tonight, but I do know a lot about her." They jokingly asked how I knew. I pointed out that she was a human being and, like everybody else, she wanted appreciation and sincere interest, and I had given her both of these things.

The same thing is true of every member of your organization and family. Everyone likes to be appreciated. What better way to express your appreciation than to share a simple, courteous "thank you" when something pleasant has been said or some simple service has been rendered. Obviously, I was not being nice to the waitress in the hope I'd get a bigger scoop of ice cream. To be honest, I didn't need the bigger scoop—I needed the smaller one. But by feeding her needs, she responded in the only way she could—which was to dig deeper and get a bigger scoop of that ice cream. I believe that in helping others to become Top Performers by teaching them to be thoughtful, kind, and considerate of the other person, we are teaching them to dig deeper and get a bigger scoop out of life.

Not a "Pollyanna" Philosophy

The December 6, 1982 issue of the *Wall Street Journal* carried the following article by Jack Falvey entitled, "To Raise Productivity, Try Saying Thank You." I believe you will benefit from these concepts, which have been italicized for emphasis.

> *People work for love and money. Few of us ever seem to get enough of either. There are no great behavioral science secrets to good management.* If you will give top priority to supporting and paying your people, you will be blessed with results beyond your dreams.

> *Managers often think of themselves as systems specialists or problem solvers or functional experts.* They lose sight of the common-sense practicality of getting others committed to doing things for them willingly. The essence of good management is letting people know what you expect, inspecting what is done, and supporting those things that are done well. *The experts acknowledge that we don't know the design limitations of a human being. All we do know is that even the most committed people seldom exceed 15% or 20% of their brain capacity in a normal day's work. Average people can double or triple their output with increased confidence, more encouragement, better organization, a deeper commitment,*

and a surprisingly small amount of effort. Additionally, if managers would begin thinking in terms of doing things for their people—instead of to them—we would see productivity increases off the scales. . . .

Here are a few things you can do right now with no increase in budget, but with big returns.

Make a list of everyone who works for you. Before the week is out, tell each one personally what he has contributed this week and how much you appreciate his efforts. Criticism is to be avoided at all costs (there is no such thing as constructive criticism, all criticism is destructive). If you must correct someone, never do it after the fact. Bite your tongue and hold off until he is about to do the same thing again and then challenge him to make a more positive contribution. If you can do that consistently, you will be earning your pay as a professional manager.

Set up informal visits with your people. Listen and use your eyes to pick up on what is going on. Don't look for problems, look for strengths and things done well. Make something out of every positive thing you can find. As a manager, your words and actions carry impact much greater than you expect. Just a small effort with these techniques will have almost immediate effect. A concentrated, disciplined, and sustained thrust in these directions will produce incredible returns. Publish everything positive you can find. Print is cheap. Its rewards are long-lasting.

Put positive notes on solid productive efforts and send them back to the producers. . . .

How innovative can you be? Do you realize the impact you have on others? Can you reduce or eliminate the negatives in your dealings with your people? Will you do the searching and analysis necessary to uncover positive contributions? Can you name the strengths of all your people? Can you say something complimentary to everyone by the end of this week?

As simple and as straightforward as all this is, it is really a tremendously difficult professional challenge. Just how good are you as a professional manager? If results are produced by committed people, just how much love and money can you spread around to build that commitment and those results? Go, do something nice for someone or say something nice to someone right now.

Recognizing Top Performance

Most managers would like to have employees and co-workers who take PRIDE in their careers. Now since PRIDE means many things to many people, let's look at a workable definition for our purposes.

To me, PRIDE is *Personal Responsibility In Daily Effort*. If we are going to encourage those around us to take Personal Responsibility In Daily Effort, we must recognize the importance of RECOGNITION in this process.

Mary Crowley, the extremely successful businesswoman who founded Home Interiors and Gifts (a half-billion-dollar company), says that *everyone* carries a sign which is constantly on display: MAKE ME FEEL IMPORTANT! If we can do this (make others feel important)—*sincerely*—then we have taken a giant stride in developing Top Performers.

Everyone needs recognition. The blue-collar worker is recognized for being the family provider; the white-collar workers are recognized for having great potential; the sales-marketing person is recognized for having high-income earning power. The point is that some people's recognition needs are very basic while the needs of others may be quite complex. The Top Performers in the world are BUILDERS, DOERS, and COMPETITORS, and they want to, and even need to, make a contribution to whatever they do. They must know when they are contributing, and how much they are contributing. Those who manage Top Performers develop a "scoring" system that keeps *everyone* informed on how they are doing. Please remember that negative scoring should be done in private and positive scoring should be done publicly.

Developing Enthusiastic Optimism

To develop Top Performers we must teach them how to be enthusiastic about life, how to graciously deal with other people, and how to encourage others.

When you develop a pleasing personality by being a little more friendly and outgoing, it can be enormously helpful to you socially, professionally, and for that matter spiritually. Let me share an incident with you which demonstrates some important concepts.

I never realized just how tough working on a cafeteria line could be until my youngest daughter, at age sixteen, tried to find a job—and the only one she could find was on a cafeteria line. As I watched what she had to do and contend with, from both customers and management, I promised myself I would never again go down a cafeteria line without saying something pleasant, gracious, optimistic, and enthusiastic to every person on the serving line. And I still do this today.

Recently, one particularly hot August day, after the lunch-hour crowd had departed, a friend of mine and I were going down the cafeteria line and I was "doing my thing." The gentleman in front of me was apparently from the same school of thought and he, too, was giving pleasant greetings and encouragement. This worked quite well until he got to the meat department and made the mistake of saying something about the day. The woman serving the meat put her hands on her hips, then wiped her forehead with her right hand and literally slung the perspiration to the floor as she proclaimed, "Yes, this is one of *those* days!"

Now I'd like to point out that she was not talking to me, but when you understand the business I'm in and the reputation I have as a positive thinker, combined with the fact that I had an associate with me, you must understand that my reputation was at stake. So, though it definitely was none of my business, I proceeded to stick my big nose in and say, "Yes, today is absolutely beautiful, isn't it?" With that she looked at me with disgust and said, "You have been out in the sun too long!" I replied, "No, actually I've just come back from overseas—and I've seen grown men and women without anything to eat, small children without any clothes to wear, sanitary conditions which are impossible to describe, and poverty beyond your wildest imagination. And I look at you today. You're young, pretty, employed, and an American citizen. I know for a fact that you could take this job, do it to the best of your ability, and someday you could well be the manager of this place. For that matter, if you really bought into the American Dream, with all its possibilities, you could eventually own a place of your own."

Personally, I thought it was a superb, impromptu, off-the-cuff speech, and I was reasonably confident she wanted to express her appreciation for my willingness to share with her those words of hope and encouragement. However, for fear she might miss her lead-in, I decided I'd better assist her a little, so I paused and said, "Now you feel lots better, don't you?" This time she looked at me with even more disgust and said, "You—are—sick!"

Stinkin' Thinkin' at Its Worst

As we'd say down home, you win some, you lose some, and some get rained out! This lady was hard-core negative. Her stinkin' thinkin' had gone into an advanced case of hardening of the attitudes, which gave every indication of being terminal. I meekly walked on down the serving line, getting the rest of my food and picking up my ticket. My buddy and I sat down to have our lunch and, after a few minutes, ran out of tea. A little lady who was at least sixty—and she could well have been seventy—came by, serving the extra tea. I don't recall ever seeing anyone her age with as much of a twinkle in her eye, so I smiled pleasantly and asked my famous question: "How ya doin'?" She literally took a half-step, half-jump, half-dance backward, grinned very broadly, and said, "Honey, if it was any better I'd think the deck was stacked!" I laughed and said to her, "Well, why don't you go tell the ladies on the serving line what you just told me?" In mock horror she threw up her hands and said, "Oh, no! I don't want to have anything to do with those girls! If I fool around with them very much, I'll end up being just like they are!"

I don't know where the lady learned her psychology, but she's right on the button. The way I read my Bible, it teaches, "Be not deceived—evil companions corrupt good morals." It's an established fact that your associates do have a strong bearing on your feelings, attitudes, moral values, and conduct. The classic example which I often use is this: You can take a Southern boy or girl and send him or her up North or out West and, after a period of time, he or she will end up with an accent. Or, you can take a Northern or Western boy or girl and send him or her into the South and pretty soon we'll have them talking normally! (Yes, I expect you Northerners and Westerners to turn this example around.) You need to be careful who you associate with, because we do become part of what we are around.

Chances are about 4000 to 1 that if you were given the choice of being with or around either the girl on the serving line cutting the beef or the older lady serving the tea, you would, without hesitation, choose to be around the lady serving the tea. This book is written so that you can help others to be Top Performers, and you do so by helping them become more like the senior citizen serving the tea and not like the young cynic on the serving line. You affect this important dimension of the Top Performer's life by recognizing outstanding performance.

Bees, Fleas, and Trees

In June of 1984, we determined that our company needed a formal recognition program. Since outstanding programs recognize the qualities that are pertinent to company and individual employee success and "sell" them, we began by deciding what qualities we wanted to foster. Based on our needs and beliefs, we determined it was important that our employees come to work regularly with a good attitude and demonstrate leadership qualities that show they are "part owners" in the company. Top Performers must realize that while the boss may sign their checks, the employee determines the amount.

Our basic needs—attendance, attitude, leadership, and loyalty have evolved into four recognition awards which we distribute quarterly. Here is the information we present in our employee manual:

The Zig Ziglar Recognition Program is based on the premise that "what gets recognized and rewarded is clearly what the company values." Our philosophy challenges each team member to look for the good in others. The Zig Ziglar Corporation Recognition Program allows us to find that good and recognize exceptional performance. There are four areas considered.

Attendance . . . The "Chinese Bamboo Tree" Award. Those who are at work, on time, for the full day throughout the quarter receive a $50 cash award and a certificate of merit. Increased productivity and less dollars spent on replacement personnel makes this award a real "bonus builder" for the Zig Ziglar Corporation. The name comes from the Chinese Bamboo Tree, which shows no sign of growth for five years . . . then grows approximately 90 feet in a six-week period. The years of watering and fertilizing when no progress is seen are what causes the tree to grow. This quarterly award allows an employee to be recognized in a single quarter, or in all four quarters.

Attitude . . . The "Bumble Bee" Award. You have read that aerodynamically the Bumble Bee cannot fly; its body is too heavy and its wings are too light . . . but the Bumble Bee doesn't read—it flies. This I CAN attitude is what the Zig Ziglar Corporation clearly values. This award is voted on by the entire People Building Team. The winner has his or her picture prominently displayed in the foyer, receives a plaque, a $50 cash award, has his or her picture in our At the Top newsletter, and has lunch with the president and executive vice-president of the Zig Ziglar Corporation.

Criteria for the Bumble Bee Award:

A. This person must actively demonstrate the physical, mental, and spiritual ideals that the Zig Ziglar Corporation embraces.

B. This person responds rather than reacts in difficult situations.

C. This person helps others' attitudes and lifts spirits when others come in contact with him or her.

Leadership . . . *The "Flea Trainer" Award. Flea Trainers teach others to jump out of the jar (overcome limitations) and keep others from becoming "S.N.I.O.P.s" (Susceptible to the Negative Influence of Other People). This leadership comes from all positions in the organization and does not necessarily have to be a supervisor or department head. These leaders strongly discourage gossip, criticism, and negative talk from their areas in the office. This award is nominated by the entire People Building Team (our staff), and determined by the president, executive vice-president, and divisional vice-president. The winner receives the same rewards and recognition as the Bumble Bee Winner.*

Criteria for the Flea Trainer Award:

A. *This person must actively demonstrate the physical, mental, and spiritual ideals that ZZC embraces.*

B. *This person "looks for the good" in others and shows it through written and verbal feedback.*

C. *This person demonstrates leadership in a way that helps others grow.*

D. *This person leads others in such a way that placing their picture on the wall will encourage others to emulate them.*

Loyalty . . . *Loyalty and Perseverance are recognized as follows:*

A. *5 years of service = employee's choice of pin, ring, or watch.*

B. *10 years of service = paid vacation trip.*

C. *15, 20, 25, etc., years of service = will be determined by the Executive Committee.*

Recognition Awards are shared on a quarterly basis. Any ties or questions will be settled by the Executive Committee.

As you can see, we have spent a great deal of time determining what we want and selling the importance of specific criteria.

How Do You Make It Happen?

If you agree that *everyone* needs recognition, and are ready to make a commitment to "making it happen" with your group or organization, here is a step-by-step procedure:

1. Determine what you want and need to be recognized. Involve as many people as possible in this process. You may choose an employee survey (written or verbal), an open forum discussion, or individual conferences. The key is to find what employees think is important to their success. This will give you great insight into employee values, as well as allow them to participate in "ownership" of the recognition program. According to an article in the April 1982 issue of the *New York Times*, in 1981, workers at a GM bearings plant in New Jersey purchased it to prevent the plant's closing. Now *productivity is up 80 percent* and the percentage of defective parts has dropped from 10 percent to 7 percent. Grievances have plummeted from a one-time high of two thousand pending to a recent total of only three. And the workers, now the owners, have agreed to new work rules to increase flexibility. Good things happen when employees are aware of shared ownership.

2. "Sell" the program. Employees *must* believe in the recognition program and see that it is administered fairly. Talk to them in terms of benefits they will enjoy by participating and "talking up" the program.

3. Control the "competitiveness and popularity contest" aspects of the program. Mary Kay Ash's Cosmetic Corporation recognizes *all* who qualify for recognition at varying "levels." Thus her people do not compete as much with one another as they do with themselves—in other words, internal competition. One of the real dangers of doing damage to our self-esteem is when we compare ourselves to others. We must remember to "be the best that we can be . . ." compared with our capabilities—not compared with others!

4. Judgment must be carefully used when establishing criteria for award winners. The policies must be as objective as possible. For example, what are the manifestations of a good attitude? Can you develop and identify "specific and observable behaviors" that demonstrate the qualities you want to recognize? Obviously, a sales volume award winner is much more objectively chosen than an attitude or leadership award winner. But are the latter awards less important? Attach as much specific criteria to the awards as possible.

5. Recognize winners regularly and promptly. Don't delay, postpone, or cancel recognition programs.

6. Do not recognize inferior performance. If there is no winner in a particular category, it is much better to say so than to award someone undeserving.

What Happens Without Recognition?

According to pollster Daniel Yankelovich, who was quoted in *Psychology Today* magazine, over the ten-year period from 1972–1982, workers keeping on-the-job diaries reported that they had been working 10 percent less. That's enough of a change to account for the *entire* drop in national productivity. But before we start blaming workers, he cautions, his own surveys have shown that the "work ethic" is stronger than ever — workers want to work hard and do a good job. He explains the paradox with the result of another survey, showing that workers don't believe that they themselves benefit from increasing productivity. Because they think greater productivity benefits only management, consumers, and shareholders, workers have no incentive to be more productive. The answer, says Yankelovich, is to *directly reward workers for their productivity gains.*

Rewards

Usually when we think of rewarding people we think of money. *Incentive motivation* is a much-debated form of motivation and for many organizations a viable alternative, especially the sales field. One of the important things to remember about incentive motivation is, "Today's fringe benefits are tomorrow's expectations." This means that in incentive motivation, we must constantly be willing (and able) to "sweeten the pot" to come up with truly motivational incentives. *Sales and Marketing Management* magazine selected several very successful incentive programs in their September 10, 1984 issue so that we could learn from the experience of others. The following is taken from the article entitled "Getting a Kick from Experience."

> When it comes to planning, announcing, and implementing sales incentive programs, executives are letting the past be their guide. By analyzing what has worked best, as well as what has failed, they are, to paraphrase the old song, accentuating the positive and eliminating the negative to get the most kick out of incentives. . . .
>
> • Rather than tie incentives to total sales volumes, managers try to match programs to specific products or objectives.
>
> • More managers regard merchandise and travel incentives as the most effective motivators, although some still prefer cash incentives.

Reprinted by permission of *Sales and Marketing* magazine, September 10, 1984.

- *Careful attention to the timing of incentive programs can affect such areas as production and shipping that are crucial to the total sales and marketing effort.*

- *Continuous reminders or teasers relating to continuing programs can help maintain enthusiasm.*

- *Incentive programs should be easy to understand and participate in so that they offer something to everyone. . . .*

While matching incentives with production can become a lesson in logistics, choosing the type of incentive that works best is a subject for debate. To say, as one executive does, that "different things motivate different people," is just not enough. Although experience has taught some managers that certain incentives work better than others for them, the decision between merchandise, travel, or cash programs—or some combination of the three—is a subjective one. . . .

Another major lesson reportedly learned by sales and marketing executives is that incentive programs, like the products they motivate salespeople to sell, must be properly promoted and supported. . . .

If there is one overall lesson that experience teaches managers, it is that incentive programs must be carefully thought out, planned, and executed. Even if programs include administrative headaches, such as splashy announcements at sales meetings and regular follow-up promotions, they should remain simple enough for everyone to understand and want to participate in enthusiastically. . . .

Another way to get salespeople involved in incentive programs is to simply ask what motivates them. Look at how a specific incentive impacts an individual. Speak with individuals to let them know what you're trying to do and to find out what kinds of incentives they'd like to see. . . .

Positively affecting the role of the salesperson perhaps sums up management's overall intent when designing incentive programs. The ways and means of doing so, however, are as varied as the experiences of the executives involved. Actually, this may be a good sign. It shows that managers are willing to try new ideas in their attempts to motivate salespeople.

In the legal world the competent attorney asks probing questions to get at the heart of the problem. In medicine the effective, sensitive physician largely depends on his questions to the patient to uncover the problem. The minister or counselor follows the same approach, as does the professional salesperson when calling on prospective customers. With these facts in mind, let's take a look at some questions professional managers need to ask about incentive programs.

Incentive Program Questionnaire

1. What has been the most effective form of incentive motivation I have used in the past? Will it work in this instance?

2. Have I spent enough time in planning this incentive program to get the best results?

3. Have I tied the incentive to the most beneficial and measurable area (product, objective, instead of sales volume)?

4. What is the best incentive: cash, merchandise, travel, or personal choice?

5. Is the timing of this program going to benefit all areas of the company (production, shipping, sales, and so forth)?

6. How am I going to constantly remind everyone involved about the contest so I can maintain enthusiasm?

7. Is this contest explained in as simple and understandable a form as possible?

8. What impact will the contest have on the business when the contest is over?

Now, let's take a look at an unusual incentive program created and used by an imaginative middle school administrator.

It Doesn't Have to Be Real Money

In the summer of 1981, Charlie Pfluger from Indianapolis, Indiana, attended one of our BORN TO WIN Seminars for Educators. He really got motivated about the positive approach to education and what could be done with the right attitude under almost any circumstances. Charlie was particularly enthused because he was the principal of an inner-city school which was just one year away from closing its doors. He went back home with a tremendous amount of enthusiasm and with the wholehearted support of his principal and the staff, they devised a game plan for the coming year.

Charlie took a silver dollar and used it for the outline of a neat little project. On one side he wrote I CAN and on the other side he put PLA MONEY. As you can see from the diagram on page 552, we've fancied it up a bit and made it out of plastic for greater durability.

Charlie's original version was cut from a sheet of paper and was fairly crude, but enormously effective. He reproduced them by the hundreds and gave each teacher a supply. When a youngster was "caught" doing something good, such as picking up paper in the school yard without instructions, cleaning the blackboard without someone ordering him to do it, welcoming new students to the school, returning "lost and found" articles, and a host of other things, the student was given an I CAN by the teacher.

When a student received one hundred of these I CANs he or she was awarded an I CAN T-shirt. Out of a student body of 594, 587 of them won an I CAN T-shirt. It truly became a status symbol. Charlie smilingly says it got to be slightly ridiculous to see a sheet of paper blowing across the school yard with five kids out there running it down!

Some of the students helped old ladies across the street who did not want to cross the street, and when a new student showed up, he was individually greeted by about ninety-seven students. In short, the entire school got involved in the project.

There are some who might contend that 587 T-shirts was expensive and, of course, they are right. However, when you consider the results, it's got to rate as the finest investment the school ever made. First of all, there was not a single case of vandalism for the entire year. There was not a single drug bust for the year. Attendance for the year was measurably better; grades were better (in many cases, substantially so); and perhaps best of all, for the first time parents, teachers, and students felt they all were on the same team seeking the same objective.

Role Models

The primary role of leadership is to create a team headed by someone the team can follow because they respect his or her integrity and leadership abilities. Our example from the educational world achieved that objective. The principle will work just as effectively in the business world, as you can see from the following article:

Question: What do Tom Selleck, Brooke Shields, and Farrah Fawcett have in common with Lee Iacocca, William Norris, and Malcolm Forbes?

Answer: Not much. But they are all models.

The fact of the matter is that the first three have been, are, and will be supermodels in the world of fashion. Each is known by millions of fashion aficionados, television watchers, and moviegoers from Kansas to Kenya. Each is easily recognized and admired by throngs eager to emulate the "look" that these supermodels have created. Each represents excellence in his or her field of work.

On the other hand, the latter three are neither dashing, smashing, nor particularly debonaire. They, too, are known by millions. Each is easily recognized. Each represents excellence in his field of work. These men are role models.

A supermodel is someone we aren't and someone we will never be. A role model is someone we aren't and someone we can be. Today, unfortunately, our society seems to be brimming with an affinity and affection for supermodels rather than role models. We are actively striving for something we will never be when we should in fact be pursuing something that we ought to be. *In short, we have systematically replaced our true American heroes of yore with The Hulk, Strawberry Shortcake, and Papa Smurf!*

The simplest and most direct route to excellence is to emulate, shadow, and replicate what works. Unfortunately, the media has a somewhat morbid preoccupation with failure or success. So we must be content to peruse advertising pages of periodicals inhabited by supermodels rather than role models.

Printed by permission from Dr. Michael H. Mescon, Dean, College of Business Administration, Georgia State University, and Holder, Ramsey Chair of Private Enterprise, and Dr. Timothy S. Mescon, Assistant Dean, School of Business Administration, University of Miami, and published by Mescon Group, Inc., Atlanta, Georgia.

We are inundated with form not function, with quantity not quality, with illusion not substance.

What characterizes a role model? *What rings a tone of excellence that is loud and clear? What separates the role model from the rest? Let's look at one:*

Nicola Iacocca immigrated to the United States from Southern Italy in 1902 and eventually settled in Allentown, Pennsylvania, where he built a small auto-rental business. His son, Lee, surrounded by cars all his life, aspired to work for Ford. With a Bachelor's degree from Lehigh and a Master's from Princeton, Lee joined Ford Motor Company in 1946. By 1970, only the grandson of Henry Ford held a higher position in the company than Iacocca. On July 13, 1978, thwarted by Ford's obsession with nepotism, Iacocca was fired. On October 30, 1978, Lee Iacocca was named president of the Chrysler Corporation; on that same day, Chrysler announced its largest-ever quarterly loss.

On Thursday, April 21, 1983, The New Chrysler Corporation triumphantly announced it earned $172.1 million in the first quarter, the highest quarterly profit in the automaker's history. Initially, many dismissed Iacocca as a hypersalesman. After all, the demise of Chrysler was imminent. Wall Street laughed, the public taunted, Congress scrutinized, and Iacocca persevered. After effectively cutting the size of the company in half, Iacocca went to work on the people at Chrysler.

His managerial style has been described as charming, demanding, arrogant, ruthless, and confident. The truth is that Lee Iacocca demands no more than he gives. He is the ideal role model. He sets quarterly goals for Chrysler, for himself, and for his management team. Iacocca exudes confidence. He is impeccably tailored and groomed . . . and literally oozes assuredness. He is a winner. . . .

Three A's for Excellence

There is, indeed, a common thread of excellence that weaves its way through men like Lee Iacocca. Not surprisingly, although these men are involved in completely unrelated businesses, there is a remarkable degree of common factors among them. These common factors, these ingredients for success, represent our three A's for excellence: Attitude, Aggressiveness, and Appearance.

Attitude. Excellence is a mind-set. You must believe. *Each person who achieves success seems to have an unwavering commitment and belief in his own abilities. They adhere to a very basic tenet of business: rely on no one. Their beliefs, their mind-sets, their attitudes are communicable. This is a top-to-bottom phenomenon in organizations. We all want to believe. But when the CEO believes and that belief is transmitted throughout the organization, the belief is catchy. Says Chrysler St. Louis plant manager, John Burkhart: "All of us at Chrysler believe in the man. . . ."*

Aggressiveness. *Our society today is overcome with a national lethargy that has reached epidemic proportions. In a multinational, hypercompetitive business environment we can no longer afford this luxury. The global business community is populated by competitors who are both hungry and aggressive. Perhaps we, too, are hungry, simply not hungry enough. The search for excellence is a top-to-bottom aggressive process. It is a preemptive strike on the business community. First you win, second you lose.*

Appearance. *A brilliant student could not find a job. He mailed resumes to dozens of businesses. Many responded favorably, invited the student to visit and interview for a position. The student visited a number of firms but no offers were forthcoming. The student wanted to know why.*

"Are you absolutely certain you want to know why?" his professor asked. "I am," replied the student. The professor then responded, "You look like you've been on a six-month camping trip." The student indignantly responded, "Are you referring to my hair and my beard?" The professor answered, "Yes, and your clothes and your shoes, and your breath." The student said, "That's not fair." And the professor patiently replied, "You didn't ask if it was fair, you simply asked why."

Fair or not, the business community responds to appearance. Naturally, appearance must be fortified with substance but, nevertheless, appearance is important. You must reek of excellence. *Much of the initial high marks received by the Reagan administration were based not on substance but simply on appearance; the White House once again appeared "Presidential." Reagan and his staff looked the part. The sartorial splendor of Iacocca is not an act. The third A is simply a visual manifestation of attitude and aggressiveness. . . .*

Special Recognition: Treat Everyone as if They Are Hurting

Role models can be found everywhere, if you just look for them. Several years ago at one of our BORN TO WIN seminars, I had a moving experience. At the end of one particular session, a beautiful black woman from the Midwest asked if she could speak with me for a moment. When everyone else had departed, she and I sat down for a visit.

Let me qualify this by saying that had anyone asked me to identify the one person in the class who "had it all together," I would have quickly identified this lady as being that person. She was a beauty queen, and she walked, talked, and acted like one. Although her voice was feminine, it was strong and clear, and she could easily be heard in a large room. She was a college graduate and a very successful businesswoman. She truly gave every indication of having it all together.

As we sat down, the young woman started to talk slowly and quietly, almost hesitantly at first, as she said, "You know, I finally found out this afternoon why I came to attend this seminar." Then she paused and had to compose herself before she could continue. She said, "You know, in my lifetime, I believe you're the first person who ever looked right at me and told me you loved me and I did not have a feeling anything was involved other than the fact that I was a human being and I, like all others, needed to be loved." She finished with tears in her eyes. That day I learned a vitally important lesson: If I treat everyone as if they are hurting, I will be treating most of them right. As my good friend Pastor Bill Weber says, "You can go up to anyone on the street and say to them, 'I heard about your problem,' and they will reply, 'Who told you?' "

I'm not implying that as managers and leaders we can go around as mother confessors or father counselors, but I am suggesting that many people are hurting, and if a person hurts in his or her personal life, he's not going to be as productive as he could be in his business life. A sensitivity to the needs of others will make us more effective in leadership roles.

If you will give *everyone* the recognition, rewards, and role models he or she deserves, both of you have taken a giant step toward becoming Top Performers!

PERFORMANCE PRINCIPLES

1. Everyone needs recognition.

2. Pride = *Personal Responsibility In Daily Effort.*

3. Outstanding recognition programs recognize the qualities *that are pertinent to company and individual success and reward these qualities.*

4. The six-step Recognition Program setup:
   a. Determine what you want and need to recognize
   b. "Sell" the program
   c. Control the "competitiveness and popularity contest" aspects of the program
   d. Evaluate carefully the criteria for award winners
   e. Recognize winners regularly and promptly
   f. Do not recognize inferior performance just for the sake of giving an award

5. The three A's for Excellence are:
   a. Attitude
   b. Aggressiveness
   c. Appearance

6. Treat everyone as if they were hurting in some area of their lives and you will help them to function more happily and more productively.

10

GETTING TO KNOW YOU . . . AND ME, TOO!

> The primary skill of a manager consists of knowing how to make assignments and picking the right people to carry out those assignments.
>
> Lee Iacocca

HAVE YOU EVER WONDERED why you hit it off so well with one person and never could seem to get along with another? Why is it that your new boss seems to be so much more difficult to deal with than the last one? What is it that really accounts for the difference in personality types and styles? The person who can unlock the key to these questions has a definite advantage in understanding himself and others.

What does this have to do with Top Performance? Quite a bit. Top Performers know themselves and know how to deal effectively with different personality types. We don't treat everyone the same. The manager who says, "I treat my people all the same," is going to be very ineffective. If you can recognize some of the basics of different personality types, you will be surprised at the difference it will make in your ability to deal with people.

There is a great deal of information on the market today that gives us insight into the personality types of ourselves and others. Psychologists administer the Briggs-Meyer Analysis; Dr. Carl Jung, the Swiss psychoanalyst, wrote in *Psychological Types* in the 1920s, "What really accounts for personality differences is that every individual develops a primacy in major behavioral functions." He went on to elaborate on the inherited and developed traits we all possess. Here at the Zig Ziglar Corporation we have used two types of analysis in our hiring procedures for several years. Walter V. Clarke and Associates has an analysis called "The Activity Vector Analysis," which has been an exceptionally good tool for us. In many of our seminars and consulting opportunities we use the Personal Profile System from Performax Systems International, Inc.

The more we know about ourselves and others, the better suited we are to deal with people in our complex society. Ten years ago I would not have considered using a personality profile in hiring employees, and today I cannot imagine hiring anyone without this tool—not just for our sake, but for the sake of the employee as well. Let me give you two specific examples.

When Ron Ezinga was considering my offer to become president of the Zig Ziglar Corporation, we agreed that it would be wise for us to be tested for compatibility. Neither of us was interested in getting involved in a business relationship that was anything less than a permanent one, because joining our firm meant Ron would have to resign the presidency of a larger company and move his family over a thousand miles to Dallas. It also meant major changes in our company and a substantial change of direction for me personally. Our getting together seemed natural, because I was speaking over two hundred times a year and was substantially less than effective in running our business. Ron's job was financially rewarding but did not permit him full use of his creative skills, organizational abilities, and management expertise. We wanted to get together but we wanted it to be "right" for our families and our careers.

As prudent decision-making businessmen, Ron and I went through extensive testing and found that we really had the potential for an excellent business partnership. My style is to be quick to act and make decisions, while Ron's is to be very deliberate and gather the facts. The psychologists said, "Zig, if you can speed Ron up a little, and he can slow you down a little, you guys are gonna be really successful!" There were many areas where it seemed his strengths compensated for my weaknesses and my strengths for his weaknesses. The scientific tools validated what we both suspected and prayed would be the answer—that we could successfully work together. And I can tell you that I am so grateful God led Ron to our company. Under his effective and imaginative direction we have moved into many new areas and are currently reaching five to ten times as many people as we were before Ron joined our team.

The second example I would like to share pertains to a young lady we hired as a backup receptionist. She was very pleasant and quite good on the phone; however, she was never in her seat when it came time for her to "back up" on the phones. She had so much energy that "sitability" came hard for her. We had reached the point that we were considering asking her to find other employment when we got involved in "Activity Vector Analysis." From the analysis we saw that *she* wasn't the problem—*we* were! We had completely misplaced her. Fortunately, we had an opening at the time for an assistant office manager. The job required that about fourteen different projects be handled at one time (ordering office supplies, getting office machines repaired, hosting visitors to our offices), and she was magnificent! She was one of the best we have ever had in the position. We all shed a tear when her husband's career called for them to relocate.

The point is this: With scientific validation we can get reinforcement for making career decisions—both in hiring and in choosing a profession. Am I recommending that your organization get involved with one of these personality profile analyses? The answer is yes and we even list the addresses of some excellent companies at the end of this book. We also have a consulting team which specializes in developing personalized personnel programs for your organization.

A *Voyage* in *"Self"* and *"Other"* Discovery

A personality analysis is somewhat like the analysis of the notes on a musical score. This analysis will reveal the nature, even the quality, of the performance. Every musical instrument and every human being is different. Take any group of people who interact together in pursuit of some common goal and you will see that each possesses personality traits different from the others. Each of these people is motivated differently, and the differences can result in effective performance (as with Ron Ezinga and me), or in complete discord. This does not necessarily mean that one person is right and the other is wrong—just that we are different. And that's good! If we always agree, then one of us isn't necessary.

The beauty of the personality analysis (regardless of the system used), is that not only does it enable you to understand why you and those around you behave as you do but it also enables you to take advantage of this knowledge (not take advantage of the people) so that you might channel energies and focus talents in existing relationships for the better. Understanding personality differences helps people appreciate each other more and, consequently, work together more effectively.

Here's how it works: Most of the studies we have done categorize behavioral style into four broad dimensions. Obviously, no one person's personality can be defined as belonging totally to one of these four categories. We are, after all, human beings and not computerized mechanisms. Our personalities reflect many subtle differences of tone and texture, and we all have some of all degrees of each of the characteristics. However, some characteristics are dominant and will surface on a regular basis.

How Aggressive Are Your Employees?

Think of four beakers of liquid that you might find in a chemistry laboratory.

Each beaker represents a personality characteristic. Let's call the first beaker our *Aggression* container. If the Aggression container is filled below the midline, the person usually is willing to let others make decisions and glad to reach decisions by consensus. This individual is often quiet and unassuming and is perceived as being mild-mannered in dealing with others, and usually modest about personal achievements.

To motivate these people, place them in low-pressure situations and allow them to lead with a "let's do it together" style instead of a demanding style. Incentive motivation will do little to motivate these good-natured individuals who are turned off by pressure. They are willing and unselfish, which is one reason they are sometimes taken advantage of by more aggressive people.

People who have their Aggression containers filled above the midline are often perceived as strong-willed, task-oriented "doers." They have a tendency to drive themselves and others and enjoy change and challenge. You recognize these people by their "steely eyed" (stern and intense) expression and clenched fists that pound the table for emphasis (or pointed finger for the same effect). They "stride" rather than walk, and always seem to be going somewhere with a purpose and in a hurry.

You motivate these people by challenging them and granting authority. The less tied down they are, the more effective they become. Give them direct answers and stick to business when in the business environment. When you disagree with them, take issue with the facts and not the person. The more you refer to objectives and results and provide facts about success probability, the more you have their attention.

These people will be turned off if you continually require documentation or require them to follow policies and procedures. They are pioneers, not followers. If you question their authority or place a ceiling on their earning potential and advancement possibilities, they will go to work for someone else.

One of the key concepts to remember when looking at personality characteristics is that *our weaknesses are often extensions of our strengths.* These individuals are goal achievers who are forceful, decisive, confident, persistent, and strive to achieve. This may lead to impatience, workaholism, lack of attention to detail, abrasive interaction with co-workers, and overstepping of privileges.

Who Are the "People" People?

The next container is our *People* container. If the container is filled below the midline, it usually indicates a person who is willing to spend time without other people. Others may perceive him or her as aloof and pessimistic. This person is usually slow to speak out and at times is suspicious of the motives of others. He is usually very conscious about the way he handles himself in the social and work environment and is careful about his appearance.

You motivate this person by providing a work environment free from social contacts. Allow this individual to think out a problem by himself. He is at his best on projects requiring logical analysis. Superficial and loud people really turn him off.

This congenial though rather reserved person can be quite a problem solver, but if placed in a position of solving "people" problems, will be quite uncomfortable.

The person who has his People container filled above the midline is normally a very spontaneous person. He is enthusiastic, friendly, and good at persuading others to join him. He is perceived as being poised, charming, emotional, and optimistic. You will recognize him by his ready smile and relaxed and friendly manner. He is very expressive with arms and hands and, if you are around him for any extended period of time, he will hug you or pat you on the back, shoulder, or hand.

To motivate these people, give them time to socialize and talk. Let them express their opinions and ideas, especially those regarding people. Help them by being supportive of them in relationships.

These people are turned off by work with long periods of intense concentration, record-keeping, and criticism of their friends. Put them

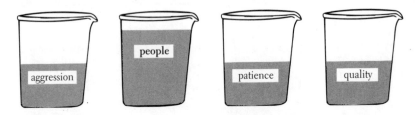

in a nonparticipative environment (computer terminal, accounting tasks) and you won't be able to keep them for long. These "People" people are trusting, sociable, generous, popular promoters. But if you go too far in extending these strengths, it may result in more concern with popularity than results, overselling, problem avoidance, and heart-over-mind decisions.

A Measure of Patience

The next container is our *Patience* container. If the container is below the midline, the person is usually actively involved and prefers an unstructured environment. He or she is frustrated by the status quo and invites change. Impulsive, ready to move about, and good at initiation, he is excitable and anxious to get the job done.

You motivate this individual by giving him a variety of activities and the freedom to move about on the job. The nervous energy he brings to the work force can be very positive when channeled; however, if left undirected, anxiety, nervousness, and tension will result. The strength of this person lies in the initiative he is willing to take. This becomes a weakness when he initiates so many projects that none are completed.

People who have their Patience containers filled above the midline are very stable and have "sitability." They are recognized for being kind, patient, quiet, disciplined, and service-oriented. You recognize these people by their willingness to listen to others and by their friendly countenances. They appear to be relaxed; body movement is smooth and effortless. To motivate these people, give them time to adjust, few changes, and *no* surprises. If you show sincere appreciation for tasks completed, these folks will be extremely loyal to you. Create a secure environment and allow them to develop work patterns for maximum productivity.

These people will be turned off by pressure placed upon them. New tasks and new people presented on a regular basis will produce diminished productivity. These people are loyal, team players, deliberate, sincere, hardworking, consistent, and dependable. Their strengths become weaknesses when they procrastinate or are asked to initiate projects.

They may have trouble meeting deadlines. They always finish the project—they just like to do it on their own time schedule.

Quality, Not Quantity

The last container is our *Quality* container. If the Quality container is below the midline, people may be perceived by others as being strong-willed (that's a nice way of saying stubborn). People who are low in this container are normally very independent and couldn't care less about details. Quantity wins out over quality with these folks.

You motivate these people by letting them do a job their own way, and granting autonomy. They are persistent and will stick to a chosen course of action. This strength becomes a weakness when they stick to a project which would be better off given up.

The people who have their Quality container filled above the midline are known for conscientiousness and concern for detail. They are intuitive and sensitive to the environment. These cautious individuals insist on competence and accuracy. You recognize them as thinkers who are seeking facts. They are not highly animated in gestures and are uncomfortable with those who easily show emotions.

To motivate this person, give him personal attention, exact job descriptions, and a controlled work environment. If you allow him to be part of a group or team and provide solid, tangible evidence for your position in discussions, you can win a friend. He is turned off by those who demand quick decisions on important matters and don't allow him enough time to check for accuracy. If you place him in an unstructured environment where no performance guidelines exist, he will find somewhere else to work.

These quality-conscious people are normally mature, accurate, logical, precise folks with high standards. If they take their strengths to the lengths that they become weaknesses, they may overanalyze and get "paralysis of analysis," become inflexible and bound by procedures and methods. They may have a tendency to get bogged down in details and hesitate to act without precedent.

How Are You Doing?

I hope that as we've been looking at each of these containers, you've been doing a little self-evaluation. On a scale of 1 to 10, with 1 being very little and 10 ready to overflow, how would you rate your *Aggression, People, Patience,* and *Quality* containers on the chart below? How would your parents rate you? How would you be rated by your employees? And so on, down the list. Let me remind you of something I said earlier. We all have *some* of each of these qualities. There are times when our containers seem almost empty and other times they are almost full. However, I think you can see that each of us has dominant characteristics.

Aggression	*People*	*Patience*	*Quality*
I say____	I say____	I say____	I say____
Parents____	Parents____	Parents____	Parents____
Employees____	Employees____	Employees____	Employees____
Spouse____	Spouse____	Spouse____	Spouse____
Children____	Children____	Children____	Children____
Boss____	Boss____	Boss____	Boss____

Another Method for Comparison

If we take each of these containers and line them up next to one another, we can get a comparison of how we stand in each area. Remember that the further away from the midline, the stronger the characteristics are perceived by others.

	Aggression	*People*	*Patience*	*Quality*
10	Direct	Enthusiastic	Predictable	Perfectionist
9	Daring	Persuasive	Relaxed	Accurate
8	Risk Taker	Emotional	Nondemonstrative	Systematic
7	Decisive	Trusting	Deliberate	Conscientious
6	competitive	Sociable	Stable	High Standards

— — — — — — — — — *Midline* — — — — — — — — — —

	Aggression	*People*	*Patience*	*Quality*
4	Calculated Risk taking	Reflective	Outgoing	Opinionated
3	Self-critical	Factual	Eager	Persistent
2	Weighs +/−	Controlled	Fidgety	Independent
1	Peaceful	Self-conscious	Restless	Rigid
0	Quiet	Suspicious	Active	Firm

Some of you (those in the upper half of the Quality container and lower half of the People container) have noticed the overlapping characteristics. These feed each other. In other words, the person rating himself a 3 in People and an 8 in Quality have the ability to analyze and should excel in positions allowing them to use these strengths. To place them in a public-relations role might not be advisable for long-term consideration. It is not that they could not perform in this position. The question is, for how long and at what cost could they do that job?

The beauty of these tools when they are applied in a scientific manner is that for hiring purposes you get the round pegs into the round holes and the square pegs in the square slots. When they are used after people are already in position, they allow you to help the employee take advantage of his strengths by working in a position which he can not only enjoy but can also excel in.

The information shared in this chapter is meant to be an introduction to the scientific tools and not to replace them. You have operated strictly on "guesstimates." The research that has gone into making the kind of tool I am talking about is enormous. I don't pretend to be able to understand the mathematical formulas and data-based information that make these analyses valid.

One idea must be reinforced: *There are no right or wrong characteristics, no good or bad characteristics. We are where we are and what we are because of what has gone into our minds. We change where we are and what we are by changing what goes into our minds.* Don't be satisfied with the broad generalities we are forced to work with in this book. If this area of personality characteristics interests you, find a good counselor who can give you information on yourself and those with whom you work.

Let me emphasize again: there is no wrong character for management, and no wrong type for achievement and Top Performance. Every profession seems to have its stereotypes . . . hard-driving, goal-oriented stockbrokers; laid back, people-oriented social workers, etc., and you may want to take those stereotypes into consideration when making career or employment choices. Yet even though different industries or companies may tend to breed a particular type of personality, you will find variations and degrees everywhere. Remind yourself that different management styles are appropriate to different times and situations. If you are directing the fire drill, don't call for a consensus vote on exit plans. But don't grimly demand that people be creative in a brainstorming session, either. Their ideas will simply dry up.

It's worth reviewing the ways in which your character type generally works best. Are you a Theory X manager or a Theory Y manager? Each can get the job done with and through people. Which works best for you? When? Here are some of the positive and negative aspects of each style of management.

Self-Oriented

- Maintains control and makes decisions, but may not get the input of others.
- Has confidence that his views are valid, but may be intolerant of other views.
- Goal-oriented and demanding in work objectives, but may make others feel he is overbearing.
- Driving and competitive, but may use excessive pressure for attaining objectives or excessive discipline on those who don't do the job in exactly the prescribed manner.
- Willing to work hard to gain recognition, but may not give recognition to others.
- Is decisive and able to confront poor performance, but expects no criticism from subordinates and will not allow his ideas or decisions to be questioned.

Other-Oriented

- Rarely makes major decisions without getting input and helping others feel a "shared" ownership, but works more slowly.
- Has enough confidence in himself to be willing to listen to others, but may not have the confidence to drive home his own decisions.
- Focuses on stimulating creativity and encourages team to take the initiative, but may not take initiative himself.
- Coaches his team and acts as a facilitator and producer who leads by example, but may not want to carry the ball.
- Seeks every opportunity to provide proper and positive recognition, but may not take enough credit himself.
- Values the ideas of others and considers the team more important than any individual (including himself), but may not allow Top Performers to stand out.
- Competitive with himself in constantly striving to do a better job, but may avoid competition with others.

So you see that both styles of management have strengths and weaknesses. The best manager uses both styles at the appropriate time with the appropriate people.

Self-Oriented Leadership
Can Be Properly Used When:

A. employees misuse or abuse their authority
B. organizational policies are neglected
C. new employees don't completely understand their objectives
D. an emergency situation exists, such as when people's safety is at stake
E. the manager/leader is solely responsible for project completion

Other-Oriented Leadership Can Be Best Used When:

A. people have become competent in carrying out their routine, daily objectives
B. creative problem solving is needed
C. the manager needs to motivate the highly qualified personnel
D. conducting "ongoing" planning for the organization
E. there is a need for creative work and "co-ownership" in ideas

One of the men who best exemplifies the correct combination of all the characteristics we have been sharing in this chapter is Robert W. Woodruff of Coca-Cola. He was nicknamed "Mr. Anonymous" despite being the CEO of the Coca-Cola Company. Here is the text of a leaflet he carried in his pocket that summarizes a solid business and personal philosophy.

Life is pretty much a selling job. Whether we succeed or fail is largely a matter of how well we motivate the human beings with whom we deal to buy us and what we have to offer.

Success or failure in this job is thus essentially a matter of human relationships.

It is a matter of the kind of reaction to us by our family members, customers, employers, employees, and fellow workers and associates. If this reaction is favorable we are quite likely to succeed. If the reaction is unfavorable we are doomed.

The deadly sin in our relationship with people is that we take them for granted. We do not make an active and continuous effort to do and say the things that will make them like us, and believe in us, and trust us, and that will create in them the desire to work with us in the attainment of our desires and purposes. Again and again we see both individuals and organizations perform only to a small degree of their potential success, or to fail entirely, simply because of their neglect of the human element in business and life. They take people and their reactions for granted. Yet it is these people and their responses that make or break them.

It is believed that these words are those of Mr. Woodruff's friend Bernard F. Gimbel, the late chairman of Gimbel Brothers, Inc. So greatly was he impressed by the message in these words that he had the pamphlet reprinted to pass out among the key men in his organization. You might say that over the years these words have almost become the spirit of Coca-Cola. These are words that all Top Performers would do well to live by.

PERFORMANCE PRINCIPLES

1. The more I understand myself, the more effectively I can work with others.

2. Personality profiles are valuable tools for getting the round pegs into the round holes and the square pegs into the square slots.

3. Self-evaluation (with a scientific tool) is more valuable than self-condemnation.

4. Our weaknesses are often extensions of our strengths.

5. There are no good/bad, right/wrong profiles—they simply help us evaluate where we are so we can determine where we want to go.

6. You are what you are and where you are because of what has gone into your mind; you change what you are and where you are by changing what goes into your mind.

11

MANAGEMENT GEMS

Find the essence of each situation, like a logger clearing a log jam. The pro climbs a tall tree and locates the key log, blows it, and lets the stream do the rest. An amateur would start at the edge of the jam and move all the logs, eventually moving the key log. Both approaches work, but the "essence" concept saves time and effort. Almost all problems have a "key" log if we learn to find it.

Fred Smith

THROUGHOUT *TOP PERFORMANCE*, we have made every effort to give credit where credit is due. We have painstakingly tracked down every traceable bit of information to keep from claiming originality when there was none. In this final chapter in "The Science of Top Performance," we want to share with you some "management gems" that frankly are difficult to credit. These are timeless truths that have really been shared by most, if not all, effective managers. Hopefully you will find some "key logs" in these concepts and formulas that will answer your "opportunities" to solve problems more efficiently and effectively.

Formula for Top Performance Management

1. Show honest and sincere appreciation at every opportunity—make the other person feel important.
2. Don't criticize, condemn, or complain.
3. Make your cause bigger than your ego.
4. Work for progress, not perfection.
5. Be solution conscious, not problem oriented.

6. Invest time in the activity that brings the highest return on investment according to the priority list of responsibilities — effort alone doesn't count; results are the reasons for activity.
7. Fulfilling responsibility is a good reason for work; discipline is the method.
8. Recognize and accept your own weaknesses.
9. Make checklists and constantly refer to them.
10. *Always* show the people in your life the humility of gratitude.

Six Action Steps for Performance-Oriented Managers

1. Give regular, specific, and observable behavior feedback on performance.
2. Respect the lines of communication and authority.
3. Make timely decisions.
4. Be accessible.
5. Encourage creative ideas.
6. Provide personal support.

The Ten "Double Win" Rules That Lead to Top Team Performance

When dealing with others:
1. Remember that a *smile* is the most powerful social tool we have at our disposal.
2. Listening is the most neglected *skill* in business (or home) today. The person who listens controls the final outcome of the discussion. Encourage others to talk, and then consciously remove any barriers to your good listening skills.
3. Talk in terms of the other person's interest. You will find a "uniqueness" and "specialness" in every individual you meet. Others are interesting when discovered; check out the other person's point of view.
4. Ask questions you already know the answer to and you will get to see the other person's perspective. Most ideas are more palatable if we "discover" them ourselves. People who truly care about others lead them down the "discovery path."
5. "What you are speaks so loudly I can't hear what you say." Remember to model the behavior and attitude you want the other person to have.
6. Give assignments that allow you to express faith and confidence that the other person can successfully perform in the task assigned.

7. Always make requests, never give orders.
8. Develop your ability to use the narrative story and the meaningful analogy—these are powerful teaching tools.
9. Always be respectful of others. Show your respect by being on time for meetings or letting others know why you must be late.
10. Return phone calls and letters immediately—there is no excuse for not doing so.

Exploding Some "Management Myths"

1. *Manipulation and Motivation are often the same thing.* Absolutely not! Manipulation is getting people to act for you in ways that may not necessarily be for their own good. Motivation is helping people recognize mutual interests and getting them to join the "cause" because there is a benefit for them as well as you.
2. *Making your best effort is all that really counts.* No! Too many people substitute effort for accomplishment. The reason for working is to get *results*. The person who gets the most results with less effort is working smarter and harder. Fatigue is not an indicator of success.
3. *Delegation is the key to management success.* Wrong again! Delegation is not telling someone what you want, when you want it, and how it is to be done. This is *direction*. Delegation means assigning the *results* you expect and designing a follow-up system that allows you to *inspect* what you *expect*. New employees get direction, experienced employees get delegation. Determining which employees need direction, giving it to them, and delegating results and the authority to get those results is an important key to management success.
4. *Managers are normally superior physically, mentally, and spiritually.* Nope! Very few managers are "normal"! And, there is nothing in the books that says a manager is a "superior." Very simply put, managers are people willing to take responsibility and work through others to achieve results. As Fred Smith says, "An executive is not a person who can do the work better than others, rather, he is one who can get others to do the work better than he can." Are you trying to be a "supervisor" or "superworker"?
5. *Managers must control all circumstances.* No way! Managers deal with problems and situations, and there is a distinct difference between the two. A situation exists because you cannot control it—people get ulcers trying to control the uncontrollable. A problem is something you can take action on. Excellent managers learn the

difference between the two, take action on problems, and stop worrying about situations.

Your Challenge

There really are no "great revelations" in this brief summary chapter. However, professionals don't need to be told, but they are glad to be reminded. If you will read these few pages every day for twenty-one days, your career will be greatly enhanced by the principles you will be putting into action.

PERFORMANCE PRINCIPLES

1. Reread the principles listed in this chapter daily for twenty-one days!

PART THREE

MOTIVATING THE
TOP PERFORMER

It is motive alone that gives character
to the actions of men.

Bruyére

12

A FORMULA FOR MOTIVATION

You can't sweep people off their feet, if you can't be swept off your own.

Clarence Day

ONE EVENING an associate and I flew back into Love Field in Dallas and got on the shuttle bus to take us to the outlying parking lot to pick up our car. As we stepped aboard, a client of mine warmly and enthusiastically greeted me. We exchanged a few pleasantries and then, to no one in particular and yet to everyone on the shuttle bus, he said, "From time to time I bring Zig in to talk to my organization. He's enthusiastic and optimistic and he gets 'em all charged up and convinces 'em that everything's going to be fine and that they need to have a good, positive mental attitude." Then he continued by saying, "Of course, I look at things a little bit differently. I tell 'em exactly how it is and from time to time I chew 'em out pretty good!"

A passenger on the bus entered the conversation at that point and said, "In other words, Ziglar is unrealistic because he's so optimistic, and you're realistic in your approach." With this, I turned to the man and said, "Friend, let me ask you a question. What percentage of the bad things you expect to happen actually happen?" At that point another passenger entered the picture and said, "About five or ten percent of them." Then I commented, "In other words, over ninety percent of the time the expected negative events just don't happen. This is realistic *and,* according to the experts, factual. From my perspective, the conclusion is obvious. *It's completely unrealistic to be negative and totally realistic to be positive.*" However, it *is* unrealistic to deny that problems do exist, so let's take a serious look at a major problem and then look at some positive solutions.

Bridging the Gap

The general trend in business in the last five years has been toward growing employee dissatisfaction, according to many of the research associations and news magazines which study business climate. Workers at all levels—hourly, clerical, professional, and even managerial personnel—are down on employers. Gripes have less to do with money and more to do with the work environment.

Now, if you are wondering what this "less than cheerful" news is doing in such a positive book, let me explain that we should look for the positive in all situations. However, that must not keep us from identifying obstacles to becoming even more positive. Just because the ostrich buries its head in the sand does not make the trouble disappear. As a matter of fact, until and unless you specifically identify the problem in a company, you cannot solve it any more than your doctor could successfully treat you for an illness until he has correctly identified the illness. Identifying obstacles or problems is the first step toward discovering solutions. *The key is to be solution-conscious and not problem-oriented.*

One study shared by *Research Institute Report* showed that four classes of workers were surveyed: managers, professionals, clerical, and hourly. For three of the four categories, over 20 percent fewer people are satisfied with their companies now, compared to twenty years ago. Seven percent fewer professionals are satisfied with their companies. The problem is not in the work; rather the problem lies in *those who create and manage the work environment.* And, though some attitudes toward employers have begun to improve, according to Opinion Research Corporation of Princeton, New Jersey, it will be a long time before most employers regain the favor the workers felt ten to twenty years ago.

What this means to us is that there is a *growing gap between managers and workers.* A major objective of *Top Performance* is to close that gap and substantially improve employee job satisfaction, which is a *must* for greater productivity. In order to reach that lofty goal, we need to examine some of the facts and *attitudes* discovered in the research:

- Age had little to do with the study—all ages showed a decline in satisfaction.
- Only professionals rated "sense of accomplishment" high . . . clerical, hourly, and even *managers* don't feel a sense of accomplishment.
- Everyone was less contented with benefits and job security.
- All except professionals showed less respect for supervisors and most workers charged that their superiors don't know the job.

- All classes were down on whether they get sufficient information and advancement opportunities.
- Only two in ten employees believed performance and pay are related.
- The "grapevine" was described as the source of information for most employees. All said they preferred to get information from supervisors and management.
- *Fully 50 percent of managers felt top management had lost touch with employees. Among all others, over 75 percent voted the same way.*

What Are We Going to Do?

Obviously, we need to take constructive measures to reverse this trend. The answer lies in this statement:

Management's imperative is to cultivate its human resources!

And, since you are involved in *Top Performance*, obviously you realize the importance of your greatest resource, your people. Here are some suggestions from researchers which we are reinforcing and expanding throughout *Top Performance:*

- *Show respect for a job well done.* Get rid of second-class job citizenship regardless of pay differences. Real job equality is feeling we have a stake in our company's success.
- *We must* involve *employees.* This means providing opportunities to make decisions and give useful input. This does not mean surrendering basic decision-making powers. It does mean giving employees a chance to participate, to be involved, *and* to hold them accountable.
- *As a company leader, keep skid chains on your tongue.* Talking about others may be destructive and probably is just gossip unless it's specifically designed to help.
- *Cultivate a calm, persuasive voice. How* you say it is often more important than *what* you say. In any type discussion or confrontation, your objective is to "win them over" . . . not "win over them."
- *Make certain you are short on promises to your people and long on fulfillment.* Action does speak louder than words.

- *Be interested in the goals, welfare, homes, and families of those with whom you work.* People have many facets in their lives. Don't be a one-dimensional supervisor. You may not supervise their private lives, but you can let them know you *really care.*
- *Keep an open mind on all debatable questions* (being the boss doesn't necessarily mean you are always right). Discuss but don't argue. The mark of superior minds is to be able to disagree without being disagreeable.
- *Be careful of employees' feelings.* Wit, put-down, and any form of ethnic or racial digs are no-no's. Leaders instinctively know that when someone is resentful and has a chip on his shoulder, the best way to remove the chip is to let him take a bow.
- *Since employee morale is affected by many factors in and outside the work place, those who have confidence in management's integrity are most likely to deliver their best work and to do so consistently.* The best way management can build this confidence in itself is to *communicate its abilities honestly, confidently, and directly. A well-run company is the best employee morale-builder available.*

In summary, what the researchers and their statistics say is very important; however, what they *don't* say is even more important:

> *What the work force really wants is management leadership whose competence and concern they can trust.*

The work force desires and feels it deserves an opportunity to grow mentally, socially, spiritually, and physically, while sharing in the financial recognition and security rewards which come as a result of their growth and effort as part of the team.

Andrew Carnegie once said, "A man can succeed at almost anything for which he has unlimited enthusiasm." Lonnie Shealey, president of Lone Star Builders, adds, "Whatever we call it—enthusiasm, motivation, ambition, drive, desire, or energy—it's a quality which plays a major role in success. *People who are unable to motivate themselves must be content with mediocrity, no matter how impressive their other talents.*" Now let's take a sobering look at why he makes that statement and why motivation is a must in our personal and corporate lives.

Our Wasted Time

One shocking statistic which costs America and its people a great deal of money and countless lost opportunities is the incredible amount of time which is wasted. The December 9, 1985, issue of *U.S. News & World Report* cites one estimate that in a year American workers will "steal" $160 billion from their employers by arriving late, leaving early, and misusing time on the job. That's a lot of corporate dollars, but the truly big loss is the individual's, because Emerson was "right on" when he said, "The right performance of this hour's duties will be the best preparation for the hours or ages that follow it."

Professor Tor Dahl, an internationally respected productivity expert from the University of Minnesota, and president of his own consulting firm, has done considerable study in the area of time utilization and productivity. He says that well over 40 percent of the time spent on the job is wasted. One of the biggest time wasters on the job is smoking. The average smoker, according to Dr. William L. Weis in an article published in the *Personnel Administrator* May 1981, is absent 2.2 days per year more than a nonsmoker and "steals" over 30 minutes per day, which translates into 18.2 more days per year. Prediction: Since the dollar loss averaged $4611 in 1981 dollars for the employer, by the end of this decade the young person entering the job market as a smoker will find it difficult—if not impossible—to get a really good job.

The most conservative nationwide survey I saw revealed that the average worker wastes nine full work weeks a year simply putting off or postponing work that should be done. Burke Marketing Research, Inc. conducted the survey for Accountemps, an accounting, bookkeeping, and data processing personnel organization. The survey was based on interviews with vice-presidents and personnel directors of one hundred of America's one thousand largest companies. Those responding to the survey estimated that *the average employee procrastinates 18 percent of the time, or nine full thirty-five-hour work weeks each year.* Why? Well, the last survey question was: "What do you believe are the main reasons for procrastination in business?" The answers make up the following list. Read it and see if you agree that motivation could be the most important ingredient leadership can bring to a company.

- unwillingness or inability to make a decision
- failure to understand responsibilities
- lack of communication
- boredom
- low morale

- lack of interest in the job or particular task
- absence of clear-cut goals or objectives
- fear of failure or of making a mistake
- too large work load
- lack of discipline
- poor self-esteem

To this list we must add the thought that far too many people get carried away with what Charles E. Hammel identifies as the "tyranny of the urgent," and permit the "urgent" things to crowd out the "important" things. Basically, we have a *prioritizing* problem and not a *time* problem.

The proper utilization of our time and resources, according to Thomas K. Connellan, president of the Management Group, Inc., of Ann Arbor, Michigan, involves some truths which are so simple and basic that many people miss them completely. First, we need to understand that *there is no point in doing well that which you should not be doing at all.* When you take on a task, you should ask yourself if this is something you should be doing, or is it something someone else should be doing. Focus on *effective* use of time rather than *efficient* use of time.

Efficiency is doing things right.
Effectiveness is doing the right things.

According to Mr. Connellan, 10–15 percent of the tasks managers are personally handling should be delegated and 10–15 percent should be eliminated.

Question: What happens to these effective people who take their jobs seriously and use their time wisely? Answer: According to a December 10, 1985, Associated Press release, they get promoted:

> CHICAGO   *Dull people may not be the first invited to parties, but they are usually the first in line for promotion, according to a research team at a medical college here. The team made a study of eighty-eight executives and found that those people with a "low pleasure capacity" make the most successful executives. This is because they can concentrate on their work without being distracted. . . . Executives who were categorized as "fun seeking" tended to have lower salaries. [Author's note: The key word is* seeking. *You should, even must, enjoy your work and have fun performing your job.]*

There is something else about those men and women who were promoted. They were masters of the utilization of their time. My friend Dan Bellus from San Diego, California, is—in my judgment—the number-one time-management authority in our country. Dan, president of Human Development Unlimited, says this:

"When the Colonists declared their independence from Great Britain, a statement was written: 'All men are created equal.' There has been a lot of discussion about the truth of that statement since the time it was written. I don't propose I can clear it all up, but this I *do* know— everyone is equal in the amount of time he or she receives.

"Everyone gets twenty-four hours a day—sixty minutes for every hour and sixty seconds for every minute. No one can get more; no one can get less. You can't play the 'army' game with time: if you know the guy who's handing out the chow you can say, 'I want more.' Not so with time. You can't build a bigger time pipeline and say, 'I want more.' No one can live more than one second at a time. In this sense, then, everyone is truly equal. Now this one fact alone makes time the most precious of all commodities. This factor forces us to an inescapable conclusion: We've got to make our time work for us—it's the most perishable and nonnegotiable possession we have. We have to get production out of every second.

"Now, if we're low on money we can go to our friendly banker and borrow a little bit. If we have a surplus of money we can save it for a rainy day. Not so with time. If our factory is capable of producing more than we can use on a daily basis, we can stockpile our merchandise; we can place it in inventory; we can use it later. Not so with time. If we have a great idea we can write it down, save it for the future. Not so with time. If we want to be totally dishonest we can counterfeit money—we can print our own. Not so with time. We can steal merchandise, we can plagiarize written material. Not so with time. Time is the only commodity we deal with which cannot be counterfeited, stolen, plagiarized, obtained by fraud, stockpiled, or placed in inventory. And no force on earth can change that. When we make a deal with the old man with the scythe, he has a little sign right up above his cash register: ALL SALES FINAL—NO EXCHANGES, NO RETURNS, NO REFUNDS. We can't bring our sales slip back and exchange it for anything. If we don't get what we want when we trade that time, there's no way we can change the transaction."

Dan goes on to say that all activity, all work, all productivity is at the same level as the planning and organization which precedes it. "*We can't work at a high level of productivity and a low level of planning.* If we're going to travel that highway of productivity, the highway of planning must lead into it. We've got to plan to use every second that's available to us and use it in the proper proportion." Dan then adds a thought which, if we buy into it, will certainly increase our productivity and effective use of our time:

> *Why is it we never have time to do it right, but we always have time to do it over?*

Dan sums it up beautifully and eloquently when he says, "It appears we must take four building-block steps: (1) realize the true value and perishable nature of time; (2) draw up a plan for the physical handling of our time; (3) understand that a one-shot attack will not work because our attitude regarding time must change, our habits of thinking and doing must change; and (4) for this change to take place, a decision and a commitment must be made.

"Perhaps the most important two words we'll say here and now are those two: *decision* and *commitment*. All of the rules in the world, all of the techniques known to man, all of the tools that were developed, all of the plans ever made, all of the ideas we have suggested for you here— none of these will be worth today's nickel, none of these will produce one fraction of a second in time gained, unless and until we make the decision that *they* will and make the commitment that *we* will. It will be easy in the white heat of inspiration; it will be simple in the desire of the moment, to envision a wealth of time gained, a wealth of time in which we can do all of these things we've always wanted to do, but without a firm, irrevocable decision, without a genuine commitment, nothing can and nothing will happen. The decision must be—the commitment must be—to develop attitudes that will make time serve us, that will get for us every second's worth of living out of every second of life. Such commitment can be made; such an attitude can be developed. The knowledge is ours, the capability is within us—not outside in some magic formula but within us, where rests all potential for our own development.

"The following ad appeared in the want-ad section of a newspaper:

LOST *Somewhere between sunrise and sunset—one golden hour encrusted with sixty silver minutes, each studded with sixty diamond seconds. No reward is offered. They are lost and gone forever.*

"Did you run that ad? Will you have to run it again tomorrow?"
I don't know how that hits you, but to me it's inspiring and motivating, as well as challenging. Yes, I believe motivation is important. I

believe we have to be motivated to clearly accept and understand that tremendously significant advice Dan Bellus is sharing with us.

The Successful Know About Attitude

Allan Cox, author of the widely acclaimed book *Confessions of a Corporate Headhunter,* talks a great deal about attitude and, as a result of a survey of 1,173 executives in 13 corporations, has some strong opinions and factual information. He says, "Attitude determines strength. It determines direction. American executives by and large believe that having a positive attitude is responsible for career advancement." In his survey he asked the question "What was your finding concerning the impact of positive thinking?" Among top executives, 49 percent said it affected their own success very strongly and 46.5 percent said it was a "significant" factor. In a nutshell, 95.5 percent of these men and women said their attitude played a very strong or significant part in their success. The rest were neutral on the question. On the other side, Cox points out that *no one with whom leaders deal is given such short shrift as the negative thinker.*

Mr. Cox points out that positive thinking is not manipulating or being manipulated. It is not being grandiose, it is not being naive. It is not being falsely enthusiastic or optimistic. Most important, perhaps, it is not to deny periodic, normal bouts of discouragement. Thinking positively is not *legislated experience,* either. By this he means you cannot practice it merely because someone tells you to, nor can you extend it selectively, say to life at home, and exclude it from work. He points out that life constantly presents us with obstacles and opportunities. Positive thinking is the means for dealing constructively with both of them.

An Important Gift You Can Give Others

One of the most important and positive things we can give others is *hope* with direction, encouragement, and believability—hope that the future is going to be bright for them, regardless of where they are at the moment. Never will I forget an incident at a hotel on Marco Island, Florida, several years ago. A speaker friend and I were visiting in my room when the maid knocked and asked permission to clean the room. Since this did not present a problem, we invited her to go ahead.

She had been working less than a minute when our conversation stopped and I started watching her in action. Though she was large and substantially overweight, she moved with amazing speed. In three fast movements she stripped the blanket and linens from the bed. With each of her hands working, she removed the pillowcases from both pillows simultaneously. She took the sheet which covers the mattress and quickly put it on one side. Next she put the light blanket on top of that, followed by the cover sheet and the bedspread. Then she put the pillowcase on the pillow and completed that one side of the bed.

At that point she quickly moved to the other side and finished that side of the bed in record time. How she handled the next little maneuver is an absolute mystery to me, but somehow from the opposite side of the bed she flipped the bedspread and the pillow (which she had neatly tucked on the other side) over in the correct spot and, with two more quick movements on her side, the bed was complete.

I don't exaggerate when I say she had made that bed in less than half the time of anyone I have ever seen. Since I served two years in the navy and made a few hundred bunks myself, I consider myself knowledgeable on the subject. But this lady was far and away the best I've ever seen.

Curiosity demanded that I get some information, so I asked her whether she minded if I asked her some questions. She cheerfully responded, "No, go right ahead," but in the meantime she was doing the other things needed to clean the room. First I asked her whether she worked on an hourly basis or if she were paid by the room. She told me she was paid by the room. I smilingly asked, "I'll bet you do all right, don't you?" For the first time she stopped and said, "Well, to tell you the truth, I have a large family and I am the only one to support them so I have to work hard." Then she grinned from ear to ear and said, "And yes, I do all right."

Where You Start Is Not Important

I'd like to complete this story by saying I got her name and address and two years later I wrote to discover she was the manager of the hotel. Unfortunately—and for me, amazingly—I did not even get her address, so I cannot finish her story on that kind of note. However, I'll bet she's still doing "all right."

About a year later I was speaking in Zanesville, Ohio, and had lunch with the manager of a Holiday Inn and the president of the Chamber of Commerce, along with a personal friend. As we visited, I told the story of this lady and the manager of the Holiday Inn said, "Well, obviously that was not me, but it could have been." She pointed out that when she finished high school she got married and had to go to work. The only job available was to serve as the housekeeper at the Holiday Inn and her job was cleaning rooms. However, she determined that she was going to work as hard as possible and be the best at what she did. The net result was that within six months she was manager of that floor of the Holiday Inn. A few months later she was manager of the entire housekeeping department. About a year later they moved her into the restaurant, first as assistant manager and shortly after as manager. A couple of years later she was manager of the Holiday Inn in Zanesville, Ohio, and served in that capacity for several years. This lady, Mrs. Nan Gump, could easily have been immobilized by where she had to start . . . instead she realized that *where you finish* is much more important. I remind you, that's in essence what I said about my coauthor at the beginning of this book.

Can You "Stand" Motivated?

Of all the subjects on this earth, surely one of the most exciting and confusing is the subject of motivation. The next example opens the door and deals with just one facet of this intriguing subject.

I don't know how you "stand" when you're waiting in a line or waiting for something to happen, but I shall never forget a little incident which took place in Washington, D.C., which fairly well describes the average person's concept of what motivation is and what a motivated person does. I had spoken for the National Federation of Parents for Drug-Free Youth, and the response had been very gratifying. The audience laughed at the appropriate places, nodded in agreement at the right spots, applauded at the high spots, and gave me an enthusiastic standing ovation when it was all over. Compliments flowed thick and fast. Had my wife been there, she would have loved everything they said about me! My children would have been a little embarrassed about it, and my mother would have *believed* every word. In short, it was an "up" occasion for me.

The next morning, I was in the restaurant waiting for the host to seat the guest who preceded me. I was quietly standing, awaiting his return. As I stood there, three women who had been present at my talk the night before joined the people behind me who were waiting in line. These three women obviously thought I was out of earshot or would not be tuned in to what they were saying. However, here's the conversation I picked up. First lady: "There is our speaker from last night." Second lady: "Yes, and he is obviously a 'night' person." Third lady: "He must be, because he sure doesn't look motivated to me!"

Now to be real honest, I don't know how you either "look" motivated or "stand" motivated. I suppose the women thought I should have had an ear-to-ear grin on my face, or perhaps I should have been bouncing up and down and waving to the people in the restaurant. If that's their idea of a motivated person, all I can say is they are way, way off base.

The question I am most often asked is, "Are you always so 'up'?" And the answer, of course, is, "No, I'm not always 'up.'" But I am "up" about 95 percent of the time. Usually if I am not "up," it is because I am exhausted as a result of a grueling schedule. Common sense and experience then dictate to me that I either need to take a nap or go jogging—which is exactly what I do if it's humanly possible.

I should explain, however, that there is a vast difference between being "up" and being "on." Anyone who is "on" twenty-four hours a day is "on" something which is deadly. In short order he will suffer from burnout and probably end up as a depressed, perhaps even psychotic, individual. Either that, or efforts to always be "on" could lead to a tragic dependency on drugs, which has claimed far too many (even one is too many) of our young people who are deluded into believing that you must always be "on" and having a marvelous time.

Just Who Is Motivated?

Unfortunately, too many people think of the "motivated" person as the loudly enthusiastic, turned-on extrovert who is making noise and is the center of attention, whether he is in a crowd of ten or ten thousand. This is not necessarily motivation, but probably falls under the banner of "hysteria" and hysteria is giving motivation a bad reputation. I'm not saying that the extrovert is not motivated because he *could* be, but being loud certainly doesn't necessarily mean being motivated. Some of the most "up" and motivated people I've ever known are quiet and unassuming. Obvious point: You can be "up" and motivated while quietly jogging, reading, praying, thinking, holding hands with your mate, or even sleeping.

As I wrote that last paragraph, the Redhead was waiting to take a walk in the Botanic Gardens along the Brisbane River in Brisbane, Australia. What an "up" experience it was! The greenery, shrubs, flowers, rocks, plants, birds, boats, water, and people were beautiful, fascinating, and quiet. At no time during the walk would anyone have accused us of being "on," especially when we sat on the bench to watch the ducks and birds in their never-ending quest for food. However, it was definitely an "up" experience and is permanently recorded in my memory bank as a most enjoyable, motivating interlude.

I might also add that this process helps to clean out the garbage and the cobwebs from the yesterdays of life, so that you really are clearing the decks for more effective action today. Another benefit is that this kind of *meditation* will help eliminate lots of *medication.*

Yes, life can be—even *should* be—sprinkled from time to time with "up" experiences. For me, a jog with one of my granddaughters or daughter Cindy, a game of golf with my wife or son, a moving sermon, inspiring semiclassical music, hymns of the faith, or a drama about real life depicting the good guy winning over the bad guy is always an "up" experience. These events turn me on when I need to be turned on to do the speaking and writing which my profession requires.

My guess is you are pretty much the same way, and like me, you have certain things that *do not* get you as motivated as your best performance demands. It may be a certain aspect of your job, such as the paperwork or long and tedious meetings. It might be making cold calls on unmotivated buyers. It might be dealing with and trying to manage other people's frustrations when you feel you have enough of your own aggravations to last a lifetime. The question should be, "Is it possible to be motivated about something that I am *not* motivated about right now?" The answer is a definite YES! Especially if you understand that most small problems, when nourished with procrastination, will grow bigger and bigger.

It will be even easier when you understand a simple formula which I call the *Three-A Formula to develop motivation.* The next three chapters are dedicated to this formula.

Before we really get into this concept of motivation, let me make one more point. You may be as motivated as you ever want to be. The chances are good, however, that there is someone in your life who is not as motivated as you would like for him or her to be. So, as you read the next chapters, don't forget that you are reading from two perspectives: (1) How will this information help me to be a Top Performer? (2) How will this information help me to help others be Top Performers? You will be pleased with the answers you find to both questions—I guarantee it!

PERFORMANCE PRINCIPLES

1. You must understand motivation to consistently motivate others.

2. Management's imperative is to cultivate its human resources.

3. What the work force really wants is management leadership whose competence and concern they can trust.

4. One of the most important things we can give others is *hope*, with direction, encouragement, and believability.

5. Where you start is not as important as where you finish.

6. You can be "up" without being "on."

13

WHY YOU MANAGE . . .
WHY THEY FOLLOW

The true motives of our actions, like the real pipes of
an organ, are usually concealed. But the gilded and
the hollow pretext is pompously placed in the front for
show.

Charles Caleb Colton

| Awareness |

Analysis

Action

THE FIRST A in our Three-A Formula stands for *Awareness*. When I am
talking about awareness, I am talking about answering the question
Why? Why are you reading this book? Why are you continuing to work
in your job? Why are you continuing to be involved in the day-to-day
activities that fill your life? The *honest* answer to the question *Why?* is
also the answer to your *personal* motivation. This is not motivation that
has been imposed upon you by anyone else; it's your personal motivation. One of the early success writers suggested we take the word *motivation* and make a slash between the *v* and the *a*—and if you've got just a
little bit of imagination, you can see two words. The word on the left is
motive, and the word on the right is *action*. People who are motivated
have a motive; they have a reason, a purpose, or a cause. And then they
take action on that reason, purpose, or cause. Question: *Have you given
it any thought at all?*

A friend of mine, attending college, was placed in a 7:30 A.M. English
class that met on Saturdays. In his words, "The counselors saw me
coming, didn't they? They must have said, 'This guy looks like he just
fell off the turnip truck! Let's put him in that 7:30 A.M. Saturday English
class and he'll probably show up!' They did—and I did!"

motiv/ation

He went on to tell me that the teacher walked to the front of the room and immediately gave an assignment. The class was to write a short theme on "Why I Am Going to College." The students dutifully got down to business, but after about ten minutes, one of them got up and left the room. When the class was over, several of his friends walked out to the quadrangle to find the student who had left early. Sure enough, Ray was sitting in front of the library. "Ray, what are you doing?" his puzzled friends asked.

"Funny, I never thought about it before," Ray said, "but I don't want to go to college! The only reason I'm here is that you guys are here and my other friends are here and my mom and dad wanted me to go to college. I don't want to go to college. I want to go to work at the plant where my dad works, get married, have a family, play slow-pitch softball at night, and spend time with my family on the weekends. I just never thought about it until that teacher asked the question."

The real irony of this true story is that Ray was a straight-A high school student, and the chances are good he could have gone on to be whatever he studied to be. However, with that attitude, he would have been a mediocre doctor, lawyer, scientist, teacher, manager, or anything else. He would have been mediocre because he had not identified his own personal reasons, purposes, or causes. If we are to motivate ourselves, we must honestly face up to the real reasons we do the things we do.

If we want to motivate other people, we have got to find out what their reason, purpose, or cause is. People are not going to be motivated for *your* reasons. They are going to be motivated for their own reasons. We must understand that *everyone* listens to the *same* radio station. The station is WII-FM and the call letters stand for What's *In It For Me?* If you want to motivate others, this is the information you need to share. You've got to find out their motive, reason, and cause—and then encourage them to take action.

The first time you attempt to discover what another person's motives are, you will probably get an answer he or she thinks you would like to hear. If you continue to probe, you will get an answer that someone very close to that person would like to hear. And if you continue to probe, you might get the *truth.* Now, people don't mean to be deceitful. It's just that they haven't given much thought to what really is important to them. You see, money doesn't motivate anyone. If you had a million dollars and stacked it in the shape of a coffee table for your living room, initially you would be excited and invite all your friends and neighbors over to see your "million-dollar coffee table." After about three weeks, you would probably be bored with the "green monstrosity" in the living area. Money is not a motivator . . . what we *can do with the money* is what really motivates us and others. Whether it's the biggest home on the street or the largest donation to the orphanage, our motives vary greatly. Honest realization of our motives (or those of others) is the first step in understanding motivation.

Fear Motivation

Motivation comes in three forms. The first is *fear motivation.* Fear motivation works for some people some of the time. In most cases, it is temporary, but there are occasions when it is effective. When the economy is extremely tight and there are more workers than jobs, many workers will consciously make a much greater effort to be extremely productive, in an effort to ensure their jobs. They will arrive earlier, stay later, and do more while they are there. However, if this is their only motive, the chances are excellent that over a period of time they will grow weary of well-doing and revert back to their old habits and, if the economy is still bad, will ultimately end up losing their jobs. Temporarily, however, it will work and effect an increase in productivity for them.

Fear motivation is also effective on a toddler who continues to reach for things which he can destroy or which might be dangerous to him. A few light slaps of the hand will convince him, in most cases, that it is not in his best interests to pursue that course of action and he will desist. Fear motivation also works for a six-, seven-, or eight-year-old when it comes to acquiring bad habits such as smoking. A threat on the part of the parents to "wear his britches out" if they catch him with a cigarette is very effective and will keep that cigarette out of his mouth. However, the same approach for a fifteen-year-old would be worthless and might even have the opposite effect.

In the marketplace, fear motivation sometimes is temporarily effective to keep workers in line, have them become team players, cooperate with, and on occasion even be subservient to their superiors. But again, the results are temporary and over the long haul can even backfire.

Incentive Motivation

The second kind of motivation is *incentive motivation*. All of us in our business careers have seen the familiar picture of the donkey pulling the cart with a carrot dangling in front of him. The donkey's motivation to pull is obviously to reach and take a bite of that carrot. For this incentive to work, the load has got to be light enough for him to pull; the donkey's got to be hungry enough so that he wants to take a bite of that carrot; and the carrot has got to be desirable enough so that he wants to take a bite. However, if he does not eventually have his bite of carrot, he's going to recognize that it's a "con game" and he will stop pulling.

The only problem is, when you give the donkey a big enough bite of the carrot, he is no longer going to be hungry and, consequently, his motivation to pull is dramatically reduced. At this point, the only way you can get him to pull is to lighten the load, shorten the stick, and sweeten the carrot. The problem here is that in the business world we have a load which is fairly well dictated by market conditions and, if you lighten it too much, or if you give the donkey too big a bite of the carrot (or the profit generated by the free-enterprise system), the operation no longer becomes profitable and we ultimately end up out of business. Remember: Today's fringe benefits are tomorrow's expectations. So what do you do? Answer: Change the donkey to a thoroughbred and make him *want* to run.

Change or Growth Motivation

This brings us to the third kind of motivation, which is *growth motivation*. The primary purpose of growth motivation is to change the thinking, the capacity, and the motivation of the worker. We must make him want to pull that cart (do his job). We must give him reasons for doing what we want him to do *and* which *he* wants to do. In other words, we must work with employees to the degree that we can help them get the things they want in life. That's a major purpose of *Top Performance*: to give specific methods, procedures, and techniques for helping each individual grow and inspiring them so they will want to do a better job—not just for the benefit of the company but for their own benefit as well. As I've said before, in reality we are all "on the same team," and consequently, we have the same objectives. When management and labor both clearly understand that we are on the same side, then both sides will be willing, even anxious, to cooperate.

When I was a small boy my friends and I frequently walked on an abandoned section of the railroad tracks. Each of us attempted to keep our balance and walk the farthest, but inevitably, after a few steps, we would fall. Had we but realized it, two of us could have gotten on opposite rails, reached across and held hands and, together, could have walked indefinitely.

I'm convinced that in the business world, when management and labor, employer and employee, fully understand that they are on the same side and have the same objectives, if they will "hold hands" and work together, all will benefit. Then we are not only developing our maximum potential as individuals but we're also achieving the maximum productivity in our company, which ensures the stability and growth of that company. That's the kind of thinking and motivation which will bring optimum results and permanent benefits for labor and management.

I'm convinced that everyone is motivated at some time in their lives about something. Winners are motivated a high percentage of the time. *Winning leaders* are motivated most of the time and *almost* always when the chips are down. My friend Gene Lewis, one of the great common-sense leaders it has been my privilege to work with, shares this analogy, which clearly points out what happens to entirely too many people:

A glowworm does its fishing not in water, but in the air. It spins and lets down fine glutinous threads. When a gnat or other small insect, attracted by the light, collides with one of these strange fishing lines, it is caught and held. The glowworm reels in the line and consumes the captive. If its hunger is satisfied, the glowworm puts out its light. Otherwise, it drops another line for another tidbit. The soft light that gives the glowworm its unearthly beauty is not produced by the "contented" glowworm. The scintillating lights come from the glowworms that are hungry and indeed earnest about their fishing.

Unique creatures though they are, these glowworms have qualities in common with human beings. With us, as with them, the full stomach too often brings about a state of complacency that dims desire for accomplishment.

The young man starting out in life is spurred on by powerful "bread and butter" incentives. To be sure of eating regularly, he must pass certain tests. He must be able to master the fundamentals of his business, and to adapt himself to the conditions that make for success in that business. Hungry with desire for life's necessities, he "fishes" in that business in dead earnest, and if he has the right qualities, his "glow" attracts success.

But, after he has met with a measure of success, he faces a different kind of test. Is he still impelled by a strong inner drive to fish hard for the really big stakes?

Many who pass the initial tests brilliantly are stopped by this secondary test. They stall at the top of the first hill. They are so eager to enjoy the fruits of their success that they are unwilling to put forth the efforts to augment their education, acquire specialized training, or do whatever else may be necessary to reach still greater heights of service and personal advancement.

Obviously, Gene is not talking about *leaders* in that last paragraph. True leaders who are really motivated will use one success to build to an even bigger one. A leader knows that he *is* the example his subordinates look to for guidance and direction. *As a manager, he knows he will be measured and judged by the number of his subordinates who surpass him.* He clearly understands that the mark of greatness is the ability to develop it in others.

A Most Misunderstood Ingredient

If you are going to be a consistent Top Performer, it's important that you understand what happiness really is. Many people maintain they'll be happy *when*—they win the trip to Hawaii, New York, or Bermuda. Many people say they'll be happy when they get the new house, but they won't. Then they'll be happy when the landscaping is completed, but they won't. Then they say they'll be happy when the new draperies are up—but that's not true, either. Then they'll be happy when the mortgage is paid off, but again, they're wrong. They'll be happy when they've added the new room to the house, but that's not true. Then they'll be happy when they build that little place out on the lake—but again, it simply is not so.

Happiness is not a when—it is a NOW! It is not what you *have* that makes you happy, it is what you *are* that's going to make you happy! Material things are never going to make us happy. As I pointed out earlier, Adam and Eve had the whole world (including, as far as I know, the mineral rights). God gave them everything and authority over it— with the exception of one tree. He carefully instructed them not to eat the fruit of that tree. With all the material possessions they had, what was the one thing they wanted? You guessed it: the fruit of that tree.

Money and Position Won't Make You Happy

Many people say, "When I get a million dollars, then I'll be happy because I'll have security," but that's not necessarily so. Most people who acquire a million dollars want another and then another. Or they could be like a good friend of mine who made and lost every dime of a million dollars. It didn't bother him a bit. He wasn't excited about it, but he explained to me, "Zig, I still know everything necessary to make another million dollars, and I've learned what to do not to lose it. I'll simply go back to work and earn it again." He proceeded to do exactly that—and more. No, security is not based on money. General Douglas MacArthur said that security lies in our ability to produce—and I believe he's right.

Many people say, "I'll be happy when I get to be head of the company, because that represents security—when I'm the person in charge." That's not true. As you well know, you can even get to be the president of the United States and if you don't handle the job properly, you're going to lose it! No, if we are to have happiness, security, and continue to be motivated, we must understand that security comes from within. It lies in our ability to produce. In my mind, one of the best ways to be certain that we will continue to produce even when our needs have long ago been met is to continue to apply these principles and procedures we advocate in *Top Performance*.

Happy and Successful People Have a Reason for What They Do

A very wealthy west Texan had a daughter of marriageable age, and he determined to give her a "coming out" party.* This simply meant that he was going to invite all the eligible bachelors in the area over to his home so that he could have a good look at them—you sales folks

* I told this story in *Raising Positive Kids in a Negative World.*

would call that "group prospecting." His reason was obvious: he wanted the very best for his daughter.

When all the eligible young men arrived from a hundred-mile radius of his two-hundred-thousand-acre ranch (with scores of fully producing oil wells and thousands of head of cattle), he called them all out by the Olympic-size swimming pool, which he had the amazing foresight of stocking with water moccasins, alligators, and other vicious beasts. He told the young men that the first one who jumped into the pool and swam the length would be given his choice of three things: one million dollars in cash, ten thousand acres of his best land, or the hand of his beautiful daughter in marriage. He even pointed out that his daughter was his only heir and that when he and his wife passed on, all of this big spread would belong to her and to the man who became her husband.

No sooner were the words spoken than there was a loud splash at one end of the pool, followed almost immediately by the emergence of a dripping wet young man from the other end of the pool. He had set a world's record that would never be approached, much less broken, in swimming the length of that pool.

As the crowd of young men and the girl's father rushed down to the other end of the pool to congratulate the young man, he stood there in eager anticipation. The host excitedly said, "Well, son, you've got your choice. Do you want the million in cash?" The young man responded, "No, sir." Then the host asked, "Do you want the ten thousand acres of my best land?" The young man responded, "No, sir." Finally the host said, "Then I guess you want the hand of my beautiful daughter in marriage!" To this the young man replied, "No, sir." Somewhat puzzled and a little frustrated, the host demanded, "Well, son, what *do* you want?" The young man responded, "What I want is to know the name of the dude that pushed me into the swimming pool!"

Now quite obviously this young man had a reason for what he was doing. It might not be what you originally expected it to be, but he had a reason. Question: Do you have a reason for what you do? Have you clearly identified your *reason, purpose, cause* . . . your MOTIVE? Are you willing to take action on that reason, purpose, or cause?

An equally important question: If you are trying to motivate others, have you *clearly* identified *their* reason, purpose, or cause? Or are you trying to get them to take action on *your* motives? Successful people who motivate themselves and others are aware of and *honestly* identify their motives—or those of the ones they would motivate—and then take the action steps necessary for success. Good managers encourage others to take the steps necessary for their personal success!

PERFORMANCE PRINCIPLES

1. Do you know *why* you do what you do?

2. Motivation = the motives we take action on.

3. Happiness is not a where or a when, it is a here and a now.

4. To motivate yourself, identify your motives and take action on them; to motivate others, identify their motives and encourage them to take action.

14

EDUCATION TO OVERCOME MANAGEMENT PARALYSIS

Only the educated are free.
Epictetus

Awareness
Analysis
Action

THE SECOND A in our Three-A Formula is *Analysis*. When I'm talking about analysis, I'm talking about education. There are three great immobilizers that keep you from succeeding and, as a matter of fact, keep all of us from accomplishing what we are capable of. The *only* way to overcome these immobilizers is through analysis and education. The immobilizers are FEAR, DOUBT, and WORRY. These are three negative uses of our imagination.

Let's take a closer look at this concept of FEAR: *False Evidence Appearing Real*. I could take a piece of cloth and my finger and chances are good I could come into your town and rob your bank. I could use the piece of cloth as a handkerchief to cover my face. Then I could put my finger in my coat pocket, giving it the appearance of a gun when I point it at a person. If I aimed it at the teller and said, "Give me your money!" I can guarantee you her palms would get sweaty and her heart would beat fast. At that point, she would give me the money. All the evidence would be false, but because it would appear to be real, the teller would act as if it were real.

You might have read about the young Cuban who hijacked a plane to Cuba with nothing but a bar of soap. He placed the soap in a shoe box, went up to the flight attendant, and said, "Hey, I've got a bomb in here." She said, "Oooooohhhh, you need to see the pilot!" He went to see the pilot and said, "Hey, I've got a bomb in here and I'd like to go to Cuba."

They went to Cuba. All the evidence was false, but because it *appeared* to be real, the captain acted as if it were real.

A Challenge for You

I want to challenge you to write down in the space provided your ten greatest fears, doubts, and worries. Now some of you might say, "I need more than ten blank spaces!" No, I said your ten *greatest* fears, doubts, and worries. If you have the courage to write them down, here is what you will find: Out of the ten items you listed, seven or eight will already have happened or cannot happen. Of the remaining items, you have absolutely no control over one or two of them. And you will find that only one or two items are within your control.

Question: Does it make sense to dissipate your energies over a long list of things you cannot control instead of focusing your energies on the one or two things you can effectively handle? Since the answer is obviously no, why do we fail to focus our energies on solvable problems?

My 10 Greatest
Fears, Doubts, & Worries

1. _____

2. _____

3. _____

4. _____

5. _____

6. _____

7. _____

8. _____

9. _____

10. _____

Answer: We refuse to focus our energies only on solvable problems because we are creatures of habit. We have an everyday routine that we are involved in, and if the routine is changed, it upsets us and can even spoil our whole day.

Unfortunately for our society, one of our most destructive habits is the habit of griping, complaining, and moaning. Or, as my associate Bryan Flanagan says, "We become members of the moan, groan, and carry on club!" Did you realize that some people would rather complain than succeed? If that sounds absurd to you, prove me wrong. Try eliminating the complaining and see if it doesn't help you move toward success more quickly. We live in a society which is used to being negative more than positive. For example, as my speaker friend Don Hutson says, economists have predicted eighteen of the last two recessions! People find fault as if there is a reward for it! Too many people look for the worst in others and never pass up the chance to cut down or criticize others.

Negative Use of the Imagination

As a general rule, I board an airplane from two to ten times each week. Obviously, I know that from time to time there are airplane crashes, so I recognize there is danger for me when I get aboard that aircraft. But realistically, there is even more danger for the airplane, because when airplanes come down faster than they go up, their trade-in value drops to virtually nothing. I mean, you just can't swap them at all!

Interestingly enough, however, though there is danger when the plane leaves the ground, there is even more danger if the plane remains *on* the ground. Engineers will quickly tell you that the plane will rust out sitting on the runway faster than it will wear out flying in the heavens—which is what airplanes are built for. When the ship leaves the harbor, there is certainly danger involved because, from time to time, ships do sink. But there's even more danger if the ship stays in the harbor. Again, the experts tell us that if it stays at anchor in the harbor it will collect barnacles and become unseaworthy faster than if it is sailing the high seas, which is why the ship was built in the first place.

If you rent out your home, you take a chance that the person you rent it to will damage it. In some cases, renters simply do not have pride of ownership and will not take as good care of your home as you would. However, my real estate friends assure me the house is in greater danger if you leave it empty. They tell me it will deteriorate faster standing empty than it will if someone is living in it, and besides, homes are built to be lived in.

Obviously, there is a certain amount of danger in doing anything, but in management there is generally even more danger in doing *nothing*. Man and nature are exact opposites in at least one respect: *We deplete nature's resources by using them up. We deplete man's natural resources by not using them at all.*

Oliver Wendell Holmes was right when he said the great tragedy in America is not the destruction of our natural resources, though that tragedy is great. He said the truly great tragedy is the destruction of our human resources by our failure to fully utilize our abilities, which means most men and women go to their graves with their music still in them. This tragedy is compounded when those of us in leadership positions do not utilize our abilities to properly direct and inspire those in our sphere of influence to become all they are capable of becoming.

The "subtitle" to our company name is "The People Builders," because our corporate purpose, our reason for being in business, is to help people recognize, develop, and use their abilities. One of the vehicles we use to accomplish this is the I CAN course, developed by Mrs. Mamie McCullough. This course is based on the philosophy I espouse in my book *See You at the Top*, and it has positively affected over three million students and teachers all over the United States and Canada.

Several years ago in Rockford, Illinois, a young lady named Marcie Lemaree was taking the I CAN class. I say "taking the class," but actually she literally had to be almost dragged into the classroom, screaming and kicking her feet. She was such a disruption that the teacher finally said, "Marcie, if you will go to the library and listen to the tapes that go along with the I CAN course, I won't turn you in to the principal." Well, that sounded a lot better than sitting in class, so she listened to the tapes and as she listened, some things started to make sense to her. Gradually her attitude changed. Marcie became involved in her school; she became aware of why her attitude was so important; she analyzed and got instruction on how she could be more effective; she became a manager of the basketball team and lettered in girls' track. She also placed fourth out of seven on the rifle team.

Now that might not sound like a big deal to you, but when I share with you (as Paul Harvey would say) "the rest of the story," it might make a difference. Marcie is legally blind. She had difficulty telling darkness from light. When she fired the rifle for the rifle team someone would say, "No, Marcie, you're a little low and to the left, you need to come up and to the right." Did Marcie have reason to FEAR, DOUBT, and WORRY? You bet she did! Did she overcome those FEARS, DOUBTS, and WORRIES? You bet she did! How? The same way you and I overcome our FEARS, DOUBTS, and WORRIES . . . through ANALYSIS and EDUCATION! Needless to say, she changed her input, which dramatically changed her output.

It Has Probably Happened to You

I think if you will search your memory bank you will be able to identify with this example. The ladies will obviously have a different perspective, but fellows, think back to the time you called a girl for your first date. You remember, you attempted to pick up the telephone and the receiver weighed a ton! You couldn't have lifted it with a crane! So you chickened out for the moment and decided that you would stop by that special person's home the next day after school. Remember how you felt as you sashayed up to that door, and just as you got ready to ring the bell you could feel the confidence draining—so much so that you didn't have the strength to ring that doorbell or knock on the door? Remember how you heard some rustling around inside and ran away because you didn't want the girl or her mother to find some "oddball" out on the porch?

But that series of events really made you *determined!* You charged directly to your home, snatched the phone off the hook, got the right person on the phone . . . and then you couldn't make an intelligible sound!

Now you really were more determined than ever! What embarrassment could be worse than not being able to speak? So you snatched up the phone again, got the special one on the phone, invited her to go out with you, and were told, "No, thank you."

As you hung up the phone you noticed you were still breathing and, to your complete shock and astonishment, your heart was still beating (admittedly faster, but still beating!). Remember saying, "Hey, it didn't kill me to get turned down, so I'll call somebody else"? So you called and called until the law of averages worked in your behalf and you finally persuaded someone to go out with you. Some of you even went on to get married after all that. The reason you were able to make the second and third call was that you overcame your fear, doubt, and worry through learning that it wasn't going to kill you to be turned down.

Managing Motivation Education

Most management books spend some time looking at behavioral scientists' view of motivation, and this can be so technical it is difficult to understand. My approach will seem to some an oversimplification, but as I have often said, some of the greatest truths in life are the simplest. For that reason, I generally speak and write at the seventh-grade, third-month level. I've also found that if I keep it at this level, even college professors will be able to keep up with me. But as my good friend Dr. Steve Franklin, a college professor from Emory University in Atlanta, Georgia, who gave me the preceding line, says, "The great truths in life are the simple ones. You don't need three moving parts or four syllables for something to be significant."

Steve pointed out to me that there are only three pure colors—but look at what Michelangelo did with those three colors! There are only seven notes, but look what Chopin, Beethoven, and Vivaldi did with those seven notes! (For that matter, look what Elvis did with two!) Lincoln's Gettysburg Address contained only 262 words and 202 of them were one syllable. Think of the impact those simple, direct words have had on our society! I know many of our problems are complex, but I believe a simple (not simplistic), direct approach, worded in simple, understandable terms, is the best and most effective way to get results. Now let's look at what three world-renowned behavioral scientists say about three important areas of our life.

Maslow—McGregor—Herzberg

The three most often quoted behavioral scientists are Abraham Maslow, who dealt with man's *needs* and the order in which they must be met; Douglas McGregor, who dealt with *personalities, values, and assumptions*; and Frederick Herzberg, who dealt with man's *reaction*—or *response*—to what his work is all about.

The truth is that managers and employees are constantly moving in and about these areas, and to understand and successfully complete our tasks, we must have a basic understanding of all three. Let's start with Maslow's theory.

Abraham Maslow believed that motivation is an "inside" job and is not determined by external factors. The internal factors begin with *basic needs* such as food, shelter, water, and air. The net level is the need for *security* or safety—to feel protected from danger. The third level of motivation is *social* in nature and deals with our need to belong to the team and to have the respect of others. The fourth level is the *ego* level where self-esteem, status, and recognition come into the picture. And finally, there is *self-actualization*, which is realizing our personal potential and becoming all we can become.

Maslow said these needs were *hierarchical,* which is just a fancy way of saying they must be met in order, one through five. However, an interesting aspect of his theory stated:

Once the need is satisfied it is no longer a motivator.

How can we help others through Maslow's theory? To meet a person's *basic needs* in the workplace, we must: (Now *slow down.* These are to be read and *acted* upon, not just read and agreed with.)

1. Create as pleasant and comfortable a working environment as possible.

2. Provide an adequate income so the person can provide for immediate creature needs, while creating the possibility of increased financial opportunity for additional creature comforts.

To meet a person's *security* or *safety needs* in the workplace, we must:

1. Not lose sight of the importance of *basic needs* being met.

2. Provide orderliness and consistency in relationships with superiors.

3. Provide protective rules, regulations, and policies.

4. Provide fringe benefits and seniority protection.

5. Provide clear and consistent Foundational Performance levels.

To meet a person's *belonging needs* in the workplace, we must:

1. Not lose sight of the importance of *basic needs* and *safety needs* being met.

2. Provide an opportunity to be a "member of the team."

3. Provide opportunities for developing relationships and being accepted and appreciated by team members.

4. Provide sincere concern for each team member and encourage him or her to do likewise.

To meet a person's *ego-status needs* in the workplace, we must:

1. Not lose sight of the importance of *basic needs, safety needs,* and *belonging needs* being met.

2. Provide a Recognition Program which rewards what the company sees as foundational concepts to company success.

3. Provide a Recognition Program which allows the person to be singled out for special recognition.

4. Provide a Recognition Program with different levels of recognition so that different levels of performance are recognized and employees compete with themselves and not always with one another.

5. Provide the opportunity for an employee to move up in areas of responsibility and be placed in "high profile" assignments to show skills.

6. Involve the person in planning activities; get his opinion.

To meet a person's *self-actualization needs* in the workplace, we must:

1. Not lose sight of the importance of *basic needs, safety needs, belonging needs,* and *ego-status needs* being met.

2. Allow the person the opportunity for more challenging work, and the freedom to be creative.

3. Reinforce a sense of personal growth in taking action.

4. Allow the work to become an "art" or mission.

5. Grant autonomy.

We looked at Douglas McGregor's Theory X and Theory Y in chapter 4, but let's take another look at how this can specifically apply to motivation. You will remember that Theory X is the basic *negative management assumption.* According to Theory X, workers inherently dislike work and will avoid it if possible, so management must coerce, control, direct every move, and threaten a lack of cooperation with punishment. Workers want to be led, according to this theory, and are without ambition, avoid responsibility, and seek only security. This means that as managers we must:

1. Lay out rigid and inflexible job standards.
2. Determine objectives without employee input.
3. Reward only those who stay within the system and punish those who don't.

Theory Y is the basic *positive management assumption*. According to Theory Y, workers feel that work is as natural as play and recreation. They are committed when properly rewarded, especially when rewarded for areas which promote self-respect and personal growth. Most workers are creative and actually seek more responsibility. This means as managers we must:

1. Provide high expectations and high standards.
2. Be even more reward and recognition conscious.
3. Be firm, fair, and consistent with standards.

Now I want to share something *profound* (just thought it would only be fair to warn you). Obviously, there is some of both of these workers in all of us . . . the key is not the ability in the worker but what the *assumption* does to the manager. Our *assumptions* lead to our *attitudes*, which lead to our *behavior*.

Management assumptions + management attitudes = management behavior

The third of our behavioral scientists is Frederick Herzberg, and to understand his concepts we need to understand the difference between dissatisfiers/demotivators and satisfiers/motivators. The motivators include interesting work, challenging work, personal achievement, recognition, and the opportunity for increased responsibility. This level has no ceiling and can continue to grow.

By contrast, the dissatisfiers are working relationships, company policies, working conditions, supervision, and compensation. And here is the key: Although you can achieve satisfaction in those areas, *satisfaction does not increase your motivation*. For example, poor company policies will create dissatisfaction; however, good policies will only create satisfaction, not motivation. Dissatisfiers cause different levels of dissatisfaction, but not different levels of motivation. For example, your idea of a good salary changes over a period of time, making dissatisfaction a reasonable possibility in the future.

Let's translate all this to some specific actions the manager might take and see if we can figure out what motivators are involved:

Action	Motivator
• take less control	• opportunity for growth/ responsibility/achievement
• establish more accountability	• responsibility/recognition/ rewards
• give job autonomy	• responsibility/achievement/ recognition
• provide more information	• internal recognition/ego satisfaction
• assign new and increasingly difficult tasks	• personal growth/career growth/financial growth

As *Top Performers*, our challenge is to understand all three areas and mix, match, and mold them to meet our personal needs and ambitions.

The next example out of the book of life pretty well sums up what this chapter is all about.

A Top Performer With Real Education

After reading this much of *Top Performance*, it might not surprise you that when I think of one of the smartest and most educated people I have ever known, I think of a person with a fifth-grade education. That person is my mother. I want to share a story with you that may seem a little unusual coming on the heels of the likes of Maslow, McGregor, and Herzberg, but I think it combines the best of all these men.

I shall never forget an incident which took place when I was a small boy in Yazoo City, Mississippi. Periodically I was given a chance to do a few odd jobs for an elderly couple who lived several blocks from us. They ran a small dairy and were probably in their late sixties or early seventies. The man was blind. We needed the extra money because things were desperately tight financially in the thirties.

I forget some of the details of the incident, but the bottom line is that something went astray. The lady berated me unmercifully and said I had not done what I had said I was going to do (she apparently subscribed to

Theory X) and therefore she was not going to pay me for the consider-able amount of work I had done.

When I went home in tears to tell my mother I was not going to be paid for what I had done, she was understandably unhappy. However, my mother was the most loving, wise, and gentle person I've ever known (the epitome of a Top Performer and the symbol of all the positive management skills taught in this book). She also had great faith and was most supportive and loyal. When I finished my story, she calmly took off her apron and said, "Let's go and talk with them, son."

My mother was a small lady. She was nearly fifty years old and all the years of her hard work had taken their toll. When we approached the couple, the lady proceeded to tell my mother in no uncertain terms that I had not done what she'd expected me to do, that I was not dependable, that I had lied to her, and any number of other things. My mother, as all good managers do, patiently heard her out, listening very, very carefully and quietly until the woman had finally finished.

Then my mother said, "Well, let me remind you that I was present when you hired my son to do this work. I remember exactly what you told him you wanted him to do in your yard and garden. Before I knocked on the door I made it a point to come by your garden. I can tell you that not only has my son done everything you hired him to do, but in my opinion he has done a real good job and thrown in some extras as well. My son did not lie to you about this and I want you to know that my son would never lie to you on any occasion about anything." Then my mother summed it up: "You owe my son the money, but whether you pay him or not is entirely up to you. I just wanted to make it very clear to you that my son is honest. If you don't pay him for what he has done, we will be able to live without the money, but are you going to be able to live with the money and the knowledge that you've unjustly accused my son of a wrong which he did not do? I leave it up to you as to whether or not you're going to pay him."

As nearly as I can recall, the lady was still adamant that I had not done what she had hired me to do and my mother closed the conversation by saying, "That's all right. We can get along without the money. You just let your conscience be your guide."

A few days later the lady stopped by the house with the money and apologized to both my mother and to me.

That was a particularly significant event in my life because my mother had stood by me and though it was many, many years ago, I shall never forget how grateful I was for the support she gave me. I believe incidents like this made a dramatic difference in my life. As managers and leaders, the support we give to our people when they are right is extremely important, and even when they are wrong we can defend their integrity while not agreeing with some of their actions.

Two of my mother's favorite sayings were, "It's not *who's* right, but *what's* right" . . . and, "If you've got the right person, what they're going to be doing is going to be right." Yes, my mother was a magna cum laude graduate of the school of life. If you will use the principles we are discussing in *Top Performance*, which she role modeled so effectively, then you, too, will be recognized as a manager who helps employees overcome Fear, Doubt, and Worry, and one who gets Top Performance from your people!

PERFORMANCE PRINCIPLES

1. Fear, Doubt, and Worry will immobilize you and your associates without the proper education.

2. Once a need is satisfied, it is no longer a motivator . . . satisfaction does not increase motivation.

3. Management Assumptions plus Management Attitudes equals Management Behavior.

15

THE SECRET TO MANAGEMENT MOTIVATION

Action often precedes the feeling.
Anonymous

Awareness

Analysis

Action

THE THIRD A in our Three-A Formula is *Action!* You are a person of *action.* It started this morning. You were lying in bed and that "opportunity" clock (negative folks call it an alarm clock!) went off. You reached over and shut it off, and in the process that cool air hit your elbow. And then you did what comes naturally . . . you quickly pulled your elbow back under the covers! Now you have a very basic decision to make: "Am I going to put *all* of me out there in that cold air, or am I going to keep *all* of me right here under these nice warm covers where I belong?" Because you are a responsible person with all the success characteristics we discussed in the first part of this book, the battle between *what you want to do* and *what you are committed to do* is won by the *what you are committed to do,* and you roll out of bed. It's obvious to you and to every other success-oriented person that nothing happens until you take that first step—nothing happens until you get the action habit.

I want to share with you one phrase which I honestly believe is worth the price of this book. Now, just in case you're thinking, *Well, why didn't you put it on the first page and leave the rest out?* the answer is, "I don't want you to just get your money's worth . . . I want you to get a bargain." The reason is partly benevolent and partly selfish. As stated earlier, I firmly believe that you can have everything you want in life if you will just help enough other people get what they want. So why do I want you to get so much from this book? Answer: The more you get, the more people you will tell about the book, which simply means the sale of more books. Now, here's that powerful magic statement:

> *Logic will not change an emotion, but ACTION will!*

Or, phrased another way:

> *Action often precedes the feeling!*

For example, I hate to be the one to break the news to you, but there are going to be days when you won't want to get out of bed and go to work. I know it will surprise some of you, but there really are going to be those days. However, sometimes the best work is done by people who don't want to do the things they have to do, but they have the old-fashioned guts, gumption, and sense of responsibility to get up and go! Who are the successful people? They are the people who do the things unsuccessful people refuse to do! They understand that every task they handle is a self-portrait of the person who performed it, and they have committed themselves to autograph every job with excellence.

As I stated in my book *See You at the Top*, one year I finished second in a national organization which employed over seven thousand sales-people. Later I finished first in another national organization that had over three thousand people in sales. I can state without reservation that there were many days when I did not feel like going to work, but actually started to feel like working after I got into action. Here is a key point: Not once in that year when I was number two of seven thousand did I finish in the top twenty in sales for a single week. Not once in that time did I finish in the top twenty for a single month. Yet at the end of the year I was second in the organization. How did this happen? Simple! I disciplined myself to start *every* day by being in front of a prospect by no later than 9:00 A.M. The net result was *some* business *every* week, so that by the end of the year the cumulative total was enough to put me in second place.

As you well know, big jobs are accomplished by taking lots of small steps. Question: How do you eat an elephant? One bite at a time! How do you lift a cow? By lifting a baby calf every day of its life! How do you lose 37 pounds? By losing 1.9 ounces per day for ten months. How do you effectively lead your people to greater accomplishments and move steadily up the ladder of success? By steadily, on a daily basis, giving your job a "best effort." The only way to coast is downhill, isn't it?

You've Heard It Before—Take One Step at a Time

My sister-in-law, Eurie Abernathy, has had multiple sclerosis (MS) for many years. In 1985 she spent several days with us over the Christmas holidays. It was her first visit in our new two-story home. Because of the MS, I assumed she could not make it up the stairs to the second floor, so I was surprised when I returned home one day and found the Redhead and her seated in our bedroom, enjoying a chat. After a few minutes, Eurie decided to go back downstairs. As a precaution, I walked in front of her so that if she should start to fall I could catch her. As we made our way downstairs, I expressed surprise that she had been able to go up the stairs, which are relatively steep. She quickly responded with a simple but profound statement: "Yes, I can do anything I want to do, as long as I take it one step at a time." The opportunity for greatness, according to the late sales trainer Charlie Cullen, does not come cascading down like a torrential Niagara Falls. Rather it comes slowly, one drop at a time!

10 *ACTION* Steps to Success

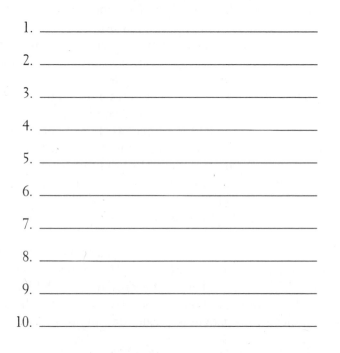

1. _____

2. _____

3. _____

4. _____

5. _____

6. _____

7. _____

8. _____

9. _____

10. _____

Here is your challenge: Make a list of your ten most important Action Steps to Success. Not what someone else must do to succeed, not what someone else thinks *you* should do to succeed, but what *you know you must do every day!* I fully understand that you do more than ten things daily, but what are the ten most important activities that translate to success for you?

At the time I set the sales records I spoke of, I was selling cookware. I was conducting demonstration parties, cooking with the heavy-duty waterless cookware I was encouraging people to buy. Many times it would be 1:00 A.M. before the kitchen was cleaned and everyone was gone, but number one on my list was to be face-to-face with a prospect at 9:00 A.M. the next day. Regardless of the fact that the baby kept us up until 3:30; despite the fact that the car had a flat tire or wouldn't start; regardless of any excuses, I was to be face-to-face with a live prospect at 9:00 A.M. *every morning!* When we set our goals and break them into bite-size pieces, there is no limit to what will be accomplished. A commitment to *start* each day at the same time and in the same way is really a commitment to finish, because starting is obviously the first step in arriving. The Chinese were right: A journey of a thousand leagues begins with a single step.

What's Holding You Back?

It is an established fact that the largest and most powerful locomotive in the world can be held in place by a one-inch block of wood. Placed in front of the eight drive wheels of the locomotive, the block will hold it completely motionless. Yet that same locomotive, with a full head of steam, can crash through a steel-reinforced concrete wall that is five feet thick. That is what getting the action habit can do for us! This next example by William Moulton Marston is from the world of sports, but it certainly applies to us in the world of business.

Hitting the Ball

I asked Babe Ruth what was the most exciting moment of his career, and he told me it was during the third game of his last World Series in Chicago. He was in a batting slump, his team was behind, and two strikes had been called on him. The crowd turned against the Babe and began to boo. Ruth's desire to win rose to meet this emergency and he flashed into action. He pointed to a distant spot in the outfield and yelled back at the howling fans, "I'll knock it out there for you!"

Babe smashed the next ball to that precise spot. It was a home run, the longest hit ever made in Wrigley Field. I asked him what he thought about when the ball was pitched.

"What'd I think about?" he snorted. "Why, what I always think about—just hittin' the ball!"

There's your champion, the man who keeps his attention riveted upon his present act and who responds positively to every crisis or desire with all there is in him. With the outcome of a World Series and his own contract for next year hanging in the balance, Ruth thought about hitting the ball. And because he wanted to win more than he ever had before, he hit the ball hard.

The next time you find yourself in a jam, with a string of mistakes behind you and everything hanging on your next move, forget both past and future. Remember Babe Ruth and think about just one thing—hitting the ball.

Let yourself go—give everything you have to your desire to win before the crisis passes. It will be the best performance you ever produced because of the emotional steam behind it. Every crisis offers you extra desired power.

Personal Conviction: Positive Thinking and Positive Believing

When we talk about being people of action, we recognize that action takes courage. Gerhard Gschwandtner of Fredericksburg, Virginia, publishes an excellent sales publication called *Personal Selling Power*, which I highly recommend. One of my favorite parts of Gerhard's format is the interview with action-oriented people. In a recent issue, Mo Siegel was the "interviewee." Now, Mo Siegel is the founder and former owner (he recently sold the business) of Celestial Seasonings, the herbal tea company which captured a major portion of the multimillion-dollar tea industry. He based his organization on a value system he equates with the four legs on a stool. The first leg is *love of product*. Mo Siegel surrounded himself with people who really loved herbal tea and believed it to be valuable to the consumer. The second leg of the stool was *love of customer* (which, in the case of Celestial Seasonings, was distributors). Celestial Seasonings put the customer first in quality-control decisions. The third leg of the stool was *love of art and beauty*, which led Mo Siegel to develop one of the most detailed (and expensive) packaging programs in retail sales. The fourth leg of the stool was *dignity of the individual*. Celestial Seasonings treated everyone (including employees) with the dignity every human being deserves. Any time a serious question arose within the organization, Mo Siegel said the solution would lie within the answers to two more questions: (1) Is the customer happy? (2) Are we making the best possible product?

The answer to that second question led him to commission "blind tea taste tests" in which his product consistently beat the major "black tea" or nonherbal teas which have the major share of the market. Despite overwhelming evidence that Celestial Seasonings had a superior product, Mo Siegel refused to use the concept in an advertising campaign. His personal convictions led him to spend his time and resources in serving the customer better. He stated, "I decided I did not want to make a fortune by bad-mouthing anybody!"

With the current trend in advertising doing exactly that, Mo Siegel's decision was one requiring courage and integrity. Siegel went on to say that "an organization values what it dedicates its time and resources to." In his case it is obvious that he values integrity. He also stated that the reason he was able to grow so big so quickly was his commitment to training. He said that managers need a minimum of thirty hours of training per year and salespeople need even more. I might add I agree with him that training is tremendously important, because it helps change a person from a "positive thinker" to a "positive believer."

Here's the difference: Positive thinking is the optimistic hope—not necessarily based on any facts—that you can move mountains or accomplish other seemingly impossible tasks. I've seen positive thinking and positive thinkers accomplish some incredible things. I've also seen some people get into serious trouble because all they had was positive thinking and enthusiasm. They had no foundations, no skills, no training. Consequently, they let their enthusiasm carry them away and they ended up in serious difficulties. (Someone has said that positive thinking and enthusiasm is like running in the dark—it might get you there, but you might get killed along the way!) Add training to that positive thinking and enthusiasm and you turn on the lights for your trip to the top—which means you will arrive alive.

Positive believing is the same optimistic hope as positive thinking, but it is based on solid reasons for believing you can move mountains or accomplish other seemingly impossible tasks. I've seen positive believers accomplish far more than positive thinkers. Positive believers have even more enthusiasm than positive thinkers because their enthusiasm is based on solid reasons, which gives them the motivation for the long haul, even when things are not going well at the moment.

A good training program—which is obviously what Mo Siegel was talking about—gives the members of his organization solid reasons for believing they can accomplish much with their lives. They believe in their company, they believe in their product, and training enables them to believe in their ability to communicate that belief to others who will, in turn, take action by buying.

I might add this simple example to further illustrate the difference between positive thinking and positive believing: If you are a positive thinker, you probably feel you could set sail for France today and successfully sell your product in that country. If your product is a highly sophisticated one that is sold only in the big cities to successful businesspeople, the odds would be fairly favorable because most of those people would also speak a second language—probably English—and you would be able to communicate with them. However, if your product is one which is sold in the rural areas, the odds are great they would only be able to speak French. With only "positive thinking" on your list of skills, you would have serious difficulty communicating the merits of your product to those prospects. A positive believer, however, would be one who knew the French language and understood something of the culture and the thinking of the people. Consequently, if you were to study the language and the culture and prepare yourself properly to deal with the situations you would encounter in rural France, your chances of being successful would be dramatically increased.

Positive thinking is always important and it certainly will enable you to accomplish more than negative thinking will—but positive believing will enable you to do infinitely more than just positive thinking will. That's why in *Top Performance* we give so many steps, procedures, and actions to follow so that, as a leader and as a manager, you move more and more into the positive-believing realm.

A Very "Moving" Experience

In April and May of 1985, the Zig Ziglar Corporation headquarters was relocated. We had outgrown our building located on Alpha and Omega because in approximately five years we had grown from less than fifteen employees to over sixty employees. About now some of the more astute of you readers are wondering why it took nearly two full months to move a company of less than one hundred employees! To be very honest with you, I had the same question myself!

Due to circumstances beyond our control, we needed to vacate the building we owned and had sold at Alpha and Omega by March 31. However, our new facility wasn't to be ready until May 15. Six to eight weeks without office space is not the best way to run a business. There was every opportunity for "stinkin' thinkin' " to creep into the attitude of our staff. However, due to the excellent leadership of Ron Ezinga, ZZC president, and Den Roossien, ZZC executive vice-president, and our divisional leaders, these two months became the two largest dollar-volume months to that point in the history of our company! Everyone worked from their homes with the exception of a skeleton crew which handled the computer and order-processing station we kept at our old building, and a valiant crew who manned the phones in the new building. I say "valiant" because the only space available in the new building was an area designed to be used for storage that measured approximately ten-by-fourteen feet. Initially there was no electricity or heating in this area.

For about a week these brave ladies answered phones by the natural light of a partially open door. They wrapped themselves in blankets and stocking caps to ward off the cold. After the first week, we got electricity into the room and the door could be kept shut, though there still was no heat except from portable units. There was *never* any grousing or complaining by this group (who, by the way, had volunteered to take care of the phones). They worked the phones and coordinated activities between two locations for offices and approximately forty-five or fifty homes.

Every person in our company *had* to pitch in to make the move work, and frankly most of us would have been glad just to keep from losing a large amount of business. But I am proud to be able to report to you that our "People Building Team" worked together to prove that they are "products of our product" and turned a potentially losing problem into a winning opportunity!

The "Team" Concept

A great deal of emphasis is almost always given to the team concept in superior management books. At the Zig Ziglar Corporation we believe in and stress this concept. As a matter of fact, each leadership unit functions as a team and is given a team name. Our organizational chart looks like this:

The Customer: Everyone's check ultimately signed by the customer. The customer allows us to stay in business so he belongs at the top of our chart.

The People Building Team: This is the name we give to our staff. The People Building Team works for the customer.

The Leadership Team: This is the name we give our department heads and divisional leaders. Their responsibility is to give leadership and direction to the company, and they work for the People Building Team.

The Development Team: This is the name we give our corporate officers. Their responsibility (in addition to leading their respective areas of the company) lies in long-range planning and development. They work for the Leadership Team.

Zig Ziglar: This is my name. My "title" is Chairman of the Board. My responsibility is to speak and write and give "vision" and "direction" to our organization. I work for all these people!

Most people would say that our triangle is upside down. I think that after getting this far into *Top Performance* you understand that this is the best way for a company to reach its full potential. At a recent People Building Team meeting we shared the following article, "From 9–5." Because it does such a great job of summarizing this team concept, I wanted to share it in full with you.

"Have You Joined the Team?"

Most of us work in departments as part of a network of people who make up our company's team. If our company's service or product is good, there are others to share the credit. If it's poor, there are people to share the blame. But if we believe the old saying that a chain is only as strong as its weakest link, we know that our company's performance is only as good as ours.

Each of us makes a choice as to the role we'll play on the team. We either join it as an actively caring member, or we go through the motions from the sidelines. When we choose to join the team, we have a better, surer shot at work that brings us satisfaction. The choice is ours. Here are the key attitudes that take us off the sideline.

I make a difference here. *I know that what I do makes it possible for my office to run smoothly. The effort I put into my job shows up in the quality of my office's services and in my company's earnings.*

I'm part of what outsiders see when they judge my organization. With every letter, every phone conversation, every personal contact, I make a statement about the caliber of service we offer. In the course of a year, I make hundreds of valuable business contacts for us.

How I feel on a given day affects the people I work with. I help to set the tone here. I know that when I bring real enthusiasm to the job, I make a contribution few others can equal.

I take responsibility for what bothers me. *When a situation is causing me trouble at work, I approach it as my problem. Whether it's a procedure which isn't working, a practice I feel is unfair, or a person I'm having difficulty working with, I do what I can to change the situation. Sometimes it takes patience. More often than not, it takes knowing when to speak up and when to wait, and how to coolly and rationally use my powers of persuasion.*

When I can't get a situation changed, I look for ways to minimize its effect on me. Most important, I remember that I've chosen to work here, and so long as I'm here, I'll give my best.

I take an interest in my company. *I know that an organization is greater than the sum of its parts; it has a life and personality of its own. I'm interested in how this company got to be what it is today, and how the people in it have grown as it has.*

My knowledge of the workings of the company not only helps me in my work, but also makes the work more interesting. It's part of what makes me a valuable employee here; and it helps me set my own career goals and plan my future.

I try to see the big picture—to think beyond my particular job to the kind of product or service I'd like to receive as a customer or client. Because I'm interested in what makes us successful, I notice what's happening in business, politics, or technology that's going to affect us.

I'm proud to be a strong, reliable member of my company's team. I know that my success, as well as my company's, depends on it.

Action completes our Three-A Formula. Action brings Awareness and Analysis to fruition. Top Performance as a person or as a manager depends on all three. If you will take Action on the concepts we have talked about in this chapter and consciously make a decision to join the team, then you will become even more of a Top Performer.

PERFORMANCE PRINCIPLES

1. More people act their way into thinking than think their way into acting.

2. Logic won't change an emotion, but action will.

3. Action often precedes the feeling.

4. If the first three principles sound a great deal alike, Congratulations! You are catching on!

16

IT TAKES TIME

There can be no persevering industry without a deep sense of the value of time.

Lydia H. Sigourney

THE UNFORTUNATE TRUTH is that far too many executives are so gung ho and goal-oriented from a career point of view that they often lose perspective and balance as far as their personal, family, and social lives are concerned. The prime reason for this chapter, which I consider the most important one in the book, is to encourage you to become a Top Performer in your personal, family, and social life as well as in your business career. Interestingly enough, when you live the balanced life in your personal, home, and community life, in the long run you will do better in your business career. Yes, I know what you're thinking: *But Ziglar, there are only twenty-four hours in the day.* I agree that it takes time and, as a matter of fact, that is the title of this chapter, so let's get on with it.

Take Time to Get Started

The chances are better than good that you have fallen victim to that great American habit of sleeping as late as is humanly possible and then, when that "opportunity clock" sounds off, you hop out of bed and go through all the procedures which are so popular in America today.

We generally get up at least thirty minutes too late, turn on the coffeemaker, the radio, the television, rush in to shave and shower or apply our makeup. We awaken the kids in a big, big bustle, get them out of bed telling them to "hurry, hurry, or we're going to be late!" It generally takes about two trips, however, to get them up and the second trip is not even as pleasant as the first one. They're sleepy and in most cases slow-moving. We finally get them half-dressed, rush them into the den, plop a bowl of sugar-rich, nutritionless cereal in front of them, encourage them to hurry while we're drinking our coffee and eating our piece of toast or a generally inadequate breakfast.

We hustle to get dressed, quickly put the dishes in the sink or in the dishwasher, make certain the cat has been fed and put outdoors, bundle the kids up, rush out to the car, back out the driveway fighting for every traffic break, silently most of the time but vociferously some of the time, fussing at those people who delay our progress toward our assigned goal. We dump the kids out at school, drive hurriedly or madly on down to the office, where we're in a hurry-hurry environment all day long.

In a nutshell, it's a serious mistake to start your day that way because the way you start your day often determines how that day is going to go and will ultimately play a part in *how many* days you have.

With that in mind, I urge you to start your day in an organized but pleasant and relaxed way. You should do one of three things, and all of them involve getting up earlier.

One option you have is to start the day quietly in one of two ways. Select a quiet nook in your home, such as an office, a library, the den, or someplace away from the flow of traffic. As a leader and manager in your company, you need to start the day refreshed and prepared for the day's activities. From my personal experience, I can tell you that when I rise early and have that quiet time, my day goes better—much better. This excerpt from an article by Eugene Peterson in the November 8, 1985 issue of *Christianity Today* puts it in proper perspective:

In Herman Melville's Moby Dick *there is a violent, turbulent scene in which a whaleboat scuds across the frothing ocean in pursuit of the great white whale, Moby Dick. The sailors are laboring fiercely, every muscle taut, all attention and energy concentrated on the task. The cosmic conflict between good and evil is joined: the chaotic sea and demonic sea monster versus the morally outraged man, Captain Ahab.*

In this boat there is one man who does nothing. He does not hold an oar; he does not perspire; he does not shout. He is languid in the crash and the cursing. This man is the harpooner, quiet and poised, waiting. And then this sentence: "To insure the greatest efficiency of the dart, the harpooners of this world must start to their feet out of idleness, and not from out of toil."

In the corporate world we might not be faced with the physical danger, nor have a great need for a burst of physical energy, but we are faced with different kinds of "opportunities" which are emotionally and physically draining. To move into these challenges from a time of restful rejuvenation can make a significant difference in our effectiveness.

One of my favorite methods of doing this is to start the day—especially in cold weather—in my office at home with the gas log burning. Sometimes I sit there quietly, thinking through a planned project or agenda, wrestling with the best and most creative way to handle an "opportunity," quoting Scripture or thinking on inspirational thoughts or messages. The first few minutes are the toughest. The temptation to get up and move around is sometimes overwhelming, but I can assure you that if you will quietly sit there, some very creative, inspiring thoughts and ideas will be yours by the time you rise.

You also can, without any notes, quietly work through some situations in which you've been involved. Maybe there's a problem or a puzzle you've been unable to solve. As you are sitting there (in most cases not totally awake), you're still in the "alpha" level of consciousness. At this level your creativity is at its very, very best—a marvelous, extremely productive way to start the day!

The second option you have in starting your day also involves getting up earlier and this option includes reading something of an inspirational nature, such as the Bible or an inspirational book, or listening to recordings which are motivational in nature. Reading or listening are both marvelous ways to get "up" for the day. As a matter of fact, some psychologists have determined that your first encounter of the day has a more direct bearing on your attitude for that day than your next five encounters. Now, I'm not speaking about a "hello" encounter; I'm talking about a significant encounter where you spend time with a person. With this in mind, if you set aside fifteen to thirty minutes early in the morning to "encounter" someone of your choice, either to listen to an inspirational recording or dig into an inspirational book, you will have made a deliberate choice of starting your day with someone who will lift you and inspire you. With that kind of start, it's much easier to keep the momentum going.

The third option for the day, and a very effective way to start it, is with exercise. Later in this chapter I will give you the whys of an exercise program, but it is sufficient to say that one of the most exciting ways to start your day is with physical exercise of some kind. This can involve calisthenics, a swim or bicycle ride, a walk, or it could involve jogging. At any rate, a good exercise program gets the adrenaline flowing and those endorphines to hoppin', and you've got the day off to a flying start.

Yes, I'm absolutely convinced that when you start your day in one of these three ways, and then awaken the other members of the family, your prospects for a productive day are infinitely greater. Your mate will be especially appreciative and you can enhance your family relationship if you awaken him or her with that steaming cup of coffee (or better yet, herbal tea), and a few minutes of getting reacquainted in the morning. Then casually and lovingly awaken the children and while one team member prepares breakfast, the other one can help the kids get ready for school.

Since breakfast is such an important part of the day, both physically and emotionally, husband and wife (and children, if there are any) should sit down and, at a more leisurely pace, have a nutritious breakfast together. It properly starts the kids' day, the family's day, and your day on a high note. It will make an overall difference in your own attitude and your own physical well-being—not to mention what it will do for the kids and your mate. When this happens, more harmony in the family will develop.

One thing that is becoming more and more obvious is that when there is harmony in the family, the effectiveness of the manager on the job is noticeably enhanced. As part of this concept, we know a good, nutritious breakfast enables a person to perform more efficiently and effectively during the day. Eating together establishes bonds between family members that simply cannot be established in any other way. They are most effective. I say it again—take time to get started.

Take Time to Grow

We have emphasized throughout *Top Performance* the necessity of personal growth for maximum business success. We're all familiar with the story of the woodcutter whose production kept going down because he did not take time to sharpen his axe. As we've indicated throughout the book, the top companies, the ones with the exciting bottom lines, have training and personal growth as major corporate objectives. It's true, the companies "on the go" are also "on the grow." Individually *you* need to take time to grow.

There are many ways to do this, of course, but one of the most effective ways is the utilization of the cassette player in your car. There are literally thousands of hours of recorded material which can be enormously helpful to you while you're going to and from your work. You can learn everything from Chinese art to a foreign language. You can learn how to set goals or close sales. You can learn how to invest in real estate and save on your income tax.

As a matter of fact, a study done several years ago at the University of Southern California revealed that you can acquire the equivalent of two years of college education in just three years while you're going about your normal activities in your automobile. This is assuming you live in a metropolitan area and drive twelve thousand miles each year.

Think about it. By utilizing your time in your car you can become knowledgeable—even expert—in your chosen field and several related ones. That gives you incredible security, regardless of what happens to your company or your relationship with your company. The exciting thing is that to acquire knowledge in that method is one of the fastest, easiest, and certainly one of the most painless ways ever devised.

You also can grow through the utilization of the marvelous books which are available today. The bookstores carry an enormous assortment of books which deal with virtually any subject related to your career and specifically with any aspect of dealing with self and interpersonal relationships. Needless to say, the public library also offers a variety of books if you do not feel inclined to buy them. It is my own personal conviction, however, that as a manager and as a leader, you need to build a substantial library of your own. Personally, I would hesitate to put a price tag on the dollar value of my library, but it would run into thousands of dollars.

Let me offer a couple of suggestions about how you should read and effectively use your books. First—and I realize this sounds selfish—I encourage you to be protective with your books. Keep them for your own personal use or permit others to use them only in your library. In most cases, I encourage you to say no to anyone who wants to borrow a book. (I know for a fact that people often don't return books. For example, I have a number of books in my own library and have no idea how they got there!) If someone cannot afford the book, then do one of two things: encourage him or her to join the library or, if it's a friend, go ahead and buy the book for him. As you build your career and develop your leadership skills, you need to have at your fingertips the resources you accumulate. Needless to say, most doctors and attorneys do not loan their resource material. Your needs are fully as great and your professionalism should certainly be equal to a doctor or lawyer.

When I read a book, or *anything* else, I always have a pen in my hand and I profusely mark the parts which are important to me. I underline, circle, make notes, etc. In the front of the book I jot down page numbers of those things that are particularly important and significant and which I feel will be useful in the future. I then file the books in my library according to the categories of study. This way, when I need information on a particular subject, I go to the correct section, open the book, and find notations in front directing me exactly where to find what I need.

Of all the skills which I have acquired, I believe the ability to read and to enjoy reading is one of the most important things I've ever learned. I encourage you, as a leader, to not only teach your children how to read but also to teach them how to *enjoy* the reading—make it come alive for them and they will be better for having done it. Ditto for your associates and subordinates. As you read the good books and listen to the good tapes, you'll have a daily source of magnificent inspiration.

The third area of growth should be through meetings and seminars. There are many marvelous educational seminars around this country which can help you to hone your skills and develop them to the degree that will enable you to move up the ladder of success and happiness much faster and more effectively. As a practical matter, you should set aside at least one full week each year to go to seminars and personal-growth opportunities which enable you to develop and bring out your inherent abilities. You should also be open to attending half-day and full-day specialized seminars once or twice each month.

I say it again: To really make it big in life—in all areas of your life—you need to take time to grow. It's not a question of whether you do or do not have time. Obviously you do not have that option. You don't have time *not* to grow.

Take Time to Be Healthy

One question I often ask my audiences is if there is a person there who has a thoroughbred horse worth in excess of a million dollars. So far, no one has seriously raised a hand to indicate he has one. I then ask the question "If you *did* have a thoroughbred worth a million dollars, would you keep him up half the night, letting him drink coffee or booze, smoke cigarettes, and eat junk food?" At this everybody laughs, because they realize that not only do thoroughbreds not drink coffee or booze or smoke cigarettes, but the idea of jeopardizing the horse's health—which obviously destroys the performance of the animal—would be so ridiculous as to be beyond discussion.

Then I ask, "Suppose you had a ten-dollar dog? Would you treat him that way?" And again, there's laughter. "What about a five-dollar cat?" Then I point out that most of us would not treat a five-dollar cat like we treat our own billion-dollar bodies. As far as a million-dollar thoroughbred is concerned, if we had such an animal we would probably keep him in an air-conditioned barn in the summertime and a steam-heated one in the wintertime. We'd hire the best veterinarian money could buy to look after him, and bring in a special nutritionist to make certain he was properly fed. In addition to that, we would get the finest trainer available to develop his potential. You can count on it, you would take care of a million-dollar thoroughbred, and yet we abuse our own billion-dollar bodies.

Actually, to take care of our bodies is a reasonably simple routine. I did not say "easy." There are several factors involved and, since I'm not an expert on any of them, I will simply make some observations and aim you at some of the experts. To begin with, I would encourage you to pick up Dr. Kenneth Cooper's book *The Aerobics Program for Total Well-Being*. This deals not only with exercise but with proper nutrition as well.

One of the things you need to consider is the amount of sleep you get. Some people do quite well on four or five hours. In my own case, I've discovered that it requires seven and one-half hours of sleep for me to achieve Top Performance. Since I know that, I conscientiously work at getting that amount of sleep each evening. Now, I can get by one night with much less sleep and do fairly well the second night, but if it goes three nights in a row, I can guarantee you that by the third day I am at considerably less than my most effective best. For that reason, I work and concentrate on getting a reasonable amount of sleep.

Exercise is the second area which is extremely important. I am a jogger by choice—I literally *love* to jog. However, there are many people who do not like that particular exercise. According to Dr. Cooper, the important thing is that you keep your heartbeat up for at least twenty minutes on about four occasions each week. Fast walking is a marvelous exercise. Riding a stationary bicycle—or, for that matter, one in the streets—is excellent exercise. You might consider those rebounders where you simply bounce up and down—they do a great job. Others prefer swimming, and some experts say that is the most desirable of all exercise programs. Still others enjoy cross-country skiing or racquetball, tennis, etc. The important thing is that you keep that heartbeat up at least twenty minutes on about four days each week. Intelligent adults always begin their exercise programs by seeing their doctors. Please *do not* skip this most important step.

I am often asked, "Well, Zig, with as much as you have to do, when do you have time to exercise? When do you have time to jog?" I often tell people that I've got so much to do, I don't have time *not* to exercise. Incidentally, when I'm on the road and the weather is bad, I jog up and down the corridors of the hotel or motel where I'm staying. On occasion I go into the hotel ballroom or meeting room and run around it. On other occasions, I've jogged in the shopping malls. I am not a hero and therefore do not run around dark streets at night. If the weather's good but it's night and I'm not absolutely certain of the area, I simply run in the parking lot or the parking garage of the facility at which I am staying.

From a time point of view, let me point out that when you jog or exercise, you activate the pituitary gland. The pituitary gland floods the system with endorphines which are over two hundred times more powerful than morphine. The net result is you are on a "natural chemical high" from two to as much as four or even five hours. I have found the best time investment ever to be my time invested in exercise. An hour invested in exercise (counting time to dress, exercise, shower, cool down, etc.) returns two to four times that much high productivity time. The ideal time, according to Dr. Cooper, is in the latter part of the afternoon or early evening. By exercising then, you actually extend your effective work day by several hours.

Number three, in order to be at your healthiest, I encourage you to eat a sensible diet. By that, I mean a well-balanced diet and again, Dr. Cooper's book will be helpful. In my own diet, I concentrate on fresh vegetables, fish, chicken, and whole-grain cereals, and I seek as much roughage as possible. In addition to that, though there is widespread disagreement on this subject, I take and have been taking a natural food supplement for a number of years. Many doctors will tell you that in a well-balanced diet you will get the minimum daily requirements for your health. My point, though, is simply that I am not interested in minimum daily requirements. I am interested in maximum daily performance, and for that reason I do use a natural food supplement.

The fourth step in caring for your health is to eliminate the negatives. Smoking is a tremendous negative. Nineteen deaths out of every one hundred are directly traced to the habit of smoking. Every time you light a cigarette you have chosen to die fourteen minutes earlier. Needless to say, if you smoke cigarettes you're not going to enjoy the maximum health which you could otherwise enjoy.

Booze is another one of those elements in your life which in most cases can be enormously destructive. If you are a "casual" drinker, I would encourage you to read *Dying for a Drink* by Anderson Spickard, M.D., and Barbara R. Thompson, and it might put drinking in a different perspective. I don't pretend to be an authority on the subject, but I've seen a great deal of grief resulting from drinking and I do know that one "casual, social" drinker out of nine will eventually end up with a serious drinking problem. I also know that alcohol is a depressant and that people don't function as effectively when they've had a drink as they do without that drink.

Obviously, the other poisons you want to eliminate are those harmful legal and illegal drugs. The evidence against pot, speed, cocaine, and heroin, as well as many other drugs, is overwhelming. I cannot believe anyone with the intellectual capacity to occupy a leadership or management position would be so foolish as to ignore the overwhelming evidence as to what these substances do to a person and then deliberately "play" with them on a casual, "sometimes" basis.

Thus far in my own career I have never met a single human being who deliberately set out to become an alcoholic or who deliberately had as an objective to become a "pothead" or a drug addict. The question you need to ask yourself is, "Is it worth even a slight risk to experiment with these substances which can destroy me personally, socially, career-wise, and wreck my family all at the same time?" No, when I'm talking about taking time to be healthy, I'm talking about eliminating the poisons which some people choose to put into their systems.

Take Time to Play

Most of the gung ho businessmen and women I know set goals on acquiring new cars, getting promotions, having a certain amount of money in the bank, living at a certain residence, acquiring some educational degree, achieving that plateau of accomplishment, excelling in this area. They set goals in every area of their lives, but often they do not set their objectives properly when it comes to taking time to play. I am absolutely convinced that unless we schedule recreational activities for ourselves and for our families, our own mental, physical, social, and family relationships are going to suffer. When that happens, it's just a question of time before our careers will suffer.

When you check on the top-level executives—those who occupy positions of responsibility—you discover that one of the major problems is executive burnout. This problem can be at least partially alleviated with a willingness to take the time to play. It could be racquetball or tennis or a regularly scheduled round of golf. It could be playing on the company slow-pitch softball team or pickup basketball. My friend Dr. James Dobson, the Christian psychologist who has such an effective work through his radio ministry and through his publications, is one of the busiest men I've ever encountered. Yet he regularly sets aside time for basketball. He and his family go skiing. He takes care of his physical and family well-being by indulging in these forms of exercise.

I believe the capacity to relax and enjoy yourself is an absolute must for those who would climb the ladder and then maintain their position once they have achieved it. You bring a fresh perspective, a fresh excitement, a fresh enthusiasm to what you're doing when you are enjoying life itself. I don't mean just enjoying your job but also enjoying the fact that you are alive and well, and that you are getting more out of life than a paycheck. A move up the corporate ladder and recognition as a community leader can be, even *should* be, your objectives. Financial success and corporate ladder climbing are worthy objectives, but within themselves they do not make you happy if you're not having fun along the way. There is nothing wrong with scheduling your playtime just as enthusiastically as you schedule your work time. I'm assuming you understand that I'm not talking about playing as much as you work, but a regular game of handball or racquetball, a round of golf, or an evening with the family at the movies, theater, church, or community activity on a regular basis can make a difference in your quality of life as well as your accomplishments in life.

Take Time to Be Quiet

When I handle the next subject in my speeches, I always prepare the audiences by saying, "My next statement is probably going to surprise you, because generally speaking I am quite outgoing." I'm so "loud" from the platform that you might not realize or think in terms of my being quiet, but actually I am by nature a quiet person. Regardless of our natures, *all* of us need to take time to be quiet. I've never known anyone who accomplished major objectives in life who did not take time to be quiet.

As I indicated when I talked about "Take Time to Get Started," we do live in a busy and noisy world and there are those occasions when your batteries are simply going to run down. When that happens, no amount of superficial charging is going to restore those energy cells to their proper level unless you do take that time to be quiet. I dearly love to jog, and my favorite time to jog, particularly in the summer months, is at around nine o'clock in the evening under a bright, moonlit sky. It seems that when those conditions prevail and I'm running in the neighborhood I love so much, I have a renewal of energy that is absolutely incredible. My most productive ideas frequently come as I am doing that jogging. As a matter of fact, much of my contribution to this book was first conceived during my jogging time.

Another of my favorite quiet times is early in the morning when I get up and go into my office. During that period of time some of my most creative ideas are born. In the summer months, late at night, I also love to go out into my swimming pool, which we primarily built for the grandchildren. It's a rare occasion when I actually use it for swimming, but late at night I love to get in, dog-paddle out to the middle of the pool, quietly lay on my back, and put my mind in neutral. The purpose of going into the pool is to get ideas, and it's a rare occasion when I come out of that pool without a creative idea or some thought or concept which is helpful in my personal, business, or family life.

I strongly encourage you to take time to be quiet. There are occasions when you will want to share that quiet time with someone you love—a slow walk (this is not for exercise purposes) with a son or daughter or your mate, when you are in no hurry to do anything except be with that person. It's amazing how close you can draw to that individual as you walk, but it also is amazing how you will develop ideas when you explore with someone you love in a casual, unhurried, completely relaxed manner, a concept or idea you've been wrestling with. When talking in detail to your mate about your business, even though your mate might not have the expertise or specific knowledge you possess, you'll be astonished at how much he or she can contribute with fresh insights. Spouses are generally free of your job-related prejudices and they're not encumbered with a lot of preconceived ideas, so they can look at the overall picture and come up with ideas which are meaningful and helpful. The questions they ask can provoke creative thinking on your part and perhaps force you to take a look from a different perspective.

Take time to be quiet. It might be a few minutes puttering around in your garden, pulling weeds, or looking at great length at some of the miracles of nature which are all around us for the enjoying, if we will but take time to take a peek. Need I remind you that it was during those still, quiet moments at Valley Forge that George Washington found the strength to deal with the problems of winning our freedom and looking after freezing, starving troops? Need I remind you that it was during those still, dark moments, during that great Civil War which threatened to split our nation asunder, that Abraham Lincoln found the strength and the resolve to pull our nation together and see to it that we were reunited as one? It was during those still, quiet moments at Gethsemane that Jesus Christ found the strength to face the awful ordeal which was in front of Him. During still, quiet moments you will find resources which you might never have known existed. Take time to be quiet—and to listen.

Take Time for Those You Love

One tragic myth which permeates our society is the belief that you can't be a hard-charging, successful businessman *and* a loving, caring husband and father. That myth was exploded several years ago and reinforced in the January 13, 1986 *U.S. News & World Report* article on the one million "ordinary" millionaires. This article points out that 80 percent of them came from middle- or working-class families and that a stable home life with few outside distractions provides the ordinary millionaire with the stamina to persevere in business. Most of them have lasting marriages, often to their high school or college sweethearts, and are likely to "spoil" (be especially kind to) their spouses and children. They have often suffered adversity. Twice as many salesmen as doctors will be millionaires by age sixty, and fewer than 1 percent of the millionaires are artists, entertainers, writers, and athletes. To me, what this really says is that successful people—including successful managers—have a balanced approach to life. The next example emphasizes this point.

A couple of years ago I stopped by to congratulate the president of a major corporation on his recent promotion. He greeted me with considerable enthusiasm and insisted I sit down so he could share with me the role he said I had played in his promotion. This was entirely unexpected, since my sole purpose was to invest sixty seconds to express my congratulations, but the new president would have none of it.

"You know, Zig," he said, "I honestly believe your talk on 'Courtship After Marriage,' which we use in our video training department, played a substantial role in this promotion." Then he went ahead to tell me the story.

"Our marriage was one of those which was truly out of the book. We both came from the 'right side of the tracks,' both went to marvelous schools, both came from successful family backgrounds. Upon graduation from college we got married and I proceeded to join the 'right' clubs while my wife started serving in the 'right' charities. We were active in our church and had the 'right number' of children." (Meaning they had two. I'm glad my parents didn't feel that was the right number, since I was the tenth of twelve!)

He continued his story: "I want to emphasize, Zig, that our marriage was a good one, but over the years we had gotten a little platonic in our relationship. But as I listened to you talk about your Redhead, I realized that although I had nearly twenty fewer birthdays than you, there seemed to be more excitement in your marriage, so I determined to see if the same thing could happen in mine. I was particularly intrigued with the fact you pointed out that, according to a West German insurance company, when a man kissed his wife good-bye—*really* kissed her good-bye [not like his little sister, but as we'd say down home, really 'stropped one on 'er!'], those men lived 5.6 six years longer than the men who neglected this pleasant little interlude in their lives on a daily basis. [Fellows, your life is at stake!] Not only that, but these men earn from twenty to thirty percent more money than do the men who leave home under their own power.

"With that in mind," he said, "I decided to start really courting my wife. I started picking up the phone and giving her a call for a moment or two during coffee breaks each day. I frequently dropped a little note in the mail or bought her a neat little card or I would take a single flower home. On occasion we had those 'heavy dates' when we really went out for a marvelous time. I went back to opening all doors for her, standing up when she got up to leave the table, holding her chair when she returned—all the little things our ladies so deeply appreciate. Now Zig, I'll have to confess that the changes were not instantaneous, but in a matter of just a few weeks, excitement definitely returned to our marriage. The intriguing thing is, that excitement carried over into the marketplace and made me a happier, more productive executive. I'm absolutely convinced my efforts at the company were recognized and I was promoted to the presidency primarily because of the increase in my effectiveness, which was brought about by the excitement which returned to my marriage. So I just want to say thank you."

I left his office and headed upstairs to congratulate the chairman of the board, whose promotion had created the presidential vacancy. The president called to tell him I was on my way. The chairman was equally enthusiastic and insisted I sit down because he, too, had a story to tell. He pointed to the telephone on the back of his credenza and said, "You know, Zig, for a long time when that phone rang I was tempted to snatch it off the hook and demand to know, 'What have the little monsters done now?' Yes, I'm embarrassed to say my teenage son and teenage daughter were little monsters who were driving me up the wall. It seemed that everything my son ate turned to hair, his room was an absolute disgrace, and his stereo could be heard three blocks away. He was totally void of motivation and, even though (or was it because?) I rode him contantly, nothing was getting done. His fourteen-year-old sister had to be one of the most disrespectful, sassy children anywhere. Frankly, I was at my wits' end and I didn't realize it until later, but I was actually avoiding any kind of contact with them at this point in our lives.

"However," he said, "something you said in one of your talks really got my attention. You pointed out that, from time to time, all of us need to just close our eyes and visualize that everyone and everything we love would suddenly be taken completely out of the picture. [I learned that from my friend and fellow speaker Herb True.] When that really hit me it dawned on me that, should something happen to either of my kids, I really would be a brokenhearted man because, despite all of our communication difficulties, I deeply loved them.

"On impulse one afternoon, I picked up the phone, called my son, and asked him if he would like to go watch the Detroit Tigers play the Texas Rangers. When my son recovered from the shock he said, 'Sure, Dad.' The next day I took off an hour early, picked up my son, and we arrived at the ball park a solid hour before game time. We were able to get excellent seats behind first base and though we are not 'baseball fans' in the real sense, we really got into the act that evening. We quickly learned that we were to boo the other team and cheer the home team, that we would be wise to question the eyesight and integrity of the umpire, and that our guys were always right and the other guys were always wrong. We took the seventh-inning stretch, ate lots of peanuts, drank lots of pop, and ate numbers of hot dogs. When it was all over, we went out for a snack and it was well past one o'clock when we returned home."

He said, "I actually spent more time with my boy that night than I had spent with him in the last six months. I'm not going to tell you that everything was instantly better, but the walls did start crumbling—the communication barrier was broken. We started talking and building a relationship." With tears in his eyes he said, "You know, Zig, I relearned that not only is my son an unusually bright boy but he is also of high moral character and I'm convinced he's going to do something with his life. Strangely enough, I never said another word about his hair and yet today it is respectable in length. I never mentioned cleaning up his room and, to be honest, if the health inspector were to inspect, it would not qualify for a Grade A restaurant permit, but it is acceptable in our home. And as far as the stereo is concerned, we all now enjoy the fact that his music can be heard clearly and distinctly in his own room, but not at the next-door-neighbor's house.

"Not only that, Zig, but a few days later I called my fourteen-year-old daughter and asked her if she'd like to go out to dinner with me that evening. She was delighted, and so I told her to put on her fanciest party dress because we were going to one of those really nice restaurants where I take my important corporate clients. That evening I picked up a little corsage and she looked so pretty in her dress with that flower! We spent over three hours at dinner that evening. We ordered hors d'oeuvres, the fancy entree, and topped it off with a flaming dessert. What a delightful time we had!

"It's almost the same story as with my son. The barriers came tumbling down. I learned that not only is she a very, very bright girl but she has definite objectives in her life. I believe someday she's going to be a marvelous wife and a good mother, if she decides to go the family route, or she's going to have an outstanding career in her chosen field if she decides to concentrate on a business career. More important, Zig, I can tell you that when I leave home every day I know all I have to concentrate on is my job. I'm convinced I am currently the chairman of the board because of the fact that my family situation has straightened up so much. I can commit all my creative energy to my job when I'm on the job because I know everything is fine on the home front."

Isn't it ironic that these two enormously successful corporate executives, who were spending countless hours on their jobs and, as they often told everybody else, "I'm doing this for my family," discovered that when they neglected their families they were not nearly as effective in the corporate world. Once they got their family lives in balance, their corporate lives also improved. After beating around these old bushes for several years, I'm convinced that regardless of whether you are an athlete or an entertainer, whether you're in business for yourself or work for a major corporation, if you pay attention to the fires on the home front and keep them properly burning, you will move up faster, more effectively, and far more happily in the corporate world.

Yeah—But Where Do I Get the Energy?

I've an idea that virtually every reader will agree, at least in principle, with the idea that a good relationship with your family is helpful to your business career. However, you just might be thinking, *Yeah, but where do I get the energy to be a good family person* and *a super manager?* This next illustration should provide you with at least a partial answer.

All of us are motivated about somebody or something in our lives. That's important to understand because motivation literally creates energy. As a matter of fact, in most cases when we claim to be "tired," we are actually mentally or emotionally drained and not physically exhausted. In short, our motivational bucket is running low. Example: Have you ever had one of "those" days? You started with a flat tire which caused you to miss an important engagement. Your office manager called in sick and you had to handle an incredible number of administrative details which you intensely dislike. The air-conditioning unit malfunctioned and made an already boring meeting an impossible one. On top of that, your most productive supervisor resigned. I mean *nothing* went right, and on top of that there is some evidence that you are developing a summer cold. Finally, however, the day mercifully ends and at 5:00 P.M. *sharp* you wearily head for home and some much-needed collapsing time.

A smiling, enthusiastic wife cheerfully welcomes you home and expresses her delight that you did not have to work late because "today is the day." With some dismay you inquire, "The day for what?" Your wife responds, "Why, honey, you remember. Today is the day we've planned for three weeks. Today we're going to clean the garage." Your reaction lies somewhere between exhaustion and anger as you protest that after the trials and tribulations of the day you can't even pick one foot up— much less the four thousand boxes you need to move to clean the garage! Undaunted, your helpmate assures you that she is going to help and it will take only three or four hours.

At that moment the phone rings and, with a tremendous burst of energy, you manage to lift the receiver all the way to your ear and say hello with all the enthusiasm of a kamikaze pilot on his thirty-third mission. The voice on the other end is that of your best golfing buddy with the good news that he has a tee time at the country club in just twenty-three minutes if you feel like getting in a fast nine holes before dark. Guess what? That utterly exhausted, can't-take-another-step body of yours suddenly explodes with energy! Those formerly lifeless legs propel you out to the garage—not to clean it, but to get those golf clubs and hurry out to the country club. You are MOTIVATED!

Now, I'm not about to suggest that your golfing buddy is a better motivator than your wife, but the energy-building motivational appeal (hitting golf balls) was substantially more to your liking than was your wife's inducement ("killing" yourself cleaning that garage!). He was being an effective manager by *channeling the energies* you had in a direction you wanted to go. Effective people managers channel their own energy as well as the energies their people possess at a target they want and need to reach. You've learned how in *Top Performance*. Now do it.

PERFORMANCE PRINCIPLES

1. Take time to get started.

2. Take time to grow.

3. Take time to be healthy.

4. Take time to play.

5. Take time to be quiet.

6. Take time for those you love.

EPILOGUE
A UNIQUE OPPORTUNITY

When I was a small boy in Yazoo City, Mississippi, I worked in a grocery store. Now you must understand that in the late 1930s and early 1940s, things were dramatically different from what they are today. At that time very few kids had money to buy sweets. Molasses candy was one of the delicacies of the day. People would buy molasses and make candy from it. The molasses was kept in a big barrel at the store. When customers brought their jars or jugs in for molasses, we simply filled them from the huge barrel of molasses. From time to time one of the little guys in town who had nothing to do would come into our store to kill time and hope for a handout.

One day a little guy was in the store and thought no one was looking. He carefully took the top off the molasses barrel, stuck his finger in, and put it in his mouth. As he was licking his lips, my boss suddenly appeared and grabbed him by the shoulders, shook him, and said, "Son, don't you ever do that again! That's not sanitary and we won't stand for it!"

The boy was somewhat shaken, but as he left the store I could tell he was going to survive. A few days later he showed up in the store again. He walked around a few minutes, carefully looked, and when he did not see the owner, he removed the top of the barrel and ran his finger through the molasses. Just as he popped his finger into his mouth, suddenly, out of nowhere, my boss appeared. This time he swatted the little guy across the rear a couple of times and told him to get out of the store and never come back.

You would have thought the kid had learned his lesson, but about ten days later that sweet tooth obviously had gotten to him again and there he was, in the store. Again the owner was nowhere to be seen, so the little guy carefully, cautiously removed the top of the barrel and again ran his finger through the molasses. Just as he was putting it in his mouth, my boss mysteriously reappeared. This time he said nothing as he picked the little guy up and dropped him right into that big barrel of molasses. As he was sinking out of sight you could hear him praying, "Oh, Lord, please give me the tongue to equal this opportunity!"

Your Challenge

As I put my thoughts on Top Performance on paper, it has been my prayer *and* my plan to share some information and inspiration which will make a difference in your life. The need for both information and inspiration in our personal and corporate worlds is enormous. The opportunity to benefit many people is great. My prayer is that some idea has struck a responsive chord in you that will enable you to enjoy your life more and be even more effective today than you were yesterday.

The Penalty of Leadership

In every field of human endeavor, he that is first must perpetually live in the white light of publicity.

Whether the leadership be vested in a man or in a manufactured product, emulation and envy are ever at work. In art, in literature, in music, in industry, the reward and the punishment are always the same. The reward is widespread recognition; the punishment, fierce denial and detraction.

When a man's work becomes a standard for the whole world, it also becomes a target for the shafts of the envious few. If his work be merely mediocre, he will be left severely alone—if he achieve a masterpiece, it will set a million tongues a-wagging. Jealousy does not protrude its forked tongue at the artist who produces a commonplace painting.

Whatsoever you write, or paint, or play, or sing, or build, no one will strive to surpass, or to slander you, unless your work be stamped with the seal of genius. Long, long after a great work or a good work has been done, those who are disappointed or envious continue to cry out that it cannot be done. Spiteful little voices in the domain of art were raised against our own Whistler as a mountebank, long after the big world had acclaimed him its greatest artistic genius. Multitudes flocked to Bayreuth to worship at the musical shrine of Wagner, while the little group of those whom he had dethroned and displaced argued angrily that he was no musician at all. The little world continued to protest that Fulton could never build a steamboat, while the big world flocked to the riverbanks to see his boat steam by.

The leader is assailed because he is a leader, and the effort to equal him is merely added proof of that leadership. Failing to equal or to excel, the follower seeks to depreciate and to destroy— but only confirms once more the superiority of that which he strives to supplant.

There is nothing new in this. It is as old as the world and as old as the human passions—envy, fear, greed, ambition, and the desire to surpass. And it all avails nothing. If the leader truly leads, he remains—the leader. Master-poet, master-painter, master-work-man, each in his turn is assailed, and each holds his laurels through the ages. That which is good or great makes itself known, no matter how loud the clamor of denial. That which deserves to live—lives.

Yes, leadership has its penalties, but fortunately, it also has its rewards. Here's hoping—and believing—that the principles taught in *Top Performance* will help you reap those rewards.

RECOMMENDED READING

Management and Motivation

Alexander, Scott. *Rhinoceros Success*. Laguna Hills, California: The Rhino's Press, 1980.

Ash, Mary Kay. *Mary Kay on People Management*. New York: Warner Books, 1984.

Blanchard, Kenneth and Spencer Johnson. *The One Minute Manager*. New York: William Morrow and Company, Inc., 1982.

Blanchard, Kenneth and Robert Lorber. *Putting the One Minute Manager to Work*. New York: William Morrow and Company, Inc., 1984.

Bradford, David and Allan R. Cohen. *Managing for Excellence*. New York: John Wiley & Sons, Inc., 1984.

Brown, W. Steven. *13 Fatal Errors Managers Make*. Old Tappan, New Jersey: Fleming H. Revell Company, 1985.

Buck, Lee. *Tapping Your Secret Source of Power*. Old Tappan, New Jersey: Fleming H. Revell Company, 1985.

Carnegie, Dale and Associates. *Managing Through People*. New York: Simon & Schuster, Inc., 1978.

DeBruyn, Robert I. *Causing Others to Want Your Leadership*. Manhattan, Kansas: DeBruyn & Associates, 1976.

Gschwandtner, Gerhard. *Superachievers*. Englewood Cliffs, New Jersey: Prentice-Hall, Inc., 1984.

Hersey, Paul and Kenneth Blanchard. *Management of Organizational Behavior*. Englewood Cliffs, New Jersey: Prentice-Hall, Inc., 1982.

Hickman, Craig and Michael Silva. *Creating Excellence*. New York: New American Library, 1984.

Hunsaker, Phillip L. and Anthony J. Alessandra. *The Art of Managing People.* Englewood Cliffs, New Jersey: Prentice-Hall, Inc., 1980.

Iacocca, Lee. *Iacocca.* New York: Bantam Books, 1984.

King, Patricia. *Performance Planning and Appraisal.* New York: McGraw-Hill Book Company, 1984.

Kirkpatrick, Donald I. *How to Improve Performance Through Appraisal and Coaching.* New York: AMACOM, 1982.

Linking Employee Attitude and Corporate Culture to Corporate Growth and Profitability. Philadelphia: Hay Management Consultants, 1984.

McCormack, Mark H. *What They Don't Teach You at Harvard Business School.* New York: Bantam Books, 1984.

Margerison, Charles. *How to Assess Your Managerial Style.* New York: AMACOM, 1980.

Peters, Thomas J. and Nancy K. Austin. *A Passion for Excellence.* New York: Random House, 1985.

Peters, Thomas J. and Robert H. Waterman, Jr. *In Search of Excellence.* New York: Harper & Row, Publishers, 1982.

Smith, Fred. *Learning to Lead.* Waco, Texas: Word Books, 1986.

Inspiration and Self-Help

Carnegie, Dale. *How to Stop Worrying and Start Living.* New York: Simon & Schuster, Inc., 1975.

Carnegie, Dale. *How to Win Friends and Influence People.* New York: Pocket Books, 1982.

Conwell, Russell. *Acres of Diamonds.* Old Tappan, New Jersey: Fleming H. Revell Company, 1975.

Cooper, Kenneth, M.D. *The Aerobics Program for Total Well-Being.* New York: M. Evans, 1982.

Dobson, James. *What Wives Wish Their Husbands Knew About Women.* Wheaton, Illinois: Tyndale House Publishers, 1975.

Follett, Ken. *On Wings of Eagles.* New York: William Morrow and Company, Inc., 1983.

Glass, Kinder, and Ward. *Positive Power for Successful Salesmen.* Dallas: Crescendo, 1972.

Hayes, Ira. *Yak! Yak! Yak!* Ira M. Hayes, 1978.

Jones, Charlie. *Life Is Tremendous*. Wheaton, Illinois: Tyndale House, 1981.

Maltz, Maxwell. *Psycho-cybernetics*. New York: Pocket Books, 1970.

Mandino, Og. *The Greatest Miracle in the World*. New York: Bantam Books, 1977.

Marshall, Peter and David Manuel. *The Light and the Glory*. Old Tappan, New Jersey: Fleming H. Revell Company, 1977.

Peale, Norman Vincent. *The Power of Positive Thinking*. New York: Fawcett, 1978.

Schuller, Robert H. *Tough Times Never Last, but Tough People Do*. Nashville: Thomas Nelson Publishers, 1983.

Schwartz, David J. *The Magic of Thinking Big*. St. Louis: Cornerstone, 1962.

Smith, Fred. *You and Your Network*. Waco, Texas: Word Books, 1984.

Spickard, Anderson and Barbara R. Thompson. *Dying for a Drink*. Waco, Texas: Word Books, 1985.

Teaff, Grant. *I Believe*. Waco, Texas: Word Books, 1975.

Waitley, Denis. *Seeds of Greatness*. Old Tappan, New Jersey: Fleming H. Revell Company, 1983.

Other Books by Zig Ziglar

Confessions of a Happy Christian. Gretna, Louisiana: Pelican, 1978.

Dear Family. Gretna, Louisiana: Pelican, 1984.

Raising Positive Kids in a Negative World. Nashville: Thomas Nelson Publishers, 1985.

See You at the Top. Gretna, Louisiana: Pelican, 1974.

Steps to the Top. Gretna, Louisiana: Pelican, 1985.

Zig Ziglar's Secrets of Closing the Sale. Old Tappan, New Jersey: Fleming H. Revell Company, 1984.

For Your Continuing Education

Bits & Pieces. Published monthly by Economics Press, Inc., 12 Daniel Road, Fairfield, New Jersey 07006.

Walter V. Clark Associates, Inc., 2 Jackson Walkway, Providence, Rhode Island 02903. 401-421-2008.

Communication Briefings. Published monthly by Encoders, Inc., 860 Westminster Boulevard, Blackwood, New Jersey 08012.

Decker Communications Report. Published monthly by Magna Publications, Inc., 607 N. Sherman Avenue, Madison, Wisconsin 53704.

Front Line Management. Published by Economics Press, Inc., Fairfield, New Jersey 07006.

Guideposts. Published monthly by Norman Vincent Peale and Ruth Stafford Peale, Carmel, New York 10512.

Harvard Business Review. Published bimonthly by the Graduate School of Business Administration, Boston, Massachusetts 02163.

National Speakers Association, 4323 N. 12th Street, Suite 103, Phoenix, Arizona 85014. 602-265-1000.

On the Upbeat. Published monthly by Economics Press, Inc., 12 Daniel Road, Fairfield, New Jersey 07006.

Performax Systems International, Inc. Personal Profile Systems, 3140 Harbor Lane North, Suite 200, Minneapolis, Minnesota 55441. 612-540-5110.

Personal Selling Power. Published monthly by Gerhard Gschwandtner & Associates, P.O. Box 5467, Fredericksburg, Virginia 22403.

Reader's Digest. Published monthly by the Reader's Digest Association, Inc., Pleasantville, New York 10570.

Research Institute Marketing for Sales Executives. Published by the Research Institute of America, Inc., 589 Fifth Avenue, New York, N.Y. 10017.

Selling by Phone. Published by Economics Press, Inc., Fairfield, New Jersey 07006.

Success. Published monthly by Success Unlimited, Inc., P.O. Box 2240, Boulder, Colorado 80322.

Supervisory Management. Published monthly by the American Management Association, 135 West 50th Street, New York, N.Y. 10020.

Working Smart. Published monthly by Learning International, P.O. Box 10211, Stamford, Connecticut 06904.

Working Together. Published by the Dartnell Corporation, 4660 Ravenswood Avenue, Chicago, Illinois 60640.